This Street Atlas is the comprehensive, easy-to-use atlas of streets in Bergen, Passaic, and Rockland Counties. Featuring the **PageFinder™ Map** (*illustrated at right*), the exclusive fold-out cover is designed for quick map and page location. Also included are 36 full-color maps; an index of 28,078 street names and places; a Northern New Jersey Regional Map; ZIP code listings and an index of all communities in the Street Atlas.

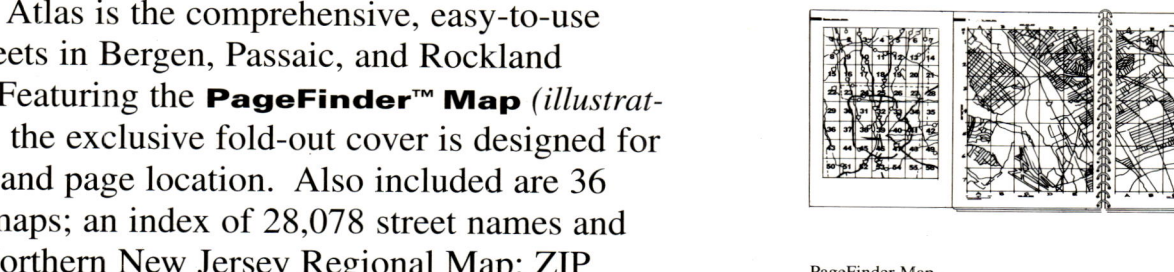

PageFinder Map

Using the Street Atlas

PageFinder Map
Located on the inside cover, the Bergen County PageFinder Map folds out for reference when using the book (*as shown in the above illustration*).

Page C in the gatefold contains the Passaic County PageFinder Map, and the Inside Back Cover has the Rockland County Map.

Example of Use
As an example of typical Street Atlas use, open the PageFinder Map to the left of the book. Assume you want to know which map Lyndhurst is on. You can quickly identify which map you need. As shown on the open PageFinder Map, Lyndhurst is on map 1. Using the PageFinder Map you can get around Bergen, Passaic, and Rockland Counties as well as the Street Atlas with ease.

Street Atlas Maps
Each map contains a letter-number grid around the edges of the map. This letter-number system provides coordinates that allow you to quickly find streets and places listed in the index. The maps also include a reference at the edges to adjoining maps. Look for neighboring areas by referring to "Continued on map..." notations.

Street Atlas Index
Starting on page 78, streets are indexed according to county. First, locate the street name alphabetically by place name. For example - Dempsey Av. in Edgewater. Turn to the page where Edgewater Streets are listed and then, alphabetically find Dempsey Av. This will give you the index and map number. The exact location of street is then simply determined by the intersection of the letter(s) and number(s).

Use Maps or Index
Locate your destination by either using the PageFinder Map or by consulting the index.

TRI-COUNTY LEGEND

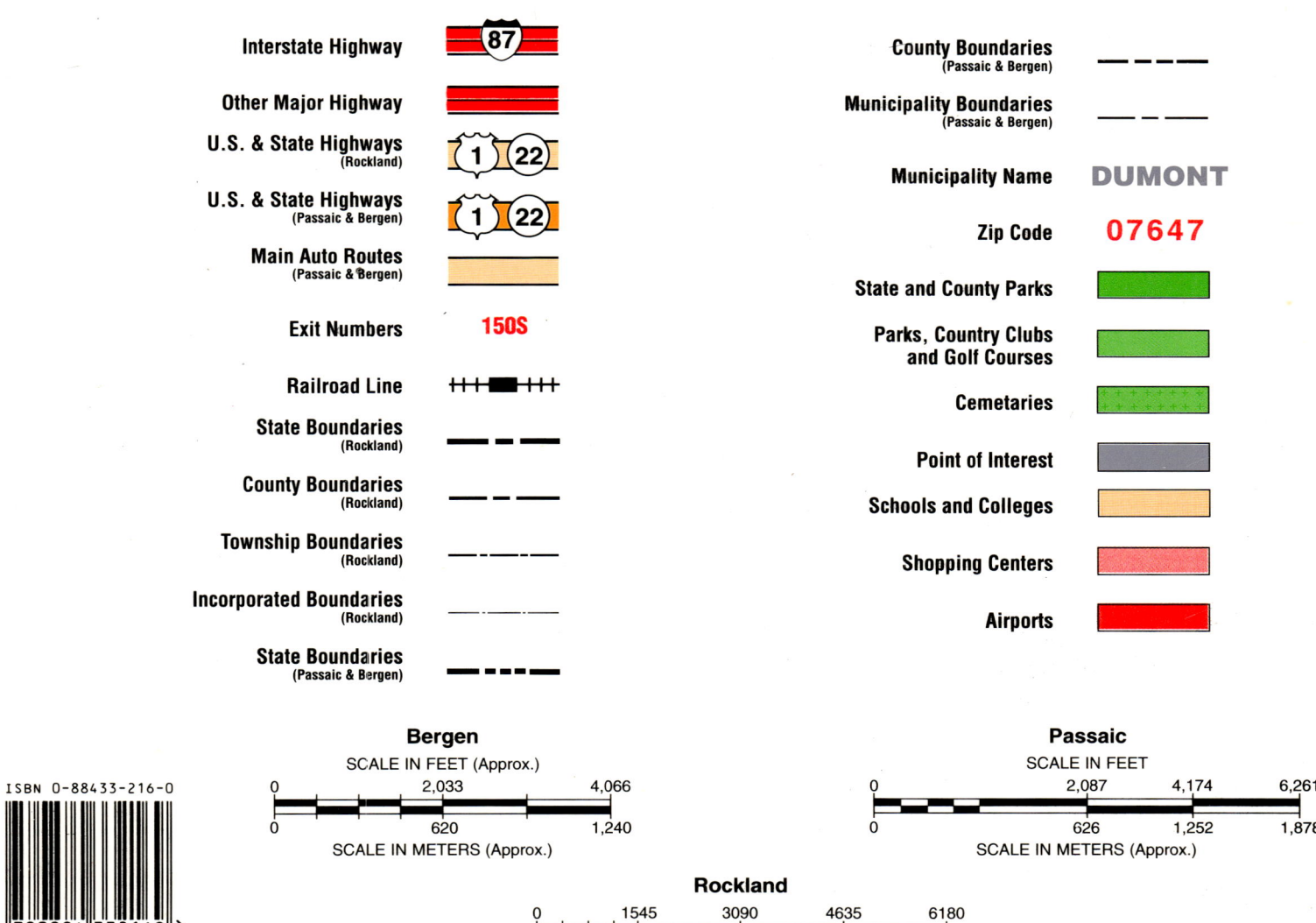

Interstate Highway	87
Other Major Highway	
U.S. & State Highways (Rockland)	1 22
U.S. & State Highways (Passaic & Bergen)	1 22
Main Auto Routes (Passaic & Bergen)	
Exit Numbers	150S
Railroad Line	
State Boundaries (Rockland)	
County Boundaries (Rockland)	
Township Boundaries (Rockland)	
Incorporated Boundaries (Rockland)	
State Boundaries (Passaic & Bergen)	

County Boundaries (Passaic & Bergen)	
Municipality Boundaries (Passaic & Bergen)	
Municipality Name	DUMONT
Zip Code	07647
State and County Parks	
Parks, Country Clubs and Golf Courses	
Cemetaries	
Point of Interest	
Schools and Colleges	
Shopping Centers	
Airports	

ISBN 0-88433-216-0

EAN
9 780884 332169 >

Bergen
SCALE IN FEET (Approx.)
0   2,033   4,066
0   620   1,240
SCALE IN METERS (Approx.)

Passaic
SCALE IN FEET (Approx.)
0   2,087   4,174   6,261
0   626   1,252   1,878
SCALE IN METERS (Approx.)

Rockland
0   1545   3090   4635   6180
SCALE IN FEET

NEW YORK
NEW JERSEY

Tappan Zee Bridge (Toll)

Suffern
13B
13A
NEW YORK STATE THRUWAY
59 14A 14
14B
15
66
Mahwah
RINGWOOD STATE PARK
14
RAMAPO STATE FOREST
287
RAMAPO VALLEY CO. RESERVATION
Ramsey
Upper Saddle River
12
BLAUVELT STATE PK.
Pearl River
Blauvelt
304 303
340 9W
Dobbs Ferry
TALLMAN MTN. STATE PK.
PALISADES INTERSTATE PARKWAY
Montvale
ROCKLAND COUNTY
BERGEN COUNTY
11
17
PASSAIC COUNTY BERGEN COUNTY
CAMPGAW MOUNTAIN RESERVATION
Allendale
507
172
Lake Tappan
503
Old Tappan
8
Northvale
Norwood
505
4
N.J. N.Y.
Franklin Lakes
Saddle River
9
168
Hillsdale
Westwood
502
Closter
501
ALPINE PK.
3
Wyckoff
BERGEN COUNTY WILDLIFE CENTER
Oakland
57 58 59
202
502
208
10
Midland Pk.
166
165
Forest
Oradell Res.
Demarest
2
7
Cresskill
YONKERS
Point View Res.
Ridgewood
507
North Haledon
Glen Rock
507
6
SADDLE RIVER PK.
163
VAN SAUM PK.
Oradell
New Milford
River Edge
Bergenfield
Madison Ave.
County Rd.
Dumont
Tenafly
9W
1
PALISADES INTERSTATE PARKWAY
HUDSON RIVER
Hawthorne
Paterson-Hamburg Tpke.
504
Fair Lawn
161
160
503
505
Englewood
4
Pompton R.
Wayne
PREAKNESS VALLEY PK.
202
23
Paterson
504
20
4
Broadway
159
Saddle Brook
17
Maywood
Washington Ave.
Teaneck
4
OVERPECK PK.
Englewood Cliffs
95 80
4
George Washington Bridge (Toll)
52 53 54 55 56 57 58 60 61 62 80
59
157
156
Elmwood Park
63 64 65
Hackensack
Bogota
66 67 68
1&9
93
46
Fort Lee
3
GARRET MTN. RES.
19
Garfield
46
Lodi
Ridgefield Pk.
18
Palisades Pk.
Ridgefield
155
154
Clifton
Passaic R.
Hasbrouck Hts.
Little Ferry
Cliffside Pk.
PASSAIC CO.
ESSEX CO.
3
Passaic
Van Houten Av.
Wood-Ridge
Teterboro Airport
Moonachie
Meadowlands Sports Complex
18W
NEW YORK
Caldwell Wright Airport
46
153
151
23
14
Carlstadt
17
TURNPIKE
N. HUDSON PK.
Caldwell
506
Montclair
Nutley
7
3
Rutherford
120
18W
North Bergen
17
3
495
Lincoln Tunnel (Toll)
Verona
Bloomfield
150
Belleville
21
17
Lyndhurst
95
Secaucus
16
1&9
95
Union City
Hoboken
WEST ESSEX PK.
527
VERONA PK.
506
149
BRANCH BROOK PK.
North Arlington
BERGEN CO.
HUDSON CO.
17
Holland Tunnel (Toll)
5
280
6
7
577
West Orange
8
148
Kearny
16 N.J.
Hackensack River
Bergen Blvd.
9
Orange
147
Harrison
17 18
1&9
PULASKI SKYWAY
Jersey City
14C
10 11
145
East Orange
12 13
14 15 16
144
Newark
510
143
21
501

5

BERGEN COUNTY

PARAMUS 07652

RIVER EDGE 07661

NEW MILFORD

ROCHELLE PARK 07662

MAYWOOD 07607

07601

HACKENSACK

RIVERSIDE SQ. MALL S.C.

BERGEN MALL

GARDEN STATE PLAZA S.C.

Farleigh Dickinson Univ

Johnson Park

Foschini Park

NEW NEW 07660

LODI 07644

BOGOTA 07603

HASBROUCK HEIGHTS 07604

TETERBORO 07608

SOUTH HACKENSACK 07606

RIDGEFIELD PARK 07660

©Geographia Map Company, Inc.

MIDLAND PARK
07432

RIDGEWOOD
07450

GLEN ROCK
07452

FAIR LAWN
07410

BERGEN COMMUNITY COLLEGE

PARAMUS GOLF AND COUNTRY CLUB

GEORGE WASHINGTON MEMORIAL PARK

ARCOLA

ELMWOOD PARK
07407

07601

SADDLE BROOK

Continued On Map 13 Of Passaic Co.

©Geographia Map Company, Inc.

WASHINGTON
07675
166

BETH-EL CEMETERY

CEDAR PARK CEMETERY

EMERSON
07630

HACKENSACK GOLF CLUB

J

EMERSON COUNTRY CLUB

07652
165
PARAMUS
WEST BROOK SCH.

PARAMUS PARK SHOPP. CTR.

N.J. VETERANS NURSING HOME

BERGEN PINES COUNTY HOSPITAL COMPLEX

COMMUNITY SERVICES BLDG

COUNTY MOSQUITO COMMISSION

ORADELL
07649
ORADELL

ORADELL RESV.

503

K

PETRUSKA PARK

RIVER DELL REGIONAL HIGH SCHOOL

L

RIDGEWOOD COUNTRY CLUB

AND GOLF CLUB

CEMETERY

163

17

RIVER EDGE

VAN SAUN COUNTY PARK

NEW MILFORD
07661

07646

CENTURY

4

161S

GARDEN STATE PLAZA S.C.

M

Continued On Map 7

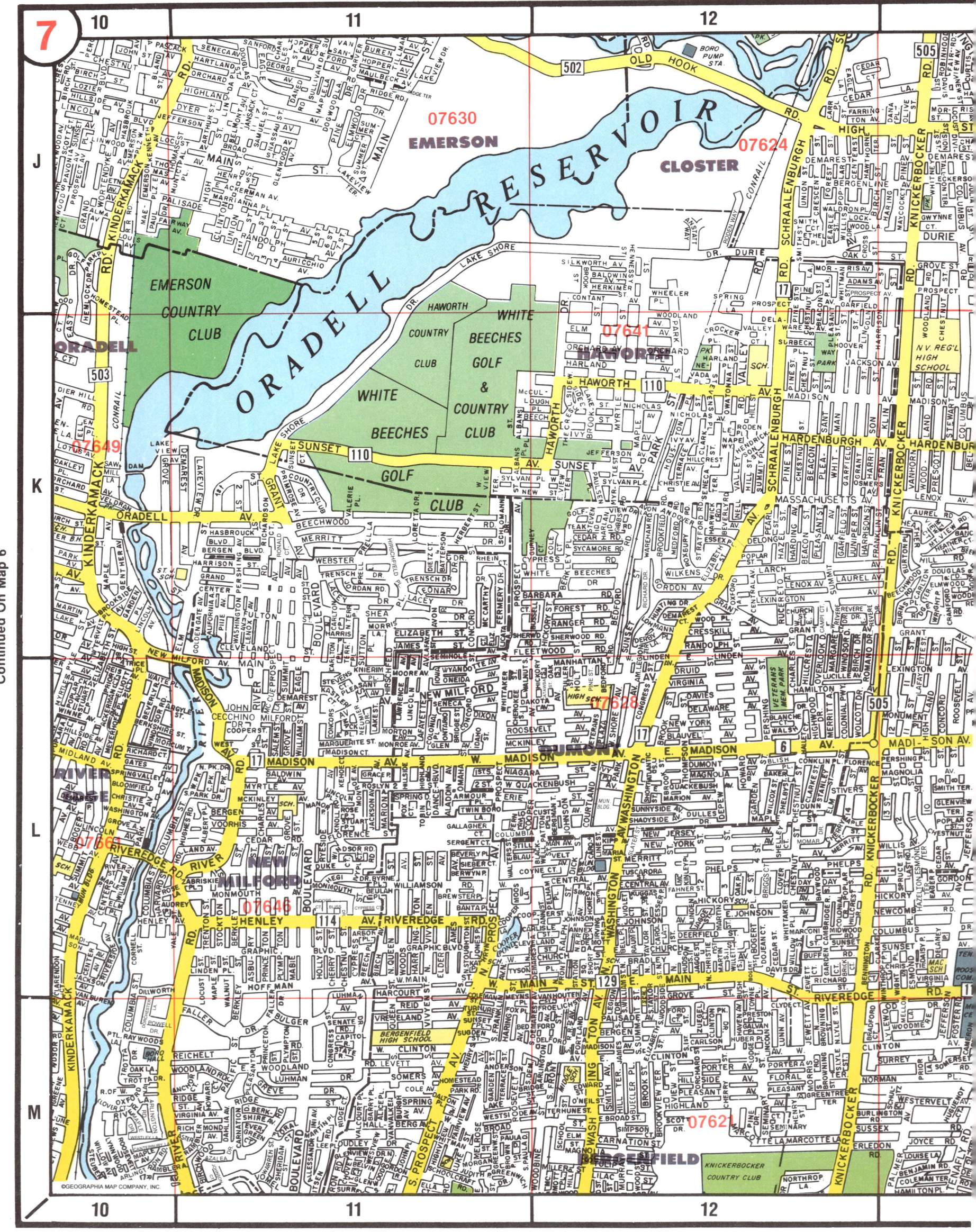

7

End Of Coverage

13　14　15

PALISADES
INTERSTATE
PARK

CAMP ALPINE
BOY SCOUTS OF AMERICA

COUNTY PARK
(UNDEVELOPED)

07624
CLOSER

BORO
PARK

Metropolitan
Green Acres

ALPINE
COUNTRY
CLUB

07627
DEMAREST

ALPINE
07620

07626
CRESSKILL

TAMCREST
COUNTRY
CLUB

MONTAMMY
COUNTRY
CLUB

Tenafly
Natural
Park

TENAFLY
07670

East Hill
Playground

GREENBROOK
POND

Alpine
Boat
Basin

Alpine
Lookout

HUDSON　RIVER

NEW JERSEY
NEW YORK

©GEOGRAPHIA MAP COMPANY, INC.

Continued On Map 13A

Continued On Map 9

8
10
11
12
13
F
G
H
J
LAKE TAPPAN
HACKENSACK WATER CO. RESERVOIR
OLD TAPPAN
07675
PARK RIDGE
07656
RIVERVALE COUNTRY CLUB
OLD TAPPAN GOLF COURSE
ROCKLAND CO.
RIVER VALE
07675
WOOD-DALE COUNTY PARK
EDGEWOOD COUNTRY CLUB
BAYLOR'S MASSACRE HIST. SITE
TOWN HALL
POLICE DPW FIRE DEPT.
HACKENSACK
HARRINGTON PARK
07640
PARK
VETS PARK
BEECH WOOD PARK
ATHLETIC FIELD
WESTWOOD
07675
PASCACK BROOK CO. PARK
PASCACK VALLEY HOSP.
PARK VALE GOLF CLUB
WESTWOOD CEMETERY
OLD HOOK CEMETERY
BORO PUMP STA.
EMERSON
07630
ORADELL RESV.
PROSPECT AV.
KINDERKAMACK RD.
RIVERVALE RD.
ORANGEBURGH RD.
OLD TAPPAN RD.
TAPPAN RD.
WASHINGTON AV.
PIERMONT AV.
WESTWOOD AV.
HARRIOT AV.
OLD HOOK RD.
SCHRAALENBURGH RD.
LAFAYETTE RD.
CRIPPLE BUSH RD.
CEDAR LA.
HARRINGTON AV.
102
104
125
17
502
503
505
106
©GEOGRAPHIA MAP COMPANY, INC.

Continued On Map 7

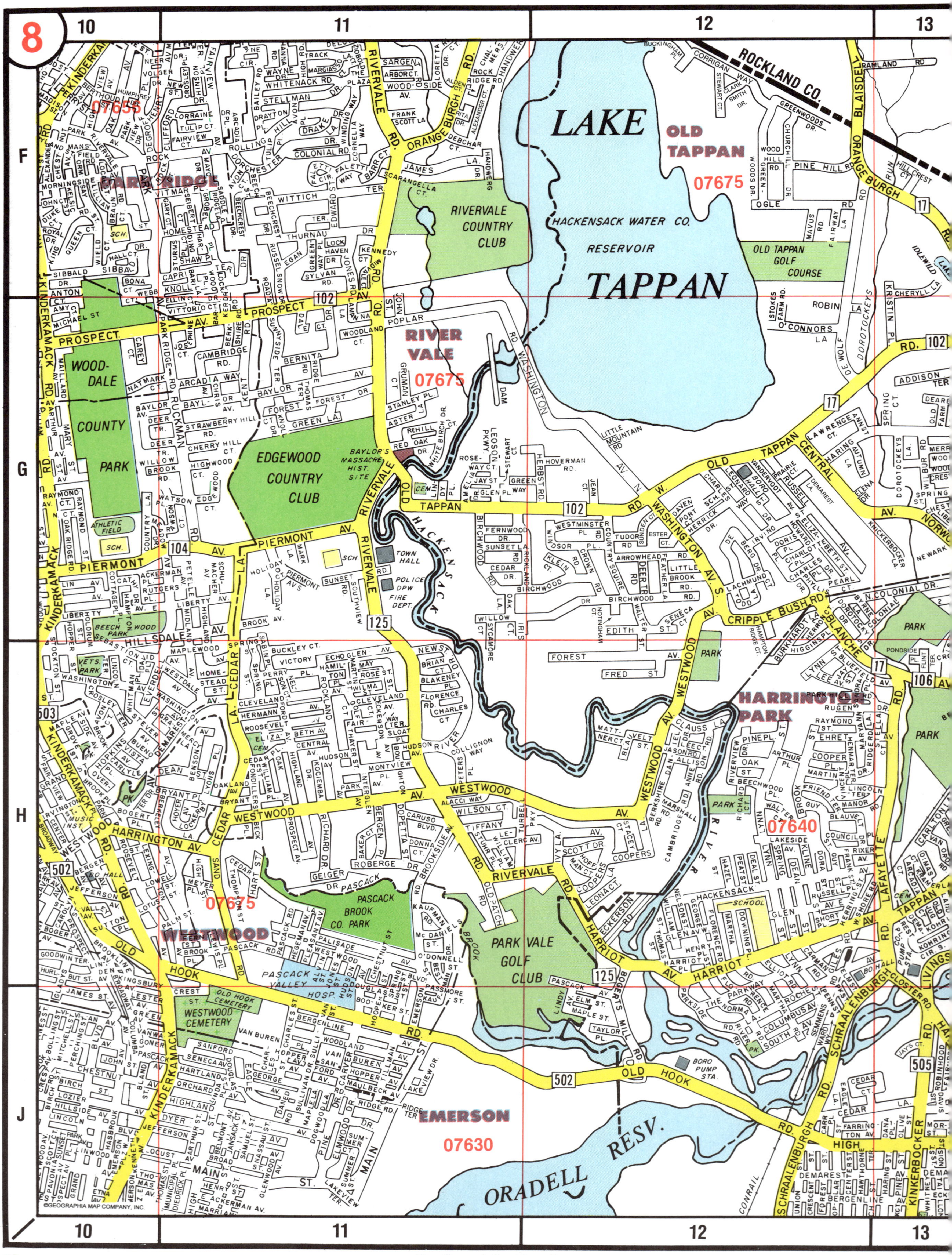

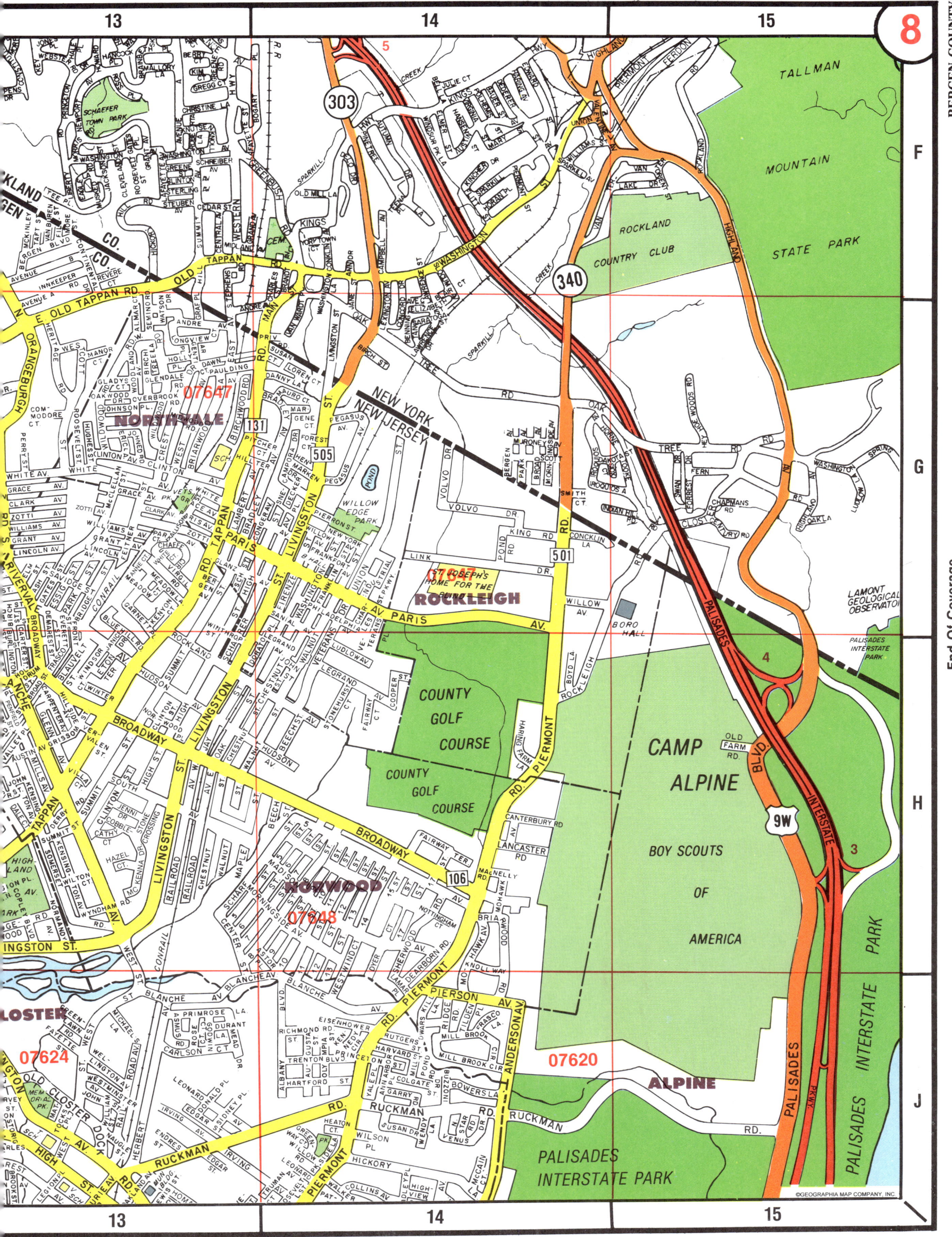

9

6 | 7 | 8

ALLENDALE
07401

SADDLE RIVER
07458

WALDWICK
07463

HO-HO-KUS
07423

MIDLAND PARK
07432

RIDGEWOOD
07450

6 | 7 | 8

22

©Geographia Map Company, Inc.

BERGEN COUNTY

PARK RIDGE
07656

WOODCLIFF LAKE
07675

WOOD CLIFF LAKE RESERVOIR

WOOD-DALE COUNTY PARK

HILLSDALE
07642

PIERMONT

WESTWOOD
07675

WASHINGTON
07675

EMERSON
07630

PARAMUS
166

BETH-EL CEMETERY

CEDAR PK. CEM.

WESTWOOD CEMETERY

OLD HOOK CEM.

GARDEN STATE PARKWAY

©Geographia Map Company, Inc.

Continued On Map 8

Continued On Map 11

10
1
2
3
F
G
H
J
RAMAPO STATE FOREST
PASSAIC CO.
BERGEN CO.
OAKLAND
07436
FRANKLIN LAKES
07417
287
208
202
108
502
4
57
58
59
FRANKLIN AV.
RAMAPO VALLEY RD.
W. OAKLAND AV.
SKYLINE DR.
LONG HILL RD.
COLONIAL RD.
HIGH MOUNTAIN RD.
FRANKLIN LAKES RD.
BREAKNECK RD.
BERDAM RD.
CRYSTAL LAKE
MIRROR LAKE
SMITH POND
CONRAD POND
WEST POND
HOPPERS CROOKED POND
BAKER'S LONG POND
VITALES POND
UPPER LAKE
LOWER LAKE
PINES LAKE
PINES LAKE PARK
COLFAX PK
LINDEN PARK
ALHTAHA PARK
FRANKLIN LAKES
POINT VIEW RESV.
VAN RIPER HOOPPER MUSEUM
HIGH MOUNTAIN
MANITOU
BERGEN
PASSAIC
CO.
CO.
CEMETERY
SCHOOL
P. SCH.
MUN. BLDG.
VALLEY SCH.
HEIGHTS SCH.
BOARD OF ED.
MANITO SCH.
©GEOGRAPHIA MAP COMPANY, INC.

Continued On Map 9 Of Passaic Co.

Continued On Map 12A Of Passaic Co.

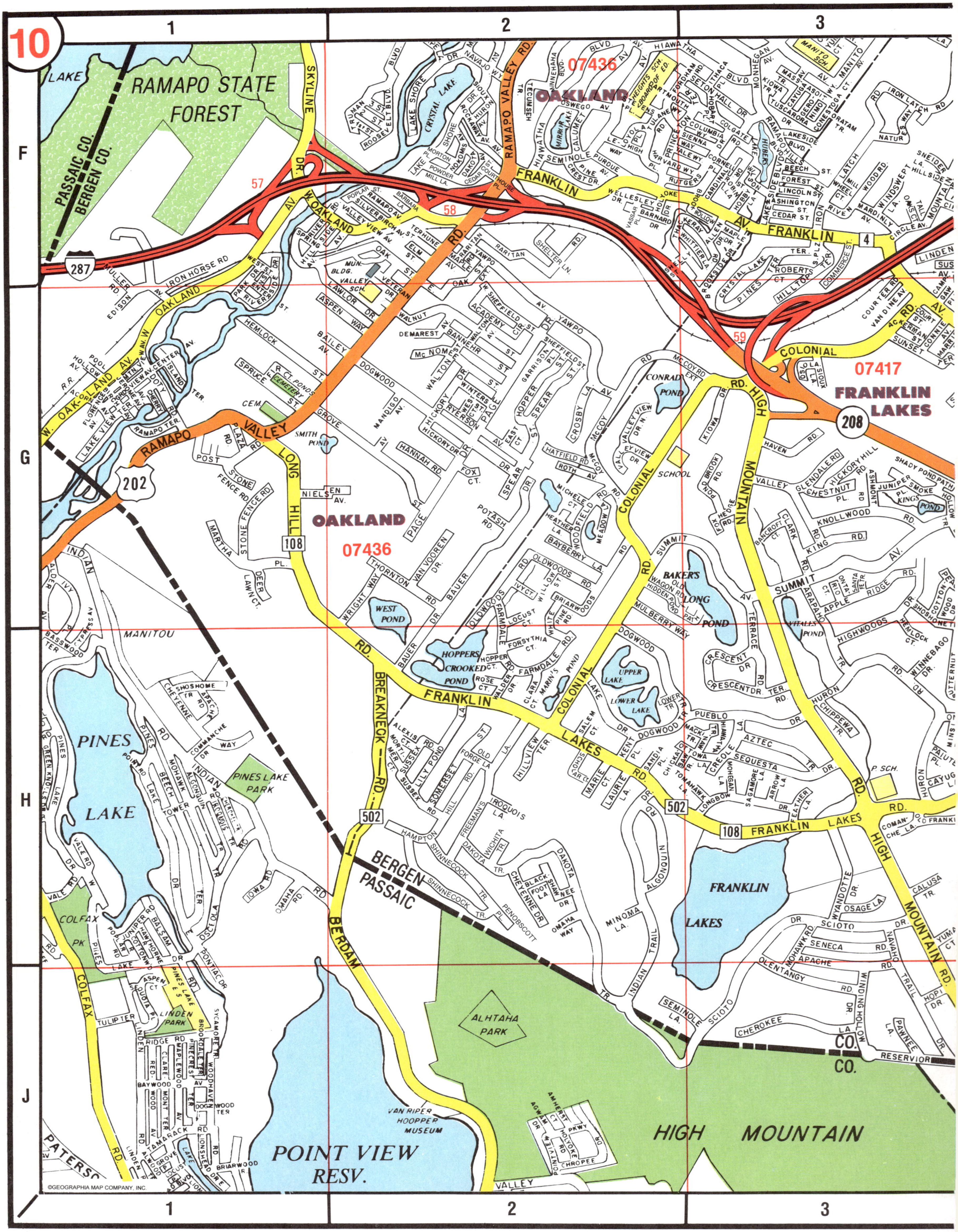

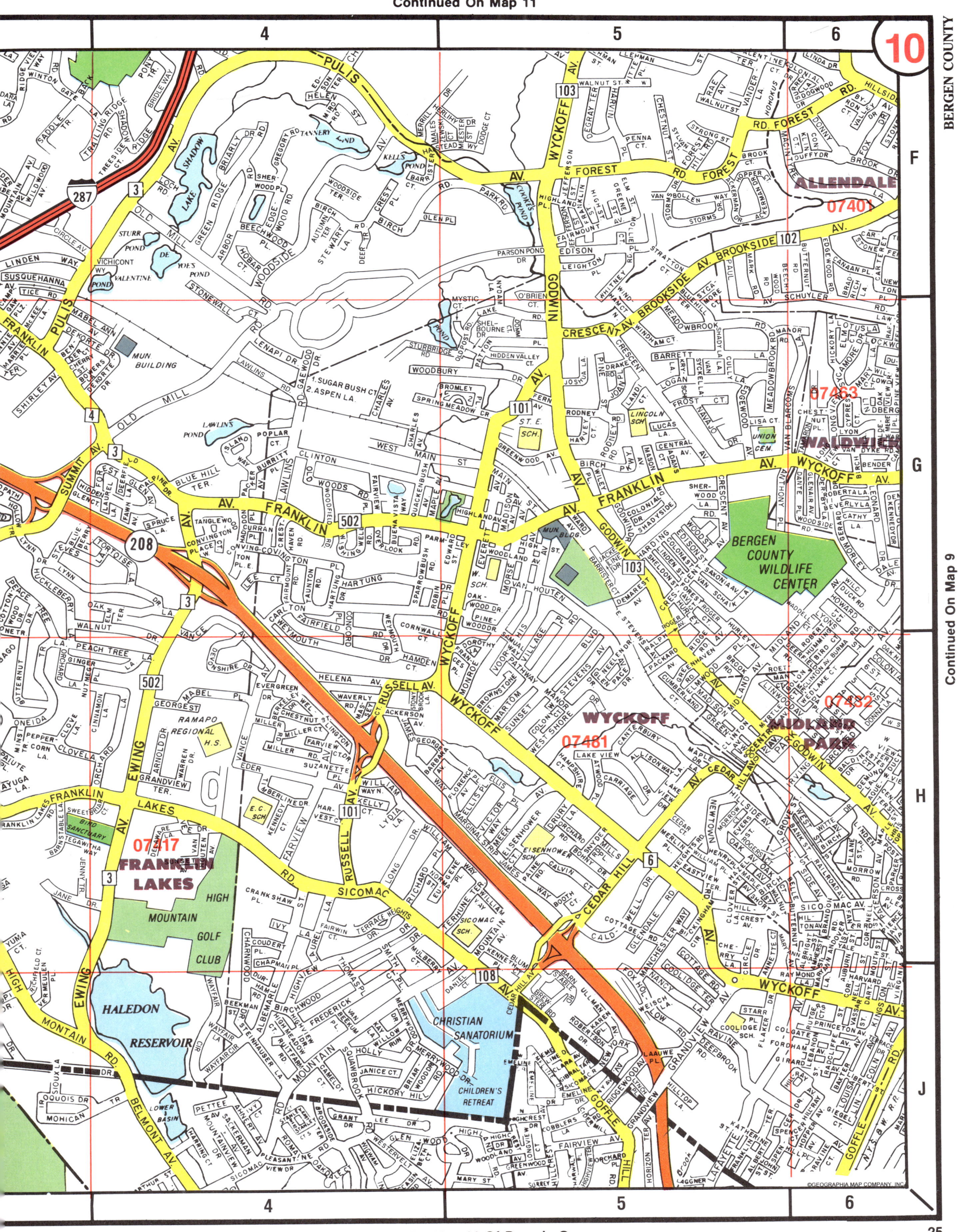

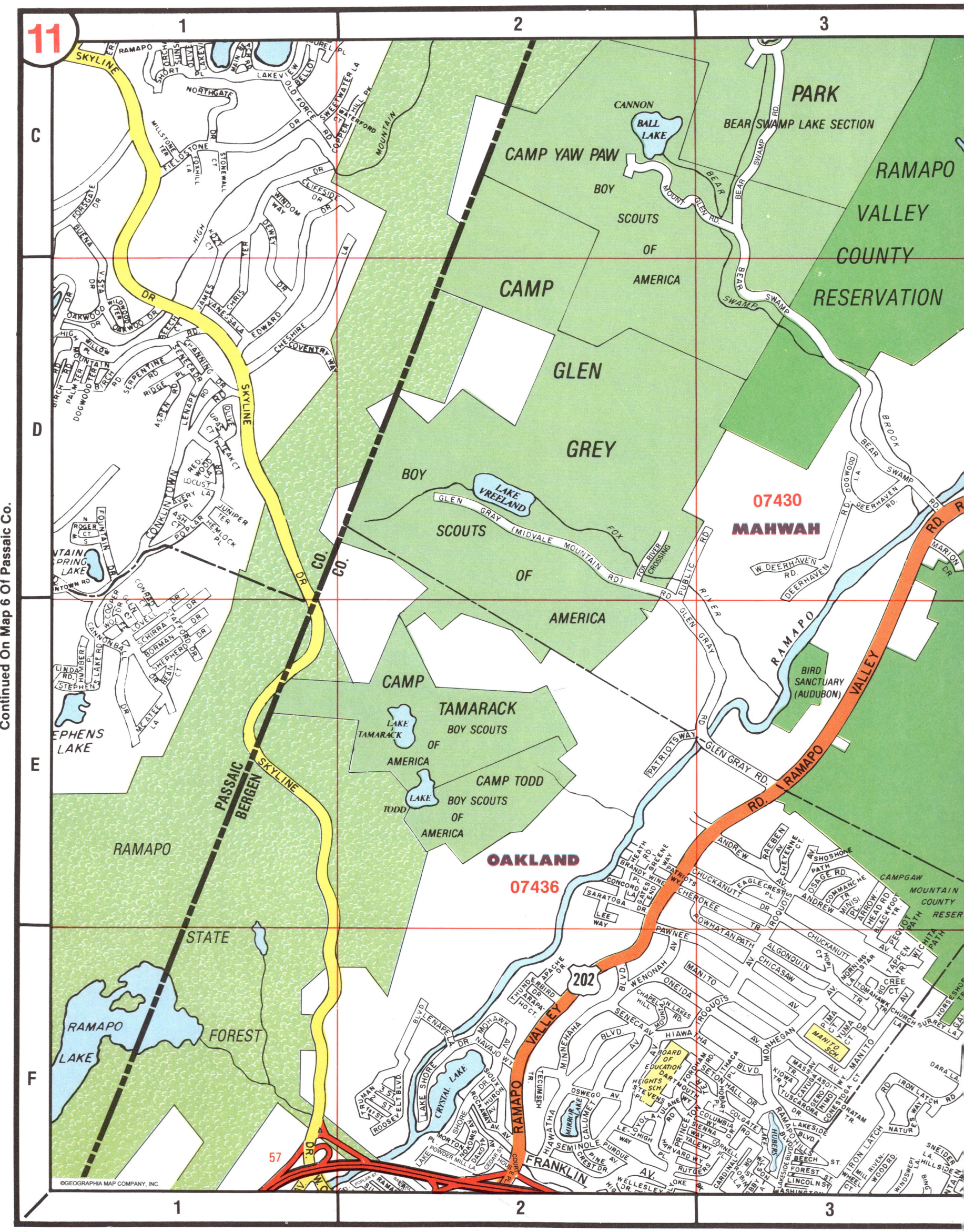

Continued On Map 6 Of Passaic Co.

Continued On Map 10

26

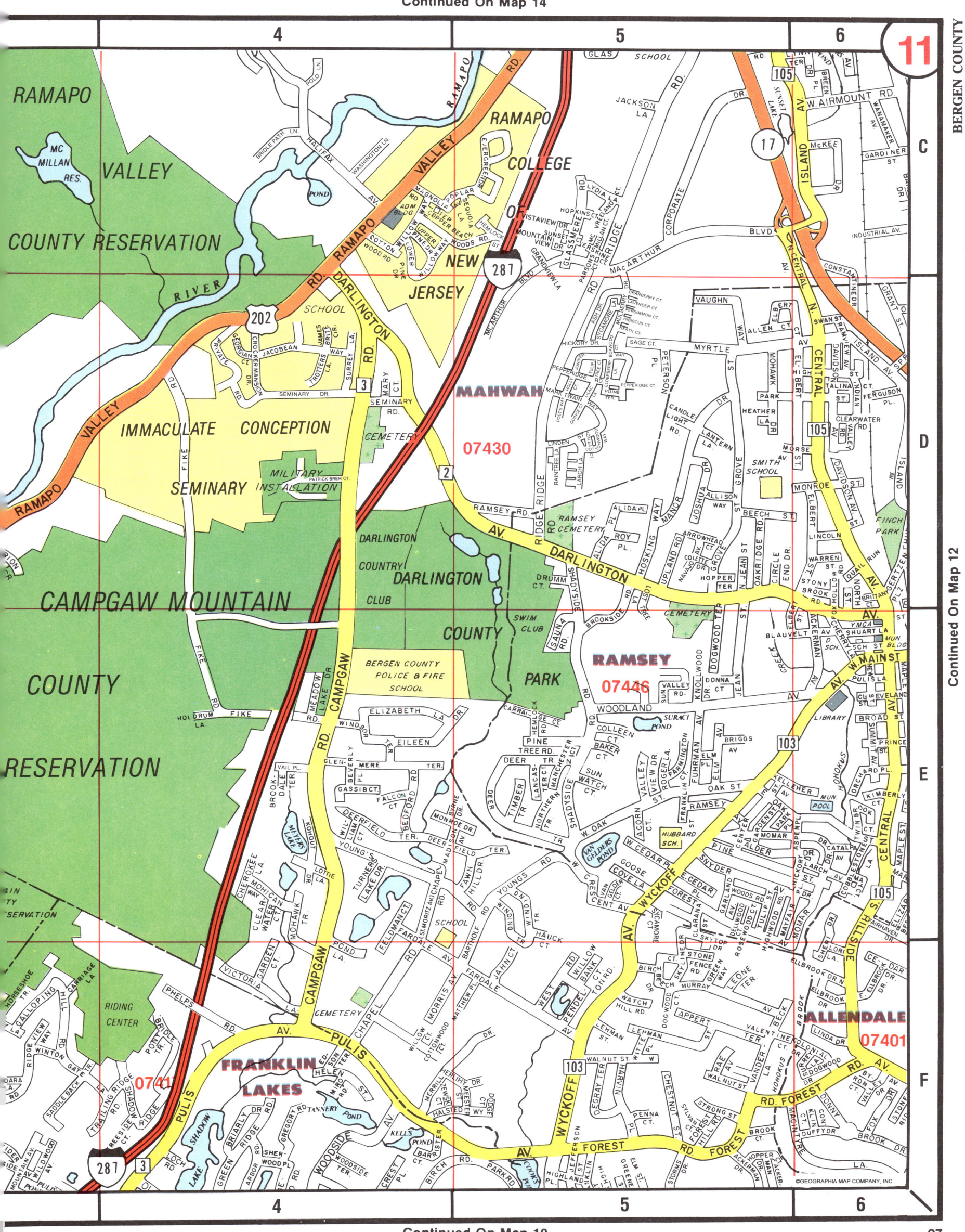

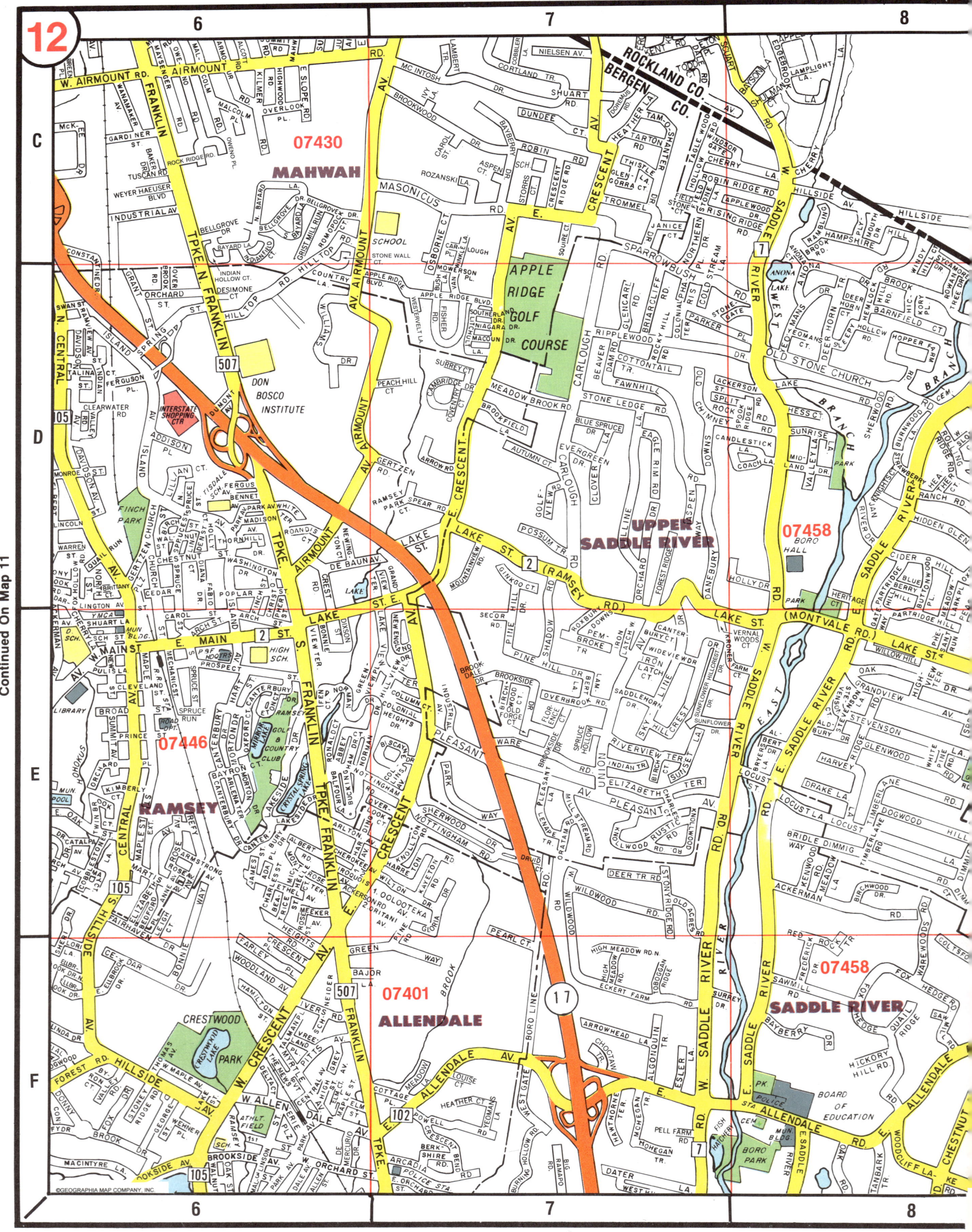

9   10

12

BERGEN COUNTY

306

45

ROCKLAND CO.
BERGEN CO.

NEW YORK
NEW JERSEY

304

109

PAROCHIAL HIGH SCH.

FLEETWOOD ELEM SCH

PASCACK BROOK TOWN PARK

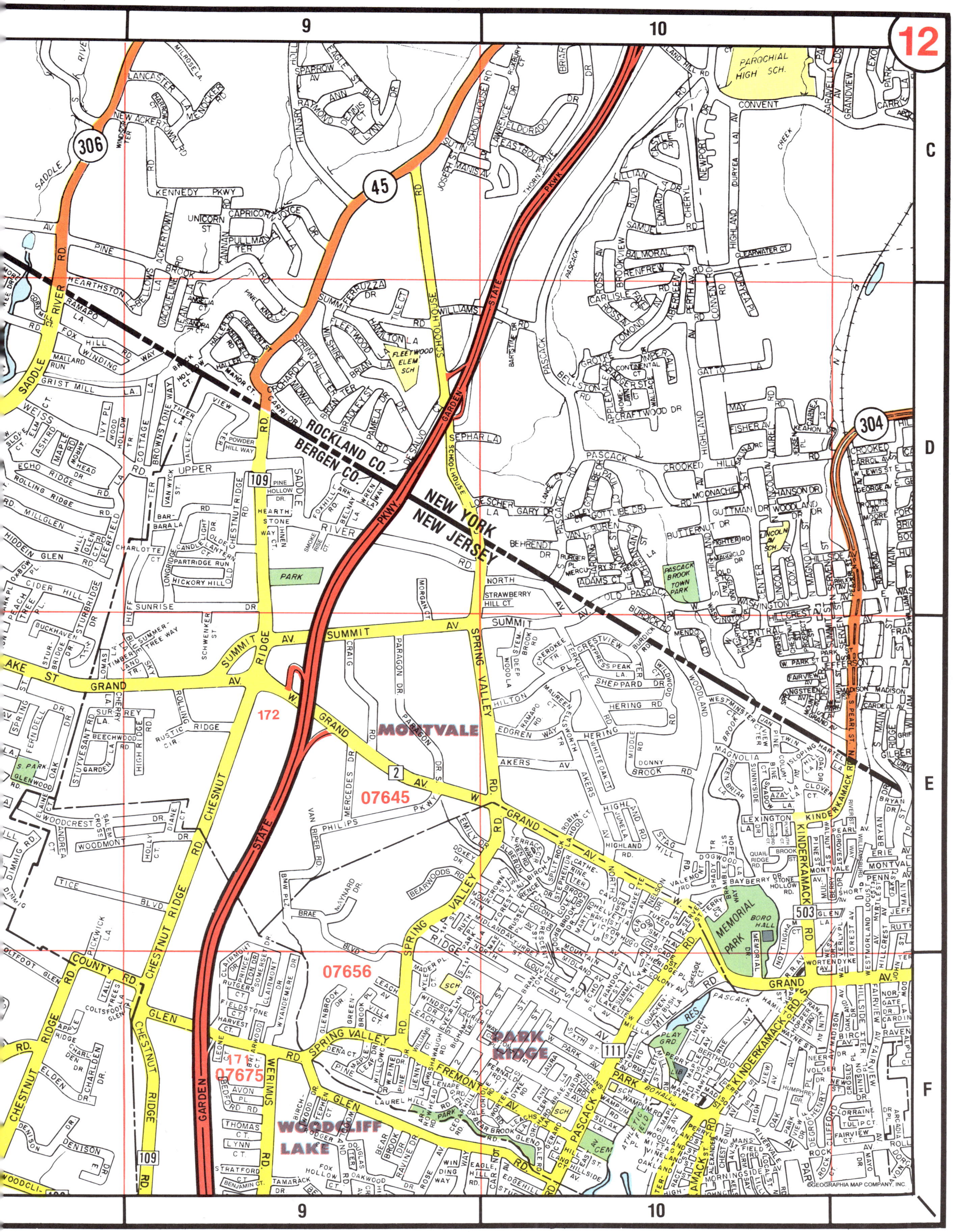

PARK

C

D

E

F

172

MONTVALE

2

07645

07656

07675

171

503

111

WOODCLIFF LAKE

PARK RIDGE

MEMORIAL PARK

BORO HALL

Continued On Map 13A

©Geographia Map Company, Inc.

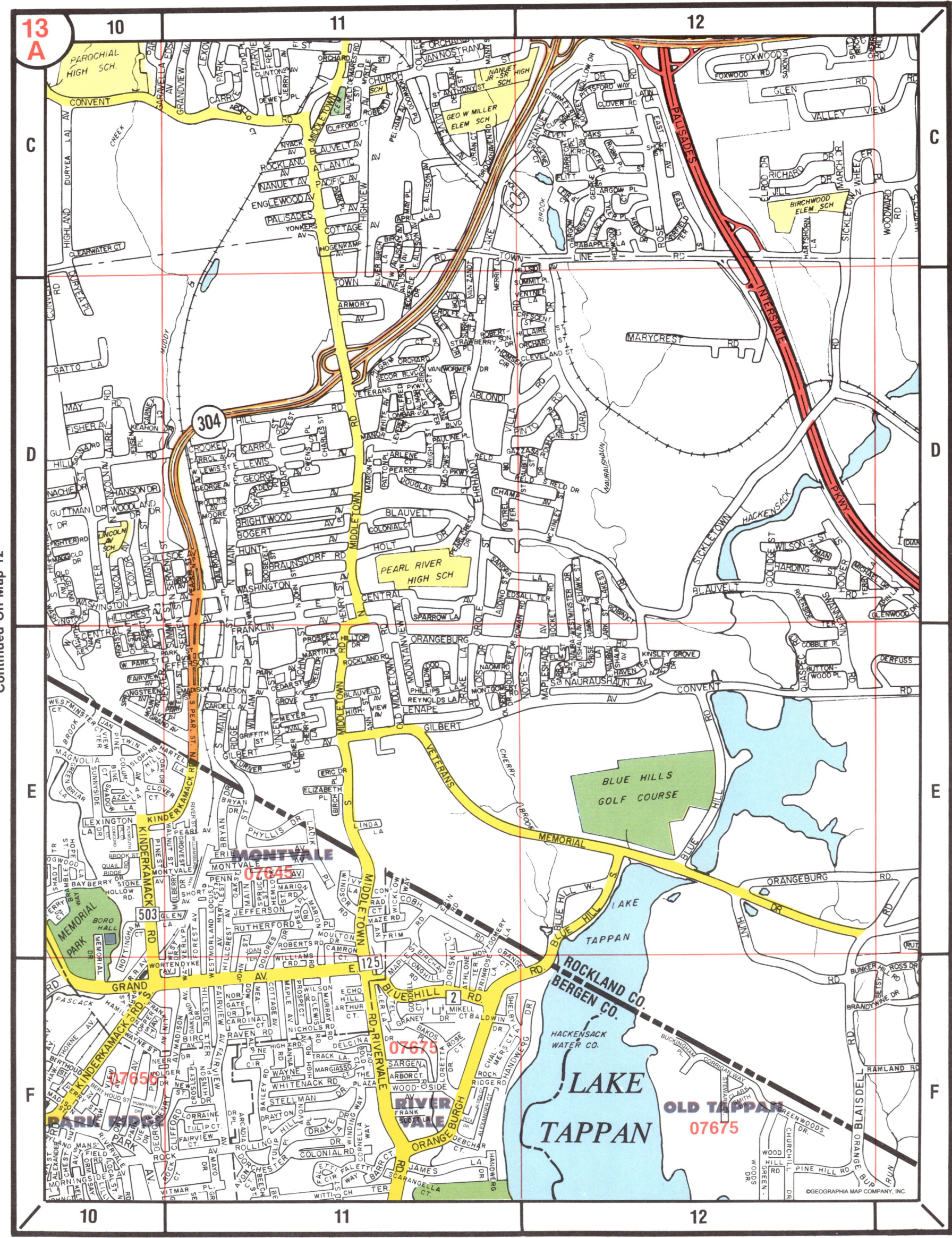

Continued On Map 12

PEARL RIVER HIGH SCH

BLUE HILLS GOLF COURSE

MONTVALE 07645

RIVER VALE

07675

07656

PARK RIDGE

LAKE TAPPAN

OLD TAPPAN 07675

ROCKLAND CO. BERGEN CO.

HACKENSACK WATER CO.

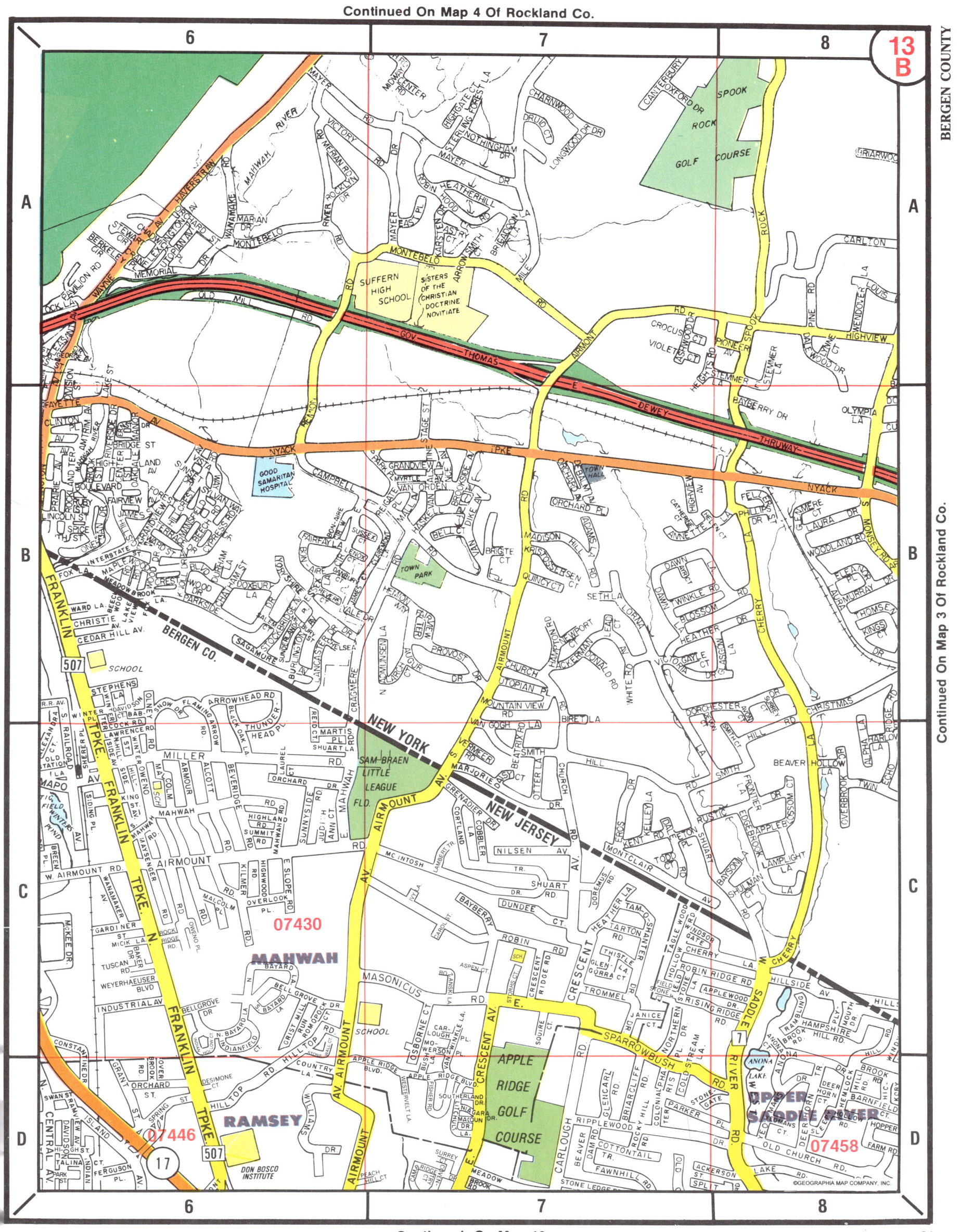

Continued On Map 3 Of Rockland Co.

07430

MAHWAH

07446

RAMSEY

UPPER SADDLE RIVER

07458

©GEOGRAPHIA MAP COMPANY, INC.

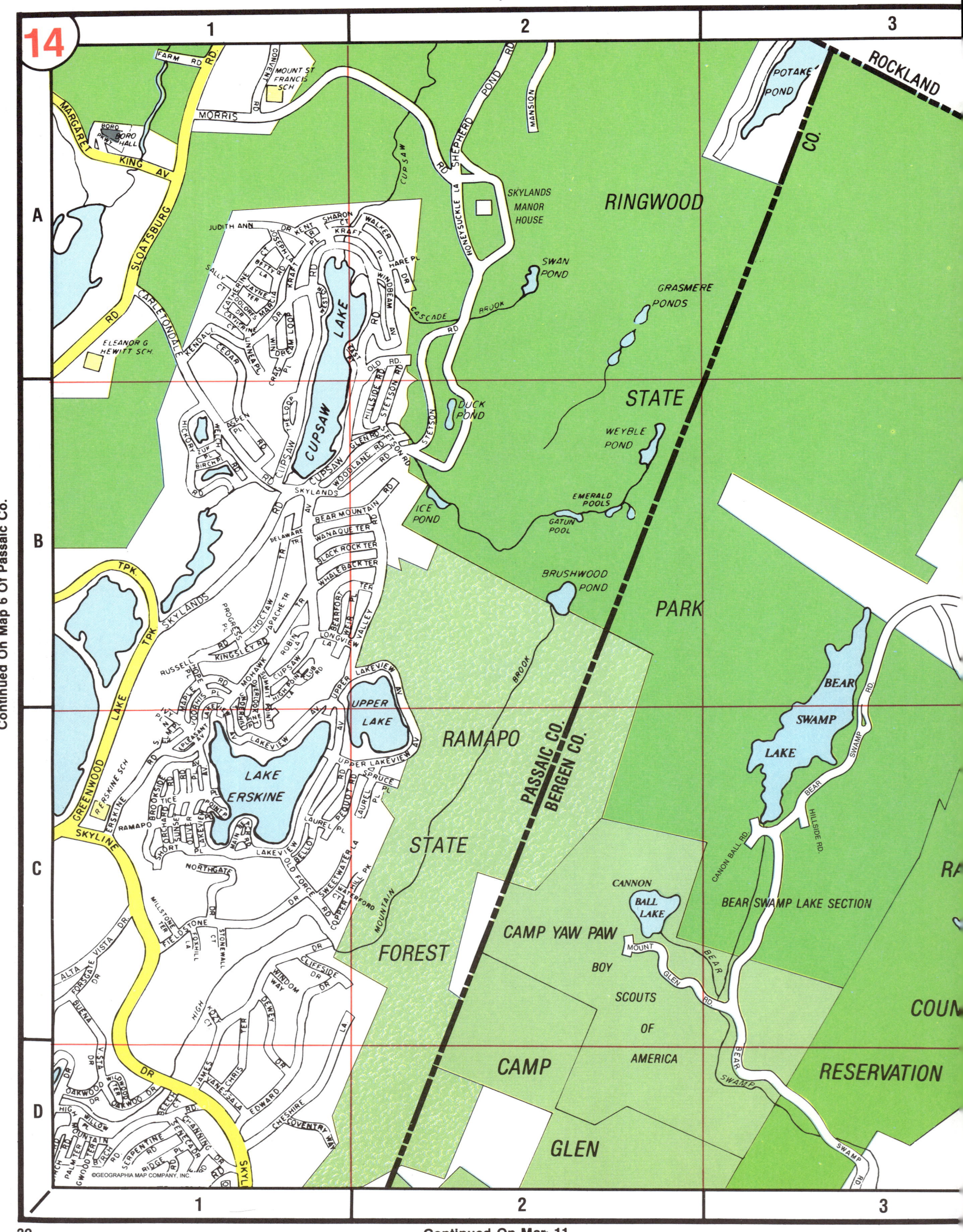

14

ROCKLAND

POTAKE POND

MOUNT ST FRANCIS SCH

FARM RD

MARGARET

MORRIS

BORO HALL

KING AV

SLOATSBURG RD

CARLETONDALE RD

ELEANOR G HEWITT SCH.

JUDITH ANN DR

KENT PL

SHARON PL

KRAFT

WALKER

HARE PL

WINDBEAM AV

SKYLANDS MANOR HOUSE

RINGWOOD

SWAN POND

GRASMERE PONDS

CO.

CUPSAW

SHEPHERD POND

MANSION RD

HONEYSUCKLE LA

CASCADE RD

BROOK

CUPSAW LAKE

HILLSIDE RD

STETSON RD

DUCK POND

STATE

WEYBLE POND

EMERALD POOLS

HICKORY

ASPEN RD

BIRCH

CUPSAW

SKYLANDS AV

WOODLAND RD

OLD RD.

ICE POND

GATUN POOL

BEAR MOUNTAIN RD

DELAWARE TR

WANAQUE TER

BLACK ROCK TER

WHALEBACK TER

SEARFORT TER

VALLEY

LONGVIEW

BRUSHWOOD POND

PARK

TPK.

SKYLANDS

PROGRESS PL

KINGSLEY RD

CHOCTAW

APACHE TR

MOHAWK

ROBIN LA

UPPER LAKEVIEW AV

BROOK

BEAR SWAMP LAKE

SWAMP RD

RUSSELL

MAPLE

IVY

PINE

UPPER LAKEVIEW AV

UPPER LAKE

RAMAPO

PASSAIC CO.

BERGEN CO.

BEAR RD

HILLSIDE RD

GREENWOOD LAKE TPK.

ERSKINE SCH

BROOKSIDE

TICE

ORCHARD

RAMAPO

LAKEVIEW

LAKE ERSKINE

SPRUCE PL

LAUREL PL

PEQUOT

STATE

CANON BALL RD

BEAR SWAMP LAKE SECTION

SKYLINE

NORTHGATE

SWEETWATER LA

OLD FORCE RD

WATERFORD

MOUNTAIN PK

CANNON BALL LAKE

MOUNT

GLEN RD

CAMP YAW PAW

FOREST

BEAR RD

RA

COUN

MILLSTONE DR

FORSGATE VISTA DR

STONEWALL

FOXHILL

CLIFFSIDE DR

WINDOM WAY

BOY

SCOUTS

OF

AMERICA

RESERVATION

ALTA

BUENA

HIGH

KOY

DEWEY

VISTA

BEECH

JANE-SALA

EDWARD

CHESHIRE

COVENTRY

CAMP

BEAR SWAMP RD

MOUNTAIN

PALMER TER

SERPENTINE RD

RIDGE

SENECA DR

SKYLINE

GLEN

4   5   6   **14**

M O U N T A I N S

ROCKLAND
BERGEN CO.

R A M A P O

SIXTH

MOUNTAIN AV

SNOW RD

STAG HILL RD

MAPLE RD
OAK RD
SPRUCE RD

PINE HILL RD
CREST RD
CREST RD

VIEW DR

SILVER LAKE

LAKE VIEW

GEIGER RD

SPLIT ROCK RD.

ECHO MOUNTAIN RD

STAG HILL RD

NEW YORK
NEW JERSEY

BOULDER AV
5TH AV
FOX ST
WILLOW ST
SUMMIT AV
CHESTNUT
HICKORY
LOCUST
OAK ST
6TH ST
SIXTH ST

1ST ST
2ND
3RD

4TH ST

BLACK LEE PL

ORANGE

RAMAPO

TERRACE AV

59

17

RAMAPO TPKE

66

287

17

EUREKA
PARK ST
MOUNTAINSIDE
TAINSIDE
HOUVENKOPF RD.

FRANKLIN

R I V E R

RAMAPO VALLEY RD.

07430

MAHWAH

HAVERMEYER RES.

MOUNTAIN RD

STAG HILL RD

VALLEY VIEW DR

VIEW DR

RIVER VIEW DR

CLOVE BROOK RD

RIVER VIEW TER

POLO LA.

202

RAMAPO

CLARK AV
GLASGOW TER

GLASGOW TER

HIGH SCHOOL

W. park av
MAPLE AV

CLINTON

JOHNSON AV
CATHERINE

STRYSK
church st
LONG
BERGEN
PL

17

RAMAPO VALLEY RD.

507

FRANKLIN TPKE.

WARD LA.
CHRISTIE
CEDAR HILL AV

505

ISLAND RD

MOUNTAIN AV

EAST VIEW AV

W. AIRMOUNT RD.

WANAMAKER

CORPORATE DR

BLVD

**RAMAPO
COLLEGE
OF
NEW
JERSEY**

BRIDLE PATH
HALIFAX

WASHINGTON LA.

POND

ADM BLDG

MAGNOLIA RD
POPLAR
SEQUOIA LA
BEECH
HEMLOCK ST

COPPER

WOODS RD.

COTTON

WOOD RD

PINE RD

MC MILLAN RES.

V A L L E Y

UNTY

RAMAPO

R I V E R

RAMAPO VALLEY RD

DARLINGTON RD.

DARLINGTON AV

SCHOOL

3
MARY

SEMINARY RD.

IMMACULATE

©GEOGRAPHIA MAP COMPANY, INC.

HOPKINS CT
LYDIA LA.
MILLAN CT
ERSKINE LA.
SUNSET

RIDGE

GLASSMERE

MAC ARTHUR
PARSONS

RIDGE RD.

VREELAND CT.

JACKSON LA.

HIBISCUS CT
HEATH CT
SAGE CT.
MULBERRY RD.
PERSIMMON CT.
LAVENDER CT.
CRANBERRY CT.

VAUGHN DR
ALLEN CT

RAMSEY

07446

HICKORY DR
ASH RD
SYCAMORE
MULBERRY DR

PEPPERIDGE RD

MARK

PLUMB TER
TULIPTREE

PETERSEN PL
MYRTLE

CENTRAL

CONSTANTINE DR

PARK

N. CENTRAL AV

07430

4   5   6

ATLANTIC OCEAN

NEW YORK CITY

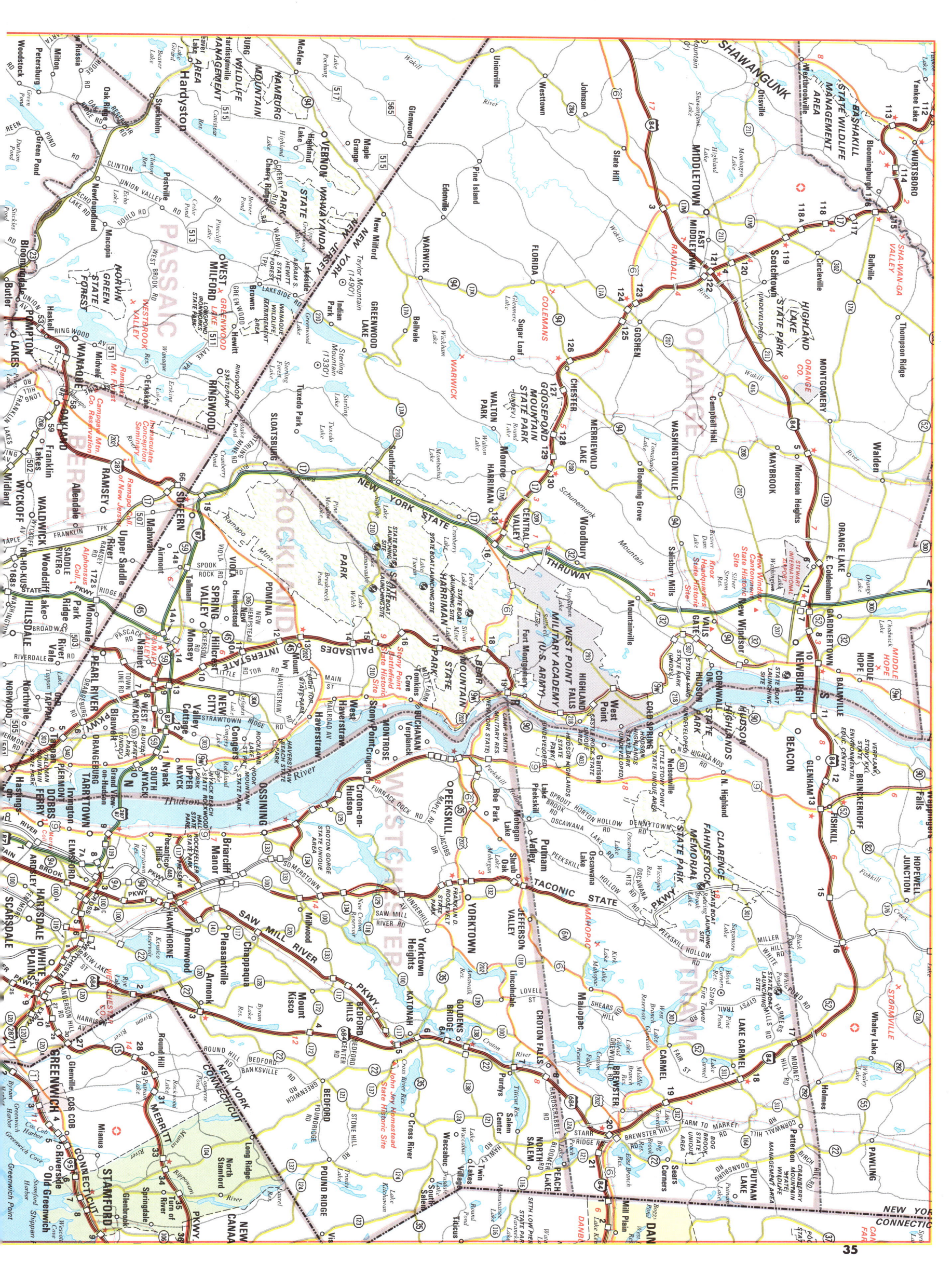

35

1

4 5 6

PASSAIC COUNTY & VICINITY

DELAWARE | GREENE | COLUMBIA | MASS.

NEW YORK

SULLIVAN | ULSTER | DUTCHESS | NEW YORK / CONNECTICUT

PENNSYLVANIA

ORANGE | PUTNAM

NEW YORK / NEW JERSEY

SUSSEX | WESTCHESTER | FAIRFIELD

NEW JERSEY | ROCKLAND

PASSAIC

WARREN | MORRIS | BERGEN

ESSEX | HUDSON | BRONX | SUFFOLK

SOMERSET | UNION | QUEENS | NASSAU

HUNTERDON | RICHMOND | BROOKLYN

PENNSYLVANIA | MIDDLESEX

MERCER | MONMOUTH

BURLINGTON | OCEAN

N

A

B

C

D

CO. CO.

SUSSEX

PASSAIC

COAL RD.

SAW MILL

CHERRY RIDGE

POND

W. MILFORD
07480

WAWAYANDA

STATE PARK

BEARFORT
WATERS

CLINTON RD.

HOLLOW RD.

WAWAYANDA

STATE PARK

BEARFORT

TERRACE POND

UPPER

GREENWOOD

LAKE

MT. LAUREL LAKE

LOOKOVER LAKE

FERBER RD.

GOLDFINCH LA.

BROOKFIELD

BROOKSIDE DR.

LOOKOVER DR.

WARWICK

BROOK RD.

DARETOWN RD.
CLERMONT RD.
BAYHEAD RD.
TRENTON RD.

WARWICK TNPK.

SHORE RD.

COLD SPRING RD.

©GEOGRAPHIA MAP COMPANY, INC.

4 5 6

1

7 8 9 10

N

ORANGE
PASSAIC

CO.
CO.

N.Y.
N.J.

Continued On Map 3

A

B

C

D

MELINDA LA.

WEST POND

SURPRISE LAKE

ABRAM S. HEWITT

STATE FOREST

GREENWOOD

FOX ISLAND

LAKE

JENNINGS

BROOK

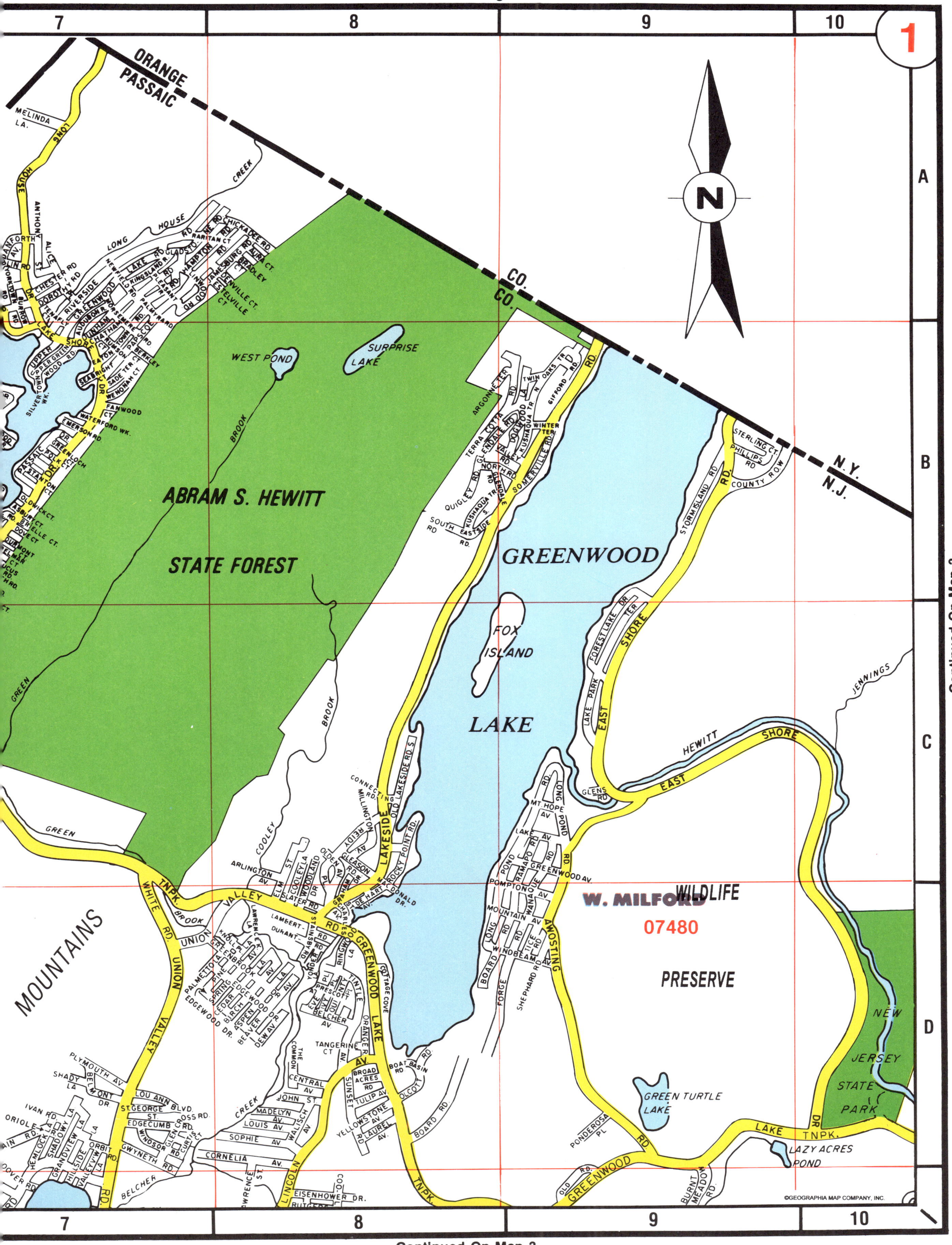

GREEN

MOUNTAINS

LAKESIDE

W. MILFORD
07480

WILDLIFE

PRESERVE

NEW JERSEY STATE PARK

GREEN TURTLE LAKE

LAZY ACRES POND

GREENWOOD LAKE

TNPK.

UNION VALLEY RD.

WHITE RD.

LAKE SHORE DR.

EAST SHORE

HEWITT

EAST SHORE DR.

FORESTLAKE DR.

AWOSTING

7 8 9 10

©GEOGRAPHIA MAP COMPANY, INC.

2

1   2   3

C

D

E

F

G

End Of Coverage

CO.

W. MILFORD

07480

SUSSEX

PASSAIC

CANISTEAR RD

HENDERSON

ELIAS LA.

CRANE LA.

PARADISE

HYDE RD.

PINEHURST RD.

CHIPPEWA TER.

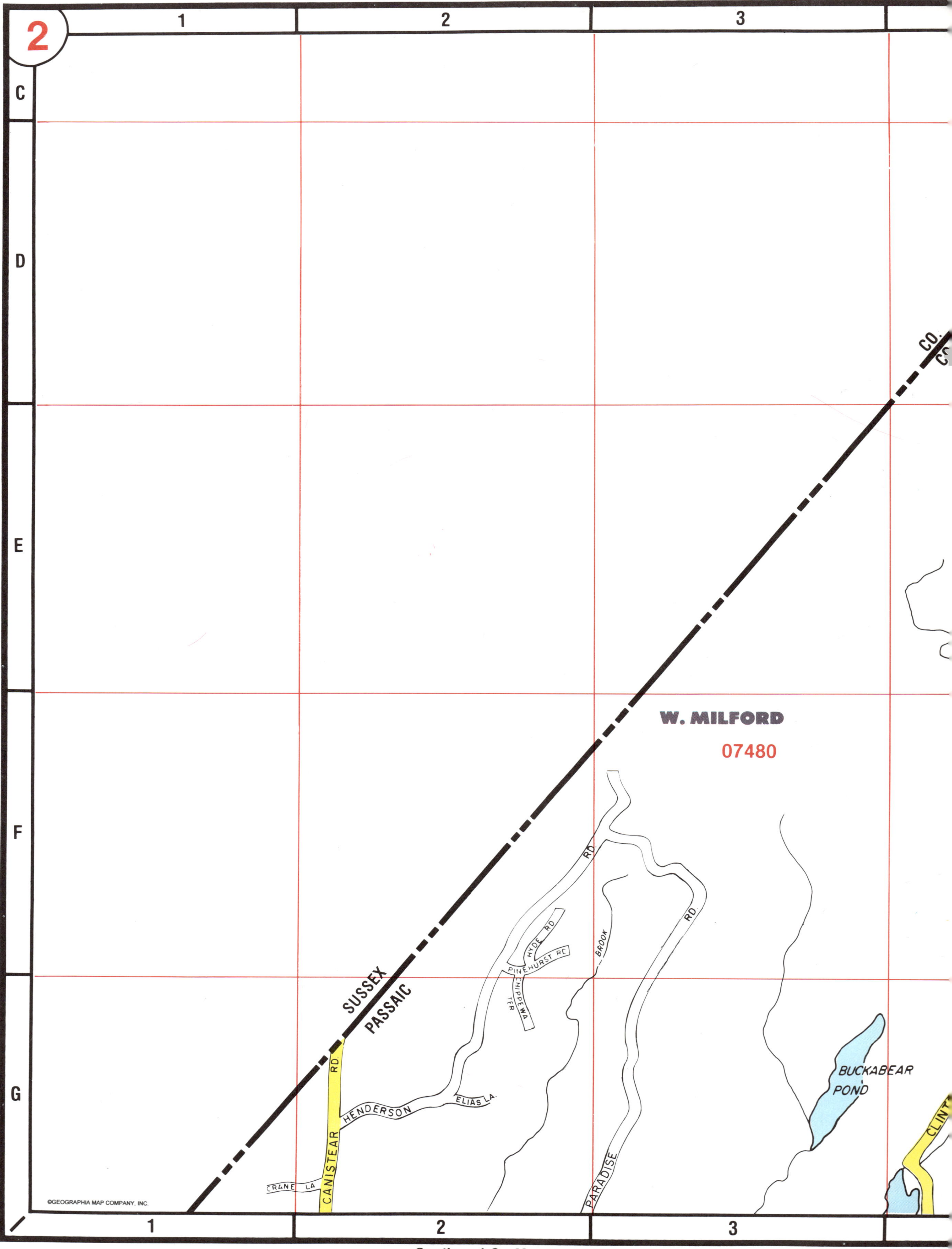

BROOK

RD

RD

BUCKABEAR POND

CLINT

©GEOGRAPHIA MAP COMPANY, INC.

1   2   3

PASSAIC COUNTY

4　5　6　7

Continued On Map 3

C

D

E

F

G

CLINTON VIEW TER.

CUTLASS

CLINTON

BROOK RD.

BROOK LA.

GREEN RD.

BROOK RD.

FERBER RD.

LA. RD.

LOOKOVER LAKE

GOLDFINCH RD.

LOOKOVER DR.

BROOKFIELD

BROOKSIDE DR.

CHERRY RIDGE

POND

COAL RD.

CO. CO.

SAWMILL

BEARFORT WATERS

WAWAYANDA

WAWAYANDA

STATE

STATE

PARK

PARK

HOLLOW RD.

BROOK

CLINTON

MOSSMANS

RD.

STEPHENS

TERRACE POND

MOUNTAINS

CLIFF RD.

TERRACE RD.

NOTCH RD.

ELL RD.

MOUNTAIN

HOOVER

ORI

JAMES RD.

BEARFORT LA.

BEARFORT RD.

PINE

CLIFF

LAKE

PARK

BINNACLE AV.

ANCHOR AV.

CAP'N

STOWAWAY

COMPASS

WILLOW LA.

PROSPECT RD.

BUSHWICK RD.

KEEL RD.

RD.

BROOK

CREEK

RD.

07480

W. MILFORD

VALLEY RD.

FAIRVIEW CT.

WILLS LA.

COLL P

REFLECTION LAKE

PETTET POND

BUNKER HILL RD.

BEACON HILL RD.

BEACON HILL

MANTRES-TER.

LEXINGTON LA.

BLACK WALNUT LA.

BELCHER

SALEM

CONCORD

AL. CONCORD RD.

FOX BORO RD.

PLYMOUTH

QUINCY

BEDFORD RD.

NEW RD.

CEDAR POND

BEARFORT

DOCKERTY

HOLLOW

QUEENS CT.

CAMELOT

KING ARTHUR

LANCELOT CT.

DR.

CARRIAGE

MAC

NEW DOCKERTY

HOLLOW

CONTINENTAL LA.

ORLEANS LA.

FLETCHER

BOURG

RENAULT

DUNKIRK

HUXTER TER.

PINECREST LAKE

ROCKLEDGE RD.

PINE CREST

ELCHARD DR.

RELIANCE LA.

PINECREST TR.

CLINTON

BROOK

UNION VALLEY RD.

CAMDEN RD.

HUNTERDON PL.

DURALEE CT.

ANDREW CT.

MORRIS PL.

MERCER PL.

OLD MILFORD RD.

LANCASTER LA.

LANCASTER LA.

MONMOUTH AV.

WARREN

SUSSEX CT.

MIDDLESEX CT.

ATLANTIC LA.

SOMERSET PL.

SUSSEX DR.

BERGEN

GREEN VALLEY LAKE

MAC GREGOR RD.

DIANE RD.

BRANCH

FREEMAN RD.

BRANCH

EAGLE ROCK

RIDGE

RYAN CT.

RIDGE RD.

VREELAND

WINDING WAY

MACOPIN

BEARFORT

©GEOGRAPHIA MAP COMPANY, INC.

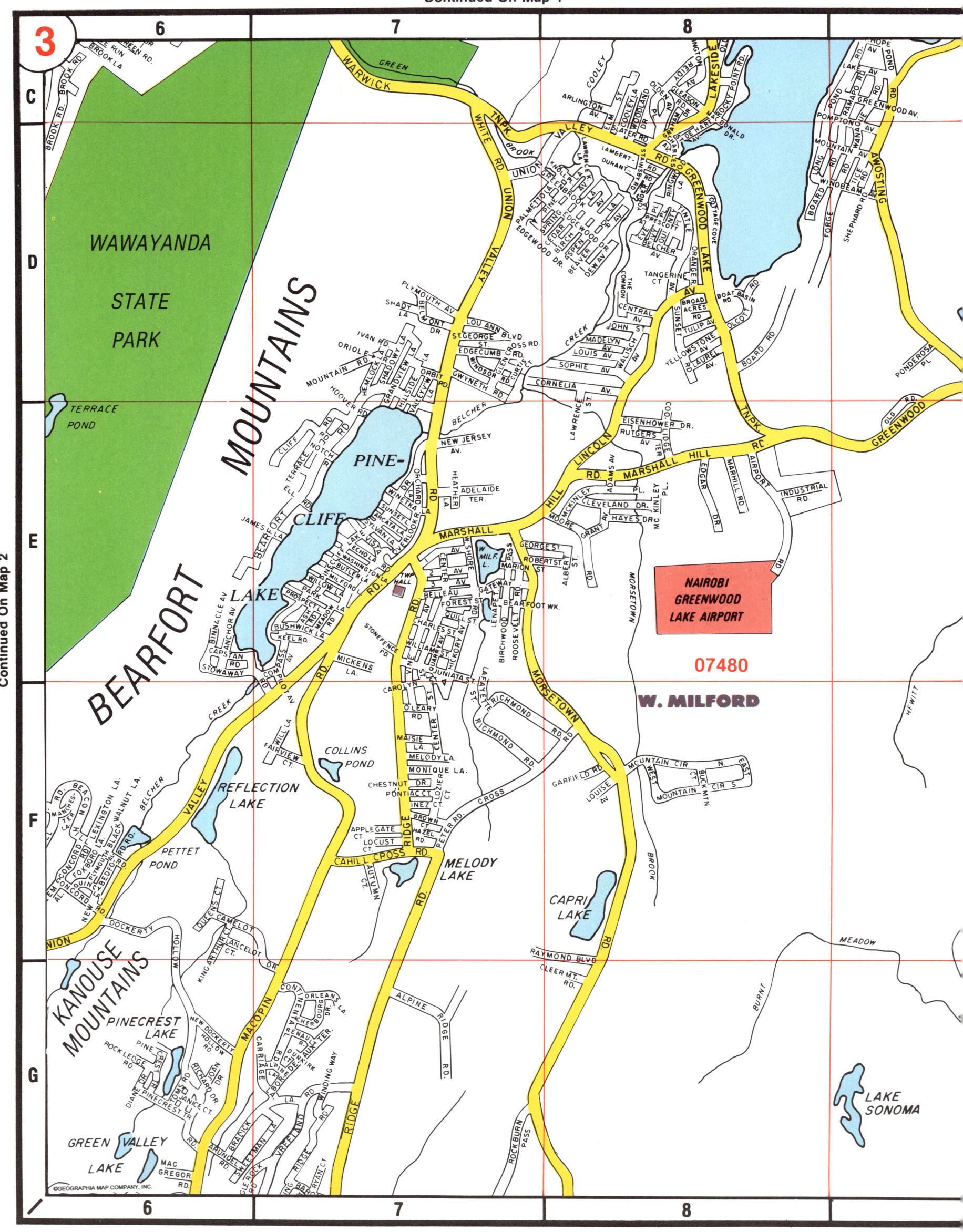

| 9 | 10 | 11 | 12 |

3

PASSAIC COUNTY

WILDLIFE PRESERVE

C

WILDLIFE

PRESERVE

NEW JERSEY

STATE

GREEN TURTLE LAKE

CABLE HOUSE RD.

PETERS

BEECH

D

PARK

RIVER

BEECH

LAKE RD.

BURNT

LAZY ACRES POND

TNPK.

VAN DUNK LA.

4 MINE RD.

CANNON MINE

VAN DUNK DR.

MILLIGAN RD.

FARM RD.

MEADOW

BROOK

GUY LA.

GREENWOOD

MARGARET

INDUSTRIAL PKWY.

PETZOLD AV.

HORSESHOE BEND RD.

AV.

MARGARET

KING AV.

E

LAKE

MINE POND

DARET DR. VAN NATTA DR.

PKWY.

DARET DR.

07456

RD.

RINGWOOD

EXECUTIVE

ELIANOR G. HEWITT SCH.

ORENGO'S LA.

MEADOW

LAKE RICONDA

SUMMIT AV.

RICKERS

WHITE RD.

DARMSTRATER DR.

F

WILLOW LA.

LAKE RICONDA DR.

SKYVIEW RD.

TNPK.

SLOATSBURG

HARRISON MTN. LAKE

HOWARD ST.

ANDERSON

RAY AV.

DAN ST.

WOODSIDE AV.

LAKE SHORE LA.

JOHN ST.

W. SHORE

ART ST.

HARRISON MT. LAKE RD.

MILLER'S LA.

LE BOUN BLVD.

STONETOWN

BURNT

GANZ RD.

G

BROOK

RD.

BURNT

MEADOW

CHERIE LA.

RESS RD.

SEMINOLE DR.

ALGON

IROQUOIS TRAIL

ARROWHEAD

TOMAHAWK PATH

WANAQUE

RESERVOIR

©GEOGRAPHIA MAP COMPANY, INC.

| 9 | 10 | 11 | 12 |

Continued On Map 4

4

12 13 14

C

ORANGE
PASSAIC

CO.
CO.

ORANGE
ROCKLAND

D

RINGWOOD

STATE PARK

CABLE HOUSE RD.
PETER'S

BROOK RD

N.Y.
N.J.

SHEPHERD POND RD

POTAKE POND

MANOR HOUSE

FURNACE

SLOATSBURG

MANOR RINGWOOD RD

BROOK

SHEPPARD POND

VAN DUNK LA.
MILLIGAN DR.
N DUNK LA.
CANNON MINE RD.
MINE RD

DAM POND

CONVENT

FARM RD

MANSION RD

POTAKE POND

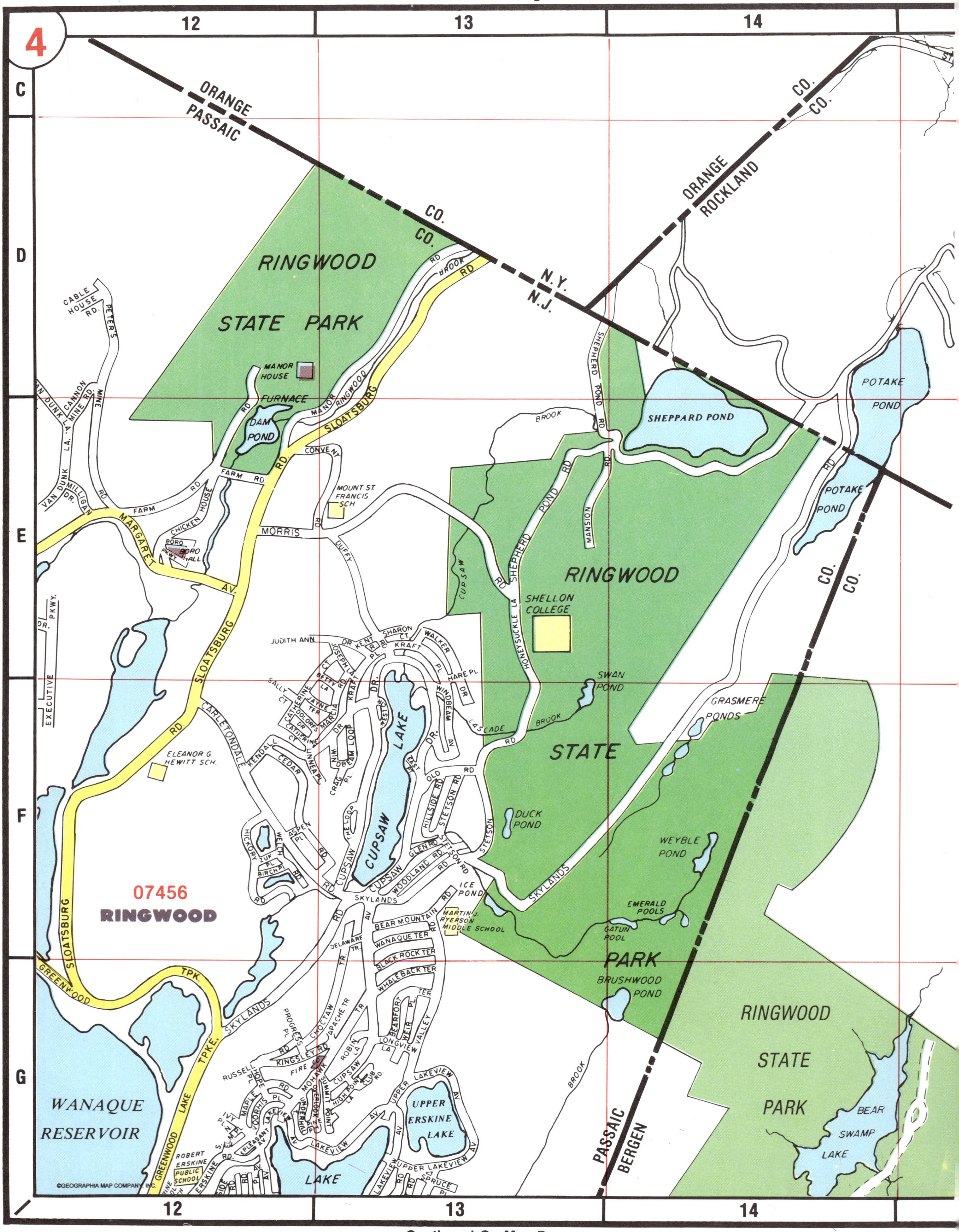

Continued On Map 3

E

MARGARET

SLOATSBURG

FARM RD

CHICKEN HOUSE RD

BORO BORO HALL

MORRIS

DUFFY

MOUNT ST FRANCIS SCH

SHEPHERD RD

CUPSAW RD

SHELLON COLLEGE

RINGWOOD

CO.
CO.

EXECUTIVE DR. PKWY.

AV.

CARLETONDALE RD

JUDITH ANN DR

JOSEPHA

KENT DR

SHARON CT
KRAFT

WALKER PL

HARE PL

WINDBEAM

HONEYSUCKLE LA

SWAN POND

GRASMERE PONDS

ELEANOR G HEWITT SCH.

SALLY
BETTY LA
CATHERINE TER
MARCIA
JAYNE TER
NICODEMUS CT
CATHERINE CT
KRAFT
LINDA
WEST

MARCIA

CRAIG PL
DREAM LOOP

KENDAL CT
CEDAR

CUPSAW LAKE

OLD

CASCADE

RD

BROOK

STATE

DUCK POND

WEYBLE POND

F

SLOATSBURG RD

HICKORY
ASPEN
TUK PL
WELTH PL
BIRCH PL

THE LOOP

CUPSAW RD

CUPSAW LAKE

GLENROY
WOODLANE
HILLSIDE RD
STETSON RD
STETSON
STEFSON RD

OLD

RD

SKYLANDS

ICE POND

EMERALD POOLS

GATUN POOL

07456
RINGWOOD

SKYLANDS

MARTIN J. RYERSON MIDDLE SCHOOL

BEAR MOUNTAIN

DELAWARE TR
WANAQUE TER

BLACK ROCK TER

WHALEBACK TER

SKYLANDS

PARK

BRUSHWOOD POND

RINGWOOD STATE PARK

G

GREENWOOD LAKE TPK.

TPKE.
SKYLANDS

PROGRESS PL
RD
KINGSLEY RD
RUSSELL
HOPE
IVY
MAPLE
PLEASANT
CODRUS PL
CHOCTAW
JAPACHE TR
MOHAWK
FIRE
ROBIN
CUPSAW
SUMMIT
OVERLOOK
LIGHT
UNDERHILL
SEARFOSS
LONGVIEW

VALLEY

BEAR

UPPER ERSKINE LAKE

PASSAIC
BERGEN

RINGWOOD STATE PARK

BEAR SWAMP LAKE

WANAQUE RESERVOIR

GREENWOOD LAKE

ERSKINE

ROBERT ERSKINE PUBLIC SCHOOL

LAKESIDE
IVY
SPRUCE PL

LAKE

UPPER LAKEVIEW AV
LAKEVIEW RD

UPPER LAKEVIEW AV

BROOK

©GEOGRAPHIA MAP COMPANY INC

12 13 14

Continued On Map 7

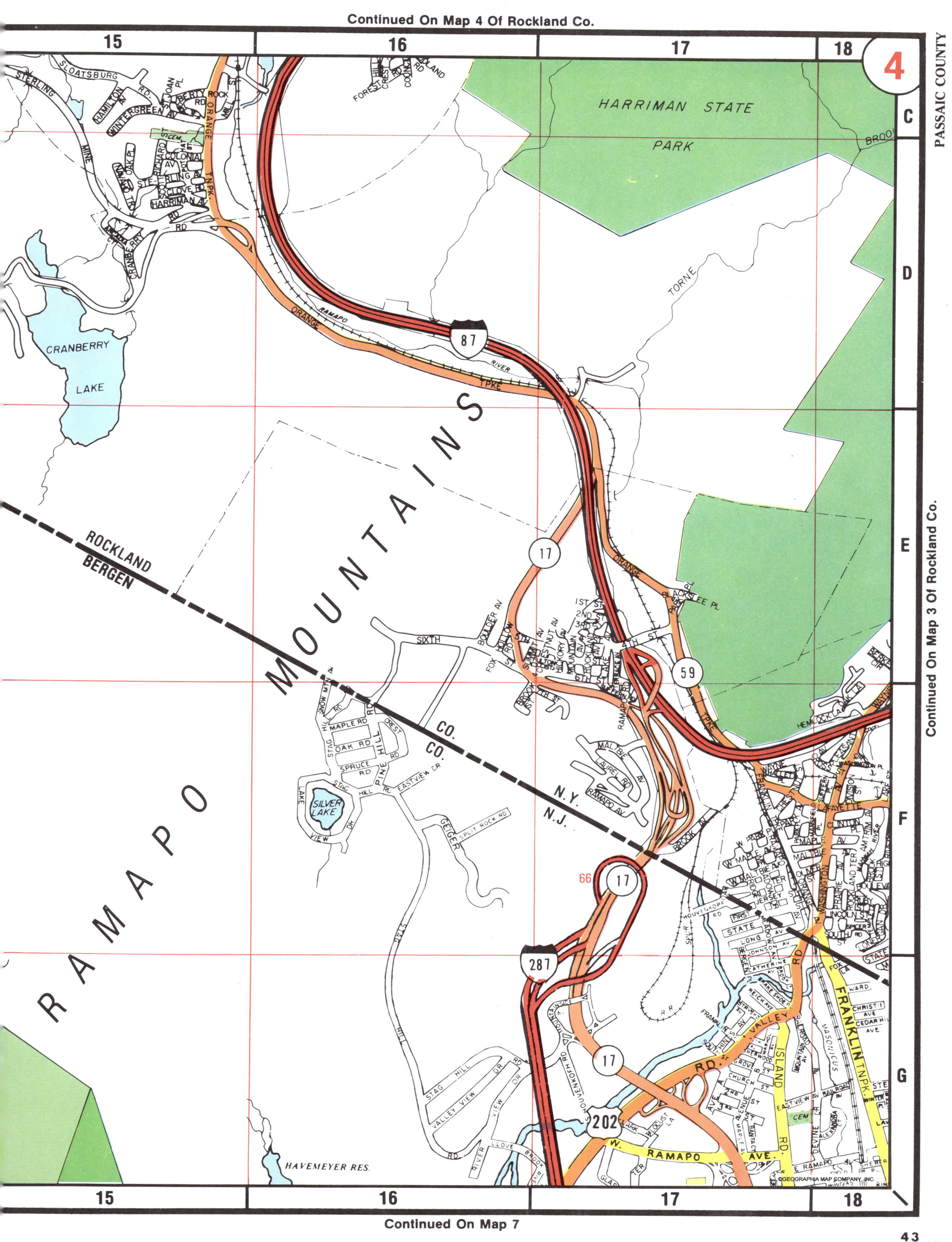

Continued On Map 3 Of Rockland Co.

HARRIMAN STATE
PARK

R A M A P O   M O U N T A I N S

CRANBERRY
LAKE

ROCKLAND
BERGEN

CO.
CO.

N.Y.
N.J.

SILVER
LAKE

HAVEMEYER RES.

FRANKLIN TPKE.

©GEOGRAPHIA MAP COMPANY, INC.

5

1   2   3

G

BUCKABEAR POND

CO. CO.

HYDE RD.
PINEHURST RD
CHIPPEWA TER
BROOK
RD

HENDERSON
ELIAS LA.

CLINTON

CRANE LA

DUNKER

PARADISE

RD

SUSSEX
PASSAIC

H

POND
DUNKERS

PARADISE

CLINTON

RESERVOIR

DUNKER POND

DUNKER

CANISTEAR

BROOK

OLD ROUTE 23

PEQUANNOCK

STICKLE RD

RD

SCHOOL HOUSE COVE RD

23

07480

RD

VAN

W. MILFORD

River

J

DUNKER

GREENDALE
CREST

SANDLOR DR
CREST LAKE

RD

GREENCREST HILL DR
GREENCALE DR

CLINTON

RD

HOPLER PL
LONGSTREAK
SUGAR

LAND OF OAKS

RD

MEADOWVIEW
POST

OLD HOOP POLE RD

DOREMUS

WOODRIDGE DR

ULYSSESS LA

BONTER

NEWLAND DR
FREMONT TER

RD

NEILSON

DAN JENNINGS RD.

LINDSAY RD

OAK RIDGE

NYS & W

ALLISON
PL

COMMUNITY

CIRCLE BLVD WEST

COVENTRY RD

RICKER MARK TER

RD

K

GREENWOOD
POND

FAIRY TALE
FOREST

DANIEL ST

AV

FAIR PL

CIRCLE BLVD
EAST
SOUTH

LARUE

CROSS

EAST

WESTBROUND

RESERVOIR

WALLACE
POND

JEFFERSON ST
WILSON ST
GROVE
HARRISON ST
PAUL ST
SPRUCE ST
WALNUT ST

COZY LAKE RD
PARADISE

RD

WESTBOUND

PIERCE AV
WILFRED
LA

APPLE TREE LA

NORMAN AV

RD

RD

COOPER

OAK

GOLD
SILVER LA

CIRCLE
OAK

DR

RIVERVIEW RD

SCENIC DR.

WALLACE CROSS RD

RD

OAK RIDGE

RR

COZY LAKE RD

RR

PEQUANNOCK

© GEOGRAPHIA MAP COMPANY, INC.

End Of Coverage

1   2   3

44

4 5 6 7 **5**

G

H

J

K

CEDAR POND

CLINTON RD.

CLINTON

UNION RD.

CAMDEN RD.

B E A R F O R T

M O U N T A I N S

M O U N T A I N

PINECREST LAKE

GREEN VALLEY LAKE

MAC GREGOR RD.

ROCKLEDGE RD.

PINE CREST

BUBBLING SPRING LAKE

VREELAND

MACOPIN

RIDGE

RIVER

HANKS POND

GOULD VALLEY RD.

WOLLEY RD.

OXBOW LA.

BROOK

WEST BUDDINGSTONE LA.

TIMBER LA.

EAST

K A N O U S E

MACOPIN

GOULD RD.

BISSET DR.

LESLIE DR.

ROGER DR.

RELDA AV.

CRAWFORD ST.

GLENDA DR.

WESLEY DR.

ALVIN DR.

EVELYN DR.

WEEDON DR.

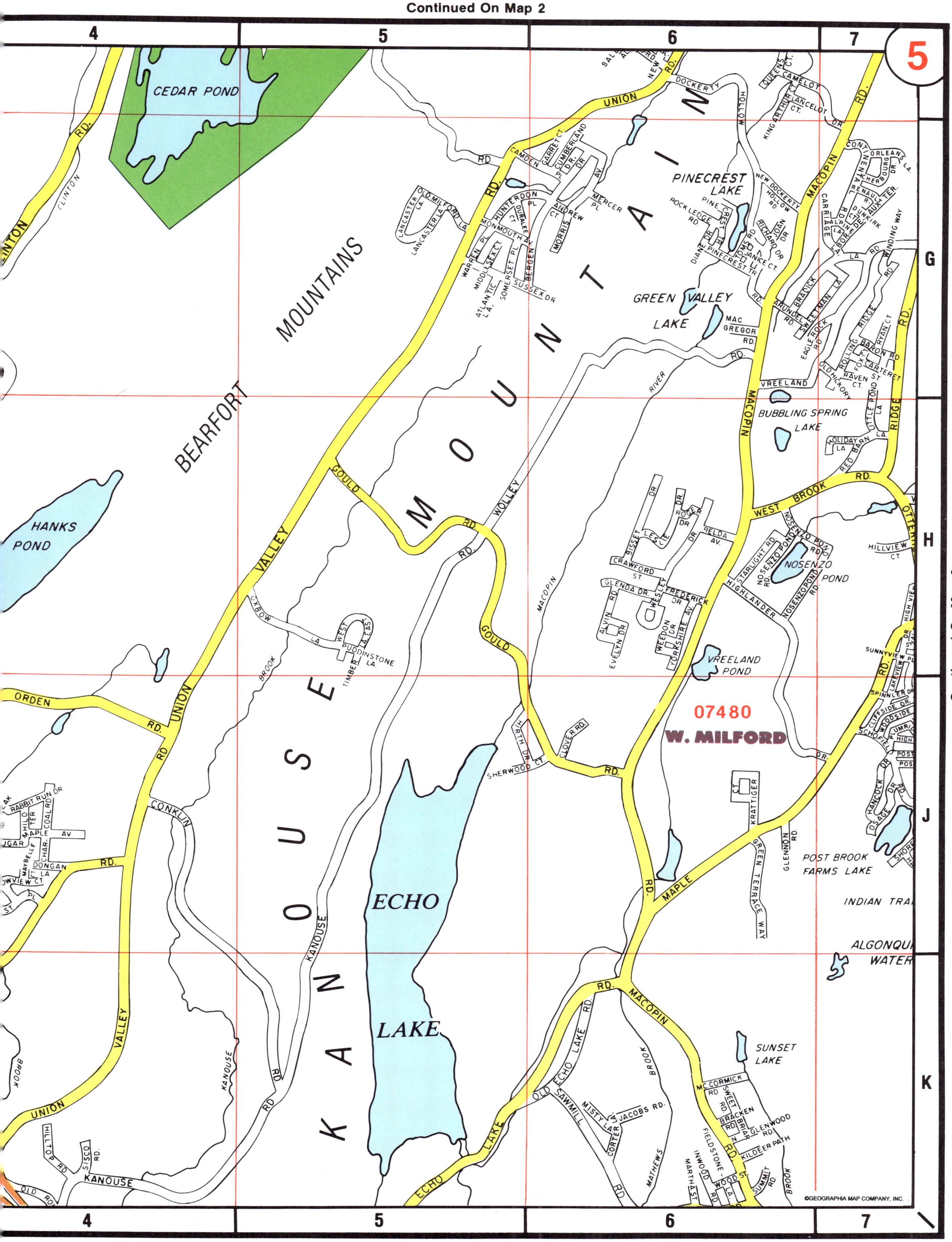

FORSHIRE AV.

FREDERICK

HIGHLANDER

STARLIGHT RD.

NOSENZO RD.

NOSENZO POND

HILLVIEW CT.

VREELAND POND

ORDEN RD.

UNION RD.

RABBIT RUN DR.

COAL RD.

MAPLE AV.

CHAR. DONGAN LA.

MAYBELLE

CONKLIN RD.

07480
W. MILFORD

HRTH DR. CT.

CLOVER RD.

SHERWOOD

SUNNYVIEW

SPINNER DR.

CLIFFSIDE DR.

WOODSIDE

KRATTIGER CT.

OSAGE

HANCOCK DR.

POST BROOK FARMS LAKE

INDIAN TRA

ALGONQUI WATER

KANOUSE RD.

ECHO LAKE

GREEN TERRACE WAY

GLENNON RD.

MAPLE RD.

MACOPIN RD.

SUNSET LAKE

UNION VALLEY RD.

HILLTOP RD.

SISCO RD.

OLD RD.

KANOUSE

ECHO LAKE RD.

OLD SAWMILL RD.

ECHO LAKE RD.

MISTY LA.

CORTER

JACOBS RD.

MATHEWS

BROOK

MCCORMICK

SWEET

BRACKEN

GLENWOOD RD.

FIELDSTONE

KILDEER PATH

INWOOD

MARTHA ST.

SUMMIT

WOOD ST.

LANCASTER PL.

OLD MILFORD LA.

LANCASTER LA.

WARREN PL.

MONMOUTH CT.

DURALEE

HUNTERDON CT.

MIDDLESEX CT.

ATLANTIC LA.

SOMERSET PL.

SUSSEX DR.

BERGEN

ANDREW PL.

MORRIS PL.

MERCER PL.

MONMOUTH AV.

DOCKERTY

HOLLOW

NEW DOCKERTY HOLLOW RD.

QUEENS CT.

CAMELOT CT.

KING ARTHUR LANCELOT CT.

RICHARD DR.

DIANE

CONTINENTAL

ORLEANS LA.

BOURG

RENAULT

DUNMARK

CARRIAGE

ARUNDEL

BRANICK

SWEETMAN

EAGLE ROCK

RIDGE

RYAN CT.

BARON RD.

CARTERET ST.

RAVEN CT.

OLD HICKORY

RED BARN LA.

HOLIDAY LA.

WEST BROOK RD.

OTTER

HILLVIEW CT.

MCCORMICK

©GEOGRAPHIA MAP COMPANY, INC.

6

Continued On Map 5

G

H

J

K

6 7 8

CAPRI LAKE

MEADOW

LAKE SONOMA

RAYMOND BLVD.

CLEER MT. RD.

BURNT

PINECREST LAKE

MACOPIN

RD.

ALPINE RIDGE RD.

ROCKBURN PASS

RHINESMITH RD.

KITCHELL LAKE

KITCHELL LAKE DR. W.

KITCHELL LAKE DR. E.

SKYVIEW RD.

MORSETOWN RD.

STONE-HEDGE WAY

GREEN VALLEY LAKE

MACGREGOR RD.

WOLLEY RD.

RIVER

MACOPIN

RIDGE RD.

VREELAND

BUBBLING SPRING LAKE

RED BARN LA.

HOLIDAY LA.

LITTLE POND LA.

WEST BROOK RD.

WEST BROOK

WEST BROOK

ROCKBURN

LAUREL HOLLOW

MARISA CT.

DEERBROOK LA.

WEST

DEBORAH LA.

WEST BROOK

BROOK

RD. WEST

SNAKE DEN

WEST BROOK RD.

HILLVIEW CT.

PONDVIEW DR.

OTTERHOLE

NOSENZO POND

NOSENZO POND RD.

STARLIGHT RD.

HIGHLANDER

CRAWFORD ST.

GLENDA DR.

FREDERICK AV.

WESLEY

WEEDON DR.

YORKSHIRE DR.

EVELYN DR.

VREELAND POND

HIGH VIEW AV.

SUNNYVIEW PL.

LINDY LAKE

LINDY'S PATH

ESSEX ST.

HUDSON

BROADWAY

CLARA ST.

LOGAN AV.

DUDLEY ST.

LOWER MOUNTAIN GLEN LAKE 07480

BOY SCOUT LAKE

W. MILFORD

UPPER MT. GLEN LAKE DR.

JOSEPH PL.

MARY ST.

VIKING RD.

ROSEMONT AV.

GILBERT

SPINNLER DR.

CLIFFSIDE DR.

WOODSIDE

SCHOFIEL DR.

BUCHANAN

LINDY'S DR.

BROADWAY

SANDERS ST.

POST BROOK RD. N.

POST BROOK RD. S.

UPPER LAKE

LARSEN RD.

OTTERHOLE RD.

GOULD RD.

KRATTIGER CT.

HANCOCK DR.

GLENNON RD.

GREEN TERRACE WAY

POST BROOK FARMS LAKE

OSAGE

SHORE

SENECA RD.

BALDWIN DR.

BRIARCLIFF DR.

BALDWIN DR.

INDIAN TRAIL LAKE

HIGHTOP

LAKE ISLE DR.

ULSTER ST.

PLEASANTVIEW ST.

ALGONQUIN WATERS

MAPLE RD.

ALGONQUIN WAY

STANLEY ST.

NEWTON

TEETER WAY

MIDWAY

MOHICAN TR.

WOODCREST ST.

BURLINGTON DR.

STONY LA.

PARK

LACKAWANNA TR.

PENMORE RD.

GRINDLE DR.

GORDON LAKES

NORVIN GREEN STATE

SUNSET LAKE

MCCORMICK RD.

SWEET BRIAR RD.

BRACKEN BR.

GLENWOOD RD.

KILDEER PATH

FIELDSTONE RD.

JACOBS RD.

SAWMILL RD.

SUMMIT RD.

MATTHEWS

INWOOD

MARTHA ST.

WOOD ST.

PORTER LA.

MACOPIN

BROOK

ARROWHEAD DOCK RD.

INDIAN DOCK RD.

CLUBHOUSE

DEER PATH

PHEASANT

POPLAR GROVE

ROBIN LA.

CHIPPY LA.

SHADY LAKE

POPLAR GROVE ST.

WILDWOOD ST.

ALLEGHENY

SUNRISE ST.

EVANS LA.

MATTHEWS LAKE

CRABTREE RD.

WEAVER RD.

OTTERHOLE RD.

©GEOGRAPHIA MAP COMPANY, INC.

46

9   10   11   12   **6**

PASSAIC COUNTY

HARRISON MTN. LAKE

DARNSTATTER RD.

WHITE RD.

SKYVIEW RD.

RINGWOOD

07456

HOWARD ST
W. SHORE RD.
TRAY AV.
ANDERSON
DAM ST.
WOODSIDE
JOHN ST.
ART ST.
HARRISON MT. LAKE RD.
LE BOUN BLVD

BROOK RD.
BURNT
MILLER'S
LA.
GANZ RD.
STONETOWN RD.
MEADOW
CHERIE LA.
RESS RD.
COLFAX DR.
IROQUOIS TRAIL
SEMINOLE
ALGONQUIN TER.
MOHICAN CT.
WINDBEAM LA.
SIOUX LA.
RD.
ARROWHEAD TR.
TOMAHAWK PATH

WANAQUE

RESERVOIR

GREENWOOD LAKE
SLOATSBURG RD.
TNPK.

G

can't get thru

★
Parking for Lake Sonoma Trail

MEADOW RD.
BURNT

LITTLE BIG HORN
CUSTER DR.
CHEYENNE WAY
WOOD TER. RD.
STONETOWN RD.
YUMA LA.

SWAMP
PAGAN TRAIL
PIMA CT.
PINEWOOD
BROOK
MAGEE

WEST BROOK

STEPHEN'S PONDS

ST.
DALE
TULIP AV.
AZALEA CT.
SHADY LA.
ELLEN ST.
SNAKE DEN
DEN ST.
ROAD WAY
TOWNSEND
W BROOK
WEST BROOK RD.
HANNAH LA.
RESERVOIR DR.
LILY
MOUNTAIN RD.
RED MINE RD.
HILLSIDE RD.

SKYLINE DR.
TPKE. SKYLINE
DEER TRAIL
KNOLLWOOD DR.
ST. CATHERINE R.C. SCHOOL & CHURCH
ALTA VISTA DR.
BUENA VISTA DR.
FORSGATE
HIGH
WILLOW
OAKWOOD DR.
BIRCH

H

GREENWOOD LAKE
HIDDEN VALLEY LAKE
BUENA VISTA
SMOKEY RIDGE RD.
FOREST
SKYLINE LAKES
LAKEVIEW
BIRCH
PALMER
DOGWOOD
FOUNTAIN
HILLTOP

J

HIDDEN VALLEY LAKE
GREENWOOD AV.
SKYLINE LA.
ARCATA
BEATTIE LA.
OAK LA.
EDGEWOOD
SYLVAN
SKYLINE
RICHARD CT.
MANNING
FOUNTAIN SPRING LAKE
ROGER CT.
OLD CONKLINTOWN RD.
FERN PL.

BLOOMINGDALE

07403

FOREST

BROOK

WANAQUE

RESERVOIR

MIDVALE DAM

GARBARINO
OAKER AV.
BELVEDERE AV.
MCKINNON
GARDEN ST.
MEADOW LA
CANTERBURY
GRAHAM
CLINFORD RD.
WILSON DR.
GARY
HELD TER.

K

STEPHENS LAKE

07465

WANAQUE

ANN ST.
HARRIET ST.
MIDVALE
WAR VETERANS
CONKLINTOWN RD.
SHERMAN
CHESTNUT
WILLOW WAY
EAST SIDE
BEAM AV.
BROOK
CEMETERY RD.
RINGWOOD AV.
GISMO
MILL RD.
CRESCENT
ELINORA
NORTHGATE
PREMONT
LORTTE TER.
FOXDEN
RONONDA PL.
LINDA RD.
EDGEWOOD CT.
HUMBERT
STEPHENS LA.
KER RD.
WOODSIDE

DEBOW AV.
GEORGE AV.
NEW ST.
N. GROVE
SHORT BROOK
FEN
ALDRIN
SCRIVAN DR.
KURUC DR.
MOLINARI DR.

MILL ST.
STEPHENS AV.
FURNACE
PROSPECT ST.
PELLINGTON ST.
MELROSE ST.
BELMONT
BELMONT
ERIE AV.
RAILROAD AV.
GROVE
COLFAX AV.
MORNINGSIDE PL.
DENA DR.
LINESA
MULLEN
HILLSIDE AV.
CROSS ST.
SMITH
RHINESMITH
CROSS

WANAQUE

RESERVOIR

©GEOGRAPHIA MAP COMPANY, INC.

9   10   11   12

Continued On Map 7

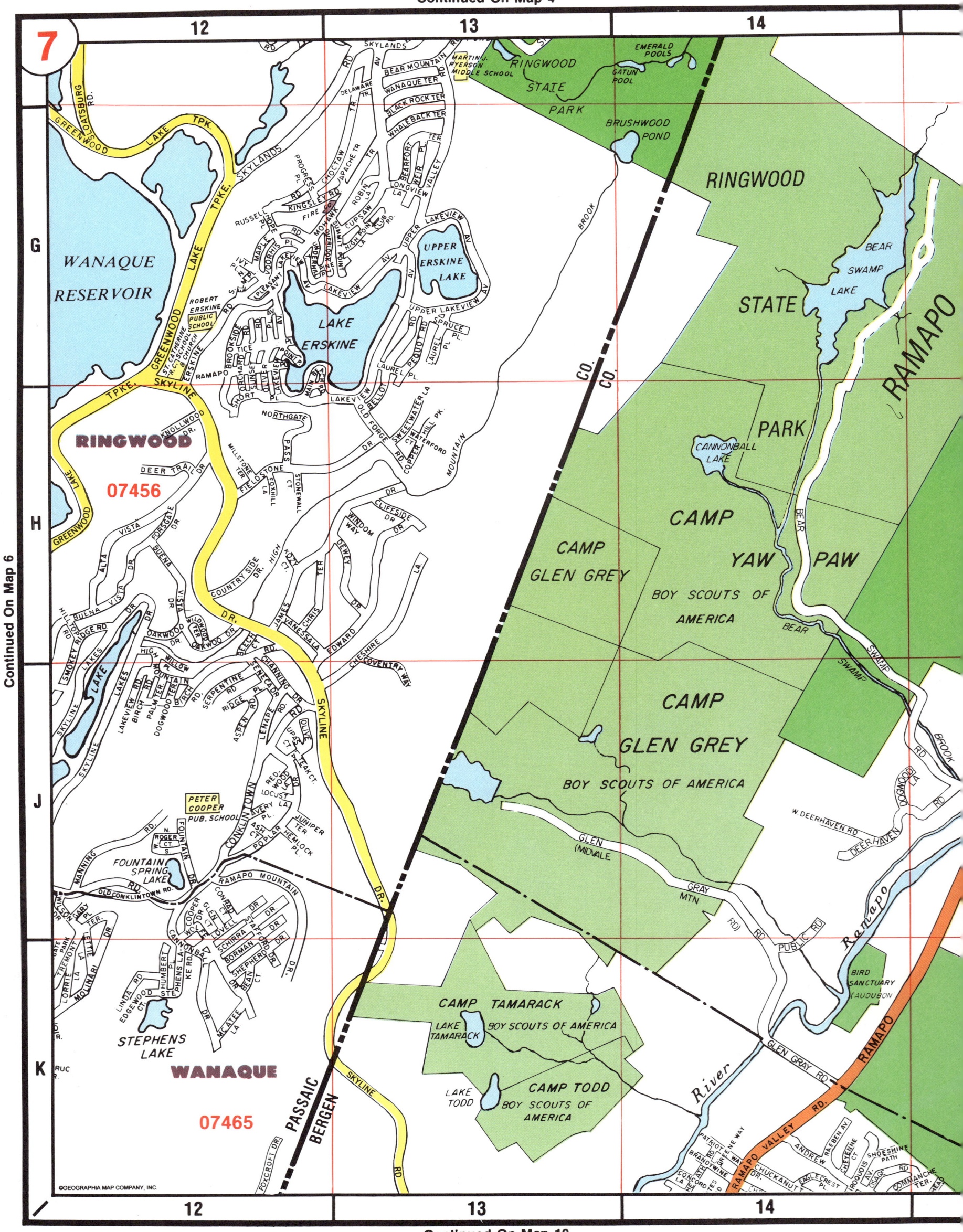

7

12 13 14

Continued On Map 6

G

WANAQUE
RESERVOIR

RINGWOOD

07456

H

J

PETER
COOPER
PUB. SCHOOL

FOUNTAIN
SPRING
LAKE

STEPHENS
LAKE

K

WANAQUE

07465

RINGWOOD
STATE
PARK

EMERALD
POOLS

GATUN
POOL

BRUSHWOOD
POND

RINGWOOD

STATE

BEAR
SWAMP
LAKE

PARK

CANNONBALL
LAKE

CAMP

CAMP
GLEN GREY

YAW PAW

BOY SCOUTS OF
AMERICA

CAMP

GLEN GREY

BOY SCOUTS OF AMERICA

GLEN
(MIDVALE)

GRAY
MTN

W. DEERHAVEN RD.

BIRD
SANCTUARY
(AUDUBON)

CAMP TAMARACK

LAKE
TAMARACK

BOY SCOUTS OF
AMERICA

CAMP TODD

LAKE
TODD

BOY SCOUTS OF
AMERICA

RAMAPO

River

Ramapo

GLEN GRAY RD.

12 13 14

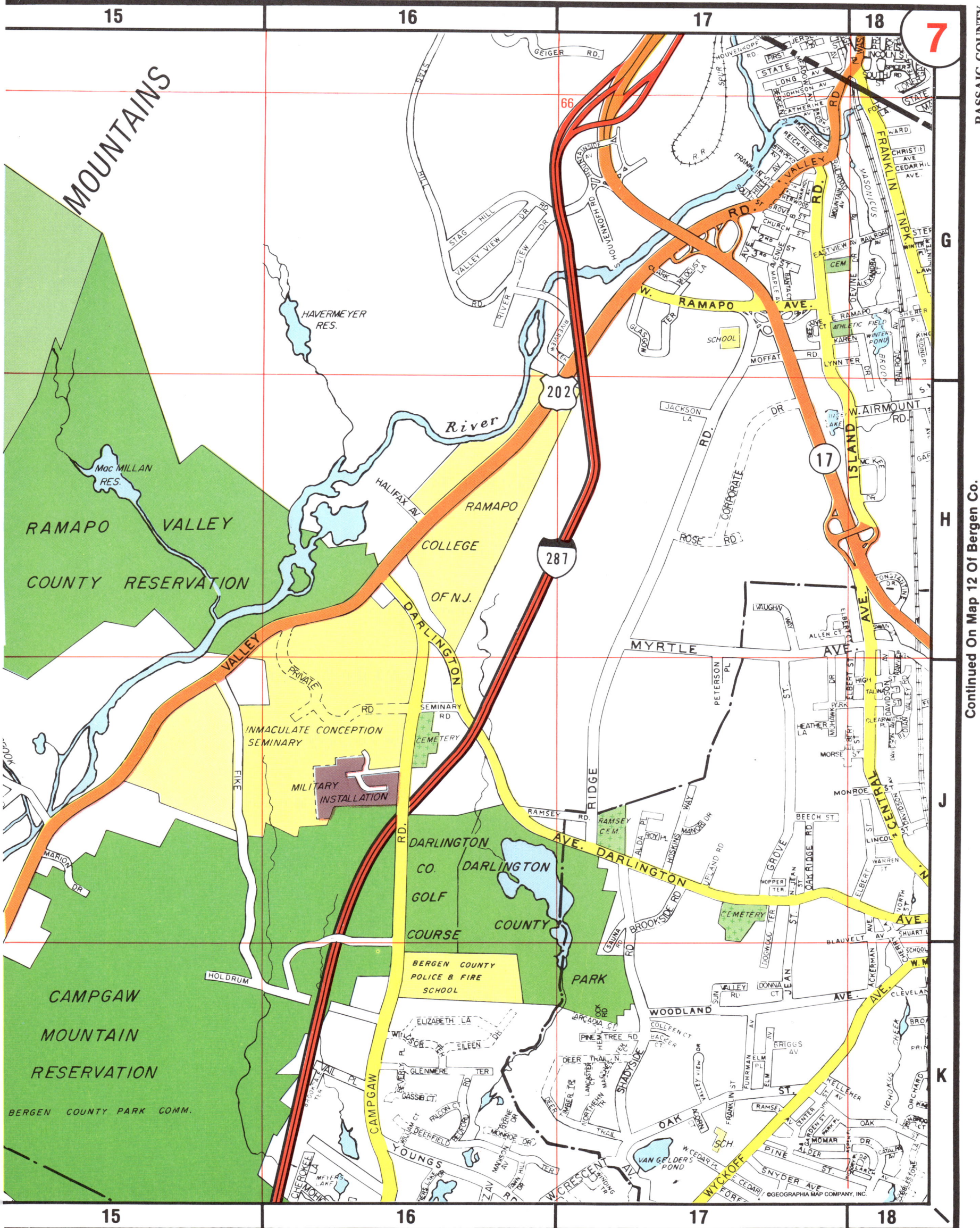

MOUNTAINS

HAVERMEYER RES.

MacMILLAN RES.

RAMAPO VALLEY

COUNTY RESERVATION

River

RAMAPO

COLLEGE

OF N.J.

IMMACULATE CONCEPTION SEMINARY

MILITARY INSTALLATION

DARLINGTON

CO.

GOLF

COURSE

DARLINGTON

COUNTY

PARK

BERGEN COUNTY
POLICE & FIRE
SCHOOL

CAMPGAW

MOUNTAIN

RESERVATION

BERGEN COUNTY PARK COMM.

©GEOGRAPHIA MAP COMPANY, INC.

Continued On Map 5

8
1
2
3
K
L
M
N
OAK RIDGE
RESERVOIR
GREENWOOD
POND
WALLACE
POND
07480
W. MILFORD
FAIRY TALE
FOREST
APPLE TREE
LA
DAN JENNINGS RD
NYS & W
RD.
COOPER
PIERCE AV
WILFRED LA
RD
OAK DR
GOLD DR
SILVER LA
CIRCLE
RESERVOIR
OAK
RIDGE
NORMAN AV.
WALLACE CROSS RD
SCENIC DR.
RIVERVIEW RD
GREEN LA
CARO DR
ALBERTINE PL
DAVENPORT RD
RR
PEQUANNOCK
PASSAIC
MORRIS
LINDSAY RD
RD.
DANIEL ST
JEFFERSON ST
WALNUT ST
ST
GROVE
WILSON AV
HARRISON ST
PAUL ST
SPRUCE ST
PARADISE
COZY LAKE RD.
ALLISON
COMMUNITY PL
AV
FAIR PL
CIRCLE BLVD WEST
EAST
SOUTH
RICKER
CLINTON RD
COVENTRY RD.
MARK TER
LARUE RD.
CROSS RD
EASTBOUND
WESTBOUND
BROOK
RIVE
1
2
3
©GEOGRAPHIA MAP COMPANY, INC.

End Of Coverage

End Of Coverage

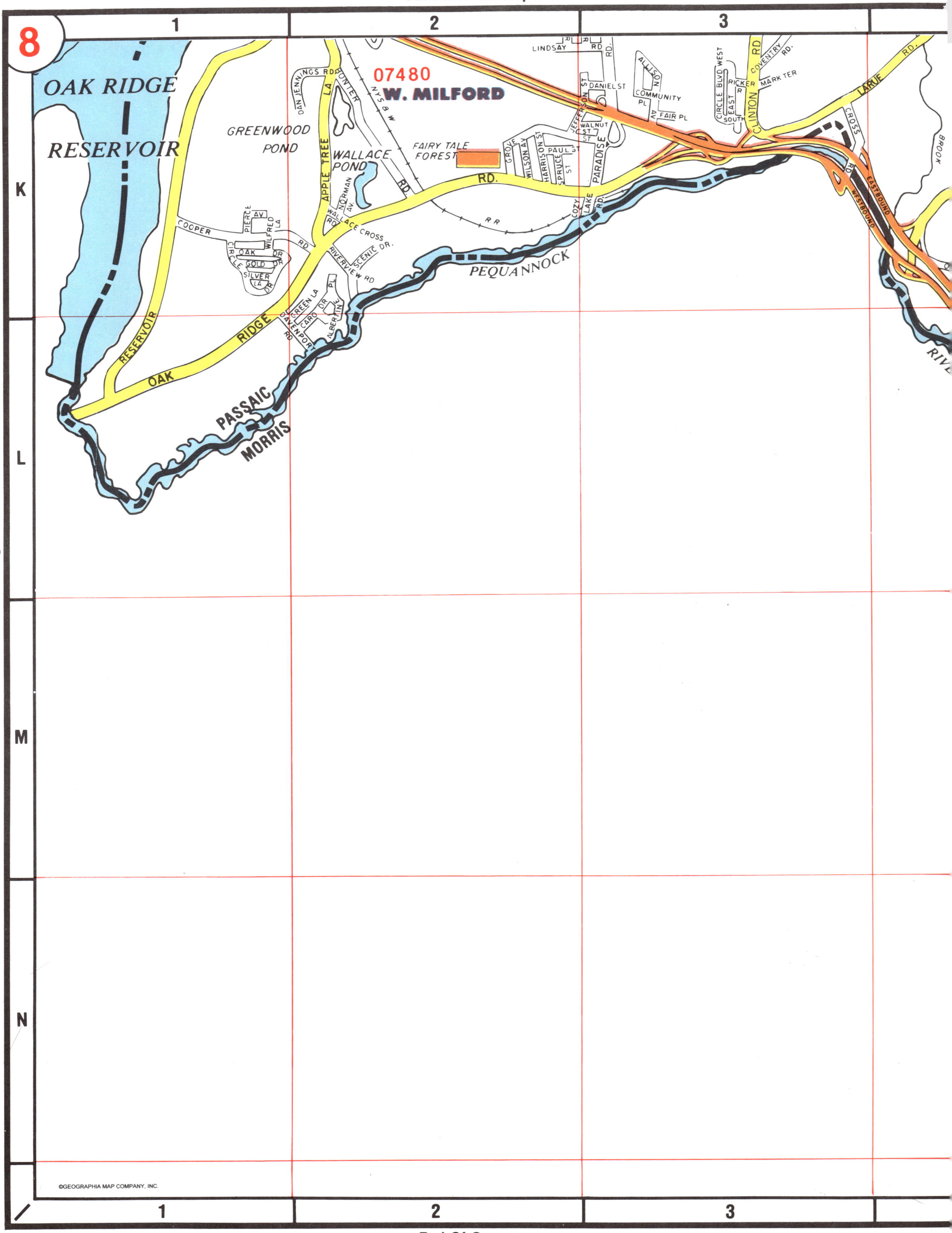

4   5   6   7   **8**

ECHO LAKE

SUNSET LAKE

UNION VALLEY RD.

CONKLIN RD.

KANOUSE

HILLTOP RD.

SISCO RD.

KANOUSE

OLD ROUTE 23

OLD ECHO LAKE RD.

OLD SAWMILL RD.

MACOPIN RD.

MISTY LA.

CORTER LA.

JACOBS RD.

MATHEWS

BROOK

McCORMICK RD.

SWEET BRIAR

BRACKEN

GLENWOOD RD.

KILDEER PATH

FIELDSTONE

INWOOD

MART. EAST

SUMMIT

WOOD ST.

WOOD LA.

BROOK

K

GERMANTOWN RD.

GENADERSO POND

WEAVER RD.

VAN

FOUNTAIN RD.

FOX TR.

WOODCOCK RD.

INDIAN

MTN. SPRINGS LAKE

LOOKOUT LA.

MOUNTAIN TR.

SPRING

ROCK SPRING TR.

N. SHORE TR.

TEAL RD.

FRONTIER TR.

CATALPA DR.

QUINCE TREE

PEACH TREE LA.

VAN NOS

W. MILFORD

07480

ECHO

LAKE

BLAKELEY LA.

RIVER

MACOPIN

HIRD LAKE

VAN NOSTRAND LA.

L

CHARLOTTEBURG

RESERVOIR

NYS & W RR

CHARLOTTESBURG RD.

TIMBERBROOK RD.

OLD ROUTE 23

23

CO. CO.

MAYFLOWER AV.

OAKWOOD

HOLLIS TER.

PECAN AV.

NELSON AV.

WALKER AV.

HIGHLAND AV.

HUNTER AV.

CYPRESS PL.

BLVD.

WONDER L.

RIDGEWOOD DR.

APSHAWA

BUTLER RESERVOIR

APSHAWA

FOREST HILL LAKE

SEMINOLE WAY

NAVAJO

MOHAWK TR.

CHEROKEE WAY

HIAWATHA

TR.

PASS

BROOK

COUNTY

HIGH CREST

CREST

HIGH

MALLORY RD.

MEETER

UPPER

HIGH CREST DR.

HIGH CREST RD.

M

JOHNS LAKE

MACOPIN RESERVOIR

EASTBOUND

WESTBOUND

NEW CITY RD.

PASSAIC

MORRIS

APSHAWA

PARK

APSHAWA

PEQUANNOCK

N

4   5   6   7

Continued On Map 9

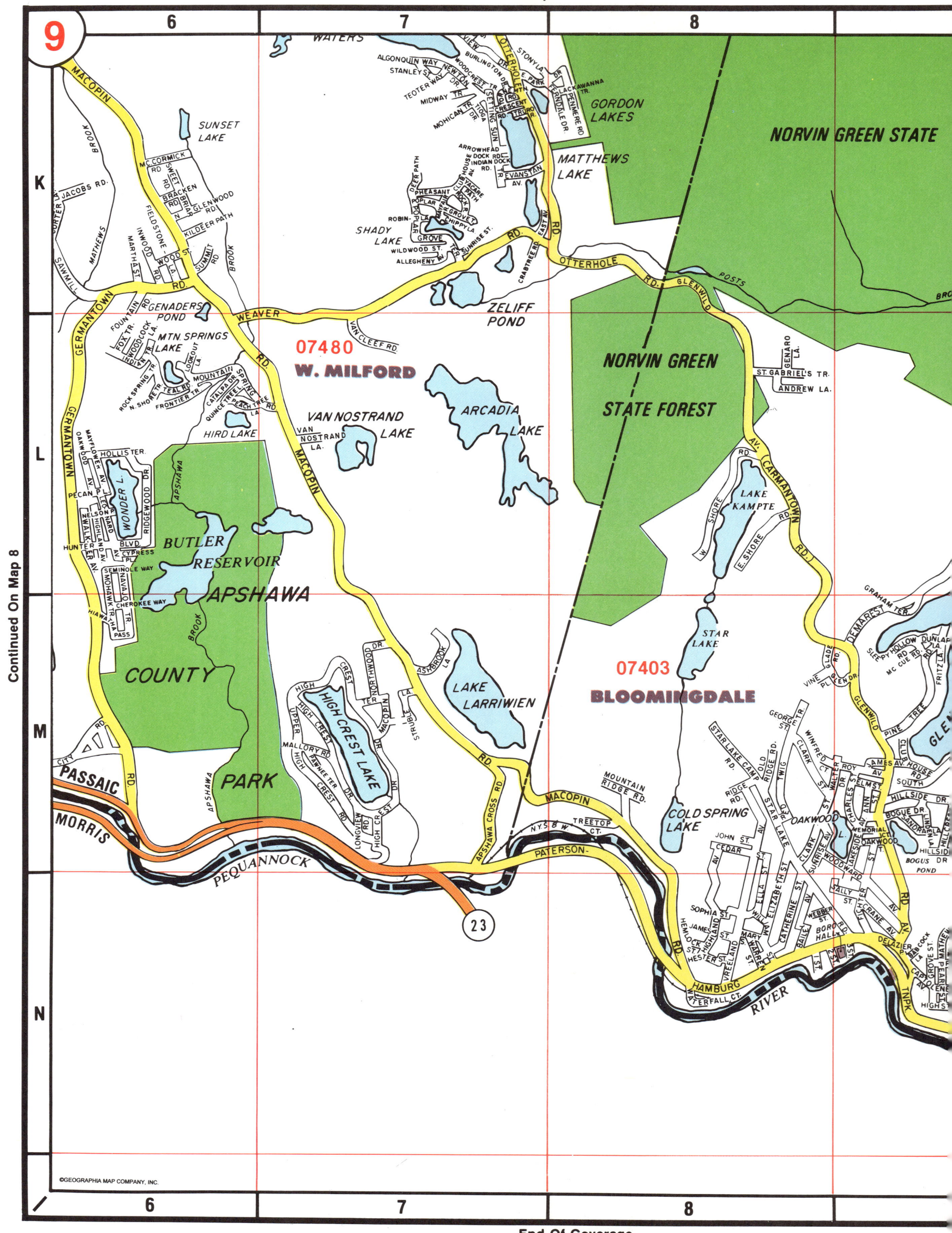

9

6 7 8

K

L

M

N

SUNSET LAKE

MACOPIN RD

GERMANTOWN RD

GENADERS POND

MTN. SPRINGS LAKE

HIRD LAKE

WONDER L.

BUTLER RESERVOIR

APSHAWA

COUNTY

PARK

PASSAIC

MORRIS

PEQUANNOCK

WEAVER RD

07480
W. MILFORD

VAN NOSTRAND LAKE

ARCADIA LAKE

HIGH CREST LAKE

LAKE LARRIWIEN

ZELIFF POND

WATERS

SHADY LAKE

MATTHEWS LAKE

GORDON LAKES

NORVIN GREEN STATE

NORVIN GREEN

STATE FOREST

LAKE KAMPTE

STAR LAKE

07403
BLOOMINGDALE

COLD SPRING LAKE

MOUNTAIN RIDGE RD.

MACOPIN RD

PATERSON-HAMBURG TNPK.

23

RIVER

GLEN

©GEOGRAPHIA MAP COMPANY, INC.

6 7 8

9

WANAQUE

RESERVOIR

07465

WANAQUE

07442

POMPTON LAKES

287

202

Continued On Map 10

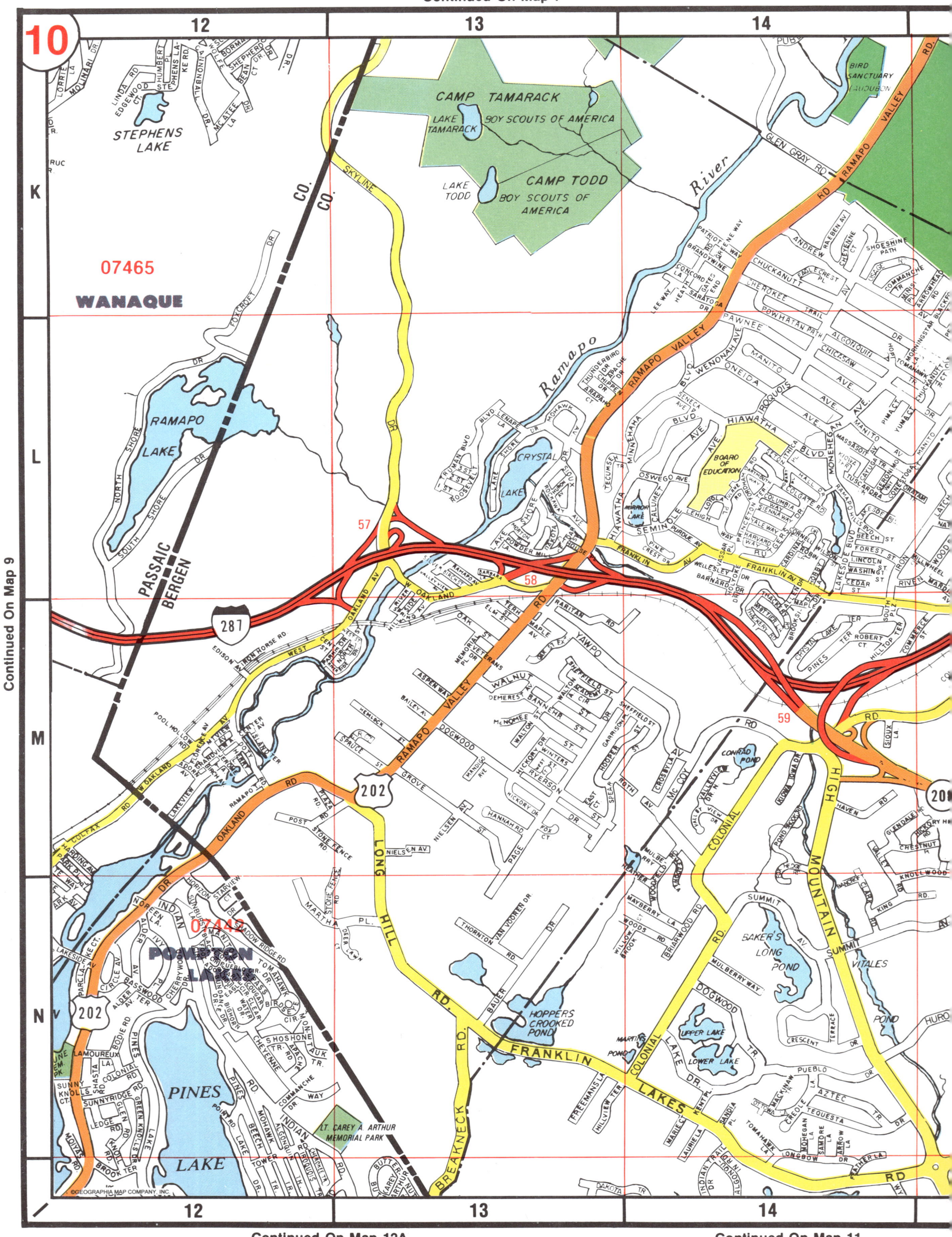

10

12 13 14

K

STEPHENS LAKE

CAMP TAMARACK
LAKE TAMARACK BOY SCOUTS OF AMERICA

BIRD SANCTUARY AUDUBON

CAMP TODD
LAKE TODD BOY SCOUTS OF AMERICA

River

GLEN GRAY RD

07465
WANAQUE

Ramapo

RAMAPO LAKE

L

CRYSTAL LAKE

BOARD OF EDUCATION

HIAWATHA

MIRROR LAKE

57

58

PASSAIC BERGEN

287

59

M

202

20

CONRAD POND

07442
POMPTON LAKES

202

LONG HILL RD.

HIGH MOUNTAIN

BAKER'S LONG POND

N

202

HOPPERS CROOKED POND

FRANKLIN LAKES DR

UPPER LAKE
LOWER LAKE

PINES LAKE

Lt. CAREY A. ARTHUR MEMORIAL PARK

BREAKNECK RD.

© Geographia Map Company, Inc.

12 13 14

Continued On Map 9

15 16 17 18 **10**

CAMPGAW
MOUNTAIN
RESERVATION

BERGEN COUNTY PARK COMM.

BERGEN COUNTY
POLICE & FIRE
SCHOOL

DARLINGTON COUNTY PARK

WOODLAND

SADDLE RIDGE
HORSEPACK
RIDING
CENTER

K

SHADOW LAKE

287

OLD MILL

CAMPGAW AVE.

PULIS AVE.

FOREST

WYCKOFF AVE.

FOREST RD.

HILLSIDE

L

FRANKLIN

PULIS

WOODSIDE RD.

PARSON POND

LAKE RD.

CREEK

WYCKOFF AVE.

CRESCENT

BROOKSIDE

GODWIN

M

W. MAIN ST.

CLINTON AVE.

FRANKLIN AVE.

WYCKOFF

GREENWOOD

WYCKOFF AVE.

BERGEN
COUNTY
WILDLIFE
CENTER

DEMAREST

N

EWING AVE.

HELENA AVE.

WYCKOFF

GODWIN

HILLSIDE

15 16 17 18

©GEOGRAPHIA MAP COMPANY, INC.

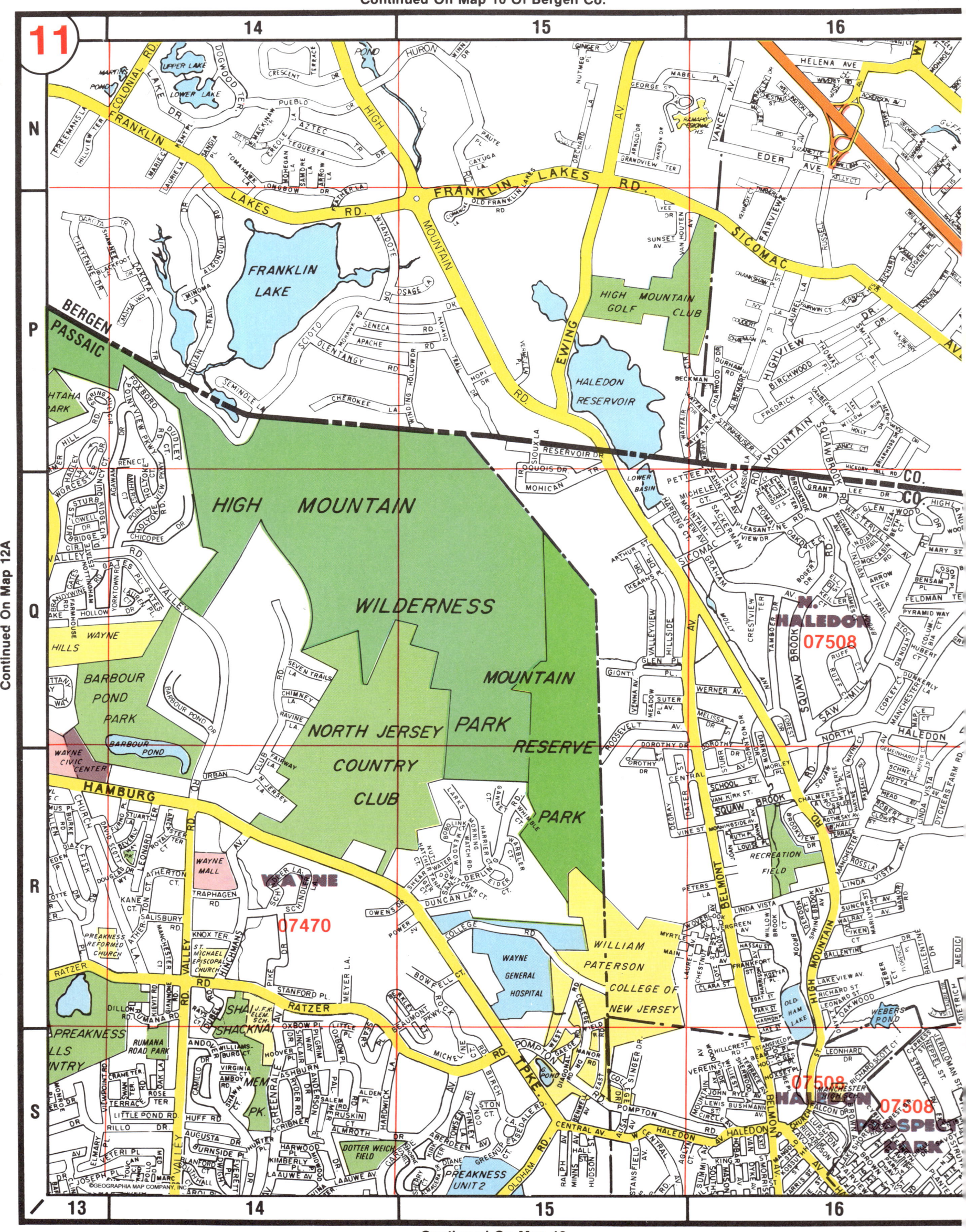

PASSAIC COUNTY

Continued On Map 9 Of Bergen Co.

07506
HAWTHORNE

PATERSON

208

©GEOGRAPHIA MAP COMPANY, INC.

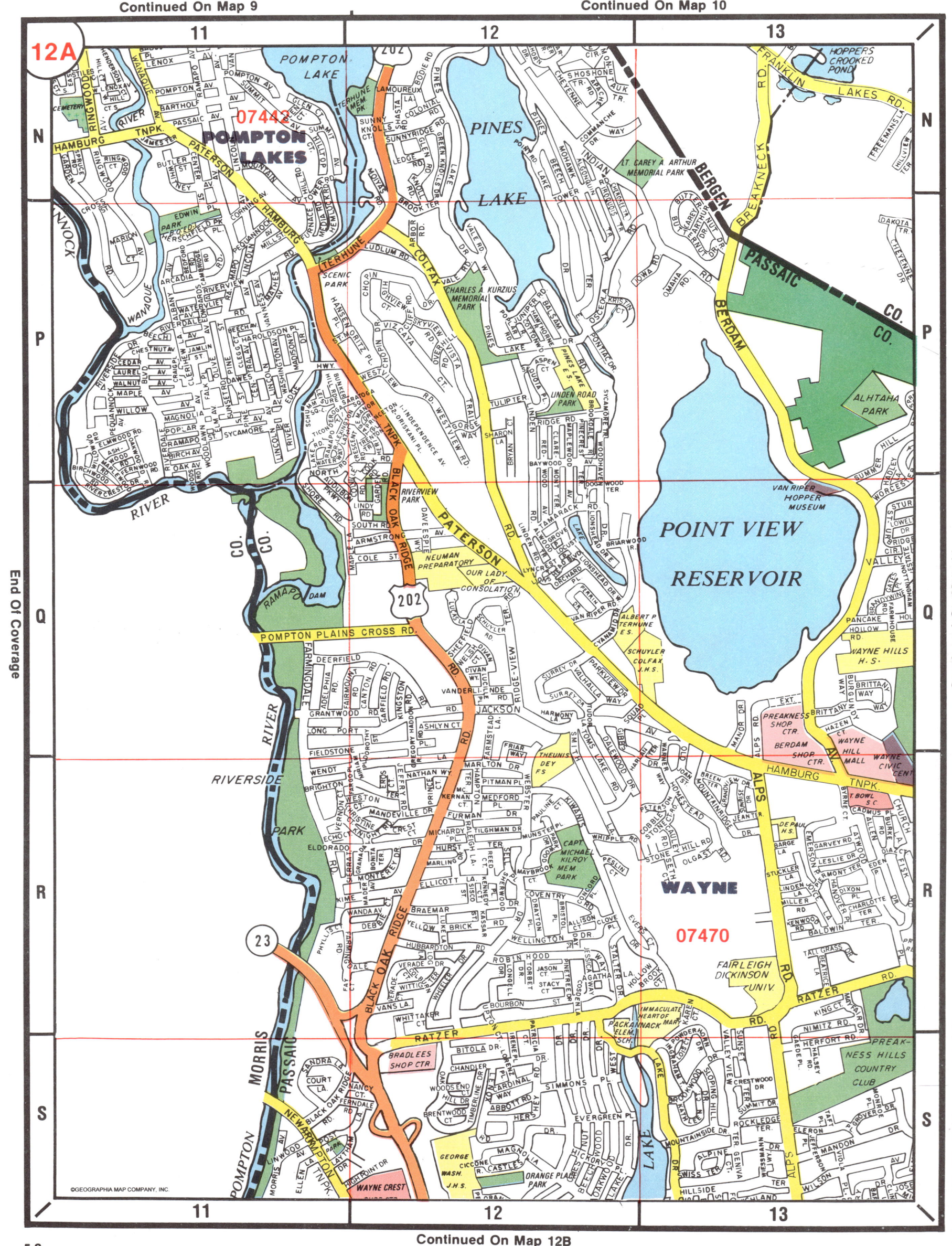

11 12 13

PASSAIC COUNTY

S S

T T

U U

V V

W W

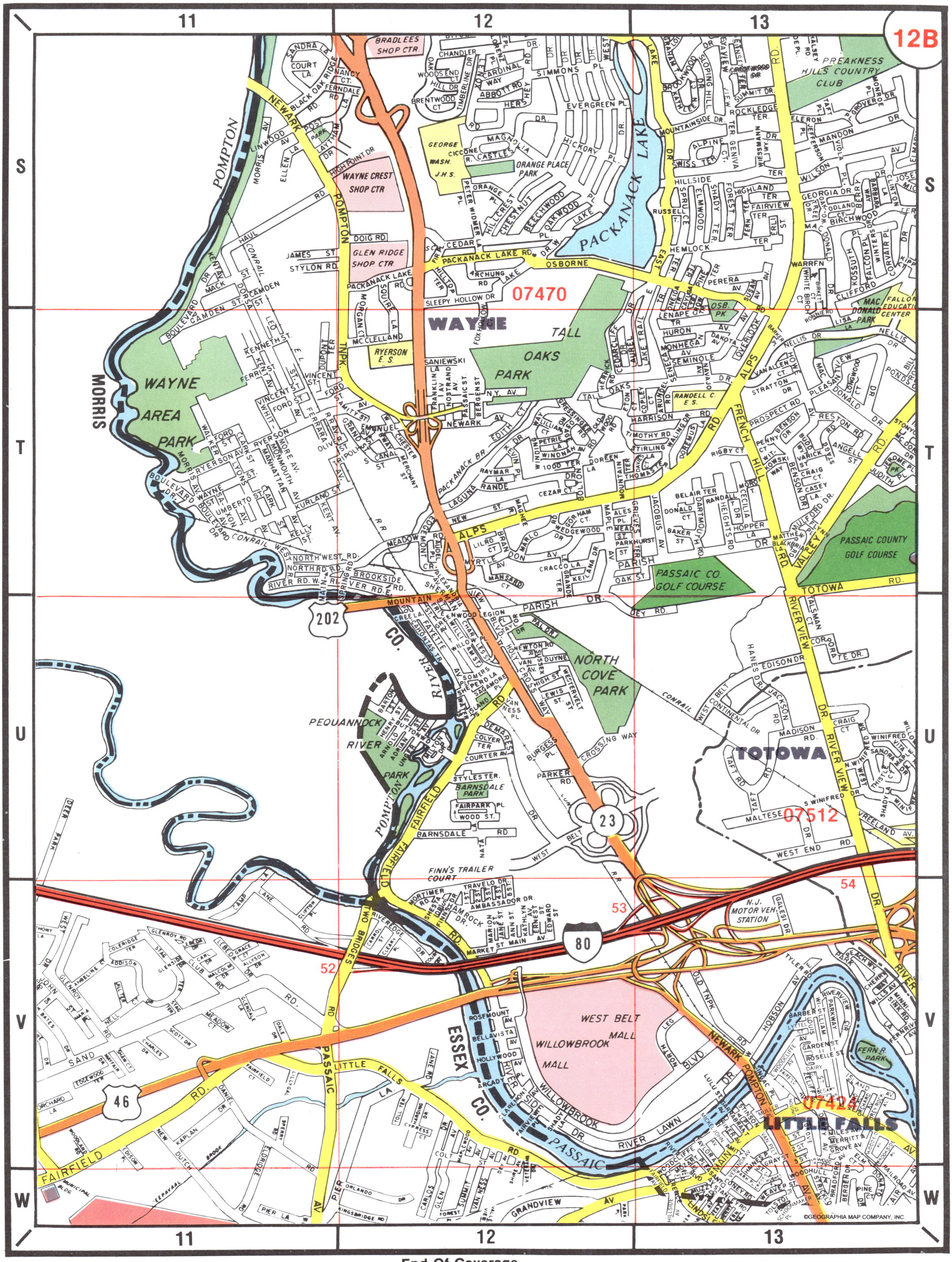

Continued On Map 13

End Of Coverage

MORRIS CO.

PASSAIC CO.

ESSEX CO.

POMPTON

NEWARK

WAYNE 07470

TOTOWA 07512

LITTLE FALLS 07424

WAYNE AREA PARK

TALL OAKS PARK

PREAKNESS HILLS COUNTRY CLUB

PASSAIC COUNTY GOLF COURSE

PASSAIC CO. GOLF COURSE

PEQUANNOCK RIVER PARK

NORTH COVE PARK

FAIRFIELD

BARNSDALE PARK

FINN'S TRAILER COURT

WEST BELT MALL / WILLOWBROOK MALL

N.J. MOTOR VEH. STATION

PACKANACK LAKE

POMPTON RIVER

PASSAIC RIVER

FERN R. PARK

BRADLEES SHOP CTR.

WAYNE CREST SHOP CTR.

GLEN RIDGE SHOP CTR.

GEORGE WASH. JR. H.S.

CICCONE R. CASTLES

ORANGE PLACE PARK

RYERSON E.S.

RANDELL C. E.S.

MAC DONALD PARK

FALLON MAC DONALD EDUCATION CENTER

OSB. PK.

Bradlees Shop Ctr.

TWO BRIDGES

202

23

80

52 53 54

46

59

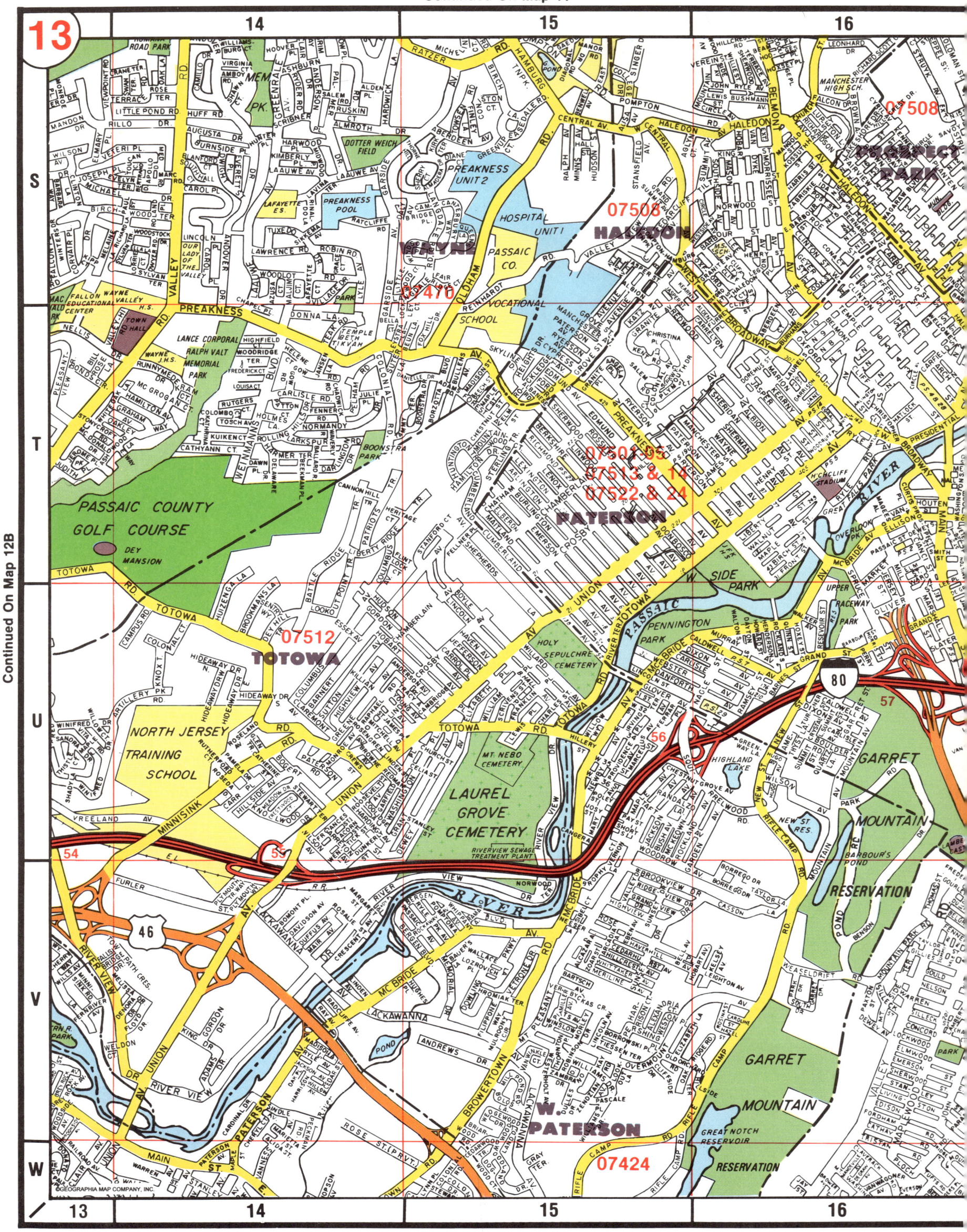

13

PASSAIC COUNTY

Continued On Map 5 Of Bergen Co.

HAWTHORNE
07506

PATERSON
07501-05
07513 & 14
07522 & 24

EAST SIDE PARK

MEM. PARK

CEDAR LAWN CEMETERY

CALVARY CEMETERY

ST. JOSEPH HOSP.

MEMORIAL PARK

FORSTMANN WOOLEN CO.

BOARD OF EDUCAT.

© GEOGRAPHIA MAP COMPANY, INC.

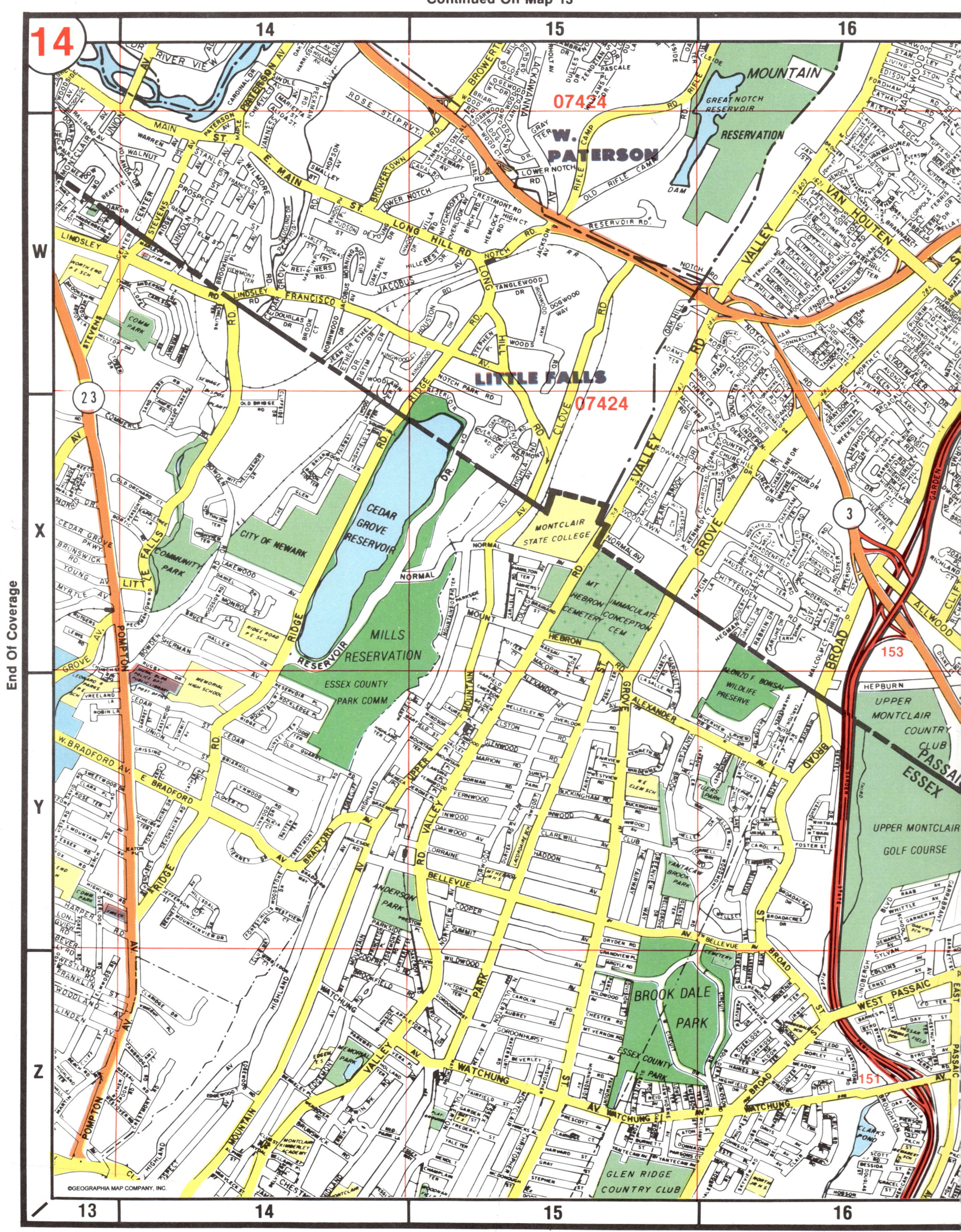

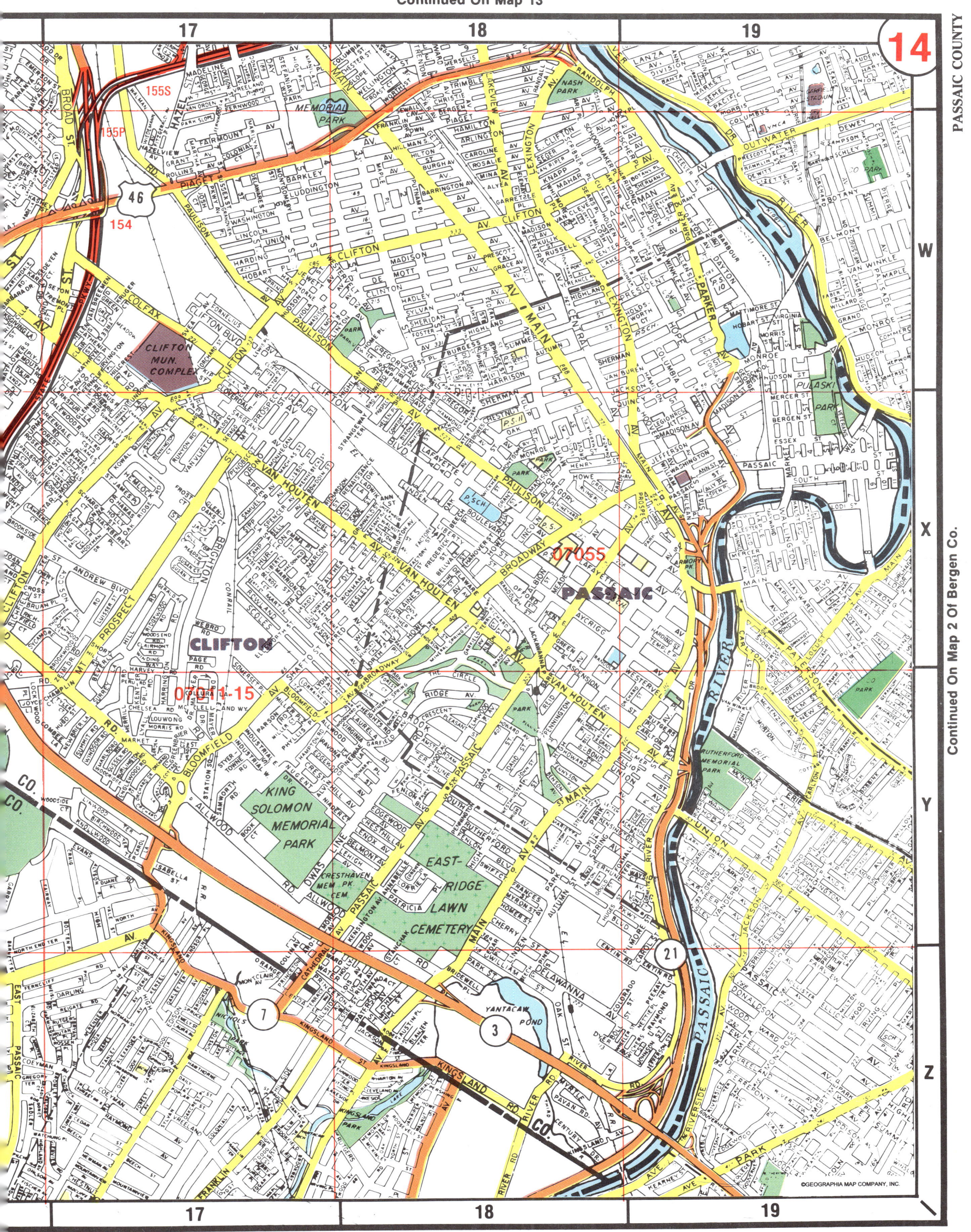

PASSAIC COUNTY

Continued On Map 2 Of Bergen Co.

BERGEN COUNTY AT A GLANCE

Bergen County was created in 1683 as one of New Jersey's four original colonies. It is located in the extreme northeastern corner of the state, bounded by the Hudson River on the east, New York State on the north, Passaic County on the west, and Essex County on the south. Access to nearby New York City is convenient via the George Washington Bridge.

The 239-square mile county has 825,380 residents, 70 municipalities (the most of any county in the state), 56 boroughs, nine townships, and three cities (Englewood, Garfield, and Hackensack).

County government maintains Bergen Pines County Hospital, health and mental health clinics, public works, housing, consumer affairs, public transportation, parks and recreation, a community college, and other services.

Bergen County has the largest number of workers and private-sector jobs and the highest per capita income in New Jersey. Five colleges in the county offer outstanding opportunity for higher education. Fine hotels and restaurants handle the needs of visitors to Bergen and to areas across the Hudson River.

Bergen County is known for its historic heritage and its variety of cultural centers. There are 18 county parks totaling 7,967 acres, providing first-class tennis facilities, golf, swimming, riding, and skiing, as well as passive areas for those seeking solitude. Excellent public transportation is available.

The Meadowlands Sports Complex offers major athletic and cultural events all year.

PASSAIC COUNTY AT A GLANCE

Passaic County is located in northern New Jersey, bordered by New York State on the north and surrounded by Sussex, Morris, Essex, and Bergen counties in New Jersey.

Although it is 18th in size (193.81 square miles) among New Jersey's 21 counties, it is the eighth most populous county in the state, with 461,382 residents in 16 municipalities. The three cities of Clifton, Passaic, and Paterson comprise about 59% of the county's population.

Passaic County has many attractions. The Great Falls at Paterson is a 70-foot waterfall where the Passaic River drops over a vertical rock shelf. Lambert Castle, a replica of an old English castle, was built in 1896---complete with observation tower---on Garret Mountain. The castle provides a breathtaking view of Paterson and the surrounding areas. The Raymond Dam at Wanaque Reservoir is situated at the southerly end of a 12-mile scenic drive around the reservoir. The Dey Mansion, in Wayne Township, is maintained in the Revolutionary War period style and contains authentic pieces from the Revolution. The new Monksville Reservoir, located along the Ringwood-West Milford boundaries, created a lake that would cover 500 acres at an average depth of 43 feet. The Monksville facility will offer boating, fishing, and swimming open to the public.

Additionally, Passaic County operates seven parks with a total land area of 3,332 acres. A 36-hole golf course, the Dey Mansion, hiking trails, and play facilities are included. Six state parks and forests, totaling 11,277 acres, are also located in the county.

The primary economic base of the county has been manufacturing; however, since 1975 there has been an increase in wholesale/retail trade, service industries, construction, finance, insurance, and real estate.

The county is served by two commuter rail lines containing eight stations, as well as over thirty bus routes. Frequent and extensive express bus service is provided to New York City.

ROCKLAND COUNTY AT A GLANCE

Rockland County is situated on the west bank of the Hudson River. Its geographical center is 33 miles north of the New York City Metropolitan business district. The county, triangular in shape, is bounded by Westchester County to the east, Orange County to the west, and New Jersey to the south.

Rockland is about 176 square miles in area. It has 265,475 residents and is enjoying population growth and a highly-educated population, with 40% of the residents 25 years old and over having completed college.

Approximately 30% of Rockland's land is devoted to parks and recreation areas. The Palisades International Park (about 30,000 acres) covers 27% of the county, with an additional 4,400 acres devoted to 13 county parks. Seven golf courses, 15 swimming areas, and 18 public and private marinas are located in Rockland. Park facilities include skiing, camping, hiking, jogging, boating, fishing, picnicking, roller skating, ice skating, biking, tennis, and wildlife sanctuaries.

The work force in Rockland continues to shift from factory employment towards professional, technical, managerial, sales, and clerical jobs. The median family income is the second highest among all counties in New York State. There are ten institutions of higher learning.

There is a comprehensive, growing public transportation system, including passenger rail service to New York via New Jersey terminals. Regional airports are within a one-hour drive.

HIGHWAY MAP

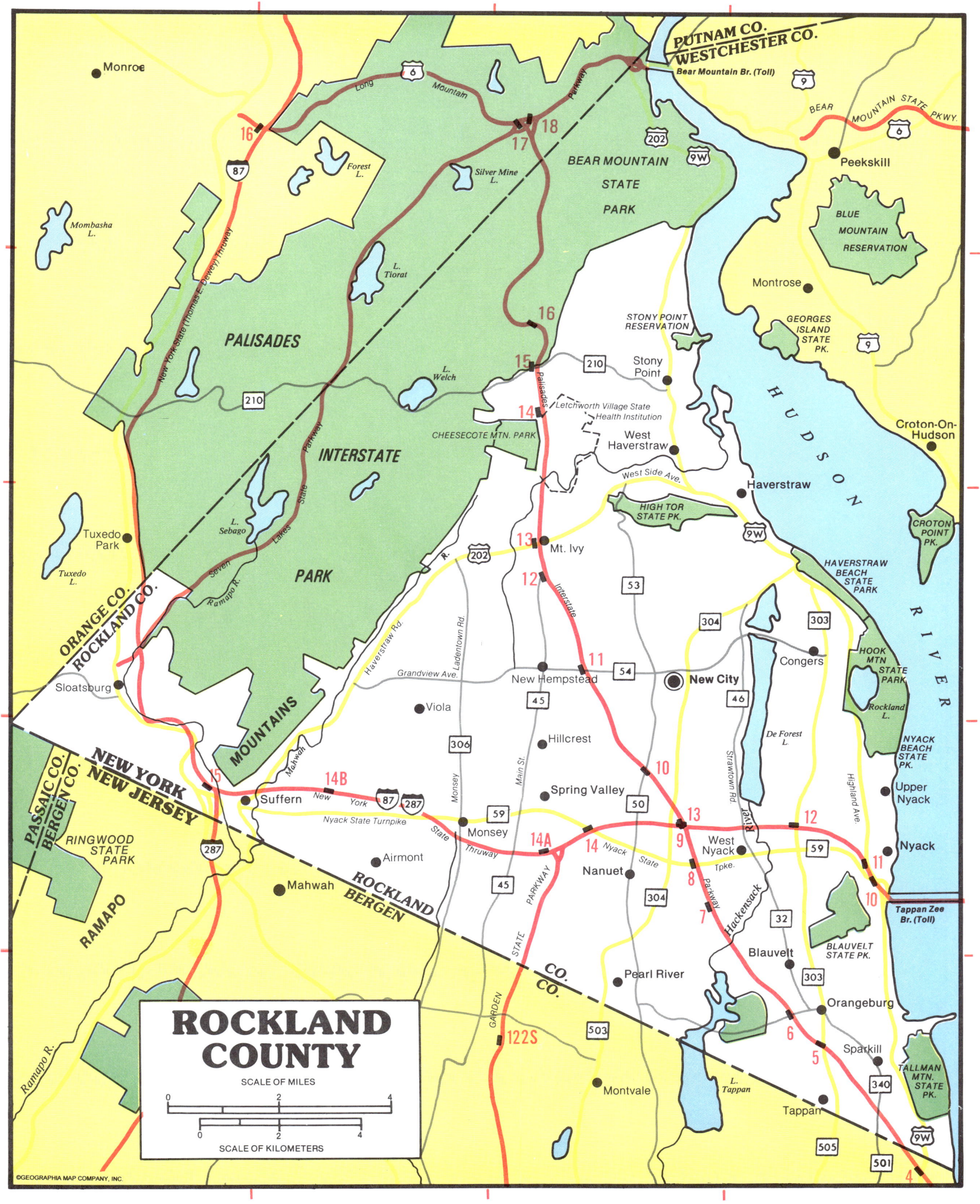

ROCKLAND COUNTY

SCALE OF MILES

SCALE OF KILOMETERS

©GEOGRAPHIA MAP COMPANY, INC.

1

8 9 10

Q

R

S

T

U

7 8 9 10

MONTVALE 07645

PEARL RIVER 10965

ORANGETOWN

Pearl River High Sch

Pearl River Middle Sch

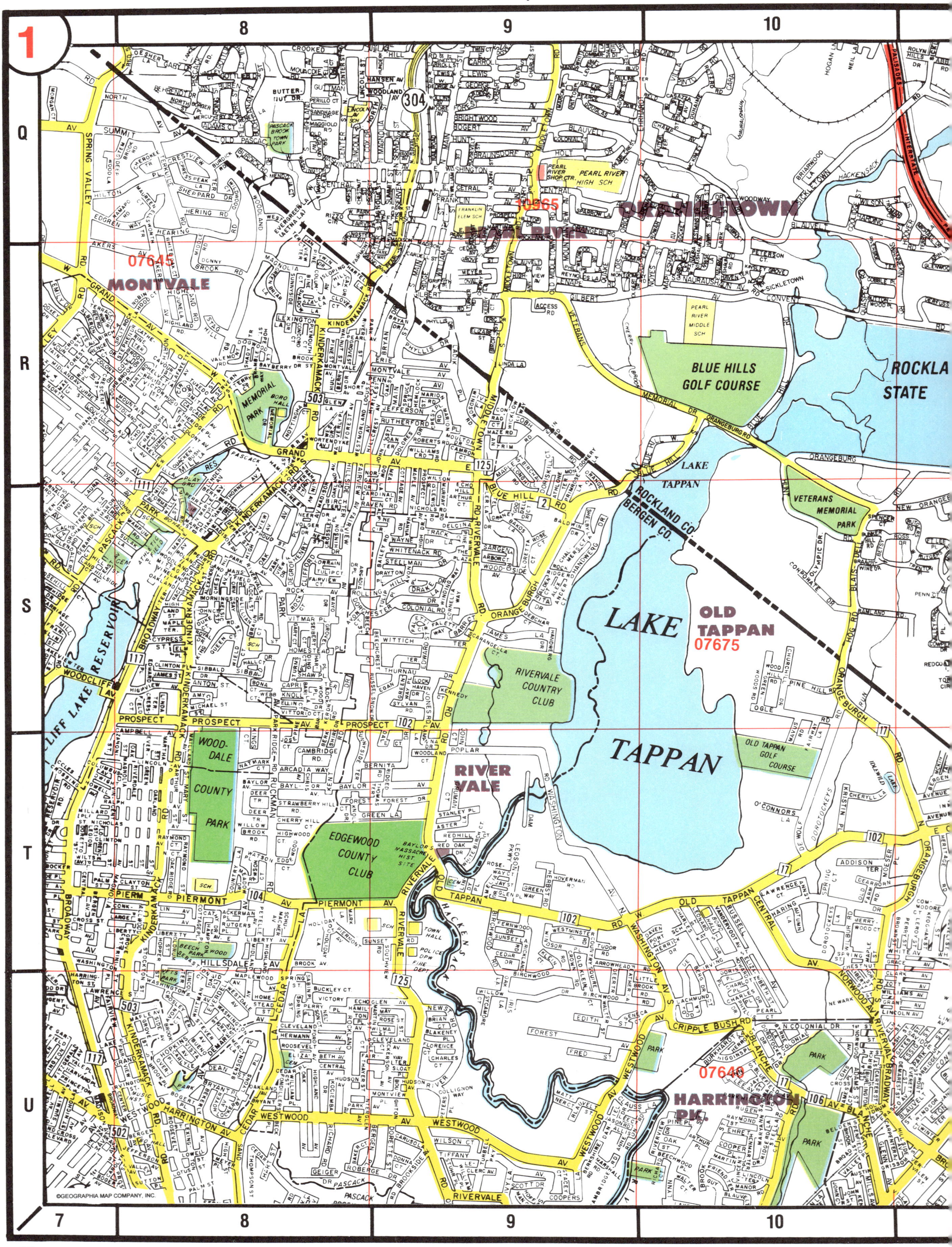

BLUE HILLS GOLF COURSE

ROCKLA STATE

LAKE TAPPAN

VETERANS MEMORIAL PARK

ROCKLAND CO. BERGEN CO.

OLD TAPPAN 07675

OLD TAPPAN GOLF COURSE

RIVERVALE COUNTRY CLUB

RIVER VALE

WOODDALE COUNTY PARK

EDGEWOOD COUNTY CLUB

CLIFF LAKE RESERVOIR

PIERMONT

HILLSDALE

HARRINGTON PK. 07640

MEMORIAL PARK

BEECH PARK

WESTWOOD

RIVERVALE

©Geographia Map Company, Inc.

66

End Of Coverage

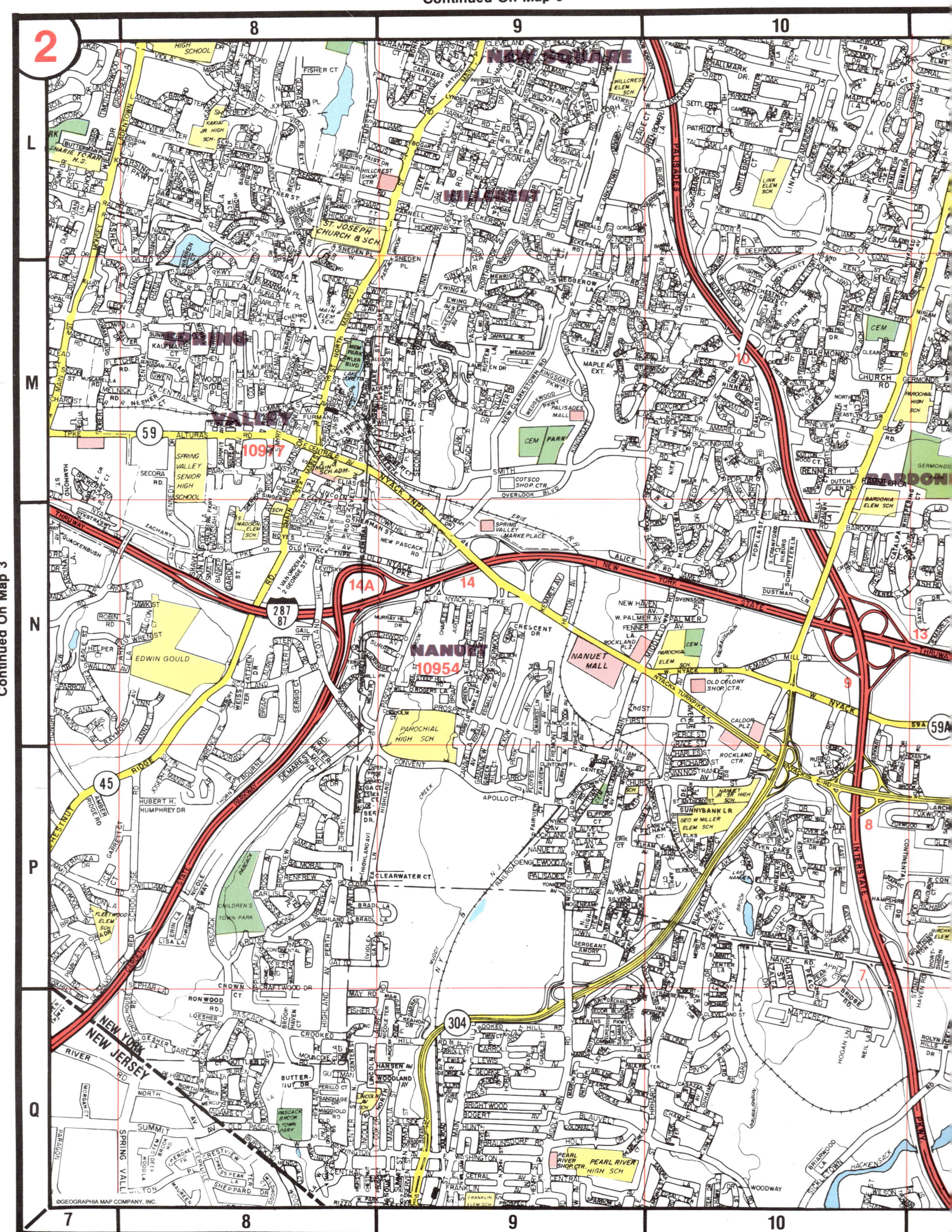

11   12   13   14   **2**

ROCKLAND COUNTY

End Of Coverage

L

M

N

P

Q

LAKE DE FOREST

CLARKS TOWN FOREST

CONGERS LAKE

SWARTWOUT LAKE

PARK

ROCKLAND LAKE

ROCKLAND LAKE STATE PARK

(GOLF COURSE)

NYACK BEACH STATE PARK

VALLEY COTTAGE 10989

NEW CITY

303

UPPER NYACK

MOUNTAINVIEW NATURE PARK

VILLAGE OF NYACK DUMP

CENTRAL NYACK

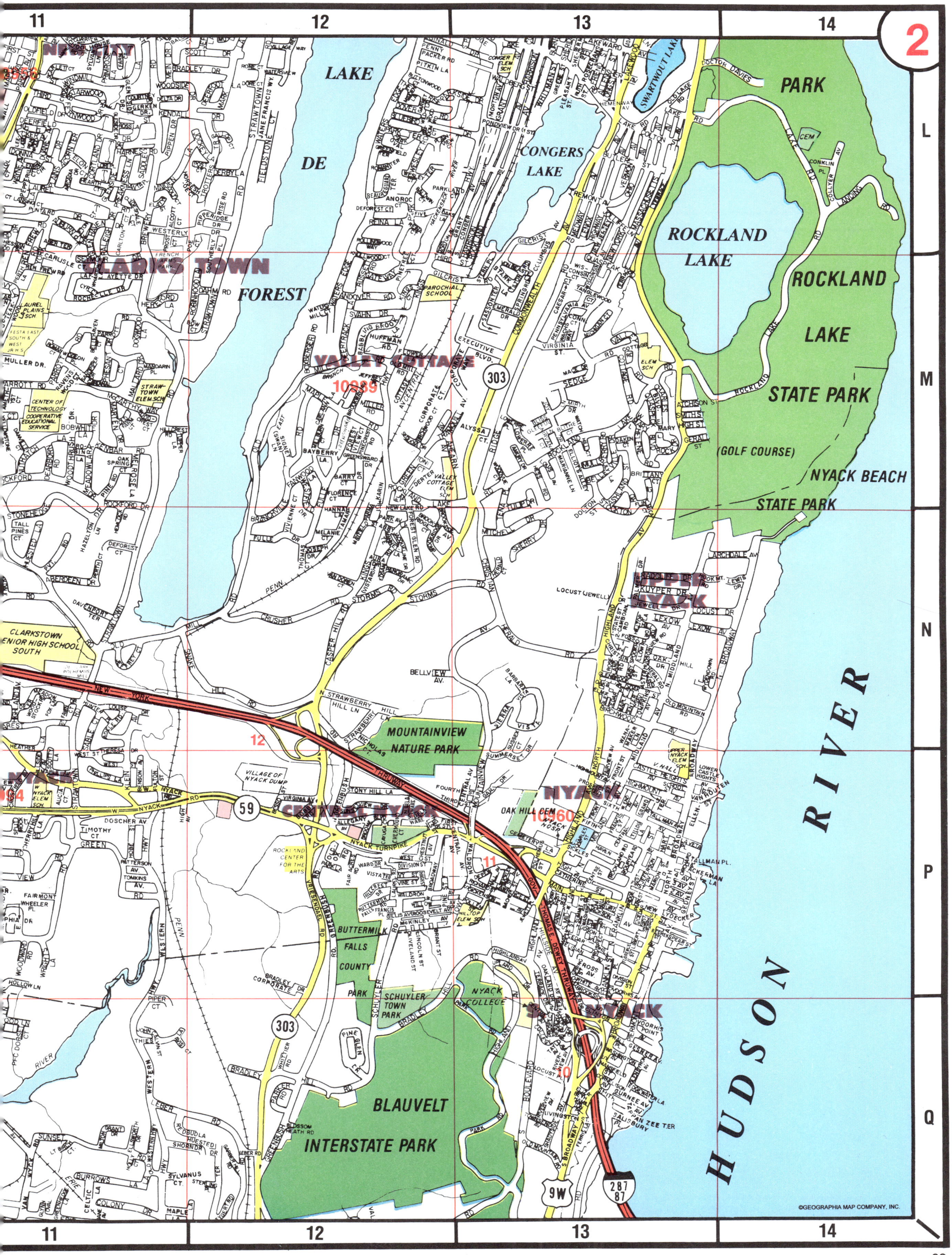

NYACK 10960

NEW YORK

12

59

11

NYACK TURNPIKE

ROCKLAND CENTER FOR THE ARTS

CLARKSTOWN SENIOR HIGH SCHOOL SOUTH

BUTTERMILK FALLS COUNTY PARK

SCHUYLER TOWN PARK

NYACK COLLEGE

SOUTH NYACK

10

BLAUVELT INTERSTATE PARK

303

9W   287 87

HUDSON RIVER

©GEOGRAPHIA MAP COMPANY, INC.

11   12   13   14

3

2 3 4

L

INSET A

ROCKLAND
BERGEN CO.
NEW YORK
NEW JERSEY

MOUNTAIN RD
MAPLE RD
STAG RD
OAK RD
SPRUCE RD
PINE HILL RD
CREST DR
VIEW DR
HILL VIEW
SILVER LAKE
SPLIT ROCK RD
GEIGER RD
ECHO MOUNTAIN RD

6

9W
202

N.Y. HESSIAN LAKE

SUFFERN
10901

FORD PLANT

6
202

59

17

GOV. THOMAS E. DEWEY THRUWAY

MONTEBELLO
RAMAPO

ERIE-LACKAWANNA

GOOD SAMARITAN HOSPITAL

M

BEAR MOUNTAIN TRAIL

ORANGE COUNTY

PERKINS MEMORIAL DR

APPALACHIAN TRAIL

SOUTH ENTRANCE

HUDSON RIVER

IONA ISLAND

VALLEY

FRANKLIN

507

SCHOOL

EAST VIEW DR

STEPHENS LA

N

SEVEN LAKES DR

BEAR MOUNTAIN TRAIL

BRIDLE PATH

LEMON RD

DOODLETOWN RD

BROOK

PALISADES

CENTRAL

BIRD SANCTUARY

SUFFERN

DOODLETOWN

TURNPIKE

INTERSTATE

OLD ROUTE NORTH

9W

LIBERTY DR

OLD ROUTE

ATHLETIC FIELD

105

W. AIRMOUNT RD

AIRMOUNT TPKE

MILLER

ISLAND

MAHWAH
07430

INDUSTRIAL AV

PARK

210

PALISADES

N.Y.

ORANGE COUNTY

P

INSET B

DON BOSCO INSTITUTE

17

507

LAKE RD

WELCH RD

JOHNSTOWN RD

INTERSTATE

FINCH PARK

AIRMOUNT AV

GERTZEN AV

Q

LAKE SEBAGO

PINE MEADOW RD

PARK

W. MAIN ST
E. MAIN

FRANKLIN TPKE

LAKESIDE

© GEOGRAPHIA MAP COMPANY, INC.

Continued On Map 14 Of Bergen Co.

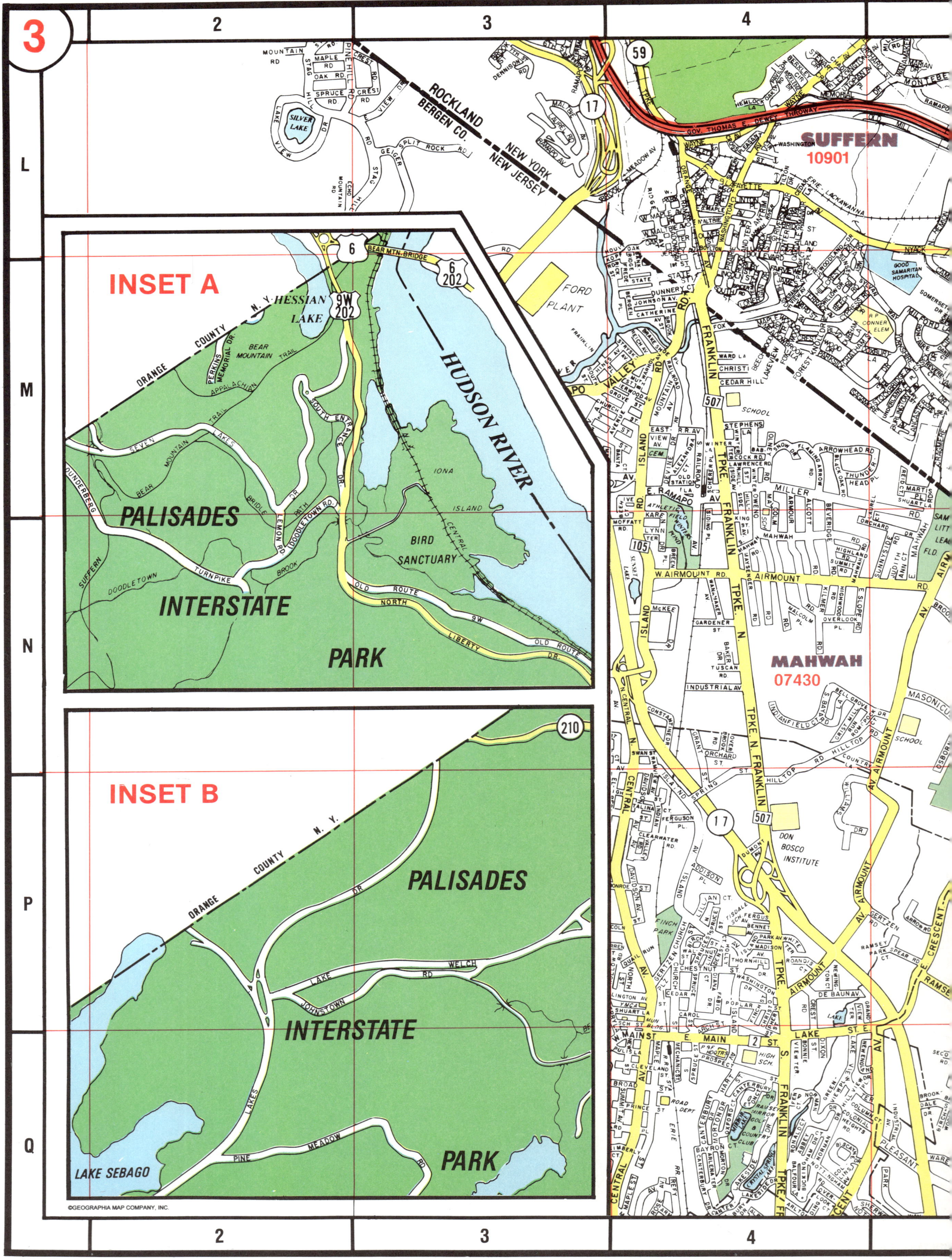

2 3 4

3

5 6 7 8

L

M

N

P

Q

ROCK TOWN GOLF COURSE

VIOLA PARK

306

HIGH SCHOOL

SUFFERN JR HIGH SCHOOL

MONTEBELLO ELEM. SCH.

14B

TALLMAN PLZ.

TALLMAN

AIRMONT SHOP. CTR.

10982

MONSEY
Albert
10952

SPRING VALLEY

59

SPRING VALLEY SENIOR HIGH SCHOOL

10977

AIRMONT

GOV. THOMAS E. DEWEY THRUWAY

MONSEY GLEN CO. PK.

ARCHDIOCESE OF NEW YORK CEM.

SADDLE RIVER POOL TOWN PARK

EDWIN GOULD

4A

287
87

BERGEN CO.

NEW JERSEY   NEW YORK

306

45

KENNEDY BLVD.

GOLF COURSE

UPPER SADDLE RIVER

07458

ROCKLAND CO.
BERGEN CO.

CHILDREN'S TOWN PARK

RAMSEY

MONTVALE

109

BORO HALL

SUMMIT AVE   SUMMIT AVE   SUMMIT AVE

5 6 7 8

Continued On Map 2

End Of Coverage

Continued On Map 4 Of Passaic Co.

4
2
3
4
G
H
J
K
L
ORANGE COUNTY
DATER MTN. COUNTY PARK
PALISADES
SLOATSBURG
10974
HILLBURN
10931
MAWAH
07430
SUFFERN
10901
POTAQUE LAKE
CRANBERRY LAKE
SILVER LAKE
ROCKLAND
BERGEN CO.
NEW YORK
NEW JERSEY
17
87
59
GOV. THOMAS E. DEWEY THRUWAY
SEVEN LAKES PKWY
STONY BROOK
TORNE BROOK
RAMAPO RIVER
ORANGE TPKE
ERIE LACKAWANNA
STERLING MINE RD
©GEOGRAPHIA MAP COMPANY, INC.

Continued On Map 3

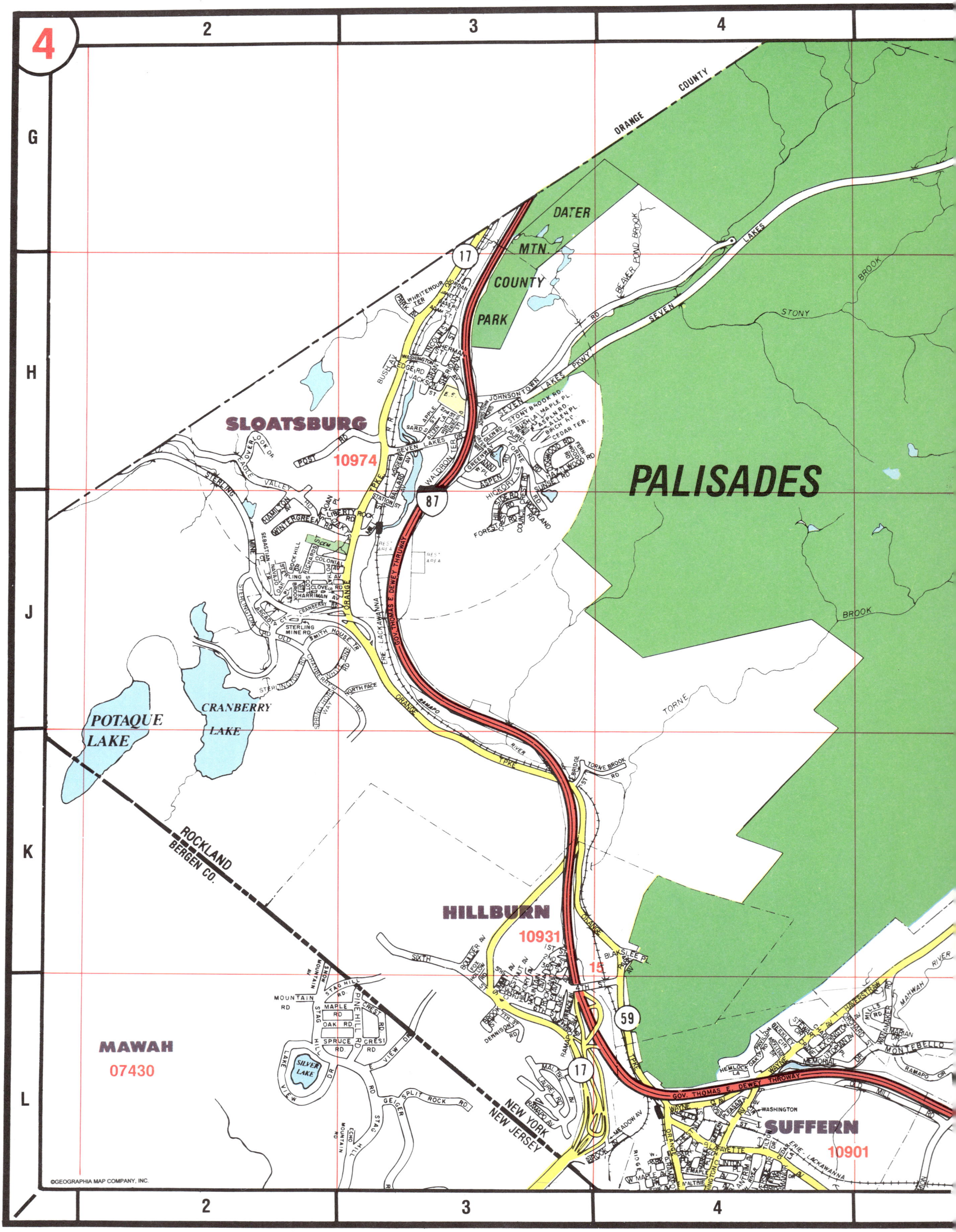

| 5 | 6 | 7 | 8 |

4

CRANBERRY LAKE

G

WANOKSINK LAKE

LADENTOWN

LAKE PINE MEADOW

PINE MEADOW

H

OLD RT 202

306

JOHN VANDEN HENDE PARK

BEAVER DAM

INTERSTATE PARK

PROSPERITY DR.

WESLEY HILLS

LIME KILN ELEM. SCH.

KAKIAT

J

COUNTY

PARK

202

DUTCH SQ.

RAMAPO

VIOLA ELEM SCH

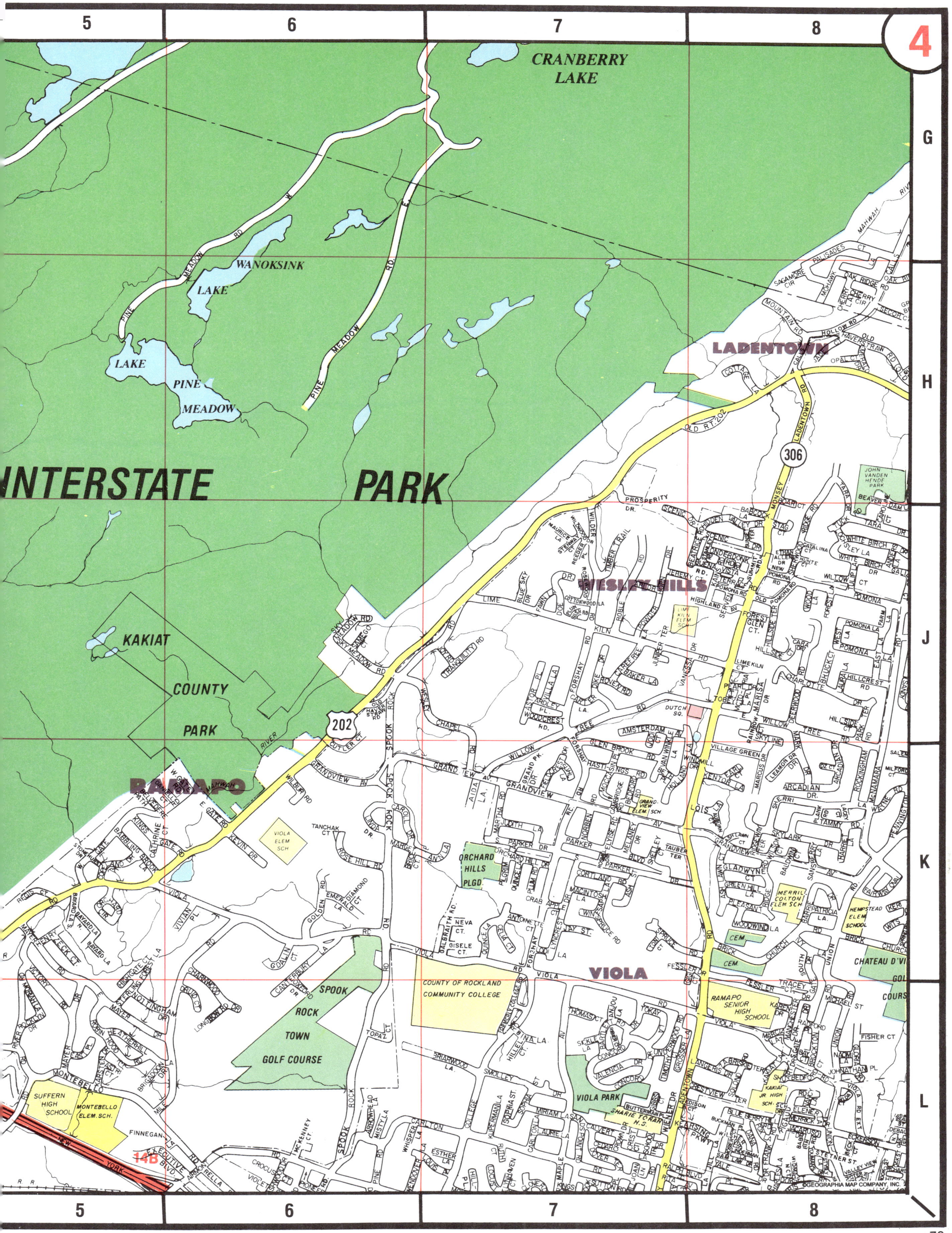

TANCHAK CT

GRANDVIEW AV

GRAND VIEW ELEM. SCH.

WINDMILL

ARCADIAN DR

K

ORCHARD HILLS PLGD.

ROSE HILL RD

EMERALD

GLADWYNE

GREEN

MERRIL COLTON ELEM SCH

NEMPSTEAD ELEM SCHOOL

CEM

CEM

CHATEAU D'VI

SPOOK

VIOLA

ROCK

COUNTY OF ROCKLAND COMMUNITY COLLEGE

RAMAPO SENIOR HIGH SCHOOL

TOWN

GOLF COURSE

KAKIAT JR HIGH SCH.

VIOLA PARK

SHARIE TORAH N.S.

L

SUFFERN HIGH SCHOOL

MONTEBELLO ELEM. SCH.

MONTEBELLO

FINNEGAN

148

YORK

| 5 | 6 | 7 | 8 |

5

8   9   10

G   PALISADES INTERSTATE PARK   STATE DEVELOPMENTAL CENTER

HAVERSTRAW

POMONA 10970

H   LADENTOWN   MT. IVY   SOUTH MOUNTAIN COUNTY PARK

Pomona Pk. Shop. Ctr.

306   HAVERSTRAW RD   PACESETTER SHOP. CTR.   Gurnee City Quarry Pk.   202

J   MT. IVY COUNTY PARK   DAVENPORT PRESERVE   KEN COU

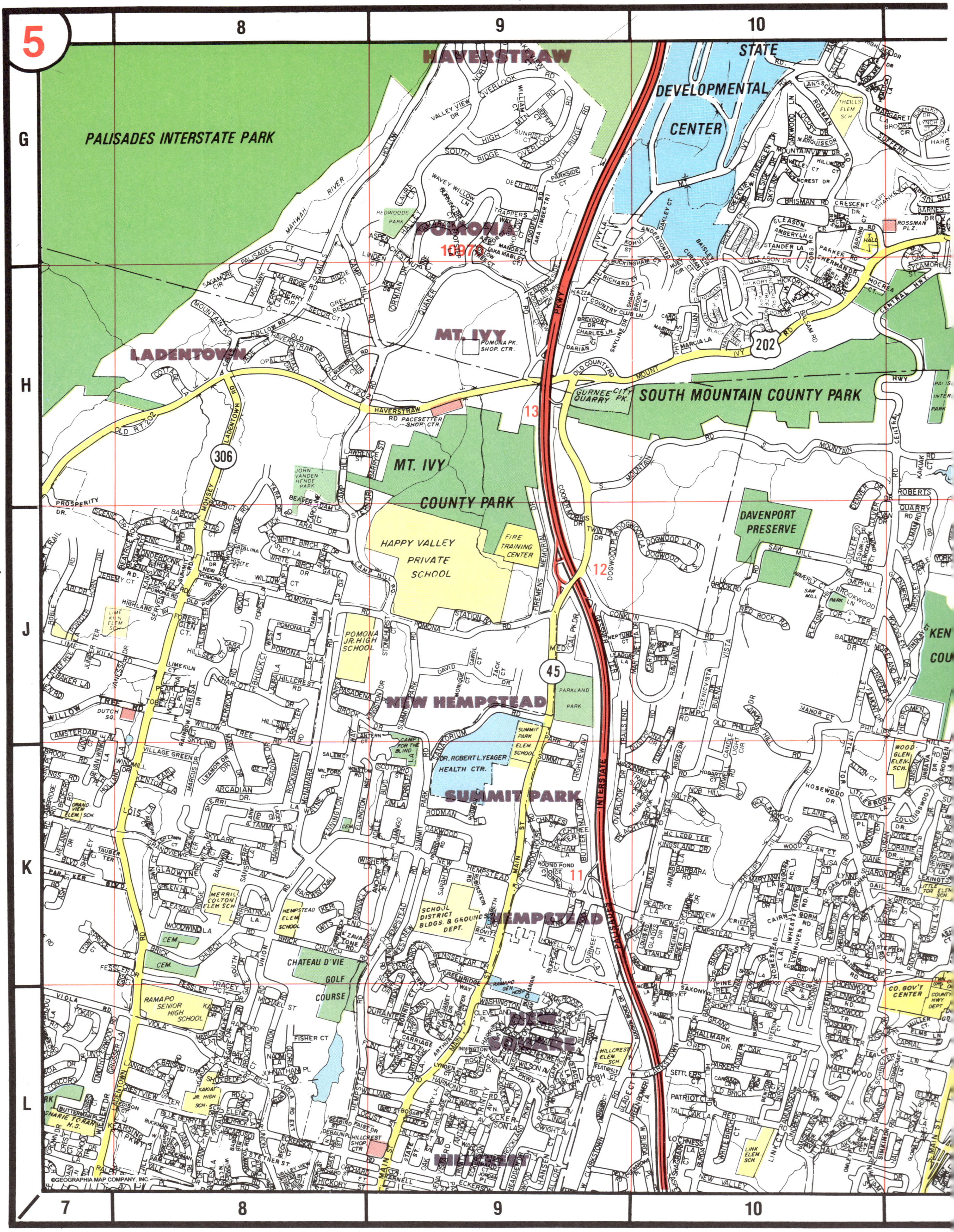

John Vanden Hende Park   HAPPY VALLEY PRIVATE SCHOOL   FIRE TRAINING CENTER

Pomona Jr. High School   45

NEW HEMPSTEAD

K   Camp For The Blind   Summit Park Elem. School   Dr. Robert L. Yeager Health Ctr.

SUMMIT PARK

Merrill Colton Elem Sch   Hempstead Elem School   HEMPSTEAD   WOODGLEN ELEM. SCH.

School District Bldgs. & Grounds Dept.

L   Ramapo Senior High School   CHATEAU D'VIE GOLF COURSE   NEW SQUARE   CO. GOV'T CENTER

Kakiat Jr. High School   Hillcrest Elem Sch   Hillcrest Shop. Ctr.   Link Elem. Sch.

HILLCREST

©GEOGRAPHIA MAP COMPANY, INC.

7   8   9   10

Continued On Map 4

11 12 13 14

5

G

H

J

K

L

End Of Coverage

HELEN HAYES HOSPITAL

W. HAVERSTRAW

10993

10923

10927

HIGH TOR

STATE PARK

HAVERSTRAW

HAVERSTRAW MARINA

HAVERSTRAW BAY

BOWLINE TOWN PARK

BOWLINE PT.

MT. REPOSE CEMETERY

HUDSON

RIVER

DELLWOOD COUNTRY CLUB

KENNEDY DELLS COUNTY PARK

THE GLEN STONE TRAIL

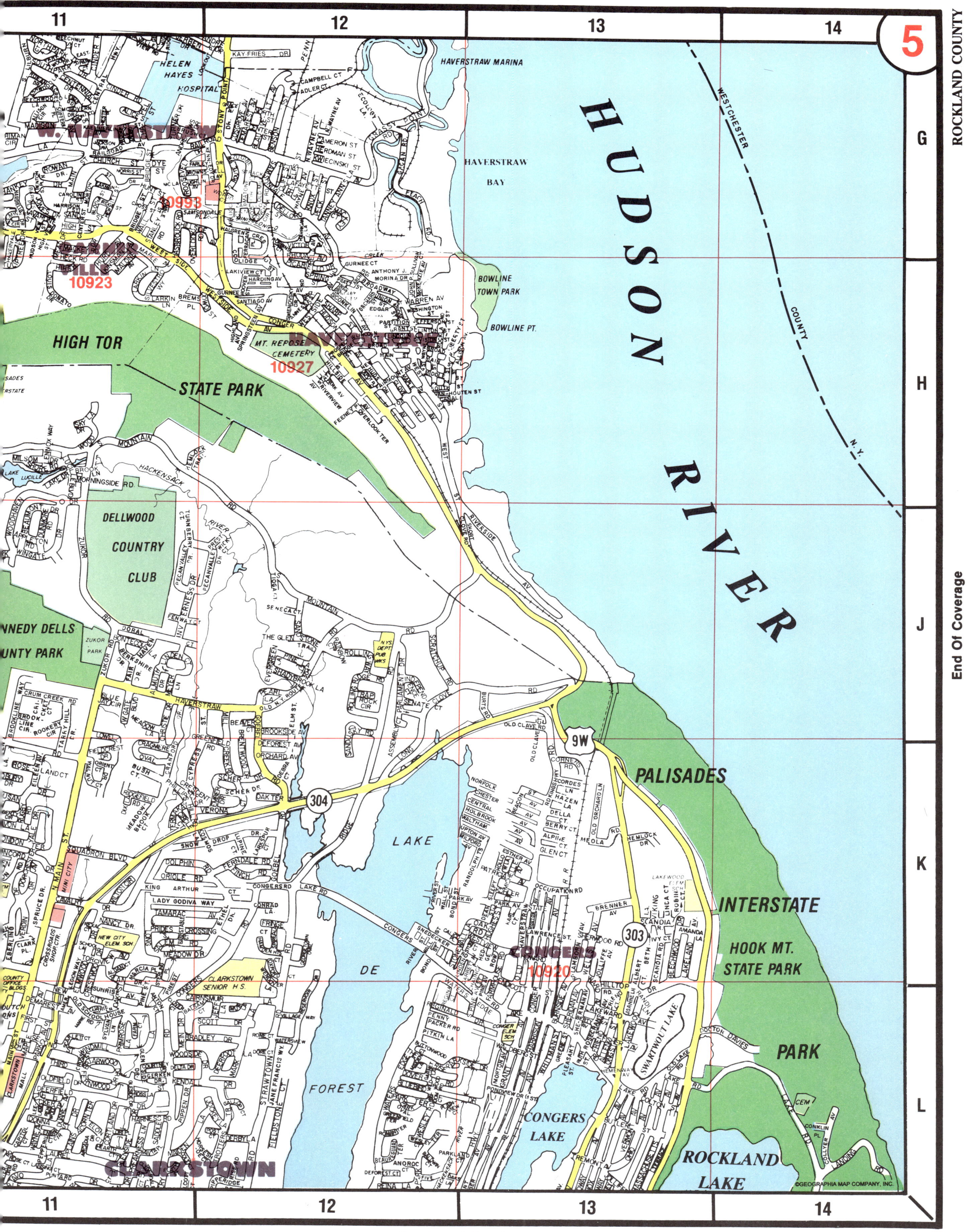

NYS DEPT PUB WKS

9W

PALISADES

INTERSTATE

HOOK MT. STATE PARK

304

LAKE

DE

FOREST

CONGERS
10920

303

PARK

NEW CITY

CLARKSTOWN SENIOR H.S.

NEW CITY ELEM SCH

CROSSROADS SHOP CTR

CLARKSTOWN

CLARKSTOWN MALL

CONGERS LAKE

SWARTWOUT LAKE

ROCKLAND LAKE

©Geographia MAP COMPANY, INC.

C

PALISADES

FLAGG MEADOW
MOUNTAIN

HARRIMAN   STATE   PARK
THE PINES

D

NAT HOUSE
MOUNTAIN

STONY

ROCKHOUSE
MOUNTAIN

GRAPE SWAMP
MOUNTAIN

POUND SWAMP
MOUNTAIN

JACKIE
MOUNTAIN

BENSON'S
POINT
CT.

210
KANAWAUKE

LAKE WELCH BEACH

IRISH
MOUNTAIN

E

LAKE

WELCH

15

VETERANS
MEMORIAL
PARK

INTERSTATE

14

LETCHWORTH
VILLAGE
LETCHWORTH VILLAGE

THEILS
10984

F

BREAKNECK POND

CHEESECOTE MT.
TOWN PARK

STATE

NORTH ROCKLAND
HIGH SCHOOL

THEILS
ELEM SCH

DEVELOPMENTAL

PARK

HAVERSTRAW

CENTER

G

©GEOGRAPHIA MAP COMPANY, INC.

11 12 13 14

6

ROCKLAND COUNTY

C

MOUNTAIN

MOUNTAIN

JONES POINT

End Of Coverage

North Liberty

TRAIL

RAMAPO

TORNE

DUNDERBERG

OVERLOOK DR.

RIVERVIEW DR.

BROOK

TOMKINS LAKE

PALISADE INTERSTATE PARK

LAKE BULLOWA

CRESTVIEW

WHITE OAK

MOUNTAIN BROOK

TOMKINS RIDGE RD.

D

NORTH LIBERTY

H·U·D·S·O·N

BUCKBERG MOUNTAIN

DEGAN'S LA.

ROSETOWN

BOULDERBERG AV.

LAKE MEAHAGH

TOMKINS COVE POINT 10986

CAMP BULLOWA BOY SCOUTS OF AMERICA

LAKE BOYCE

TOMKINS COVE

9W 202

E

STONY POINT PARK

PALISADES INTERSTATE PARK

R·I·V·E·R

WOODRUM

KEIFER

HOLLISTER CT.

STONY POINT ELEM. SCH.

STONY PT. 10980

CEM.

OLD ROUTE 210

JOHN KENNEDY

RIVERVIEW

GRANT

F

STONY POINT SHOP. CTR.

JAMES A. FARLEY JR. H.S.

210

SUNRISE

CENTRAL DR.

TOMKINS AV. EXT.

TOWN HALL

GRASSY PT.

STATE TIDAL WETLANDS

WESTCHESTER COUNTY

N.Y.

G

HELEN HAYES HOSPITAL

KAY FRIES DR.

CAMPBELL CT.

ADLER CT.

HAVERSTRAW MARINA

W. HAVERSTRAW 10993

HAVERSTRAW BAY

©GEOGRAPHIA MAP COMPANY, INC.

11 12 13 14

Bergen/Passaic/Rockland Counties

Street Index

EXPLANATION:

GRID NUMBERS:
The letters and numbers which correspond to the letters and numbers on the perimeter of the map.

MAP NUMBERS:
The numbers that indicate the map on which the respective streets can be located. (Each map consists of two pages)

HOW TO USE THE INDEX:
First, locate the street name alphabetically by place name. For example, Dempsey Av. in Edgewater, Bergen County. Turn to the page where Edgewater streets are listed unde Bergen County and then, alphabetically, find Dempsey Av This will give you the grid and map number. Turn to the Bergen County map number indicated. The exact location o the street is then determined by the intersection of the letters and numbers in the margins of that map.

NOTE:
Named streets starting with north, south, east or west are alphabetically listed by direction.

BERGEN COUNTY

Allendale, Boro of

STREET	GRID	MAP
1st St	F-6	9,12
3rd St	F-6	9,12
Ackerson Rd	E-6	12
Ada Pl	E-6	12
Allen St	E-6	12
Arcadia Rd	F-7	9,12
Arlton Av	E-6	12
Bajor Ln	F-6	9,12
Beatrice St	F-6	9,12
Bedford Pl	F-6	9,12
Beechwood Rd	F-5	10,11
Beresford Rd	F-6	9,12
Beresford Rd	G-6	9
Berkshire Rd	F-7	9,12
Birch St	F-7	9,12
Bonnie Wy	F-6	9,12
Boro Line Rd	F-7	9,12
Bradrich Ln	F-6	9,12
Brookside Av	F-5	10,11
Burtwood Ct	G-6	9
Butternut Rd	F-6	9,12
Byron Ct	F-6	9,12
Cambridge Dr	F-6	9,12
Cambridge Dr	G-6	9
Canaan Pl	F-6	9,12
Canterbury Dr	E-6	12
Carteret Ct	F-6	9,12
Carteret Rd	F-6	9,12
Cebak Ct	F-6	9,12
Cedar Dr	F-6	9,12
Ceely Ct	F-6	9,12
Central Av	F-6	9,12
Central Av	F-6	9,12
Charles St	E-6	12
Charles St	E-6	12
Cherokee Av	E-6	12
Cherokee Av	E-6	12
Chestnut St	F-7	9,12
Chestnut St	F-6	9,12
Chestnut St	F-7	9,12
Chestnut St	F-6	9,12
Colonial Dr	F-6	9,12
Colonial Dr	F-6	9,12
Commerce Dr	F-7	9,12
Conklin Ct	F-6	9,12
Cottage Pl	F-6	9,12
Cottage Pl	F-6	9,12
Cottage Pl	F-7	9,12
Crescent Bend	F-7	9,12
Crescent Pl	E-6	12
Crescent Pl	E-6	12
Crescent Pl	F-6	9,12
Crestwood Mews	F-6	9,12
Dale Av	F-6	9,12
De Mercurio Dr (Memorial Dr)	F- 6	9,12
Delta Ct	F-6	9,12
Dogwood Dr	F-6	9,12
Donny Brook Dr	F-6	9,12
Duffy Dr	F-6	9,12
Duffy Dr	F-6	9,12
East Allendale Av	F-7	9,12
East Crescent Av	E-6	12
East Crescent Av	E-7	12
East Orchard St	F-7	9,12
Edgewood Rd	F-6	9,12
Elizabeth Av	E-6	12
Ellbrook Dr	F-6	9,12
Ellbrook Dr	F-6	9,12
Ellbrook Dr E	F-6	9,12
Ellbrook Dr N	F-6	9,12
Elm Ct	F-6	9,12
Elm Ct	F-6	9,12
Elm St	F-6	9,12
Elmwood Av	F-7	9,12
Erie Plz	F-6	9,12
Erold Ct	F-6	9,12
Ethel Av	E-6	12
Ethel Av	F-6	9,12
Fairhaven Dr	F-6	9,12
Fairhaven Dr	E-6	12
Fairhaven Dr	E-6	12
Farley Pl	F-6	9,12
Forest Rd	F-5	10,11
Forest Rd	F-5	10,11
Forest Rd	F-6	9,12
Fox Dr	F-6	9,12
Franklin Tnpk	E-6	12
George St	F-6	9,12
George St	F-6	9,12
Gloria Dr	E-7	12
Green Wy	F-6	9,12
Green Wy	F-7	9,12
Grey Av	F-6	9,12
Hamilton St	F-6	9,12
Harding Av	E-6	12
Harreton Rd	E-7	12
Heather Ct	F-7	9,12
Heights Rd	E-6	12
Heights Rd	F-6	9,12
Heights Rd	E-6	12
High St	F-6	9,12
High St	F-6	9,12
Hillside Av	F-6	9,12
Hillside Av	E-6	12
Hillside Av	F-6	9,12
Homewood Av	F-7	9,12
Hubbard Ct	E-7	12
Iroquois Av	E-6	12
Ivers Rd	F-6	9,12
James St	E-6	12
Kayeton Rd	E-7	12
Knollton Rd	E-7	12
Lake St	F-6	9,12
Lakeside Dr	E-6	12
Lawrence Ln	G-6	9
Leigh Ct	E-6	12
Linda Dr	F-6	9,12
Lori Ln	F-6	9,12
Louise Ct	F-7	9,12
Macintyre Ln	F-6	9,12
Mallinson St	F-6	9,12
Maple St	F-6	9,12
Maple St	F-6	9,12
Mark Rd	F-5	10,11
Martis Av	E-6	12
Martis Av	E-6	12
McDermott Ct	G-7	9
Meadow Ln	F-7	9,12
Meeker Av	E-6	12
Midwood Av	F-7	9,12
Montrose Ter	E-6	12
Mytle Av	F-6	9,12
New St	F-6	9,12
Newton Pl	F-6	9,12
Nidd Ct	G-6	9
Oak St	F-6	9,12
Oakwood Rd	G-6	9
Oolooteka Av	E-7	12
Oolooteka Av	E-6	12
Oritani Av	E-7	12
Oritani Av	E-6	12
Park Av	F-6	9,12
Paul Av	F-5	10,11
Pearl Ct	E-7	12
Pearl Ct	F-7	9,12
Pell Farm Rd	F-7	9,12
Pine Rd	E-7	12
Pitts Av	F-6	9,12
Powell Rd	F-7	9,12
Princeton Rd	G-6	9
Refy Av	E-6	12
Rio Vista	F-7	9,12
Rozmus Ct	G-7	9
Rose St	E-6	12
Sawyer Ct	E-7	12
Schneider	F-6	9,12
Schuyler Rd	G-6	9
Schuyler Rd	F-6	9,12
Scott Ct	G-6	9
Sheri Dr	F-6	9,12
Sheri Dr	E-6	12
Stonefence Rd	F-6	9,12
Stoney Ridge Rd	F-6	9,12
Surrey Ln	F-6	9,12
Talman Pl	F-6	9,12
Thomas Av	F-6	9,12
Valley Rd	F-6	9,12
Vreeland Pl	F-6	9,12
Waibel Dr	G-7	9
Waibel Dr	F-7	9,12
Walnut Pl	F-6	9,12
Wehner Pl	F-6	9,12
West Allendale Av	F-6	9,12
West Crescent Av	G-6	9
West Crescent Av	F-6	9,12
West Maple Av	F-6	9,12
West Orchard St	F-6	9,12
Wilton Dr	E-7	12
Woodland Av	F-6	9,12
Yeomans Ln	F-7	9,12

Alpine, Boro of

STREET	GRID	MAP
Allison Rd	K-14	7
Alpine Dr	K-14	7
Alpine Dr	L-14	7
Alpine Lookout	L-15	7
Anderson Av	J-14	7,8
Anderson Av	K-14	7
Anderson Av	J-14	7,8
Autumn Ter	J-14	7,8
Autumn Ter	K-14	7
Basswood Ct	L-14	7
Berkery Pl	K-14	7
Birch Rd	K-14	7
Brenner Pl	K-14	7
Bristol Ct	K-14	7
Buckingham Dr	J-14	7,8
Buckingham Dr	K-14	7
Cambridge Wy	K-14	7
Canterbury Ct	K-14	7
Cassandra Dr	K-15	7
Cassandra Dr	K-14	7
Cemetery St	K-14	7
Charney Dr	K-14	7
Church St	L-14	7
Closter Dock Rd	K-14	7
Closter Dock Rd	L-14	7
Dock Rd	K-15	7
Dogwood Ln	K-14	7
Dubois Av	K-14	7
Duck Pond Rd	L-14	7
East Main St	K-15	7
Ellens Wy	L-14	7
Ellens Wy	K-14	7
Forest St	K-14	7
Glengoin Dr	L-14	7
Glengoin Dr	L-15	7
Graham St	L-14	7
Grant Ct	K-15	7
Haring Ln	K-14	7
Hemlock Dr	L-14	7
Henry Hudson Dr	L-15	7
Henry Hudson Dr	M-15	7
Highwood Pl	L-14	7
Hillside Av	L-14	7
Huyler Landing Rd	M-14	4,7
Litchfield Wy	K-14	7
Main St	K-14	7
Margo Wy	K-14	7
Mariane Ct	K-14	7
Marie Major Dr	K-14	7
Miles St	L-14	7
Old Farm Rd	H-15	8
Old Quarry Rd	J-14	7,8
Old Quarry Rd	K-14	7
Old Saw Mill Rd	K-14	7
Overlook Rd	K-15	7
Overlook Rd	K-14	7
Oxford Wy	K-14	7
Palisades Interstate Pkwy	H-15	8
Palisades Interstate Pkwy	K-15	8
Palisades Blvd	M-14	4,7
Palisades Blvd	L-14	7
Palisades Blvd	J-15	7,8
Pike St	L-14	7
Ridge St	K-15	7
Rio Vista Dr	L-14	7
Rionda Ct	L-15	7
Robin Ln	L-14	7
Ruckman Rd	J-14	7,8
Schaffer Rd	K-15	7
School House Ln	K-15	7
School House Ln	K-14	7
Sherwood Ct	K-14	7
Stone Tower Dr	L-14	7
Summit Rd	K-15	7
Sycamore Ln	L-14	7
Tamarack Rd	L-14	7
The Esplanade	L-14	7
Timberline Dr	K-14	7
Timberline Dr	K-15	7
Warren Ln	K-14	7
West Main St	K-15	7
West Main St	K-14	7
Wilson Dr	L-14	7

Bergenfield, Boro of

STREET	GRID	MAP
2nd St	L-12	7
3rd St	L-12	7
4th St	L-12	7
Addison Rd	M-11	4,7
Alice Pl	M-11	4,7
Ames Av	L-11	7
Anderson Av	M-11	4,7
Ann St	L-12	7
Annex Pl	L-12	7
Arlington Av	M-12	4,7
Armour Pl	L-11	7
Avon Ct	M-11	4,7
Baker Av	M-11	4,7
Banta Pl	L-11	7
Barry Pl	M-11	4,7
Baywood St	L-12	7
Bedford Av	M-12	4,7
Bedford Av	M-11	4,7
Beechwood St	M-12	4,7
Bell Pl	L-12	7
Belvin Ct	M-11	4,7
Bergen Av	M-12	4,7
Berwyn Pl	L-11	7
Beucler Pl	M-12	4,7
Beverly Pl	L-11	7
Birch Av	L-11	7
Blackwell St	L-12	7
Blauvelt Av	L-12	7
Blauvelt Av	L-11	7
Bogert Pl	L-12	7
Bradley Av	L-12	7
Brewster Pl	L-11	7
Brey La	M-11	4,7
Briarcliff Rd	M-11	4,7
Bridge Gate	M-11	4,7
Bridge St	M-11	4,7
Bridge St	M-12	4,7
Briggs Ct	L-12	7
Brook St	M-12	4,7
Brookview Ter	M-12	4,7
Brown Pl	M-11	4,7
Buecler	M-12	4,7
Bush St	M-12	4,7
Bush St	L-12	7
Byrne Pl	L-11	7
Cameron Rd	M-11	4,7
Campeau Pl	M-11	4,7
Carlisle St	L-12	7
Carlisle St	L-11	7
Carlson Pl	M-12	4,7
Carnation St	M-12	4,7
Carol Ln	L-12	7
Caroline St	L-12	7
Cedar St	L-12	7
Cherry St	M-12	4,7
Chestnut St	L-12	7
Chovet Tr	M-11	4,7
Cleveland St	L-11	7
Cleveland St	L-12	7
Clinton Park Dr	M-12	4,7
Clover St	L-12	7
Clyde Ct	M-12	4,7
Cole Av	M-11	4,7
Cole Av	M-11	4,7
Coleman St	M-11	4,7
Coleman St	L-11	7
Cooper Ln	L-11	7
Cooper St	L-11	7
Cooper St	L-12	7
Coyne Ct	L-12	7
Coyne Ct	L-11	7
Dalton Pl	M-11	4,7
Davis Dr	L-12	7
Day Av	L-12	7
De Mott Av	L-12	7
Deerfield St	L-12	7
Delford Av	M-12	4,7
Dick St	L-12	7
Do Jean Ct	L-12	7
Dover Ct	M-11	4,7
Dudley Dr	M-11	4,7
East Broad St	M-12	4,7
East Central Av	L-12	7
East Church St	L-12	7
East Clinton Av	M-12	4,7
East Johnson Av	L-12	7
East Main St	L-12	7
Edward St	M-12	4,7
Elder Av	L-11	7
Elizabeth St	M-12	4,7
Ella Ct	M-11	4,7
Elm St	M-12	4,7
Englewood Av	M-12	4,7
Esser Pl	L-12	7
Fahner St	L-12	7
Fairview Av	M-11	4,7
Floral Ter	M-12	4,7
Ford Ct	M-12	4,7
Foster St	M-12	4,7
Fox Pl	M-11	4,7
Frederick Pl	M-11	4,7
Froelich St	M-12	4,7
Fulton St	M-11	4,7
Gallagher Ct	L-11	7
Galvan Pl	M-12	4,7
Garden St	M-11	4,7
Georgian Ct	M-12	4,7
Glenview Dr N	M-11	4,7
Glenwood E	M-11	4,7
Glenwood S	M-11	4,7
Gordon Rd	M-11	4,7
Graphic Blvd	L-11	7
Greenbriar St	M-11	4,7
Greenwich Dr	M-11	4,7
Greenwich St	M-11	4,7
Greenwood St	M-11	4,7
Grove St	M-12	4,7
Grove St	L-12	7
Halberg Av	M-11	4,7
Harcourt Av	M-11	4,7
Harcourt Av	L-11	7
Haring St	M-11	4,7
Harriet Av	M-11	4,7
Harrington St	L-11	7
Haven Av	M-12	4,7
Henrietta Av	M-11	4,7
Henry St	M-11	4,7
Hickory Av	L-12	7
Highgate Ter	M-11	4,7
Highland Av	M-12	4,7
Highview Av	M-11	4,7
Hill Pl	M-12	4,7
Hillside Av	M-12	4,7
Home Pl	L-12	7
Homestead Pl	M-11	4,7
Howard Dr	M-12	4,7
Howard Morrissey Walk	M-12	4,7
Huber Pl	M-12	4,7
Hudson St	L-12	7
Hughes Rd	M-11	4,7
Hunt Walk	M-12	4,7
Irving Pl	L-12	7
Ivy Ln	M-13	4,7
Jagoe St	L-12	7
James St	M-12	4,7
John Pl	M-11	4,7
Jones Pl	L-11	7
Judith Pl	M-11	4,7
Kathryn Pl	L-11	7
Kipp Av	L-12	7
Kuggas Pl	L-12	7
Lake St	M-11	4,7
Laurel Ct	M-11	4,7
Lee Pl	M-11	4,7
Legion Dr	L-12	7
Legion Dr	M-12	4,7
Levett Av	M-11	4,7
Levitt Av	M-11	4,7
Liberty Rd	M-12	4,7
Lilac St	M-12	4,7
Lincoln Av	M-12	4,7
Linwood St	M-12	4,7
Lodge Tr	M-12	4,7
Luke St	M-11	4,7
Lunn Av	M-12	4,7
Lunn Av	M-12	4,7
Mackay Dr	M-12	4,7
Madison Av	M-12	4,7
Magnolia St	M-12	4,7
Maiden Ln	M-11	4,7
Malden Ct	M-11	4,7
Manning Pl	M-11	4,7
Marcotte Ln	M-12	4,7
Maria St	L-12	7
Martin St	L-12	7
McDermott Pl	M-12	4,7
McGrath Ln	M-11	4,7
McKinley Pl	L-12	7
Melrose Av	M-11	4,7
Merritt Av	L-12	7
Meyns Pl	M-11	4,7
Miller St	M-12	4,7
Minko Pl	L-12	7
Momar Dr	L-12	7
Moods Ln	L-11	7
Morgan St	M-11	4,7
Morgan St	M-11	4,7
Morrissey Walk	M-12	4,7
Murray Hill Ter	M-12	4,7
New Bridge Gate	M-11	4,7
New Bridge Rd	M-11	4,7
New Hampton Ct	M-11	4,7
New Jersey Av	L-12	7
New York Av	L-12	7
North Christie St	L-12	7
North Demarest Av	L-12	7
North Franklin Av	L-11	7
North Front St	L-12	7
North Prospect Av	L-11	7
North Queen St	L-11	7
North Rail Road Av	L-12	7
North Stoughton St	L-11	7
North Summit St	M-12	4,7
North Summit St	L-12	7
North Taylor St	L-12	7
North Vivyen St	L-11	7
North Washington Av	L-12	7
North William St	M-12	4,7
North William St	L-12	7
North Woodside St	M-12	4,7
North Woodside St	L-12	7
North 1st St	L-12	7
North St	M-12	4,7
O'Neil St	M-12	4,7
Oak Pl	L-12	7
Orchard St	M-12	4,7
Owen La	L-12	7
Palisade Av	M-12	4,7
Park Rd	M-11	4,7
Paula Dr	M-11	4,7
Pelham Pl	L-12	7
Phelps Av	L-12	7
Pine Dr	M-12	4,7
Pleasant Av	M-12	4,7
Porter Av	M-12	4,7
Portland Av	M-12	4,7
Preston Pl	M-12	4,7
Quincy Ln	M-11	4,7
Ralph St	L-12	7
Raum Pl	L-12	7
Rector Ct	M-11	4,7
Redwood St	M-12	4,7
Regent St	M-11	4,7
Reid Av	M-11	4,7
Rivera Way	L-12	7
Riveredge Rd	L-11	7
Roosevelt Av	M-11	4,7
School St	M-12	4,7
Schoolcraft Rd	M-11	4,7
Scott Dr	M-12	4,7
Seminary Ct	M-12	4,7
Sergent Ct	L-11	7
Shelley Ct	L-12	7
Short St	L-12	7
Sieber Ct	L-11	7

STREET	GRID	MAP
Simone Pl	L-12	7
Simpson Ct	M-12	4,7
Slater St	L-12	7
Smith Av	M-12	4,7
Somers Av	M-11	4,7
South Christie St	L-12	7
South Demarest Av	M-11	4,7
South Demarest Av	M-12	4,7
South Franklin Av	M-11	4,7
South Front St	M-12	4,7
South Jagoe St	L-12	7
South Paula Dr	M-11	4,7
South Prospect Av	M-11	4,7
South Queen St	M-11	4,7
South Rail Road Av	M-12	4,7
South Summit St	M-12	4,7
South Taylor St	M-12	4,7
South Taylor St	L-12	7
South Vivyen St	M-11	4,7
South Washington Av	M-12	4,7
South William St	L-12	7
South William St	M-12	4,7
South Woodside St	L-12	7
South Woodside St	M-12	4,7
South 1st St	M-12	4,7
Spring Av	M-11	4,7
Station Sq	L-12	7
Stillman Av	L-11	7
Stillman Av	L-12	7
Sugden St	M-11	4,7
Sunrise Ter	M-11	4,7
Sunset Pl	M-11	4,7
Surrey Ln	M-11	4,7
Sussex Rd	M-11	4,7
Sylvamdur Av	M-11	4,7
Sylvan Av	M-12	4,7
Terhune St	M-12	4,7
Terrace St	M-11	4,7
Thames Blvd	M-11	4,7
Towne Pl	L-12	7
Towne Pl	M-12	4,7
Trinity Ct	M-11	4,7
Tulip St	M-12	4,7
Turnure St	M-11	4,7
Tuscarora St	L-12	7
Twin Boro Ln	L-11	7
Tyson Pl	L-11	7
Van Court Pl	M-11	4,7
Van Houten St	M-12	4,7
Van Valkenburgh Av	M-11	4,7
Veterans Plaza	L-12	7
View St	M-12	4,7
Violet Ct	L-12	7
Vreeland Av	M-11	4,7
Walters St	M-12	4,7
Walters St	L-11	7
Warren St	M-12	4,7
West Broad St	M-11	4,7
West Central Av	L-12	7
West Central Av	L-11	7
West Church St	L-11	7
West Church St	L-12	7
West Clinton Av	M-11	4,7
West Englewood Av	M-12	4,7
West Englewood Av	M-11	4,7
West Johnson Av	L-12	7
West Main St	L-11	7
West Main St	L-12	7
West Minster Av	M-11	4,7
Westside Av	M-11	4,7
Westview Dr	M-11	4,7
Whitman St	M-11	4,7
Whittaker Pl	L-12	7
Wilbur Rd	M-11	4,7
Wildrose Av	M-11	4,7
Willett St	L-12	7
Williamson Rd	L-11	7
Willow St	L-12	7
Windsor Rd	M-11	4,7
Woodbine St	M-12	4,7
Woods Av	L-11	7
Zuegel Ct	M-12	4,7

Bogota, Boro of

STREET	GRID	MAP
1st Pl.	P-11	4
2nd Pl	P-11	4
3rd Pl	P-11	4
4th Pl	P-11	4
Beechwood Av	P-11	4
Beechwood Av	P-10	5
Bogert St	P-11	4
Bogota Gardens	P-10	5
Cane St	P-11	4
Central Av	P-11	4
Chestnut Av	Q-10	2,5
Crestview Pl	P-11	4
Cross St	P-10	5
Cypress Av	Q-10	2,5
Dunn Av	Q-11	3,4
East Broad St	P-11	4
East Grove St	P-11	4
East Main St	P-11	4
East Fort Lee Rd	P-11	4
Elm Av	P-10	5
Elmwood Av	P-10	5
Elmwood Av	P-11	4
Fairview Av	Q-10	2,5
Feller Pl	P-10	5
Fisher Av	Q-11	3,4
Gray St	P-11	4
Highview Pl	P-11	4
Hill St	P-11	4
Hill St	P-10	5
Homestead Pl	P-10	5
James St	P-11	4
Kovar St	P-11	4
Kramer Ct	P-10	5
Larch Av	P-10	5
Leonia Av	P-10	5
Leonia Av	P-11	4
Leonia Av	P-10	5
Linden Av	P-10	5
Linwood Av	P-11	4
Lynn Ct	P-10	5
Maplewood Av	Q-10	2,5
Maplewood Av	Q-11	3,4
Martin St	Q-11	3,4
McDougall Ln	P-10	5
Munn Av	P-10	5
North Av	Q-10	2,5
Oakwood Av	P-10	5
Oakwood Av	Q-11	3,4
Orchard Ter	P-10	5
Palisade Av	P-11	4
Palisade Av	Q-10	2,5
Palisade Av	P-10	5
Palisade Av	Q-11	3,4
Park Pl	P-10	5
Park Pl W	P-10	5
Pine St	P-11	4
Preston St	P-10	5
Queen Anne Rd	Q-11	3,4
Ridgefield Av	P-10	5
River Rd	P-10	5
South St	P-10	5
Summit Av	P-11	4
Summit Av	P-10	5
Walnut Av	P-10	5
West Broad St	P-10	5
West End Av	P-11	4
West End Av	P-10	5
West Fort Lee Rd	P-10	5
West Grove St	P-10	5
West Main St	P-10	5
West Shore Av	Q-10	2,5
West Shore Av	P-10	5

Carlstadt, Boro of

STREET	GRID	MAP
1st St	R-8	2
2nd St	R-8	2
3rd St	R-8	2
4th St	R-8	2
5th St	R-8	2
6th St	R-8	2
7th St	R-8	2
8th St	R-8	2
9th St	R-8	2
10th St	R-8	2
10th St	S-8	1,2
12th St	S-8	1,2
13th St	S-8	1,2
14th St	S-8	1,2
15th St	S-8	1,2
16th St	S-8	1,2
17th St	S-8	1,2
18th St	S-8	1,2
19th St	S-8	1,2
20th St	S-8	1,2
Amor Av	S-9	1,2
Asia Pl	S-9	1,2
Barell Av	S-9	1,2
Berry Av	R-8	2
Broad St	S-8	1,2
Broad St	R-8	2
Carlyle Ct	R-8	2
Center St	R-8	2
Central Av	R-8	2
Commerce Rd	S-10	1,2
Commerce Rd	S-9	1,2
Commerce St	R-8	2
Commercial Av	S-9	1,2
Dae Woo Pl	S-9	1,2
Dell Rd	S-9	1,2
Division Av	R-8	2
Eastern Av	S-9	1,2
Floral Ln	R-8	2
Franklin St	R-8	2
Fritsch Av	R-8	2
Garden St	R-8	2
Garden St	R-7	2
Gotham Pkwy	S-9	1,2
Grand St	R-9	2
Hoboken Rd	R-8	2
Industrial Rd	R-8	2
Interstate Pl	R-8	2
Jefferson St	R-8	2
Jony Dr	S-9	1,2
Kero Rd	S-9	1,2
Lilac Ln	R-8	2
Lincoln St	R-8	2
Madison St	R-8	2
Marsan Av	R-8	2
Meadow Ln	S-9	1,2
Michele Pl	S-9	1,2
Monroe St	R-8	2
Moonachie Av	S-9	1,2
Oehler Pl	S-9	1,2
Orchard St	R-8	2
Out Water Pl	T-9	1
Palmer Ter	S-9	1,2
Park Ln	R-8	2
Passaic Av	R-8	2
Paterson Plank Rd	S-8	1,2
Paterson Plank Rd	S-9	1,2
Small St	R-8	2
South Commercial Av	S-9	1,2
Starke Rd	S-9	1,2
Summit Av	R-8	2
Terminal Ln	S-9	1,2
Terminal Ln	S-10	1,2
Triangle Blvd	S-9	1,2
Union St	R-8	2
Universal Pl	S-9	1,2
Veterans Blvd	S-9	1,2
Washington Av	S-9	1,2
Washington St	R-8	2

Cliffside Park, Boro of

STREET	GRID	MAP
1st St	S-12	3
2nd St	S-12	3
3rd St	S-12	3
Accommando Pl	T-12	3
Adolphus Pl	S-12	3
Anderson Av	S-12	3
Aurora Av	R-12	3
Baar Pl	T-12	3
Bagley Pl	S-12	3
Bender Pl	T-12	3
Brandon Pl	S-12	3
Cecelia Av	S-12	3
Cecilia Pl	S-12	3
Cedar St	T-12	3
Center Ln	S-12	3
Claremont Av	S-12	3
Clark Ter	S-12	3
Cliff Ln	S-12	3
Cliff St	S-12	3
Columbia Av	S-12	3
Columbus Pl	T-12	3
Commercial Av	S-12	3
Cottage Ln	S-12	3
Courtland Pl	S-12	3
Crescent Av	S-12	3
Crescent La	S-12	3
Day Av	T-12	3
De Soto Pl	T-12	3
Delia Pl	S-12	3
Dewey Av	S-12	3
Division St	S-12	3
Edgewater Av	S-12	3
Edgewater Rd	S-12	3
Edgewood Ln	S-12	3
Esplanade Pl	S-12	3
Esplanade Rd	T-12	3
Esplanade Rd	S-12	3
Everett Pl	S-12	3
Fairview Ln	R-12	3
Florence	R-12	3
Florence	S-12	3
Fox Ter	S-12	3
Franklin Av	S-12	3
Fulton Ter	S-12	3
Gigante Ter	T-12	3
Glen St	S-12	3
Gorge Rd	S-12	3
Gorge Rd	T-12	3
Grant Av	S-12	3
Green Mount Av	S-12	3
Grove Av	S-12	3
Harvard Pl	R-12	3
Highbridge Av	S-12	3
Highland Av	S-12	3
Highland Av	T-12	3
Highridge Av	S-12	3
Hillside Av	S-12	3
Hilltop Pl	S-12	3
Holley Terr	S-12	3
Hudson Pl	T-12	3
Hudson Ter	S-12	3
Inwood Ter	R-12	3
Jefferson Av	S-12	3
Jersey Av	S-12	3
John St	S-12	3
Kearney Av	S-12	3
Knox Av	S-12	3
Lafayette Av	S-12	3
Laird Av	T-12	3
Laird Pl	T-12	3
Lawton Av	S-12	3
Lincoln Av	S-12	3
Lindberg Av	S-12	3
Long View Av	S-12	3
Longview Pl	S-12	3
Main St	T-12	3
Main St	S-12	3
Manhattan Pl	T-12	3
Marion Av	S-12	3
Morningside Av	S-12	3
Nagel St	S-12	3
Nelson Av	S-12	3
Newmans Ln	S-12	3
Norman Dr	S-13	3
Oakdene Av	S-12	3
Oakwood Av	T-12	3
Olympia Av	S-12	3
Oncrest Ter	S-12	3
Oregon Av	S-12	3
Overlook Av	S-12	3
Palisade Av	S-12	3
Palisade Av	T-12	3
Palisade Plz	T-12	3
Park Av	S-12	3
Pine St	T-12	3
Pleasant Av	S-12	3
Prospect Av	T-12	3
Reynolds La	S-12	3
River View Av	S-12	3
Riverivew Pl	T-12	3
Rothwell Av	T-12	3
Saint Paul Av	S-12	3
Shannon Pl	S-12	3
Summit Av	T-12	3
Summit Ter	S-12	3
Vetean Pl	S-12	3
Walker St	S-12	3
Warren Av	S-12	3
Washington Av	S-12	3
Washington Pl	T-12	3
Wayne Av	S-12	3
West End Av	S-12	3
West End Av	R-12	3
West View Av	S-12	3
Wheeler St	S-12	3
Wilfred Ter	S-12	3
William Pl	S-12	3
William Ter	S-12	3
Williams Pl	S-12	3
Winston Dr	S-13	3
Winterburn Grove	S-12	3

Closter, Boro of

STREET	GRID	MAP
1st St	J-13	7,8
1st St	J-13	7,8
2nd St	J-13	7,8
2nd St	J-13	7,8
3rd St	K-13	7
4th St	K-13	7
5th St	K-13	7
11th St	H-14	8
Albany Blvd	J-14	7,8
Alpine Dr	J-14	7,8
Anderson Av	K-14	7
Ann Arbor Pl	J-14	7,8
Arnold Av	J-14	7,8
Arthur Ct	K-14	7
Asmus Rd	J-13	7,8
Augusta St	J-14	7,8
Auryansen Ct	J-14	7,8
Bergenline Av	J-13	7,8
Bethany Cir	J-12	7,8
Birch St	J-12	7,8
Blanche Av	J-14	7,8
Bogert St	J-13	7,8
Bowers Ln	J-14	7,8
Bradley Pl	J-14	7,8
Brodil Ct	J-14	7,8
Brook St	J-13	7,8
Buzzoni Dr	J-14	7,8
Buzzoni Dr	J-14	7,8
Campbell Av	J-13	7,8
Carlson Ct	J-13	7,8
Carr Pl	J-12	7,8
Cedar Ln	J-12	7,8
Cedar Ct	J-12	7,8
Center St	J-12	7,8
Charles St	J-13	7,8
Chestnut Av	J-13	7,8
Church Ct	J-14	7,8
Clarke St	J-13	7,8
Cleveland St	J-13	7,8
Closter Rd	J-13	7,8
Colgate St	J-14	7,8
Collins Av	J-14	7,8
Columbus Av	J-13	7,8
Crescent St	J-12	7,8
Cross St	J-12	7,8
Curtis Pl	J-13	7,8
Dana Pl	J-13	7,8
Davis St	J-13	7,8
Demarest Av	J-12	7,8
Division St	J-13	7,8
Donald Pl	J-13	7,8
Durant Ln	J-13	7,8
Durie Av	J-13	7,8
Eagle Ln	J-12	7,8
Eckerson Av	J-13	7,8
Edgar St	J-13	7,8
Eisenhower Rd	J-14	7,8
Endres St	J-13	7,8
Ethel Pl	J-12	7,8
Everett St	J-13	7,8
Fairview Av	J-13	7,8
Farrington Av	J-12	7,8
Fayette St	J-13	7,8
Flambrook Rd	K-14	7
Forest St	J-12	7,8
Garry Rd	J-14	7,8
Giletta Ct	J-14	7,8
Godwin Ct	J-13	7,8
Green Way Ct	J-14	7,8
Greenlawn Rd	J-13	7,8
Grove St	J-13	7,8
Gwynne Ct	J-13	7,8
Halsey Ln	J-14	7,8
Haring St	J-13	7,8
Harrington Av	J-13	7,8
Hartford St	J-14	7,8
Harvard St	J-14	7,8
Harvey St	J-13	7,8
Hawthorne Ter	J-12	7,8
Heaton Ct	J-14	7,8
Henmar Dr	K-14	7
Herbert Av	J-13	7,8
Hickory Ln	J-14	7,8
High St	J-12	7,8
High St	J-13	7,8
Highview Ct	J-14	7,8
Homans Av	J-13	7,8
Homans Av	J-14	7,8
Irene Ct	K-14	7
Irving Av	J-13	7,8
Jane St	J-13	7,8
Jason Woods Rd	K-14	7
Jay's Ct	J-13	7,8
John St	J-13	7,8
Johnson Ct	K-14	7
Julia St	J-13	7,8
Kennedy Cir	J-14	7,8
King Pl	J-14	7,8
Kinkaid Av	J-14	7,8
Knickerbocker Rd	J-13	7,8
Lake Rd	K-14	7
Lawrence Ct	J-14	7,8
Legion Pl	J-13	7,8
Leonard Av	J-14	7,8
Leonard Av	J-13	7,8
Lewis St	J-13	7,8
Lindberg	J-13	7,8
Lindberg	J-14	7,8
Linderman Av	J-13	7,8
Lockwood Ln	J-12	7,8
Locust St	J-13	7,8
MacArthur Av	J-14	7,8
Madison St	J-13	7,8
Maple Av	J-13	7,8
Maple Av	K-13	7
Maplewood Rd	K-14	7
Mattocks Pl	J-13	7,8
Mattocks Pl	J-13	7,8
Maycock Ct	J-13	7,8
McCain Ct	J-14	7,8
McKinley St	J-13	7,8
Mead Dr	J-13	7,8
Meadows Ln	K-14	7
Michael Ln	J-13	7,8
Mill Pond Rd	J-14	7,8
Morrison St	J-13	7,8
Naugle St	J-13	7,8
New St	J-13	7,8
North Star Rd	J-14	7,8
O'Shaughnessy Ln	K-14	7
Oak St	J-12	7,8
Oakland Av	J-13	7,8
Old Closter Dock Rd	J-13	7,8
Old Hook Rd	J-12	7,8
Olive St	J-13	7,8
Olympia St	J-14	7,8
Parkside Ln	J-14	7,8
Parsells Ct	J-14	7,8
Parsells Ln	K-14	7
Patton Cres	J-14	7,8
Patton Ln	J-14	7,8
Pearle St	J-12	7,8
Perry St	J-13	7,8
Piermont Rd	J-13	7,8
Pine Hill Rd	K-14	7
Pine St	J-13	7,8
Poplar St	J-12	7,8
Primrose Ln	J-13	7,8
Princeton St	J-14	7,8
Rail Road Av	J-13	7,8
Ranch Ln	K-14	7
Reuten Dr	J-13	7,8
Richard Ct	K-14	7
Richmond St	J-14	7,8
Robinhood Rd	J-13	7,8
Roden Wy	J-12	7,8
Roosevelt St	J-14	7,8
Rose Ct	J-13	7,8
Ruckman Rd	J-13	7,8
Ruckman Rd	J-14	7,8
Rutgers St	J-14	7,8
Ryerson Pl	J-13	7,8
Schraalenburgh Rd	J-12	7,8
Sherman Av	J-14	7,8
Sidney Pl	J-13	7,8
Smith Ct	J-12	7,8
Station Ct	J-13	7,8
Storig Av	J-13	7,8
Susan Dr	J-14	7,8
Tallon Ter	J-13	7,8
Taylor Dr	J-14	7,8
Tenakill St	J-13	7,8
Trautwein Cres	J-14	7,8
Trenton Blvd	J-14	7,8
Truman Ct	J-14	7,8
Union St	J-12	7,8
Van Sciver St	J-13	7,8
Venus Dr	J-14	7,8
Vervalen St	J-13	7,8
Vivian Ln	K-14	7
Vivian Ln	K-13	7
Wainwright Av	J-14	7,8
Wainwright Ct	J-14	7,8
Waldron Pl	J-12	7,8
Walker Av	J-14	7,8
Walnut St	J-13	7,8
Wellington Av	J-13	7,8
Wendy Ln	J-14	7,8
West Minster Av	J-13	7,8
West Wind Ct	H-14	8
West Wind Ct	J-14	7,8
West St	J-13	7,8
Westervelt Av	J-13	7,8
Whitne St	J-13	7,8
William St	J-13	7,8
Willis Dr	J-12	7,8
Willow Rd	J-14	7,8
Wilson Pl	J-14	7,8
Yale Pl	J-14	7,8

Cresskill, Boro of

STREET	GRID	MAP
2nd St	L-13	7
3rd St	L-13	7
4th St	L-13	7
5th St	L-13	7
6th St	L-13	7
7th St	L-13	7
8th St	L-13	7
9th St	L-13	7
10th St	L-13	7
11th St	L-13	7
11th St	K-13	7
12th St	L-13	7
13th St	L-13	7
14th St	L-12	7
Ackerman Pl	L-13	7
Adams Dr	L-14	7
Adele Av	K-13	7
Allen St	L-13	7
Bancroft	K-13	7
Beechwood Rd	K-13	7
Beekman	K-13	7
Bergen Ter	K-13	7
Broadway	L-13	7
Brookside Av	L-13	7
Buckingham Rd	L-13	7
Burns Pl	K-13	7
Burton Pl	K-13	7
Carlton Ter	K-13	7
Cedar St	L-13	7
Center St	L-13	7
Cherry Ct	L-12	7
Chestnut St	L-13	7
Churchill Rd	L-13	7
Clark St	K-13	7
Concord St	L-13	7
Cottage Pl	L-13	7
County Rd	L-13	7
Cranford Pl	K-13	7
Cresskill Av	L-13	7
Crest Dr E	L-13	7
Crest Dr N	L-13	7
Crest Dr S	L-13	7
Davenport Av	L-13	7
Deacon Pl	K-13	7
Delmar Av	L-13	7
Delmar Av	K-13	7
Devon Pl	L-14	7
Devon Pl	L-13	7
Devonshire Rd	L-13	7
Devonshire Rd	L-13	7
Devonshire Rd	L-14	7
Division St	L-13	7
Dogwood Ln	L-13	7
Douglas Dr	K-13	7
Eager Pl	L-13	7
East Madison Av	L-13	7
East Madison Av	L-14	7
East Hill Ct	L-14	7
Edgewood Ct	K-13	7
Eisenhower Dr	L-14	7
Elmore Pl	L-13	7
Elmwood Tr	K-13	7
Emerson St	L-13	7
Engle St	L-13	7
Engleside St	L-13	7
Esmond Ter	L-13	7
Evans Rd	K-13	7
Evergreen Av	L-13	7
Fairway Ct	L-14	7
Fenway Ct	K-13	7
Florence Av	L-12	7
Gilmore Av	K-13	7
Gilmore Av	L-13	7
Glenview Ter	L-13	7
Godfrey Pl	K-13	7
Grant Av	L-13	7
Grant Av	K-13	7
Haight Pl	K-13	7
Harvard St	K-13	7
Heather Hill Ct	K-13	7
Heather Hill Rd	K-13	7
Hemlock Dr	L-14	7
Highland St	L-13	7
Hillside Av	L-14	7
Hillside Av	L-13	7
Holly Ln	K-13	7
Hoover Dr	L-14	7
Hoover Dr	L-14	7
Huyler Landing Rd	L-14	7
Jackson Av	L-14	7
Jefferson Av	L-13	7
Johnson Ct	L-14	7
Kenilworth St	L-13	7
Kenilworth St	L-13	7
Kennedy Rd	L-14	7
Knickerbocker Rd	L-12	7
Knoll Rd	L-13	7
Lafayette St	L-13	7
Lafayette St	K-13	7
Lambs Ln	L-14	7
Lancaster Ct	L-14	7
Last Rd	L-13	7
Legion Dr	L-13	7
Lexington Av	L-13	7
Lincoln Dr	L-13	7
Lincoln Dr	K-13	7
Linwood Av	L-13	7
Loman Ct	L-14	7
Madison Av	L-13	7
Magnolia Av	L-13	7
Maple St	L-12	7
Margie Av	L-13	7
McGrath Dr	L-14	7
Meadow St	K-13	7
Merrifield Wy	K-13	7
Merritt Av	L-12	7
Mezzine Dr	K-13	7
Mezzine Dr	K-13	7
Michelle Ct	L-13	7
Milton St	L-13	7
Monroe Av	L-13	7
Monument Pl	L-13	7
Morningside Av	L-13	7
Mount View Ct	K-13	7
Mount View Rd	K-13	7
New St	L-13	7
Oak St	L-13	7
Oxford Pl	L-13	7
Palisade Av	L-13	7
Palisades Ct	L-13	7
Park Av	L-13	7
Pershing Pl	L-13	7
Phelps Av	L-12	7
Pierce Av	K-13	7
Piermont Rd	L-13	7
Piermont Rd	K-13	7
Poplar St	L-13	7
Prospect Av	L-13	7
Ridge Rd	K-13	7
Roosevelt St	L-13	7
Rose St	L-13	7
Short Pl	L-13	7
Smith Ter	L-13	7
South St	K-13	7
Spring St	L-13	7
Spruce St	L-13	7
Stivers St	L-12	7
Sycamore St	L-13	7
Tenakill Rd	L-13	7
Truman Dr	L-14	7
Union Av	L-13	7
Van Buren Ct	L-14	7
Washington St	L-13	7
Waverly Pl	L-13	7
Weil Pl	L-13	7
Wells Ct	K-13	7
West Morningside Av	K-13	7
Westervelt Pl	L-13	7
Willis Av	L-13	7
Willow St	L-13	7
Wilson Dr	L-14	7
Woodland Rd	K-13	7
Wright Pl	K-13	7

Demarest, Boro of

STREET	GRID	MAP
Achilles St	K-13	7
Adele Av	K-13	7
Alpine Ct	K-14	7
Anderson Av	K-14	7
Arthur Ct	K-13	7
Belmar St	K-13	7
Blanche Av	K-13	7
Bogert Rd	K-13	7
Brenner Pl	K-14	7
Broad St	K-13	7
Brook Wy	K-13	7
Brookside Av	K-13	7
Carlotta Wy	K-13	7
Carol Ct	K-14	7
Central Av	K-13	7
Chestnut St	J-13	7,8
Chestnut St	K-13	7
Christie St	K-13	7
Columbus Rd	K-14	7
Country Club Wy	K-14	7
County Rd	L-13	7
County Rd	K-13	7
Cross St	K-13	7
Cypress Pl	L-14	7
Deerhill Rd	L-14	7
Demarest Av	K-13	7
Devon Pl	L-13	7
Devon Pl	L-14	7
Dogwood Ln	K-13	7
Donny Brook Dr	J-13	7,8
Drury Ln	K-13	7
Duane Ln	K-14	7
Duck Pond Rd	L-14	7
Eastview Ter	J-13	7,8
Eastview Ter	K-13	7
Edgewood Ct	K-13	7
Edward St	K-13	7
Elm Pl	L-13	7
Emily Ct	K-14	7
Emily Ct	K-13	7
Eric Pl	K-13	7
Everett Rd	K-13	7
Evergreen Pl	K-13	7
Fairfield Ct	K-13	7
Fairfield Ct	L-13	7
Ford St	K-13	7
Forest Rd	K-13	7
Glenwood Av	L-14	7
Glenwood Av	K-13	7
Grove St	J-13	7,8
Grove St	J-13	7,8
Hardenburgh Av	K-14	7
Hardenburgh Av	K-13	7
Heather Hill Rd	K-13	7
Heritage Ct	K-13	7
High St	K-13	7
Highland Av	L-13	7
Highland Av	L-14	7
Holland Av	L-13	7
Holland Av	L-14	7
Insley St	K-13	7
Irene Ct	K-14	7
Isabella Wy	K-13	7
John St	K-13	7
Knickerbocker Rd	K-13	7
Lake Rd	K-13	7
Lake Rd	K-14	7
Laurel Rd	K-13	7
Lenox Av	K-13	7
Liberty Rd	K-13	7
Lincoln St	K-13	7
Lois Av	K-13	7
Madison Av	K-13	7
Maple Av	K-13	7
Margaret Ct	K-13	7
Mayforth Ter	K-13	7
Meadow St	K-13	7
Meredith Rd	K-13	7
Merrifield Wy	K-13	7
Mount View Ct	K-13	7
Mount View Rd	K-13	7
Myrtle Av	K-13	7
Northwood Av	K-13	7
Oak Pl	L-14	7
Old Country Rd	K-13	7
Old Stable Rd	K-13	7
Orchard Rd	K-13	7
Palisade Blvd	K-13	7
Park St	K-13	7
Piermont Rd	K-13	7
Pine Av	J-13	7,8
Pine Ter	K-13	7
Pine Ter	K-14	7
Poplar Rd	K-14	7
Prescott St	K-13	7
Prospect St	J-13	7,8
Robin Rd	K-13	7
Rodney Pl	K-13	7
Ross Av	L-13	7
Ruth Ln	K-13	7
Serpentine Rd	K-13	7
South St	K-13	7
Spring Ln	K-13	7
Spruce Pl	L-14	7
Stelfox St	K-13	7
Stewart St	K-13	7
Stratford Ct	K-13	7
Sunset Rd	K-13	7
Van Horn St	K-13	7
Village Ct	L-13	7
Village Ct	K-13	7
Wakelee Dr	K-13	7
Wakelee St	K-13	7
Wells Ct	K-13	7
Wellwood Rd	K-13	7
William St	K-13	7
Woodland Rd	J-13	7,8
Woodland Rd	K-13	7

Dumont, Boro of

STREET	GRID	MAP
Aladdin Av	L-11	7
American Legion	L-12	7
American Legion Ter	L-12	7
American Legion Ter	K-12	7
American Legion	K-12	7
Andover Av	K-12	7
Armour Pl	L-11	7
Atlantic St	L-12	7
Avon Ln	K-12	7
Baker Ln	L-12	7
Barbara Rd	K-12	7
Barbara Rd	K-11	7
Beacon St	K-12	7
Bedford Rd	L-12	7
Bedford Rd	K-12	7
Bergman Ter	L-12	7
Berkley Pl	K-12	7
Beverly Rd	K-12	7
Birch Dr	L-12	7
Birch Dr	K-12	7
Blanche Ct	L-12	7
Blauvelt Av	L-12	7
Blish Pl	L-12	7
Bridge St	L-11	7
Brook St	L-12	7
Brookfield Rd	K-12	7
Bussell Ct	K-12	7
Campi Ct	K-12	7
Catawba St	L-12	7
Cedar Rd	K-12	7
Central Av	K-12	7
Charles St	L-12	7
Charles St	K-12	7
Cherokee St	L-11	7
Chestnut St	L-12	7
Church St	K-12	7
Church St E	K-12	7
Church St W	K-12	7
Clarke St	L-12	7
Cole Ct	K-12	7
Colonial Pkwy	L-12	7
Colonial Pl	L-11	7
Columbia Av	L-12	7
Columbia Av	L-11	7
Concord St	L-11	7
Congress St	L-12	7
Conklin Pl	L-12	7
Cooper Av	L-11	7
Cooper Av	L-12	7
Courtland Av	L-12	7
Cresskill Av	K-12	7
Cypress Rd	K-12	7
Cypress Rd	K-11	7
Dakota Av	L-11	7
Dakota Av	L-12	7
Dance Blvd	L-11	7
Davies Av	L-12	7
Delaware Av	L-12	7
Delong Av	K-12	7
Demarest Ct	K-12	7
Depew St	L-12	7
Derby Ln	K-12	7
Dixon Av	L-11	7
Druid Av	L-12	7
Dulles Dr	L-12	7
Dumont Av	L-12	7
Dunn Pl	L-12	7
East Linden Av	L-12	7
East Linden Av	K-12	7
East Madison Av	L-12	7
East Quackenbush Av	L-12	7
East Revere Dr	K-12	7
Elizabeth St	K-12	7
Elm St	L-12	7
Erie St	L-11	7
Essex Pl	K-12	7
Fern Av	L-11	7
Fleetwood Rd	K-11	7

BERGEN COUNTY

STREET	GRID	MAP
Fleetwood Rd	K-12	7
Florence Av	L-12	7
Forest Rd	K-12	7
Fox Ct	L-11	7
Franklin St	K-12	7
Franklin St	K-13	7
Fuller St	L-12	7
Garden St	L-12	7
Garfield St	K-12	7
Gibbs Rd	K-12	7
Glen Av	L-11	7
Golf View Dr	K-12	7
Gordon Av	K-12	7
Grant Av	K-12	7
Gurney Ct	K-12	7
Gurney Ct	K-11	7
Hallet Ct	L-12	7
Hamilton Av	L-12	7
Harding Av	K-12	7
Harlan Dr	K-12	7
Harrison St	K-12	7
Harwick Rd	K-12	7
Hazel St	K-12	7
Hickory St	K-12	7
Hickory St	L-12	7
Highland Av	L-11	7
Highwood Dr	L-12	7
Hillcrest Dr	L-12	7
Hillcrest Dr	K-12	7
Hillside Av	L-11	7
Holt St	L-12	7
Howard St	L-12	7
Hunting Dr	K-12	7
Idaho St	L-11	7
Iowa	L-11	7
Ivy Pl	L-12	7
Johnson Av	L-12	7
Juniper St	K-12	7
Knickerbocker Rd	K-13	7
Lafayette Av	L-11	7
Larch Av	K-12	7
Laurel Av	K-12	7
Lawrence Av	L-11	7
Lenox Av	K-12	7
Lexington Av	K-12	7
Lincoln Av	L-11	7
Locust Av	L-11	7
Locust Av	L-12	7
Lohmann Pl	K-12	7
Lucille Av	L-12	7
Magnolia Av	L-12	7
Manhattan Tr	L-12	7
Maple St	L-12	7
Margaret Ct	L-12	7
Margaret Ct	K-12	7
Marion Av	L-12	7
Massachusetts Av	K-12	7
McKinley Av	L-12	7
McKinley Av	L-11	7
Medford Rd	K-12	7
Merritt Av	L-12	7
Monroe Av	L-11	7
Moore Av	L-11	7
Morton Av	L-11	7
Neil Ct	K-12	7
New Milford Av	L-11	7
New York Av	L-12	7
Niagara St	L-12	7
Niagara St	L-11	7
Oak St	L-12	7
Omaha St	L-11	7
Oneida Av	L-11	7
Ontario	L-11	7
Overlook Dr	K-12	7
Overlook Dr	L-12	7
Oxford Av	K-12	7
Park Av	L-12	7
Patton Pl	L-12	7
Pearl St	K-12	7
Pershing St	L-12	7
Pine St	L-12	7
Pleasant St	K-12	7
Poplar St	K-12	7
Prospect Av	K-11	7
Prospect Av	L-11	7
Randolph Av	K-12	7
Ranger Rd	K-12	7
Revere Dr	K-12	7
Richard Dr	K-12	7
Romano Dr	L-12	7
Romano Dr	K-12	7
Roosevelt Av	L-12	7
Roosevelt Av	L-11	7
Roxbury Rd	K-12	7
Rucereto Av	K-12	7
Seminole Av	L-11	7
Seminole Av	K-11	7
Seneca Av	L-11	7
Shadyside Av	L-12	7
Shelby St	L-12	7
Sherwood Rd	K-11	7
Sherwood Rd	K-12	7
Short St	L-12	7
Slater St	L-12	7
Spring Dr	L-11	7
Stanley St	L-12	7
Steven Dr	K-12	7
Stivers St	L-12	7
Stratford Rd	K-12	7
Summit Av	K-12	7
Sunnyside Av	L-12	7
Sunset St	K-12	7
Sycamore Rd	K-12	7
Teak Rd	K-12	7
Thompson St	L-12	7
Tobin Ct	L-11	7
Twin Boro Ln	L-11	7
Veterans Plz	L-12	7
Virginia Av	L-12	7
Walnut St	L-11	7
Walsh Dr	L-12	7
Walters St	L-11	7
Washington Av	L-12	7
West Linden Av	L-12	7
West Madison Av	L-12	7
West Madison Av	L-11	7
West Quackenbush Av	L-11	7
West Quackenbush Av	L-12	7
West Revere Dr	K-12	7
West Shore Av	K-12	7
White Beeches Dr	K-11	7
White Beeches Dr	K-12	7
Whittaker St	L-11	7
Wilcox St	L-12	7
Wilkens Dr	K-12	7
Windsor Dr	L-12	7
Windsor Dr	K-12	7
Wolcott Dr	L-12	7

East Rutherford, Boro of

STREET	GRID	MAP
Ann St	S-8	1,2
Atkins Tr	R-7	2
Bobbink Tr	R-7	2
Boiling Springs Av	S-8	1,2
Branca Rd	S-8	1,2
Brook Ter	R-7	2
Carlton Av	R-7	2
Central Av	R-7	2
Chadwick St	R-7	2
Clinton Pl	R-7	2
Cornelia St	S-8	1,2
Cottage Pl	R-7	2
DuBois St	S-8	1,2
East Union Av	S-8	1,2
Edison Pl	S-8	1,2
Elm St	R-7	2
Enoch St	S-8	1,2
Erie Av	R-8	2
Everett Pl	S-8	1,2
Everett Pl	S-7	1,2
Francis St	S-8	1,2
Franklin Pl	R-7	2
Garden St	R-8	2
Garden St	S-8	1,2
George St	R-8	2
Glenn Ct	R-7	2
Grant St	R-7	2
Grove St	R-7	2
Hackensack St	S-8	1,2
Herman St	R-7	2
Herrick St	R-7	2
High St	S-8	1,2
High St	R-8	2
Hillside Tr	R-7	2
Hoboken Rd	R-8	2
Hope St	R-7	2
Humbolt St	R-7	2
Humbolt St	S-7	1,2
Jane St	S-8	1,2
Jersey St	R-7	2
John St	R-7	2
Landing Pl	S-8	1,2
Laurel Pl	R-8	2
Lincoln Pl	R-8	2
Lincoln Pl	S-8	1,2
Locust Ln	R-7	2
Madison Circle Dr	S-8	1,2
Madison St	R-7	2
Main St	S-8	1,2
Main St	S-7	1,2
Manor Rd	S-8	1,2
Mansion St	S-8	1,2
Maple St	R-7	2
Margood Ct	R-7	2
McKenzie Av	R-7	2
Morton St	R-7	2
Mozart St	R-7	2
Murray Hill Pkwy	S-8	1,2
New St	R-7	2
Oak St	R-7	2
Orchard St	S-8	1,2
Park Av	S-8	1,2
Paterson Av	R-7	2
Paterson Av	R-8	2
Paterson Plank Rd	S-9	1,2
Paterson Plank Rd	S-8	1,2
Poplar St	R-7	2
Prospect St	S-8	1,2
Prospect Ter	R-8	2
Rail Road Av	R-7	2
Rail Road Av	S-7	1,2
Rail Road Av	S-8	1,2
Randolph Av	R-8	2
River St	R-7	2
Rose St	R-7	2
Shepard Ter	R-7	2
Spring St	R-7	2
Stanley St	S-8	1,2
Summer St	S-8	1,2
Swan Ct	R-7	2
Uhland St	S-8	1,2
Uhland St	S-7	1,2
Union Av	S-8	1,2
Union Pl	R-7	2
Union St	R-7	2
Van Winkle St	R-7	2
Van Winkle St	S-8	1,2
Vreeland St	S-8	1,2
Wall St	R-7	2
Washington Pl	R-8	2
Whelan Rd	S-8	1,2
White Tr	R-7	2
William St	S-8	1,2
Willow St	R-7	2
Willow Wood Ct	R-7	2
Windsor Av	R-8	2
Winter Pl	S-8	1,2
York St	R-7	2

Edgewater, Boro of

STREET	GRID	MAP
Adelaid Pl	S-13	3
Annette Av	R-13	3
Archer St	S-12	3
Archer St	S-13	3
Arlington Ter	R-13	3
Beverly Pl	S-13	3
Burdett Ct	S-13	3
Casta Ln	S-13	3
Colony Rd	S-13	3
Columbia Ter	S-13	3
Dempsey Av	S-13	3
Edgewater Rd	S-12	3
Edgewater Rd	S-12	3
Garden Pl	S-13	3
Glenwood Av	R-13	3
Glenwood Ln	R-13	3
Hilliard Av	S-13	3
Hooks Ln	R-13	3
Hudson Ter	S-13	3
Hudson Ter	R-13	3
Lasher Ln	R-13	3
Leary Ln	R-13	3
Manatauck Av	S-13	3
Manatauck Av	R-13	3
Maple St	R-13	3
Massa Ln	R-13	3
McCurry Ln	S-13	3
Myrtle Av	R-13	3
North St	R-13	3
North Glen La	R-13	3
Oakdene Av	S-13	3
Old River Rd	T-12	3
Old Wood Rd	S-13	3
Orchard St	R-13	3
Palisade Plaza	R-13	3
Palisade Ter	R-13	3
Panorama Dr	S-13	3
Park St	R-13	3
River Rd	T-12	3
River Rd	R-13	3
River Rd	S-13	3
Rockwood Pl	R-13	3
Russell Av	S-13	3
Shore Rd	R-13	3
Sterling Pl	R-13	3
Undercliff Av	S-13	3
Undercliff Av	R-13	3
Valley Pl	S-13	3
Veterans Wy	R-13	3
Vista La	R-13	3
Vreeland Ter	S-13	3
Washington Ln	R-13	3
Winter Burn Pl	S-13	3
Yorkview Ter	R-13	3

Elmwood Park, Boro of

STREET	GRID	MAP
1st St	N-6	5
2nd St	N-7	5
2nd St	N-6	5
3rd St	N-7	5
13th Av	M-7	5,6
13th Av	M-7	5,6
14th Av	M-7	5,6
14th Av	M-7	5,6
15th Av	M-7	5,6
15th Av	M-7	5,6
16th Av	M-7	5,6
16th Av	M-7	5,6
17th Av	M-7	5,6
17th Av	M-7	5,6
18th Av	M-7	5,6
18th Av	M-7	5,6
Ackerman Av	M-6	5,6
Ann St	P-6	5
Arena Ct	N-7	5
Augusta St	N-7	5
Bank St	N-7	5
Bank St	P-7	5
Bart Pl	N-7	5
Beech St	N-7	5
Beechwood Av	M-6	5,6
Bellevue Av	M-7	5,6
Birchwood Dr	N-7	5
Birchwood Dr	N-6	5
Boulevard	N-7	5
Boulevard	M-7	5,6
Boulevard	M-7	5,6
Bredder Ct	N-7	5
Broadway	M-6	5,6
Broadway	M-7	5,6
Brookside Av	N-7	5
Bushes Ln	N-7	5
Cadmus Av	N-7	5
Cedar St	N-7	5
Center St	N-7	5
Chamberlain Av	N-6	5
Chamberlain Av	N-7	5
Chestnut St	N-7	5
Chobot Ln	N-7	5
Church St	N-7	5
Coates St	N-7	5
Cole	N-7	5
Cole St	N-7	5
Columbia St	M-6	5,6
Columbia St	M-7	5,6
Court Pl	N-7	5
Court St	N-7	5
Craig Ct	N-7	5
Dapp Ct	M-7	5,6
Donor Av	M-6	5,6
Doremus Pl	M-7	5,6
Dye Av	N-7	5
Dye Blvd	N-7	5
East Phillip Av	N-7	5
East Pkwy	N-7	5
East Washington Av	M-7	5,6
East 52nd St	M-7	5,6
East 53rd St	M-7	5,6
East 54th St	M-7	5,6
East 55th St	M-7	5,6
Echo Pl	N-7	5
Edward H Ross Dr	N-7	5
Elizabeth Av	M-7	5,6
Elm St	M-6	5,6
Elm St	N-6	5
Elmhurst St	N-7	5
Elmwood Dr	M-6	5,6
Elmwood Dr	M-7	5,6
Elmwood Ter	M-6	5,6
English Av	M-7	5,6
Falmouth Av	N-7	5
Falmouth Av	N-6	5
Fencsak Av	N-7	5
Florence Pl	M-7	5,6
Fournier Cres	N-7	5
Franklin St	N-7	5
Fredericks Ct	P-6	5
Fredericks Ct	P-7	5
Gall Av	N-7	5
Gantner Av	N-6	5
Gantner Av	N-7	5
Garden Dr	N-7	5
Garden Dr	N-6	5
Garden Dr	P-6	5
Garden State Pkwy	N-7	5
Garners Ln	N-7	5
Garuth Av	N-7	5
Garvey Pl	N-7	5
Gate Wy	N-7	5
Gate Wy	P-7	5
Gilbert Av	N-6	5
Glenwood Av	M-6	5,6
Godwin Av	M-7	5,6
Grant St	N-7	5
Greenwood Av	M-6	5,6
Gregory Ct	N-7	5
Grove St	N-7	5
Grove St	N-6	5
Halstead Pl	N-7	5
Hamilton Av	M-7	5,6
Henry St	N-7	5
Herman St	N-7	5
Hillman Dr	N-7	5
Homestead Rd	N-7	5
Homestead Rd	N-6	5
Iozia Ter	M-7	5,6
James Ct	N-7	5
Jan Ct	N-7	5
Jefferson St	N-7	5
Kipp Av	P-6	5
Lee St	N-7	5
Lee St	N-6	5
Legion Pl	N-7	5
Leliarts	M-7	5,6
Lincoln Av	M-7	5,6
Lincoln Av	M-6	5,6
Linden Av	N-7	5
Linwood Av	M-6	5,6
Livi Ct	N-7	5
Locust St	M-7	5,6
Locust St	M-6	5,6
Magnolia St	M-6	5,6
Main Av	N-7	5
Maltese Av	N-7	5
Maple St	N-7	5
Maplewood Av	M-6	5,6
Marginal Rd	N-7	5
Market St	N-6	5
Market St	N-7	5
Martha Av	N-7	5
Martha Av	P-7	5
Martha Av	P-6	5
Martha Av	N-6	5
Memorial Pl	N-7	5
Meyer St	N-7	5
Midland Av	N-7	5
Miles St	P-7	5
Miles St	N-7	5
Mill	N-7	5
Mill St	N-7	5
Miller Av	N-6	5
Miller Av	N-7	5
Molnar Dr	N-7	5
Mulberry St	N-7	5
New St	N-7	5
Norris St	N-6	5
North Van Riper Av	N-7	5
North St	N-7	5
Oak	N-7	5
Obal Av	N-7	5
Orange Av	M-6	5,6
Orange Av	M-6	5,6
Orchard St	N-6	5
Page St	P-7	5
Page St	N-7	5
Palsa Av	N-7	5
Parkview Av	M-6	5,6
Paterson St	N-6	5
Paul Kohner Pl	N-7	5
Paul Ct	M-7	5,6
Philip Av	N-6	5
Phillip St	M-7	5,6
Pine St	N-7	5
Plant Av	N-6	5
Ray St	N-7	5
Ray St	P-7	5
Reihl St	N-7	5
Rena Ct	N-7	5
River Dr	P-6	5
River Dr	N-6	5
River Rd	N-6	5
Roosevelt Av	N-6	5
Roosevelt Av	N-7	5
Rosedale Av	M-6	5,6
Rosemont Av	M-6	5,6
Roth St	N-7	5
Rudolph Av	N-7	5
Russel Ct	M-6	5,6
Sabo Ct	N-7	5
Slater Dr	N-6	5
Slauhterdam Rd	N-6	5
South Center St	N-7	5
Speidel Av	M-7	5,6
Spruce St	N-7	5
Spruce St	M-7	5,6
Staedler Ln	N-7	5
Stefanic Av	N-7	5
Steinway Ln	N-7	5
Sterling St	M-6	5,6
Steuli Ct	N-7	5
Stone Av	N-7	5
Summit Av	N-7	5
Susan Ct	N-7	5
Terrace St	N-7	5
Tina Ct	N-7	5
Tuella Av	N-7	5
Van Riper Av	N-7	5
Veterans Pl	N-7	5
Viviney St	M-6	5,6
Viviney St	N-7	5
Viviney St	M-6	5,6
Wallace St	N-7	5
Walnut St	N-7	5
Washington Av	M-6	5,6
Wenzel St	N-7	5
West Pkwy	N-7	5
West St	N-7	5
Willow St	M-6	5,6

Emerson, Boro of

STREET	GRID	MAP
1st St	J-11	7,8
2nd St	J-11	7,8
3rd St	J-11	7,8
4th St	J-11	7,8
5th St	J-11	7,8
6th St	J-11	7,8
7th St	J-11	7,8
Ackerman Av	J-10	6,9
Adams Ct	J-10	6,9
Alan Rd	J-10	6,9
Alma Av	J-10	6,9
Arthur St	J-11	7,8
Auricchio Av	J-11	7,8
Belmont Av	J-11	7,8
Birch St	J-10	6,9
Bland St	J-10	6,9
Bolling St	J-10	6,9
Briarwood Ct	J-10	6,9
Broad St	J-11	7,8
Broadway	J-10	6,9
Brook St	J-10	6,9
Carver Av	J-11	7,8
Chandler Dr	J-10	6,9
Charles St	J-11	7,8
Chestnut Av	J-10	6,9
Cindy Ln	J-10	6,9
Clinton St	J-11	7,8
Colonial Rd	J-10	6,9
Columbia Av	J-10	6,9
Congress Rd	J-10	6,9
Crest Rd	J-10	6,9
Daned Rd	J-11	7,8
Demorest Av	J-10	6,9
Diedrick Pl	J-11	7,8
Dogwood Ln	J-11	7,8
Dorchester Rd	J-10	6,9
Douglas St	J-11	7,8
Dyer Av	J-11	7,8
Eagle Dr	J-11	7,8
East Ackerman Av	J-11	7,8
Elmwood Dr	J-11	7,8
Emerson Plz E	J-10	6,9
Emerson Plz W	J-10	6,9
Erie Av	J-10	6,9
Etna Av	J-10	6,9
Fairway Av	J-10	6,9
Fairway Av	J-11	7,8
Forest Av	J-10	6,9
Franklin Ct	J-9	6,9
Franklin Ct	J-10	6,9
Furman Dr	J-10	6,9
George St	J-11	7,8
Glenwood Av	J-11	7,8
Golf Club Rd	J-10	6,9
Grand Blvd	J-10	6,9
Grand Blvd	J-10	6,9
Greta Pl	J-10	6,9
Haines St	J-10	6,9
Hancock St	J-10	6,9
Hartland Av	J-11	7,8
Hasbrouck Av	J-10	6,9
Henry St	J-11	7,8
High St	J-11	7,8
Highland Av	J-11	7,8
Hill Rd	J-10	6,9
Hillcrest Av	J-10	6,9
Hillside Av	J-10	6,9
Hollywood Av	J-10	6,9
Hopper Av	J-11	7,8
Huyler St	J-10	6,9
Huyler St	K-10	6
Jansack Ct	J-11	7,8
Jefferson Av	J-10	6,9
Jefferson Av	J-11	7,8
John St	J-10	6,9
Jordan Rd	J-10	6,9
Karen Ln	J-10	6,9
Kenneth Av	J-10	6,9
Kensington Av	J-10	6,9
Kinderkamack Rd	J-10	6,9
Lakeview Dr	J-11	7,8
Lakeview Ter	J-11	7,8
Lee Ct	J-10	6,9
Lee Ct	J-9	6,9
Lexington Av	J-10	6,9
Lincoln Blvd	J-10	6,9
Linda Pl	J-11	7,8
Linden Av	J-10	6,9
Linwood Av	J-10	6,9
Locust Av	J-10	6,9
Locust Av	J-11	7,8
Longview Dr	J-10	6,9
Louis Av	J-10	6,9
Lozier Av	J-10	6,9
Maepaul Dr	J-10	6,9
Main St	J-11	7,8
Maple Ln	J-11	7,8
Marriana Pl	J-11	7,8
Maulbeck Av	J-11	7,8
Mitchell St	J-10	6,9
Municipal Pl	J-11	7,8
Municipal Pl	J-10	6,9
Munsey Rd	J-10	6,9
Nassau St	J-11	7,8
Nimando Pl	J-10	6,9
Oakland Av	J-10	6,9
Orchard Av	J-11	7,8
Overlook Av	J-10	6,9
Palisade Av	J-10	6,9
Palisade Av	J-11	7,8
Park Av	J-10	6,9
Parker Dr	J-10	6,9
Pascack Av	J-10	6,9
Pascack Av	J-10	6,9
Pavonia Av	J-10	6,9
Pershing St	J-10	6,9
Pine Dr	J-11	7,8
Powell Rd	J-9	6,9
Powell Rd	J-10	6,9
Rail Road Av	J-10	6,9
Randolph Av	J-11	7,8
Remington Av	J-10	6,9
Revere Av	J-10	6,9
Ridge Rd	J-11	7,8
Ridge Ter	J-11	7,8
Ridge Pl	J-10	6,9
Ross Av	J-10	6,9
Samuel St	J-11	7,8
Sanford Av	J-11	7,8
Scott Ct	J-10	6,9
Seneca Av	J-11	7,8
Sherwood Ct	J-10	6,9
Soldier Hill Rd	K-10	6
Spruce Av	J-10	6,9
Sullivan Dr	J-11	7,8
Summer Ct	J-11	7,8
Summer St	J-11	7,8
Sunset Pl	J-10	6,9
Sycamore Av	J-10	6,9
Tarnapoll Rd	J-10	6,9
Thomas Av	J-10	6,9
Thomas St	J-11	7,8
Thomas St	J-10	6,9
Tillman St	J-11	7,8
Union St	J-11	7,8
Valley Brook Av	J-10	6,9
Van Wagoner Av	J-10	6,9
Vivian Av	J-10	6,9
Walnut Av	J-10	6,9
Washington Av	J-10	6,9
Woodside Av	J-10	6,9
Wortendyke Av	J-10	6,9

Englewood Cliffs, Boro of

STREET	GRID	MAP
1st St	Q-13	3,4
1st St	P-13	4
2nd St	Q-13	3,4
3rd St	Q-13	3,4
5th St	Q-13	3,4
6th St	Q-13	3,4
7th St	Q-13	3,4
8th St	Q-13	3,4
Alfred St	P-13	4
Allison Dr	N-14	4
Allison Rd	P-14	4
Alpine Ct	P-13	4
Anderson St	P-13	4
Arthur Av	P-13	4
Ash St	P-13	4
Barbara Dr	N-14	4
Bayview Av	Q-13	3,4
Berkshire Pl	N-14	4
Beverly Rd	P-13	4
Birch St	P-13	4
Bolz St	P-13	4
Booth Av	N-13	4
Cambridge Pl	N-13	4
Cambridge Pl	N-14	4
Camner St	Q-13	3,4
Carol Dr	N-14	4
Casper Rd	P-13	4
Castle Dr	P-13	4
Cathy Terr	N-14	4
Center St	P-13	4
Charlotte Pl	P-13	4
Charlotte St	P-13	4
Chestnut St	N-13	4
Churchill Rd	N-13	4
Churchill Rd	N-14	4
Clendinen Pl	P-14	4
Cliff Rd	P-13	4
Clifton Ter	P-14	4
Connor Dr	N-14	4
Deborah Tr	Q-13	3,4
Deborah Tr	P-13	4
Deborah Tr	Q-13	3,4
Deborah Tr	P-13	4
Demarest Av	P-13	4
Demarest Ct	P-13	4
Dillingham Pl	P-13	4
Dorchester Rd	P-13	4
Eagan Pl	P-14	4
Elisa Dr	P-13	4
Ellington Pl	N-14	4
Ellington Pl	N-13	4
Elm St	P-13	4
Fairview Av	N-13	4
Floyd Ct	P-13	4
Floyd St	P-13	4
Forest Dr	P-13	4
Geraldine Ct	N-14	4
Geraldine Rd	N-14	4
Hammet Av	Q-13	3,4
Henry Hudson Dr	Q-14	3,4
Henry Hudson Dr	P-14	4
Henry Hudson Dr	N-14	4
Henry Hudson Dr	Q-14	3,4
Henry St	Q-13	3,4
Hickory St	P-13	4
Hollywood Av	N-14	4
Hudson Ter	Q-13	3,4
Irving Av	P-13	4
Jane Dr	N-14	4
Jean Dr	N-14	4
Jenkins Dr	P-13	4
John St	P-13	4
Johnson Av	N-13	4
Johnson Av	N-14	4
Karens Ln	P-13	4
Kathy Ter	N-14	4
Kimhunter Rd	P-13	4
Knox Dr	N-14	4
Laurie Dr	N-14	4
Leighton St	Q-13	3,4
Loretta Ct	P-13	4
Lyncrest Rd	N-14	4
Lyncrest Rd	N-13	4
Lynn Dr	N-14	4
Maple St	N-13	4
Marietta St	P-13	4
Marilyn Dr	N-14	4
Marjorie Ter	P-13	4
Martin Ct	P-13	4
Mauro Rd	P-13	4
Mercer Av	P-13	4
Mercer Av	Q-13	3,4
Middlesex Av	P-13	4
Neal Dr	N-14	4
New St	P-13	4
North Virginia Ct	N-14	4
Oak Hill Ter	P-13	4
Oakwood Ln	P-13	4
Palisade Av	P-13	4
Palisades Interstate Pkwy	Q-13	3,4
Palisades Interstate Pkwy	Q-14	3,4
Pershing Rd	N-13	4
Priscilla Ln	N-14	4
Proposed Route 1	P-13	4
Raymond St	P-14	4
Raymond St	P-13	4
Reiner Pl	N-14	4
Reiner Pl	N-13	4
Ridge Rd	P-13	4
Roberts Rd	N-14	4
Rock Rd	P-13	4
Ropes Rd	P-13	4
Rose Av	P-13	4
Rossett St	Q-13	3,4
Sage Rd	N-14	4
Samford Dr	N-14	4
Sherwood Av	P-13	4
Skyline Dr	P-13	4
Snyder Rd	P-13	4
South Virginia Ct	N-14	4
Stephen Dr	N-14	4
Stratford Rd	P-13	4
Summit Av	P-13	4
Sylvan Blvd	P-13	4
Sylvan Blvd	Q-13	3,4
Toni Dr	P-13	4
Van Nostrand Av	P-13	4
Van Wagoner Dr	N-14	4
Vine St	N-14	4
West Bayview Av	P-13	4
West Bayview Av	Q-13	3,4
Westervelt Pl	P-13	4
Willow Dr	N-14	4
Wittefield Ct	N-14	4
Wood Rd	P-13	4

Englewood, City of

STREET	GRID	MAP
1st St	N-12	4
2nd St	N-12	4
3rd St	N-12	4
4th St	N-12	4
Adam Dr	N-12	4
Adele Ct	P-13	4
Alden Pl	N-12	4
Allison Ct	P-13	4
Arch Rd	P-13	4
Armory St	N-12	4
Audubon Rd	P-13	4
Balsam St	N-12	4
Bancker St	P-12	4
Barling St	M-13	4,7
Beech Rd	P-13	4
Belmont Av	N-12	4
Belmont St	N-12	4
Bennett Rd	N-12	4
Bergen St	N-13	4
Bilmar Pl	N-12	4
Booth Av	N-13	4
Brayton St	N-13	4
Brinckerhoff Ct	N-13	4
Broad Av	P-12	4
Brook Av	N-13	4
Brookside Av	P-12	4
Brookway Av	N-12	4
Brookway Av	N-12	4
Brownes Ter	N-13	4
Cambridge Av	M-12	4,7
Cambridge Av	M-13	4,7
Cambridge Av	N-13	4
Cape May St	P-13	4
Cedar Ln	P-12	4
Cedar St	N-13	4
Central Av	N-12	4
Chamin Plz	N-12	4
Charles St	N-12	4
Chester Pl	N-13	4
Chester Pl	P-13	4
Chestnut St	N-13	4
Church St	N-13	4
Cleveland St	N-12	4
Cliff Dr	P-13	4
Columbus Av	P-12	4
Concord Pl	M-13	4,7
Conrad Rd	M-12	4,7
Coolidge Av	N-12	4
Coolidge Av	P-12	4
Cottage Pl	N-12	4
Crescent Ct	N-13	4
Cross Creek Dr	P-13	4
Cross Creek Dr	P-12	4
Cross St	N-12	4
Culver St	P-13	4
Cumberland St	P-13	4
Curry Av	N-13	4
Curry Av	M-13	4,7
Dana Pl	P-13	4
Daniel Cir	P-13	4
Davidson Pl	N-13	4
De Mott St	N-13	4
Decatur Av	P-12	4
Depot Sq S	N-13	4
Devika Dr	P-13	4
Division St	N-13	4
Douglas St	N-13	4
Dow Pl	P-12	4
Durie Av	N-13	4
Dwight Pl	P-13	4
Eagles Notch Dr	P-13	4
East Nordhoff Pl	P-12	4
East Roosevelt Sq	N-13	4
Eastwood Ct	N-13	4
Edgewood Rd	Q-13	3,4
Egan Pl	N-13	4
Elkwood Ter	N-13	4
Elm Rd	P-13	4
Elmore Av	N-12	4
Engle St	N-13	4
Englewood Av	N-13	4
Englewood Av	N-12	4
Epps Av	P-12	4
Eton St	P-13	4
Everett Pl	M-12	4,7
Fairfield St	N-12	4
Fairview Av	N-13	4
Florence St	P-12	4
Forest Av	N-12	4
Fountain Rd	P-13	4
Fox Run Dr	P-13	4
Franklin Rd	P-12	4
Franklin St	N-12	4
Garden St	N-12	4
Garrett Pl	N-12	4
Genesee Av	N-12	4
Gentry Dr	P-12	4
Glenbrook Pkwy	N-12	4
Glenwood Rd	N-12	4
Gloucester St	P-13	4
Grand Av	P-12	4
Grandview Pl	Q-13	3,4
Grant St	P-12	4
Green St	N-12	4
Greenleaf Av	N-12	4
Grove St	N-12	4
Haase Pl	P-12	4
Hamilton Av	N-13	4
Haring Pl	N-12	4
Harold Av	P-12	4
Hedgerow Dr	P-13	4
Henry St	N-13	4
Henry St	N-12	4
Herzo Pl	P-12	4
Hidden Ledge Rd	P-13	4
Highland Av	M-13	4,7
Highland St	N-13	4
Highview Rd	N-13	4
Highwood Av	M-13	4,7
Hillcrest Rd	N-13	4
Hillside Av	N-13	4
Hirliman Rd	N-12	4
Holland Ln	M-12	4,7
Honeck St	P-12	4
Howard Pl	P-13	4
Howell Rd	N-12	4
Howland Av	N-12	4
Hudson Av	M-12	4,7
Hudson Av	M-13	4,7
Huguenot Av	P-13	4
Humphrey St	N-12	4

BERGEN COUNTY

BERGEN COUNTY

STREET	GRID	MAP
Barbara Ln	F-2	10,11
Barnstable Ln	H-3	10
Barrister Ct	F-4	10,11
Bayberry Ln	G-2	10
Beech St	F-3	10,11
Beechwood Pl	F-4	10,11
Bender Ct	G-3	10
Bentley Dr	F-4	10,11
Birch Rd	F-4	10,11
Birdsong La	G-2	10
Black Foot Ln	H-2	10
Black Hawk La	G-3	10
Blue Berry Pl	G-3	10
Blue Hill Ter	G-4	10
Bowers Ln	G-3	10
Breakneck Rd	H-2	10
Briarly Dr	F-4	10,11
Briarwoods Rd	G-2	10
Bridle Wy	F-4	10,11
Burritt Pl	G-4	10
Butternut Dr	H-3	10
Calusa Tr	H-3	10
Campgaw Plz	G-3	10
Campgaw Plz	F-3	10,11
Carriage Ln	F-3	10,11
Carriage Ln	G-3	10
Cayuga Ln	H-3	10
Cedar St	F-3	10,11
Cedar St	F-2	10,11
Cherokee Ln	J-3	10
Cherry St	G-3	10
Chestnut Pl	G-3	10
Cheyenne Dr	H-2	10
Chickasaw Tr	H-2	10
Chickasaw Tr	H-3	10
Chippewa Tr	H-3	10
Church Ln	F-3	10,11
Cinnamon Ln	H-4	10
Cinnamon Ln	H-3	10
Circle Av	F-3	10,11
Clara Ct	H-2	10
Clark Rd	G-3	10
Clove Ln	H-3	10
Colonial Rd	G-4	10
Colonial Rd	H-3	10
Colonial Rd	G-3	10
Comanche Ln	H-3	10
Commerce St	G-3	10
Connie Av	G-3	10
Convington Pl E	G-4	10
Convington Pl W	G-4	10
Cottontail Path	G-3	10
Cottonwood Dr	G-3	10
Court St	G-3	10
Courter Rd	G-3	10
Courthouse Pl	F-2	10,11
Creole Ln	H-3	10
Crescent Dr	H-3	10
Crest Pl	F-4	10,11
Crystal Lake Ter	F-3	10,11
Crystal Lake Ter	G-3	10
Curran Pl	G-4	10
Dakota Tr	H-2	10
Dara Ln	F-3	10,11
De Korte Dr	G-3	10
De Korte Dr	G-4	10
Deer Tr	F-4	10,11
Deerfield Ln	G-4	10
Delaware Ln	H-4	10
Devonshire Dr	H-4	10
Dogwood Tr	H-2	10
Edgewood Rd	F-4	10,11
Edson Ter	F-4	10,11
Elm Tr	G-4	10
Ewing Av	J-3	10
Ewing Av	H-4	10
Farmdale Rd	H-2	10
Farmdale Rd	G-2	10
Fawn Av	G-4	10
Feather Ln	H-3	10
Fieldstone Ct	G-3	10
Forest Glen Av	G-4	10
Forest St	F-3	10,11
Forsythia Ct	H-2	10
Fox Hedge Rd	G-3	10
Franklin Av	F-3	10,11
Franklin Av	G-3	10
Franklin Farms Ct	G-2	10
Franklin Lakes Rd	H-2	10
Franklin Lakes Rd	H-4	10
Franklin Lakes Rd	H-3	10
Freeman's Ln	H-2	10
Gaewood Dr	G-4	10
Galloping Hill Rd	F-3	10,11
George St	H-4	10
Ginger Ln	H-3	10
Glen Pl	F-4	10,11
Glendale Rd	G-3	10
Grandview Ter	H-4	10
Green Ridge Rd	F-4	10,11
Gregory Rd	F-4	10,11
Haddon Pl	G-4	10
Hampton Hill	H-2	10
Hampton Hill Rd	H-2	10
Harriet Pl	G-3	10
Haven Rd	G-3	10
Heather Ln	G-2	10
Helen Ct	F-4	10,11
Hemlock Ct	H-3	10
Hemlock Ct	G-3	10
Hiawatha Tr	H-3	10
Hickory Hill Rd	G-3	10
Hidden Glen Ct	G-3	10
Hidden Pond Path	G-2	10
High Mountain Rd	H-3	10
Highwoods Dr	G-3	10
Highwoods Dr	H-3	10
Hillside Av	F-3	10,11
Hilltop Ter	F-3	10,11
Hilltop Ter	G-3	10
Hillview Tr	H-2	10
Hobar Ct	F-4	10,11
Hopi Dr	J-3	10
Hopper Ct	H-2	10
Horsehorse Tr	F-3	10,11
Huckleberry Ln	G-3	10
Huron Rd	H-3	10
Indian Trail Dr	H-2	10
Indian Trail Dr	J-2	10
Iron Latch Rd	F-3	10,11
Iroquois Ln	H-2	10
Island Wy	G-4	10
Ivy Ct	G-2	10
Jane Dr	H-3	10

STREET	GRID	MAP
Jenny Tr	H-3	10
Juniper Pl	G-3	10
Kent Pl	H-2	10
King Rd	G-3	10
Kings Pointe Tr	F-4	10,11
Kiowa Dr	G-3	10
Knollwood Rd	G-3	10
Kuliana Ct	H-3	10
Lake Dr	H-2	10
Lake Shore Dr	F-2	10,11
Lake Side Blvd	F-3	10,11
Laurel Ln	G-4	10
Laurie Ln	H-2	10
Lawlins Rd	G-4	10
Lenapi Dr	G-4	10
Lenel La	H-3	10
Lily Pond Ln	H-2	10
Lincoln St	F-3	10,11
Linden Av	F-3	10,11
Linden Wy	F-3	10,11
Loch Rd	F-4	10,11
Locust Ct	G-2	10
Longbow Dr	H-3	10
Lower Tr	H-2	10
Lynn Dr	G-3	10
Mabel Ann Av	G-3	10
Mabel Ann Av	G-4	10
Mabel Pl	H-4	10
Mackinaw Tr	H-3	10
Mardinly Av	F-3	10,11
Marie Ct	H-2	10
McCoy Rd	G-2	10
McCoy Rd Ext	G-2	10
McCoy Rd Ext	G-3	10
McKee Ln	G-3	10
Meadow Ln	G-2	10
Michele Ct	G-2	10
Millwheel Ct	F-3	10,11
Minoma Ln	H-2	10
Minsi Tr	G-2	10
Minsi Tr	H-3	10
Miro Rd	F-4	10,11
Mockingbird La	G-2	10
Mohawk Rd	H-3	10
Mohegan Ln	H-3	10
Mortimer Ct	H-2	10
Morton Pl	F-2	10,11
Mountain Av	F-3	10,11
Mulberry Wy	G-3	10
Natures Wy	F-3	10,11
Navaho Trail Dr	J-3	10
Navaho Trail Dr	H-3	10
Nicholas Ct	H-3	10
Nutmeg Pl	H-3	10
Oak Ln	G-4	10
Oak Ln	G-3	10
Old Forge Ln	H-2	10
Old Mill Rd	F-4	10,11
Old Wagon Rd	G-2	10
Old Woods Rd	G-2	10
Olentangy Rd	J-3	10
Olentangy Rd	H-3	10
Omaha Wy	H-2	10
Oneida Tr	H-3	10
Ontario Ct	G-3	10
Orchard Ln	H-4	10
Orchard Ln	H-3	10
Osage Ln	H-3	10
Osio Ln	G-3	10
Ottowa Ln	H-3	10
Ottowa Ln	H-2	10
Packer Av	G-4	10
Paiute Pl	H-3	10
Park Rd	F-5	10,11
Parson Pond Dr	F-5	10,11
Pawnee Ln	J-3	10
Peach Tree Ln	H-3	10
Peach Tree Ln	G-3	10
Penobscott Pl	H-2	10
Peppercorn Ln	H-3	10
Pequot Pl	G-3	10
Phelps Rd	F-4	10,11
Pinecroft Ct	G-3	10
Pines Ter	F-3	10,11
Pines Ter	G-3	10
Pond Brook Rd	G-3	10
Pony Tr	F-4	10,11
Poplar St	F-3	10,11
Powder Mill Ln	F-2	10,11
Pueblo Dr	H-3	10
Pullis Av	F-4	10,11
Pullis Av	G-3	10
Reservoir Dr	J-3	10
Richfield Ct	G-3	10
Richfield Ct	H-3	10
Ridge View Wy	F-3	10,11
Riven Wood Rd	F-3	10,11
Roberts Ct	F-3	10,11
Rose Ct	H-2	10
Roth Av	G-2	10
Ryerson Rd	F-4	10,11
Saber Dr	H-4	10
Saddle Back Tr	F-3	10,11
Sagamore Ln	H-3	10
Salem Ct	H-2	10
Sandia Pl	H-3	10
Santa Fe Tr	G-3	10
Scholar Ct	H-2	10
Scioto Dr	J-3	10
Scioto Dr	H-3	10
Seider Ln	F-3	10,11
Seminole Ln	J-2	10
Seminole Ln	J-3	10
Seneca Rd	H-3	10
Shadow Ridge Rd	F-4	10,11
Shawnee Dr	H-2	10
Shelter Ln	F-2	10,11
Sherwood Pl	F-4	10,11
Shinnecock Tr	H-2	10
Shirley Av	G-3	10
Shoshone Tr	G-3	10
Sioux Ln	G-3	10
Skyridge Rd	H-2	10
Smoke Hollow Tr	G-3	10
Somerset St	H-2	10
South Plz	F-3	10,11
Spruce Ln	G-4	10
Steves Ln	G-3	10
Stewart Ln	F-4	10,11
Stokes Farm Rd	H-3	10
Stonewall Ct	F-4	10,11
Stonewall Ct	G-4	10
Summit Av	G-2	10
Summit Av	G-3	10

STREET	GRID	MAP
Sunset Av	H-4	10
Sunset Ter	G-3	10
Surrey Ln	F-3	10,11
Susquehanna Av	F-3	10,11
Sussex Rd	H-2	10
Sweetbriar Ct	H-3	10
Sweetbriar Ct	H-4	10
Tall Oaks Ct	F-3	10,11
Tanglewood Ct	G-4	10
Tegawitha Wy	H-3	10
Tequesta Dr	H-3	10
Terrace Rd	H-3	10
Terrace Rd	G-3	10
Tice Rd	F-3	10,11
Tomahawk Ln	H-2	10
Tomahawk Ln	H-3	10
Tortoise Ln	G-4	10
Trailing Ridge Rd	F-3	10,11
Trailing Ridge Rd	F-4	10,11
Treeside Ct	F-4	10,11
Tulip La	G-3	10
Valen Ct	F-4	10,11
Valley Rd	G-3	10
Valley View Dr	G-2	10
Van Dine Av	H-4	10
Van Houten Av	H-4	10
Vance Av	H-4	10
Vance Av	G-4	10
Vassar Pl	F-2	10,11
Vee Dr	H-4	10
Vermeulen Pl	J-3	10
Vichiconti Way	F-4	10,11
Walder Dr	H-2	10
Walnut Dr	G-4	10
Walnut Dr	G-3	10
Warren Dr	H-4	10
Washington St	F-3	10,11
Waterview Dr	H-3	10
Wayfair Cir	J-4	10
Wayfair Ln	J-4	10
White Pine Rd	H-2	10
White Pine Rd	G-2	10
Wichita Tr	H-2	10
Wildwood Av	F-3	10,11
Willow St	G-2	10
Willowbrook St	G-2	10
Winding Hollow Dr	J-3	10
Windswept Ln	F-3	10,11
Winnebago Dr	H-3	10
Winton Gate Ln	F-3	10,11
Wooded Trail	G-2	10
Wooded Trail Est	G-2	10
Woodfield Rd	G-2	10
Woodside Av	F-4	10,11
Woodside Ter	F-4	10,11
Wyandotte Dr	H-3	10
Yuma Ct	H-3	10

Garfield, City of

STREET	GRID	MAP
1st St	P-8	5
2nd St	P-8	5
Alaska St	P-7	5
Albert St	P-7	5
Alpine St	P-7	5
Ann St	P-7	5
Arnot St	P-8	5
Atlantic Av	Q-7	2,5
Banta Av	P-7	5
Barthold St	P-7	5
Beech St	P-7	5
Bellport Pl	P-8	5
Belmont Av	P-7	5
Bergen St	P-7	5
Blakely Pl	Q-7	2,5
Bloomingdale Av	Q-7	2,5
Bogart Av	Q-7	2,5
Botany St	P-7	5
Cambridge Av	Q-7	2,5
Carl St	P-7	5
Cedar St	P-7	5
Center St	P-7	5
Charles St	P-7	5
Charles St	P-8	5
Cherry St	P-7	5
Chestnut St	P-7	5
Clark St	P-7	5
Columbus Av	P-7	5
Commerce St	Q-7	2,5
Cottage Pl	P-6	5
Dahnerts Park Ln	P-7	5
Davison St	P-7	5
Dewey St	P-7	5
Dewitt St	P-7	5
Division Av	P-6	5
Division Av	P-7	5
Dolphine Pkwy W	P-7	5
Dye Av	N-7	5
Dye Blvd	N-7	5
East Garden Ct	P-7	5
East Willow St	P-7	5
Elizabeth St	P-8	5
Elizabeth St	P-7	5
Elm St	P-7	5
Emanuel St	P-8	5
Erie St	P-7	5
Faber Pl	Q-7	2,5
Farnham Av	Q-8	2,5
Franklin Av	P-7	5
Frederick St	P-8	5
Frederick St	P-7	5
Garfield Av	Q-8	2,5
Garwood Ct E	P-7	5
Garwood Ct N	P-7	5
Garwood Ct S	P-7	5
Gaston Av	P-8	5
Grace Av	P-7	5
Grand St	Q-7	2,5
Grand St	Q-8	2,5
Harding Ct	P-7	5
Harrison Av	Q-7	2,5
Harrison Av	P-8	5
Hartmann Av	P-7	5
Hazel St	P-7	5
Henrietta Ct	P-7	5
Hepworth Pl	Q-7	2,5
Herman St	N-7	5
Herman St	P-7	5
High St	P-8	5
Highland Av	P-7	5
Hillside Ter	P-8	5
Hobart Pl	Q-7	2,5
Hudson St	Q-7	2,5
Irving Pl	P-8	5
Jacob St	P-7	5
Jefferson St	N-7	5
Jewell St	P-7	5
Joanne Ter	P-8	5
John St	P-7	5
Karl St	P-7	5
Krakow St	P-8	5
Lanza Av	P-6	5
Lanza Av	P-7	5
Laurel St	P-7	5
Leonard St	P-8	5
Liberty St	P-7	5
Lincoln Pl	Q-7	2,5
Lizette St	P-7	5
Louise St	P-7	5
MacArthur Av	Q-7	2,5
MacArthur Av	P-8	5
MacDonald St	P-8	5
Madeline Av	P-7	5
Madonna Pl	P-7	5
Main St	P-7	5
Maitland Pl	P-7	5
Malcolm Av	P-8	5
Manner Av	P-8	5
Maple Av	P-7	5
Market St	P-7	5
Marsellus Pl	Q-7	2,5
Mattausch Pl	P-7	5
Midland Av	P-7	5
Midland Av	Q-7	2,5
Monroe St	Q-7	2,5
Morrell Pl	P-7	5
Morrell Pl	P-8	5
Morris Av	P-7	5
New Garden Ct	P-7	5
New Schley St	P-7	5
North View Ct	P-8	5
Oak St	P-7	5
Orchard St	P-7	5
Outwater Ln	P-7	5
Pacific Av	P-7	5
Palisade Av	P-7	5
Park Av	P-8	5
Passaic Av	Q-8	2,5
Passaic St	Q-7	2,5
Passaic St	Q-8	2,5
Pershing St	P-7	5
Pierre Av	P-7	5
Plaudeville Av	P-7	5
Pleasant Av	P-7	5
Prescott Av	P-7	5
Prospect St	P-7	5
Rail Road Pl	P-7	5
Ray St	P-7	5
River Dr	P-6	5
River Dr	Q-7	2,5
Riverside Pl	Q-7	2,5
Sampson St	P-7	5
Schley St	P-7	5
Scudder St	P-7	5
Seifert St	N-7	5
Semel Av	P-7	5
Shafto St	P-7	5
Shafto St	P-8	5
Shaw St	P-7	5
Sherman Pl	Q-7	2,5
Somerset St	Q-7	2,5
South Garden Ct	P-7	5
Spencer Pl	Q-7	2,5
Spring Gardens Ln	N-7	5
Spring Gardens Ln	P-7	5
Spring St	P-7	5
Spruce St	P-7	5
Steinberg Av	P-7	5
Summit Av	P-7	5
Terrace Pl	Q-8	2,5
Terrace Pl	Q-7	2,5
Union Av	P-7	5
Van Bussum Av	N-7	5
Van Bussum Av	P-7	5
Van Winkle Av	P-7	5
Victor St	P-8	5
Walnut St	P-7	5
Washington Pl	Q-7	2,5
Wendy Ter	P-8	5
Wessington Av	P-7	5
Westervelt Pl	P-8	5
Westervelt Pl	Q-8	2,5
Westminster Pl	Q-8	2,5
Willard St	Q-7	2,5
William St	P-7	5
Willow St	P-7	5
Wilson St	P-7	5
Wood St	P-7	5
Wright Pl	P-7	5

Glen Rock, Boro of

STREET	GRID	MAP
Abbington Ter	K-6	6
Aberdeen Pl	K-6	6
Ackerman Av	J-7	6,9
Alan Av	K-7	6
Amherst Ct	K-7	6
Amherst Ct	J-7	6,9
Andover Ter	K-7	6
Argyle Rd	K-6	6
Ashton Pl	J-7	6,9
Austin Pl	K-6	6
Bedford Pl	J-6	6,9
Bedford Pl	K-7	6
Beech Rd	J-7	6,9
Beekman Pl	K-7	6
Belmont Rd	K-7	6
Belvidere Rd	K-6	6
Belvidere Rd	K-7	6
Benson Rd	K-7	6
Bergen St	J-7	6,9
Bergen St	J-6	6,9
Berkely Pl	K-7	6
Berry Pl	K-6	6
Berwyn Rd	K-6	6
Beverly Rd	K-6	6
Birchwood Rd	K-6	6
Bradford St	K-6	6
Broad St	J-6	6,9
Broad St	J-6	6,9
Brook Pl	K-6	6
Brookfield Av	K-6	6
Buckingham Pl	K-7	6
Cambridge Pl	K-6	6
Carlton Pl	K-7	6
Carol Ct	K-7	6
Catherine St	K-5	6
Catherine St	K-6	6
Cedar St	K-5	6
Central Av	K-7	6
Chadwick Av	K-7	6
Chadwick Pl	K-7	6
Chatham Pl	J-6	6,9
Chestnut Dr	K-7	6
Clifton Pl	J-7	6,9
Clinton Pl	J-6	6,9
Clinton Pl	J-7	6,9
Concord Av	K-6	6
Corn Wall Rd	K-7	6
Cornelia Pl	K-6	6
Cranford Rd	K-7	6
Crestwood Dr	K-7	6
Cumberland Rd	K-6	6
De Boar Dr	K-6	6
De Young Rd	K-7	6
Dean St	J-7	6,9
Delmar Av	K-7	6
Demarest St	J-6	6,9
Devonshire Pl	K-7	6
Diamond Ct	K-6	6
Doremus Av	K-6	6
Driscoll Pl	K-7	6
Dunham Pl	J-6	6,9
East Gramercy Pl	K-7	6
Edgemont Rd	K-6	6
Elizabeth St	J-7	6,9
Ellsworth Ter	K-7	6
Elmwood Av	K-7	6
Emerson Rd	K-7	6
Eton Pl	K-6	6
Fairmount Av	K-7	6
Fairview Av	K-6	6
Ferguson Pl	K-7	6
Ferndale Av	K-6	6
Fieldmere Av	K-7	6
Forest Rd	J-7	6,9
Forest Rd	K-7	6
Franklin Pl	K-7	6
Garret Pl	K-7	6
Garvey Pl	K-7	6
Gaynor Pl	K-7	6
George Rd	K-7	6
Gibson Pl	K-7	6
Glen Av	K-6	6
Glen Blvd	J-6	6,9
Glen Blvd	K-6	6
Glendale Rd	J-7	6,9
Glenfair Rd	K-7	6
Godfrey Ter	K-7	6
Goodviet Pl	K-6	6
Gordon Pl	K-7	6
Graham Pl	K-7	6
Gramercy Pl	K-7	6
Gramercy Pl	K-6	6
Grandview Av	K-6	6
Green Way Rd	J-6	6,9
Gregory Pl	K-6	6
Griswold Pl	K-7	6
Grove Av	J-7	6,9
Grove St	J-7	6,9
Grover Ter	K-7	6
Hamilton Av	K-6	6
Hanover Pl	K-6	6
Harding Plz	K-6	6
Harding Rd	K-6	6
Harristown Rd	K-6	6
Harristown Rd	K-7	6
Hazelhurst Av	K-6	6
Healthcote Rd	K-6	6
Heather Ln	K-6	6
Henry St	J-7	6,9
Herold Dr	K-7	6
High St	J-7	6,9
Highland Rd	K-7	6
Highwood Av	J-7	6,9
Highwood Ter	J-7	6,9
Hillman Av	K-7	6
Hillside Av	K-6	6
Hillview Ter	K-6	6
Holt Av	K-6	6
Holt Ct	K-6	6
Hudson Pl	K-6	6
Iona Pl	K-6	6
Iris Cir E	K-6	6
Iris Cir N	K-6	6
Iris Cir W	K-6	6
Isabella Pl	J-6	6,9
Isabella Pl	K-6	6
Jennifer Ct	K-6	6
Jennifer Pl	K-6	6
Jerome Av	K-7	6
Keith Pl	K-7	6
Kenmore Pl	K-6	6
Kent Rd	K-6	6
Kirkwood Pl	K-7	6
Lehigh Pl	J-7	6,9
Leigh Ter	K-7	6
Leone Ct	J-6	6,9
Lincoln Av	K-6	6
Locust Rd	K-7	6
Lowell Pl	J-6	6,9
Lowell Rd	J-6	6,9
Malvern Pl	J-6	6,9
Manor Ct	K-7	6
Maple Av	K-6	6
Marinus Pl	K-6	6
Marlboro Rd	K-7	6
McKinley Pl	J-6	6,9
Midwood Rd	J-7	6,9
Midwood Rd	K-7	6
Monmouth Rd	K-7	6
Mortlock Pl	K-6	6
Norwood Av	J-7	6,9
Nottingham Rd	K-7	6
Oak Knoll Rd	J-6	6,9
Oak Knoll Rd	K-6	6
OaklynPl	K-6	6
Orchard Pl	K-7	6
Oxford Pl	K-7	6
Pamrapo Ct E	K-6	6
Pamrapo Ct W	K-6	6
Park Av	J-7	6,9
Park View Pl	K-7	6
Pembroke Pl	J-6	6,9
Pinelynn Rd	K-7	6
Plymouth Rd	J-6	6,9
Princeton Pl	K-6	6
Prospect St	J-7	6,9
Prospect St	K-7	6
Radburn Rd	K-7	6
Ridge Rd	K-7	6
Robert Ct	K-6	6
Robinson Av	K-7	6
Rock Rd	K-6	6
Rock Rd	K-7	6
Rockingham Pl	K-7	6
Rodney St	K-6	6
Romary Ct	K-6	6
Roxbury Pl	K-6	6
Rutland Rd	J-6	6,9
Salem Ct	K-6	6
Serafin Pl	K-6	6
Somerset Ct	K-6	6
South Boro Ln	K-6	6
South Broad St	J-7	6,9
South Highland Av	J-7	6,9
South Highland Av	K-7	6
Spottswood Rd	K-7	6
Spruce Ct	K-6	6
Sterling Pl	K-6	6
Stillwell Pl	J-7	6,9
Stonefield Rd	K-6	6
Sycamore Ter	K-7	6
The Boulevard	K-6	6
Thornbury Av	K-6	6
Thurston Ter	K-7	6
Tilghman Dr	K-7	6
Tonawanda Rd	K-6	6
Van Allen Rd	J-6	6,9
Van Allen Rd	K-6	6
Wadsworth Rd	K-7	6
Wadsworth Rd	K-6	6
Waldron Av	K-6	6
Warren Pl	J-7	6,9
Wellesley Rd	J-6	6,9
West Main St	K-6	6
West Plz	K-6	6
West Valley Rd	K-6	6
William Pl	K-6	6
Wilson St	K-6	6
Windham Pl	J-6	6,9
Winslow Ter	K-7	6
Woodvale Rd	K-7	6
Yardley Ct	K-7	6

Hackensack, City of

STREET	GRID	MAP
1st St	N-9	5
2nd St	N-10	5
2nd St	P-9	5
3rd St	N-9	5
Ackerson St	P-10	5
Ackerson St	M-10	5,6
Allen St	M-10	5,6
American Legion Dr	N-9	5
American Legion Dr	P-9	5
Ames St	P-9	5
Anderson St	N-10	5
Anderson St	N-9	5
Arcadia Rd	P-9	5
Atlantic St	P-10	5
Atlantic St	P-9	5
Bank St	Q-10	2,5
Banta Pl	P-10	5
Beech St	P-9	5
Berdan Pl	N-10	5
Bergen St	P-10	5
Berry St	P-10	5
Berry St	N-10	5
Berry St	N-9	5
Bershire Pl	P-9	5
Blanchard Ter	N-9	5
Blauvelt Pl	Q-10	2,5
Bloom St	P-10	5
Bloom St	Q-10	2,5
Bonhommer Av	P-10	5
Bridge St	P-10	5
Briscolina St	P-10	5
Broadway	P-10	5
Brook St	N-9	5
Buckingham Dr	P-9	5
Burlews Ct	N-10	5
Byrne St	N-9	5
Cambridge Ter	P-9	5
Camden St E	P-10	5
Campbell Av	P-10	5
Carmen Pl	M-10	5,6
Catalpa Av	M-10	5,6
Cedar Av	M-10	5,6
Central Av	N-9	5
Charles St	P-9	5
Church St	P-10	5
Clarendon Pl	N-10	5
Clark St	P-9	5
Clay St	N-10	5
Cleveland St	P-10	5
Clinton Pl	N-10	5
Club Wy	N-9	5
Coles Av	M-10	5,6
Collidge Pl	N-9	5
Colonial Ter	N-9	5
Commerce Wy	M-10	5,6
Conklin Pl	N-10	5
County Pl	P-10	5
Court St	P-10	5
Crestwood Av	N-9	5
Daniel St	P-9	5
Davis Av	M-10	5,6
De Wolf Pl	N-10	5
Dean St	P-9	5
Demarest St	P-10	5
Devoe Pl	N-10	5
Dewitt Pl	P-10	5
Division St	P-10	5
Division St	P-9	5
Dorchester Rd	N-9	5
Dorchester Rd	P-9	5
Dyatt Pl	N-10	5
East Anderson St	N-10	5
East Atlantic St	P-10	5
East Broadway	P-10	5
East Kansas St	P-10	5
East Kennedy St	Q-10	2,5
East Lafayette St	P-10	5
East Moonachie Rd	Q-10	2,5
East Pleasantview Av	P-9	5
East Railroad Av	P-10	5
Eileen Tr	P-9	5
Elizabeth St	P-9	5
Elizabeth St	P-10	5
Elm Av	N-9	5
Emerald St	N-10	5
English St	P-10	5
Essex St	P-9	5
Euclid Av	N-10	5
Fair St	P-10	5
Fairmount Av	N-10	5
Franklin Pl	N-10	5
Franklin St	Q-10	2,5
Frederick St	Q-10	2,5
Fuller Pl	N-10	5
Gamewell St	P-10	5
Gardner Pl	Q-10	2,5
George St	P-10	5
Golf Pl	N-9	5
Gracie Pl	P-10	5
Grand Av	M-10	5,6
Grand Av	N-10	5
Green St	P-9	5
Grove St	P-10	5
Hackensack Av	N-10	5
Hamilton Pl	N-10	5
Hamilton Pl	N-9	5
Haynes St	N-10	5
Heath Pl	N-9	5
Henry Pl	Q-10	2,5
Henry St	P-9	5
Herman St	N-10	5
High St	N-9	5
High St	N-10	5
Hillside Pl	P-9	5
Hobart St	P-10	5
Hoffman St	Q-10	2,5
Holt St	Q-10	2,5
Holt St	P-10	5
Hooper St	P-9	5
Hudson St	P-10	5
Huyler St	P-10	5
Ise St	Q-10	2,5
Ises Ln	Q-10	2,5
Jackson Av	Q-10	2,5
Jackson Av	P-10	5
James St	N-10	5
Jay St	Q-10	2,5
Jefferson St	M-10	5,6
Jersey Pl	P-9	5
Johnson Av	N-10	5
Kansas St	P-10	5
Kaplan Av	P-9	5
Kennedy St	Q-10	2,5
Kenneth St	P-9	5
Kent St	P-9	5
Kinderkamack Rd	M-10	5,6
Kinderkamack Rd	N-10	5
King St	P-9	5
King St	P-9	5
Knapp Pl	N-10	5
Kotte Pl	N-10	5
Krone Pl	N-10	5
Lawrence St	P-10	5
Lawton St	N-10	5
Lee Pl	P-9	5
Lehigh St	P-9	5
Lexington Av	P-10	5
Lexington Av	P-9	5
Liberty St	P-9	5
Lincoln St	N-10	5
Linden St	N-10	5
Lodi St	P-10	5
Lodi St	P-9	5
Longview Av	P-9	5
Lookout Av	N-10	5
Lookout Av	N-9	5
Louis St	N-10	5
Madison St	M-10	5,6
Maiden Ln	Q-10	2,5
Main St	P-10	5
Main St	N-10	5
Maple Dr	P-9	5
Marginal Rd	Q-10	2,5
Marion St	P-10	5
Marlatt	P-9	5
Martin Ter	N-10	5
Marvin Av	P-9	5
Mary St	P-9	5
McKinley St	P-9	5
McKinley St	P-10	5
Meadow St	P-10	5
Mercer St E	P-10	5
Michael St	P-10	5
Midtown Bridge Ext	P-10	5
Midtown Pl	P-10	5
Moonachie Rd	Q-10	2,5
Morningside Pl	P-9	5
Myer St	P-10	5
New St	P-10	5
Newman St	P-9	5
Newman St	P-10	5
North Constitution Sq	P-10	5
North Euclid Av	N-10	5
Oak St	N-10	5
Old Hoboken Rd	Q-10	2,5
Old River St	P-10	5
Orchard St	N-10	5
Overlook Av	P-9	5
Owens Rd	P-9	5
Pang Born Pl	N-10	5
Park St	P-10	5
Park St	N-10	5
Parker Av	P-9	5
Parkway	P-9	5
Passaic St	N-9	5
Peters Rd	P-10	5
Pine St	N-10	5
Pink St	P-10	5
Polifly Rd	P-9	5
Poor St	P-10	5
Poplar Av	N-10	5
Porter Av	P-10	5
Prospect Av	N-10	5
Prospect Av	P-10	5
Pulaski Pl	Q-10	2,5
Rail Road Pl	P-10	5
Reilly Ct	Q-10	2,5
Ricardo St	P-10	5
River St	Q-10	2,5
River St	P-10	5
Romaine Ct	M-10	5,6
Ross Av	N-10	5
Rowland Av	P-9	5
Russel St	P-9	5
Shaffer Pl	Q-10	2,5
Simons Av	P-9	5
South Constitution Sq	P-10	5
South Euclid Av	N-9	5
South Euclid Av	N-10	5
South Lake Dr	M-10	5,6
South Newman St	P-9	5

BERGEN COUNTY

STREET	GRID	MAP
South Prospect Av	P-9	5
South State St	P-10	5
South Summit Av	P-9	5
South St	P-9	5
Spring Valley Av	N-10	5
Standish Av	P-9	5
Stanley Pl	N-10	5
State St	P-10	5
Summit Av	N-10	5
Summit Av	P-10	5
Sussex St	P-10	5
Sutton Av	P-9	5
Taylor St	Q-10	2,5
Temple Av	N-10	5
Terheun Pl	N-10	5
Terrace Pl	N-10	5
The Esplanade	N-9	5
Thompson St	P-9	5
Tracy Pl	N-9	5
Trinity Pl	P-10	5
Troost St	P-10	5
Union St	P-10	5
University Plaza Dr	N-10	5
Van Orden Pl	N-10	5
Van Wetering Pl	P-10	5
Vanderbeck Pl	N-10	5
Vincent Av	P-9	5
Voorhis Ln	N-10	5
Voorhis Pl	N-10	5
Vreeland Av	Q-10	2,5
Ward St	N-10	5
Warren St	P-10	5
Washington Av	P-10	5
Washington Av	Q-10	2,5
Washington Av	P-10	5
Water St	P-10	5
West Anderson St	N-9	5
West Franklin St	Q-10	2,5
West Pleasantview Av	P-9	5
West Railroad Av	N-10	5
West Railroad Av	P-10	5
West St	P-10	5
Williams St	Q-10	2,5
Willow Av	M-10	5,6
Wilson St	N-10	5
Winchester Pl	P-9	5
Winchester Pl	N-9	5
Woodridge Av	N-10	5
Worth St	Q-10	2,5
Wysoki Pl	Q-10	2,5
Zabriskie St	N-10	5

Harrington Park, Boro of

STREET	GRID	MAP
1st St	G-13	8
2nd St	G-13	8
3rd St	G-13	8
Adams St	H-13	8
Adams St	G-13	8
Arcadia Ct	H-13	8
Arthur Pl	H-12	8
Beechwood Pl	H-12	8
Blanche Av	H-12	8
Blanche Av	G-12	8
Bluefield Av	H-12	8
Bogerts Mill Rd	J-12	7,8
Bogerts Mill Rd	H-12	8
Brook St	H-12	8
Burkhardt Ln	H-12	8
Burkhardt Ln	G-12	8
Byrne Ln	G-12	8
Carlton Ln	H-13	8
Carman Rd	H-12	8
Closter Rd	H-13	8
Closter Rd	J-13	7,8
Columbus Av	J-12	7,8
Cooper Pl	H-12	8
Copley Blvd	H-13	8
Council Dr	H-12	8
Council Pl	H-12	8
Cross St	H-13	8
Deal St	H-12	8
Demarest Pl	H-13	8
Dimas Ct	H-13	8
Dora St	H-12	8
Dorotocky Dr	G-12	8
Downing Pl	H-12	8
Eckerson Rd	H-12	8
Edgewood Rd	H-13	8
Ehret Av	H-12	8
Elliot Rd	H-12	8
Elm St	H-12	8
Flint Ter	H-13	8
Florence Rd	H-12	8
Florence Rd	J-12	7,8
Frank St	H-12	8
Friend Ter	H-12	8
George St	H-12	8
Giles Rd	H-12	8
Glen Av W	H-12	8
Glen Av E	H-12	8
Green Wy	H-13	8
Guy St	H-12	8
Hackensack Av	H-12	8
Harriot Av	H-12	8
Hazel St	H-12	8
Henmar Ter	H-12	8
Henry Pl	H-12	8
Herring St	H-12	8
Herron Ct	G-12	8
Higgins Pl	G-12	8
Higgins Pl	H-12	8
Highland Av	H-13	8
Jay St	H-12	8
Kline St	H-12	8
Kohring Cir N	H-13	8
Kohring Cir S	H-13	8
Kramer Ln	H-13	8
La Roche Av	J-12	7,8
Lafayette Rd	H-13	8
Lakeside Av	H-12	8
Lee Av	H-12	8
Legion Av	H-13	8
Lincoln Ter	H-12	8
Livingston St	H-13	8
Livingston St	J-13	7,8
Lohns Pl	G-13	8
Lohns Pl	H-13	8
Lynn St	H-12	8
Manor Rd	H-12	8
Martha Rd	H-12	8
Martha Rd	J-12	7,8
Martin Dr	H-12	8
Maryann Ln	H-12	8
Names Ct	H-13	8
Nelson St	H-12	8
Norma Rd	J-12	7,8
Normandy Av	H-13	8
North Colonial Dr	G-13	8
North Colonial Dr	G-12	8
Norwood Av	G-13	8
Oak St	H-12	8
Old Hook Rd	J-12	7,8
Old Jug Ct	H-13	8
Park Hill Rd	H-12	8
Park St	J-12	7,8
Parkside Rd	J-12	7,8
Pascack Av	J-12	7,8
Pascack Av	H-12	8
Peat St	H-12	8
Penn St	J-12	7,8
Pine Pl	H-12	8
Pondside Pl	H-13	8
Railroad Av	J-12	7,8
Raymond St	H-12	8
Richard Ct	H-12	8
Ridge Rd	H-12	8
Riker Av	H-12	8
River Rd	J-12	7,8
Riverview Dr	H-12	8
Rixer Av	H-12	8
Rugen Dr	H-12	8
Russell Pl	H-12	8
Sandra Pl	H-12	8
Schraalenburgh Rd	H-13	8
Schraalenburgh Rd	J-12	7,8
Semmens Rd	J-12	7,8
Short Pl	H-12	8
South Av	J-12	7,8
South Colonial Dr	G-12	8
South Colonial Dr	G-13	8
Spring St	H-12	8
Stella Ct	H-13	8
Tappan Rd	H-13	8
Taylor Pl	J-12	7,8
Thomas St	H-12	8
Van Orden Rd	H-13	8
Vincent Pl	H-12	8
Walter Ct	H-12	8
Ward Wy	J-12	7,8
West Shore Rd	H-12	8
Wicks Dr	H-13	8
William St	H-12	8

Hasbrouck Hts., Boro of

STREET	GRID	MAP
2nd St	R-9	2
3rd St	R-9	2
4th St	R-9	2
4th St	Q-9	2,5
Alger Av	Q-9	2,5
Austin Pl	Q-8	2,5
Baldwin Av	P-9	5
Bell Av	Q-9	2,5
Berkshire Rd	Q-9	2,5
Boulevard	Q-8	2,5
Burr Pl	Q-9	2,5
Burton Av	Q-8	2,5
Burton Ter	Q-9	2,5
Central Av	Q-8	2,5
Charlton Av	Q-9	2,5
Church St	Q-9	2,5
Clark Ct	P-9	5
Cleveland Av	Q-8	2,5
Collins Av	Q-9	2,5
Columbus Av	Q-8	2,5
Coolidge Av	P-9	5
Division Av	Q-8	2,5
Field Av	Q-9	2,5
Franklin Av	Q-8	2,5
Garrison Av	Q-9	2,5
George Ct	P-9	5
Hamilton Av	Q-8	2,5
Hasbrouck Av	Q-9	2,5
Henry St	Q-8	2,5
Hillcrest Av	R-8	2
Hillside Av	Q-9	2,5
Hillside Dr	Q-9	2,5
Industrial Av	R-9	2
Jefferson Av	Q-8	2,5
Kepp Av	Q-8	2,5
La Salle Av	Q-8	2,5
Lawrence Av	Q-9	2,5
Lincoln Av	Q-8	2,5
Lincoln St	R-8	2
Longview Av	P-9	5
Longview Pl	P-9	5
Longworth Av	Q-9	2,5
Madison Av	Q-8	2,5
Main St	R-8	2
Meyers Av	Q-9	2,5
Michigan Av	Q-9	2,5
Moonachie St	R-9	2
Oak Grove Av	Q-8	2,5
Old Field Av	Q-9	2,5
Ottawa Av	Q-8	2,5
Ottawa Av	Q-9	2,5
Pasadena Av	Q-9	2,5
Passaic Av	Q-8	2,5
Paterson Av	Q-9	2,5
Plant Rd	R-9	2
Prospect St	Q-9	2,5
Railroad St	R-9	2
Ravine Av	Q-9	2,5
Raymond St	Q-8	2,5
Roosevelt Av	Q-8	2,5
Springfield Av	Q-8	2,5
Stanley Av	Q-9	2,5
Summit St	R-8	2
Summit St	Q-8	2,5
Valley Blvd	R-8	2
Walter Av	Q-8	2,5
Washington Pl	Q-8	2,5
Webb Pl	R-8	2
Williams Av	Q-9	2,5
Wood St	Q-8	2,5
Woodland Dr	Q-8	2,5
Woodside Av	Q-8	2,5

Haworth, Boro of

STREET	GRID	MAP
Adams Av	J-12	7,8
Anstatt Wy	J-12	7,8
Baldwin Av	J-12	7,8
Beacon St	J-12	7,8
Beacon St	K-12	7
Beech St	K-11	7
Beech St	K-12	7
Brook St	J-12	7,8
Brook St	K-12	7
Chestnut St	J-12	7,8
Chestnut St	K-12	7
Christie Av	K-12	7
Clark St	K-12	7
Massachusetts Av	K-12	7
McCullough Pl	K-11	7
McCullough Pl	K-12	7
Morris Av	J-12	7,8
Myrtle St	K-12	7
Nevada Pl	K-12	7
New St	K-11	7
New St	K-12	7
Nicholas Av	K-12	7
Orchard Av	K-12	7
Orchard Pl	K-12	7
Osmers Av	K-13	7
Osmers Av	K-12	7
Owatonna St	K-12	7
Park St	K-12	7
Paulson Pl	K-12	7
Pine Ln	J-12	7,8
Pine St	K-12	7
Pine St	J-12	7,8
Pleasant Ln.	J-12	7,8
Pleasant Ln	K-12	7
Pleasant St	K-12	7
Pleasant St	J-12	7,8
Prospect Av	J-12	7,8
Roden Pl	K-12	7
Roden Wy	J-12	7,8
Saint Albans Pl	K-11	7
Schraalenburgh Rd	K-12	7
Seneca Ter	K-12	7
Silkworth Av	J-12	7,8
Sprin Ln	J-12	7,8
Stevens Pl	K-12	7
Summit Pl	K-12	7
Sunset Av	K-11	7
Sunset Av	K-12	7
Sunset Ct	K-11	7
Surbeck Pl	K-12	7
Terrace St	K-12	7
The Crescent St	K-12	7
Valley Rd	K-12	7
Valley Ct	K-12	7
View Ter	K-12	7
West View Ter	K-11	7
Wheeler Pl	J-12	7,8
Whitman St	J-12	7,8
Whitman St.	K-12	7
Woodland Av	J-12	7,8
Woodland Av	K-12	7

Hillsdale, Boro of

STREET	GRID	MAP
Ackerman P	G-10	9
Ackerman P	G-11	8
Allwood Pl	G-10	9
Alpine Ter	G-9	9
Appeld Ct	H-10	9
Apple Tree Ln	G-9	9
Arcadia Wy.	G-11	8
Arden Pl	H-9	9
Arthur St	G-10	9
Avon Ct	H-10	9
Baylor	G-11	8
Baylor	G-10	9
Beach St	H-9	9
Bedford Rd	G-9	9
Beech St	H-9	9
Beechnut St	G-9	9
Beechwood Dr	H-10	9
Bergen Av	G-10	9
Berkshire Rd	G-11	8
Beverly Rd	H-9	9
Beverly Rd	G-9	9
Birchwood Dr	G-9	9
Bluefield Ct	G-9	9
Boulevard S	H-10	9
Briarcliff Rd	G-9	9
Briarcliff Rd	G-10	9
Broadway	G-10	9
Brookside Pl	G-10	9
Brookview Ter	G-9	9
Buena Vista Av	H-10	9
Buff Ln	G-9	9
Cambridge Rd	G-11	8
Carlyle Pl	H-10	9
Catherine Ct	H-10	9
Cathy Dr	G-10	9
Cedar Ln	H-11	8
Cedar St	H-10	9
Center Dr	H-10	9
Central Av	G-10	9
Chadwick Rd	G-9	9
Chadwick Rd	G-10	9
Chelsea Ct	G-9	9
Cherry Hill Ct	G-11	8
Cherry Pl	H-9	9
Chestnut St	H-9	9
Chris Av	G-11	8
Church Rd	G-10	9
Church Rd	G-9	9
Clayton St	G-10	9
Clinton Av	G-10	9
Coles Crossing Rd	G-10	9
Colonial Blvd	H-9	9
Colonial Blvd	G-9	9
Columbus Av	G-10	9
Conlin Av	G-10	9
Cottage Pl.	G-10	9
Country Ln	G-10	9
Craig Rd	G-8	9
Crest Rd	H-10	9
Crestwood Pl	G-9	9
Crosley Ter	H-10	9
Cross St	G-10	9
David Pl	H-10	9
Deer Tr	G-11	8
Deer Tr	G-10	9
Demarest Av	H-10	9
Demarest Av	H-11	8
Douglas Dr	G-9	9
Douglas Dr	G-8	9
Dwight Av	G-10	9
East Liberty Av	G-10	9
East Liberty Av	G-11	8
Edgewood Ct	G-11	8
Elaine Ct	G-9	9
Elfhill Ct	H-9	9
Ell Rd	H-9	9
Ell Rd	G-9	9
Ellen Ct	G-9	9
Elm St	H-10	9
Elm St	H-9	9
Esplanade Dr	G-10	9
Everdell Av	H-10	9
Everdell Av	H-11	8
Evergreen St	G-10	9
Fairhaven Dr	G-9	9
Fairview Av	H-10	9
Fernwood Av	H-9	9
Fernwood Av	H-10	9
Florence St	G-10	9
Forest Dr	G-9	9
Glen Hook Rd	G-8	9
Glen Hook Rd	G-9	9
Glen Ln	G-9	9
Glen Ln	H-9	9
Glendale Dr	H-10	9
Gramercy Ln	H-11	8
Grove St	G-10	9
Grove St	H-10	9
Hampton Pl	G-10	9
Harrington St	H-10	9
Hazelwood Av	G-10	9
Hazelwood Av	H-10	9
Heritage Ct	G-9	9
Highland Av	G-11	8
Highwood Ct	G-11	8
Hillsdale Av	G-10	9
Hillsdale Av	G-9	9
Hillsdale Av	G-11	8
Hillsdale Ct	G-9	9
Holdrum St	G-10	9
Homestead St	H-11	8
Hooper St	H-10	9
Hooper St	G-10	9
Hopkins St	H-10	9
Hopper Av	G-10	9
Hopper St	G-10	9
Horizon Ter	G-9	9
Howell Av	G-10	9
Hunters Ct	G-9	9
Jan Ct	H-9	9
Jane Ct	G-9	9
Jolen Dr	G-9	9
Josephine Ct	G-11	8
Kent Rd	G-11	8
Kenwood Dr	G-9	9
Kinderkamack Rd	H-10	9
Kinderkamack Rd	G-10	9
King Ct	G-9	9
Knickerbocker Av	G-10	9
Lafayette Av	H-10	9
Lake Dr	G-10	9
Langerfield Rd	G-9	9
Large Av	G-10	9
Lawrence St	H-10	9
Legion Pl	G-10	9
Lesa Ln	G-9	9
Liberty Av	G-10	9
Lincoln Av	G-10	9
Lincoln Ter	H-10	9
Loretta St	G-10	9
Lynne Pl	G-9	9
Magnolia Av	G-10	9
Mansion Pl	G-10	9
Maple Av	H-9	9
Maplewood Av	H-11	8
Maria Dr	G-9	9
Maria Dr	G-10	9
Marilyn Ln	G-9	9
Mary St	G-10	9
Meadow Dr	G-11	8
Meadow Dr	G-10	9
Melville Rd	G-8	9
Melville Rd	G-9	9
Midland Av	G-11	8
Millard Pl	G-10	9
Morris Dr	G-10	9
Mountain View Ter	G-9	9
Nancy Dr	G-10	9
New St	G-10	9
North Ct	G-10	9
North Ramapo Ln	G-9	9
North Ramapo Ln	G-10	9
Oak St	H-10	9
Oak Trail Rd	G-9	9
Oakland St	G-10	9
Oakridge Rd	G-10	9
Orchard Ln	G-9	9
Orchard St	G-10	9
Overbrook Pl	H-10	9
Palm St	G-10	9
Park Av	G-10	9
Park Ridge Rd	G-11	8
Parkview Dr	G-10	9
Pascack Rd	H-9	9
Pascack Rd	G-9	9
Patterson St	G-10	9
Paul Ct	G-9	9
Pawn Pl	G-10	9
Petelle Av	G-11	8
Piermont Av	G-10	9
Plymouth Pl	G-10	9
Prospect Pl	G-10	9
Queen Court Dr	G-10	9
Queen Court Dr	G-9	9
Ralph Av	G-10	9
Ramapo Ln	G-9	9
Rawson Ct	G-11	8
Raymond Ct	G-10	9
Raymond St	G-10	9
Reservoir Rd	G-1	10
Ridge Ct	G-9	9
Riverdale St	G-10	9
Riverside Dr	H-10	9
Royal Park Ter	G-9	9
Ruckman Rd	G-11	8
Rutgers Pl	G-11	8
Rutgers Pl	G-10	9
Saddle Ranch Ln	G-9	9
Saint Nicholas Av	G-10	9
Sandlewood Dr	G-10	9
Schumacher Av	G-11	8
Sebastion Ct	G-10	9
Sebastion Ct	H-10	9
Shadyside Ln	G-9	9
Sherwood Dr	G-9	9
Sierra Ct	G-9	9
Sierra Ct	G-8	9
Standish Rd	G-9	9
Stever Av	H-10	9
Stockton St	H-10	9
Stockton St	G-10	9
Stony Ridge Dr	G-9	9
Strawberry Hill Rd	G-11	8
Summit St	H-10	9
Sunrise Dr	G-9	9
Sunrise Dr	G-8	9
Sycamore Av	G-10	9
Sycamore Av	H-10	9
Taylor St	H-10	9
Trinity Pl	H-10	9
Upper Brook Ln	G-9	9
Valley St	G-10	9
Van Pl	H-9	9
Vincent St	G-10	9
Vorrah Pl	H-9	9
Vorrah Pl	H-10	9
Washington Av	H-10	9
Washington Av	H-11	8
Watson Pl	G-11	8
West St	G-10	9
Westdale Av	H-11	8
White Beaches Dr	H-9	9
Whitman Pl	H-10	9
Wierimus Ln	G-9	9
Wierimus Rd	G-8	9
Wierimus Rd	G-9	9
William St	G-10	9
Willow Brook Rd	G-10	9
Willow Brook Rd	G-11	8
Wilts Av	G-10	9
Windham Rd	G-9	9
Winthrop Rd	G-9	9
Woodhill Rd	G-9	9
Yesler Wy	H-10	9

Ho-Ho-Kus, Boro of

STREET	GRID	MAP
1st St	H-7	9
Academy Rd	G-8	9
Academy Rd	H-8	9
Ackerman Av	G-7	9
Addison Pl	H-7	9
Arbor Dr	H-7	9
Ardmore Rd	G-7	9
Arrow Ln	H-8	9
Barnett St	H-7	9
Beechwood Rd	H-7	9
Bernard Pl	H-7	9
Birch Ln	H-8	9
Blanchfield Ct	H-7	9
Blanchfield Ct	G-7	9
Blauvelt Av	G-7	9
Bogert Rd	H-8	9
Boiling Spring Rd	G-8	9
Boiling Spring Rd	H-8	9
Braeburn Rd	G-7	9
Brandywine Rd	H-8	9
Bridle Wy	H-8	9
Bridle Wy	G-8	9
Brook View Ct	G-8	9
Brookside Av	H-7	9
Brown Ln	G-8	9
Carlton Av	H-7	9
Chestnut Pl	H-8	9
Clearwater Dr	H-8	9
Cleverdon Rd	H-8	9
Cliff St	H-7	9
Conifer Ln	H-8	9
Crescent Pl	H-7	9
Deerhill Dr	H-8	9
Dogwood Ln	H-8	9
Duncan Rd	G-7	9
East Franklin Tnpk	H-7	9
East Gate Rd	H-8	9
East Saddle River Rd	G-8	9
East Saddle River Rd	H-8	9
Edgewood Dr	H-7	9
Elmwood Av	H-7	9
Enos Pl	H-7	9
Fairlawn St	G-7	9
Fairlawn St	H-7	9
Ferris Ct	G-7	9
Fox Run	H-8	9
Garden Ct	G-7	9
Gilbert Rd	G-7	9
Glendon Rd	G-7	9
Gordon Rd	H-8	9
Hollis Dr	G-7	9
Hollywood Av Relocation	H-8	9
Hollywood Av Relocation	H-7	9
Hollywood Av	H-7	9
Hollywood Pl	H-7	9
Hollywood Pl	G-7	9
Jacquelin Av	G-8	9
Jacquelin Av	H-8	9
Knollwood Dr	H-7	9
Lakewood Av	H-7	9
Linden Rd	H-7	9
Linden Rd	H-8	9
Lloyd Rd	H-7	9
Maple Av	H-7	9
Marion Ct	H-8	9
Mill Rd	G-8	9
Nauset Ln	H-7	9
Normandy Ct	G-8	9
North Franklin Tnpk	G-7	9
North Franklin Tnpk	H-7	9
North Saddle Brook Rd	H-8	9
North Saddle Brook Rd	G-8	9
Orville Ct	H-7	9
Paddock Rd	G-8	9
Pinecrest Rd	G-7	9
Pitcairn Av	H-8	9
Powder Horn Rd	H-8	9
Prescott Rd	H-8	9
Race Track Rd	H-8	9
Race Track Rd	H-7	9
Riverview Ln	G-7	9
Riverview Ln	G-8	9
Road A	G-7	9
Road B	G-7	9
Rosencrantz Ln	G-7	9
Ross Pl	H-7	9
Saddle Brook Dr	H-8	9
Saddle Ridge Rd	G-8	9
Saddle Ridge Rd	H-8	9
Sargent Rd	G-7	9
Sheridan Av	H-7	9
Sherwood Rd	H-7	9
Sleepy Hollow Dr	H-8	9
Spruce Pl	H-7	9
Spruce Pl	H-8	9
Stone Ridge Ln	G-7	9
Stone Wy	H-8	9
Stone Wy	G-8	9
Stouts Ln	G-7	9
Stratford Ln	H-8	9
Sutton Dr	G-7	9
Sycamore Av	H-7	9
Thomas Ln	G-8	9
Timberline Rd	H-8	9
Valley Forge Wy	H-8	9
Valley Stream	H-8	9
Valley Stream	G-8	9
Van Dyke Dr	H-8	9
Warren Av	H-7	9
Washington Av	H-8	9
Wayne Ct	H-8	9
Wayne Rd	H-8	9
Wearimus Rd	H-8	9
West Saddle River Rd	G-8	9
West Saddle River Rd	H-8	9
Whispering Pines Rd	G-8	9
Whispering Pines Rd	H-8	9
Wickham Wy	H-8	9
Wyncote Rd	G-7	9

Leonia, Boro of

STREET	GRID	MAP
Allaire Av	Q-12	3,4
Ames Av	Q-12	3,4
Beechwood Pl	Q-12	3,4
Birch Ln	Q-12	3,4
Borough Pl	Q-12	3,4
Broad Av	Q-12	3,4
Brook Tr	P-12	4
Charles Pl	Q-12	3,4
Chestnut St	Q-12	3,4
Christie Heights St	P-12	4
Christie Heights St	Q-12	3,4
Christie St	Q-12	3,4
Coover St	Q-12	3,4
Cottage Pl	Q-12	3,4
Crescent Av	Q-12	3,4
Cumley Tr	Q-12	3,4
Dogwood Ct	Q-12	3,4
Eastview Av	P-12	4
Edgewood Rd	Q-13	3,4
Elizabeth Terr	Q-12	3,4
Elm Pl	Q-13	3,4
Elm St	Q-13	3,4
Fairway Dr	Q-13	3,4
Ferber Rd	Q-13	3,4
Fort Lee Rd	Q-13	3,4
Gladwin Av	Q-13	3,4
Glenwood Av	Q-13	3,4
Golf Course Dr	Q-13	3,4
Grand Av	Q-13	3,4
Grandview Ter	Q-13	3,4
Greenway Dr	Q-13	3,4
Harold Av	Q-13	3,4
Harrison St	Q-13	3,4
Hawthorne Tr	Q-13	3,4
Hazlitt	Q-13	3,4
High St	Q-13	3,4
Highland St	Q-13	3,4
Highwood Av	Q-13	3,4
Hillcrest Av	Q-12	3,4
Hillcrest Av	P-12	4
Hillside Av	Q-12	3,4
Hilltop Av	Q-12	3,4
Hoefleys Ln	Q-12	3,4
Howard Ter	Q-12	3,4
Irving St	Q-12	3,4
Kingsley St	Q-12	3,4
Knapp Ter	Q-12	3,4
Lakeview Av	P-12	4
Leonia Av	Q-12	3,4
Lester St	Q-12	3,4
Leyland Dr	Q-12	3,4
Linden Tr	Q-12	3,4
Longview Av	P-12	4
Lowe St	Q-12	3,4
Magnolia Pl	Q-12	3,4
Maple St	Q-12	3,4
Meadowview Ct	Q-12	3,4
Moore Av	Q-12	3,4
Nordhoff Dr	Q-12	3,4
North St	Q-12	3,4
Oak Tree Pl	Q-12	3,4
Oakdene Av	Q-12	3,4
Oratam Ter	Q-12	3,4
Orchard Pl	Q-12	3,4
Overbrook Av	P-12	4
Overlook Av	P-12	4
Overlook Tr	Q-12	3,4
Palisade Av	Q-12	3,4
Palmer Pl	Q-12	3,4
Park Av	Q-12	3,4
Paulin Blvd	Q-12	3,4
Pine Hill Rd	Q-12	3,4
Prospect St	Q-12	3,4
Ray Av	P-12	4
Reldyes Av	Q-12	3,4
Richmond Pl	Q-12	3,4
Ridgeland Ter	Q-13	3,4
Romaine Pl	Q-12	3,4
Schor Av	Q-12	3,4
Spring St	Q-12	3,4
Station Pkwy	Q-12	3,4
Summit Av	Q-12	3,4
Sylvan Av	Q-12	3,4
Van Orden Av	Q-12	3,4
Van Orden Av	P-12	4
Warwick Ln	Q-12	3,4
Washington Ter	Q-12	3,4
Western Blvd	P-12	4
Westview Av	Q-12	3,4
Willow Tree Rd	Q-12	3,4
Winthrop Pl	Q-12	3,4
Wood Ter	Q-12	3,4
Woodland Pl	Q-12	3,4
Woodridge Pl	Q-12	3,4
Yalden Ter	Q-12	3,4

Little Ferry, Boro of

STREET	GRID	MAP
1st St	Q-10	2,5
Abend St	R-10	2
Adams St	R-10	2
Alfred Pl	Q-10	2,5
Alley Rd	Q-10	2,5
Alsan Wy	Q-10	2,5
Ann St	Q-10	2,5
Backiel St	Q-10	2,5
Baker Ct	Q-9	2,5
Baker Ct	Q-10	2,5
Beech St	R-10	2
Bergen Tnpk	Q-10	2,5
Bertoletto Av	R-10	2
Birch St	R-10	2
Brandt St	Q-10	2,5
Brandt St	R-10	2
Carlson St	R-10	2
Centre St	R-10	2
Chamberlain Av	R-10	2
Chapman Dr	R-10	2
Charles St	Q-10	2,5
Christina St	R-10	2
Claremont Av	R-10	2
Claremont Av	R-9	2
Columbus Av	R-10	2
Couchon Dr	Q-10	2,5
Crescent St	R-10	2
Dietrichs St	R-10	2
Eckel Rd	R-10	2
Elizabeth Ct	R-10	2
Franklin St	Q-10	2,5
Franklin St	R-10	2
Frederick St	R-10	2
Frederick St	Q-10	2,5
Fulton St	Q-10	2,5
Garden St	Q-10	2,5
Garden St	R-10	2
Garfield Pl	Q-10	2,5
Garfield St	Q-10	2,5
Gates Rd	R-10	2
Gertz Av	R-10	2
Grand St	Q-10	2,5
Grand St	R-10	2
Grant St	Q-10	2,5
Grove St	R-10	2
Harding Av	Q-10	2,5
Hartwick St	R-10	2
Helen St	R-10	2
Henches Pl	R-10	2
Herman St	R-10	2
Hester St	R-10	2
Heuer St	R-10	2
Indian Lake Dr	Q-10	2,5
Industrial Av	R-10	2
Jackson St	R-10	2
Jefferson St	R-10	2
John St	R-10	2
Joseph St	R-10	2
Katherine St	R-10	2
Kaufman Av	R-10	2
Kaufman Av	Q-10	2,5
Kavrik St	R-10	2
Kinzley St	Q-10	2,5
Kleber Pl	R-10	2
Kleber Pl	R-9	2
La Rosa	R-10	2
Lafayette St	R-10	2
Lakeview Av	Q-10	2,5
Lamker Ct	R-10	2
Liberty St	R-10	2
Lincoln St	R-10	2
Lorena St	R-10	2
Louis St	R-10	2
Ludwig St	R-10	2
Madison St	R-10	2
Maiden Ln	R-10	2
Main St (Lodi Av)	Q-10	2,5
Maple St	R-10	2
Mariani Dr	R-10	2
Marshall Av	R-10	2
McCabe Ct	R-10	2
Mehrhof Ln	R-10	2
Mehrhof Rd	R-10	2
Millo Ct	Q-10	2,5
Monnett St	Q-10	2,5
Monroe St	R-10	2
Nicholas St	R-10	2
Niehouse Av	R-10	2
Park Av	R-10	2
Paroubek St	R-10	2
Paroubek St	Q-10	2,5
Peterslige Dr	R-10	2
Pickens St	R-10	2
Poplar Av	R-10	2
Porcaro Dr	R-10	2
Prospect Av	R-10	2
Red Neck Av	R-10	2
Robby Rd	R-10	2
Romanko Av	R-9	2
Romanko Av	R-10	2
Roosevelt St	R-10	2
Rose St	R-10	2
Sabina St	R-10	2
Saint John St	R-10	2
Sandhill Ct	Q-10	2,5
Seiler Ct	R-9	2
Sievers Ln	Q-10	2,5
Summit Cir	Q-10	2,5
Summit Pl	Q-10	2,5
Sylvan Av	R-10	2
Sylvan Av	Q-10	2,5
Taylor St	Q-10	2,5
Treplow St	R-10	2
Union St	R-10	2
Union Av	R-10	2
Valley Rd	Q-10	2,5
Van Buren St	Q-10	2,5
Velock Dr	R-10	2
Vogt Ln	R-10	2
Warren St	R-10	2
Washington Av	R-10	2
Werneking Pl	R-10	2
Werneking Pl	R-10	2
West Gate	Q-10	2,5
William St	R-10	2
Wilson St	Q-10	2,5
Wilson St	R-10	2
Woodland Av	Q-10	2,5

Lodi, Boro of

STREET	GRID	MAP
1st St	N-8	5
Adams Pl	Q-8	2,5
Aida Ct	P-9	5
Annette Ter	P-8	5
Arlene Grove	P-8	5
Arlene Grove	P-9	5
Arnot St	P-8	5
Austin Pl	Q-8	2,5
Autumn St	P-8	5

BERGEN COUNTY

STREET	GRID	MAP
Autumn St	Q-8	2,5
Avenue A	P-8	5
Avenue B	P-8	5
Avenue D	P-8	5
Avenue E	P-8	5
Avenue F	P-8	5
Barbara Ct	Q-9	2,5
Bel Vista Ct	P-8	5
Bell Av	Q-8	2,5
Bernice Pl	P-8	5
Blueridge Rd	P-8	5
Borig Pl	P-8	5
Boyd St	P-8	5
Branca St	P-9	5
Brook Pl	P-8	5
Brook St	P-8	5
Brookside Av	P-8	5
Brookside Av	Q-8	2,5
Bruce Ct	P-9	5
Bryant Pl	P-8	5
Burns Av	P-8	5
Calvin Av	N-8	5
Calvin Av	P-8	5
Central Av	Q-8	2,5
Charles Ct	P-9	5
Charles St	P-8	5
Charlton Av	P-9	5
Chestnut St	Q-8	2,5
Christie St	P-8	5
Christopher Ct	P-9	5
Christopher St	P-9	5
Church St	P-8	5
Church St	Q-9	2,5
Circle Dr	Q-8	2,5
Clark Ct	P-9	5
Clinton Av	N-9	5
Columbia Av	P-9	5
Columbia Ln	P-8	5
Constant Av	P-8	5
Corabelle Av	P-8	5
Davis Dr	P-9	5
Dellglen Av	P-8	5
Division St	P-9	5
East Gate Ct	P-8	5
East Pl	P-8	5
Edward Ct	P-8	5
Essex St	N-8	5
Essex St	N-9	5
Farnham Av	N-8	5
Ferndale Ct	N-8	5
Ford St	N-9	5
Franklin Av	N-8	5
Galanti Pl	N-8	5
Garden St	P-8	5
Garfield Av	Q-8	2,5
Garfield Av	P-8	5
Garibaldi Av	P-8	5
Graham Ln	P-8	5
Grant St	P-8	5
Green Ct	P-8	5
Greenlawn Dr	N-9	5
Greenlawn Dr	P-9	5
Gregg St	P-9	5
Grove St	Q-8	2,5
Gunther Av	N-8	5
Hamilton Av	P-8	5
Hancock St	P-9	5
Hancock St	P-8	5
Hansen St	N-8	5
Harrison Av	P-8	5
Henry St	Q-8	2,5
Hillcrest Av	Q-8	2,5
Hillside Pl	P-8	5
Hoehn St	Q-9	2,5
Home Pl	P-8	5
Hope St	P-8	5
Howard St	P-8	5
Hughes St	P-8	5
Hunter St	Q-8	2,5
Industrial Rd	P-8	5
Industrial Rd	P-8	5
Jackson Pl	Q-8	2,5
James Ct	P-9	5
James Pl	P-8	5
James Pl	P-9	5
James St	P-8	5
Jefferson Av	Q-8	2,5
John St	P-8	5
Joseph Blvd	P-8	5
Keasler Av	P-8	5
Kimming Av	P-8	5
Kipp Av	Q-8	2,5
Lafayette Pl	P-8	5
Lafayette Pl	Q-8	2,5
Lawrence Av	P-8	5
Lawrence Av	Q-8	2,5
Leo Pl	P-8	5
Leo Pl	P-9	5
Liberty St	P-9	5
Lincoln Pl	Q-8	2,5
Lincoln St	P-8	5
Logan Pl	P-8	5
Long Valley Rd	P-9	5
Lorelei Ter	P-9	5
Louis St	Q-9	2,5
Lucille Dr	N-9	5
Lucille Dr	N-8	5
MacArthur Av	P-9	5
Madison St	Q-8	2,5
Main St	P-8	5
Marion St	P-8	5
Marion Pepe Dr	Q-8	2,5
Marvin Av	P-9	5
Mary St	Q-8	2,5
Massey St	P-8	5
McGuire Pl	P-8	5
McKinley Av	Q-8	2,5
Memorial Dr	P-8	5
Mercer Pl	P-8	5
Mercer St	P-8	5
Mercer St N	P-8	5
Meta Ln	P-9	5
Mill St	P-9	5
Millbank St	P-8	5
Mitchell St	P-8	5
Money St	P-8	5
Monroe St	Q-8	2,5
Myrtle St	P-8	5
Needles Ln	P-8	5
Norwood Av	Q-8	2,5
Oratio Pl	P-8	5
Orchard Ct	P-9	5
Orchard St	P-8	5
Orchard St	Q-8	2,5
Outwater Ln	P-8	5
Park Av	P-8	5
Park Pl	P-8	5
Pasadena Av	P-9	5
Passaic St	Q-8	2,5
Paterson Av	Q-8	2,5
Patton St	Q-8	2,5
Pauline Ter	P-9	5
Pearl Ct	P-9	5
Pine St	P-9	5
Plescia Ln	P-8	5
Plescia Ln	Q-8	2,5
Porter Av	P-9	5
Prince St	P-8	5
Prospect St	Q-8	2,5
Putnam St	P-8	5
Ragonese St	P-8	5
Redstone Ln	P-9	5
Rennie Pl	P-8	5
Richard St	Q-8	2,5
River St	P-8	5
Riverview Av	P-8	5
Riverview Av	N-8	5
Robert Av	Q-9	2,5
Robinson Rd	P-9	5
Roosevelt Av	Q-8	2,5
Roosevelt Pl	P-8	5
Roosevelt Pl	P-9	5
Rosell Av	N-8	5
Savoie St	P-9	5
Shady Ln	P-9	5
Sheridan St	Q-8	2,5
Sherman Av	P-8	5
Short St	P-8	5
Sidney St	P-8	5
South Main St	Q-8	2,5
South Pl	P-8	5
Spring St	P-8	5
Stokes St	P-8	5
Stokes St	P-9	5
Summer St	P-8	5
Terhune St	Q-8	2,5
Terrace Av	Q-8	2,5
Trudy Dr	P-8	5
Union St	P-8	5
United Dr	P-8	5
Victor St	P-8	5
Vreeland St	P-8	5
Walnut Pl	P-8	5
Warren St	P-8	5
Washington St	P-8	5
Westervelt Pl	P-8	5
Westminster Pl	P-8	5
White Oak Dr	P-8	5
White Oak Dr	P-9	5
Willard St	P-8	5
Wilson St	N-8	5
Wisse Ct	P-9	5
Wisse St	P-9	5
Woodside Av	Q-8	2,5
Woodside Av N	P-8	5
Yolanda Pl	P-9	5

Lyndhurst, Boro of

STREET	GRID	MAP
1st St	T-7	1
2nd Av	T-7	1
3rd Av	T-7	1
3rd St	T-7	1
Adams St	T-6	1
Alder St	T-6	1
Anthony Ct	T-6	1
Ash St	T-6	1
Baldwin Av	T-7	1
Beech St	T-6	1
Belmount Av	U-6	1
Bloomfield Pl	T-7	1
Bogle Dr	T-6	1
Brisbin Av	T-7	1
Cassidy Ct	T-6	1
Castel St	T-7	1
Cedar	T-6	1
Chase Av	T-6	1
Chase Av	T-7	1
Chubb Av	T-8	1
Chubb Av	T-7	1
Circle Dr	Q-8	2,5
Circle Dr	Q-8	2,5
Clark Ct	P-9	5
Clay Av	T-7	1
Cleveland Av	T-7	1
Clinton Av	N-9	5
Clinton Tr	T-7	1
Commercial St	T-6	1
Copeland Av	T-6	1
Court Av	T-7	1
Court Av	S-6	1,2
Delafield Av	T-7	1
Elizabeth Av	T-7	1
Elm St	T-6	1
Ewing Av	U-7	1
Fern Av	T-6	1
Forest Av	T-6	1
Freeman St	T-7	1
Furman Pl	T-7	1
Garland Wy	T-7	1
Grant Av	T-6	1
Grant Av	T-7	1
Green Av	T-6	1
Guthell Pl	T-7	1
Harding Av	T-6	1
Harrington Av	T-7	1
Hazel St	T-6	1
Irving Pl	T-7	1
Jackson Pl	T-7	1
Jauncey Av	T-6	1
Jay Av	S-6	1,2
Jay Av	T-6	1
Jenness Pl	T-7	1
Kearney St	S-7	1,2
Kearney St	S-6	1,2
Kennedy Ct	T-7	1
Kingsland Av	T-6	1
Lafayette Av	T-6	1
Lafayette Pl	T-7	1
Lake Av	S-7	1,2
Laurel Ln	T-7	1
Lewandowski St	T-7	1
Lincoln Av	T-7	1
Lincoln Av	T-6	1
Lincoln St	T-6	1
Livingston Av	S-7	1,2
Livingston Av	T-6	1
Livingston Av	T-7	1
Louis Ct	T-7	1
Lyndhurst Av	T-6	1
Madison St	T-7	1
Manor Ct	S-7	1,2
Maple Av	T-6	1
Marin Av	T-7	1
Meadow Rd	T-7	1
Meyer Av	T-6	1
Milburn Av	T-7	1
Milton Av	T-7	1
Monroe St	T-6	1
Mountain Wy	T-7	1
Nelson St	T-7	1
New Jersey Av	T-7	1
New York Av	T-7	1
New St	T-6	1
Newark Av	T-7	1
Oak St	T-7	1
Oak St	T-6	1
Octavia Pl	T-7	1
Octavia Pl	T-6	1
Olive St	T-7	1
Orient Wy	T-7	1
Oriental Pl	T-6	1
Page Av	T-6	1
Park Ridge Dr	U-6	1
Park Av	S-6	1,2
Park Pl	T-6	1
Park St	T-6	1
Paul Pl	T-7	1
Peabody Av	S-6	1,2
Pennsylvania Av	T-7	1
Pine St	T-6	1
Pine St	T-7	1
Polito Av	T-7	1
Post Av	T-7	1
Post Av	T-6	1
Prospect St	T-6	1
Regina Ct	T-7	1
Ridge Rd	T-7	1
Ridge Rd	T-6	1
Riverside Av	T-6	1
Roosevelt Av	T-6	1
Rudolph Pl	T-7	1
Sanford Av	T-6	1
Schuyler Av	T-7	1
Sollas Ct	T-7	1
Stuyvesant Av	T-6	1
Stuyvesant Av	S-7	1,2
Summer Av	T-6	1
Summit Av	T-6	1
Swayne Av	U-7	1
Ten Eyck Av	T-6	1
Thomas Av	T-6	1
Tontine Av	T-6	1
Travers Pl	T-6	1
Tyler St	T-6	1
Union Av	T-7	1
Valley Brook Av	T-7	1
Valley Brook Av	T-6	1
Van Buren St	T-6	1
Van Eyck Ct	T-6	1
Warren St	T-7	1
Watson Av	T-6	1
Weart Av	T-6	1
Webster Av	S-6	1,2
Webster Av	T-6	1
Wiederman	T-6	1
Willow Av	T-6	1
Wilson Av	T-6	1

Mahwah, Twp of

STREET	GRID	MAP
1st St	B-5	14
2nd St	B-5	14
2nd St	B-5	14
3rd St	C-5	11
Ackerman Dr	F-5	10,11
Adirondack Ct	C-5	14
Airmount Av	C-6	12,13B
Airmount Av	D-6	12,13B
Airmount Av	C-7	12,13B
Alcott Rd	C-6	12,13B
Alexandra Ct	C-6	12,13B
Anderson Dr	B-4	14
Apache Ct	C-5	14
Appert Ter	F-5	10,11
Apple Ridge Blvd	D-7	12,13B
Armour Rd	C-6	12,13B
Arrowhead Rd	B-6	13B
Ash Dr	D-5	11
Aspen Ct	C-7	12,13B
Aspen Ct	C-7	12,13B
Avenue A	B-5	14
Avenue B	B-5	14
Azalea Ct	D-5	11
Babbit Bridge Rd	F-5	10,11
Babcock Rd	B-6	13B
Baker Dr	C-6	12,13B
Bank Ridge	B-5	14
Banta Ct	C-5	11
Bartholf Ln	F-5	10,11
Bartholf Rd	F-5	10,11
Bartholf Rd	E-5	11
Bayard Ln	C-6	12,13B
Bayberry Dr	C-7	12,13B
Bear Swamp Rd	C-3	11
Bear Swamp Rd	D-3	11
Bedford Rd	E-4	11
Beech Dr	F-5	10,11
Beech Ive Ct	C-5	11
Beechwood Rd	B-6	13B
Bell Grove Dr	C-6	12,13B
Bellgrove Dr	C-6	12,13B
Belmont Pl	D-6	12,13B
Belmont Pl	D-7	12,13B
Bergen Pl	B-5	14
Beveridge Rd	C-6	12,13B
Beverly Pl	E-4	11
Birch Ct	F-5	10,11
Black Oak Ln	C-6	12,13B
Black Oak Ln	B-6	13B
Blue Ridge Ln	C-6	11
Blueberry Ct	F-4	10,11
Boulder Trail	C-6	12,13B
Boxwood Ct	D-5	11
Brake Shoe Pl	B-5	14
Brams Hill Dr	D-4	11
Breen Pl	C-6	12,13B
Bridle Path	C-4	11
Bridle Path Ln	C-4	11
Brook Ct	F-5	10,11
Brook St	B-5	14
Brookdale Ter	E-4	11
Bush Ln	D-7	12,13B
Byrne Dr	E-5	11
Cambridge Ct	C-6	12,13B
Campgaw Rd	F-4	10,11
Campgaw Rd	E-4	11
Canon Ball Rd	C-3	11
Carlough Pl	C-7	12,13B
Carol St	C-7	12,13B
Cascade Ct	C-5	14
Castle Rd	C-6	12,13B
Catherine Av	B-5	14
Cedar Hill Av	B-6	13B
Chapel Rd	F-4	10,11
Cherokee Ln	E-4	11
Chestnut St	F-5	10,11
Christie Av	B-6	13B
Church St	B-5	14
Clarana St	E-5	11
Clark Av	C-5	11
Clear Water Ct	E-4	11
Clearwater Rd	D-6	12,13B
Clove Brook Rd	C-5	11
Cobbler Ln	C-7	12,13B
Constance Dr	C-6	12,13B
Constance Dr	D-6	12,13B
Cooke St	C-6	12,13B
Copper Beach Ter	C-4	11
Copper Beach Ter	C-5	11
Cornwall Rd	C-6	12,13B
Corporate Dr	C-5	11
Cortland Tr	C-7	12,13B
Cottonwood Ct	F-4	10,11
Cottonwood Rd	C-4	11
Cottonwood Wy	D-5	11
Country Ln	D-6	12,13B
Cranberry Ct	D-5	11
Crescent Av	C-7	12,13B
Crescent Ridge Rd	C-7	12,13B
Crest Rd	A-4	14
Crocker Mansion Dr	D-4	11
Crown Ct	C-6	12,13B
Darlington Av	D-4	11
Davidson Ct	B-6	13B
Day Ct	F-5	10,11
Decker Ct	E-4	11
Deerfield Ter	E-5	11
Deerfield Ter	E-4	11
Deerhaven Rd	D-3	11
DeGraaf Ct	D-4	11
Degray Ter	F-5	10,11
Delhagen Ct	F-4	10,11
Demedu Ct	F-4	10,11
Devine Dr	C-6	12,13B
Devon Ct	C-6	12,13B
Diablo Ct	C-5	14
Division Pl	E-5	11
Dodge Ct	F-5	10,11
Dogwood Ct	F-5	10,11
Dogwood Ln	D-3	11
Doremus Rd	C-7	12,13B
Dundie Ct	C-7	12,13B
East Crescent Av	C-7	12,13B
East Crescent Av	D-7	12,13B
East Crescent Av	C-7	12,13B
East Mahwah Rd	C-6	12,13B
East Ramapo Av	C-6	12,13B
East View Av	C-5	11
East View Av	B-5	14
East View Dr	A-4	14
Echo Mountain Rd	B-4	14
Edison Pl	F-5	10,11
Eileen Dr	E-4	11
Elderberry Ln	D-5	11
Elizabeth Ln	E-4	11
Elm St	F-5	10,11
Erskine Ct	C-5	11
Eureka Pl	B-5	14
Evergreen Dr	C-5	11
Fairmount Av	F-5	10,11
Falcon Ct	E-4	11
Fardale Av	F-5	10,11
Fardale Av	E-4	11
Fardale Av	F-4	10,11
Faulkner Ct	D-5	11
Fawn Hill Dr	E-5	11
Feldman Ct	F-4	10,11
Feldman Ct	E-4	11
Fieldstone Dr	F-4	10,11
Fike Rd	E-4	11
Fisher Rd	D-7	12,13B
Flaming Arrow Rd	B-6	13B
Flaming Arrow Rd	C-6	12,13B
Forest Hill Rd	F-5	10,11
Forest Rd	F-5	10,11
Fox Ln	B-6	13B
Fox River Crossing	D-2	11
Frank Ct	F-4	10,11
Franklin Pl	B-5	14
Franklin St	F-5	10,11
Franklin Tnpk	C-6	12,13B
Franklin Tnpk	B-6	13B
Frederick St	B-5	14
Furman Ct	E-5	11
Fyke Rd	D4,E-4	11
Garden Ct	F-4	10,11
Gardiner St	C-6	12,13B
Garrison Ct	C-6	12,13B
Gassib Ct	E-4	11
Geiger Rd	B-4	14
Georgian Ct	D-4	11
Glasgow Ter	C-5	11
Glassmere Rd	C-5	11
Glen Gray Rd	E-3	11
Glen Gray Rd	D-2	11
Glen Gray Rd (Midvale Mountain Rd)	E-3	11
Glen Gray Rd (Midvale Mountain Rd)	E-2	11
Glen Gray Rd(Midvale Mountain Rd)	D-2	11
Glengorra Ct	C-7	12,13B
Glenmere Ter	E-4	11
Godwin Av	F-5	10,11
Godwin Av	F-5	10,11
Grandview Ln	C-5	11
Great Hall Rd	D-4	11
Green Mountian Rd	C-5	14
Green Wy	F-5	10,11
Greene St	F-5	10,11
Grenadier Dr	C-7	12,13B
Grist Mill Run	C-6	12,13B
Grove St	B-5	14
Halifax Rd	C-4	11
Halifax Rd	C-4	11
Halstead Wy	F-5	10,11
Halsted Wy	F-4	10,11
Halsted Wy	F-5	10,11
Hampshire Rd	D-4	11
Haring Ln	C-6	12,13B
Harvin Pl	F-5	10,11
Hauck Ct	E-5	11
Hawthorne Ln	D-5	11
Heath Ct	D-5	11
Heather Ln	C-7	12,13B
Hemlock St	C-5	11
Hemmingway Ln	D-5	11
Herlihy Dr	F-4	10,11
Hetzel Dr	F-4	10,11
Hibiscus Ct	D-5	11
Hickory Dr	D-5	11
Hickory Ln	D-5	11
High St	F-5	10,11
Highland Pl	F-5	10,11
Highland Rd	C-6	12,13B
Highland St	F-5	10,11
Highwood Rd	C-6	12,13B
Hillside Av	C-6	12,13B
Hillside Rd	C-3	11
Hilltop Rd	D-6	12,13B
Hilltop Rd	C-6	12,13B
Hines Av	B-5	14
Holdrum Ln	E-4	11
Holly Ct	D-5	11
Homespun Ct	C-6	12,13B
Hopkins Ct	C-5	11
Hopper Ct	F-5	10,11
Houvenkoph Rd	B-5	14
Hutton Dr	F-5	10,11
Hyde Park Rd	C-6	12,13B
Indian Hollow Ct	C-6	12,13B
Indianfield Ct	C-6	12,13B
Industrial Av	C-6	12,13B
Island Av	C-6	12,13B
Ivy Ln	C-7	12,13B
Jackson Ln	C-5	11
Jacobean Wy	D-4	11
Jaguar	C-5	14
Jahn Ct	F-5	10,11
James Brite Cir	F-4	10,11
Janice Ct	C-7	12,13B
Jefferson St	F-5	10,11
Jersey Av	B-5	14
Johnson Av	B-5	14
Judith Ann Ct	C-6	12,13B
Juniper Wy	D-5	11
Karen Dr	D-5	11
Karen Dr	C-6	12,13B
Kiersted Pl	C-6	12,13B
Kilmer Rd	C-6	12,13B
King St	C-6	12,13B
Knichel Rd	F-5	10,11
Kohout Dr	E-4	11
Konight Ct	F-4	10,11
Lake View Dr	B-4	14
Lakeview Rd	B-6	13B
Lambert Tr	C-7	12,13B
Laramie Ln	C-5	14
Larch Ln	D-5	11
Laurel Ct	C-6	12,13B
Lavender Ct	D-5	11
Lawrence Rd	C-6	12,13B
Lehman St	F-5	10,11
Leighton Pl	F-5	10,11
Leisure Ln	B-5	14
Leona Tr	F-5	10,11
Lilac Ln	D-5	11
Linden St	D-5	11
Litchult Ln	D-7	12,13B
Locust Ln	F-5	10,11
Long Av	B-5	14
Lost River Ct	C-5	14
Lottie Ln	E-4	11
Lower Pine Dr	C-4	11
Lydia Ln	C-5	11
Lynn Ter	C-5	11
Lynn Ter	C-6	12,13B
Mable Ct	F-4	10,11
MacArthur Blvd	C-5	11
MacMillan Ct	C-5	11
Macoun Dr	D-7	12,13B
Madison Av	E-4	11
Madison Av	E-5	11
Magnolia Rd	C-4	11
Mahogany Ct	C-5	14
Mahwah Rd	C-6	12,13B
Malcolm Pl	C-6	12,13B
Males Zewski Ct	F-5	10,11
Maleszewski Ct	F-4	10,11
Maple Rd	A-4	14
Marion Dr	D-3	11
Mark Twain Way	D-5	11
Martis Pl	C-6	12,13B
Mary Ct	D-4	11
Masonicus Rd	C-6	12,13B
Masonicus Rd E	C-7	12,13B
Masonicus Rd E	C-6	12,13B
Matthew Pl	F-5	10,11
May Ct	C-7	12,13B
Maysenger Rd	C-6	12,13B
McArthur Blvd	C-5	11
McArthur Blvd	C-5	11
McIntosh Dr	C-7	12,13B
McKee Dr	C-6	12,13B
Meadow Av	B-5	14
Meadow Lakes Dr	E-4	11
Meadowbrook Ln	B-6	13B
Meester St	F-5	10,11
Meldisco	C-5	14
Melville Ct	D-5	11
Merril Dr	F4,F-5	10,11
Meyers Rd	E-4	11
Midvale Mountain R (Glen Gray Rd)	E-2	11
Midvale Mountain Rd (Glen Gray Rd)	D-2	11
Midvale Mountain Rd (Glen Gray Rd)	E-3	11
Miller Rd	C-6	12,13B
Moccasin Ct	C-6	12,13B
Moffatt Rd	C-5	11
Mohawk Tr	E-4	11
Mohican Wy	R-3	11
Mollie Ct	F-5	10,11
Monroe Dr	E-5	11
Monroe Dr	E-4	11
Moramarco Ct	F-5	10,11
Morris Av	F-4	10,11
Mount Glen Rd	C-2	11
Mountain Av	B-5	14
Mountain Rd	B-4	14
Mountain Rd	A-4	14
Mountainside Av	B-5	14
Mountainview Dr	C-5	11
Mulberry Dr	D-5	11
Murray Av	F-5	10,11
Muth St	B-5	14
Nielsen Av	C-7	12,13B
North Central Av	C-6	12,13B
North Central Av	D-6	12,13B
North Glasgow Ter	C-5	11
North Hillside Av	C-6	12,13B
Northerly Dr	F-4	10,11
Oak Rd	A-4	14
Oak Ter	B-5	14
Old Lane	D-4	11
Old Station Ln	C-6	12,13B
Old Wood Ct	C-5	14
Olney Rd	B-6	13B
Orchard Dr	C-6	12,13B
Osborne Ct	D-7	12,13B
Osborne Ct	C-7	12,13B
Overlook Pl	C-6	12,13B
Oweno Pl	C-6	12,13B
Oweno Rd	C-6	12,13B
Oxford St	C-6	12,13B
Paddington Park Rd	C-6	12,13B
Paddington Rd	C-6	12,13B
Park St	B-5	14
Parsloe Ct	F-5	10,11
Parsons Ct	D-5	11
Patrick Brem Ct	D-4	11
Patriots Wy	E-2	11
Pelz Farm Ct	D-6	12,13B
Pelz Farm Ct	D-7	12,13B
Pendelton Rd	F-5	10,11
Penna Ct	F-5	10,11
Pepperidge Ct	D-5	11
Pepperidge Rd	D-5	11
Persimmon Ct	D-5	11
Petersen Pl	D-5	11
Pierson Ct	C-6	12,13B
Pine Hill Rd	A-4	14
Plumb Ter	D-5	11
Pocono Ct	C-5	14
Poet's Wy	D-5	11
Polo Ln	C-4	11
Pond Ln	F-4	10,11
Poplar Av	C-5	11
Public Rd	D-2	11
Pulis Av	F-4	10,11
Quince Ct	D-5	11
Rae Av	F-5	10,11
Railroad Av	B-6	13B
Railroad Av	C-6	12,13B
Railroad Av	B-5	14
Railroad Av	C-5	11
Raintree Ln	D-5	11
Ramapo Brae	B-4	14
Ramapo Ln	C-5	14
Ramapo Valley Rd	E-3	11
Ramapo Valley Rd	B-5	14
Ramapo Valley Rd	C-4	11
Ramapo Valley Rd	D-3	11
Ramapo Valley Rd	E-3	11
Ramsey Rd	D-5	11
Reich Av	B-5	14
Reid Ct	B-6	13B
Reid Ct	C-6	12,13B
Reid Ct	B-6	13B
Richmond Rd	C-6	12,13B
Ridge Rd	C-5	11
Ridge Rd	D-5	11
River View Dr	C-5	11
River View Ter	C-5	11
Robin Rd	C-7	12,13B
Rock Ridge Rd	C-6	12,13B
Romopock Ct	C-6	12,13B
Rozanski Ln	C-7	12,13B
Rutherford Rd	C-6	12,13B
Sage Ct	D-5	11
Sage Ct	D-4	11
Saint Moritz Av	E-4	11
Santiago Ct	C-5	14
Sassafras Ct	D-5	11
Scherer Pl	C-6	12,13B
Seminary Dr	D-4	11
Seminary Rd	D-4	11
Sequoia Ln	C-5	11
Seton La	D-4	11
Shadow Mountian Rd	C-5	14
Sherwood Av	B-5	14
Shuart Ln	C-6	12,13B
Shuart Rd	C-7	12,13B
Siding Pl	C-6	12,13B
Sierra Ct	C-5	14
Skyline Dr	F-5	10,11
Skytop Dr	E-5	11
Skytop Dr	F-5	10,11
Snow Dr	B-6	13B
Snow Mountain Av	A-4	14
South Bayard Ln	C-6	12,13B
South Houvenkoph Rd	C-5	11
South Houvenkoph Rd	B-5	14
South Mahwah Rd	C-6	12,13B
South Railroad Av	C-6	12,13B
South Slope Rd	C-6	12,13B
South St	B-5	14
Southerly Dr	F-4	10,11
Sparrowbush Rd	C-7	12,13B
Spruce Rd	A-4	14
Stag Hill Rd	B-4	14
Stag Hill Rd	A-4	14
Stag Hill Rd	B-5	14
State St	B-5	14
Stephens Ln	B-6	13B
Stephens Ln	B-6	13B
Stone Fence Rd	F-5	10,11
Stone Wall Ct	C-7	12,13B
Stonewall Ct	C-6	12,13B
Storrs Ct	C-7	12,13B
Stowe Ln	D-5	11
Strong St	F-5	10,11
Strysko Av	B-5	14
Summit Rd	C-6	12,13B
Sunny Side Rd	C-6	12,13B
Sunset Ct	C-5	11
Suzeski Ct	F-4	10,11
Swiatek Ct	F-4	10,11
Switzer Rd	F-5	10,11
Sycamore Ln	D-5	11
Tam O'Shanter Dr	C-7	12,13B
Tartan Rd	C-7	12,13B
Thistle Ln	C-7	12,13B
Thunderhead Pl	C-6	12,13B
Trommel Dr	C-7	12,13B
Tulip Tree Ct	D-5	11
Tuliptree Ct	D-5	11
Turner Lake Dr	E-4	11
Tuscan Rd	C-6	12,13B
Upper Pine Dr	C-4	11
Vail Pl	E-4	11
Valentine Ct	F-5	10,11
Valley View Dr	C-4	11
Valley View Dr	B-5	14
Van Brookhaven Ct	F-5	10,11
Van Mulen St	F-5	10,11
Vanderbeck Ln	F-5	10,11
Victoria Ln	F-4	10,11
Vista View Dr	C-5	14
Vistaview Dr	C-5	11
Vreeland Ct	C-5	11
Wagon Trail	C-6	12,13B
Walnut St	F-5	10,11
Walsh Dr	D-4	11
Wanamaker Av	C-6	12,13B
Ward Ln	B-6	13B
Warhol Av	B-5	14
Washington Ln	C-4	11
Watch Hill Rd	F-5	10,11
West Airmount Rd	C-6	12,13B
West Crescent Av	E-5	11
West Deerhaven Rd	D-3	11
West Ramapo Av	C-5	11
West Rd	F-5	10,11
Westervelt Ln	D-7	12,13B
Weyer Haeuser Blvd	C-6	12,13B
Whitney Rd	F-5	10,11
Whittier Ct	D-5	11
William Ct	E-4	11
Willow Bank Ct	F-5	10,11
Willow Wy	C-4	11
Wilmuth St	B-5	14
Winding Tr	E-5	11
Windsor Ter	E-4	11
Winter Ln	B-6	13B
Winter St	C-6	12,13B
Winter Ter	B-6	13B
Witte Pl	F-5	10,11
Woods Rd	C-5	11
Wyckoff Av	F-5	10,11
York St	C-6	12,13B
Young's Rd	E-4	11
Young's Rd	E-5	11
Zewski Ct	F-4	10,11

Maywood, Boro of

STREET	GRID	MAP
Ackerman St	N-9	5
Albert St	N-9	5
Beech St	N-9	5
Belle Av	N-9	5
Bergen Av	N-9	5
Berry Ct	N-9	5
Briarcliff Av	M-9	5,6
Brook Av	N-9	5
Brookdale St	N-9	5
Buckingham Ct	P-9	5
Buckingham Ct	N-9	5
Byron Pl	N-9	5
Cedar Av	M-9	5,6
Central Av	N-9	5
Clinton St	N-9	5
Coles St	N-9	5
Collingwood Av	M-9	5,6
Concord Dr	N-9	5
Conklin Av	M-9	5,6
Coolidge Av	M-9	5,6
Cumming Av	M-9	5,6
Davison St	N-9	5
De Soto Av	N-9	5
De Soto Av	M-9	5,6
Demarest Pl	P-9	5
Duvier Pl	N-9	5
East Fairmount Av	M-9	5,6
East Forest Av	N-9	5
East Hunter Av	N-9	5
East Magnolia Av	N-9	5
East Pleasant Av	N-9	5
Edell Av	N-9	5
Edgewood Pl	N-9	5
Elizabeth Ct	N-9	5
Elm St	N-9	5
Essex Ct	P-9	5
Essex St	P-9	5
Fairway	N-9	5
Felter Av	M-9	5,6
Forest Av	M-9	5,6
Forest Pl	N-9	5
Garden St	N-9	5
Golf Av	N-9	5
Grant Av	M-9	5,6
Grove Av	N-9	5
Hammel Pl	N-9	5
Hampton Ct	P-9	5
Harding Pl	M-9	5,6
Hartwich St	N-9	5
Hergesell Av	N-9	5
Hill St	N-9	5
Howcroft Rd	N-9	5
Jaeger Av	N-9	5
Jersey Av	N-9	5
Lafayette Av	N-9	5
Latham St	N-9	5
Lawrence St	N-9	5
Lenox Av	N-9	5
Lethbridge Ln	N-9	5
Lincoln Av	N-9	5
Locust Dr	M-9	5,6
Loughlin Pl	M-9	5,6
Louis St	N-9	5
Maple Av	N-9	5
Marlboro Ct	P-9	5
Maybrook Dr	P-9	5
Maywood Av	P-9	5
Maywood Av	N-9	5
Mendez Av	N-9	5
Mount Vernon Ct	N-9	5
North Edel Av	M-9	5,6
North Lincoln Av	M-9	5,6
North Wyoming Av	M-9	5,6
Oak Av	N-9	5
Orchard Pl	N-9	5
Palmer Av	M-9	5,6
Palmer Av	N-9	5
Park Av	N-9	5

BERGEN COUNTY

STREET	GRID	MAP
Parkway	M-9	5,6
Parkway	N-9	5
Passaic Ct	N-9	5
Passaic St	N-9	5
Paterson Av	M-9	5,6
Pleasant Ct	N-9	5
Poplar Av	N-9	5
Prospect Av	N-9	5
Ramapo Av	N-9	5
Romaine Av	N-9	5
Roosevelt Pl	M-9	5,6
Rosalie St	N-9	5
Rutherford Av	M-9	5,6
Sanzari Pl	M-9	5,6
Sininger Pl	N-9	5
Spring Valley Av	M-9	5,6
Spring Valley Rd	M-9	5,6
Spring Valley Rd	N-9	5
Stavola Pl	M-9	5,6
Stelling Av	M-9	5,6
Stewart St	N-9	5
Stone St	N-9	5
Taplin Av	N-9	5
Terrace Av	N-9	5
The Esplanade	N-9	5
Thoma Av	N-9	5
Van Cleve St	N-9	5
Walnut Rd	M-9	5,6
Walnut Rd	M-10	5,6
Ward St	M-9	5,6
Washington Av	M-9	5,6
Washington Av	N-9	5
West Fairmount Av	M-9	5,6
West Grove Av	N-9	5
West Hunter Av	N-9	5
West Magnolia Av	N-9	5
West Pleasant Av	N-9	5
Wilhelm Pl	N-9	5
William St	N-9	5
Windsor Ct	N-9	5
Windsor Ct	P-9	5
Woodland Av	N-9	5
Wyoming Av	N-9	5
Wyoming Av	M-9	5,6
Zuber Pl	M-9	5,6

Midland Park, Boro of

STREET	GRID	MAP
1st St	H-6	9
2nd St	H-6	9
3rd St	H-6	9
4th St	H-6	9
5th St	H-6	9
6th St	H-6	9
Aqueduct Av	H-6	9
Arminda Av	H-6	9
Baldwin Ct	H-6	9
Baldwin Dr	H-6	9
Balsam St	H-6	9
Balsam St	G-6	9
Bank St	H-6	9
Belle Ct	H-6	9
Birch St	H-6	9
Birch St	H-5	10
Brandon Rd	H-6	9
Brautigam Ln	H-6	9
Busteed Dr	H-6	9
Butternut Av	H-6	9
Canterburt Dr	H-6	9
Cardar St	G-6	9
Center St	H-6	9
Central Av	H-5	10
Chamberlain Pl	H-6	9
Chestnut St	H-6	9
Christopher St	H-6	9
Clinton Av	H-5	10
College Rd	H-6	9
Colonial Dr	H-6	9
Colonial Rd	H-6	9
Cornell St	H-6	9
Cottage St	J-6	6,9
Crest Dr	H-6	9
Cross Av	H-6	9
Cross St	H-6	9
Cyphers Ln	H-6	9
Dairy St	H-6	9
Demund Ln	H-6	9
Donna Ln	H-6	9
Drews Ln	H-6	9
East Center St	H-6	9
East Payne Av	H-6	9
East Summit Av	H-6	9
Erie Av	H-6	9
Estes Ct	H-6	9
Evergreen St	G-6	9
Fairhaven St	G-6	9
Faner Rd	H-6	9
Floral Ln	G-6	9
Foster Ct	H-6	9
Franklin Av	H-6	9
Garret Pl	H-6	9
Glen Av	H-6	9
Gobel Terr	H-6	9
Godwin Av	H-6	9
Goffle Av	J-6	6,9
Golon Ter	H-6	9
Golon Ct	H-6	9
Greenwood Av	H-5	10
Grove St	H-5	10
Grove St	H-6	9
Habben Av	H-6	9
Hampshire Rd	H-6	9
Heights Rd	H-6	9
Hemlock Pl	G-6	9
Hemlock St	G-6	9
Hiawatha Av	H-6	9
Highland Av	H-6	9
Highwood Av	H-6	9
Hill Av	H-5	10
Hill St	H-6	9
Hillside Av	H-6	9
Hillside Av	H-5	10
Hillton Av	H-6	9
Irving St	H-6	9
Kew Ct	H-6	9
Lake Av	J-6	6,9
Lake Av	J-6	6,9
Lakeview Dr	J-6	6,9
Linden Pl	H-6	9
Linwood Av	H-5	10
Linwood Av	H-6	9
Logan Dr	H-6	9
Madison Av	H-5	10
Maltbie Av	J-6	6,9
Maltbie Av	J-6	6,9
Maple Av	H-5	10
Maple St	H-6	9
Meadow Ct	H-6	9
Meadow Ct	G-6	9
Meda Pl	H-6	9
Midland Av	H-5	10
Miedama Pl	H-6	9
Millington Dr	H-6	9
Morrow Rd	H-6	9
Mountain Av	J-6	6,9
Mulders Ln	H-6	9
Myrtle Av	H-5	10
Oak Av	H-5	10
Oak Hill Rd	H-6	9
Orchard St	H-6	9
Park Av	H-5	10
Park Av	H-6	9
Parker Pl	H-6	9
Paterson Av	H-6	9
Patricia Ct	H-6	9
Payne Av	H-6	9
Pierce Av	H-6	9
Pine St	G-6	9
Plane St	H-6	9
Pleasant Av	H-6	9
Post St	H-6	9
Princeton Av	H-6	9
Prospect St	H-6	9
Railroad Av	H-6	9
Rea Av	J-6	6,9
Roetman Ct	H-5	10
Roetman Ct	H-6	9
Rogers Ct	H-6	9
Rubble St	H-6	9
Short St	H-5	10
Sicomac Av	H-6	9
Smith Ln	H-6	9
Smithfield Rd	G-6	9
South Rea Av	J-6	6,9
Spruce St	G-6	9
Stonecroft Rd	J-6	6,9
Sunset Av	H-6	9
Susan Av	G-6	9
Tice Ct	H-6	9
Van Blarcom Av	H-6	9
Vreeland Av	H-6	9
Waldo Av	G-6	9
Walnut St	H-5	10
Wedlake Ct	H-6	9
West End Av	J-6	6,9
West Summit Av	H-6	9
West View Pl	H-6	9
West View Ter	H-6	9
West St	H-6	9
Westbrook St	H-6	9
Witte Dr	H-6	9
Woodside Av	H-6	9
Wostbrook Ln	H-6	9
Zimmer Av	H-6	9
Zimmer Av	G-6	9
Zimmerman Ct	H-6	9

Montvale, Boro of

STREET	GRID	MAP
Ackers Av	E-10	12
Akers Av	E-10	12
Alpine Cir	F-11	13A
Antrim Rd	E-11	13A
Arthur Ct	F-11	13A
Azalia Ln	E-10	12
Barbara Ln	D-9	12
Bayberry Dr	E-10	12
Beechwood Rd	E-9	12
Belnay Ln	D-9	12
Birch Av	F-11	13A
Blue Sky Ln	E-9	12
BMW Plz	E-9	12
Bramble Wy	E-10	12
Brook St	E-10	12
Bryan Dr	E-11	13A
Burdick Rd	E-10	12
Camron Ct	E-11	13A
Candlelight Dr	D-9	12
Cardinal Ct	F-11	13A
Charlotte Ct	D-8	12,13B
Charlotte Ct	D-9	12
Cherokee Tr	E-10	12
Cherry Ln	E-8	12
Chestnut Ridge Rd	E-9	12
Clover Ct	E-11	13A
Clover Ct	E-10	12
Columbine Ct	E-10	12
Conrad Ct	E-11	13A
Cottage Av	F-11	13A
Craig Rd	E-9	12
Crest Rd	E-11	13A
Crestview Ter	E-10	12
Cypress Peak Ln	E-10	12
Deepwood Ln	E-10	12
Dogwood Ln	E-10	12
Dolores Dr	E-11	13A
Dolores Dr	F-11	13A
Donny Brook Rd	E-10	12
East Grand Av	F-10	9,12
Echo Hill	F-11	13A
Edgren Wy	E-10	12
Ellsworth Tr	E-10	12
Erie Av	E-11	13A
Fairview Av	F-11	13A
Forest Av	E-11	13A
Fox Hill Rd	D-9	12
Franklin Av	F-10	9,12
Garden Ln	E-8	12
Glen Ln	E-10	12
Glen Ln	E-11	13A
Grand Av	E-8	12
Green Briar Ln	E-10	12
Green Wy	D-9	12
Grove St	E-11	13A
Hamilton St	F-10	9,12
Hartel Ln	E-10	12
Hartel Ln	E-11	13A
Hearing Rd	E-10	12
Hearth Stone Wy	D-9	12
Hemlock St	E-11	13A
Hering Rd	E-10	12
Hickory Hill	D-9	12
High Ridge Rd	E-9	12
Highland Rd	E-10	12
Hillcrest Av	E-11	13A
Hillcrest Av	F-11	13A
Hillside Ter	F-11	13A
Hilton Pl	E-10	12
Holly Hill Ct	D-10	12
Hope St	E-10	12
Hopper Av	F-10	9,12
Huff Ter	E-9	12
Huff Ter	D-8	12,13B
Huff Ter	E-8	12
Huff Ter	D-9	12
Ihnen Ct	D-9	12
Ivy Ln	E-11	13A
Jan Ct	E-10	12
Jefferson Pl	E-11	13A
Joan Ter	E-11	13A
John St	F-11	13A
John Ter	E-11	13A
June Ln	E-10	12
Kinderkamack Rd	E-10	12
Kinderkamack Rd S	F-10	9,12
Kinderkamack Rd	E-11	13A
Ladik Pl	E-11	13A
Lark Ln	D-9	12
Lewis Rd	F-11	13A
Lexington Ln	E-10	12
Locust St	E-11	13A
Lomas Ln	E-8	12
Longridge Rd	D-9	12
Madison Av	F-11	13A
Magnolia Av	E-10	12
Main St	E-11	13A
Maple Av	F-11	13A
Marion Av	E-11	13A
Maureen Ct	E-10	12
Maze Rd	E-11	13A
Meadow Ln	F-11	13A
Memorial Dr	F-10	9,12
Memorial Dr	E-10	12
Mercedes Dr	E-9	12
Middle Rd	E-10	12
Middletown Rd	E-11	13A
Montvale Av	E-11	13A
Montvale Av	E-10	12
Morgan Ct	D-9	12
Moulton Dr	E-11	13A
Mulberry Dr	E-11	13A
Murray Rd	F-11	13A
Myrtle St	E-11	13A
Nichols Rd	F-11	13A
Norgate Dr	F-11	13A
North Av	D-10	12
Nottingham Ct	E-10	12
Nottingham Ct	F-10	9,12
Oak St	E-11	13A
Oakland Dr	F-11	13A
Old Chestnut Ridge Rd	D-9	12
Old Lantern Ct	D-9	12
Paragon Dr	E-9	12
Paragon Dr S	E-9	12
Park St	F-10	9,12
Partridge Run	D-9	12
Pearl Av	E-11	13A
Penn Av	E-11	13A
Philips Pkwy	E-9	12
Phyllis Dr	E-11	13A
Pine Hollow Dr	D-9	12
Pine View Ter	E-10	12
Pine St	E-10	12
Plymouth Place Ct	E-10	12
Powder Hill Wy	D-9	12
Prospect Av	F-11	13A
Quail Ridge Rd	E-10	12
Rail Road Av	F-10	9,12
Ramapo Rd	E-10	12
Raven St	F-11	13A
River St	E-11	13A
Roberts Rd	E-11	13A
Robin Hood Ct	E-10	12
Rolling Ridge	E-9	12
Rustic Cir	E-9	12
Rutherford Pl	E-11	13A
Schwenker St	E-9	12
Shadow Ln	E-10	12
Shady Tr	E-10	12
Sheppard Dr	E-10	12
Short Av	E-11	13A
Sloping Hill Ln	E-10	12
Smoke Rise Ct	D-9	12
Spring Valley Rd	E-10	12
Spring Valley Rd	D-10	12
Spring Valley Rd	E-9	12
Spring Valley Rd	D-9	12
Spruce St	E-11	13A
Stag Hill	E-10	12
Stem Brook Rd	E-10	12
Stone Hollow Rd	E-10	12
Strawberry Hill Ct	D-10	12
Stuyvesant Rd	E-8	12
Summer Tree Wy	E-9	12
Summit Av	E-10	12
Summit Av	E-9	12
Sunnyside Dr	E-10	12
Sunrise Dr	D-9	12
Surrey Ln	E-8	12
Surrey Ln	E-9	12
Terkuile Rd	E-10	12
Terry Ct	E-10	12
Thier Ln	D-9	12
Timber Land Tr	E-8	12
Timber Land Tr	E-9	12
Twin Oak Dr	E-10	12
Twin Dr	E-10	12
Upper Saddle River Rd	D-9	12
Valemont Rd	E-10	12
Valley View Ter	D-9	12
Van Riper Rd	E-9	12
Van Wyck St	D-9	12
Walnut St	E-11	13A
Walnut St	F-11	13A
Waverly Pl	E-11	13A
Waverly Pl	F-11	13A
Wayne St	F-10	9,12
West Grand Av	E-9	12
West Grand Av	E-10	12
West Dr	E-11	13A
West Dr	F-11	13A
Westminster Ct	E-10	12
Westmoreland Av	E-11	13A
Westmoreland Av	F-11	13A
White Oak Ct	E-10	12
Wildwood Ct	E-10	12
Williams Rd	E-11	13A
Williams Rd	F-11	13A
Williamsburg Wy	E-11	13A
Wilson Rd	E-11	13A
Wilson Rd	F-11	13A
Windsor Rd	E-11	13B
Woodland Rd	E-10	12
Wortendyke Av	F-10	9,12
Wren Wy	D-9	12

Moonachie, Boro of

STREET	GRID	MAP
Albert St	R-10	2
Anderson Av	R-9	2
Barrett Av	R-9	2
Barrett St	R-9	2
Berger St	R-8	2
Billy Diehl Rd	R-9	2
Broad St	R-10	2
Bruno St	R-10	2
Caesar Pl	R-9	2
Capitol Dr	R-10	2
Carol Pl	R-10	2
Central Blvd	S-10	1 2
Charles St	R-10	2
Charles Lindberg Blvd	R-9	2
Christiana St	R-9	2
Commercial Av	R-9	2
Commercial Av	S-9	1 2
Concord St	R-9	2
Congress Dr	R-10	2
Congress Dr	S-10	1 2
Craig St	R-9	2
Daniel St	R-10	2
Diamond Wy	R-10	2
Division St	R-8	2
Division St	R-9	2
Edstan Dr	R-10	2
Empire Blvd	S-10	1,2
Francis St	R-10	2
Frederick St	R-10	2
Garden St	R-10	2
Grand St	R-9	2
Graphic Pl	R-10	2
Henry St	R-10	2
Horizon Blvd	S-10	1,2
Industrial Av	R-9	2
Jackson Pl	R-9	2
Jefferson Pl	R-9	2
Jefferson Pl	R-10	2
Joseph St	R-10	2
Jubilee Pl	R-10	2
Knickerbocker Rd	R-9	2
Lincoln Pl	R-9	2
Lladro Dr	R-10	2
Maple St	R-10	2
Mavus Pl	R-9	2
Molinari St	R-10	2
Monte Pl	R-9	2
Moonachie Av	R-9	2
Moonachie Rd	R-10	2
Oak St	R-8	2
Oxford Dr	R-10	2
Park St	R-10	2
Purcell Ct	R-9	2
Ramella Av	R-10	2
Redneck Rd	R-9	2
Romeo St	R-9	2
Rooney Pl	R-10	2
Roosevelt Pl	R-10	2
Roosevelt Pl	R-9	2
Sedita Pl	R-9	2
Sony Dr	R-10	2
Sova Pl	R-9	2
State St	S-10	1,2
Teresa Ct	R-10	2
Truman Pl	R-10	2
Union St	R-9	2
Union St	R-8	2
Wash Pl	R-9	2
West Commercial Av	R-9	2
West Commercial Av	S-9	1,2
Willow St	R-9	2

New Milford, Boro of

STREET	GRID	MAP
Albert Pl	L-11	7
Alessandrini Av	M-11	4,7
Anchor Ct	M-11	4,7
Anchor Ct	M-10	5,6
Arbor Pl	L-11	7
Arlington Rd	M-10	5,6
Asbury St	L-11	7
Audrey Pl	L-10	6
Audrey Pl	L-11	7
Avon Pl	K-11	7
Azalea Dr	M-11	4,7
Baldwin Av	L-11	7
Batterson Ct	K-11	7
Beech Pl	L-11	7
Bergen Av	L-11	7
Berkley St	L-11	7
Berkley St	M-11	4,7
Berkshire Av	M-11	4,7
Birch Av	L-11	7
Birchwood Rd	M-11	4,7
Bliss Dr	L-11	7
Boulevard	M-11	4,7
Boulevard	K-11	7
Boulevard	L-11	7
Bulger Av	M-11	4,7
California Av	K-11	7
Canterbury Ln	M-10	5,6
Capitol Rd	M-11	4,7
Carlton Pl	L-11	7
Carlton Pl	K-11	7
Carnation Dr	M-11	4,7
Cedar Rd	L-11	7
Center St	K-11	7
Central Park Dr	L-11	7
Charles St	L-11	7
Cherry St	L-11	7
Chestnut St	L-11	7
Cleveland St	K-11	7
Clinton St	M-10	5,6
Clover Ct	M-10	5,6
Columbia St	L-10	6
Columbia St	M-10	5,6
Concord St	K-11	7
Concors Pl	L-11	7
Congress St	M-11	4,7
Cooper St	L-11	7
Cornell St	L-10	6
Cypress Ct	L-11	7
Dahlia Av	M-11	4,7
Demarest Av	L-11	7
Dietz Ct	K-11	7
Dillworth Rd	L-10	6
Dorchester Ln	M-10	5,6
Duke Ct	L-11	7
Duke Rd	L-11	7
Eagle Av	L-11	7
East Park Dr	L-11	7
East Woodland Rd	M-11	4,7
Elizabeth Ct	K-11	7
Elizabeth St	K-11	7
Evergreen Ct	M-11	4,7
Faller Dr	M-11	4,7
Fermery Dr	K-11	7
Floral Ct	M-11	4,7
Florence St	L-11	7
Fulton St	K-11	7
Golden Gate Av	K-11	7
Grace Pl	L-11	7
Grand St	K-11	7
Graphic Blvd	L-11	7
Greve Dr	M-11	4,7
Grix Ct	L-11	7
Grove St	L-11	7
Harris Pl	K-11	7
Harrison St	K-11	7
Harvard St	L-10	6
Hegi Dr	L-11	7
Henley Av	L-10	6
Henley Av	L-11	7
Hirschfield Pl	K-11	7
Hirschfield Pl	L-11	7
Hoffman Av	L-11	7
Holly St	L-11	7
Howard Ct	M-11	4,7
Hughes Rd	L-11	7
Huguenot Dr	M-10	5,6
Huguenot Dr	M-11	4,7
Ivy Pl	L-11	7
Jackson Av	L-11	7
James St	K-11	7
John Cecchino Dr	L-11	7
Johnson Ct	M-11	4,7
Jordan Rd	K-11	7
Kastler Ct	L-11	7
Kehoe Ct	L-11	7
Knierim Pl	L-11	7
Knoll Rd	L-11	7
Korfitsen Rd	M-11	4,7
Lacey Dr	K-11	7
Lafayette St	K-11	7
Lake St	L-11	7
Lee Pl	M-11	4,7
Lenox Av	K-11	7
Leonard Dr	K-11	7
Licala Av	K-11	7
Lincoln Pl	K-11	7
Linden Pl	L-11	7
Locust St	L-11	7
Locust St	M-11	4,7
Luhman Dr	M-11	4,7
Lynnwood Av	M-10	5,6
Mabie St	L-11	7
Mack Pl	L-11	7
Mack Pl	K-11	7
Madison Av	L-11	7
Madison Ct	L-11	7
Main St	L-11	7
Manor Pl	L-11	7
Maple Av	M-10	5,6
Maple St	M-11	4,7
Maple St	L-11	7
Marguerite St	L-11	7
Marion Av	L-11	7
Martin Pl	M-11	4,7
McCarthy Dr	K-11	7
McCue Ln	L-11	7
McKinley Av	L-11	7
Milford Av	L-11	7
Monmouth Av	L-11	7
Monroe Av	L-11	7
Moore Av	L-11	7
Morris Ln	K-11	7
Myrtle Av	L-11	7
Neumier Dr	L-11	7
New Bridge Rd	M-11	4,7
New Bridge Rd	M-10	5,6
New Milford Av	L-11	7
North Carlton Pl	K-11	7
North Park Dr	L-11	7
North Terrace Pl	K-11	7
Oak Ln	M-10	5,6
Old New Bridge Rd	M-10	5,6
Oxford Ln	M-10	5,6
Pacific St	M-11	4,7
Pershing Av	K-11	7
Pine Av	K-11	7
Pleasant Av	L-11	7
Pleasant Dr	M-11	4,7
Plympton St	L-11	7
Plympton St	M-11	4,7
Powell Dr	M-10	5,6
Prell Ln	K-11	7
Princeton St	L-11	7
Princeton St	M-11	4,7
Prospect Av	K-11	7
Prospect Av	L-11	7
Rambler Av	M-10	5,6
Rambler Av	M-11	4,7
Ray Woods Ln	M-10	5,6
Reichelt Rd	M-10	5,6
Reichelt Rd	M-11	4,7
Rhein Ct	K-10	6
Richmond Av	M-11	4,7
Ridge Ct	M-11	4,7
Ridge St	M-11	4,7
Ridge St	M-11	4,7
Ridge St	M-10	5,6
River Ln	M-10	5,6
River Rd	M-10	5,6
River Rd	L-11	7
Riveredge Rd	L-10	6
Roosevelt Av	M-10	5,6
Rose Ln	L-10	6
Rose Pl	L-11	7
Rosse Av	M-10	5,6
Ryeside Av	L-11	7
Salem St	K-11	7
Senate Rd	M-11	4,7
Shea Dr	K-11	7
Sheridan St	M-11	4,7
South Park Dr	L-11	7
State Rd	M-11	4,7
Steuben Av	M-10	5,6
Stevens Ct	L-11	7
Stockton St	L-11	7
Stuart Pl	L-11	7
Summit Av	L-11	7
Summit Av	K-11	7
Sutton Pl	K-11	7
Sutton Pl	L-11	7
Terrace Pl	K-11	7
Terrace Pl	L-11	7
Trensch Dr	K-11	7
Trenton St	L-11	7
Trotta Dr	M-10	5,6
Virgina Av	M-11	4,7
Vomel Dr	M-11	4,7
Voorhis Av	L-11	7
Walnut St	L-11	7
Walnut St	M-11	4,7
Warren St	M-11	4,7
Warren St	M-11	4,7
Washington Av	K-11	7
Webster Dr	K-11	7
West Park Dr	L-11	7
West St	L-11	7
Westley Ln	M-10	5,6
William St	L-11	7
Willow Av	M-10	5,6
Windsor Ct	L-11	7
Windsor Rd	L-11	7
Woodland Rd	M-10	5,6
Woodland Rd	M-11	4,7
Woods Ct	L-11	7
Yale St	L-10	6
Zabriskie Pl	L-11	7

North Arlington, Boro of

STREET	GRID	MAP
1st St	U-7	1
2nd St	U-7	1
3rd St	U-7	1
4th St	U-6	1
5th St	T-6	1
6th St	U-6	1
7th St	T-6	1
8th St	T-6	1
9th St	T-6	1
Abbott Pl	U-6	1
Albert St	U-6	1
Allan Dr	U-6	1
Argyle Pl	U-6	1
Arlington Av	U-6	1
Arlington Blvd	U-6	1
Astor Av	U-6	1
Avon Pl	U-6	1
Avon Pl	V-6	1
Baltimore Av	U-6	1
Baltimore Av	T-6	1
Barnard Pl	U-6	1
Barnard Pl	U-7	1
Bathurst Av	U-6	1
Bayliss St	U-6	1
Beaver Av	U-6	1
Beech St	U-6	1
Belleville Tnpk	U-6	1
Belmont Av	U-6	1
Bergen Av	U-6	1
Bergen Av	T-6	1
Bernice Rd	U-7	1
Biltmore St	U-6	1
Birchwood Dr	U-6	1
Bogle Av	T-6	1
Bogle Av	U-6	1
Bond Pl	U-6	1
Boston Av	T-6	1
Brandenberg Pl	T-6	1
Canterbury Av	U-6	1
Canterbury Av	U-7	1
Canterbury Av	U-7	1
Carrie Pl	U-7	1
Cary Av	U-7	1
Cedar St	U-6	1
Chestnut St	U-6	1
Church Pl	U-6	1
Clinton Pl	U-7	1
Coupe Pl	U-6	1
Crystal St	U-6	1
Devon St	U-6	1
Eagle St	U-6	1
Eckhardt Ter	U-7	1
Elm St	U-6	1
Ewig Av	U-6	1
Exton Av	U-6	1
Fairmount Av	U-6	1
Fisher Pl	U-6	1
Forest St	V-6	1
Forest St	U-6	1
Franklin Pl	U-6	1
Front St	U-6	1
Garden Ter	U-6	1
Geraldine Rd	U-7	1
Gold St	U-6	1
Greco Tr	U-6	1
Halsey Pl	U-6	1
Halsey Pl	U-7	1
Harding Av	U-6	1
Hedden Ter	U-6	1
Hendel Av	U-6	1
High St	U-6	1
Hillside Pl	U-6	1
Hoover St	U-7	1
Hull Av	V-7	1
Hull Av	U-7	1
Ilford Av	U-6	1
Inman Pl	U-6	1
Jason Wy	U-7	1
Jauncey Av	T-6	1
Legion Pl	U-6	1
Leonard Pl	U-7	1
Lincoln Av	T-6	1
Locust Av	U-6	1
Lorrigan Pl	U-6	1
Madison Av	U-7	1
Melrose Av	U-6	1
Millar Pl	T-7	1
Millar Pl	T-6	1
Moore Pl	U-6	1
Moore Pl	U-7	1
Morgan Pl	U-6	1
Morton Pl	V-6	1
Morton Pl	U-6	1
Noel Dr	U-6	1
Norwood Tr	T-6	1
Park Ridge Dr	U-6	1
Park Av	U-6	1
Pershing Pl	U-6	1
Pine St	U-6	1
Porete Av	V-6	1
Prospect Av	U-6	1
Pulaski Dr	U-6	1
Renner Pl	U-6	1
Ridge Park Dr	U-6	1
Ridge Rd	U-6	1
River Rd	U-6	1
Riverview Av	T-6	1
Riverview Av	U-6	1
Roosevelt St	U-6	1
Rutherford Pl	U-6	1
Schuyler Av	U-6	1
Sherman Av	U-7	1
Shields Pl	U-6	1
Stevens Pl	U-6	1
Stover Av	U-6	1
Stratford Pl	U-6	1
Sunset Av	U-6	1
Sylvia Pl	U-7	1
Truman Rd	U-7	1
Union Av	T-7	1
Union Pl	U-6	1
Vanderbilt Pl	U-6	1
Vanderbilt Pl	U-7	1
Verhoeff Pl	U-7	1
Verhoeff Pl	U-7	1
Veteran Pl	T-6	1
Webster St	U-7	1
Wesley Pl	U-6	1
West St	U-6	1
William St	U-6	1
Willis Rd	U-6	1
Wilson Pl	T-6	1
York Rd	U-6	1

Northvale, Boro of

STREET	GRID	MAP
Allison St	G-13	8
Almar Ct	G-13	8
Andre Av	G-13	8
Argenti Pl	G-13	8
Birchtree Ln	G-13	8
Birchwood Rd	G-13	8
Bradley Av	G-13	8
Bradley Av	G-14	8
Briarwood Ln	G-13	8
Campora Dr	G-14	8
Charles St	G-14	8
Chestnut St	H-14	8
Clinton Av	G-13	8
Conger Av	G-14	8
Cooper St	H-14	8
Crest Dr	G-13	8
Danny Ln	G-14	8
Dawn Ct	G-13	8
Doranto Pl	H-14	8
Doranto Pl	H-13	8
East Av	G-13	8
Eric Ln	G-13	8
Fairway Ct	H-14	8
Feitner St	G-13	8
Firenze St	G-14	8
Forest Ct	G-14	8
Frankfort Av	G-14	8
Franklin St	G-14	8
Gladys Ct	G-13	8
Glanz Av	G-13	8
Glendale Rd	G-13	8
Grace Av	G-13	8
Graf Pl	G-13	8
Henmarken Dr	G-14	8
High St	G-13	8
Hill Ter	G-13	8
Holly Pl	G-13	8
Hughes St	G-13	8
Industrial Pkwy	G-14	8
John St	H-14	8
Johned Rd	G-13	8
Johnson Pl	G-13	8
Lambert Av	G-13	8
Legrand Av	H-14	8
Livingston St	G-14	8
Longview Ct	G-13	8
Loren Ct	G-13	8
Ludlow Av	H-14	8
Margene Ct	G-14	8
Mauro Ct	G-14	8
McClellan St	G-13	8
Midwood Rd	G-13	8
New York Av	G-14	8
Oakwood Dr	G-13	8
Old Tappan Rd	F-13	8
Overbrook Rd	G-13	8
Paris Av	G-13	8
Paulding Av	G-13	8
Pegasus Av	G-14	8
Philadelphia Av	G-14	8
Pierron St	G-14	8
Pitcher Ct	G-13	8
Pitcher Ct	G-14	8
Private Rd	G-14	8
Roosevelt St	G-13	8
Sanial Av	G-14	8
Scharer Av	G-13	8
Scharer Av	H-13	8
School St	G-13	8
Semino Rd	G-13	8
Snedecker Pl	G-14	8
Stonehurst Ct	H-14	8
Susan Ct	G-14	8
Tappan Rd	G-13	8
Union St	G-14	8
Veterans Pl	G-14	8
Veterans Pl	H-14	8
Walnut St	H-14	8
Washington St	G-14	8
Watson Dr	G-13	8
West Wildwood Rd	G-13	8
West Av	G-13	8
White Av	G-13	8
Wildwood Rd	G-13	8
Willow Av	G-14	8
Winthrop St	H-13	8
Winthrop St	G-13	8
Woodland Av	G-13	8
Zotti Av	G-13	8

Norwood, Boro of

STREET	GRID	MAP
1st St	G-13	8
2nd St	G-13	8
3rd St	G-13	8
4th St	G-13	8
5th Av	H-14	8
5th St	H-14	8
5th St	H-13	8
6th St	H-13	8
6th St	H-14	8
7th St	H-14	8

BERGEN COUNTY

STREET	GRID	MAP
7th St	H-13	8
8th St	H-14	8
8th St	H-13	8
9th St	H-14	8
10th St	H-14	8
11th St	H-14	8
12th St	H-14	8
13th St	H-14	8
14th St	H-14	8
15th St	H-14	8
17th St	H-14	8
20th Av	G-13	8
Adams St	G-13	8
Anderson Av	J-14	7,8
Anderson Av	H-14	8
Anne Ct	G-13	8
Ash St	G-13	8
Astor Pl	H-14	8
Austin Av	H-13	8
Beech St	H-14	8
Belden Pl	H-13	8
Bergen Av	G-13	8
Birch St	G-13	8
Blanche Av	H-13	8
Blanche Av	J-13	7,8
Blanche Av	J-14	7,8
Blauvelt St	H-13	8
Blue Hill Rd	H-13	8
Blue Hill Rd	G-13	8
Briarwood Rd	H-14	8
Bridge St	G-13	8
Broad St	H-13	8
Broadway	H-14	8
Broadway	H-13	8
Brook St	H-13	8
Burlington St	H-13	8
Burlington St	G-13	8
Canterbury Rd	H-14	8
Carpenter Av	H-13	8
Carter St	G-13	8
Carter St	H-13	8
Cathy Ct	H-13	8
Center St	H-13	8
Chaffee Cir	G-13	8
Chestnut St	H-13	8
Chestnut St	H-14	8
Clark Av	G-13	8
Clinton St	H-13	8
Cobblestone Crossing	H-13	8
Cross St	H-13	8
Dale Ct	H-13	8
Dearborn Rd	J-14	7,8
Dearborn Rd	H-14	8
Demarest St	G-13	8
Demarest St	H-13	8
Derby Rd	H-13	8
Dwars Kill Ln	J-14	7,8
Dyer Ct	H-14	8
Elm St	G-13	8
Elton Ter	H-13	8
Essig St	G-13	8
Everett St	G-13	8
Everett St	H-13	8
Fairway Ter	H-14	8
Feitner St	G-13	8
Frasco Av	H-13	8
Frasco Ln	J-14	7,8
Front St	H-13	8
Front St	G-13	8
Garnett Pl	G-13	8
Gates St	G-13	8
Glenn Av	H-13	8
Grace Av	G-13	8
Grant Av	G-13	8
Grissom St	H-13	8
Hazel Ct	G-13	8
High St	H-13	8
Hillside Av	H-13	8
Holdrum St	H-13	8
Hudson Av	H-14	8
Hudson Av	H-13	8
Janice Dr	G-13	8
Janice Dr	H-13	8
Jay St	H-13	8
Jenni Dr	H-13	8
John Cir	H-13	8
John St	H-13	8
Kensington Av	H-13	8
Kenyon Ct	G-13	8
Knoll Wy	H-14	8
Lamar Pl	J-14	7,8
Lancaster Rd	H-14	8
Lincoln Av	G-13	8
Livingston St	H-13	8
MacNelly Rd	H-14	8
Madison Av	H-14	8
Maple St	H-13	8
McClellan St	G-13	8
McKenna Dr	G-13	8
Meadow Ct	G-13	8
Meadow Ln	G-13	8
Mill Brook Cir	J-14	7,8
Mills Av	H-13	8
Mohawk Av	H-14	8
Mohawk Av	J-14	7,8
Morningside Av	H-13	8
Morningside Av	H-14	8
Nottingham Ct	H-14	8
Oak St	H-13	8
Park Ct	G-13	8
Park St	G-13	8
Penfield St	G-13	8
Piermont Rd	H-14	8
Piermont Rd	J-14	7,8
Pierson Av	J-14	7,8
Ridge Rd	J-14	7,8
Riverdale Av	G-13	8
Rockland Av	H-13	8
Savidge St	G-13	8
Scharf St	H-13	8
Sherwood Rd	H-14	8
Somerset Rd	H-13	8
South Av	H-13	8
Summit St	H-13	8
Tappan Rd	H-13	8
Tilden Pl	J-14	7,8
Valley Pl	H-13	8
Vervalen St	H-13	8
Villa Ct	H-13	8
Virgil Rd	G-13	8
Walnut St	H-13	8
Walnut St	H-14	8
West St	H-13	8
Westwind Ct	H-14	8
Westwind Ct	J-14	7,8
White Ct	G-13	8
Williams Av	G-13	8
Wilton Ct	H-13	8
Winter	H-13	8
Winthrop St	H-13	8
Winthrop St	G-13	8
Wyndham Rd	H-13	8

Oakland, Boro of

STREET	GRID	MAP
1st St	F-2	10,11
2nd St	F-2	10,11
3rd St	F-2	10,11
Academy Cir	G-2	10
Acorn Av	G-1	10
Algonquin Tr	F-3	10,11
Allen Dr	F-3	10,11
Andrew Av	E-3	11
Apache Dr	F-2	10,11
Arapaho Ct	F-2	10,11
Arrowhead Rd	E-3	11
Aspen Wy	G-1	10
Aspen Wy	G-2	10
Bailey Av	G-1	10
Bailey Av	G-2	10
Bannehr St	G-2	10
Barbara Ln	F-2	10,11
Barnard Dr	F-2	10,11
Bauer Dr	H-2	10
Bauer Dr	G-2	10
Beech St	F-3	10,11
Birch Av	G-1	10
Blackfoot Tr	E-3	11
Brandy Wine Pl	E-2	11
Breakneck Rd	H-2	10
Brook Hollow	F-3	10,11
Brookside Dr	F-3	10,11
Calumet Av	F-2	10,11
Cardinal Dr	F-3	10,11
Cayuga Av	F-3	10,11
Cedar St	F-2	10,11
Center Av	F-2	10,11
Chapel Hill	F-2	10,11
Cherokee Tr	E-3	11
Cherokee Tr	E-2	11
Cherry Av	G-1	10
Cheyenne Ct	E-3	11
Chicasaw Dr	F-3	10,11
Chuckanutt Dr	E-3	11
Church Ln	F-3	10,11
Colgate Rd	F-3	10,11
Columbia Wy	F-3	10,11
Commanche Tr	E-3	11
Concord Ln	E-2	11
Conestoga Ct	F-3	10,11
Cornell Pl	F-3	10,11
Court House Pl	F-2	10,11
Cree Ct	F-3	10,11
Crosby Ln	G-2	10
Dakota Av	F-2	10,11
Dartmouth Wy	F-2	10,11
Deer Lawn Ct	G-1	10
Demarest Av	G-2	10
Dogwood Dr	G-2	10
Doty Rd	G-1	10
Eaglecrest Pl	E-3	11
East Oak St	F-2	10,11
East Ct	G-2	10
Edison Av	G-1	10
Elm St	F-2	10,11
Enter St	G-1	10
Enter St	F-1	10
Fir Ct	G-1	10
Florence Av	G-1	10
Fordham Rd	F-2	10,11
Fordham Rd	F-3	10,11
Forest St	F-3	10,11
Fox Ct	G-2	10
Franklin Av	F-2	10,11
Garrison Pl	G-2	10
Gates End	E-2	11
Geronimo Wy	F-3	10,11
Glen Gray Rd	E-3	11
Glen Gray Rd(Midvale Mountain Rd)	E-3	11
Grandview Av	G-1	10
Greene Wy	E-2	11
Grove Av	G-2	10
Grove St	G-2	10
Grove St	G-1	10
Hannah Rd	G-2	10
Harvard Wy	F-2	10,11
Hatfield Rd	G-2	10
Health Rd	E-2	11
Hemlock St	G-1	10
Hiawatha Blvd	F-2	10,11
Hiawatha Blvd	F-3	10,11
Hickory Dr	G-2	10
Hillside Av	F-1	10
Hobart Pl	F-3	10,11
Hobby Ln	F-3	10,11
Holyoke Dr	F-2	10,11
Hopi Ct	F-3	10,11
Hopper St	G-2	10
Huron Av	F-2	10,11
Iron Horse Rd	F-1	10
Iroquois Av	F-3	10,11
Iroquois Av	E-3	11
Island Ter	G-1	10
Ithaca Pl	F-3	10,11
Jerome Av	G-1	10
Kiowa Tr	F-3	10,11
Lake Shore Dr	F-2	10,11
Lake View Ter	G-1	10
Lakeside Blvd	F-3	10,11
Lawlor Dr	G-2	10
Lehigh Wy	F-2	10,11
Lenape Ln	F-2	10,11
Long Hill Rd	G-1	10
Loyola Pl	F-2	10,11
Mandigo Av	G-2	10
Manito Av	F-2	10,11
Manito Av	F-3	10,11
Maple Av	F-2	10,11
Maple Dr	F-3	10,11
Martha Pl	G-1	10
Massasoit Tr	F-3	10,11
McCoy Rd	G-2	10
McNomes St	G-2	10
Minisi Pl	E-3	11
Minnehaha Blvd	F-2	10,11
Minsi Ter	G-2	10
Minsi Pl	E-3	11
Mohawk Av	F-2	10,11
Monhegan Av	F-3	10,11
Morningstar Ln	F-3	10,11
Morton Pl	F-2	10,11
Mountain Lakes Rd	F-2	10,11
Mountain View Av	G-1	10
Muller Rd	F-1	10
Navajo Wy	F-2	10,11
Nielsen Av	G-1	10
Nokomis Av	F-2	10,11
North St	F-1	10
Oak St	F-2	10,11
Oneida Av	F-2	10,11
Oratam Tr	F-3	10,11
Osage Rd	E-3	11
Oswego Av	F-2	10,11
Page Dr	G-2	10
Park Dr	F-1	10
Park Dr	G-1	10
Patriots Wy	E-2	11
Pawnee Av	E-2	11
Pequot Path	E-3	11
Pequot Path	E-3	11
Pima Ct	F-3	10,11
Pine Crest Dr	F-2	10,11
Plaza Rd	G-1	10
Pool Hollow Av	G-1	10
Poplar St	F-2	10,11
Post Rd	G-1	10
Potash Rd	G-2	10
Powder Mill Ln	F-2	10,11
Powhatan Path	E-3	11
Prinston Pl	F-2	10,11
Prinston Pl	F-3	10,11
Purdue Av	F-2	10,11
Raeben Av	E-3	11
Ramapo Av	F-2	10,11
Ramapo Hills Blvd	F-3	10,11
Ramapo Ter	G-1	10
Ramapo Valley Rd	F-2	10,11
Ramapo Valley Rd	G-1	10
Raritan Rd	F-2	10,11
River Rd	F-1	10
Riverside St	F-1	10
Riverside St	G-1	10
Robin Ln	F-3	10,11
Rockaway Av	F-2	10,11
Roosevelt Blvd	F-2	10,11
Rutgers Dr	F-2	10,11
Rutgers Dr	F-3	10,11
Ryerson Av	G-2	10
Saratoga Dr	E-2	11
Seminole Av	F-2	10,11
Seneca Av	F-2	10,11
Seton Hall Dr	F-3	10,11
Sheffield St	G-2	10
Shelly Ct	F-3	10,11
Shelly Ct	F-2	10,11
Shoshone Path	E-3	11
Sienna Wy	F-3	10,11
Silver Birch Av	F-2	10,11
Sioux Av	F-2	10,11
Skyline Dr	E-1	11
Spear St	G-2	10
Spring Av	F-1	10
Spruce St	G-1	10
Stevens Pl	F-2	10,11
Stonefence Rd	G-1	10
Tappen Tr	F-3	10,11
Tecumseh Tr	F-2	10,11
Terhune St	F-2	10,11
Thackery Rd	F-2	10,11
Thackery Rd	F-3	10,11
Thornton Rd	G-2	10
Thunderbird Dr	F-2	10,11
Tomahawk Tr	F-3	10,11
Truman Blvd	F-2	10,11
Tulane Rd	F-2	10,11
Tuscarona Dr	F-3	10,11
Valley View Av	F-2	10,11
Van Vooren Dr	G-2	10
Vassar Pl	F-2	10,11
Veteran Dr	F-2	10,11
Veteran Dr	G-2	10
Walnut St	G-2	10
Walton Av	G-2	10
Walton St	G-2	10
Wellesley Dr	F-2	10,11
Wenonah Av	F-2	10,11
West Oakland Av	F-2	10,11
West Oakland Av	G-1	10
West Oakland Av	F-1	10
West Sheffield St	G-2	10
West Ct	G-2	10
West St	F-1	10
Whittier Ln	F-3	10,11
Wichita Path	E-3	11
Wichita Path	F-3	10,11
Wilson St	F-3	10,11
Winters St	G-2	10
Wright Wy	G-2	10
Yale Wy	F-3	10,11
Yale Wy	F-2	10,11
Yampo Av	F-2	10,11
Yampo Av	G-2	10
Yuma Ct	F-3	10,11

Old Tappan, Boro of

STREET	GRID	MAP
Addison Ter	G-13	8
Amelia Dr	G-11	8
Ann St	G-12	8
Arrowhead Rd	G-12	8
Autumn Ln	G-12	8
Avenue A	G-13	8
Avenue B	F-13	8
Bergen Blvd	F-13	8
Birchwood Rd	G-11	8
Birchwood Rd	G-12	8
Buckingham Pl	F-12	7,8
Cedar Dr	G-11	8
Central Av	G-12	8
Charles Pl	G-12	8
Charlotte Pl	G-12	8
Cheryll Ln	F-13	8
Cheryll Ln	G-13	8
Chestnut Av	G-13	8
Churchill Dr	F-12	7,8
Clark Smith Dr	F-12	7,8
Clark Av	G-13	8
Commodore Ct	G-13	8
Continental Dr	F-13	8
Corrigan Wy	F-12	7,8
Country Squire Rd	G-12	8
Cripple Bush Rd	G-12	8
Davenport Ct	G-12	8
De Berg Dr	G-12	8
De Wolf Rd	G-12	8
Dearborn Dr	G-13	8
Deer Trail Rd	G-12	8
Demarest Ln	G-12	8
Doris Pl	G-12	8
Dorotokeys Ln	G-13	8
East Old Tappan Rd	F-13	8
East Old Tappan Rd	G-13	8
Edith St	G-12	8
Elena Dr	G-12	8
Elizabeth St	G-12	8
Ester Ct	G-12	8
Fairway Ln	F-12	7,8
Feather Ln	G-12	8
Fernwood Dr	G-11	8
Fernwood Dr	G-12	8
Filmore St	F-13	8
Forest Av	H-12	8
Fred St	H-12	8
Glen Pl	G-11	8
Grace Av	G-13	8
Grant Av	G-13	8
Green Wy	G-12	8
Green Wy	G-11	8
Greenwoods Dr	F-12	7,8
Hampton Ct	G-12	8
Hampton Ridge Ct	G-12	8
Haring Dr	G-12	8
Herbst Rd	G-12	8
Heritage Rd	G-13	8
Herrick Dr	G-12	8
Hill Crest Ct	F-13	8
Hort St	G-13	8
Hoverman Rd	G-12	8
Howard Dr	G-12	8
Innkeeper Rd	F-13	8
Iris Ct	G-11	8
Irving St	G-12	8
Jay St	G-11	8
Jean Ct	G-12	8
Karyn Ct	G-13	8
Klein Ct	G-12	8
Knickerbocker Ln	G-13	8
Kristin Pl	G-13	8
Kristin Pl	F-13	8
Lachmund Ct	G-12	8
Lawrence Ct	G-12	8
Leonard Dr	G-12	8
Leoson Pkwy	G-11	8
Liberty St	G-13	8
Lindy Pl	G-11	8
Little Brook Rd	G-12	8
Little Mountain Rd	G-12	8
Manor Ct	G-13	8
Maple St	G-13	8
Mavus Rd	F-12	7,8
McKinley St	F-13	8
Merrywood Ct	G-13	8
Moeser Pl	G-13	8
Newark St	G-13	8
Norwood Av	G-13	8
Nottingham Ct	G-12	8
O'Connors Ln	G-12	8
Oak Ln	G-11	8
Ogle Rd	F-12	7,8
Old Crown Rd	G-12	8
Old Farm Rd	G-13	8
Old Tappan Rd	G-11	8
Orangeburgh RdN	F-12	7,8
Orangeburgh RdN	F-13	8
Orangeburgh RdS	G-13	8
Pearl Ct	G-12	8
Perry St	G-13	8
Phyllis Dr	G-12	8
Pine Hill Rd	F-12	7,8
Prairie Ct	G-12	8
Revere Ct	F-13	8
Rickland Rd	G-12	8
Robin Ln	F-12	7,8
Roseway Ct	G-11	8
Russell Av	G-12	8
School St	G-12	8
Seneca Ct	G-12	8
Spring Ct	G-13	8
Stewart Ct	G-11	8
Stewart Ct	F-12	7,8
Stokes Farm Rd	G-12	8
Sunden Ct	G-12	8
Sunset Ln	G-11	8
Sycamore Ct	H-11	8
Sycamore Ct	G-11	8
Taft St	F-13	8
Todd Ln	G-12	8
Tudor Rd	G-12	8
Van Buren St	F-13	8
Vandervoot Av	G-12	8
Walter St	G-12	8
Way St	G-12	8
West Old Tappan Rd	G-12	8
Westcott St	G-13	8
Westminster Pl	G-12	8
Westwood Av	H-12	8
White Av	G-13	8
Wilbur Rd	G-13	8
Williams Av	G-13	8
Willow Dr	G-11	8
Windsor Pl	G-12	8
Wood Hill Rd	F-12	7,8
Woodcrest Ln	G-13	8
Zotti Av	G-13	8

Oradell, Boro of

STREET	GRID	MAP
1st St	K-11	7
2nd St	K-11	7
3rd St	K-11	7
Ackerman Av	L-10	6
Amaryllis Av	K-10	6
Amelia Ct	K-10	6
Amelia Ct	K-9	6
Argyle St	L-11	7
Argyle St	L-10	6
Atlantic St	K-10	6
Austin Av	K-10	6
Battel Pl	K-10	6
Beatrice Pl	L-10	6
Beech Av	L-10	6
Beechwood Rd	K-11	7
Bellis Pkwy	K-10	6
Bergen Blvd	K-11	7
Berkshire St	L-10	6
Beverly Rd	L-10	6
Birchtree Rd	K-10	6
Blauvelt Dr	K-10	6
Briarwood Ct	J-10	6,9
Briarwood Ct	K-10	6
Brookside Av	K-10	6
Cambridge Cir	K-10	6
Camden St	K-10	6
Carol Pl	J-10	6,9
Carolina Dr	K-10	6
Center St	K-10	6
Center St	K-11	7
Chapin Ct	K-10	6
Church Ct	K-10	6
Clinton Av	K-10	6
Commander Black Dr	K-10	6
Cooper Av	K-10	6
Cordes Ct	K-10	6
Country Club Dr	K-11	7
De Marrais Av	K-10	6
De Marrais Pl	K-10	6
Deerfield Ct	K-10	6
Deerfield Ct	K-9	6
Delford Av	K-10	6
Delford Av	L-10	6
Demarest Av	K-11	7
Dinsmore Pl	K-10	6
East Dr	K-10	6
Elizabeth St	L-10	6
Elizabeth St	K-10	6
Ellen Pl	K-10	6
Elliot Ct	L-10	6
Ellis Pl	K-10	6
Elm St	K-11	7
Elm St	K-10	6
Essex St	K-10	6
Fletcher Av	L-10	6
Fletcher Av	K-10	6
Forest Av	K-9	6
Francis Ct	K-10	6
Garden Pl	K-10	6
Genther Av	K-10	6
Glenside Ct	K-10	6
Golf Pl	J-10	6,9
Gordon Ct	K-10	6
Grand St	K-11	7
Grant Av	K-11	7
Green Tree Ln	K-10	6
Grove St	K-10	6
Hague Ct	K-10	6
Harrison St	K-11	7
Hasbrouck Blvd	K-11	7
Hemlock Dr	J-10	6,9
Henniger Av	K-10	6
Henniger Pl	K-10	6
Hensler Ln	K-10	6
Herbert St	K-11	7
Hickory Av	L-10	6
High St	K-10	6
Hirschfield Pl	K-11	7
Homestead Pl	J-10	6,9
Howard Ct	L-10	6
Howard Ct	K-10	6
Iroquois St	K-10	6
John St	K-10	6
Kinderkamack Rd	K-10	6
Lake Shore Dr	K-11	7
Lake Av	K-10	6
Lakeview Av	K-10	6
Lakeview Dr	K-11	7
Laurel Dr	K-10	6
Lenox Av	K-10	6
Leonard Young St	K-10	6
Lincoln Av	K-10	6
Loretta Dr	K-11	7
Lotus Av	K-10	6
MacKay Av	L-10	6
Maple Av	K-10	6
Marggraff Ct	K-10	6
Marggraff Ct	K-9	6
Martin Av	K-10	6
Merritt Dr	K-11	7
Meyerhoff Pl	L-10	6
Midland Rd	K-10	6
Mildred Pl	K-10	6
Mill La	K-10	6
Morcum Tr	L-10	6
Morcum Tr	L-10	6
Morris St	K-10	6
Neill Ct	K-10	6
New Millford Av	K-10	6
New Millford Av	L-11	7
O'Connell Pl	K-10	6
Oakley Pl	K-10	6
Oaktree Rd	K-10	6
Oradell Av	K-10	6
Orchard St	K-10	6
Oxford Cir	K-10	6
Park Av	K-10	6
Park Pl	J-10	6,9
Pershing Av	K-11	7
Phyllis Ln	K-10	6
Poplar Av	L-10	6
Prell Ln	K-11	7
Primrose Av	K-11	7
Prior Ct	L-10	6
Prospect Av	K-10	6
Pyle St	L-10	6
Reis Av	L-10	6
Richardson Ct	K-11	7
Ridgewood Av	K-10	6
River Dell Rd	K-10	6
Ronald Ct	K-11	7
Rustic Rd	K-10	6
Sawmill Ln	K-10	6
Schaeffer Av	K-10	6
Schirra Dr	J-10	6,9
Schlomann Dr	K-11	7
Seminole St	K-10	6
Sherwood Ct	K-10	6
Soldier Hill Rd	K-10	6
Spring Valley Rd	K-10	6
Stuart Pl	L-10	6
Summit Av	K-10	6
Sussex St	K-10	6
Taylor Av	K-10	6
Union St	K-10	6
Valerie Pl	K-11	7
Van Antwerp Av	K-10	6
Van Antwerp Pl	K-10	6
Veldran Av	K-10	6
Village Rd	K-10	6
Waite Pl	L-10	6
Wannamaker Av	K-10	6
Wendel Pl	K-10	6
Westervelt Pl	K-10	6
Wildwood Rd	K-10	6
Windsor Rd	L-10	6
Winne Av	L-10	6
Woodlawn Av	K-10	6

Palisades Park, Boro of

STREET	GRID	MAP
1st St	R-12	3
2nd St	R-12	3
3rd St	R-12	3
4th St	R-12	3
5th St	R-12	3
6th St	R-12	3
7th St	R-12	3
8th St	R-12	3
9th St	R-12	3
10th St	R-12	3
11th St	R-12	3
12th St	R-12	3
13th St	R-12	3
14th St	R-12	3
Abbott Av	R-12	3
Ackerman Pl	Q-12	3,4
Alliotts Pl	R-12	3
Bell View Pl	R-12	3
Bergen Blvd	R-12	3
Boro Ln	R-12	3
Brinckerhoff Ter	R-12	3
Broad Av	R-12	3
Burr Pl	Q-12	3,4
Central Pl	R-12	3
Centre Pl	R-12	3
Chateau Rd	R-12	3
Cleveland Pl	R-12	3
Columbus Av	R-12	3
Columbus Av	R-11	3
Commercial Av	R-12	3
Commercial Av	R-11	3
Delia Av	R-12	3
East Brinkerhoff Av	R-12	3
East Central Blvd	R-12	3
East Columbia Av	R-12	3
East Edsall Av	R-12	3
East Edsall Blvd	R-12	3
East Edsall Blvd	Q-12	3,4
East Harriet Av	R-12	3
East Harwood Av	R-12	3
East Homestead Av	R-12	3
East Palisades Blvd	R-12	3
East Ruby Av	R-12	3
East Washington Pl	R-12	3
Fair St	Q-12	3,4
Fairview St	R-11	3
Glen Av	R-12	3
Grand Av	R-12	3
Grantwood Blvd	R-12	3
Henry Av	R-12	3
Henry St	R-11	3
Highland Av	R-12	3
Hillside Av	R-12	3
Lawn Av	Q-12	3,4
Liberty Pl	Q-12	3,4
Lincoln St	Q-12	3,4
Lincoln St	R-12	3
Morningside Ln	R-12	3
Norman Rd	R-12	3
Northwood Wy	R-12	3
Oakdene Av	R-12	3
Oakdene Av	Q-12	3,4
Oakwood Ln	R-12	3
Orchard Av	Q-12	3,4
Palisades Blvd	R-12	3
Perrome Pl	R-12	3
Princeton Pl	R-12	3
Prospect St	R-11	3
Rail Road Av	R-11	3
Railroad Av	Q-12	3,4
Ravenhill Pl	R-12	3
Roff Av	R-12	3
Roosevelt St	R-11	3
Roosevelt St	R-12	3
Shetland Ln	R-12	3
Sunset Pl	R-12	3
Trafalgar	R-12	3
Union St	R-12	3
Union St	Q-12	3,4
West Central Blvd	R-12	3
West Columbia Av	R-11	3
West Columbia Av	R-12	3
West Edsall Av	R-12	3
West Edsall Blvd	Q-12	3,4
West Harriet Av	R-12	3
West Harwood Av	R-12	3
West Homestead Av	R-12	3
West Palisades Blvd	Q-12	3,4
West Palisades Blvd	R-12	3
West Ruby Av	R-11	3
West Ruby Av	R-12	3
West Washington Pl	R-12	3

Paramus, Boro of

STREET	GRID	MAP
A & S Dr	K-9	6
Abbott Rd	K-8	6
Acorn Dr	K-9	6
Adams Ln	K-9	6
Addison Pl	L-9	6
Adler Way	K-9	6
Alan Dr	L-9	6
Alberta Dr	K-9	6
Albradt St	K-8	6
Albright La	K-8	6
Alcorn Dr	K-9	6
Alden Rd	J-8	6,9
Alpine Dr	L-8	6
Amherst Ct	M-9	5,6
Andrea Ct	M-9	5,6
Ann Ct	M-8	5,6
Arbor Rd	J-9	6,9
Arbor Wy	M-9	5,6
Arcadian Av	M-8	5,6
Arcola Av	M-8	5,6
Ardale Rd	M-9	5,6
Arnot Pl	L-9	6
Arthur Ter	K-9	6
Arundel Rd	J-8	6,9
Ashley Pl	L-9	6
Aspen Ct	L-9	6
Aster Ct	J-8	6,9
Azalea St	J-8	6,9
Bailey Rd	L-10	6
Bailey St	L-10	6
Bancroft Pl	J-8	6,9
Barbard Rd	M-9	5,6
Bay Ct	J-8	6,9
Beasley Ter	J-8	6,9
Bedford Rd	J-9	6,9
Beech Av	L-10	6
Beech Ln	K-8	6
Beechwood Dr	L-9	6
Behnke Av	L-9	6
Benton Rd	K-8	6
Berkley Pl	L-9	6
Berry Ln	K-9	6
Beverwyck Pl	J-8	6,9
Birch Ln	J-8	6,9
Birchwood Rd	K-8	6
Bluebell Ct	J-9	6,9
Bogert Pl	L-9	6
Bona Ln	J-8	6,9
Boyd Rd	J-9	6,9
Briarcliff Ln	K-9	6
Bridle Wy	M-8	5,6
Broad Av	L-9	6
Broad Ter	L-9	6
Broadway Blvd	K-10	6
Brook St	K-8	6
Brookfield Av	M-9	5,6
Brown Cir	M-9	5,6
Brown Cir	M-10	5,6
Bruce Rd	K-9	6
Bryant St	J-8	6,9
Bryn Mawr Ct	K-9	6
Buchanon Ct	J-8	6,9
Budd Rd	L-9	6
Buehler Pl	L-9	6
Bullard Av	L-9	6
Burke Pl	J-9	6,9
Burlington Rd	L-10	6
Burnet Pl	L-9	6
Bush Pl	J-9	6,9
Bush Rd	J-9	6,9
Buttonwood Dr	L-9	6
Cadmus Av	L-9	6
Cambridge Rd	K-9	6
Cambridge Rd	J-9	6,9
Cardnial Pl	K-8	6
Carl Pl	J-8	6,9
Carletta Ct	K-9	6
Carlough Dr	M-9	5,6
Caroline Rd	L-9	6
Carter Ln	J-8	6,9
Cathy Ann Ct	J-9	6,9
Cedar Av	L-10	6
Cedar Ln	K-8	6
Central Av	K-8	6
Century Rd	L-8	6
Century Rd	L-9	6
Century Rd Ext	L-8	6
Century Rd N	L-9	6
Chadwick Dr	J-9	6,9
Chelsea St	L-9	6
Chelsea St	K-9	6
Chestnut St	L-10	6
Chestnut St	S-7	1,2
Chimes Rd	J-8	6,9
Circle Dr	L-9	6
Circle Ln	S-7	1,2
Clark Av	R-7	2
Clark Ct	R-7	2
Clark Rd	K-10	6
Clarkson Ct	L-10	6
Clauss Av	J-8	6,9
Clayton Tr	L-9	6
Cleenput Ter	L-9	6
Cleveland Av	M-8	5,6
Clinton Rd	K-9	6
Clover Rd	L-9	6
Cloverdale Av	M-9	5,6
Coe Rd	K-9	6
Colby Pl	K-10	6
Colgate Av	M-9	5,6
College	S-7	1,2
College Rd	L-8	6
Colorado Rd	L-9	6
Columbia Ter	K-10	6
Columbine Rd	K-9	6
Columbine Rd	K-8	6
Concord Dr	L-9	6
Continental Av	L-10	6
Coolidge Pl	K-8	6
Coombs Dr	L-9	6
Cooper Pl	L-10	6
Copper Pl	R-7	2
Cornell Rd	K-9	6
Cottonwood Ct	J-9	6,9
Country Club Ln	L-8	6
Courier Pl	R-7	2
Courier St	R-7	2
Crabtree Ln	J-8	6,9
Crabtree Ln	J-9	6,9
Craig Av	J-8	6,9
Craig Av	K-8	6
Crain Rd	J-9	6,9
Crane Av	T-7	1
Crest Dr	M-9	5,6
Croton Pl	L-9	6
Curley Ct	K-8	6
Curry Ln	J-9	6,9
Cypress Ln	J-9	6,9
Daisy Wy	M-9	5,6
Daniel Av	S-7	1,2
Daniels Av	S-7	1,2
Dansen Av	M-8	5,6
Dansen Av	M-9	5,6
Dartmouth Ct	L-10	6
Darwin Av	R-7	2
De Graff Ln	K-9	6
Dean Ct	S-7	1,2
Deborah Ct	L-10	6
Decker Pl	J-8	6,9
Delafield Av	S-7	1,2
Demarest Rd	K-9	6
Demarest Rd	K-8	6
Denver Rd	L-9	6
Diane Pl	L-9	6
Diaz Pl	K-8	6
Dogwood Ct	L-9	6
Donaldson Av	S-7	1,2
Doremus Av	M-8	5,6
Dorothy Av	M-9	5,6
Douglass Dr	J-8	6,9

BERGEN COUNTY

STREET	GRID	MAP
Dover St	K-8	6
Drew Av	K-9	6
Drexel Rd	K-9	6
Duke Dr	M-9	5,6
Dunkerhook Rd	K-8	6
East Beverly Wyck Pl	J-8	6,9
East Brook Dr	L-9	6
East Dr	K-9	6
Eastern Wy	S-7	1,2
Edgewood Av	M-8	5,6
Edmund Ter	K-10	6
Edstan Wy	L-10	6
Ehret St	L-9	6
Eisenhower Dr	L-8	6
Elden St	L-9	6
Elizabeth Ct	J-9	6,9
Elizabeth St	S-7	1,2
Ellen Pl	L-10	6
Elliot Pl	S-7	1,2
Elliot Pl	L-9	6
Elm St	S-7	1,2
Elmwood Dr	L-9	6
Elycroft Pkwy	T-7	1
Elycroft Pkwy	S-7	1,2
Emerald Ct	J-8	6,9
Engle Rd	K-8	6
Erie Av	R-7	2
Erie Av	S-7	1,2
Erie Rd	J-9	6,9
Essex Rd	L-8	6
Estate Pl	S-7	1,2
Eton Ct	L-10	6
Ettrick	S-7	1,2
Evans Av	S-7	1,2
Evans St	J-8	6,9
Evelyn St	L-9	6
Evergreen Pl	K-8	6
Fairfield Dr	M-9	5,6
Fairmount Pl	M-9	5,6
Fairview Av	S-7	1,2
Fairview Ter	M-9	5,6
Fairway Ter	L-8	6
Falmouth Av	J-8	6,9
Falmouth Av	L-9	6
Farview Av	K-9	6
Farview Av	M-9	5,6
Farview Av	L-9	6
Fern Pl	J-9	6,9
Ferndale Rd	K-8	6
Feronia Wy	S-7	1,2
Filippe Ct	M-9	5,6
Fillmore Ct	J-8	6,9
Flint Pl	J-8	6,9
Fordham Pl	K-10	6
Forest Av	K-9	6
Forest Av	J-10	6,9
Forest Av	M-9	5,6
Forest Av	K-9	6
Forsythia Ln	M-9	5,6
Francisco Av	S-7	1,2
Franklin Pl	K-9	6
Franklin Pl	S-7	1,2
Frederick St	L-9	6
Freeland Av	J-8	6,9
Freeland Av	K-8	6
Frisch Ct	M-10	5,6
Frisch Ct	M-9	5,6
Frisch Ct	M-10	5,6
From Rd	K-9	6
Galda Rd	J-9	6,9
Garden Wy	J-8	6,9
Garfield Pl	S-7	1,2
Garry St	L-9	6
Gary Ter	L-9	6
Geering Ter	L-9	6
Georgian Ct	J-9	6,9
Gerald St	J-8	6,9
Geranium Ct	L-9	6
Gertrude Av	M-9	5,6
Gettysburg Pl	J-9	6,9
Gilbert Av	L-9	6
Glen Av	J-8	6,9
Glen Rd	S-7	1,2
Godwin Rd	J-8	6,9
Golf Pl	L-8	6
Gordon Dr	L-9	6
Gouverneur Av E	S-7	1,2
Gouverneur Av W	S-7	1,2
Grand Av	R-7	2
Grant Pl	K-9	6
Green Valley Rd	K-8	6
Greenbriar Rd	J-8	6,9
Greglawn Dr	K-9	6
Gregory Rd	K-9	6
Grist Tr	J-8	6,9
Grist Tr	K-8	6
Grove St	S-7	1,2
Haase Av	L-9	6
Hackett Pl	S-7	1,2
Halco Dr	L-9	6
Hall Rd	K-8	6
Halsey St	L-9	6
Hamilton Ct	K-8	6
Hampshire Rd	J-8	6,9
Harmon Dr	L-9	6
Harold St	J-8	6,9
Harrison St	L-9	6
Harvey Av	M-8	5,6
Harwood Pl	L-9	6
Hasbrouck Pl	R-7	2
Hastings Av	R-7	2
Hawthorne St	R-7	2
Haywood Dr	L-9	6
Heather Ln	M-9	5,6
Hebberd Av	L-9	6
Heights Rd	L-9	6
Helen Av	M-9	5,6
Helhoski Dr	K-9	6
Hemlock Dr	L-9	6
Henry St	L-9	6
Herbert Pl	L-9	6
Hickory Av	L-10	6
Highfield Ln	S-7	1,2
Highland Av	J-9	6,9
Highland Cross	S-7	1,2
Highland Ct	J-9	6,9
Highview Ter	J-9	6,9
Hillcrest Dr	L-9	6
Hillside Av	L-9	6
Hilton Pl	J-8	6,9
Hobart Av	R-7	2
Hobart Rd	K-10	6
Hollister Av	S-7	1,2
Holly Av	L-10	6
Hollybrook Rd	J-8	6,9
Home Av	S-7	1,2
Homestead Rd	K-9	6
Hoover Ct	M-9	5,6
Hoppers Ln	K-8	6
Howland Av	M-9	5,6
Idaho St	K-10	6
Industrial Av	K-9	6
Industrial Dr	T-8	1
Industrial Dr	T-7	1
Insley Av	R-7	2
Iona Pl	M-9	5,6
Iris Ct	K-8	6
Irving Pl	S-7	1,2
Island Rd	K-8	6
Ivanhoe Dr	K-9	6
Iversen Ct	L-10	6
Ivy Pl	L-10	6
Ivy Pl	S-7	1,2
Jackson Av	R-7	2
Jackson Pl	K-9	6
Janet Av	L-10	6
Jasper Rd	K-9	6
Jay Dr	J-8	6,9
Jefferson Av	K-9	6
Jenness Pl	S-7	1,2
Jerome Av	K-9	6
Jersey Pl	J-8	6,9
Johnson Ct	L-8	6
Jolene Ct	L-9	5
Jonquil Ct	K-8	6
Josephine Av	M-8	5,6
June Dr	J-8	6,9
Juniper Ln	J-8	6,9
Kalisa Wy	K-9	6
Kaywin Rd	L-9	6
Kearney Pl	J-9	6,9
Kendrick St	K-8	6
Kennedy Ct	M-9	5,6
Kenwood Rd	L-10	6
Keystone Pl	K-9	6
King Rd	K-9	6
Kip Av	S-7	1,2
Knollwood Dr	K-9	6
Knox Pl	M-9	5,6
Koman Dr	J-8	6,9
Kossuth St	K-8	6
Kramer Dr	J-8	6,9
Lafayette St	J-8	6,9
Lambert Pl	J-8	6,9
Lambert Pl	J-9	6,9
Larch Rd	J-8	6,9
Laurel Ct	M-9	5,6
Lawrence Dr	L-9	6
Lawson Pl	L-9	6
Lee Pl	K-9	6
Legion Pl	J-8	6,9
Lentz Av	L-9	6
Leonard Pl	L-9	6
Lilac Ln	M-9	5,6
Lincoln Av	S-7	1,2
Lincoln Dr	K-9	6
Linden St	J-8	6,9
Linwood Av	J-8	6,9
Livingston Ct	J-9	6,9
Lockwood Dr	L-9	6
Locust Av	L-10	6
Longview Ct	L-9	6
Lotus Ln	M-9	5,6
Lozier Ct	L-9	6
Lucky Hollow Dr	L-9	6
Lyncrest Dr	J-8	6,9
Lynn Ct	T-7	1
Lynn Dr	L-9	6
Mackay Av	M-8	5,6
Mackcentre Dr	K-9	6
MacKinley Blvd	K-9	6
Madison Av	M-9	5,6
Maitland Av	M-9	5,6
Manchester Way	J-9	6,9
Manning Rd	K-8	6
Maple St	S-7	1,2
Maple St	M-9	5,6
Maplewood Dr	L-9	6
Marginal Rd	K-9	6
Marginal Rd	S-7	1,2
Maril Ct	L-10	6
Marion Ln	K-9	6
Marquett Ct	L-9	6
Mary Ann Ct	L-9	6
Maryland Rd	J-9	6,9
Mason Pl	K-8	6
Mayfair Rd	K-8	6
Mazur Av	J-8	6,9
Mazur Av	K-8	6
McHenry Dr	L-9	6
Meadow Ln	M-9	5,6
Meadow Rd	S-8	1,2
Melton Pl	K-8	6
Middlesex Av	L-9	6
Midland Av	K-9	6
Midland Av	K-8	6
Midwood Rd	K-8	6
Mildred Av	M-9	5,6
Mill Run	K-8	6
Millar Ct	M-9	5,6
Milton Ct	S-7	1,2
Minogue Ter	J-9	6,9
Monona Av	R-7	2
Monroe Av	K-9	6
Montana St	L-10	6
Montross Av	S-7	1,2
Morningside Av	M-8	5,6
Morningside Rd	K-8	6
Morris Town Pl	J-8	6,9
Morse Av	R-7	2
Mortimer Av	S-7	1,2
Mountain Wy	S-7	1,2
Mulberry Ln	K-8	6
Myrna Pl	J-8	6,9
Myrtle St	R-7	2
Nelson Av	J-8	6,9
Nevada St	K-10	6
Nevins St	S-7	1,2
Nevins St	T-7	1
Newell Av E	S-7	1,2
Newell Av W	S-7	1,2
Nichols Dr	J-9	6,9
Nichols Dr	J-8	6,9
Nimitz Rd	L-9	6
Norman Wy	M-9	5,6
Norman Wy	M-10	5,6
Nugent St	J-8	6,9
Oakwood Dr	L-9	6
Oliver Rd	J-8	6,9
Olympia Blvd	J-8	6,9
Oradell Av	K-9	6
Orchard Pl	M-8	5,6
Oregon St	K-10	6
Orient Wy	S-7	1,2
Orient Wy	T-7	1
Otto Pl	K-8	6
Owen Pl	J-9	6,9
Oxford Ct	K-8	6
Palm Ct	J-9	6,9
Paramus Rd	L-8	6
Paramus Rd	K-8	6
Paramus Rd	J-8	6,9
Park Av	S-7	1,2
Park Pl	K-8	6
Park Pl	S-7	1,2
Parkside Dr	L-10	6
Pascack Rd	J-9	6,9
Pascack Rd	K-9	6
Passaic Av	S-7	1,2
Passaic Av E	S-7	1,2
Passaic Av W	S-7	1,2
Paul Ct	J-9	6,9
Pepperidge Rd	K-8	6
Pierce Dr	J-8	6,9
Pierrepont Av	S-7	1,2
Plaza Wy	M-8	5,6
Polly Ann Ter	K-9	6
Pond Pl	M-8	5,6
Powers Dr	L-9	6
Preble Pl	S-7	1,2
Prescott Pl	J-8	6,9
Prescott Pl	J-9	6,9
Primrose Ln	M-9	5,6
Princeton Ter	K-10	6
Prospect Pl	S-7	1,2
Prospect St	M-9	5,6
Purdue Ct	K-8	6
Ramile Ct	M-9	5,6
Raymond Av	R-7	2
Redwood Rd	K-9	6
Reeder Rd	J-9	6,9
Regis Ct	K-8	6
Reid Wy	J-8	6,9
Richard Av	M-9	5,6
Ridge Rd	S-7	1,2
Ridgeland Rd	M-9	5,6
Ridgewood Av	K-10	6
Ridgewood Av	J-8	6,9
Ridgewood Av	J-9	6,9
Ridgewood Av	K-9	6
Ring Rd	K-9	6
River Oaks Dr	S-7	1,2
Riverside Av	S-7	1,2
Riverside Av	R-7	2
Riverside Ter	S-7	1,2
Riverview Av	S-7	1,2
Robert St	L-9	6
Robin Rd	L-8	6
Roedel Pl	K-9	6
Roliver St	S-7	1,2
Roosevelt Blvd	K-8	6
Rose Dr	K-8	6
Rosemont Ct	J-8	6,9
Ross Dr	K-9	6
Ross Rd	K-8	6
Rutgers Pl	J-9	6,9
Rutgers Pl	K-9	6
Rutherford Av	S-7	1,2
Saint Clair Av	R-7	2
Salem St	K-10	6
Sandor Ct	J-9	6,9
Santiago Av	R-7	2
Sayre Ln	J-8	6,9
Schimmel St	M-9	5,6
School St	M-9	5,6
Schubert Ln	M-9	5,6
Seagull Dr	K-9	6
Sears Dr	K-9	6
Seaton Hall Dr	K-10	6
Seneca Ct	J-8	6,9
Sette Dr	K-9	6
Shelby Av	M-9	5,6
Shelby Ct	M-9	5,6
Shepherd Way	M-9	5,6
Sherwood Dr	L-9	6
Short Wy	L-9	6
Sidney Av	R-7	2
Silver Rod Ct	L-10	6
Skie Dr	K-8	6
Skylark Ct	K-8	6
Soldier Hill Rd	J-9	6,9
Soldier Hill Rd	J-10	6,9
Sorbello Rd	K-8	6
South Dr	K-9	6
South Terhune Av	L-10	6
Southcrest Av	M-9	5,6
Southcrest Av	M-8	5,6
Sparrow Ln	K-8	6
Spencer Pl	K-8	6
Spring Ln	K-9	6
Spring Valley Av	M-9	5,6
Spring Valley Rd	L-10	6
Spring Valley Rd	M-9	5,6
Spring Wy	L-9	6
Springfield Av	L-9	6
Springfield Av	S-7	1,2
Standish Rd	K-9	6
Stella Ct	J-9	6,9
Stevens Ct	J-8	6,9
Stony Ln	J-8	6,9
Stuart St	L-9	6
Stuyvesant Av	S-7	1,2
Summer Ct	M-9	5,6
Summer Ln	M-9	5,6
Summit Dr	L-8	6
Sunderland Av	R-7	2
Sunflower Av	J-8	6,9
Surrey Ln	L-10	6
Swan Ct	M-9	5,6
Swathmore Ln	K-9	6
Sweet Briar Pl	K-9	6
Sycamore St	K-8	6
Sylvan St	S-7	1,2
Taft Ct	L-10	6
Talbright Ln	K-8	6
Taylor Rd	K-9	6
Terhune Av	L-10	6
Terrace Rd	K-9	6
Tether Ln	K-8	6
Thomas Dr	L-9	6
Timothy Pl	L-9	6
Trinity Ct	M-9	5,6
Troast Rd	J-8	6,9
Truman Ter	K-8	6
Tryon Pl	K-9	6
Tuers Ln	K-8	6
Tuffs Ct	L-10	6
Tulane Ct	K-10	6
Tulip Ln	K-9	6
Tyler Rd	K-8	6
Union Av	R-7	2
University Wy	L-10	6
Utah St	K-10	6
Valley View Av	K-9	6
Valley View Av	L-9	6
Van Binsberger Blvd	K-8	6
Van Ness Av	S-7	1,2
Van Riper Av	S-7	1,2
Van Riper Av	T-7	1
Van Winkle Pl	S-7	1,2
Vanderbilt Ct	K-10	6
Vanderburgh Av	R-7	2
Vassar Dr	M-9	5,6\
Vera Pl	L-10	6
Vermont Dr	J-8	6,9
Verona Wy	L-10	6
Veronica Ct	K-9	6
Veterans Blvd	T-8	1
Victoria Av	J-8	6,9
Victoria Ter	J-8	6,9
Village Cir	M-9	5,6
Villanova Dr	K-8	6
Viola Wy	L-9	6
Virginia Ct	L-9	6
Vivien Ct	L-9	6
Vreeland Av	S-7	1,2
Wagner Ct	K-9	6
Walnut St	J-8	6,9
Walnut St	R-7	2
Walter Ct	T-7	1
Washington Av	R-7	2
Washington Av	K-9	6
Weaton Pl	S-7	1,2
Webster St	J-8	6,9
Wedgewood Dr	L-9	6
Wells Pl	R-7	2
Wendy Ann Ct	J-9	6,9
West Beverly Wyck Pl	J-8	6,9
West Dr	K-9	6
Westbrook Ct	K-9	6
Westview Av	M-9	5,6
Willard Rd	L-9	6
William St	S-7	1,2
Willowbrook Ct	K-8	6
Wilsey Ct	K-9	6
Wilson Av	K-9	6
Wilson Av	S-7	1,2
Windsor Rd	K-8	6
Wingra Av	R-7	2
Winslow Pl	M-9	5,6
Winslow Pl	S-7	1,2
Winters Ln	K-9	6
Wood St	S-7	1,2
Woodcrest Rd	L-9	6
Woodland Av	S-7	1,2
Woodland Av	J-8	6,9
Woodward Av	S-7	1,2
Wynetta Pl	J-8	6,9
Wyoming Rd	L-9	6
Yahara Av	R-7	2
Yale Ct	L-10	6
Yorktown Pl	J-8	6,9
Yuhas Dr	K-9	6
Zabriskie Pl	J-8	6,9

Park Ridge, Boro of

STREET	GRID	MAP
1st St	E-9	12
2nd St	F-9	9,12
3rd St	F-9	9,12
3rd St	F-10	9,12
3rd St	F-10	9,12
4th St	F-10	9,12
6th St	F-10	9,12
Alberon Dr	E-10	12
Alexander St	F-10	9,12
Ann Ter	F-10	9,12
Arrowhead Rd	F-9	9,12
Awashawaugh Rd	F-9	9,12
Bari Ln	F-11	8,13A
Barker Ct	G-11	8
Bear Brook Rd	F-10	9,12
Bearwoods Rd	E-9	12
Berkshire Rd	G-11	8
Berthoud St	F-10	9,12
Bigham Tr	F-9	9,12
Birch Ln	E-10	12
Bona Ct	F-10	9,12
Brae Blvd	E-9	12
Brae Mar Dr	F-10	9,12
Branton St	F-10	9,12
Braun Ct	F-10	9,12
Broadway	F-10	9,12
Brook Rd	E-10	12
Brook Dr	E-10	12
Camelot Gate	E-9	12
Capri Ter	F-11	8,13A
Cascade St	E-10	12
Cascade St	F-10	9,12
Catherine Ter	E-10	12
Cavour St	E-10	12
Cedarhill Rd	F-9	9,12
Chadwick Ct	F-10	9,12
Chestnut Av	F-10	9,12
Circle Dr	E-10	12
Clayton Pl	F-10	9,12
Clifford Dr	F-11	8 13A
Cole Brook Rd	E-10	12
Colony Av	E-10	12
Crescent St	F-10	9,12
Crescent St	E-10	12
Crosley Pl	F-11	8 13A
Crown St	E-10	12
Cypress Av	F-10	9,12
Cypress St	F-10	9,12
Degroff Pl	F-10	9,12
Dena Ct	F-9	9,12
Dibella Dr	F-9	9,12
Doxey Dr	E-9	12
Duke Ct	F-10	9,12
East Av	F-10	9,12
Echo Pl	F-10	9,12
Ellin Dr	F-11	8,13A
Ellin Dr	G-11	8
Elm Pl	F-10	9,12
Emily Dr	E-9	12
Etheridge Pl	F-10	9,12
Evelyn St	F-9	9,12
Fairview Av	F-11	8,13A
Fairview Ct	F-11	8,13A
Fernald Rd	F-10	9,12
Forest St	E-10	12
Forester Dr	E-9	12
Fremont Av	F-9	9,12
Gary Ct	F-11	8,13A
Gerard Ct	F-10	9,12
Glenbrook Dr	E-9	12
Glendale Rd	F-9	9,12
Glendale Rd	F-10	9,12
Grand Av W	E-10	12
Greenbrook Pl	E-9	12
Grobel Pl	F-11	8,13A
Hall Ct	F-10	9,12
Harding Ct	F-11	8,13A
Hawthorne Av	F-10	9,12
Helvetia St	E-10	12
Henry Av	F-10	9,12
High View Av	F-10	9,12
Highland St	F-10	9,12
Hill St	F-10	9,12
Hillside Av	F-10	9,12
Hillside Ter	F-11	8,13A
Hinson Pl	F-11	8,13A
Homestead Pl	F-11	8,13A
Humphrey Dr	F-10	9,12
Jenny Ln	F-9	9,12
John Ct	F-10	9,12
Johnsvale Rd	F-10	9,12
Kelsic St	F-10	9,12
Kinderkamack Rd	F-10	9,12
King Rd	F-10	9,12
Knoll Dr	F-11	8,13A
Kyle Ct	F-9	9,12
Lafayette Av	E-10	12
Lakeside Ct	F-10	9,12
Lakeview Ln	F-10	9,12
Lang Ct	F-10	9,12
Laura Ln	F-10	9,12
Laurel Hill Rd	F-9	9,12
Laurence Ct	E-10	12
Laurier Wy	F-9	9,12
Lawn St	F-10	9,12
Leach Av	F-9	9,12
Leachs Ln	F-10	9,12
Lenape Rd	F-9	9,12
Lillian St	F-10	9,12
Linden Av	F-10	9,12
Local St	F-10	9,12
Lockwood Pl	F-11	8,13A
Lorraine Dr	F-11	8,13A
Louville Av	F-10	9,12
Mader Pl	F-9	9,12
Madison St	F-10	9,12
Mae Ct	E-10	12
Mallon Ct	F-10	9,12
Mansfield Rd	F-10	9,12
Maple Leaf Dr	F-9	9,12
Maple Ter	F-10	9,12
Market St	F-10	9,12
Marti Rd	E-10	12
Maynard DR	E-9	12
Mayo Dr	F-11	8,13A
Midland Av	F-10	9,12
Midland Av	E-10	12
Mill Ln	F-10	9,12
Mill Rd	F-10	9,12
Mittag Pl	F-10	9,12
Morningside Av	F-10	9,12
Mountain Av	E-9	12
Mountain Av	E-10	12
Mountain Av	F-10	9,12
Mountain Av	F-9	9,12
Neer Dr	F-11	8,13A
Neer Dr	F-10	9,12
Nelson Dr	E-10	12
New St	F-11	8,13A
North Maple Av	F-10	9,12
North 5th St	E-10	12
North 5th St	F-10	9,12
North Av	E-10	12
North Av	F-10	9,12
Oak Av	F-10	9,12
Oakland St	F-10	9,12
Oneto Ct	F-10	9,12
Oneto Ct	F-9	9,12
Orchard Ln	F-10	9,12
Oriole Rd	F-10	9,12
Ormsay St	F-10	9,12
Park View Dr	F-10	9,12
Park Av	F-10	9,12
Park Ln	E-9	12
Pascack Rd	F-10	9,12
Perry St	F-10	9,12
Perryland St	F-10	9,12
Pine Dr	F-9	9,12
Prospect Av	G-11	8
Quackenbush Ln	F-10	9,12
Queen Ct	F-10	9,12
Randolph St	F-10	9,12
Ray Ct	E-10	12
Ridge Av	F-9	9,12
Ridge Av	E-9	12
Rivervale Rd	F-10	9,12
Rock Av	F-10	9,12
Rock Av	F-11	8,13A
Rock Ct	F-10	9,12
Rock Ct	F-11	8,13A
Roland St	F-10	9,12
Royal Dr	F-10	9,12
Russet Pl	E-10	12
Ruth Pl	E-9	12
Saddle Ridge Ln	F-11	8,13A
Seibert Ct	F-11	8,13A
Serven St	E-10	12
Shaw Pl	F-11	8,13A
Sibbald Dr	F-10	9,12
Smith Av	E-10	12
South Maple Av	F-10	9,12
South 1st St	F-9	9,12
South 5th St	F-10	9,12
Spring Valley Rd	E-9	12
Spring Valley Rd	F-9	9,12
Stephen Dr	E-10	12
Storms Av	F-10	9,12
Sturms Pl	F-11	8,13A
Sulak Ln	F-10	9,12
Sulak Ln	F-10	9,12
Summit St	F-10	9,12
Terrace Cir	E-10	12
Terrace St	F-10	9,12
Tulip Ct	F-11	8,13A
Turret St	E-10	12
Turret St	F-10	9,12
Tuxedo Av	E-10	12
Victor Hugo St	E-10	12
Villa Ct	F-9	9,12
Vineland St	F-10	9,12
Vitmar Pl	F-11	8,13A
Vittorio Ct	G-11	8
Volger Dr	F-11	8,13A
Volger Dr	F-10	9,12
Wampum Rd	F-10	9,12
Warren Rd	E-10	12
Webb Ct	F-10	9,12
West Park Av	F-10	9,12
West Pine Dr	F-9	9,12
Wield Ct	F-10	9,12
Willett St	F-10	9,12
Williams Ct	F-9	9,12
Willow Ct	F-9	9,12
Windsor Dr	F-9	9,12
Woodland St	F-10	9,12
Wortendyke Rd	F-10	9,12

Ramsey, Boro of

STREET	GRID	MAP
Abbey Ct	E-6	12
Ackerman Av	E-6	12
Acorn Ct	E-5	11
Addison Pl	D-6	12,13B
Airmount Av	D-6	12,13B
Alder Dr	E-5	11
Alexander Ct	D-7	12,13B
Alida Pl	D-5	11
Allen Ct	D-5	11
Allison Wy	D-5	11
Amanda Ct	D-6	12,13B
Anne Av	E-6	12
Arch St	E-6	12
Arlena Ter	E-6	12
Arlton Av	E-6	12
Armstrong Av	E-6	12
Arrow Rd	D-7	12,13B
Arrowhead Ct	D-5	11
Aspen Pl	E-6	12
Baker Ct	E-5	11
Balfour Ln	E-6	12
Bayron Ct	E-6	12
Bedford Pl	E-6	12
Beech St	D-5	11
Bennet Av	D-6	12,13B
Birch St	D-6	12,13B
Birchwood Ln	E-5	11
Biscayne Dr	E-7	12
Blauvelt Av	E-5	11
Blauvelt Av	E-6	12
Bonnie View Ter	E-6	12
Boro Line Rd	F-7	9,12
Briggs Av	E-5	11
Brittany Ct	D-6	12,13B
Broad St	E-6	12
Brookdale Dr	E-7	12
Brookfield Ln	D-7	12,13B
Brookside Dr	E-7	12
Brookside Rd	E-5	11
Buckingham Dr	E-6	12
Cambridge Dr	D-7	12,13B
Candlelight Rd	D-5	11
Canterbury Dr	E-7	12
Carol St	E-6	12
Carriage Ct	E-5	11
Carriage Ln	E-5	11
Catalpa Av	E-6	12
Cedar St	D-6	12,13B
Center St	E-5	11
Cherry Ln	E-6	12
Chestnut St	D-6	12,13B
Christopher St	E-6	12
Christopher St	D-6	12,13B
Church St	D-6	12,13B
Circle End Dr	D-5	11
Clarana St	D-5	11
Clearwater Pl	D-6	12,13B
Clearwater Pl	D-6	12,13B
Cleveland St	E-6	12
Cobblestone Ln	E-6	12
Colleen Ct	E-5	11
Collette Dr	D-5	11
Collins Av	E-7	12
Colonial Heights Dr	E-7	12
Column Ct	E-7	12
Constance Dr	C-6	12,13B
Constance Dr	D-6	12,13B
Coventry Ct	D-7	12,13B
Cranberry Ct	E-7	12
Crescent Hollow	E-7	12
Crest Rd	D-6	12,13B
Cypress Ct	D-6	12,13B
Darlington Av	D-5	11
Davidson Av	D-6	12,13B
De Baun Av	D-6	12,13B
Deer Tr	E-5	11
Deer Tr N	E-5	11
Dellwood Ct	E-5	11
Desimone Ct	D-6	12,13B
Diana Ct	D-6	12,13B
Dixon St	E-6	12
Dixson St	E-6	12
Dogwood Ter	E-5	11
Donna Ct	E-5	11
Druid Ct	E-7	12
Drumm Ct	D-5	11
Duck Pond La	D-6	12,13B
Dumont Av	D-6	12,13B
East Cedar Pl	E-5	11
East Crescent Av	D-6	12,13B
East Crescent Av	D-7	12,13B
East Crescent Av	E-7	12
East Crescent Av	E-6	12
East Main St	E-6	12
East Oak St	E-5	11
Elbert Ct	E-5	11
Elbert St	D-6	12,13B
Elbert St	E-5	11
Elbert St	E-6	12
Elbert St	E-5	11
Elizabeth Av	E-6	12
Elm Av	E-5	11
Elm Pl	E-5	11
Eton Ct	E-6	12
Evergreen Rd	D-6	12,13B
Fabio Dr	D-6	12,13B
Fairfax Ct	D-7	12,13B
Farmington Ct	E-5	11
Fawn Hill Ct	E-5	11
Fen Ct	E-6	12
Fergus Av	D-6	12,13B
Ferguson Pl	D-6	12,13B
Finch St	D-6	12,13B
Finch St	E-6	12
Forest Av	E-5	11
Fox Hollow Rd	D-6	12,13B
Franklin St	E-5	11
Fuhrman Av	E-5	11
Garden St	E-5	11
Garland Av	E-5	11
Garrison Dr	D-6	12,13B
Georgetown Rd	D-7	12,13B
Gertzen Plz	D-6	12,13B
Gertzen Rd	D-7	12,13B
Goose Cove Ln	E-5	11
Grandview Ter	D-6	12,13B
Grandview Ter	D-7	12,13B
Grant St	D-6	12,13B
Greenview Pl	E-6	12
Grove St	E-5	11
Hart St	E-6	12
Heather Ln	D-5	11
Hemlock Rd	E-5	11
Hickory Pl	E-6	12
High St	D-6	12,13B
Highwood Rd	E-5	11
Highwood Rd	F-5	10,11
Hilltop Rd	D-6	12,13B
Hillview Pl	E-7	12
Holly Ct	D-6	12,13B
Hooper Ter	D-5	11
Hosking Wy	D-5	11
Hubbard School Rd	E-5	11
Indian Valley Rd	D-6	12,13B
Island Av	E-6	12
Island Av	D-6	12,13B
Island Park Ave	D-6	12,13B
Jean St	D-5	11
Joshua Dr	D-5	11
Kate Ct	E-5	11
Kelleher Av	E-6	12
Kelleher Av	E-5	11
Kimberly Ct	E-6	12
Knollwood Dr	E-5	11
Lake St	E-6	12
Lake St E	E-6	12
Lake View Ter	E-6	12
Lake View Ter	E-7	12
Lakeside Dr	E-6	12
Lancaster Ct	E-5	11
Lantern Ln	D-5	11
Larch Av	E-6	12
Lillian Ct	D-6	12,13B
Lincoln St	D-6	12,13B
Linden St	D-6	12,13B
Lost Tree Ln	E-5	11
Madison Av	D-6	12,13B
Magnolia Rd	D-6	12,13B
Manchester Ct	E-5	11
Manor Dr	D-5	11
Maple Ct	E-6	12
Maple St	E-6	12
Maple St Ext	E-6	12
Martis Av	E-6	12
May Ct	E-6	12
Mayfair Dr	E-5	11
Mayfair Dr	E-6	12
Meadow Brook Rd	D-7	12,13B
Mechanic St	E-6	12
Mohawk Dr	D-5	11
Momar Dr	E-5	11
Momar Dr	E-6	12
Monroe St	D-6	12,13B
Morse Av	D-6	12,13B
Morse Av	D-5	11
Morton Dr	E-6	12
Mulberry Rd	D-6	12,13B
Myrtle Av	D-5	11
Navajo Av	D-5	11
New England Dr	E-7	12
New St	E-6	12
Newington Ct	D-6	12,13B
Newport Dr	D-7	12,13B
Norman Dr	E-6	12
North Central Av	D-6	12,13B
North Franklin Tnpk	D-6	12,13B
North Jean St	D-5	11
North Spruce St	D-6	12,13B
North St	D-6	12,13B
Northern Tr	E-5	11
Nottingham Rd	E-6	12
Nottingham Rd	E-7	12
Oak Ridge Rd	D-5	11
Oak St	E-5	11
Oakland Ct	D-6	12,13B
Orchard Pl	D-6	12,13B
Orchard St	D-6	12,13B
Overbrook Rd	D-6	12,13B
Overlook Ct	E-6	12
Overlook Ct	E-7	12
Oxford Ct	E-6	12
Park Pl	E-5	11
Park St	D-5	11
Partridge Ct	D-7	12,13B
Peach Hill Ct	D-6	12,13B
Peach Hill Ct	D-7	12,13B
Pine St	E-5	11
Pine Tree Rd	E-5	11
Poplar St	D-6	12,13B
Prince St	E-6	12
Prospect St	E-6	12
Pulis Ln	E-6	12
Quail Run	D-6	12,13B
Ramsey Av	E-5	11
Ramsey Park Ct	D-7	12,13B
Ramsey Park Ct	D-6	12,13B
Ramsey Rd	D-5	11
Ramview Av	D-6	12,13B
Redwood Ct	D-6	12,13B
Refy Av	E-6	12
Richmond Ct	D-7	12,13B
Ridge Rd	D-5	11
Roandis Ct	D-6	12,13B
Roanoke Ct	D-7	12,13B
Roger Ln	E-5	11
Ronald Ct	E-6	12
Rose Av	E-6	12
Rosewood Ct	E-5	11
Rosewood Ct	F-5	10,11
Roy Pl	D-5	11
Sauna Rd	E-5	11

STREET	GRID	MAP
Schierloh Ct	E-5	11
School St	E-6	12
Shadyside Rd	D-5	11
Shadyside Rd	E-5	11
Sherwood Dr	E-7	12
Shuart Ln	E-6	12
Snyder Av	E-5	11
Somerset Ct	D-7	12,13B
South Central Av	E-6	12
South Franklin Tnpk	E-6	12
South Spruce St	E-6	12
Spear Rd	D-7	12,13B
Spring St	D-6	12,13B
Spruce St	D-6	12,13B
Stony Brook Rd	D-6	12,13B
Summit Av	E-6	12
Sun Valley Rd	E-5	11
Sun Watch Ct	E-5	11
Surrey Rd	D-7	12,13B
Swan Hollow	D-7	12,13B
Swan St	D-6	12,13B
Sycamore Ct	E-5	11
Talina Ct	D-6	12,13B
Thornhill Dr	D-6	12,13B
Timber Tr	E-5	11
Tulip St	E-5	11
Twin Brook Ct	E-6	12
Upland Rd	D-5	11
Valley View Dr	E-5	11
Van Gelder Ct	E-5	11
Vaughn Dr	D-5	11
Vaughn Wy	D-5	11
Walnut St	D-6	12,13B
Warren St	D-6	12,13B
Washington Dr	D-6	12,13B
West Cedar St	E-5	11
West Crescent Av	E-5	11
West Main St	E-6	12
West Oak St	E-5	11
West Side Plaza	E-6	12
White Ter	D-6	12,13B
Williams St	D-6	12,13B
Woodland Av	E-5	11
Woods Rd	E-5	11
Wyckoff Av	E-5	11

Ridgefield, Boro of

STREET	GRID	MAP
Abbott Av	S-11	3
Abbott Av	R-12	3
Alexander Av	R-11	3
Alan Pl	R-12	3
Alpine Ct	R-11	3
Art Ln	S-12	3
Aurora Av	R-12	3
Bagley Pl	S-12	3
Banta Pl	R-11	3
Bell Dr	R-11	3
Bergen Blvd	S-12	3
Bergen Tnpk	R-11	3
Bernard Pl	S-12	3
Birch St	R-11	3
Brewster Av	R-11	3
Brinkerhoff St	R-11	3
Broad Av N	R-11	3
Broad Av S	S-11	3
Bruce St	R-8	2
Bruce St	S-8	1,2
Bryant Pl	R-11	3
Bryant Pl	R-12	3
Carpenter Pl	S-12	3
Center St	S-12	3
Challenger Av	R-11	3
Charlotte Ter	S-11	3
Chestnut St	S-12	3
Chestnut St	R-11	3
Church Av	R-11	3
Clark Av	S-12	3
Clinton Av	S-11	3
College Pl	R-11	3
Columbia Av	S-12	3
Columbia Ct	S-11	3
Day Av	S-12	3
De Lalla Ter	S-11	3
Dwight Pl	R-11	3
East Edgewater Av	S-12	3
East Winant Av	R-11	3
Edgewater Av	S-11	3
Edgewater Av W	R-11	3
Edison St	R-11	3
Edison St	S-12	3
Edwards Ter	S-11	3
Elite Ct	R-12	3
Elizabeth St	S-11	3
Elm Av	R-12	3
Elm Av	R-11	3
Elm St	S-11	3
Emerson St	R-11	3
Eucker St	R-11	3
Euclid Av	R-11	3
Fairview Ter	S-12	3
Florence Av	R-12	3
Fulton St	R-11	3
Garden St	R-11	3
Grand Av	R-11	3
Green Mount Av	S-12	3
Hamilton St	S-12	3
Hendricks Cswy	R-11	3
Henry St	R-11	3
Hillcrest Av	S-12	3
Hillie Pl	R-11	3
Hillside Av	R-11	3
Hillside St	R-11	3
Howard Pl	R-11	3
Hoyt Av	R-11	3
Hudson Av	S-11	3
Industrial Av	R-11	3
Island Av	S-11	3
Jacobus St	R-12	3
Kingsland Ln	R-12	3
Kingsland Ln	R-11	3
Lancaster St	S-11	3
Lancaster Rd	S-12	3
Laurel St	R-11	3
Lawton Av	S-12	3
Liberty Pl	R-12	3
Liberty Pl	S-11	3
Lincoln Av	S-12	3
Linden Av	R-11	3
Linden Av	R-11	3
Linden Ct	S-11	3
Lloyd St	R-12	3
Lowe Av	R-11	3
Main St	R-11	3
Major Dr	S-12	3
Maple Av	R-12	3
Maple St	R-11	3
Marion Av	S-11	3
Martling Pl	S-12	3
Mayer Ct	S-11	3
Meuter Pl	S-12	3
Monroe Pl	S-11	3
Morningside	R-12	3
Morse Av	S-11	3
Nelson Av	S-11	3
Norman Rd	S-12	3
North Sketch Pl	S-12	3
Oak St	R-11	3
Oak St	S-12	3
Oakdene Av	S-12	3
Oakdene St	S-11	3
Oakwood Ln	R-12	3
Orchard St	R-11	3
Oritan Av	R-11	3
Pembroke Wy	R-12	3
Pleasantview Ter	S-11	3
Prospect Av	R-11	3
Prospect Av	S-11	3
Rail Road Av	S-11	3
Ravenhill Pl	R-12	3
Ray Av	R-12	3
Ray Av	R-11	3
Remsen Pl	S-11	3
Ridge Ct	S-12	3
Ridgefield Av	S-11	3
Ridgefield Ter	S-12	3
River St	R-11	3
Russel Av	S-11	3
Shalber Blvd	S-11	3
Shannon Pl	S-12	3
Shetland Ln	R-12	3
Slocum Av	S-12	3
Slocum Av	S-11	3
South Sketch Pl	S-12	3
South St	S-11	3
Stewart Av	S-12	3
Studio Rd	S-12	3
Sunset Ct	S-11	3
Teaneck Rd	R-11	3
Trafalgar Rd	R-12	3
Truit St	R-11	3
Van Courtland Pl	S-11	3
Van Rensselaer Ct	S-11	3
Victoria Ter	R-11	3
Victory Av	R-12	3
Victory Av	S-12	3
Virgil Av	R-12	3
Virgil Av	R-11	3
Voct St	S-11	3
Voorhees Pl	R-11	3
Walnut St	S-12	3
Washington Av	S-12	3
West Pleasantview Ter	S-11	3
West View Av	S-12	3
Winant Av	R-11	3
Witt Av	R-11	3

Ridgefield Park, Boro of

STREET	GRID	MAP
1st St	Q-10	2,5
2nd St	Q-10	2,5
3rd St	Q-10	2,5
4th St	Q-10	2,5
5th St	Q-10	2,5
6th St	Q-10	2,5
7th St	Q-10	2,5
8th St	Q-10	2,5
Arthur St	Q-11	3,4
Austin St	Q-11	3,4
Barnes Dr	Q-11	3,4
Barnes Dr E	Q-11	3,4
Barnes Dr W	Q-11	3,4
Bergen Av	Q-11	3,4
Brinkerhoff St	Q-11	3,4
Cedar St	Q-11	3,4
Central Av	Q-10	2,5
Christie St	Q-11	3,4
Cutter St	Q-11	3,4
Edwin St	Q-11	3,4
Ehler Ct	Q-11	3,4
Euclid Av	Q-11	3,4
Gordon St	Q-11	3,4
Grand Av	Q-11	3,4
Grove St	Q-11	3,4
Hackensack Av	Q-10	2,5
Hackensack Av	Q-11	3,4
Hazelton St	Q-11	3,4
Herbert St	Q-11	3,4
Highland Pl	Q-11	3,4
Hobart St	Q-11	3,4
Homestead Pl	Q-11	3,4
Hudson Av	Q-11	3,4
Industrial Av	Q-10	2,5
Lincoln Av	Q-11	3,4
Main St	Q-11	3,4
Morningside Ln	Q-11	3,4
Mount Vernon St	Q-11	3,4
North Av	Q-11	3,4
North Av	Q-10	2,5
North Av	Q-11	3,4
North Av	Q-10	2,5
North Av	Q-11	3,4
North Av	Q-10	2,5
North Av	Q-11	3,4
North Av	Q-10	2,5
North Av	Q-11	3,4
Overlook Av	Q-11	3,4
Overpeck Av	Q-11	3,4
Park St	Q-11	3,4
Paulison Av	Q-11	3,4
Pershing Av	Q-11	3,4
Pine St	Q-11	3,4
Pleasantview Ter	S-11	3
Poplar St	Q-11	3,4
Preston St	Q-11	3,4
Rail Road Av	Q-10	2,5
Roosevelt Av	Q-11	3,4
Scott Ct	Q-11	3,4
Spruce Av	Q-11	3,4
Summit St	Q-11	3,4
Summit St	Q-11	3,4
Summit St	Q-10	2,5
Teaneck Rd	Q-11	3,4
Union Pl	Q-11	3,4
Victory Ln	Q-11	3,4
Webster St	Q-11	3,4

Ridgewood, Village of

STREET	GRID	MAP
2nd St	H-7	9
Abbey Ct	H-7	9
Ackerman Av	J-6	6,9
Adams St	H-7	9
Addison Pl	J-7	6,9
Alanon Rd	J-7	6,9
Alanon Rd	J-8	6,9
Albert Pl	J-7	6,9
Albert Pl	H-7	9
Albin Ct	H-8	9
Allen Pl	H-7	9
Allison Ct	H-8	9
Alpine Ter	H-7	9
Amsterdam Av	J-7	6,9
Amsterdam Av	K-7	6
Andover Ter	G-6	9
Arcadia Rd	J-7	6,9
Arcadia Rd	K-7	6
Arden Ct	J-7	6,9
Arrow Ln	J-8	6,9
Avondale Rd	H-7	9
Banta Dr	H-8	9
Barnes Dr	G-6	9
Barnett Pl	H-7	9
Barrington Rd	H-7	9
Bartell Pl	K-8	6
Bartell Pl	K-7	6
Bedford Rd	H-6	9
Beechwood Rd	H-6	9
Bellair Rd	J-6	6,9
Belmont Rd	H-7	9
Bennington Ter	H-8	9
Bergen Ct	J-8	6,9
Berkshire Rd	K-7	6
Best Ct	J-8	6,9
Betty Ct	H-8	9
Beveridge Rd	J-7	6,9
Beverly Rd	J-7	6,9
Bingham Rd	H-8	9
Bogert Av	H-7	9
Bogert Av	J-7	6,9
Boyce Pl	J-7	6,9
Boyce Pl	J-7	6,9
Brainard Pl	J-7	6,9
Brian Ct	H-8	9
Briarcliff Rd	J-6	6,9
Brookmere Ct	H-7	9
Brookside Av	J-7	6,9
Brookside Av	H-7	9
Bryden Pl	H-7	9
Burnside Pl	H-7	9
California St	H-7	9
Cambridge Rd	H-8	9
Cambridge Rd	H-7	9
Cameron Ln	H-7	9
Canterbury Pl	H-7	9
Cantrell Rd	J-6	6,9
Carlisle Rd	J-7	6,9
Carlton Ter	H-7	9
Carolina Pl	J-8	6,9
Cathleen Pl	J-8	6,9
Cedar Av	H-7	9
Cedarcroft Rd	J-6	6,9
Cherry Ln	H-7	9
Chesterfield St	H-7	9
Chestnut St	H-7	9
Christopher Pl	J-7	6,9
Circle Av	J-7	6,9
Claremont Rd	J-6	6,9
Claremont Rd	J-7	6,9
Cliff St	H-7	9
Clinton Av	H-7	9
Collingwood Pl	J-7	6,9
Colonial Rd	J-7	6,9
Colwell Ct	H-7	9
Concord Rd	H-7	9
Corella St	K-7	6
Corona Pl	H-8	9
Corsa Ter	H-8	9
Cottage Pl	J-7	6,9
Coventry Pl	J-7	6,9
Crest Rd	H-8	9
Crest Rd	J-7	6,9
Darby Ct	H-8	9
Dayton St	J-7	6,9
Deerfield St	H-7	9
Delaware Av	K-7	6
Demarest St	H-7	9
Devon St	H-7	9
Dorchester Rd	K-7	6
Doremus Av	J-7	6,9
Doris Pl	J-8	6,9
Douglas Pl	H-7	9
Downing St	H-7	9
Downs St	H-7	9
Durar Av	J-7	6,9
East Gate Rd	H-8	9
East Glen Av	H-7	9
East Glen Av	H-7	9
East Ridgewood Av	J-7	6,9
East Saddle River Rd	H-8	9
East Side Av	J-8	6,9
Eastbrook Rd	H-8	9
Eastern Ct	J-8	6,9
Edgewood Pl	J-7	6,9
Edwards St	J-7	6,9
Elaine Ter	J-8	6,9
Eldon St	H-7	9
Ellington Rd	K-7	6
Elmsley Pl	H-7	9
Emker Ter	J-8	6,9
Emmett Pl	J-8	6,9
Essex St	J-7	6,9
Ethelbert Pl	J-7	6,9
Eton Ct	H-7	9
Evergreen Pl	J-7	6,9
Fairfield Av	H-7	9
Fairfield St	H-7	9
Fairview St	H-6	9
Fairway Rd	J-7	6,9
Fernwood Ct	H-6	9
Ferris Pl	J-7	6,9
Floyd St	K-8	6
Floyd St	J-7	6,9
Foster Ter	J-7	6,9
Fox Ct	J-8	6,9
Fox Ter	J-7	6,9
Franklin Av	H-7	9
Franklin Tnpk	H-7	9
Frederick St	J-8	6,9
Garber Sq	J-7	6,9
Gardiel Pl	J-6	6,9
Gardiel Pl	J-6	6,9
Gardner Pl	J-6	6,9
Gateway Rd	J-8	6,9
George St	H-7	9
Gilbert St	J-7	6,9
Glenread Ct	J-8	6,9
Glenview Rd	G-7	9
Glenwood Rd	H-7	9
Glenwood Rd	H-6	9
Glenwood Rd	J-6	6,9
Godwin Av	J-6	6,9
Goffle Rd	J-6	6,9
Gordon Rd	J-7	6,9
Grandview Cir	J-7	6,9
Grant St	J-6	6,9
Graydon Ter	J-7	6,9
Greenway Rd	J-6	6,9
Grove St	J-7	6,9
Hamilton Rd	H-6	9
Hamilton Rd	H-7	9
Hammond Rd	J-8	6,9
Hampshire Rd	H-8	9
Hampton Pl	J-7	6,9
Hanks Av	J-7	6,9
Hawthorne Pl	J-7	6,9
Heermance Pl	J-7	6,9
Heights Rd	H-7	9
Heights Rd	H-7	9
Hempstead Rd	J-6	6,9
Henrietta Ct	H-8	9
Hickory St	H-8	9
Highland Av	J-6	6,9
Highview Ter	J-6	6,9
Highwood Av	J-6	6,9
Hillcrest Rd	H-7	9
Hillcrest Rd	G-6	9
Hillcrest Rd	G-7	9
Holly Pl	J-6	6,9
Hope St	J-7	6,9
Hopper Av	J-7	6,9
Houston Ln	K-7	6
Howard Rd	H-8	9
Hudson St	J-7	6,9
Hunter St	H-7	9
Ivy Pl	J-7	6,9
Jackson St	H-6	9
James St	K-8	6
James St	J-8	6,9
Jeffer Ct	J-8	6,9
Jeffer St	J-8	6,9
Jefferson St	H-8	9
Jefferson St	H-8	9
Jemco Pl	K-7	6
John St	H-7	9
Katherine Rd	J-6	6,9
Katherine Rd	J-6	6,9
Kemah Rd	H-6	9
Kemah Rd	H-7	9
Kenilworth Rd	J-7	6,9
Kenwood Rd	H-8	9
Kesington Dr	H-7	9
Kingsbridge Ln	H-7	9
Knickerbocker Rd	J-7	6,9
Knickerbocker Rd	J-6	6,9
Knollwood Rd	J-6	6,9
Lake Av	J-7	6,9
Lakeview Dr	J-6	6,9
Laurel Rd	J-7	6,9
Lawrence Ct	H-7	9
Lenox Av	J-6	6,9
Leonard Pl	J-7	6,9
Leroy Pl	J-7	6,9
Libby Av	H-7	9
Liberty St	J-8	6,9
Library Pl	J-7	6,9
Lincoln Av	J-6	6,9
Linden St	J-7	6,9
Linwood Av	J-7	6,9
Litchfield St	H-7	9
Lockwood Rd	J-7	6,9
Lotte Rd	J-6	6,9
Lotus Rd	J-7	6,9
Lucille Ct	K-7	6
Lynn St	H-8	9
Macksoud Cir	J-7	6,9
Madison Pl	J-6	6,9
Madison Pl	J-7	6,9
Maltbie Av	J-7	6,9
Manchester Rd	H-6	9
Marshall St	J-7	6,9
Mary Ann Pl	J-8	6,9
Mastin Pl	H-7	9
Maxwell Pl	J-7	6,9
Maynard Ct	H-7	9
McGuire Ct	J-8	6,9
McKinley Pl	J-7	6,9
Meadowbrook Av	H-7	9
Melrose Pl	J-8	6,9
Midvale St	J-6	6,9
Midwood St	K-7	6
Midwood Rd	K-8	6
Monte Vista Av	J-6	6,9
Monte Vista Av	J-6	6,9
Morningside Rd	H-6	9
Morningside Rd	H-7	9
Mountain Av	H-7	9
Mulberry St	H-7	9
Nagle St	H-7	9
Nagle St	H-8	9
Nauset Ln	H-7	9
Newcomb Rd	K-7	6
Newcomb Rd	K-8	6
Norgate Dr	H-8	9
Norman Dr	H-8	9
North Broad St	J-7	6,9
North Hillside Pl	H-6	9
North Hillside Pl	J-6	6,9
North Irving St	H-7	9
North Maple Av	H-7	9
North Monroe St	H-7	9
North Monroe St	J-6	6,9
North Murray Av	H-6	9
North Murray Av	J-6	6,9
North Pleasant Av	H-7	9
North Van Dien Av	J-7	6,9
North Walnut St	H-7	9
North Rd	H-8	9
Northern Pkwy	J-7	6,9
Northern Pkwy	J-7	6,9
Oak St	J-7	6,9
Oak St	J-7	6,9
Old Stone Rd	H-6	9
Olivia St	J-6	6,9
Orchard Pl	J-6	6,9
Orville Pl	J-8	6,9
Orville Pl	H-7	9
Overbrook Rd	J-7	6,9
Oxford Ct	H-8	9
Oxford Pl	H-7	9
Palmer Ct	H-6	9
Paramus Rd	J-8	6,9
Park Slope	J-6	6,9
Park Slope	J-7	6,9
Parsons Rd	H-7	9
Passaic St	J-7	6,9
Patricia Ct	H-6	9
Paul Ct	J-6	6,9
Pearsall Av	H-7	9
Pearsall Av	H-7	9
Pershing Av	J-8	6,9
Phelps Rd	J-7	6,9
Phoenix Av	J-7	6,9
Pine St	J-7	6,9
Pomander Walk	J-7	6,9
Ponfield Pl	H-7	9
Preston Pl	H-7	9
Prospect St	J-7	6,9
Quackenbush Pl	H-8	9
Quackenbush Pl	J-8	6,9
Queens St	H-8	9
Race Track Rd	J-8	6,9
Race Track Rd	H-8	9
Randolph St	J-6	6,9
Randolph Pl	J-7	6,9
Red Birch Ct	J-8	6,9
Red Rock Ct	H-7	9
Reynen Ct	J-7	6,9
Richards Rd	J-6	6,9
Richards Rd	H-7	9
Richmond Av	J-6	6,9
Ridge Ct	J-7	6,9
Rivara Ct	J-8	6,9
Robert St	K-7	6
Robinson Ln	J-7	6,9
Rock Rd	H-7	9
Rose Ct	H-7	9
Rugby St	J-7	6,9
Salem Ln	H-8	9
Shadow Bridge Rd	H-8	6,9
Sheffield Rd	H-7	9
Shelbourne Ter	H-6	9
Shelton Rd	J-6	6,9
Sheridan Ter	H-6	9
Sherman Pl	J-7	6,9
Sherman Pl	J-8	6,9
Sherwood Rd	H-7	9
Smith Pl	J-8	6,9
Sollas Ct	J-8	6,9
Somerville Rd	J-6	6,9
South Broad St	J-7	6,9
South Hill Rd	H-7	9
South Hillside Pl	J-6	6,9
South Irving St	H-7	9
South Maple Av	J-7	6,9
South Monroe St	J-7	6,9
South Murray Av	J-6	6,9
South Pleasant Av	K-7	6
South Van Dien Av	J-7	6,9
South Walnut St	J-7	6,9
Southern Pkwy	J-7	6,9
Spencer Pl	H-7	9
Spring Av	J-6	6,9
Standish Pl	J-8	6,9
Stanley Pl	J-7	6,9
Stanley Pl	J-6	6,9
Steilen Av	J-6	6,9
Steilen Av	J-8	6,9
Sterling Pl	H-7	9
Stevens Av	K-7	6
Stillwell Pl	J-7	6,9
Stonycroft Rd	J-6	6,9
Stratford Rd	H-7	9
Stuart St	H-7	9
Summit St	H-7	9
Sunset Av	H-7	9
Sunset Av	J-7	6,9
Taylor Rd	H-8	9
Terhune Rd	J-7	6,9
Terrace Dr	J-6	6,9
Theyken Pl	H-7	9
Thompson Pl	H-7	9
Unadilla Rd	H-7	9
Undercliff Ct	H-7	9
Union St	H-7	9
Upper Blvd	H-7	9
Valley View Av	H-7	9
Van Buren St	H-7	9
Van Dyke St	H-7	9
Van Emburgh Av	J-8	6,9
Van Emburgh Av	H-7	9
Van Neste Sq	J-7	6,9
Vesta Ct	J-7	6,9
Virginia Pl	H-7	9
Waiku Rd	J-7	6,9
Waiku Rd	H-6	9
Wall St	J-7	6,9
Wallington Ter	J-7	6,9
Walthery Av	J-6	6,9
Walton St	J-7	6,9
Warren Pl	H-7	9
Washington Pl	J-6	6,9
Washington Pl	H-7	9
Wastena Ter	J-7	6,9
Waverly Rd	H-6	9
Wellington Rd	H-6	9
Wenrob Ct	J-6	6,9
West End Av	J-6	6,9
West Glen Av	H-7	9
West Glen Av	H-7	9
West Ridgewood Av	J-6	6,9
West Saddle River Rd	H-8	9
West Av	H-6	9
Westbrook Rd	H-8	9
Westfield Ct	H-8	9
Westgate St	H-8	9
Wickham Wy	H-8	9
Wild Wood Rd	J-8	6,9
William St	J-8	6,9
William St	H-7	9
Willow St	J-7	6,9
Wilsey Sq	J-7	6,9
Wilson St	H-7	9
Windsor Ter	H-7	9
Witthill Rd	J-8	6,9
Woodbine Ct	J-7	6,9
Woodfield Ct	G-6	9
Woodland Av	H-6	9
Woodland Dr	H-7	9
Woodside Av	J-7	6,9
Woodside St	J-7	6,9
Wyndemere Av	J-8	6,9
Wyndemere Av	J-7	6,9

River Edge, Boro of

STREET	GRID	MAP
3rd Av	L-10	6
4th Av	L-10	6
5th Av	M-10	5,6
5th Av	L-10	6
5th Ct	M-10	5,6
6th Av	L-10	6
7th Av	L-10	6
8th Av	L-10	6
Ackerson St	M-10	5,6
Adams Av	L-10	6
Adrian Way	L-10	6
Beech Ct	M-10	5,6
Beech North Dr	M-10	5,6
Beech South Dr	M-10	5,6
Berkeley St	M-10	5,6
Bloomfield Av	L-10	6
Bogert Rd	L-10	6
Bogert Rd	M-10	5,6
Center Av	L-10	6
Cherry Ln	M-10	5,6
Cherry News	M-10	5,6
Christie Av	L-10	6
Clarendon Ct	L-10	6
Cleveland Pl	M-10	5,6
Coles St	M-10	5,6
Colonial St	M-10	5,6
Concord Dr	L-10	6
Continental Av	L-10	6
Demarest Pl	L-10	6
Dorchester Rd	M-10	5,6
Eastbrook Dr	M-10	5,6
Elizabeth St	M-10	5,6
Elm Av	M-10	5,6
Elm Av	L-10	6
Elm Pl	L-10	6
Erskinel Av	M-10	5,6
Gates Av	L-10	6
Grand Av	M-10	5,6
Greene Av	M-10	5,6
Greenway Ter	L-10	6
Grove Av	L-10	6
Hillside Av	L-10	6
Howland Av	M-10	5,6
Irene Ct	M-10	5,6
Jackson Av	L-10	6
Jefferson Av	L-10	6
Johnson Av	M-10	5,6
June	L-10	6
Kamack Rd	M-10	5,6
Kensington Rd	M-10	5,6
Kenwood Rd	L-10	6
Kimberly Wy	L-10	6
Kinderkamack Rd	L-10	6
Lafayette Av	L-10	6
Lakeview St	M-10	5,6
Laurel Av	L-10	6
Lee Av	M-10	5,6
Lexington Dr	M-10	5,6
Lincoln Av	L-10	6
Lozier Ter	M-10	5,6
Madison Av	L-10	6
Magnolia Av	L-10	6
Main St	M-10	5,6
Manchester Rd	M-10	5,6
Manning Av	L-10	6
Maple Pl	L-10	6
Mercer Av	M-10	5,6
Midland Av	M-10	5,6
Millbrook Rd	L-10	6
Mohawk Av	M-10	5,6
Monroe Av	L-10	6
Monroe Ct	L-10	6
Monroe St	L-10	6
North Dr	M-10	5,6
Oak Av	M-10	5,6
Oak Av	L-10	6
Olympia Dr	M-10	5,6
Oneida Dr	M-10	5,6
Oswego Pl	M-10	5,6
Oxford Ter	M-10	5,6
Park Av	L-10	6
Poplar Av	L-10	6
Princeton Dr	M-10	5,6
Reservoir Av	L-10	6
Richard Ct	L-10	6
River St	L-10	6
Riveredge Rd	L-10	6
Riverside Av	L-10	6
Rutgers St	M-10	5,6
Springvalley Av	M-10	5,6
Summit Av	L-10	6
Surrey Ln	L-10	6
Taft Ct	M-10	5,6
Taft Rd	M-10	5,6
Tenney Av	L-10	6
The Fenway Ct	M-10	5,6
Valley Rd	M-10	5,6
Van Buren Av	M-10	5,6
Van Saun Av	M-10	5,6
Van Saun Dr	L-10	6
Voorhis Av	L-10	6
Wales Av	L-10	6
Warwick Dr	M-10	5,6
Washington Av	L-10	6
Wayne Av	M-10	5,6
Webb Av	L-10	6
Westview St	L-10	6
William Av	L-10	6
Willow Av	L-10	6
Windsor Rd	M-10	5,6
Woodland Av	L-10	6
Zabriskie Pl	M-10	5,6

River Vale, Twp of

STREET	GRID	MAP
Alacci Wy	H-11	8
Alden Ct	F-11	8,13A
Alexander Ct	F-11	8,13A
Allison Rd	H-12	8
Alpine Cir	F-11	8,13A
Anne Rd	H-12	8
Antrim Rd	E-11	13A
Arbor Ct	F-11	8,13A
Arcadia Pl	F-11	8,13A
Aster Ln	G-11	8
Athlone Ter	F-11	8,13A
Avon Ct	F-11	8,13A
Avon Pl	F-11	8,13A
Bailey Rd	H-11	8
Baker Ct	H-11	8
Bakos Ln	F-11	8,13A
Bakos Pl	F-11	8,13A
Baldwin Dr	F-11	8,13A
Barr Ct	F-11	8,13A
Baylor Av	G-11	8
Beck Pl	H-11	8
Beech St	F-11	8,13A
Beechcrest Dr	F-11	8,13A
Bergen Pl	H-11	8
Berkshire Rd	H-12	8
Bernita Dr	F-11	8
Birch Av	E-11	13A
Birch Av	F-11	8,13A
Blakeney Pl	H-11	8
Blauvelt St	H-11	8
Blue Hill Rd	F-11	8,13A
Boughton Av	H-11	8
Brian Ct	H-11	8
Brook Av	G-11	8
Brookside Av	H-11	8
Bryant Pl	H-11	8
Buckingham Pl	FJ-12	7,8
Buckley Ct	H-11	8
Cambridge Rd	H-12	8
Caruso Blvd	H-11	8
Cedar Ln	H-11	8
Cedar Pl	H-11	8
Central Av	H-11	8
Chalmers Ct	F-11	8,13A
Charles Ct	H-11	8
Clark Smith Dr	FJ-12	7,8
Clauss Av	H-11	8
Cleveland Av	H-11	8
Cobb Rd	E-11	13A
Collignon Wy	H-11	8
Colonial Rd	F-11	8,13A
Coopers Ln	H-12	8
Cornelia Wy	F-11	8,13A
Corrigan Wy	FJ-12	7,8
Dale Ct	G-11	8
Daniel Dr	H-12	8
Debchar Ct	F-11	8,13A
Delcina Dr	F-11	8,13A
Donna Ct	H-11	8
Dorchester Dr	F-11	8,13A
Doretta St	H-11	8
Doriskill Ct	E-11	13A
Doriskill Dr	F-11	8,13A
Drake Ln	F-11	8,13A
Drayton Pl	F-11	8,13A
Echo Glen Av	H-11	8
Eckerson Av	H-11	8
Eckerson Ct	H-11	8
Edward St	F-11	8,13A
Egan Ter	F-11	8,13A
Elizabeth Av	H-11	8
Ellen La	H-11	8
Elm St	J-12	7,8
Erin Rd	E-11	13A
Fairway Ter	H-11	8
Faletti Cir	F-11	8,13A
Faletti Ct	F-11	8,13A
Faletti Wy	F-11	8,13A
Florence Ct	H-11	8
Florence Rd	H-11	8
Fondiller St	H-11	8
Ford Av	H-11	8
Forest Ct	G-11	8
Forest Dr	G-11	8
Frank Scott Ln	F-11	8,13A
Geiger Dr	H-11	8
Golf Ct	H-11	8
Goodell Ct	F-11	8,13A
Graney Dr	F-11	8,13A
Green Ln	G-11	8
Greenway Pl	F-11	8,13A
Gruman Ct	H-11	8
Hamilton Dr	H-11	8
Handwerg Dr	F-11	8,13A
Handwerg Dr	FJ-12	7,8
Hanna Rd	F-11	8,13A
Haring Farm Rd	G-11	8
Hermann Av	H-11	8
High Rd	F-11	8,13A
Highland Av	H-11	8
Hoffman Ct	H-12	8
Holiday Ct	H-11	8
Holiday Ln	H-11	8
Hudson Av	H-11	8
Interglen Av	H-11	8
Ivy Ln	H-11	8
James Ln	F-11	8,13A
Jason Rd	G-11	8
John St	G-11	8
John Shine Ct	H-11	8
Jones Rd	F-11	8,13A
Keenan Ct	H-11	8
Kennedy Ct	F-11	8,13A
Kociemba Dr	H-11	8
Lamanna Ln	G-11	8
Leclerc Av	H-11	8
Leclerc Av	H-12	8
Lee Ct	H-11	8
Leona Ct	H-12	8
Lindy Av	J-12	7,8
Lockhaven Dr	F-11	8,13A
Longhill Rd	F-11	8,13A
Loretta Dr	F-11	8,13A
Maple St	E-11	13A
Maple St	F-11	8
Maple St	J-12	7,8
Margiasso Ct	F-11	8,13A
Mark Ln	G-11	8
Marshall Rd	H-12	8
Martin St	H-11	8
Mattner Ct	H-12	8
May St	E-11	13A
Maze Rd	E-11	13A
Middletown Rd	E-11	13A
Middletown Rd	E-11	13A
Midell Ct	F-11	8,13A
Midvale Ct	F-11	8,13A
Montgomery Ln	E-11	13A
Montview Pl	H-11	8
Nelson Ct	H-11	8
New St	H-11	8
Oak Av	H-11	8

STREET	GRID	MAP
Oakland Av	H-11	8
Old Patch Rd	H-11	8
Orange Ct	E-11	13A
Orange Ct	F-11	8,13A
Orangeburgh Rd	F-11	8,13A
Park Av	H-11	8
Pascack Av	H-12	8
Pascack Av	J-12	7,8
Patriot La	G-11	8
Paul Ct	H-11	8
Perry Pl	H-11	8
Peters Pl	H-11	8
Piermont Av	G-11	8
Piermont Av S	G-11	8
Poplar Rd	G-11	8
Primrose Ln	F-11	8,13A
Prospect Av	H-11	8
Prospect Av	G-11	8
Red Oak Dr	G-11	8
Rehill Ct	G-11	8
Richard Dr	H-11	8
Ridge Rd	G-11	8
Rita Dr	F-11	8,13A
River Dr	H-11	8
Rivervale Rd	G-11	8
Rivervale Rd	H-11	8
Rivervale Rd	F-11	8,13A
Road A	G-11	8
Road A	F-11	8,13A
Roberge Dr	H-11	8
Rockland Av	H-11	8
Rockridge Rd	F-11	8,13A
Rolling Hill Dr	F-11	8,13A
Roosevelt Av	H-11	8
Rose Ct	F-11	8,13A
Rose St	H-11	8
Russel Snow Dr	F-11	8,13A
Sabin Pl	H-11	8
Sabin Pl	G-11	8
Saint Uhr Pl	H-11	8
Sargent Rd	F-11	8,13A
Sargent Rd	F-11	8,13A
Scarangella Ct	F-11	8,13A
Scott Dr	H-12	8
Shelby Ln	F-11	8,13A
Sloat Pl	H-11	8
Southview Rd	G-11	8
Spring St	G-11	8
Spring St	H-11	8
Stacey Ct	H-12	8
Stanley Pl	G-11	8
Stellman Dr	F-11	8,13A
Stewart Ct	FJ-12	7,8
Sunnyside Ter	G-11	8
Sunset Rd	G-11	8
Sylvan Rd	F-11	8,13A
Teller Ln	F-11	8,13A
Thayer St	H-11	8
The Plaza	F-11	8,13A
Thomas Ter	G-11	8
Thurnau Dr	F-11	8,13A
Tiffany Av	H-11	8
Track Ln	F-11	8,13A
Tulip Pl	F-11	8,13A
Turbell Pkwy	H-12	8
Victory Pl	H-11	8
Wayne Dr	F-11	8,13A
Westwood Av	H-11	8
Westwood Av	H-12	8
White Birch Dr	G-11	8
Whitenack Rd	F-11	8,13A
Wicklow Wy	E-11	13A
William Pl	H-11	8
William St	H-11	8
Wilma St	H-11	8
Wilson Ct	H-11	8
Winding Wy	F-11	8,13A
Wittich Ter	F-11	8,13A
Woodland Ct	G-11	8
Woodside Av	F-11	8,13A
Ziobold Ct	F-11	8,13A

Rochelle, Park, Twp of

STREET	GRID	MAP
Becker Av	N-8	5
Bennett Av	M-8	5
Berdan St	M-8	5
Berdan St	N-8	5
Berdan St	M-8	5
Brooks Av	N-8	5
Catherine St	N-9	5
Cedar Dr	M-8	5
Central Av	N-8	5
Central Av	N-9	5
Chestnut Av	N-9	5
Chestnut St	M-8	5
Chestnut St	N-8	5
Colling Av	N-9	5
Crescent St	N-9	5
Dorothy Av	M-9	5
Dorothy Av	N-9	5
Durand Pl	N-9	5
East Forest Pl	N-8	5
East Terrace Av	N-8	5
East Terrace Av	N-9	5
El Dorado Ct	M-8	5
Essex St	N-9	5
Essex St	N-8	5
Fairfield Dr	M-9	5
Forest Pl	N-8	5
Gertrude Av	M-9	5
Gertrude Av	N-9	5
Grove Av	N-9	5
Hahn Av	M-8	5
Harvey Av	M-8	5
Hazley Ct	M-8	5
Hazley St	M-8	5
High St	N-9	5
Hobart Ct	M-8	5
Hoffman Av	M-8	5
Howard Av	M-8	5
James St	M-8	5
Lakeview Av	M-8	5
Legion Pl	M-9	5
Lexington Av	N-9	5
Lexington Av	N-8	5
Lincoln Av	N-9	5
Lincoln Dr	N-9	5
Madison Av	N-9	5
Marian Av	N-9	5
Marinus St	N-9	5
Meakin Av	M-8	5
Midland St	N-9	5
North Dr	M-8	5
Oak St	N-8	5
Oldis St	M-8	5
Oldis St	M-9	5
Oldis St	N-9	5
Oldis St	N-8	5
Overlook Av	M-9	5
Paramus Rd	M-8	5
Park Wy	N-8	5
Park Wy	N-9	5
Parker Av	M-8	5
Passaic St	M-8	5
Patton Ct	M-8	5
Peek St	N-9	5
Plaza Wy	M-8	5
Pleasant Av	M-9	5
Powell Av	M-8	5
Prospect Av	N-9	5
Rail Road Av	N-8	5
Ridgefield Rd	M-9	5
Rochelle Av	N-9	5
Roosevelt Av	M-8	5
Saint Ann Pl	N-8	5
Schlosser Dr	M-8	5
Somerville St	M-8	5
South Dr	M-8	5
Susquehanna Av	N-9	5
Terrace Av	N-8	5
Theim Av	N-8	5
Ward St	N-9	5
West End St	N-9	5
West End St	N-8	5
West Oldis St	M-8	5
West Oldis St	N-8	5
Whittman St	M-8	5
William St	N-8	5
Woodland Av	N-9	5

Rockleigh, Boro of

STREET	GRID	MAP
Anderson Av	H-14	8
Bergen Av	G-14	8
Boyd Ln	H-14	8
Brooklawn Pt	H-14	8
Concklin Ln	G-14	8
Haring Farm Ln	H-14	8
King Rd	G-14	8
Link Dr	G-14	8
Paris Av	G-14	8
Piermont Rd	H-14	8
Pond Rd	G-14	8
Rockleigh Rd	H-14	8
Volvo Dr	G-14	8
Willow Av	G-14	8

Rutherford, Boro of

STREET	GRID	MAP
Addison Av	S-7	1,2
Agnew Pl	S-7	1,2
Altman Dr	T-8	1
Alwyn Pl	S-7	1,2
Ames Av	S-7	1,2
Arthur Dr	T-7	1
Ayer Pl	S-7	1,2
Barrows Av	T-7	1
Beckwith Pl	S-7	1,2
Beckwith Pl	R-7	2
Beech St	R-7	2
Belford Av	R-7	2
Belford Av	S-7	1,2
Borough St	S-8	2
Bryan Ct	R-7	2
Carlton Pl	R-7	2
Carmita Av	S-7	1,2
Carneer Av	R-7	2
Chesnut St	S-7	2
Circle Ln	S-7	2
Clark Ave	R-7	2
Clark Ct	R-7	2
College	S-7	1,2
Copper Pl	R-7	2
Couier Pl	R-7	2
Courier St	R-7	2
Crane Av	T-7	1
Daniel Av	S-7	2
Daniels Av	S-7	1,2
Darwin Av	R-7	2
Dean Ct	S-7	1,2
Delafield Av	S-7	1,2
Donaldson Av	S-7	1,2
Eastern Wy	S-7	1,2
Edgewood Pl.	S-7	1,2
Elizabeth St	S-7	1,2
Elliot Pl	S-7	1,2
Elm St	S-7	1,2
Elycroft Pkwy	S-7	1,2
Elycroft Pkwy	T-7	1,2
Erie Av	R-7	2
Erie Av	S-7	2
Estate Pl	S-7	1,2
Ettrick	S-7	1,2
Evans Av	S-7	1,2
Fairview Av	S-7	1,2
Feronia Wy	S-7	1,2
Francisco Av	S-7	1,2
Franklin Pl	S-7	1,2
Garfield Pl.	S-7	1,2
Glen Rd	S-7	1,2
Gouvemeur Av E.	S-7	1,2
Gouvemeur Av W.	S-7	1,2
Grand Av	R-7	2
Grove St	S-7	1,2
Hackett Pl	S-7	1,2
Hasbrouck Pl	R-7	2
Hastings Av	R-7	2
Hawthorne St	R-7	2
Highfield La	S-7	1,2
Hobart Av	R-7	2
Hollister Av	S-7	1,2
Home Av.	S-7	1,2
Industrial Dr	T-7	1
Industrial Dr	T-8	1
Insley Av	R-7	2
Irving Pl	S-7	1,2
Ivy Pl	S-7	1,2
Jackson Av	R-7	2
Jenness Pl	S-7	1,2
Kip Av	S-7	1,2
Linclon Av	S-7	1,2
Lynn Ct	T-7	1
Maple St	S-7	1,2
Marginal Rd	S-7	1,2
Meadow Rd	S-8	2
Milton Ct.	S-7	1,2
Monona Av	R-7	2
Montross Av	S-7	1,2
Morse Av	R-7	2
Mortimer Av	S-7	1,2
Mountain Wy	S-7	1,2
Myrtle St	R-7	2
Nevins St	S-7	1,2
Nevins St	T-7	1,2
Newell Av E.	S-7	1,2
Newell Av W	S-7	1,2
Orient Wy	S-7	1,2
Orient Wy	T-7	1,2
Park Av	S-7	1,2
Park Pl	S-7	1,2
Passaic Av	S-7	1,2
Passaic Av E.	S-7	1,2
Passaic Av W	S-7	1,2
Pierrepont Av	S-7	1,2
Preble Pl	S-7	1,2
Prospect Pl	S-7	1,2
Raymond Av	R-7	2
Ridge Rd	S-7	1,2
River Oaks Dr	S-7	1,2
Riverside Av.	R-7	2
Riverside Av.	S-7	1,2
Riverside Ter	S-7	1,2
Riverview Av	S-7	1,2
Roliver St	S-7	1,2
Rutherford Av	S-7	1,2
Saint Clair Av	R-7	1,2
Santiago Av	R-7	2
Sidney Av	R-7	2
Spring Dell	S-7	1,2
Springfield Av	S-7	1,2
Stuyvesant Av	S-7	1,2
Summit Cross.	S-7	1,2
Sunderland Av.	R-7	2
Sylvan St	S-7	1,2
The Terrace	S-7	1,2
Union Av	R-7	2
Van Ness Av	S-7	1,2
Van Riper Av	S-7	1,2
Van Riper Av	T-7	1,2
Van Winkle Pl	S-7	1,2
Vanderburgh Av	R-7	2
Veterns Blvd	T-8	1
Vreeland Av	S-7	1,2
Walnut St	R-7	2
Walter Ct	T-7	1
Washington Av	R-7	2
Weaton Pl	S-7	1,2
Wells Pl	R-7	2
William St.	S-7	1,2
Wilson Av.	S-7	1,2
Wingra Av	R-7	2
Winslow Pl	S-7	1,2
Wood St	S-7	1,2
Woodland Av	S-7	1,2
Woodward Av	S-7	1,2
Yahara Av	R-7	2

Saddle Brook, Twp of

STREET	GRID	MAP
1st St	P-7	5
2nd St	P-8	5
3rd St	P-8	5
4th St	P-8	5
5th St	P-8	5
5th St	N-8	5
6th St	P-8	5
6th St	N-8	5
7th St	N-8	5
7th St	P-8	5
8th St	P-8	5
9th St	P-8	5
10th St	P-8	5
Ackerman Av	N-8	5
Adams Av	N-8	5
Adriana St	N-8	5
Albany St	N-8	5
Alberta Dr	M-8	5,6
Anthony Ct	N-8	5
Ardmore Ct	M-8	5,6
Ash Av	M-7	5,6
Avon Ln	M-8	5,6
Beech Av	M-7	5,6
Beech Av	M-8	5,6
Bell Av	N-8	5
Bell Av	M-7	5,6
Bellavista Av	N-8	5
Belli Av	M-7	5,6
Birk St	N-8	5
Blanche St	N-8	5
Boulevard N	N-8	5
Boulevard St	N-8	5
Brook St	M-8	5,6
Burgess Dr	M-8	5,6
Caldwell Av	N-8	5
Cambridge Av	M-7	5,6
Capitol St	P-8	5
Catherine Av	N-8	5
Central Av	N-8	5
Chelsea Dr	N-8	5
Christy Tr	M-7	5,6
Claire Pl	M-7	5,6
Claremont Av	N-8	5
Clover Ct	M-7	5,6
Coger St	N-8	5
Colonial Av	M-7	5,6
Colonial Av	N-7	5
Congress St	N-8	5
Cozy Glen	N-8	5
Cypress Av	M-8	5,6
Daniel Ct	M-8	5,6
Daniel Pl	M-8	5,6
Danna Wy	M-8	5,6
Dewey Av	N-7	5
Dewey Av	N-8	5
Dyer Pl	M-8	5,6
East Lanza Ct	N-8	5
Elm Av	M-7	5,6
Erie St	N-7	5
Evans Pl	M-7	5,6
Fairlawn Pkwy	M-7	5,6
Fairview Av	N-8	5
Finnigan Av	N-8	5
Floral Ln	M-7	5,6
Franklin Av	N-8	5
Garden St	N-8	5
George St	M-7	5,6
Glen Rd	N-8	5
Grace Av	N-8	5
Graham Ct	M-8	5,6
Graham Ter	M-8	5,6
Grunauer Av	N-8	5
Harley Pl	M-8	5,6
Harrison Av	N-8	5
Harrop Av	N-8	5
Hayes Dr	M-7	5,6
Hemstrand Ct	M-7	5,6
Henry St	N-8	5
Herbert Ter	M-7	5,6
Hickey Ter	N-8	5
Hickory Av	M-8	5,6
Hiemstrand Ct	N-8	5
Hilda Tr	M-7	5,6
Hillside Av	N-8	5
Hobson Av	N-8	5
Hobson Av	N-7	5
Hollywood Av	N-8	5
Hutter St	M-7	5,6
Jamros Ter	M-8	5,6
Jefferson Av	P-7	5
John Ochs Dr	M-8	5,6
John Ochs Pl	M-8	5,6
John St	N-8	5
Kenny Pl	N-7	5
Kenwood Ct	N-8	5
Kern Pl	M-7	5,6
Kuhn Ct	M-8	5,6
Kuhn Dr	M-8	5,6
Lanza Av	P-7	5
Lanza Av	N-8	5
Larch Av	M-7	5 6
Legregni Ct	N-8	5
Leswing Av	N-8	5
Liberty St	N-8	5
Lincoln Av	N-8	5
Louis St	M-8	5 6
Lyndon Pl	M-7	5 6
Lyster Av	N-7	5
Madeline Av	N-7	5
Madison Av	N-8	5
Maple Av	M-7	5 6
Marie Pl	M-8	5 6
Market St	N-8	5
Martin Pl	M-7	5 6
Mayhill St	N-8	5
McArthur Dr	N-8	5
McKenzie St	N-8	5
Midland Av	P-7	5
Miller St	N-8	5
Monte Mura S	M-7	5,6
Montemuro St	M-7	5,6
Nedellec Dr	M-7	5,6
Nightingale Rd	M-8	5,6
North Lanza Ct	N-8	5
North Leswing Av	N-8	5
North Midland Av	M-7	5,6
Oak Av	M-7	5,6
Outwater Ln	P-8	5
Oxford Av	M-7	5,6
Pehle Av	N-8	5
Pehle Av	N-7	5
Pine Av	M-7	5,6
Platt Av	N-8	5
Poplar St	N-8	5
President St	P-8	5
Rail Road Av	N-8	5
Riverview Av	N-8	5
Rochelle Pkwy	N-8	5
Roosevelt Blvd	N-8	5
Rosario Ct	M-7	5,6
Rosedale Av	N-8	5
Rosemont Av	N-8	5
Rosol Ln	M-7	5,6
Rugby Rd	M-8	5,6
Saddle River Ct	M-8	5,6
Saddle River Rd	M-8	5,6
Saddle River Rd	N-8	5
Sampson St	N-8	5
Santa Lucia Ct	N-8	5
Scheele Pl	M-8	5,6
Schepis Av	M-7	5,6
Sherry La	N-7	5
Skillman Ter	M-8	5,6
South Lanza Ct	N-8	5
South Leswing Av	N-8	5
South Rd	M-7	5,6
South St	N-8	5
Spindler Tr	M-8	5,6
Spruce Av	M-7	5,6
Steinway Rd	M-7	5,6
Steinway Rd	N-8	5
Sterling Pl	N-8	5
Strathmore Tr	M-8	5,6
Susan Ln	M-8	5,6
Sylvan St	N-8	5
Taggart Wy	M-8	5,6
Urma Pl	N-7	5
Van Luyn Tr	N-8	5
Van Orden St	N-8	5
Victor St	N-7	5
Victor St	N-8	5
Washington St	N-8	5
Welcome Rd	N-8	5
Weller Ter	M-8	5,6
West St	N-8	5
Westminster Av	N-8	5
Westminster Av	P-8	5
Williams St	N-8	5
Willow Av	M-8	5,6
Wilson Ct	M-7	5,6
Wilson St	M-7	5,6
Woodcrest Pl	N-7	5
Woodcrest Pl	M-7	5,6
Woodward St	N-8	5
Youngs Pl	M-8	5,6
Yves Ct	M-7	5,6

Saddle River, Boro of

STREET	GRID	MAP
Ackerman Rd	E-8	12
Adams Rd	G-7	9
Algonquin Tr	F-7	9 12
Apple Ridge	F-8	9 12
Arrowhead Ln	F-7	9 12
Baldwin Rd	G-8	9
Bayberry Dr	F-8	9,12
Beechwood Dr	G-8	9
Big Ramapo Rd	F-7	9,12
Birchwood Dr	E-8	12
Boro Line Rd	F-7	9,12
Bridle Wy	E-8	12
Burning Hollow Rd	G-7	9
Cameron Rd	F-7	9,12
Cameron Rd	G-7	9
Charlden Dr	F-8	9,12
Chestnut Ridge Rd	F-9	9,12
Chestnut Ridge Rd	G-8	9
Chestnut Ridge Rd	F-8	9,12
Chipmunk Ct	G-7	9
Choctaw Tr	F-7	9,12
Christopher Pl	F-7	9,12
Coltsfoot Glen	E-8	12
Coltsfoot Glen	F-8	9,12
Country Squire Rd	G-7	9
County Rd	F-8	9,12
Dater Ln	F-7	9,12
Deer Trail Rd	E-7	12
Denison Dr	F-8	9,12
Denison Dr E	F-8	9,12
Dogwood Dr	F-8	9,12
East Allendale Rd	F-8	9,12
East Prospect St	G-7	9
East Saddle River Rd	F-8	9,12
Eckert Farm Rd	F-7	9,12
Elden Dr	F-8	9,12
Esler Ln	F-7	9,12
Eugene Dr	G-7	9
Fox Hedge Rd	F-8	9,12
Frederick Dr	F-8	9,12
Frederick Dr	E-8	12
Frederick Dr	F-8	9,12
Glenwood Dr	G-8	9
Hawthorne Ter	F-7	9,12
Hedger Dr	F-7	9,12
Hickory Hill Rd	F-8	9,12
High Meadow Rd	F-7	9,12
High Meadow Rd N	F-7	9,12
Kenwood Rd	E-8	12
Locust Ln	E-8	12
Locust St	E-8	12
Lookout Dr	G-8	9
Lower Cross Rd	G-8	9
Lower Cross Rd	G-7	9
Malcolm St	G-8	9
Meadow Ln	E-8	12
Mill Rd	G-8	9
Mohegan Tr	F-7	9,12
Normandy Dr	G-8	9
North Church Rd	G-8	9
Oak Rd	F-8	9,12
Old Acres Rd	E-7	12
Old Farm Rd	G-8	9
Old Woods Rd	G-8	9
Overlook Rd	F-7	9,12
Pell Farm Rd	F-7	9,12
Pine Tree Rd	G-7	9
Pitch Pipe Rd	G-7	9
Plymouth Ln	G-8	9
Raiff Rd	G-7	9
Red Rock Tr	F-8	9,12
Red Rock Tr	E-8	12
Ridge Crest Rd	F-8	9,12
River Farm Ln	G-8	9
Rock Ledge Rd	F-8	9,12
Sawmill Rd	F-8	9,12
Shefler Dr	F-8	9,12
South Pond Rd	G-7	9
Spruce Rd	F-7	9,12
Stonewall Rd	F-7	9,12
Stonewall Rd	G-7	9
Stony Ridge Rd	E-7	12
Surrey Dr	F-7	9,12
Surrey Dr	F-8	9,12
Tall Trees Ln	F-8	9,12
Tanbark Tr	F-8	9,12
Twin Brook Rd	G-8	9
Warewoods Rd	E-8	12
Warewoods Rd	F-8	9,12
Werimus Brook Rd	G-8	9
Werimus Brook Rd	G-9	9
West Church Rd	G-8	9
West Gate	F-7	9,12
West Saddle River Rd	G-9	9
West Saddle River Rd	F-9	9,12
West Wildwood Rd	E-7	12
West Hill Rd	F-7	9,12
Westerly Rd	F-8	9,12
Westwind Ct	G-7	9
Wildwood Rd	E-7	12
Willow Pond Rd	G-7	9
Winding Wy	G-8	9
Woodcliff Lake Rd	F-8	9,12
Woodfield Ln	G-8	9

South Hackensack, Twp of

STREET	GRID	MAP
1st St	Q-10	2,5
4th Av	Q-10	2,5
Agar Pl	Q-10	2,5
Bruce Ct	Q-10	2,5
Caliconeck Rd	Q-10	2,5
Central Blvd	S-10	1,2
Chestnut Av	Q-10	2,5
Chippewa St	Q-10	2,5
Christopher St	Q-9	2,5
Dinallo St	Q-10	2,5
Division St	P-9	5
Division St	P-10	5
Dyer Av	Q-10	2,5
East Wesley St	Q-10	2,5
Florence St	Q-10	2,5
Florida St	Q-10	2,5
Francis Ln	Q-10	2,5
Franklin St	Q-10	2,5
Garfield Pl	Q-8	2,5
Georgia St	Q-9	2,5
Georgia St	Q-10	2,5
Gilbert St	Q-8	2,5
Green St	P-9	5
Green St	Q-9	2,5
Grove St E	Q-10	2,5
Grove St	Q-10	2,5
Hegner Ct	Q-10	2,5
Hoffman St	Q-10	2,5
Horizon Blvd	S-10	1,2
Huyler St	Q-10	2,5
Ise St	Q-10	2,5
Jackson Av	Q-10	2,5
James St	P-9	5
James St	Q-9	2,5
John St	Q-10	2,5
Leuning Av	P-9	5
Lincoln St	Q-10	2,5
Louis Ct	Q-10	2,5
Louis St	Q-10	2,5
Maple Av	Q-10	2,5
Michael St	P-10	5
Milano Ct	Q-10	2,5
Milano Ln	Q-10	2,5
Millo Ct	Q-10	2,5
Millo Pl	Q-10	2,5
Moonachie Rd	Q-10	2,5
North Taylor St	Q-10	2,5
North Veprek Ln	Q-10	2,5
North Av	Q-10	2,5
North Av	Q-11	3,4
Park St	Q-10	2,5
Phillips Av	Q-10	2,5
Ramanelli Av	P-9	5
Rossi Ct	Q-10	2,5
Ruta Ct	Q-10	2,5
Saddle River Av	Q-8	2,5
Schriefer St	P-9	5
Schriefer St	Q-9	2,5
Sievers Ln	Q-10	2,5
South Main St	P-10	5
South Main St	Q-10	2,5
Taylor Av	Q-10	2,5
Taylor St	Q-10	2,5
Tuve Ln	Q-10	2,5
Veprek La	Q-10	2,5
Virginia St	Q-10	2,5
Vreeland Av	Q-10	2,5
Wesley St	Q-9	2,5
West St	P-10	5
West St	Q-10	2,5
Wilks St	Q-10	2,5
Williams Av	Q-10	2,5
Wilson St	P-10	5
Wilson St	Q-10	2,5
Worth St	Q-10	2,5
Worth St	P-10	5

Teaneck, Twp of

STREET	GRID	MAP
Academy Ln	N-11	4
Albin St	P-11	4
Aldred St	P-12	4
Alfred Av	P-12	4
Alicia Av	N-11	4
Allan Ct	P-11	4
Alma Ter	P-11	4
Alpine Dr	P-11	4
Alrich Ct	P-11	4
American Legion Dr	P-11	4
Amsterdam Av	N-12	4
Amsterdam Av	N-11	4
Anna St	N-11	4
Ardsley Ct	N-12	4
Argonne Ct	N-12	4
Arlington Av	N-12	4
Armory Pl	M-12	4,7
Aspen Tr	N-12	4
Audubon Rd	P-12	4
Audubon Rd	P-11	4
Ayers Ct	N-11	4
Azalea Ct	P-12	4
Balsam St	N-12	4
Barbara Dr	P-12	4
Barr Av	P-11	4
Bayard St	P-12	4
Beatrice St	N-11	4
Beaumont Av	N-11	4
Bedford Av	N-12	4
Beech St	P-11	4
Belle Av	N-11	4
Belle Av	P-11	4
Bennett Rd	P-11	4
Bergen Av	Q-11	3,4
Berkeley St	N-12	4
Berwick Av	N-11	4
Beveridge St	N-12	4
Beverly Rd	N-10	5
Beverly Rd	N-11	4
Billington Rd	N-11	4
Bilton St	N-11	4
Birch St	N-11	4
Blauvelt St	Q-11	3,4
Bogert St	N-11	4
Briarcliff Rd	N-11	4
Briarcliff Rd	M-11	4,7
Brinkerhoff Av	P-11	4
Broad St	P-11	4
Bromley Av	N-11	4
Bryant Av	P-12	4
Buckingham Rd	M-11	4,7
Buffet Tr	N-12	4
Bying St	N-12	4
Cadmus Ct	P-10	5
Cambridge Rd	N-11	4
Campertown Av	N-11	4
Cane St	P-11	4
Canterbury Ct	P-11	4
Canterbury Ct	P-12	4
Carlton Ter	N-11	4
Carrol Pl	P-11	4
Catalpa Av	N-10	5
Catalpa Av	P-10	5
Cedar Ln	N-10	5
Center Pl	P-10	5
Chadwick Rd	P-11	4
Champlin Sq	N-12	4
Cherry Ln	P-11	4
Cherry Ln	N-11	4
Chestnut Av	P-11	4
Chestnut Pl	P-11	4
Church St	N-11	4
Churchill Rd	M-11	4,7
Circle Driveway	N-12	4
Claremount Av	N-11	4
Clinton Pl	M-12	4,7
Club Rd	P-11	4
Colonial Ct	N-11	4
Columbus Dr	P-12	4
Commonwealth Dr	P-11	4
Congress Av	N-12	4
Cooper Av	N-12	4
Cooper Av	P-12	4
Copley Av	P-11	4
Cornwall Av	N-10	5
Cornwall Av	N-11	4
Cottage Pl	M-10	5
Cottage Pl	M-11	4,7
Country Club Dr	P-12	4
Court St	N-11	4
Cranford Pl	N-11	4
Crescent Av	N-12	4
Crestview Pl	P-11	4
Cumberland Av	N-11	4
Darien Tr	P-12	4
Dartmouth St	N-11	4
Dearborn St	M-11	4,7
Decatur Av	P-12	4
DeGraw Av	P-11	4
Delavan St	P-12	4
Demarest Rd	P-11	4
Demott Av	P-11	4
Dewey Pl	N-11	4
Dickerson Rd	N-11	4
Dogwood Ln	P-12	4
Dohrmann Av	P-11	4
Dover Ct	M-11	4,7
Downing St	M-11	4,7
East Cedar Ln	P-11	4
East Forest Av	N-12	4
East Lawn Ct	P-12	4
East Maple St	Q-11	3,4
East Oakdene Av	P-12	4
East Oakdene Av	P-11	4
East Sherwood Av	Q-11	3,4
East Walnut St	Q-11	3,4
Eastlawn Dr	P-12	4
Eastview	Q-11	3,4
Edgemont Pl	P-11	4
Edgemont Ter	N-11	4
Edgewood Av	N-11	4
Elizabeth Av	N-11	4
Elm Av	P-11	4
Elm Av	N-11	4
Elmer Pl	M-12	4,7
Emerson Av	N-11	4
Endicott Tr	N-12	4
Englewood Av	N-12	4
Essex Rd	N-11	4
Ester Av	N-11	4
Evergreen Pl	N-11	4
Fabry Tr	P-12	4
Fairfield St	N-12	4
Fairidge Ter	N-11	4
Fairview Av	N-12	4
Falmouth Av	N-11	4
Farragut Ct	P-12	4
Farragut Dr	P-12	4
Farragut Ter	P-11	4
Fayette St	N-11	4
Fenimore Rd	P-11	4
Forest Av	N-11	4
Fort Lee Rd	P-11	4
Frances St	P-11	4
Frank W Burr Blvd	P-11	4
Franklin Rd	N-12	4
French Ct	P-12	4
Frycke Ln	P-11	4
Gail Ct	P-11	4
Galway Pl	N-12	4
Galway Pl	N-11	4
Garden St	N-12	4
Garrison Av	N-11	4
Gaylor Tr	N-12	4
Genesee Av	N-12	4
George St	P-11	4
Gifford Pl	P-11	4
Glen Ct	P-12	4
Glenwood Av	P-12	4
Golf Ct	P-11	4
Grace Tr	N-11	4
Graham Pl	N-11	4
Gramercy Pl	N-12	4
Grange Ct	P-11	4
Grange Rd	P-11	4
Grant Ter	P-11	4
Gray St	P-11	4
Grayson Pl	N-11	4
Green Ct	N-10	5
Greenville Av	N-11	4
Greenwood Rd	P-12	4
Griggs Av	P-11	4
Grove St	P-11	4
Haddon Pl	N-11	4
Hamilton Ln	M-12	4,7
Hamilton Ln	N-12	4
Hamilton Rd	N-12	4
Hancock Av	P-12	4
Hanover St	M-11	4,7
Harding Av	P-12	4
Hargreaves Av	N-12	4
Hartwell St	P-11	4
Hastings St	N-11	4
Hawthorne Av	P-12	4
Helen St	N-11	4
Hemlock Tr N	P-12	4
Hemlock Tr S	P-12	4
Henry St	P-11	4
Herrick Av	P-11	4
Hickory St	P-11	4
Highwood St	P-11	4
Hill St	N-11	4
Hillcrest St	P-10	5
Hillside Av	P-11	4
Hirliman Rd	N-12	4
Hobson Pl	N-11	4
Holland Tr	P-11	4
Home St	P-11	4
Home St	P-12	4
Howard St	P-11	4
Howland Av	N-12	4
Hubert Tr	N-12	4
Hudson Rd	N-11	4
Intervale Rd	N-12	4
Irene Ct	N-12	4
Iris Ct	P-12	4
Irvington Rd	M-12	4,7
Ivy Ct	M-12	4,7
Ivy Ln	M-12	4,7
James St	P-11	4
Jasper St	Q-11	3,4
Jefferson St	M-11	4,7
Jefferson St	N-11	4
Jerome Pl	N-12	4
John St	P-11	4
Johnson Av	P-11	4
Johnson Ct	P-11	4
Joseph Ct	P-11	4
Julia St	N-11	4
Katherine St	N-11	4
Kensington Rd	N-11	4
Kent Av	P-10	5
Kenwood Pl	P-10	5
Kilmurray Dr	P-12	4
Kings Ct	N-11	4
Kipp St	P-11	4
Kipp St	P-10	5
Lakeview Ter	P-12	4
Lambert Rd	N-11	4
Larch Av	P-10	5
Laurel Tr	N-11	4
Laurelton Pkwy E	N-11	4
Laurelton Pkwy W	N-11	4
Lees Av	Q-11	3,4
Lerome Pl	M-12	4,7
Letter Av	P-12	4

BERGEN COUNTY

STREET	GRID	MAP
Morris Av	R-7	2
Mount Cedar Av	R-7	2
Mount Pleasant Av	R-7	2
Muller St	R-7	2
Narcissus Dr	R-7	2
Orchard St	Q-7	2,5
Orchid Dr	R-7	2
Park Row	Q-7	2,5
Park Wy	Q-7	2,5
Parkview Dr	R-7	2
Paterson Av	R-7	2
Pine St	Q-8	2,5
Pleasant View Ter	R-7	2
Primrose Dr	R-7	2
Pulaski Av	Q-7	2,5
Reservoir Av	Q-7	2,5
Reservoir Av	R-7	2
Reservoir Rd	R-7	2
Roehrs Dr	R-7	2
Rose St	R-7	2
Spring Ct	R-8	2
Spring St	R-8	2
Stein Av	Q-7	2,5
Strong St	R-7	2
Strong St	Q-7	2,5
Tulip Pl	R-7	2
Turs Ct	R-7	2
Tuttle St	R-7	2
Union Blvd	R-7	2
Van Dyke St	R-7	2
Van Winkle Av	Q-7	2,5
Veterans Ct	R-7	2
Wadsworth St	R-7	2
Wagner Av	Q-8	2,5
Wagner Av	Q-7	2,5
Wallington Av	R-7	2
Wallington Av	Q-7	2,5
Washington Pl	R-7	2
Washington Pl	Q-7	2,5
William St	R-7	2
Willow Av	Q-8	2,5

Washington, Twp of

STREET	GRID	MAP
Adams Pl	H-9	9
Amherst Dr	H-9	9
Andrea Ln	J-8	6,9
Andrea Ln	J-8	6,9
Arden Pl	H-9	9
Barry Dr	H-8	9
Barry Dr	H-9	9
Beech St	H-9	9
Beech St	H-8	9
Beechwood Dr	H-9	9
Bergen Av	J-9	6,9
Berkley Ct	H-9	9
Birch Av	H-10	9
Birch Av	H-9	9
Boulevard St	H-10	9
Braeburn Dr	H-9	9
Bridge St	H-9	9
Brook Av	J-9	6,9
Burger Pl	J-9	6,9
Burger Pl	J-10	6,9
Burke St	H-9	9
Calvin St	H-9	9
Calvin St	H-10	9
Calvin St	J-9	6,9
Cambridge Dr	H-9	9
Carriage Ct	H-9	9
Celia Ct	H-9	9
Chestnut St	H-9	9
Chimney Ridge Ct	J-9	6,9
Clark Av	H-9	9
Clayton Ct	J-9	6,9
Cleveland Av	H-9	9
Clinton Av	H-9	9
Colonial Blvd	H-9	9
Colonial Blvd	J-9	6,9
Columbus Sq	H-9	9
Concord Ln	H-9	9
Coolidge Av	H-9	9
Cosman St	J-9	6,9
Cottage Pl	H-9	9
Cottage Pl	H-10	9
Crest Pl	H-9	9
Crestwood Ter	H-10	9
Cross St	H-9	9
Curtis Pl	H-9	9
Cypress St	H-9	9
Danbury Ct	H-9	9
Darlene Ter	H-10	9
Dartmouth Dr	H-9	9
Dawes Av	H-10	9
Dawes Av	H-9	9
Devon Rd	H-9	9
Donald Av	H-9	9
Douglas Dr	H-9	9
East Glen Av	J-9	6,9
East View Ter	H-9	9
Edgewood Dr	J-8	6,9
Edgewood Dr	J-9	6,9
Edison St	H-9	9
Elfhill Ct	H-9	9
Ellen Pl	J-9	6,9
Eton Rd	H-9	9
Eugene Ct	J-9	6,9
Fairfield Ct	J-9	6,9
Fern St	H-9	9
Fern St	J-9	6,9
Fillmore Dr	H-9	9
Forsgate Ct	H-9	9
Gabriel Wy	J-8	6,9
Garden Ct	J-9	6,9
Garden Ct	J-9	6,9
Garden State Pkwy	H-9	9
Garibaldi Pl	H-9	9
Gorga Pl	H-8	9
Grace Ct	J-10	6,9
Halsey St	H-9	9
Hampshire Rd	H-8	9
Hampton Ct	J-9	6,9
Harrison St	H-9	9
Hemlock Dr	J-9	6,9
Hering Pl	H-10	9
Hering Pl	H-9	9
Hickory St	J-9	6,9
Hickory St	H-10	9
Hickory St	H-9	9
Hickory St	J-9	6,9
High View Ter	J-9	6,9
Hillcrest Rd	H-9	9
Honeysuckle Dr	J-9	6,9
Hoover Av	H-9	9
Horizon Ct	H-8	9
Howard St	H-10	9
Howard St	J-9	6,9
Howard St	H-9	9
Howard St	H-9	9
Hudson Av	H-9	9
Hull Ter	H-10	9
Jackson Av	H-9	9
Jacob Rd	H-8	9
Jacquelyn Rd	H-9	9
Jefferson Av	H-9	9
Johnson Pl	H-8	9
Katharina Pl	H-8	9
Kennedy Dr	H-9	9
Kennedy Ter	H-10	9
Kenneth St	H-9	9
Koch Peak Av	H-10	9
Lafayette Av	J-10	6,9
Lafayette Ter	H-10	9
Leigh Ter	H-9	9
Lexington Ct	H-9	9
Lincoln Av	H-9	9
Lincoln Pl	H-9	9
Lindenwood Ct	H-9	9
Linwood Av	J-8	6,9
Madeline Ct	J-9	6,9
Manhattan Av	H-9	9
Maple Av	J-9	6,9
Mariann Pl	H-9	9
McKinley Av	H-9	9
Meisten St	H-9	9
Melba Wy	H-9	9
Monroe Av	H-9	9
Morgan Ct	H-10	9
Mountain Av	J-9	6,9
Mountain Av	H-9	9
Northgate Rd	H-9	9
Oakwood Av	H-9	9
Oxford Pl	H-9	9
Palm St	H-9	9
Park Pl	H-9	9
Park Pl	H-10	9
Parkway Ct	J-8	6,9
Parkway Ct	J-9	6,9
Pascack Rd	H-9	9
Pershing Av	J-9	6,9
Pine Lake Dr	H-9	9
Pine Lake Dr	J-9	6,9
Pond Ter	J-9	6,9
Pond Ct	J-9	6,9
Pond Dr	J-9	6,9
President Rd	J-9	6,9
Prospect Av	J-9	6,9
Reagan Wy	H-9	9
Ridgewood Blvd	H-9	9
Ridgewood Rd	J-9	6,9
Roberts Ct	J-8	6,9
Robinwood Rd	H-9	9
Ruby Ct	H-10	9
Salem Rd	H-8	9
School St	H-9	9
South Chestnut St	H-9	9
Spice Dr	H-9	9
Spruce Av	H-9	9
Standish Rd	J-8	6,9
Stratford Ct	H-9	9
Sunset Ln	H-10	9
Sussex Rd	H-9	9
Sutton Ct	J-9	6,9
Sycamore Ln	H-9	9
Taylor Rd	H-8	9
Taylor St	H-10	9
Times Sq	H-9	9
Tulane Ct	H-9	9
Valley Ct	H-9	9
Van Emburgh Av	H-8	9
Van Pl	H-9	9
Viola Ter	H-9	9
Walnut St	H-9	9
Walnut St	J-9	6,9
Washington Av	H-8	9
Washington Av	H-9	9
Wayne Pl	H-9	9
Webster Av	J-9	6,9
West Pl	H-9	9
Westgate Rd	H-9	9
White Beeches Dr	H-9	9
White Birch Rd	H-9	9
Willow St	H-9	9
Wilson Av	H-9	9
Winchester Ct	H-9	9
Windsor Cir	H-9	9
Woodbury Ct	H-9	9
Woodfield Rd	H-9	9
Yorktown Ct	H-9	9

Westwood, Boro of

STREET	GRID	MAP
1st Av.	H-10	9
2nd Av	H-10	9
3rd Av	J-10	6,9
4th Av	J-10	6,9
5th Av	H-10	9
6th Av	H-10	9
7th Av	H-10	9
8th Av	H-10	9
Ackerman Av	J-10	6,9
Addicks Rd	J-10	6,9
Alvin St	H-11	8
Ash St	H-10	9
Beech St	H-10	9
Benson Av	H-11	8
Berdais Ct	H-10	9
Bergen St	H-10	9
Bergenline Av	J-11	7,8
Berkeley Av	H-10	9
Berkeley Av	H-11	8
Best St	H-11	8
Bogert Av	H-10	9
Bogert Pl	H-10	9
Booker St	J-11	7,8
Boulevard	H-10	9
Brickell Av	H-10	9
Broadway	H-10	9
Brook Pl	H-11	8
Brookline Av	H-10	9
Brookside Av	H-10	9
Bryant Pl	H-11	8
Bryant Pl	H-10	9
Burger Pl	J-10	6,9
Burger Pl	J-9	6,9
Cardinal Ln	J-10	6,9
Carl Pl	J-10	6,9
Carolyn St	H-10	9
Carver Av	J-11	7,8
Cedar Ln	H-11	8
Center Av	H-10	9
Charles St	J-11	7,8
Chestnut St	H-11	8
Clairmont Av	H-10	9
Clinton Av	H-10	9
Cottage Pl	J-10	6,9
Cottage Pl	H-10	9
Crest St	J-11	7,8
Cypress St	H-10	9
David Hooper Pl	H-10	9
Dean St	H-11	8
Dogwood	J-10	6,9
Douglas St	J-11	7,8
Elm St	H-10	9
Emerson Rd	J-11	7,8
Emwood Av	J-10	6,9
Euclid Av	H-10	9
Fairview Av	H-10	9
Fern St	H-11	8
Fitzgerald Av	H-10	9
Forest Av Ext	J-10	6,9
Garden Pl	H-10	9
Garfield Av	H-10	9
Gladys Pl	H-10	9
Gladys Pl	J-10	6,9
Glenn Ct	H-10	9
Goodwin Ter	H-10	9
Grand St	H-10	9
Green Av	J-10	6,9
Gritman Ct	J-10	6,9
Grove St	H-10	9
Harding Av	H-10	9
Harrington Av	H-10	9
Harrington Av	H-11	8
Hart St	H-11	8
Harvard Pl	H-10	9
Hegeman Av	H-11	8
High St	H-11	8
Hillcrest Av	J-10	6,9
Hillside Av	H-10	9
Hooper St	J-11	7,8
Hopper Av	J-11	7,8
Hoyer Av	H-11	8
Hudson St	J-11	7,8
Hudson St	H-11	8
Hurlbut St	H-10	9
Irvington St	H-10	9
James St	J-10	6,9
James St	H-10	9
Jefferson Av	H-10	9
Jones St	H-11	8
Kaufman Dr	H-11	8
Kaufman Rd	H-11	8
Kennedy Ter	H-10	9
Kinderkamack Rd	H-10	9
Kingsberry Av	J-10	6,9
Kingsberry Av	H-10	9
Lafayette Av	H-10	9
Lafayette Av	J-10	6,9
Lafayette Ter	H-10	9
Lake Dr	J-10	6,9
Lake St	H-10	9
Langner Pl	J-10	6,9
Lester Av	J-10	6,9
Lewis Pl	H-11	8
Lexington Av	H-10	9
Lincoln Av	H-10	9
Lincoln Blvd	J-10	6,9
Linden Av	H-10	9
Lindenmann Ln	H-10	9
Lockerby Ln	H-11	8
Lotus St	H-10	9
Lowell St	H-10	9
Lowell St	H-11	8
Lyons Pl	H-11	8
Madison Av	H-10	9
Maple Av	H-10	9
Maulbeck Av	J-11	7,8
McDaniels St	H-11	8
McKinley Av	H-10	9
Meadow Rd	J-10	6,9
Meyer Pl	H-11	8
Mill St	H-10	9
Mountain Av	H-10	9
Newark Av	H-10	9
Nugent Pl	H-10	9
O'Donnell St	H-11	8
O'Neill Ct	J-10	6,9
O'Toole St	J-10	6,9
Oakland Av	H-10	9
Old Hook Rd	H-11	8
Old Hook Rd	H-10	9
Palisade Av	H-11	8
Palm St	H-11	8
Park Av	H-10	9
Park Pl	H-10	9
Pascack Rd	H-11	8
Passmore St	J-11	7,8
Pine St	H-10	9
Pleasant Av	H-11	8
Polin Pl	H-10	9
Princeton Pl	H-10	9
Prospect Av	H-10	9
Repetti St	J-10	6,9
Ring Rose Ct	H-10	9
Roosevelt Av	H-10	9
Ruckner Rd	J-10	6,9
Saint Nicholas Av	H-10	9
Sand Rd	H-11	8
Scott Pl	J-10	6,9
Sealy St	J-10	6,9
Siemers Ln	J-10	6,9
Spring St	H-11	8
Spring St	J-11	7,8
Steinbach Pl	J-10	6,9
Steuben Av	H-10	9
Stratton Av	H-10	9
Sullivan St	J-11	7,8
Summit Av	H-10	9
Sutton Pl	H-10	9
Sycamore Ct	J-10	6,9
Taco Av	J-10	6,9
Terrace Dr	H-10	9
Thompson St	H-11	8
Tillman St	J-11	7,8
Trenton Av	H-10	9
Valley Av	H-10	9
Van Buren Av	J-11	7,8
Van Buren Pl	J-11	7,8
Ward Av	J-10	6,9
Washington Av	H-10	9
Wellington Pl	H-10	9
West End Av	H-10	9
Westervelt Pl	H-10	9
Westwood Av	H-10	9
Westwood Blvd	H-11	8
Wheeler Av	H-10	9
Whelan Ct	J-10	6,9
William St	J-10	6,9
Woodcliff Av	J-10	6,9
Woodland Av	J-11	7,8
Woodland Cross	H-10	9
Woodside Av	J-10	6,9
Yale Pl	H-10	9

Wood-Ridge, Boro of

STREET	GRID	MAP
1st St	R-8	2
2nd St	R-8	2
3rd St	R-8	2
4th St	R-8	2
5th St	R-8	2
6th St	R-8	2
7th St	R-8	2
8th St	R-8	2
9th St	R-8	2
10th St	R-8	2
11th St	R-8	2
12th St	R-8	2
13th St	R-8	2
14th St	R-8	2
Anderson St	R-8	2
Arnot Pl	R-8	2
Berger St	R-8	2
Blum Blvd	R-8	2
Burton Pl	R-8	2
Center St	R-8	2
Charter Oak St	R-8	2
Cliff St	R-8	2
Columbia Blvd	R-8	2
Columbia St	R-8	2
Concord St	R-8	2
Division St	R-8	2
Ethel Blvd	R-8	2
Floral Ln	R-8	2
Franklin St	R-8	2
Fritsch Av	R-8	2
Garden St	R-8	2
Hackensack St	R-8	2
Helm Av	Q-8	2,5
Highland Av	R-8	2
Hill St	R-8	2
Hillcrest Av	R-8	2
Humbolt St	R-8	2
Industrial Rd	R-8	2
Innes Rd	Q-8	2,5
Innes Rd	R-8	2
Jay St	R-8	2
Jefferson St	R-8	2
Jocelyn Av	Q-8	2,5
Laurel Dr	R-8	2
Madison St	R-8	2
Main Av	R-8	2
Marlboro Rd	R-8	2
Moonachie Av	R-8	2
North Av	R-8	2
Oak St	R-8	2
Palmer Ter	R-8	2
Park Pl E	R-8	2
Park Pl W	R-8	2
Rose St	R-8	2
Ryerson Av	R-8	2
Sussex Rd	Q-8	2,5
Sussex Rd	R-8	2
Terhune St	Q-8	2,5
Union Av	R-8	2
Union St	R-8	2
Valley Blvd	R-8	2
Washington St	R-8	2
Way St	R-8	2
Willow St	R-8	2
Windsor Rd	Q-8	2,5
Windsor Rd	R-8	2
Woodbridge Av	R-8	2
Woodridge St	R-8	2

Woodcliff Lake, Boro of

STREET	GRID	MAP
Ackerman Av	G-10	9
Allen Dr	G-9	9
Amy Ct	G-10	9
Anderson Ct	G-9	9
Andrea Ct	E-8	12
Angela Ct	G-9	9
Angela Dr	G-9	9
Anton Ct	F-10	9,12
Apple Ridge	F-8	9
Apple Ridge	G-8	9
Arcadia Rd	F-9	9,12
Avon Pl	F-9	9,12
Balsam Rd	G-9	9
Bear Brook Dr	F-9	9,12
Bedford Rd	F-9	9,12
Benjamin Ct	F-9	9,12
Berkshire Rd	F-9	9,12
Birchwood Dr	F-9	9,12
Blueberry Dr	G-8	9
Bree Ct	G-9	9
Briarwood Ct	F-9	9,12
Broadway	F-10	9,12
Brookview Dr	G-9	9
Burlington Pl	G-9	9
Cambridge Rd	F-9	9,12
Campbell Av	G-10	9
Carnot Av	F-10	9,12
Carriage Ln	F-10	9,12
Carrington Ct	F-9	9,12
Centennial Way	E-8	12
Chestnut Ridge Rd	F-9	9,12
Chestnut Ridge Rd	G-8	9
Chestnut Ridge Rd	E-9	12
Chestnut Ridge Rd	E-9	12
Church Rd	G-10	9
Church Rd	G-9	9
Claire Cir	G-9	9
Clairmont Dr	F-9	9,12
Clinton Pl	F-10	9,12
Coles Crossing Rd	G-10	9
Colonial Ct	G-9	9
County Rd	F-8	9,12
Cressfield Ct	G-10	9
Cricket Ln	F-10	9,12
Daniel Ct	G-9	9
David Ln	G-9	9
Deborah Ct	G-8	9
Deer Run Ct	G-9	9
Deerfield Dr	F-9	9,12
Dennis Ct	F-9	9,12
Diane Ct	E-9	12
Dorchester Rd	F-9	9,12
Douglas Ter	F-9	9,12
Eagle Hill Rd	F-10	9,12
Eagle Hill Rd	F-9	9,12
Edgehill Ct	F-10	9,12
Edward Pl	F-10	9,12
Elane Ct	E-8	12
Ellis Ln	F-10	9,12
Elm Ter	F-10	9,12
Emery Ln	G-9	9
Evan Ct	F-9	9,12
Evergreen St	G-10	9
Fairview Av	F-9	9,12
Fairview Av	G-9	9
Fern St	G-9	9
Fieldstone Ct	F-9	9,12
Fox Hollow Ct	F-9	9,12
Franklin St	F-10	9,12
Garden State Pkwy	G-9	9
Gary Ct	G-9	9
Ginny Dr	G-8	9
Glen Rd	F-9	9,12
Greenway Ct	G-8	9
Harvest Ct	F-9	9,12
Hathaway Ct	G-9	9
Heather Hill Ln	F-9	9,12
Heather Hill Ln	G-9	9
Heidi Ln	F-9	9,12
Henke Ct	F-10	9,12
Heritage Ct	G-9	9
Highview Av	G-10	9
Hillcrest Av	F-9	9,12
Holly Ct	E-9	12
Hunter Ridge	G-8	9
Hunter Ridge	G-9	9
Indian Dr	G-8	9
Indian Dr	G-9	9
James St	F-10	9,12
Kenwood Dr	G-9	9
Kinderkamack Rd	F-10	9,12
Kinderkamack Rd	G-10	9
Kings Ct	G-10	9
Knollwood Rd	G-9	9
Knollwood Rd	G-8	9
Lakeview Ter	F-10	9,12
Leonard Ct	F-9	9,12
Leone Ct	F-9	9,12
Lincoln Av	G-10	9
Linda Ter	G-10	9
London Ct	G-9	9
Longwood Ct	G-9	9
Lori Ct	G-9	9
Lynn Ct	F-9	9,12
Lyons Ct	G-9	9
Mallard Av	G-10	9
Maple Hill Rd	F-9	9,12
Maria Rd	G-8	9
Marjo Ct	F-9	9,12
Martha St	G-10	9
Marz Dr	G-9	9
Michael St	G-10	9
Mill Rd	F-10	9,12
Mill Rd Ext	G-9	9
Mill Rd Ext	G-8	9
Natmark Ct	G-10	9
Nowak Ct	F-10	9,12
Oak Av	G-9	9
Oak St	G-10	9
Oakwood Dr	F-9	9,12
Old English Ct	G-9	9
Old Farm Rd	F-8	9,12
Old Mill Rd	G-9	9
Old Pascack Rd	G-9	9
Olde Woods Rd	F-9	9,12
Orchard St	F-10	9,12
Orchard St	G-10	9
Overlook Dr	F-9	9,12
Park Ridge Rd	G-11	8
Pascack Rd	G-9	9
Paulith St	F-9	9,12
Pickwick Ln	E-8	12
Pickwick Ln	F-8	9,12
Pinecrest Dr	G-9	9
Pond Rd	F-9	9,12
Princeton Dr	F-9	9,12
Prospect Av	G-10	9
Ravine Dr	F-9	9,12
Reeds Ln	G-9	9
Renee Ct	G-10	9
Rodger Ct	F-9	9,12
Rose Av	F-9	9,12
Ruckman Rd	F-9	912
Rutgers Ct	F-9	9,12
Saddle River Rd	F-9	9,12
Shaw Av	F-9	9,12
Shields Dr	G-8	9
Sibbald Dr	F-10	9,12
Somerset Dr	F-9	9,12
Sophie Ct	F-9	9,12
South Carnot Av	F-9	9,12
South Carnot Av	G-9	9
Springhouse Rd	G-9	9
Stacey Ct	F-9	9,12
Stephen Ct	F-9	9,12
Stonewall Ct	E-8	12
Stratford Ct	F-9	9,12
Sturbridge Dr	F-10	9,12
Sycamore Dr	G-8	9
Sylvia Ct	F-9	9,12
Taft Ct	G-9	9
Tamarack Dr	F-9	9,12
Taryn Ct	E-9	12
Thomas Ct	F-9	9,12
Tice Blvd	E-8	12
Van Riper Ln	G-9	9
Welter Av	G-9	9
Welter Pl	G-9	9
Welter Pl	G-10	9
Werimus Rd	F-9	9,12
Werimus Rd	G-9	9
West Hill Rd	G-9	9
Wierimus Ln	G-9	9
Wildwood Rd	F-9	9,12
Willow St	G-10	9
Willow St	G-9	9
Windham Ct	F-9	9,12
Winding Wy	F-9	9,12
Winthrop Dr	F-9	9,12
Woodcliff Av	G-9	9
Woodcliff Av	G-10	9
Woodcrest Dr	E-8	12
Woodland Dr	F-9	9,12
Woodland Rd	F-9	9,12
Woodmont Dr	E-8	12
Wright St N	G-9	9
Wright St S	G-9	9
Wyandemere Dr	F-9	9,12
Zononi St	G-10	9

Wyckoff, Twp of

STREET	GRID	MAP
Ackerson Av	H-4	10
Adams Ct	G-5	10
Albemarle St	J-4	10
Albert St	J-5	10
Albright St	H-6	9
Allison Wy	H-5	10
Amherst St	H-6	9
Amherst St	J-6	6,9
Andover St	H-6	9
Annette Ct	J-5	10
Annette Ct	H-5	10
Anthony Pl	G-5	10
Aspen Ln	G-4	10
Atwood Pl	H-5	10
Auburn St	H-6	9
Auburn St	J-6	6,9
Barbara Av	H-4	10
Barnstable Dr	J-5	10
Barnstable Rd	J-5	10
Barrett Ln	G-5	10
Barrister Ct	G-5	10
Baxter Av	J-6	6,9
Beekman St	J-4	10
Berkekey Dr	H-4	10
Beth Ln	G-5	10
Birch Pkwy	G-5	10
Birchwood Dr	J-4	10
Bluehill Ter	F-5	10,11
Bluehill Ter	G-5	10
Blum Ct	J-5	10
Bohny Dr	H-5	10
Booth Ct	H-5	10
Brewster Rd	J-5	10
Briarwood Dr	J-4	10
Bromley Pl	G-5	10
Brook Rd	H-5	10
Brookside Av	G-5	10
Brookside Av	F-5	10,11
Brownstone Ct	H-5	10
Buckingham Cir	H-5	10
Buena Vista Wy	G-4	10
Burma Rd	H-6	9
Burritt Pl	G-4	10
Bush Ln	J-6	6,9
Butternut Av	H-6	9
Caldwell Dr	H-5	10
Calvin Ct	H-5	10
Camelot Ct	J-4	10
Canterbury Ln	H-5	10
Carlton Rd	G-4	10
Carriage Ln	H-5	10
Cedar Ct	H-5	10
Cedar Hill Av	J-5	10
Cedar Hill Av	H-5	10
Central Av	G-5	10
Chapman Pl	H-4	10
Charles Av	G-4	10
Charnwood Dr	J-4	10
Charnwood Dr	H-4	10
Cherry Ln	H-5	10
Chestnut St	H-4	10
Circle Dr	J-5	10
Circle Dr	H-5	10
Clinton Av	G-4	10
Clover Ln	H-5	10
Coe Av	J-6	6,9
Colgate Av	J-5	10
Colgate Av	J-6	6,9
Colona St	G-5	10
Colonial Dr	G-5	10
Colony Ct	H-5	10
Concord Pl	H-4	10
Concord Pl	G-4	10
Coolidge Ter	J-5	10
Cornell St	J-5	10
Cornwall Ct	H-4	10
Cornwall Ct	G-4	10
Cottage Ct	H-5	10
Cottage Ct	J-5	10
Coudert Pl	H-4	10
Covington Pl	G-4	10
Crankshaw Pl	H-4	10
Crescent Av	G-5	10
Cresthaven Rd	G-4	10
Cull Ln	G-5	10
Cumberland Ct	H-5	10
Curran Pl	G-4	10
Dale Av	G-6	9
Daniel Ct	J-5	10
Dartmouth St	H-6	9
Dartmouth St	J-6	6,9
Deepbrook Rd	J-5	10
Deerfield Rd	H-6	9
Demarest Av	G-5	10
Domm Ct	G-5	10
Dorothy Ln	H-5	10
Drake Rd	G-5	10
Drury Ln	H-5	10
Durham Rd	J-4	10
East Stevens Av	G-5	10
East Stevens Av	H-5	10
Eastview Ter	H-5	10
Eder Av	H-4	10
Edgewood Av	G-5	10
Edison St	G-5	10
Edward St	G-5	10
Eisenhower Ct	H-5	10
Ellis Pl	H-5	10
Elmwood Pl	H-5	10
Eugene Pl	H-4	10
Eugene Pl	H-5	10
Eugene Way	H-5	10
Everett Av	G-5	10
Evergreen Dr	H-4	10
Evers St	H-5	10
Fairfield Rd	G-4	10
Fairmount Rd	G-4	10
Fairview Av	H-4	10
Fairview Ct	H-4	10
Fairview Pl	G-4	10
Farwin Ct	H-4	10
Fern Av	G-5	10
Flaker Dr	J-5	10
Florence Av	H-5	10
Fordham Av	J-5	10
Fordham Av	J-6	6,9
Forest Av	G-5	10
Fox Hollow Rd	J-5	10
Frances Pl	H-5	10
Franklin Av	G-4	10
Franklin Av	G-5	10
Franklin Ter	J-5	10
Frederick Ct	J-4	10
Frost Ct	G-5	10
Gaewood Dr	G-4	10
George Pl	H-4	10
Gerard Dr	G-6	9
Giegel Ct	J-6	6,9
Girard Av	J-5	10
Glen Dr	H-5	10
Glendale Rd	H-5	10
Godwin Av	F-5	10,11
Godwin Av	G-5	10
Goffle Rd	J-6	6,9
Grandview Av	J-5	10
Greenhaven Rd	H-5	10
Greenwood Av	G-5	10
Hamden Ct	H-4	10
Hampshire Ct	H-5	10
Harding Rd	G-5	10
Hartung Dr	G-4	10
Harvard Av	J-6	6,9
Harvest Ct	H-4	10
Harvey Ct	G-5	10
Hazel St	H-5	10
Heights Rd	H-5	10
Helena Av	H-4	10
Henry Pl	H-5	10
Hickory Hill Rd	J-4	10
Hidden Valley Ct	G-5	10
High Meadow Ct	J-4	10
High St	G-5	10
Highland Av	G-5	10
Highview Dr	J-4	10
Hill Pl	J-6	6,9
Hill Ray Av	J-6	6,9
Hillcrest Av	H-5	10
Hillside Av	H-5	10
Hilltop Ln	J-5	10
Holly Dr	J-4	10
Hopper Av	J-6	6,9
Howard St	G-6	9
Hummingbird Ct	H-6	9
Hurley Av	G-5	10
Hurley Av	H-5	10
Ivy Ln	H-4	10
Jacqueline Dr	G-5	10
James Wy	H-5	10
James Wy	H-4	10
Janice Ct	J-4	10
Joan Pl	G-5	10
John St	J-5	10
Joshua Ln	G-5	10
Karen Pl	J-5	10
Katherine St	J-5	10
Kay Ln	J-4	10
Kelly Ct	H-4	10
Kennedy Ct	H-4	10
Kenneth Pl	H-5	10
Kingston St	J-6	6,9
Krysch Ln	G-5	10
Laauwe Pl	J-5	10
Lafayette Av	J-5	10
Lake Rd	G-5	10
Lake View Dr	H-5	10
Landi Ct	G-5	10
Laurel Ln	H-4	10
Lavelle Ct	H-5	10
Lawlins Rd	G-4	10
Lawrence Ct	G-5	10
Lebanon St	J-6	6,9
Lee Ct	G-4	10
Lehigh St	J-6	6,9
Leonard Dr	G-6	9
Liberty St	J-6	6,9
Lincoln Av	J-6	6,9
Linden St	G-5	10
Lisa Ct	G-5	10
Logan Ln	G-5	10
Long Dr	H-4	10
Louisa Av	J-6	6,9
Lucas Ln	G-5	10
Lydia Ln	H-4	10
Lynch Pl	J-6	6,9
Lyons St	G-6	9
Madison Av	G-5	10
Madison Av	H-5	10
Madison Heights	H-5	10
Madowbrook Rd	G-5	10
Main St	G-5	10
Manchester Wy	H-5	10
Manchester Wy	J-5	10
Manor Rd	G-5	10
Manor Rd	G-6	9
Maple Av	G-4	10
Maple Dr	H-5	10
Maple St	H-5	10
Marginal Strip	H-5	10
Marr Av	J-6	6,9
Martom Rd	H-5	10
Maryann Ln	J-6	6,9
Mason Av	G-5	10
Massey Ct	H-4	10
Meek Av	H-5	10
Meer Ave	H-5	10
Merlin Pl	H-5	10
Merrywood Dr	J-4	10
Merrywood Dr	J-5	10
Midland Av	H-5	10
Midland Av	G-6	9
Miller Ct	H-4	10
Miller Rd	H-4	10
Mills Pl	H-5	10
Monroe Av	H-5	10
Morley Dr	G-6	9
Morse Av	G-5	10
Mountain Av	H-5	10
Mountain Av	J-4	10
Mulberry Ct	H-4	10
Mystic Ct	G-5	10
Nancy Ln	J-5	10
Navajo Dr	G-5	10
Neelen Dr	H-5	10
New York Av	J-5	10
Newton Rd	H-5	10
Norma St	H-4	10
Norma St	H-5	10
Nydam Ln	G-5	10
Nydam Ln	F-5	10,11
O'Brien Ct	F-5	10,11
Oak Av	H-5	10
Oakwood Dr	G-5	10

BERGEN COUNTY

STREET	GRID	MAP
Old Mill Ln	H-5	10
Old Post Rd	G-5	10
Old Woods Rd	G-4	10
Orchard Rd	H-5	10
Overlook Dr	G-4	10
Pace Dr	H-5	10
Packard Av	H-5	10
Paine Rd	H-5	10
Park Av	G-6	9
Parmley	G-5	10
Parmley	G-4	10
Pathway Manor	H-5	10
Patton Pl	G-5	10
Paul Ct	H-5	10
Pine St	G-5	10
Pinewood Dr	G-5	10
Poplar Ct	G-4	10
Princeton Av	J-6	6,9

STREET	GRID	MAP
Quackenbush Av	G-4	10
Radcliffe St	J-6	6,9
Ralph Av	H-5	10
Ravine Av	J-5	10
Ravine Ct	J-6	6,9
Raymond Ln	J-6	6,9
Richard Pl	H-4	10
Ridge Rd	H-5	10
Ridgewood Av	J-5	10
Robert Ct	H-6	9
Robert Ct	H-6	9
Robertson Dr	J-5	10
Robin Pl	G-4	10
Rodney Rd	G-5	10
Roger Ct	G-5	10
Ruitfarm Rd	J-4	10
Russell Av	H-4	10
Rutgers Ct	J-6	6,9

STREET	GRID	MAP
S. Woodfield Dr	G-4	10
Samuel Wy	H-5	10
Saw Mill Ln	H-5	10
Saxonia Av	G-5	10
Schlenz Ct	G-5	10
Shady Ln	G-5	10
Shadyside Dr	G-5	10
Shelbourne Dr	G-5	10
Sheldon St	G-5	10
Sherwood Ln	H-4	10
Sicomac Av	H-4	10
Smith Pl	H-4	10
Snyder Rd	H-5	10
Sparrowbush Rd	G-4	10
Spencer Ct	J-5	10
Spencer Ct	J-6	6,9
Spencer Dr	J-5	10
Spencer Dr	J-6	6,9

STREET	GRID	MAP
Springmeadow Dr	G-4	10
Springmeadow Dr	G-5	10
Squawbrook Rd	J-4	10
Starr Pl	J-5	10
Steinhauser Ln	J-4	10
Stonybrook Ln	H-4	10
Stratton Ct	F-5	10,11
Sturbridge Rd	G-4	10
Sturbridge Rd	G-5	10
Sugar Bush Ct	G-4	10
Sunset Blvd	H-5	10
Sycamore Ct	G-5	10
Sycamore Ct	F-5	10,11
Taunton Rd	G-4	10
Terhune Ter	H-5	10
Terrace Dr	J-6	6,9
Terrace Heights	H-4	10

STREET	GRID	MAP
Terrace Heights Dr	H-4	10
Thomas Pl	J-4	10
Thomas Pl	H-4	10
Timberline Dr	H-4	10
Ullman Av	J-6	6,9
Van Beekum Pl	J-4	10
Van Blarcoms Ln	G-6	9
Van Houten Av	G-5	10
Van Schaik Ln	G-5	10
Van Syckel Ln	G-5	10
Vance Av	H-4	10
Vassar St	J-6	6,9
Victor Wy	H-5	10
Virginia St	J-6	6,9
Voorhis Av	H-5	10
Waddell Ct	G-6	9
Ward Av	G-5	10

STREET	GRID	MAP
Waverly Rd	H-4	10
Wayfair Cir	J-4	10
Wayfair Ln	J-4	10
Weisch Ln	J-5	10
Wellfleet Ln	J-5	10
Wellington Dr	H-4	10
West Main St	G-4	10
West Shore Dr	H-5	10
West Stevens Av	H-5	10
Weymouth Dr	H-4	10
Weymouth Dr	G-4	10
Wiley Pl	G-5	10
William Pl	H-5	10
William Wy	H-5	10
William Wy N	H-4	10
Willow Pond Ct	H-4	10

STREET	GRID	MAP
Willow Run	J-4	10
Wilson Pl	H-5	10
Windham Ct	F-5	10,11
Windham Ct	G-5	10
Windham Ct	F-5	10,11
Wishing Well Rd	G-4	10
Wood St	G-5	10
Woodbury Dr	G-5	10
Woodbury Dr	G-4	10
Woodfield Rd	G-4	10
Woodland Av	G-5	10
Wyckoff Av	H-5	10
Wyckoff Av	J-5	10
Wyckoff Av	G-5	10
Yale St	H-6	9,10

PASSAIC COUNTY

Bloomingdale, Boro of

STREET	GRID	MAP
1st St.	N-8	9
2nd St.	N-8	9
3rd St.	N-9	9
Andrew Av.	M-9	9
Ann St.	M-9	9
Babcock Ln.	N-9	9
Bailey Av.	N-8	9
Ballston Av.	N-9	9
Birch Rd.	M-10	9
Birch St.	N-9	9
Bogue Dr.	M-9	9
Buena Vista Rd.	M-10	9
Captolene Av.	N-9	9
Carmantown Rd.	M-9	9
Carmantown Rd.	L-8	9
Catherine St.	N-8	9
Cedar St.	M-8	9
Charles St.	M-9	9
Chestnut St.	N-9	9
Clark St.	M-8	9
Clubhouse Rd.	M-9	9
Comstock Rd.	M-9	9
Cook Ct.	M-9	9
Crane Av.	N-9	9
Delazier Pl.	N-9	9
Demarest Rd.	L-9	9
Demarest Rd.	M-9	9
Doty Rd.	L-10	9
Dunlap Ln.	M-9	9
E. Buena Vista Way	M-10	9
East Shore Dr.	L-9	9
Elizabeth St.	M-8	9
Elizabeth St.	N-8	9
Ella St.	N-8	9
Elm St.	M-9	9
Fichter St.	M-9	9
Fichter St.	N-9	9
Forest Dr.	N-9	9
Fritz Ln.	M-9	9
George St.	M-8	9
Glen Dr.	M-9	9
Glade Rd.	M-8	9
Glen Rd.	M-9	9
Glenwild Rd.	L-8	9
Glenwild Rd.	M-9	9
Graham Ter.	M-9	9
Grove St.	N-9	9
Hamilton St.	N-9	9
Heather Ln.	M-9	9
Hemlock St.	N-8	9
Henion Pl.	N-9	9
Hester St.	N-8	9
High Point Rd.	M-9	9
High St.	N-9	9
Highland Av.	N-8	9
Highland Rd.	M-9	9
Hillcrest Dr.	M-9	9
Hillside Dr. E.	M-9	9
Hillside Dr. N.	M-9	9
Hillside Dr. S.	M-9	9
Hilltop Ter.	M-9	9
James Av.	M-9	9
James St.	N-8	9
Jeffrey Dr.	M-9	9
Knolls Rd.	M-9	9
Knolls Rd.	N-9	9
Lake Iosco Rd..	M-9	9
Lakeside Av.	M-8	9
Leach Dr.	M-9	9
Leary Av.	N-9	9
Linden Ln.	M-9	9
Macopin	M-8	9
Macopin	N-8	9
Maple Lake Rd.	M-10	9
Maple Av.	N-9	9
Mary St.	N-8	9
Mathews Ter.	M-9	9
Mathews Ter.	N-9	9
McCue Rd.	M-9	9
Memorial Ct.	M-9	9
Michens Ln.	M-9	9
Morse Lake Rd.	M-10	9
Morse Lake Rd.	M-9	9
Mountain Ridge Rd.	M-8	9
Natalie Ct.	M-9	9
North Rd.	L-9	9
Oak St.	N-9	9
Oakwood Ter.	M-9	9
Old Farm Rd.	N-9	9
Old Ridge Rd.	M-8	9
Orchard St.	N-9	9
Park Av.	M-9	9
Paterson-Hamburg Tnpk.	N-9	9
Paterson-Hamburg Tnpk.	N-8	9
Pearl St.	N-9	9
Pine Tree Rd.	M-9	9
Pleasantville Av.	N-9	9
Poplar St.	N-9	9
Provost Ln.	M-9	9
Raffman Rd.	M-9	9
Rafkind Rd.	M-9	9
Rafkind Rd.	N-9	9
Red Twig Tr.	M-8	9
Reeve Av.	N-9	9
Reeve Av.	M-9	9
Ridge Rd.	M-10	9
Roy Av.	M-9	9
Ryerson Av.	N-9	9
Sally St.	N-9	9
Sandra Ln.	M-9	9
Short Rd.	L-9	9
Sisco Pl.	M-9	9
Siscoe Pl.	M-9	9
Sleepy Hollow Rd.	M-9	9
Snake Den Rd.	J-9	6
Sophia St.	N-8	9
South Rd.	M-9	9
South Rd.	L-10	9
Star Lake Rd.	M-8	9
Star Lake Rd.	N-8	9
Star Lake Camp Rd.	M-8	9
Sunrise Av.	M-8	9
Sunset Rd.	M-9	9
Sycamore Rd.	M-9	9
Tice St.	N-9	9
Treetop Ct.	M8	9
Union Av.	M-10	9
Union Av.	N-9	9
Vale Rd.	M-9	9
Valleyview St.	N-9	9
Van Dam Av.	N-9	9
Vine Pl.	M-8	9
Vreeland Av.	N-8	9
Vreeland Av.	M-8	9
W. Buena Vista Way	M-10	9
Wallace Av.	N-9	9
Walnut St.	N-9	9
Walter Dr.	M-9	9
Walter Dr.	M-8	9
Warren St.	N-8	9
Webber St.	N-8	9
West Shore Rd.	L-8	9
Whitehaven Pl.	N-9	9
William St.	N-8	9
Winfield Ct.	M-8	9
Winfield Rd.	J-9	6
Wood Pl.	L-9	9
Woodlot Ct.	M-9	9
Woodlot Rd.	M-9	9
Woodward Av.	N-9	9
Woodward Av.	M-9	9

Clifton, City of

STREET	GRID	MAP
1st St.	W-18	14
2nd St.	W-18	14
3rd St.	W-18	14
4th St.	W-18	14
4th St.	W-17	14
5th Av.	V-17	13
5th St.	W-17	14
6th Av.	V-17	13
6th St.	W-17	14
7th Av.	V-17	13
7th St.	W-17	14
Abbe Ln.	W-16	14
Ackerman Av.	W-19	14
Ackerman Av.	W-18	14
Adams St.	V-17	13
Adams Ter.	W-15	14
Addison Pl.	X-17	14
Albury Rd.	X-16	14
Alfred St.	X-18	14
Allwood Av.	Y-17	14
Allwood Av.	X-16	14
Allwood Pl.	Y-18	14
Allwood Pl.	Y-17	14
Althea St.	Y-18	14
Althea St.	Y-17	14
Alvin Ct.	Y-17	14
Alyea Ter.	W-18	14
Anderson Rd.	X-16	14
Ann St.	X-18	14
Annabelle Av.	X-18	14
Arcadia Ln.	X-16	14
Ardmore Av.	Y-17	14
Arlington Av.	W-18	14
Arlington Pl.	V-18	14
Arlington Pl.	W-18	14
Arthur St.	W-18	14
Arthur St.	W-19	14
Ash St.	W-18	14
Athenia Av.	W-17	14
Atkins Ct.	W-16	14
Austin Pl.	Z-18	14
Autumn St.	Y-18	14
Avondale Av.	X-16	14
Avondale Av.	W-16	14
Baker Ct.	V-18	13
Barbara Dr.	W-16	14
Barberry Ln.	X-16	14
Barkley Av.	W-18	14
Barkley Av.	W-17	14
Barnsdale Rd.	X-17	14
Barrington Av.	W-18	14
Bart Pl.	W-16	14
Beech St.	Z-18	14
Belgrade Av.	V-16	13
Belmont Av.	Y-18	14
Belrose Ct.	X-17	14
Bender Dr.	W-16	14
Bennington Ct.	X-17	14
Bergen Av.	V-18	13
Beverly Hill Rd.	X-17	14
Birchwood Ter.	Y-17	14
Bird Av.	X-18	14
Blanjen Ter.	Z-18	14
Bloomfield Av.	Y-17	14
Blue Hill Rd.	W-16	14
Bobbink Ct.	W-16	14
Bogert Pl.	X-16	14
Boll St.	Z-18	14
Book Ct.	Y-17	14
Botany Pl.	W-19	14
Bowdoin St.	X-17	14
Brannan Ct.	W-16	14
Brantwood Pl.	X-16	14
Breen Ct.	W-16	14
Breezy Hill Ct.	X-16	14
Bridewell Pl.	Z-18	14
Brighton Rd.	Y-17	14
Brighton Rd.	X-17	14
Broad St.	V-17	14
Broad St.	X-16	13
Broad St.	V-17	13
Broad St.	X-16	14
Broad St.	W-17	13
Broad St.	W-17	14
Broadale Rd.	X-16	14
Broadale Rd.	W-16	14
Brook Hill Ter.	W-16	14
Brookside Dr.	X-16	14
Brookwood Rd.	X-17	14
Brower Av.	W-16	14
Brown Av.	W-18	14
Bruan Pl.	X-16	14
Bruan Pl.	X-17	14
Burgess Pl.	W-18	14
Burgh Av.	W-18	14
Burlington Rd.	Y-17	14
Butler St.	V-17	13
Buttel Dr.	X-16	14
Byron Pl.	X-18	14
Campbell Av.	X-17	14
Canterbury Ct.	W-16	14
Carline Dr.	X-16	14
Carol Ln.	Y-17	14
Carol St.	Z-19	14
Carol St.	Y-19	14
Caroline Av.	W-18	14
Cathay Rd.	V-16	13
Cathedral Av.	Z-17	14
Cedar Pl.	Y-18	14
Cedar Pl.	Z-18	14
Center St.	W-19	14
Center St.	W-18	14
Central Av.	W-18	14
Century Dr.	Z-18	14
Chamberlin Av.	X-17	14
Chambers Ct.	V-16	13
Champlin Ct.	Y-17	14
Charlene Dr.	X-16	14
Charles Ct.	X-16	14
Charles St.	X-16	14
Chatham Ter.	X-16	14
Chaytor St.	W-17	14
Cheever Av.	W-19	14
Chelsea Rd.	Y-17	14
Cherry St.	Y-18	14
Chester St.	V-18	13
Chestnut St.	V-17	13
Chitteden Rd.	X-16	14
Chrisbar Dr.	X-16	14
Christie Av.	V-18	13
Churchill Dr.	X-16	14
Circle Av.	V-17	13
Clair St.	W-17	14
Clairmont Rd.	X-17	14
Claverack Rd.	W-16	14
Clay St.	Z-18	14
Cliff Hill Rd.	W-16	14
Clifton Av.	W-18	14
Clifton Av.	X-16	14
Clifton Av.	X-17	14
Clifton Av.	W-17	14
Clifton Blvd.	W-17	14
Clifton Blvd.	X-18	14
Clifton Ter.	W-17	14
Clinton Av.	W-18	14
Cloverdale Rd.	W-17	14
Cloverdale Rd.	X-17	14
Colfax Av.	W-17	14
Colin Av.	Y-17	14
Collura La.	Y-17	14
Colonial Ct.	W-17	14
Colorado St.	Z-18	14
Columbia St.	V-18	13
Combee Ln.	Y-17	14
Comfort Pl.	X-18	14
Concord St.	V-16	13
Conklin Dr.	W-16	14
Conover Ct.	Y-18	14
Coppola Ct.	W-16	14
Costello Pl.	V-18	13
Cottage Ct.	Y-17	14
Cottage Ln.	X-16	14
Country Ln.	X-16	14
Coyles Ct.	X-16	14
Craig Pl.	W-16	14
Cresthill Av.	Y-18	14
Cresthill Av.	Y-17	14
Crooks Av.	V-18	13
Crooks Av.	V-17	13
Cross St.	X-16	14
Curie Av.	V-18	13
Cutler St.	W-18	14
Dalewood Rd.	X-17	14
Dan St.	X-18	14
Dando Ct.	X-16	14
Daniels Dr.	X-16	14
Davidson St.	W-19	14
Dawson Av.	X-17	14
Dawson Av.	X-18	14
Day St.	W-17	13
Day St.	V-17	13
Day St.	W-17	14
Day St.	V-17	14
De Graw Av.	W-16	14
De Mott Av.	W-18	14
De Mott Av.	W-17	14
Delawanna Av.	Z-18	14
Delaware St.	W-17	14
Dewey Av.	V-16	13
Dick St.	X-18	14
Dinne Ct.	X-16	14
Doherty Dr.	X-16	14
Donald St.	V-17	13
Donna Dr.	X-17	14
Donnalin Pl.	W-16	14
Doremus Pl.	X-17	14
Doremus Pl.	W-17	14
Duane Rd.	X-17	14
Dumont Av.	V-16	13
Durant Av.	W-19	14
Dwas Line Rd.	Y-17	14
Dwas Line Rd.	Y-18	14
Dwight Ter.	X-16	14
Dyer Av.	Z-18	14
Earnshaw Pl.	X-16	14
East 11th St.	V-18	13
East1st St.	V-18	13
East2nd St.	V-18	13
East3rd St.	V-18	13
East4th St.	V-18	13
East5th St.	V-18	13
East6th St.	V-18	13
East7th St.	V-18	13
East8th St.	V-18	13
East9th St.	V-18	13
East Clifton Av.	W-18	14
East Emerson St.	V-16	13
East Gate St.	W-16	14
East Madison Av.	W-18	14
East Pkwy.	Y-18	14
Edgewood Av.	Y-18	14
Edgewood Av.	Y-17	14
Edison Ct.	V-16	13
Edwards Ct.	V-17	13
Edwards Rd.	X-15	14
Edwards Rd.	X-16	14
Ehrle Pl.	X-16	14
Eldridge St.	V-16	13
Elemay Pl.	W-18	14
Ellsworth St.	X-17	14
Elm Hill Rd.	W-16	14
Elm St.	W-17	14
Elmwood Dr.	V-16	13
Emerson St.	V-16	13
Emma Pl.	X-17	14
Englewood Rd.	Y-17	14
Entin Rd.	Z-18	14
Entin Rd.	Z-19	14
Essex St.	Z-18	14
Everson Pl.	W-16	14
Exchange Pl.	W-19	14
Fair Hill Rd.	W-16	14
Fairfield Rd.	X-16	14
Fairmount Av.	W-17	14
Federal St.	W-18	14
Fenlon Blvd.	Y-18	14
Fenner Av.	V-16	13
Ferncliff St.	W-17	14
Fernhill Rd.	W-16	14
Fernwood Ct.	V-17	13
Fernwood Ln.	V-17	13
Ferris Dr.	W-16	14
Field Rd.	X-16	14
Filmore St.	Y-19	14
Fitzgerald Av.	W-17	14
Fleischer Pl.	W-19	14
Florence Dr.	V-17	13
Fordham Rd.	V-16	13
Forest Wy.	X-17	14
Fornelius Av.	W-17	14
Foster St.	W-18	14
Fountain St.	W-18	14
Frair Ln.	X-16	14
Frances St.	Y-18	14
Franklin Av.	W-18	14
Frederick Av.	V-16	13
Frost Ct.	X-17	14
Gail Ct.	X-17	14
Garden Ct.	X-17	14
Garfield Av.	Y-18	14
Garrabrant Rd.	W-16	14
Garret Ct.	W-16	14
Garrettsee Pl.	W-18	14
George St.	V-17	14
Gerald Av.	X-17	14
Getty Av.	W-18	14
Gilbert Pl.	W-18	14
Gillies St.	V-16	13
Gleeson Dr.	W-16	14
Glen Oaks Ct.	X-17	14
Glenwood St.	X-17	14
Godwin Pl.	X-17	14
Gordon St.	V-18	13
Goss Pl.	W-16	14
Gould St.	V-16	13
Gould Ter.	X-16	14
Gourley Av.	V-16	13
Grace Av.	W-18	14
Graham Pl.	W-16	14
Grandview Pl.	W-17	14
Grant Av.	W-17	14
Graydon Ter.	X-16	14
Green Meadow Ln.	W-17	14
Green Tree Dr.	W-17	14
Greenbrier Ct.	Y-17	14
Greendale Rd.	X-17	14
Greenlawn Av.	W-16	14
Greenlawn Av.	X-16	14
Greglawn Dr.	W-16	14
Gregory Av.	W-18	14
Grove St.	X-16	14
Grove St.	W-16	14
Grunwald St.	W-18	14
Hackberry Pl.	X-17	14
Haddenfield Rd.	X-16	14
Hadley Av.	W-18	14
Hadrys Ct.	X-17	14
Haines Av.	V-18	13
Hall St.	Z-18	14
Hamas St.	X-17	14
Hamil Ct.	W-16	14
Hamilton Av.	W-18	14
Hammond Av.	W-18	14
Hammond Av.	X-18	14
Hampton Rd.	Y-17	14
Harding Av.	W-17	14
Harding Av.	W-18	14
Harold Pl.	V-17	13
Harrington Rd.	Y-17	14
Harrington Rd.	X-17	14
Harrison Pl.	W-19	14
Harvey Rd.	Y-17	14
Harvey Rd.	X-17	14
Haussler Ter.	X-16	14
Hawthorne Av.	W-17	14
Hazel St.	V-17	13
Hazelview Av.	W-18	14
Hegman Pl.	X-16	14
Heights Rd.	Y-18	14
Helen Pl.	X-18	14
Helen St.	W-17	14
Hemlock St.	X-17	14
Henoch Av.	W-16	14
Henry St.	X-17	14
Hepburn Rd.	Y-16	14
Hibben Pl.	X-15	14
Hickory St.	X-16	14
High Peak Pl.	V-17	13
High St.	Y-18	14
Highland Av.	W-18	14
Highland Dr.	X-16	14
Highview Dr.	X-16	14
Hill Top Ct.	X-17	14
Hillcrest Av.	W-17	14
Hillman St.	W-18	14
Hilton St.	W-18	14
Hobart Pl.	W-17	14
Holden St.	W-18	14
Holly St.	X-17	14
Hollywood Av.	Y-18	14
Hollywood Av.	Z-18	14
Holster Rd.	X-16	14
Homcy Pl.	W-18	14
Home Pl.	W-18	14
Homer St.	Y-18	14
Homestead St.	W-17	14
Hooyman Dr.	X-17	14
Hope Av.	W-19	14
Howard Av.	V-18	13
Howard Av.	X-17	14
Howard Av.	X-18	14
Hudson St.	W-17	14
Huemmer Ter.	X-16	14
Hughes St.	Y-18	14
Hugo St.	Y-17	14
Huron Av.	X-17	14
Hutton Rd.	X-17	14
Independence Ct.	X-16	14
Industrial E.	Y-17	14
Industrial W.	Y-17	14
Inwood St.	V-17	13
Irvington Pl.	W-17	14
Isabella St.	Y-17	14
Ivanhoe Ln.	W-16	14
Ivy Ct.	V-17	13
Jacklin Ct.	X-17	14
James St.	W-19	14
Jani Ct	W-16	14
Janice Ter.	X-16	14
Jaskot Ln.	X-17	14
Jay St.	W-16	14
Jefferson St.	Z-19	14
Jennifer Ct.	W-16	14
Jerome Dr.	V-17	13
Jewett Av.	W-18	14
Jewett Av.	W-17	14
Joan Pl.	X-16	14
John Aldens St.	W-16	14
John St.	W-16	14
John St.	V-16	13
Johnson St.	Z-19	14
Jones Ct.	W-16	14
Josh Ct.	W-17	14
Joyce Ln.	Y-16	14
Karen Dr.	W-16	14
Kashey St.	W-16	14
Katherine Av.	X-17	14
Katherine Av.	X-18	14
Kathryn St.	W-17	14
Kehoe St.	V-18	13
Kennebeck St.	X-17	14
Kennedy Ct.	X-15	14
Kensington Av.	Y-18	14
Kenter Pl.	Y-17	14
Kenyon St.	X-17	14
Kingsland Av.	Z-18	14
Kingsland Rd.	Z-18	14
Kip St.	W-17	14
Knapp Av.	W-18	14
Knoll Pl.	W-16	14
Kowal St.	X-17	14
Kozy Ln.	W-16	14
Kruger Ct.	W-17	14
Kulik St.	W-18	14
Kuller Rd.	V-17	13
La Salle Av.	X-17	14
Ladwik Ln.	X-18	14
Lake Av.	W-18	14
Lake Av.	W-19	14
Lakeview Av.	V-18	14
Lakeview Av.	W-18	14
Lakeview Av.	W-18	13
Lakeview Av.	V-18	13
Lambert Av.	V-16	13
Landis Pl.	X-16	14
Lane	Z-18	14
Larkspur Ln.	X-17	14
Laurel Av.	Y-18	14
Lawrence Ct.	X-16	14
Layton Dr.	W-16	14
Lehigh Av.	Y-18	14
Lennon Pl.	X-16	14
Lester	X-16	14
Lewis Pl.	W-17	14
Lexington Av.	V-18	13
Lexington Av.	V-18	14
Lexington Av.	W-18	14
Lexington Av.	W-18	13
Liberty Ct.	X-17	14
Liberty St.	X-17	14
Lincoln Av.	W-18	14
Lincoln Av.	W-17	14
Lincoln Pl.	W-19	14
Lindale Ct.	X-17	14
Linden Av.	Z-18	14
Linden Av.	Y-18	14
Linwood Ter.	Y-17	14
Lisbon St.	X-17	14
Livingston St.	V-16	13
Lockwood Dr.	V-16	13
Lockwood Pl.	Y-16	14
Lois Av.	Z-18	14
Long Hill Dr.	W-16	14
Loretta St.	W-18	14
Lorraine Dr.	Y-17	14
Lorrie Ln.	Y-18	14
Lotz Hill Rd.	W-16	14
Lou Wong Dr.	Y-17	14
Louis Dr.	V-17	13
Louise St.	V-18	13
Loumar Pl.	Y-18	14
Lowry Ct.	X-16	14
Luddington Av.	W-18	14
Luddington Av.	W-17	14
Luisser St.	X-17	14
Lyall Rd.	Y-17	14
Lydia Pl.	Y-17	14
Lynn Dr.	X-17	14
MacDonald St.	X-17	14
Machias St.	X-17	14
Madeline Av.	V-17	14
Madison Av.	W-17	14
Madison Av.	W-18	14
Mahar Av.	W-18	14
Main Av.	Y-18	14
Main Av.	W-18	14
Major St.	X-17	14
Malcolm Ct.	X-16	14
Mandeville Av.	W-16	14
Manila St.	V-17	13
Manor Dr.	X-16	14
Maple Hill Rd.	W-16	14
Maple Pl.	W-18	14
Maplewood Av.	V-16	13
Marconi St.	X-17	14
Margery Ct.	X-17	14
Marie Pl.	X-17	14
Marilyn Pl.	W-17	14
Market St.	Y-17	14
Marlboro Rd.	Y-17	14
Marrion St.	X-17	14
Martha Av.	W-17	14
Martin Av.	X-17	14
Martindale Rd.	W-16	14
May St.	V-17	13
Mayfair Pl.	V-16	13
Mayflower St.	W-16	14
Mc Clelland Wy.	Y-17	14
McArthur Dr.	X-16	14
McCosh Rd.	X-15	14
McLean Rd.	X-15	14
Meadow Ln.	X-17	14
Melody Hill Rd.	W-16	14
Merrill Rd.	Y-17	14
Merselis Av.	V-18	13
Miller Ct.	Y-17	14
Miller Plz.	Y-17	14
Milosh St.	W-18	14
Milton Av.	X-18	14
Mina Av.	W-18	14
Monhegan St.	X-17	14
Montclair Av.	V-17	13
Montgomery St.	W-17	13
Morris Rd.	Y-17	13
Mount Prospect Av.	V-17	13
Mount Washington Dr.	W-16	13
Mountain Park Rd.	V-16	13
Mountainside Ter.	V-16	13
Mt. Prospect St.	X-17	14
Myron St.	Y-18	14
Myrtle Av.	Z-18	14
Nash Av.	Z-18	13
Nelson St.	V-16	13
Nettie Pl.	Z-19	14
Newbrier Ln.	Y-17	14
Niader Ct.	Y-18	14
Noll Ter	X-16	14
Normal Av.	X-15	14
Norman Av.	V-17	13
Normandy Rd.	W-16	14
North Ct.	W-16	14
Northfield Ter.	X-16	14
Norwood Av.	V-17	13
Notch Rd.	W-16	14
Notch Rd.	W-16	14
Nottingham Rd.	W-16	14
Nugent Dr.	Y-17	13
Oak Ridge Rd.	X-17	14
Oak St.	Z-18	14
Oakwood Ct.	X-17	14
Olga Ter.	X-17	14
Olympia St.	V-17	13
Orange Av.	X-17	13
Orchard Ct.	Y-17	13
Orchard Dr.	Y-17	13
Orchard St.	W-17	13
Oregon St.	V-17	13
Orono St.	X-17	14
Page Rd.	X-17	14
Paranya Ct.	V-16	13
Park Av.	Y-18	14
Park Slope	V-18	13
Park Slope	V-17	13
Park Slope	W-17	14
Park St.	Z-18	14
Parker Av.	W-19	14
Parkhill Ter.	W-16	14
Parkview Ter.	W-18	14
Parkway Av.	W-17	14
Parson Rd.	Y-17	14
Passaic Av.	Y-18	14
Paterson Av.	Z-18	14
Patricia Pl.	Y-18	14
Paulison Av.	W-17	14
Paxton St.	V-16	13
Pearl Brook Dr.	X-15	14
Peekay Dr.	Z-19	14
Pennington Av.	Y-18	14
Penobscot St.	X-17	14
Pershing Rd.	X-17	14
Peru Rd.	Y-17	14
Peterson Ct.	X-16	14
Phyllis Pl.	Y-17	14
Piaget Av.	W-18	14
Piaget Av.	W-17	14
Pilgrim Dr.	W-16	14
Pine Hill Dr.	W-16	14
Pine St.	Z-18	14
Pinebrae Ln.	Y-18	14
Pino Ct.	W-16	14
Pleasant Av.	V-18	14
Ploch Rd.	W-16	14
Plymouth Rd.	W-16	14
Pond St.	W-16	14
Portland Av.	W-18	14
Potter Rd.	W-16	14
Prescott Av.	W-18	14
Princeton St.	Z-18	14
Princeton St.	Z-17	14
Priscilla St.	W-16	14
Prospect St.	V-17	13
Prospect St.	W-18	14
Putnam Pl.	W-18	14
Rabkin Dr.	X-16	14
Randall Av.	V-18	13
Randolph Av.	V-18	13
Ravine Ct.	W-16	14
Ravona St.	Y-18	14
Raymond Pl.	Z-19	14
Renaissance Dr.	X-18	14
Richardson St.	X-17	14
Richfield St.	X-16	14
Richfield Ter.	X-16	14
Richland Ct.	X-16	14
Richmond St.	V-17	13
Ridge Ter.	W-16	14
Ridgewood Rd.	X-17	14
River Rd.	Z-18	14
Robert St.	Z-18	14
Robin Hood Rd.	W-16	14
Robinson Ter.	X-16	14
Rock Hill Rd.	W-16	14
Rodgers Pl.	W-16	14
Rolling Hills Rd.	X-16	14
Rollins Av.	W-17	14
Ronald Dr.	X-16	14
Rooney St.	V-18	13
Roosevelt Av.	V-18	13
Rosalie Av.	X-16	14
Rose St.	X-17	14
Rosedale Av.	X-16	14
Rosemawr Pl.	Y-18	14
Rowland Av.	X-17	14
Roy Ct.	X-16	14
Runyon Rd.	X-17	14
Russell St.	W-18	14
Rutgers Pl.	W-16	14
Ruth Av.	Z-18	14
Rutherford Blvd.	Y-18	14
Saco St.	X-17	14
Sade St.	X-18	14
Sago St.	X-17	14
Saint Andrew Blvd.	X-17	14
Saint James Pl.	X-17	14
Saint Michaels Pl.	X-17	14
Saint Phillips Dr.	W-16	14
Samuel Av.	X-17	14
Samworth Rd.	Y-17	14
Sanford St.	X-18	14
Sargeant Av.	X-17	14
Scharg Ct.	X-17	14
Schoonmaker Pl.	W-18	14
Scoles Av.	X-17	14
Scott Ter.	W-16	14
Scribner Pl.	W-18	14
Sears Pl.	W-18	14
Sebago St.	X-17	14
Sedeyen Ct.	W-16	14
Seger Av.	W-18	14
Serven Pl.	V-17	13
Seton Ln.	W-17	14
Sewall Av.	V-18	13
Shafto St.	X-17	14
Sheridan Av.	W-18	14
Sherman Pl.	W-19	14
Sherwood St.	V-16	13
Short Hill Rd.	X-17	14
Silleck St.	V-17	13
Silleck St.	V-16	13
Sipp Av.	X-17	14
Sisco Pl.	W-18	14
Sisco Pl.	X-18	14
Somerset Pl.	Y-17	14
South Ct.	X-16	14
South Pkwy.	Y-17	14
Southfield Ter.	X-16	14
Speer Av.	X-17	14
Speer Av.	X-18	14
Spencer Av.	X-17	14
Sperling Rd.	W-16	14
Spring Hill Rd.	W-16	14
Spring St.	W-17	14
Springdale Av.	X-16	14
Springdale Ct.	X-16	14
Stadtmauer Dr.	W-16	14
Stadtmauer Dr.	X-16	14
Stan Pl.	X-16	14
Standish Dr.	W-16	14
Stanley St.	V-16	13
Stanshak Ct.	Z-18	14
Starmond Av.	X-17	14
Station S.	Y-17	14
Stevens Rd.	W-16	14
Stony Hill Rd.	W-16	14
Strangeway Ter.	X-18	14
Stuyvesant Ct.	W-16	14
Styertowne Rd.	Y-17	14
Summer St.	X-18	14
Summer St.	W-18	14
Summit Av.	V-16	13
Summit Rd.	Y-17	14
Sundown Ln.	X-17	14
Sunnycrest Av.	X-17	14
Surrey Ln.	Y-17	14
Susan Ct.	X-17	14
Sussex Rd.	Y-13	14
Sussex St.	W-17	14
Svea Av.	W-17	14
Swift Ct.	Y-18	14
Sycamore Rd.	X-17	14
Sycamore Rd.	X-16	14
Sylvan Av.	W-18	14
Tamboer Av.	W-16	14
Tancin Ln.	X-16	14
Taylor St.	V-16	13
Thanksgiving Dr.	W-16	14
Thanksgiving Ln.	W-16	14
The Meadow	Y-17	14
Thomas St.	V-16	13
Thompson St.	V-18	13
Thornton Pl.	X-17	14
Trella Ter.	W-16	14
Tremont Pl.	W-17	14
Trenton Av.	V-18	13
Trimble Av.	V-18	13
Tristan Rd.	W-16	14
Troast Ct.	V-18	13
Tromp St.	W-18	14
Tufts Rd.	W-16	14
Tulip Ct.	W-16	14
Twain Pl.	W-17	14
Underwood Pl.	W-18	14
Union Av.	W-17	14
Union Av.	W-18	14
Urma Av.	X-16	14
Vale Av.	V-16	13
Valley Rd.	V-16	14
Valley Rd.	W-16	13
Valley Rd.	X-15	13
Valley Rd.	W-16	14
Valley Rd.	X-15	14
Valley Rd.	V-16	13
Van Breeman Dr.	W-17	14
Van Cleve Av.	W-18	14
Van Houten Av.	X-17	14
Van Houten Av.	W-16	14
Van Ness Ct.	W-16	14
Van Orden Pl.	V-17	13
Van Riper Av.	W-18	14
Van Vliet Ct.	X-17	14
Van Wagoner Av.	W-16	14
Van Winkle Av.	W-19	14
Vernon Av.	V-19	13
View Pl.	W-17	14
Village Rd.	W-17	14
Village Rd.	X-17	14
Vincent Dr.	X-16	14
Viola Av.	W-17	14
Virginia Av.	Y-18	14
Vreeland Pl.	V-17	13
Wabash Av.	V-18	13
Waldo St.	X-17	14
Walman Av.	V-17	13
Walnut St.	X-18	14
Walsh Ct.	X-16	14
Wanda Ct.	Z-18	14
Ward Av.	Z-18	14
Ward Av.	Z-17	14
Ward St.	W-18	14
Warren St.	V-16	13
Washington Av.	W-18	14
Washington Av.	W-17	14
Water St.	Z-18	14
Water St.	Z-17	14
Wayne Pl.	X-16	14
Webro Rd.	X-17	14
Weeks Ct.	X-16	14
Wellington St.	V-18	13
Wells Ct.	X-16	14
Wesley St.	X-18	14
West 1st St.	V-17	13
West 2nd St.	V-17	13
West 3rd St.	V-17	13
West 4th St.	V-17	13
West 5th St.	V-17	13
West 7th St.	V-17	13
Wester Pl.	X-16	14
Westervelt Av.	W-18	14
Wheeler St.	Z-18	14
Wheeler St.	Z-19	14
WhitmorePl.	W-18	14
Whitmore St.	W-18	14
Wickers St.	Z-19	14

PASSAIC COUNTY

STREET	GRID	MAP
Wiedemann Av.	W-17	14
Willett St.	X-18	14
William St.	Z-18	14
Wilson St.	W-18	14
Winding Wy.	X-17	14
Windsor Rd.	Y-17	14
Winsey St.	W-19	14
Witherspoon Rd.	X-15	14
Wonham St.	W-18	14
Woodlawn Av.	X-15	14
Woodridge Rd.	Y-13	14
Woods End Rd.	X-17	14
Woodside Ct.	Y-17	14
Woodward Av.	Y-17	14
Worth St.	V-18	13
Yereance Av.	W-18	14
Yorkshire Rd.	W-16	14
Zeim Dr.	X-17	14

Haledon, Borough of

STREET	GRID	MAP
Aberdeen Ct.	T-16	13
Aglyn Ct.	S-15	11
Al-Lyn Ct.	S-15	11
Al-Lyn Ct.	S-16	11
Albanese Rd.	T-15	13
Albion Av.	S-15	13
Alisa Av.	S-15	13
Avenue B	S-15	13
Avenue B	T-15	13
Avenue C	S-15	13
Avenue C	T-15	13
Avenue D	S-15	13
Avenue E	S-15	13
Avenue F	S-15	13
Barbour St.	S-16	13
Beam Pl.	S-16	13
Belmont Av.	S-16	13
Bernard Av.	S-16	13
Burhans Av.	T-16	13
Burhans Av.	S-16	13
Buschmann Av.	S-16	13
Cedarcliff Av.	S-15	13
Central Av.	S-15	13
Church St.	S-16	13
Circle Av.	S-16	13
Cliff Ct.	S-16	13
Cliff St.	S-16	13
Cliff St.	T-16	13
Clinton St.	S-16	13
College Dr.	S-15	13
Cona Ct.	S-16	13
Coolidge Pl.	S-16	13
Cypress Av.	T-15	13
Edmund Av.	T-15	13
Falcon Dr.	S-16	13
Ford Rd.	T-15	13
Geyer St.	S-16	13
Grand Summit Av.	S-16	11
Grand Summit Av.	S-15	13
Grand Summit Av.	S-15	11
Grand Summit Av.	S-16	13
Granite Av.	S-16	13
Grove St.	T-15	13
Haledon Av.	S-16	13
Haledon Ct.	S-16	13
Halsey Av.	S-16	13
Harris St.	S-16	13
Heights Dr.	T-15	13
Henry St.	S-16	13
Hillcrest Rd.	S-16	13
Hobart Av.	S-16	13
Hodges Pl.	S-16	13
Hoxsey Pl.	S-16	13
Ida St.	S-16	13
Jasper St.	S-15	13
John Ryle Av.	S-16	13
John St.	S-16	13
King St.	S-16	13
Kossuth St.	S-16	13
Lee Av.	S-16	13
Legion Pl.	S-16	13
Leonhard Dr.	S-16	11
Leonhard Dr.	S-16	13
Lewis St.	S-16	11
Lewis St.	S-16	13
Lupton La.	S-16	13
Manchester Av.	T-15	13
Mangold St.	S-16	13
Manson Av.	S-16	13
Morrissee Av.	S-16	13
Morrissee Av. Ext.	S-16	13
Mountain Av.	S-16	13
North 12th St.	S-16	13
North 13th St.	S-16	13
North 14th St.	S-16	13
North 15th St.	S-16	13
North 16th St.	S-16	13
North 17th St.	S-16	13
Norwood St.	S-16	13
Oxford Ct.	S-16	13
Oxford St.	S-16	13
Paterson Av.	T-15	13
Pompton-Hamburg Tnpk.	S-15	13
Pompton Rd.	S-15	13
Pompton Rd.	S-16	13
Post St.	S-16	13
Richard Scott Ct.	S-16	13
Richard Scott Ct.	S-16	11
Richardson Av.	S-16	13
Roe St.	S-16	13
Ryerson Av.	T-15	13
Sherwood Rd.	S-16	13
Singer Dr.	S-15	13
Skyline Dr.	T-15	13
Southside Av.	S-16	13
Standfield Pl.	S-16	13
Standsfield Av.	S-15	13
Terrace Rd.	S-16	13
Valley View Rd.	S-15	13
Van Dyke Av.	S-16	13
Verein St.	S-16	13
W. Clinton St.	S-16	13
West Broadway	S-16	13
West Broadway	T-16	13
West Haledon Av.	S-15	13
West Haledon Av.	S-16	13
Westside Av.	S-16	13
Willie St.	S-16	13
Woodside Av.	S-16	13
Zabriskie St.	S-16	13

Hawthorne, Borough of

STREET	GRID	MAP
1st Av.	R-17	11
2nd Av.	R-17	11
3rd Av.	R-17	11
3rd St.	R-17	11
4th Av.	Q-17	11
4th Av.	R-17	11
5th Av.	R-17	11
6th Av.	Q-17	11
6th Av.	R-17	11
7th Av.	R-17	11
8th Av.	R-17	11
8th Av.	R-18	11
9th Av.	R-18	11
9th Av.	Q-18	11
10th Av.	R-18	11
11th Av.	R-18	11
11th Av.	Q-18	11
11th St.	S-17	13
Alan Dr.	R-17	11
Alexandria Av.	Q-17	11
Allen St.	S-17	13
Annette Av.	R-18	11
Apple Hill Ct.	Q-17	11
Archmore Pl.	R-17	11
Arlington Av.	R-17	11
Ashley Pl.	R-17	11
Bamford Av.	R-17	11
Barker Av.	Q-18	11
Beverly Rd.	Q-17	11
Birchwood Rd.	R-18	11
Braen Av.	Q-17	11
Brian Ct.	Q-17	11
Brockhuizen Ln.	R-17	11
Brookside Av.	R-17	11
Brownstone Ter.	R-17	11
Buena Vista Av.	R-17	11
Calvo Pl.	Q-17	11
Cathy Av.	Q-18	11
Cedar Av.	R-17	11
Cedar Ln.	R-17	11
Central Av.	R-18	11
Central Av.	R-17	11
Charwalt Pl.	Q-17	11
Cherry Hill Dr.	Q-17	11
Chopin Dr.	R-17	11
Cidermill Rd.	Q-17	11
Clara Av.	P-17	11
Cobblers Ln.	Q-17	11
Columbus Av.	S-17	13
Columbus Av.	S-18	13
Coolidge Pl.	S-17	13
Cornell Av.	R-18	11
Cornell Av.	Q-18	11
Coulter St.	S-17	13
County Pkwy.	S-17	13
County Pkwy.	S-17	11
County Pkwy.	R-17	13
County Pkwy.	R-17	11
Crist Av.	R-17	11
Cynthia Ct.	Q-17	11
Debra Ct.	Q-17	11
Devoe Pl.	Q-18	11
Diamond Ridge Av.	R-18	11
Diamond Ridge Av.	R-17	11
Disepo Av.	S-17	13
Division St.	R-17	11
Dixie Av.	R-18	11
Dixie Av.	R-17	11
Dogwood Dr.	Q-17	11
Douglas Av.	Q-17	11
East Prospect St.	S-17	11
East Prospect St.	R-17	11
East Prospect St.	R-17	13
East Prospect St.	S-17	13
Ekings Av.	R-18	13
Elberon Av.	S-17	13
Emeline Dr.	P-17	11
Emeline Dr.	P-17	11
Ethel Av.	P-17	11
Ethel Av.	R-17	11
Faber Dr.	Q-17	11
Fairview Av.	Q-17	11
Florence Av.	R-17	11
Florence Av.	R-18	11
Forest Av.	R-17	11
Franklin Av.	S-17	11
Frederick Av.	R-18	11
Frederick Av.	R-17	11
Garden Av.	Q-18	11
Garfield Av.	R-17	11
Genevieve Av.	Q-17	11
Genevieve Av.	Q-18	11
Genevieve Av.	R-17	11
Gibraltar Ter.	P-17	11
Glen Ct.	Q-17	11
Goffle Hill Rd.	Q-17	11
Goffle Rd.	Q-17	11
Goffle Rd.	S-17	13
Goffle Rd.	S-17	11
Goffle Rd.	Q-17	13
Grand Av.	S-17	13
Grand Av.	S-17	11
Grand Av.	R-17	11
Grand Av.	R-17	13
Grandview Av.	Q-17	11
Greenwood Av.	Q-17	11
Harrison Pl.	S-17	13
Hawthorne Av.	R-17	11
Hawthorne Av.	R-18	11
Henry Av.	Q-18	11
Highcrest Dr.	Q-17	11
Highview Ter.	Q-17	11
Hillcrest Av.	Q-17	11
Hillock Av.	R-17	11
Hopper St.	Q-17	11
Horizon Ter.	Q-17	11
Horton Av.	R-17	11
Horton Av.	R-18	11
Hutchinson Av.	Q-17	11
Irvington St.	S-17	13
Ivan Pl.	Q-17	11
Jefferson Pl.	R-17	11
Karl Av.	R-17	13
Kaywin Av.	Q-18	11
Keith Ct.	S-17	13
Kenwood Rd.	Q-17	11
Kingston Av.	R-17	11
Kingston Av.	R-18	11
Knoble Pl.	S-17	13
Lafayette Av.	Q-17	13
Lafayette Av.	S-17	11
Lafayette Av.	S-17	13
Lafayette Av.	Q-17	11
Lafayette Av. Ext.	Q-17	11
Laggner Ct.	Q-17	11
Laurel St.	Q-17	11
Lee Av.	Q-18	11
Legion Pl.	R-17	11
Lincoln St.	S-17	13
Little St.	Q-18	11
Llewellyn Av.	S-17	13
Longview Ct.	Q-17	11
Loretto Av.	S-18	13
Lucille Dr.	R-17	11
Lynack Rd.	R-17	11
Lynne Av.	Q-18	11
MacFarlan Av.	S-17	13
Maitland Av.	Q-17	13
Mandon Ter.	Q-17	11
Mary St.	R-17	11
Mawhinney Av.	R-18	11
Mawhinney Av.	R-17	11
Mawhinney Av.	R-17	11
May St.	R-18	11
May St.	R-17	11
May St.	R-18	13
May St.	R-17	13
Mazur Av.	R-17	11
McKinley Av.	R-17	11
Metro Vista Dr.	R-17	11
Midland Av.	R-17	11
Midland Av.	R-18	11
Minerva Av.	R-18	11
Missonellie Ct.	Q-17	11
Mohawk Av.	S-17	13
Mountain Av.	R-17	11
Nelson Av.	R-17	11
New York Av.	P-17	11
New York Av.	P-17	11
Nixon Ct.	Q-17	11
Norma Ter.	R-18	11
North 10th St.	S-17	13
North 12th St.	S-17	13
North 13th St.	S-17	13
North 14th St.	S-17	13
North 15th St.	S-17	13
North 16th St.	S-17	13
North 16th St.	S-16	13
North 17th St.	S-17	13
North 17th St.	S-16	13
North 19th St.	S-17	13
North4th Av.	Q-17	11
North7th St.	S-17	13
North8th St.	S-17	13
North9th St.	S-17	13
North Ethel Av.	Q-17	11
North Highcrest Dr.	Q-17	11
North Watchung Dr.	Q-17	11
Oak Pl.	R-17	11
Old Orchard Dr.	R-17	11
Old Orchard Dr.	Q-17	11
Orchard Pl.	Q-17	11
Orchard Pl.	Q-17	11
Outlook Av.	S-17	13
Park Av.	R-17	11
Park Slope Ter.	Q-17	11
Parker Av.	R-18	11
Parker Av.	R-17	11
Parmelee Av.	R-17	11
Pasadena Pl.	Q-17	11
Pasadena Pl.	R-17	11
Passaic Av.	S-18	13
Passaic Av.	R-18	13
Passaic Av.	R-18	13
Passaic Av.	S-18	11
Peachtree Ct.	R-17	11
Peachtree Ct.	Q-17	11
Penny Ct.	R-17	11
Pocomoke Pl.	R-17	11
Post Av.	R-18	11
Post Av.	R-17	11
Prescott Av.	S-16	13
Prescott Av.	S-17	13
Prospect Av.	S-17	13
Ravine Dr.	Q-17	11
Ravine Dr. W.	Q-17	13
Raymond Pl.	R-18	13
Rea Av.	R-17	11
Rea Av.	R-18	11
Rea Av. Ext.	Q-17	11
Rea Av. Ext.	R-17	11
Regal Ct.	R-17	11
Reid Pl.	R-18	11
Ridge Rd.	Q-17	11
Ridgewood Av.	Q-17	11
Ridgewood Av.	P-17	11
Robertson Av.	Q-18	11
Rock Rd.	Q-18	11
Rockledge Rd.	Q-17	11
Roosevelt Av.	Q-17	11
Royal Av.	R-17	11
Ruth Av.	Q-18	11
Schoon St.	S-17	13
Service Rd.	S-17	13
Sherman Av.	Q-18	11
Short St.	Q-17	11
Sicomac Rd.	P-17	11
Sotnick St.	Q-17	11
South Av.	R-17	11
Stam's Alley	S-17	13
Summer St.	Q-17	11
Summit Av.	R-17	11
Sunrise Dr.	Q-17	11
Surrey Pl.	Q-17	11
Sylvester Av.	R-18	11
Sylvester Av.	R-17	11
Taylor Av.	R-18	11
Thomas Rd. N.	S-17	11
Thomas Rd. S.	S-17	11
Todd Ct.	Q-17	11
Tonia Ter.	Q-17	11
Tudor Ct.	R-17	11
Tuxedo Av.	S-17	11
Union St.	Q-17	11
Utter Av.	F-17	11
Utter Av.	F-18	11
Valley St.	Q-17	11
Van Winkle Av.	Q-18	11
Van Winkle Av.	Q-17	11
Victor Pl.	Q-18	11
Victor Pl.	R-18	11
Vincent St.	S-17	13
Vreeland Av.	R-17	11
Wagner Pl.	R-18	11
Wagraw Rd.	S-17	13
Warburton Av.	R-18	13
Warburton Av.	R-17	13
Warren Av.	R-17	11
Washington Av.	S-17	11
Washington Av.	S-17	13
Washington Av.	R-17	11
Washington Av.	R-17	13
Washington St.	S-17	13
Watchung Dr.	Q-17	13
Watchung Dr.	R-17	13
West Emeline Dr.	P-17	11
West Prospect St.	S-17	13
Westervelt Av.	S-17	13
Woodside Av.	Q-17	11

Little Falls, Township of

STREET	GRID	MAP
1st Av.	W-14	14
1st St.	V-13	12B
2nd St.	V-13	12B
3rd Av.	W-14	14
3rd St.	V-13	12B
4th Av.	W-14	14
Alida St.	W-14	14
Alida St.	V-14	14
Alida St.	W-14	13
Alida St.	V-14	13
Amity St.	V-13	12B
Arlington St.	V-13	12B
Beattie Ct.	W-14	14
Bergen Dr.	W-13	12B
Birch Rd.	W-15	14
Bogart St.	V-13	12B
Bradford Av.	W-13	12B
Brook Ct.	W-14	14
Brookhill Pl.	W-14	14
Brookside Av.	V-13	12B
Browertown Rd.	W-15	14
Browertown Rd.	W-14	14
Capalbo Av.	W-15	14
Cardinal Dr.	V-14	13
Cedar Grove Rd.	W-14	14
Cedar St.	V-14	13
Center Av.	W-14	14
Charles St.	W-14	14
Cherry St.	W-13	12B
Cheryl Ct.	V-14	13
Clarence Av.	W-13	12B
Clove Rd.	X-15	14
Clove Rd.	W-15	14
Coney Rd.	W-13	12B
Crane St.	W-14	14
Crestmont Rd.	W-15	14
Cross St.	W-13	12B
Dairy St.	V-13	12B
De Young Dr.	W-14	14
Dewey Av.	V-13	12B
Dogwood Wy.	W-15	14
Donato Dr.	W-13	12B
Douglas Dr.	W-14	14
East Woodcliffe Av.	V-13	12B
Elm Ct.	V-13	14
Elm Ct.	V-13	12B
Elm St.	W-14	14
Ethel Dr.	W-14	14
Fairfield Av.	V-13	12B
Fairfield Rd.	W-13	12B
Frances St.	W-14	14
Francisco Av.	W-14	14
Francisco Av.	W-15	14
Garden St.	V-13	12B
Garrabrant Av.	V-13	12B
Glenrock Rd.	X-15	14
Gray St.	V-13	12B
Grey Rock Av.	V-13	12B
Grove Av.	V-13	12B
Grove St.	V-13	12B
Haines Pl.	V-13	12B
Harrison St.	V-14	13
Hemlock Rd.	W-15	14
High Ct.	W-15	14
Highland Av.	X-15	14
Hillcrest Dr.	W-15	14
Hopson Av.	W-14	14
Houston Rd.	W-15	14
Houston Rd.	W-15	14
Hudson St.	W-14	14
Hughes Pl.	W-13	12B
Inwood Dr.	W-15	14
Inwood Dr.	W-14	14
Ironwood Wy.	W-15	14
Island Av.	V-13	12B
Jackson Av.	V-14	13
Jackson Av.	W-15	14
Jacobus Av.	W-14	14
Jacobus Av.	W-15	14
Jean Dr.	W-14	14
Kingwood Ct.	W-14	14
Kingwood Ct.	W-15	14
Kingwood Dr.	W-15	14
Kingwood Dr.	W-14	14
Lincoln Av.	W-14	14
Lindsley Rd.	W-14	14
Long Hill Rd.	W-14	14
Long Hill Rd.	W-15	14
Loretta Dr.	W-13	12B
Louis St.	V-13	12B
Lower Notch Rd.	W-14	14
Lower Notch Rd.	W-15	14
Lynn Pl.	W-15	14
Lyttel St.	V-13	12B
Madison Av.	V-14	13
Main St.	V-13	12B
Main St. E.	W-14	14
Maple St.	W-14	14
Marietta St.	W-14	14
Marietta St.	V-14	13
Marietta St.	V-14	14
Marietta St.	W-14	13
Martini Pl.	W-14	14
Meadow Dr.	W-13	12B
Merritt Av.	V-13	12B
Mickel John Av.	V-13	12B
Miles Av.	V-13	12B
Montclair Av.	W-13	12B
Morningside Cir.	W-14	14
Mozart St.	W-13	12B
Mozart St.	V-13	12B
Muller Pl.	V-13	12B
Muzzy Rd.	W-13	12B
Newark Pompton Tnpk.	W-13	12B
Newark Pompton Tnpk.	V-13	12B
Notch Park Rd.	W-15	14
Notch Park Rd.	X-15	14
Notch Rd.	W-15	14
Notch Rd.	W-16	14
Notchcroft Dr.	W-15	14
Oak Cres.	X-15	14
Oak Pl.	V-14	13
Oak Tree Ln.	X-14	14
Orchard St.	V-13	12B
Overlook Av.	W-15	14
Overlook Rd.	X-15	14
Overmont Rd.	X-15	14
Park Pl.	W-13	12B
Parkway	V-13	12B
Paterson Av.	V-14	13
Paterson Av.	V-14	14
Paterson Av.	W-14	14
Paul Pl.	W-13	12B
Pine Ct.	W-13	12B
Pleasant Av.	W-13	12B
Pleasant Av.	V-13	12B
Prospect St.	W-14	14
Railroad Av.	W-13	12B
Randolph Pl.	W-14	14
Reiners Rd.	W-14	14
Reservoir Dr.	X-15	14
Ridge Av.	W-14	14
Ridge Rd.	X-15	14
Ridge Rd.	W-15	14
Riker Av.	V-13	12B
Riker Rd.	W-13	12B
River Blvd.	W-13	12B
River Blvd.	V-13	12B
Riverview Cir.	V-13	12B
Robinwood Dr.	W-14	14
Rose St. (Private)	W-14	14
Roselle St.	V-13	12B
Ryle Av.	V-14	13
Schoonmaker Pl.	W-13	12B
Seugling Dr.	W-14	14
Siglim Dr.	W-14	14
Sindle Av.	W-14	13
Singac Pl.	V-13	12B
Smalley St.	W-14	14
South Grey Rock Av.	V-13	12B
Stanley Rd.	W-13	12B
Stanley St.	W-14	14
Stephen Pl.	W-15	14
Stevens Av.	W-14	14
Stewart Av.	W-15	14
Stinson Pl.	V-13	12B
Strickland Av.	W-13	12B
Tanglewood Dr.	W-15	14
Taylor Av.	V-13	12B
Thomas St.	W-14	14
Tolstoi Pl.	W-13	12B
Union Av.	W-13	12B
Union Av.	W-13	14
Union Av.	W-14	12B
Union Av.	W-14	14
Van Pelt Pl.	V-13	12B
Van Pelt Pl.	W-13	12B
Vanness Av.	W-14	13
Vanness Av.	V-14	14
Vanness Av.	V-14	13
Vanness Av.	W-14	14
Veranda Av.	W-13	12B
Veranda Av.	V-13	12B
Viewmont Ter.	W-14	14
Villa Rd.	W-15	14
Walnut St.	W-14	14
Warren St.	W-14	14
Weaver St.	W-13	12B
West End Av.	V-13	12B
William St.	V-13	12B
Willow Av.	V-14	13
Wilmore Rd.	W-14	14
Woodcliffe Av.	W-13	12B
Woodhull Av.	W-13	12B
Woodlawn Ter.	X-14	14
Woodlawn Ter.	W-14	14
Woods Rd.	W-15	14
Woods St.	V-13	12B
Woodside Av.	V-13	12B
Yolanda Dr.	W-14	14
Zeliff Av.	V-13	12B

North Haledon, Borough of

STREET	GRID	MAP
Ahnert Av.	Q-16	11
Arrow Ter.	Q-16	11
Arthur St.	Q-15	11
Ballentine Dr.	R-16	11
Bansam Pl.	Q-16	11
Belmont Av.	R-16	11
Belmont Av.	Q-15	11
Boat St.	R-16	11
Bogert Dr.	Q-16	11
Brookside Ter.	Q-16	11
Brookview Dr.	R-16	11
Buff Ct.	Q-16	11
Cassion Ln.	Q-16	11
Central Av.	R-15	11
Central Av.	R-16	11
Chalmers Av.	R-16	11
Chestnut Av.	R-16	11
Clara St.	R-16	11
Clowes St.	R-16	11
Columbia Ct.	Q-16	11
Copley Ct.	Q-16	11
Crestview Ter.	Q-16	11
Darrow Dr.	Q-15	11
Dater St.	R-15	11
Dawn Av.	R-16	11
De Roon Av.	R-16	11
Degray St.	R-15	11
Dickers Farm Rd.	R-16	11
Dietrich Ln.	R-16	11
Dorothy Dr.	Q-15	11
Dorothy Dr.	Q-16	11
Dorothy Dr.	Q-16	11
Dorothy Dr.	R-16	11
Dunkerly Ln.	Q-16	11
Edson Pl.	Q-16	11
Elizabeth Ct.	Q-16	11
Ellis Dr.	Q-16	11
Evergreen Av.	R-16	11
Feldman Ter.	Q-16	11
Florence Pl.	R-16	11
Forest Dr.	Q-16	11
Frankfort St.	R-16	11
Gemeinhardt Pl.	R-16	11
Gionti Pl.	Q-15	11
Glen Pl.	Q-15	11
Glenwood Dr.	Q-16	11
Graham Av.	Q-16	11
Grandview Dr.	Q-16	11
Grant Dr.	Q-16	11
Greenwood Av.	Q-17	11
Greenwood Av.	Q-16	11
Haring Ct.	Q-15	11
Harmon Pl.	R-16	11
Harrison Av.	R-16	11
Hartwig Pl.	Q-17	11
High Mountain Rd.	Q-16	11
High Mountain Rd.	R-16	11
Highcrest Dr.	Q-16	11
Highland Rd.	Q-16	11
Hillside Av.	Q-15	11
Hubert Ct.	Q-16	11
Indian Tr.	Q-16	11
Iroquois Dr.	Q-15	11
Ivy Ct.	Q-16	11
James Ct.	Q-16	11
Joan Pl.	R-16	11
Kearns Pl.	Q-15	11
Keiller Ct.	Q-16	11
Koster Pl.	R-16	11
Kuiken Ct.	R-16	11
Lake St.	S-16	13
Lakeview Av.	R-16	11
Laurel Av.	R-16	11
Laurel Av.	R-15	11
Laurie Dr.	R-16	11
Lee Dr.	Q-16	11
Lenox Av.	R-16	11
Leonard St.	R-16	11
Linda Vista Av.	R-16	11
Lisa Ct.	R-16	11
Louise Pl.	R-16	11
Main Av.	R-16	11
Main Av.	R-15	11
Manchester Av.	R-16	11
Manchester Av.	Q-16	11
Manor Rd.	R-16	11
Maple Ct.	Q-16	11
Marilyn St.	R-16	11
Mary St.	Q-16	11
Mead Av.	R-16	11
Meadow Pl.	Q-15	11
Medici Ct.	R-15	11
Melissa Dr.	Q-16	11
Messerve Pl.	R-16	11
Michele Ct.	Q-16	11
Moccasin Rd.	Q-16	11
Mohican Tr.	Q-15	11
Morley Pl.	R-16	11
Morningside Av.	R-16	11
Motta Av.	R-16	11
Mountainview Dr.	Q-16	11
Moyer Ct.	R-16	11
Myrtle Av.	R-15	11
Myrtle Av.	R-16	11
Nassau St.	R-16	11
North Haledon Av.	Q-16	11
Oakdale Ct.	Q-16	11
Oakwood Av.	R-16	11
Onyx Ter.	R-16	11
Park St.	R-16	11
Passaic Av.	R-16	11
Peters Ln.	R-16	11
Pettee Av.	Q-15	11
Pettee Av.	Q-16	11
Pleasantview Dr.	Q-16	11
Pyramid Wy.	Q-16	11
Reservoir Dr.	P-15	11
Richard St.	R-16	11
Ridge Rd.	R-17	11
Robert St.	R-16	11
Romaine Rd.	Q-16	11
Roosevelt Av.	Q-15	11
Ross Ln.	R-16	11
Rosslee Av.	R-16	11
Rothesay Av.	R-16	11
Ruff Ct.	Q-16	11
Ruth Pl.	R-16	11
Sackerman Av.	Q-16	11
Saw Mill Rd.	Q-16	11
Schnell Ct.	R-16	11
School St.	R-16	11
Sicomac Rd.	Q-16	11
Sioux Ln.	P-15	11
Spring Brook Av.	R-16	11
Squaw Brook Rd.	R-16	11
Squaw Brook Rd.	Q-16	11
Stanley Ct. E.	Q-16	11
Stanley Ct. N.	Q-16	11
Stanley Ct. S.	Q-16	11
Stanley Ct. W.	Q-16	11
Stockton Rd.	Q-16	11
Sturr St.	Q-16	11
Sturr St.	R-16	11
Suncrest Av.	R-16	11
Suter Av.	R-16	11
Tamboer Dr.	Q-16	11
Terrace Av.	R-16	11
Thornton Dr.	R-16	11
Valleyview Dr.	Q-15	11
Van Kirk St.	R-16	11
Venna Av.	Q-15	11
Vine St.	R-15	11
Vine St.	R-16	11
Walray Av.	R-16	11
Wayne Av.	R-16	11
Wayne Ct.	R-16	11
Wayne Ct.	R-16	11
Weber Ct.	R-16	11
Werner Av.	Q-16	11
West Overlook Av.	R-16	11
Westervelt Av.	Q-16	11
Wigwam Av.	Q-16	11
Willow Brook Ct.	R-16	11
Woodland Av.	Q-17	11
Woodland Av.	Q-16	11

Passaic, City of

STREET	GRID	MAP
1st St.	X-19	14
3rd St.	X-19	14
3rd St.	W-19	14
4th St.	X-19	14
4th St.	W-19	14
5th St.	X-19	14
6th Av.	X-18	14
6th St.	X-19	14
7th Av.	X-18	14
7th St.	X-19	14
8th Av.	X-18	14
8th St.	X-19	14
9th St.	X-19	14
10th St.	X-19	14
11th St.	X-19	14
Academy St.	X-19	14
Ackerson Pl.	Y-19	14
Albion St.	X-	14
Alfred St.	X-	
Allen St.	W-	
Alley	Y-19	14
Ally Pl.	X-19	14
Amsterdam Av.	Y-18	14
Ann St.	X-19	14
Anton St.	X-18	14
Ascencion St.	X-18	14
Ascension St.	Y-18	14
Ascension St.	Y-19	14
Aspen Pl.	X-19	14
Autumn St.	W-18	14
Autumn St.	Y-18	14
Aycrigg Av.	X-18	14
Ball Av.	X-18	14
Barbour Av.	X-19	14
Barry Pl.	Y-18	14
Barry Pl.	X-18	14
Beech St.	X-18	14
Bellvale St.	X-18	14
Belmont Pl.	Y-18	14
Benson Av.	Y-18	14
Bergen St.	Y-19	14
Blaine St.	X-18	14
Bond St.	Y-18	14
Boulevard St.	X-18	14
Bowes Pl.	X-18	14
Bradford Av.	X-18	14
Brighton Av.	X-18	14
Brinkerhoff Pl.	W-19	14
Broadway	X-18	14
Brook Av.	Y-18	14
Burgess Pl.	W-18	14
Carlton Pl.	Y-19	14
Cedar St.	X-18	14
Cedar St.	W-18	14
Central Av.	W-18	14
Century Pl.	X-18	14
Chard St.	Y-19	14
Chestnut St.	X-18	14
Clifton Blvd.	X-18	14
Columbia Av.	X-19	14
Columbia Av.	W-19	14
Cornelia Ct.	Y-19	14
Crescent Av.	Y-18	14
Crescent Pl.	X-18	14
Cronje Pl.	W-18	14
Dakota St.	Y-18	14
Dawson Av.	X-18	14
Dayton Av.	W-19	14
De Bell Ct.	Y-18	14
De Groot Pl.	W-18	14
Delaware Av.	X-18	14
Donald Av.	X-18	14
Elliot St.	Y-19	14
Elmwood Av.	Y-18	14
Essex St.	X-19	14
Exchange Pl.	X-19	14
Factory St.	X-18	14
Falstrom Ct.	Y-18	14
Federal St.	W-18	14
Forest Ct.	Y-18	14
Foxhall Ter.	Y-18	14
Frederick St.	X-18	14
Garden St.	X-18	14
Garfield Av.	X-18	14
Garfield Av.	Y-18	14
George St.	W-19	14
Gould St.	Y-18	14
Gourle St.	Y-18	14
Grace Ter.	Y-18	14
Grant St.	X-18	14
Green St.	X-18	14
Gregory Av.	X-18	14
Grove St.	X-18	14
Guenther Pl.	X-18	14
Hamilton Av.	W-19	14
Hamilton Av.	X-19	14
Hammond Av.	X-18	14
Hanover St.	X-18	14
Harding St.	X-19	14
Harrison St.	W-18	14
Henderson Pl.	X-18	14
Henry St.	X-18	14
High St.	Y-18	14
Highland Av.	W-18	14
Highland Av.	W-19	14
Hillside Av.	Z-17	14
Hillside Wy.	X-18	14
Hobart St.	W-19	14
Holdsworth Ct.	W-19	14
Hoover Av.	X-19	14
Hope Av.	W-19	14
Hope Av.	X-19	14
Howard Av.	Y-18	14
Howe Av.	Y-18	14
Hudson St.	W-19	14
Huges St.	Y-19	14
Huges St.	Y-18	14
Hughs St.	Y-18	14
Idaho St.	Y-18	14
Irving Pl.	X-18	14
Jackson St.	W-19	14
Jefferson St.	X-19	14
John St.	Y-18	14
Katherine Av.	X-18	14
Kennington Ter.	Y-19	14
Kennington Ter.	Y-18	14
Kent Ct.	X-18	14
Kent Ct. E.	X-18	14
Kent Ct. W.	X-18	14
Kreuger Pl.	X-18	14
Lackawanna Pl.	X-18	14
Lafayette Av.	X-18	14
Legion Ct.	X-19	14
Leitch Pl.	X-18	14
Leonard Pl.	X-18	14
Lexington Av.	X-19	14
Lexington Av.	W-19	14
Liberty St.	X-18	14
Lincoln St.	X-18	14
Linden St.	X-18	14
Lodi St.	X-19	14
Louisa Pl.	W-19	14
Louisa St.	X-19	14
Lucille Pl.	X-18	14
Madison Av.	X-19	14
Madison St.	X-19	14
Madison St.	X-18	14
Main Av.	X-19	14
Main Av.	Y-18	14
Main Av.	Y-19	14
Main Av. E.	X-19	14
Marietta Av.	Y-18	14
[illegible]	X-19	14
		14

PASSAIC COUNTY

STREET	GRID	MAP
Mass Ct.	Y-18	14
Mattimore St.	W-19	14
McLean St.	X-19	14
McKinley St.	W-18	14
Meade Av.	X-18	14
Mercer St.	X-19	14
Mineral Spring Av.	Y-18	14
Mineral Spring Av.	X-18	14
Monroe Av.	W-19	14
Monroe Av.	X-18	14
Montgomery St.	X-18	14
Morris St.	W-19	14
Myrtle Av.	W-18	14
Myrtle Av.	X-18	14
Oak St.	X-18	14
Offord St.	X-18	14
Onyx Ct.	X-18	14
Orth Av.	X-18	14
Palmer St.	Y-19	14
Park Av.	Y-19	14
Park Av.	W-19	14
Park Av.	Y-18	14
Park Dr.	Y-18	14
Park Pl.	X-19	14
Parker Av.	W-19	14
Parker St.	W-19	14
Parkview Pl.	X-19	14
Passaic Av.	Y-19	14
Passaic Av.	X-19	14
Passaic Av.	X-19	14
Passaic St.	X-19	14
Paulison Av.	X-18	14
Peach St.	X-18	14
Pearl St.	X-18	14
Pennington Av.	Y-18	14
Pennington Ct.	Y-18	14
Pine St.	W-18	14
Pleasant St.	Y-18	14
Poplar St.	X-18	14
President St.	W-19	14
Pretoria St.	W-18	14
Prospect St.	X-19	14
Quincy St.	W-19	14
Quincy St.	X-19	14
Randolph St.	X-18	14
Reid Av.	Y-18	14
Richard St.	X-18	14
Ridge Av.	Y-18	14
River Dr.	Z-19	14
River Dr.	X-19	14
Rosz Pl.	X-19	14
Rutgers Pl.	Y-19	14
Saint Francis Wy.	X-18	14
Scher Pl.	Y-19	14
Schneider Pl.	W-19	14
School St.	W-19	14
Scole Pl.	Y-19	14
Sherman St.	X-18	14
Sherman St.	W-18	14
Short St.	W-18	14
Slater St.	X-18	14
South St.	X-19	14
Spring St.	Y-19	14
Spring St.	Y-18	14
Spruce St.	W-18	14
State St.	X-19	14
Stewart St.	Y-18	14
Steyn Pl.	X-18	14
Summer St.	W-18	14
Sunset Ct.	Y-19	14
Temple Pl.	X-19	14
Tennyson Pl.	Y-18	14
Terhune Av.	Y-18	14
Terrace Av.	Z-17	14
Terry St.	X-18	14
The Circle	Y-18	14
Tulip St.	X-18	14
Union Av.	Y-19	14
Van Buren St.	W-19	14
Van Buren St.	W-18	14
Van Houten Av.	X-18	14
Van Houten Av.	Y-18	14
Van Winkle Av.	W-19	14
Veterans Ct.	X-19	14
Vineyard Pl.	X-18	14
Virginia St.	W-19	14
Vreeland Av.	X-19	14
Wall St.	X-19	14
Washington Pl.	X-19	14
Waverly Pl.	Y-18	14
Wayside Ct.	Y-19	14
Westervelt Pl.	Y-19	14
Westminster Pl.	Y-18	14
Wickham St.	X-18	14
Willett St.	X-18	14
William St.	X-19	14
Wilscot St.	W-18	14

Paterson, City of

STREET	GRID	MAP
1st Av.	S-18	13
2nd Av.	S-18	13
3rd Av.	S-18	13
4th Av.	S-17	13
4th Av.	S-18	13
5th Av.	S-17	13
5th Av.	S-18	13
6th Av.	S-17	13
6th Av.	S-18	13
7th Av.	S-17	13
7th Av.	S-18	13
8th Av.	T-17	13
8th Av.	T-18	13
9th Av.	T-17	13
9th Av.	T-18	13
10th Av.	T-17	13
10th Av.	T-18	13
11th Av.	T-17	13
11th Av.	T-18	13
12th Av.	T-17	13
12th Av.	T-18	13
14th Av.	T-17	13
14th Av.	T-18	13
15th Av.	T-17	13
15th Av.	T-18	13
16th Av.	T-17	13
17th Av.	U-17	13
17th Av.	U-18	13
18th Av.	U-17	13
18th Av.	U-18	13
19th Av.	U-17	13
19th Av.	U-18	13
20th Av.	U-17	13
20th Av.	U-18	13
21st Av.	U-17	13
21st Av.	U-18	13
22nd Av.	U-17	13
22nd Av.	U-18	13
23rd Av.	U-17	13
Alabama Av.	U-17	13
Albion Av.	T-16	13
Alden Ter.	T-16	13
Alois Pl.	T-18	13
Amethyst La.	U-16	13
Amity	S-17	13
Angela Pl.	T-15	13
Ann Pl.	S-17	13
Ann St.	T-17	13
Arch St.	T-16	13
Arlington Av.	T-15	13
Arlington St.	T-16	13
Atlantic St.	U-17	13
Auburn St.	T-17	13
Barbour St.	U-16	13
Barclay St.	U-17	13
Barnes St.	U-16	13
Barnett Pl.	T-16	13
Beckwith Av.	U-17	13
Beech St.	U-17	13
Belle Av.	S-17	13
Belmont Av.	T-16	13
Bergen St.	T-17	13
Berkshire Av.	T-15	13
Birch St.	T-16	13
Bleeker St.	S-17	13
Bloomfield Av.	V-17	13
Boulder Rd.	U-16	13
Branch St.	S-17	13
Braun St.	U-17	13
Bridge St.	T-17	13
Broadway	T-18	13
Buffalo Av.	V-18	13
Buffalo Av.	V-17	13
Burhans Av.	S-16	13
Burhans Av.	T-16	13
Burlington Av.	T-15	13
Butler St.	S-17	13
Butler St.	T-17	13
Caldwell Av.	U-16	13
California Av.	U-17	13
Camden St.	U-17	13
Canal St.	U-17	13
Carbon St.	S-16	13
Carlisle Av.	U-16	13
Carlisle Av.	U-15	13
Carrelton	T-16	13
Carroll St.	U-17	13
Carroll St.	T-17	13
Cedar St.	U-17	13
Chadwick St.	U-17	13
Chamberlain Av.	T-15	13
Chatham Av.	T-15	13
Chestnut St.	U-17	13
Christina Pl.	T-15	13
Christopher Ct.	T-16	13
Church St.	T-16	13
Cianci St.	T-16	13
Circle Av.	T-16	13
Clark St.	T-16	13
Cliff St.	T-16	13
Clinton St.	S-16	13
Clinton St.	T-16	13
Clover Av.	U-15	13
College Blvd.	T-17	13
College Blvd.	T-16	13
Colonial Av.	T-15	13
Colonial Pkwy.	T-16	13
Colt St.	T-17	13
Columbia Av.	V-17	13
Coral St.	T-16	13
Court St.	U-17	13
Courtland St.	U-17	13
Crooks Av.	V-17	13
Crooks Av.	V-18	13
Crosby Av.	T-15	13
Crosby Pl.	U-17	13
Cumberland Av.	T-15	13
Cumberland Av.	U-15	13
Curie	T-16	13
Curtis Pl.	T-16	13
Dakota St.	V-17	13
Dale Av.	T-17	13
Dale Av.	U-17	13
Danforth Av.	U-16	13
Danforth Av.	U-15	13
Dayton St.	U-16	13
DeGrasse St.	U-16	13
Delaware Av.	V-18	13
Delaware Av.	V-17	13
Derrom Av.	U-18	13
Derrom Av.	T-18	13
Dewey St.	T-16	13
Dey St.	V-17	13
Dixon Av.	U-16	13
Donbosco Av.	T-15	13
Doremus St.	T-16	13
Dover St.	U-17	13
Dundee Av.	V-18	13
Eagle Av.	V-17	13
East 6th St.	S-17	13
East 7th St.	S-17	13
East 11th St.	S-17	13
East 12th St.	S-17	13
East 13th St.	S-17	13
East 15th St.	T-17	13
East 15th St.	S-17	13
East 17th St.	S-17	13
East 18th St.	T-17	13
East 18th St.	S-17	13
East 19th St.	S-17	13
East 19th St.	U-17	13
East 20th St.	U-17	13
East 21st St.	U-17	13
East 21st St.	T-17	13
East 22nd St.	U-17	13
East 22nd St.	T-17	13
East 22nd St.	S-18	13
East 23rd St.	U-17	13
East 23rd St.	S-18	13
East 23rd St.	T-17	13
East 24th St.	U-17	13
East 24th St.	T-17	13
East 24th St.	S-18	13
East 25th St.	S-18	13
East 25th St.	U-17	13
East 25th St.	T-18	13
East 26th St.	S-18	13
East 26th St.	T-18	13
East 26th St.	U-17	13
East 27th St.	U-18	13
East 27th St.	S-18	13
East 28th St.	T-18	13
East 28th St.	U-18	13
East 28th St.	T-18	13
East 29th St.	U-18	13
East 29th St.	T-18	13
East 30th St.	T-18	13
East 30th St.	U-18	13
East 31st St.	T-18	13
East 31st St.	U-18	13
East 32nd St.	U-18	13
East 32nd St.	T-18	13
East 33rd St.	U-18	13
East 33rd St.	T-18	13
East 34th St.	T-18	13
East 34th St.	U-18	13
East 35th St.	T-18	13
East 35th St.	U-18	13
East 36th St.	T-18	13
East 36th St.	U-18	13
East 37th St.	T-18	13
East 37th St.	U-18	13
East 38th St.	T-18	13
East 38th St.	U-18	13
East 39th St.	U-18	13
East 39th St.	T-18	13
East 40th St.	U-18	13
East 40th St.	T-18	13
East 41st St.	U-18	13
East 42nd St.	T-18	13
East 42nd St.	U-18	13
East 43rd St.	T-18	13
East Haledon Av.	T-16	13
East Haledon Av.	T-17	13
East Main St.	T-17	13
East Railway Av.	V-17	13
East Railway Av.	U-17	13
Edmund Av.	T-15	13
Edward Av.	T-18	13
Elberon Av.	T-15	13
Elizabeth St.	U-17	13
Elk St.	V-17	13
Ellison Pl.	T-17	13
Ellison St.	T-17	13
Ellison St.	T-16	13
Elm St.	T-16	13
Emerson Av.	U-15	13
Emerson Av.	T-15	13
Erie St.	S-17	13
Essex St.	U-17	13
Fair St.	T-17	13
Florida Av.	V-17	13
Franklin St.	T-17	13
Front St.	T-16	13
Fulton Pl.	T-17	13
Fulton St.	T-17	13
Furrey Pl.	T-16	13
Garfield St.	T-16	13
Garrett St.	U-16	13
Garrison St.	T-16	13
Genesee Av.	V-17	13
George St.	V-17	13
Getty Av.	V-17	13
Getty Av.	U-17	13
Godwin Av.	T-17	13
Godwin St.	T-17	13
Godwin St.	T-16	13
Goshen St.	V-17	13
Gould Av.	V-17	13
Governor St.	T-17	13
Grand St.	U-16	13
Granite Pl.	T-15	13
Granite St.	T-15	13
Gray St.	U-17	13
Green St.	U-17	13
Grimes Pl.	S-18	13
Grove St.	V-17	13
Haldon Av.	S-16	13
Halpine St.	S-16	13
Hamilton Av.	T-17	13
Hamilton St.	T-16	13
Harris Pl.	T-18	13
Harrison St.	T-17	13
Hazel St.	V-17	13
Hemlock St.	U-17	13
Henderson	U-16	13
Henry St.	T-16	13
Highland St.	S-17	13
Highland St.	T-17	13
Hill St.	T-15	13
Hillman St.	T-17	13
Hine St.	U-17	13
Holsman St.	T-17	13
Hospital Plz.	U-17	13
Howard St.	U-16	13
Hoxey St.	U-16	13
Hudson	T-17	13
Illinois Av.	V-18	13
Illinois Av.	V-17	13
Industrial Pl.	U-17	13
Inglis Pl.	S-16	13
Iowa Av.	U-17	13
Jackson St.	U-16	13
James St.	T-16	13
Jane St.	T-16	13
Jasper St.	T-16	13
Jasper St.	S-15	13
Jefferson St.	S-16	13
Jefferson St.	T-16	13
Jelsma Pl.	T-17	13
Jersy St.	U-16	13
John St.	T-16	13
Katz	S-15	13
Katz	T-15	13
Kearny	S-16	13
Kearny St.	T-16	13
Keen St.	T-17	13
Kent Rd.	T-15	13
Kentucky Av.	U-17	13
Kiddie Pl.	U-18	13
Kipp Pl.	U-18	13
Knickerbocker Av.	V-17	13
Knickerbocker Av.	V-18	13
Lacka Pl.	U-16	13
Lafayette St.	T-17	13
Lake Av.	V-17	13
Lake St.	T-17	13
Lakeview Av.	V-18	13
Lakeview Av.	U-18	13
Laurel St.	T-16	13
Lawrence Pl.	T-17	13
Lawrence St.	T-17	13
Lee Pl.	U-16	13
Lehigh Av.	V-17	13
Lenox Av.	T-15	13
Leon St.	T-17	13
Leslie St.	U-17	13
Lewis St.	U-17	13
Lexington Av.	T-15	13
Liberty St.	T-16	13
Lily St.	S-16	13
Lincoln St.	U-15	13
Lindbergh Pl.	U-17	13
Linden Rd.	T-18	13
Linwood Av.	T-15	13
Lowe St.	S-17	13
Lyon St.	T-17	13
Madison Av.	T-17	13
Madison Av.	U-17	13
Madison St.	U-17	13
Magees Al.	T-16	13
Main St.	U-16	13
Main St.	V-17	13
Main St.	U-17	13
Main St.	T-16	13
Maitland Av.	U-15	13
Maitland Av.	T-15	13
Manchester Av.	T-16	13
Manor Rd.	T-18	13
Maple St.	T-16	13
Marion St.	T-16	13
Market St.	U-17	13
Market St.	T-17	13
Market St.	T-16	13
Marshall St.	U-16	13
Marshall St.	V-17	13
Martin Luther King Wy.	T-17	13
Martin St.	U-16	13
Mary St.	U-17	13
Maryland Av.	U-17	13
Maryland Av.	U-18	13
Matlock St.	T-16	13
May St.	S-17	13
McBride Av.	T-16	13
McBride Av.	U-16	13
McLean Blvd.	S-18	13
McLean Blvd.	U-18	13
Memorial Dr.	T-17	13
Memorial Dr.	T-16	13
Mercer St.	T-17	13
Michigan Av.	V-18	13
Michigan Av.	V-17	13
Mill St.	U-16	13
Mill St.	T-16	13
Montclair Av.	V-17	13
Montgomery Pl.	T-17	13
Montgomery St.	T-17	13
Morris St.	U-16	13
Morton St.	U-17	13
Mountain Av.	U-16	13
Murray Av.	U-16	13
Nagle St.	U-16	13
New St.	U-16	13
New York St.	T-17	13
Newark Av.	V-17	13
North 10th St.	T-16	13
North 11th St.	S-16	13
North1st St.	T-16	13
North2nd St.	T-16	13
North3rd St.	T-16	13
North4th St.	T-16	13
North5th St.	T-16	13
North6th St.	T-16	13
North7th St.	T-16	13
North8th St.	T-16	13
North9th St.	T-16	13
North Barclay St.	U-17	13
North Bridge St.	T-17	13
North Main St.	T-16	13
Oak St.	U-17	13
Overlook Dr.	T-18	13
Oxford St.	T-16	13
Pacific St.	V-17	13
Pacific St.	U-17	13
Park Av.	T-17	13
Park Av.	U-18	13
Park Dr.	U-18	13
Park Pl.	S-17	13
Park Rd.	T-18	13
Park Rd.	U-16	13
Park St.	U-17	13
Park Wy.	U-17	13
Passaic St.	T-16	13
Paterson Av.	T-16	13
Paterson Av.	T-15	13
Paterson St.	T-17	13
Paxton St.	V-17	13
Peach St.	U-17	13
Pearl St.	T-17	13
Peel St.	S-17	13
Pennington St.	U-17	13
Pennsylvania Av.	V-17	13
Pennsylvania Av.	U-17	13
Perry St.	U-16	13
Piercy St.	T-17	13
Plessinger Pl.	S-18	13
Ploch St.	U-17	13
Plum St.	U-17	13
Plymouth Dr.	T-15	13
Pope Rd.	T-18	13
Potomac Av.	V-18	13
Preakness Av.	T-16	13
Preakness Av.	T-15	13
Presidential Blvd.	T-16	13
Prince St.	U-17	13
Prospect St.	T-16	13
Putnam St.	T-17	13
Quinn St.	U-16	13
Railroad Av.	U-17	13
Ramsey St.	U-16	13
Raritan Av.	V-18	13
Redwood Av.	T-16	13
Reservoir Av.	U-16	13
Reservoir St.	U-16	13
Richmond Av.	T-15	13
Ridge Ter.	T-18	13
River St.	S-17	13
River St.	U-15	13
River St.	T-17	13
Robert St.	V-17	13
Rockland St.	U-16	13
Rosa Parks Blvd.	U-17	13
Rosa Parks Blvd.	T-17	13
Rose St.	U-17	13
Rossiter Av.	T-15	13
Rye St.	S-17	13
Ryerson Av.	T-15	13
Ryle Av.	T-16	13
Ryle Rd.	T-16	13
Salem Rd.	T-15	13
Sassafras St.	S-17	13
Seeley St.	U-17	13
Shady St.	S-17	13
Sheridan Av.	T-16	13
Sherman Av.	T-16	13
Sherwood Av.	T-15	13
Short St.	S-17	13
Slater St.	U-17	13
Slater St.	U-16	13
Smith St.	T-16	13
Southard St.	U-17	13
Sparrow St.	S-17	13
Sparrow St.	T-17	13
Spring St.	U-16	13
Spruce St.	U-16	13
State St.	U-17	13
Stout St.	T-17	13
Straight St.	T-17	13
Straight St.	U-17	13
Summer St.	U-17	13
Summer St.	T-17	13
Summit St.	U-16	13
Sussex St.	V-17	13
Swinburn St.	U-17	13
Temple St.	T-16	13
Thomas St.	V-17	13
Timothy St.	V-17	13
Totowa Av.	T-16	13
Totowa Av.	U-15	13
Trenton Av.	U-18	13
Trenton Av.	V-18	13
Turner St.	U-16	13
Tyler St.	T-17	13
Union Av.	T-16	13
Union Av.	U-15	13
Union Av.	T-15	13
Valley Rd.	U-17	13
Van Blarcom St.	T-17	13
Van Houten St.	T-17	13
Van Houten St.	T-16	13
Van Winkle Av.	U-17	13
Vernon Av.	U-18	13
Vernon Av.	V-18	13
Vesper St.	V-17	13
Veterans Pl.	T-16	13
Vreeland Av.	U-18	13
Wabash Av.	U-17	13
Wait St.	S-17	13
Wait St.	T-17	13
Walker Av.	U-16	13
Wall Av.	T-18	13
Walnut St.	T-16	13
Walton St.	U-16	13
Ward St.	T-16	13
Warren St.	T-17	13
Washington Av.	U-17	13
Washington St.	T-16	13
Watson St.	T-17	13
Wayne Av.	T-16	13
Webster Av.	U-15	13
Webster Av.	U-16	13
Weiss St.	U-17	13
Welcome St.	T-16	13
West Broadway	T-16	13
West Railway Av.	V-17	13
White St.	T-16	13
William St.	T-17	13
Wood St.	S-17	13
Woodruff Pl.	T-16	13

Pompton Lakes, Borough of

STREET	GRID	MAP
Ackerman Pl.	N-10	9
Adrian St.	N-11	9
Albert St.	N-11	9
Arcadia Rd.	P-11	9
Babbit Pl.	M-11	9
Babcock Pl.	N-11	9
Barbara Dr.	M-11	9
Bartholf Av.	N-11	9
Beam St.	N-11	9
Broad St.	N-10	9
Broad St.	N-11	9
Broadway	N-11	9
Butler St.	N-11	9
Cannon Ball Rd.	N-11	9
Carr St.	M-11	9
Cedar St.	N-11	9
Center St.	N-11	9
Chalen Ct.	N-11	9
Circle Av.	N-11	9
Colfax Rd.	N-11	9
Colfax Rd.	M-12	9
Colfax Rd.	N-11	9
Colfax Rd.	M-12	9
Dupont Av.	M-11	9
Dupont Pl.	M-11	9
Durham St.	M-11	9
Durham St.	N-11	9
Edwards Av.	M-11	9
Fairview Pl.	N-11	9
Federal Hill Rd.	N-10	9
Furnace Hill Rd.	P-11	9
Furnace Hill Rd.	N-11	9
Garden Rd.	P-11	9
Garden Rd.	N-11	9
Glen Ct.	N-11	9
Grant Av.	N-11	9
Grove St.	N-11	9
Harding Av.	M-12	10
Henderson Ct.	N-11	9
Hershfield Park Pl.	P-11	9
Hershfield St.	N-10	9
Hill Ct. S.	N-11	9
Hill Ct. W.	N-11	9
Hilltop Ct.	N-11	9
Howard St.	M-11	9
Howard St.	N-11	9
Hunter Pl.	N-11	9
Ivy St.	N-11	9
James Ter.	N-11	9
Jefferson Av.	N-11	9
Hershfield St.	N-10	9
Kluge St.	N-10	9
Kluger St.	N-11	9
Lake Av.	N-12	10
Lakeside Av.	N-11	9
Lambert St.	N-11	9
Laura St.	N-11	9
Laurel Av.	P-11	12A
Legion St.	N-11	9
Lenox Av.	N-11	9
Lincoln Av.	N-11	9
Lincoln Av.	P-11	12A
Lincoln Av.	N-11	12A
Lincoln Av.	P-11	9
Locust Av.	N-11	9
Madison Pl.	P-11	12A
Magnolia Av.	P-11	12A
Mandeville St.	N-11	9
Maple Av.	P-11	12A
Maple St.	N-11	9
Maplewood Rd.	P-11	12A
Maplewood Rd.	Q-11	12A
Marion Ct.	P-11	12A
Mathes Av.	P-11	12A
Media Rd.	P-11	12A
Midland Av.	N-10	9
Mill St.	P-11	12A
Montclair Av.	N-10	9
Mountain Av.	N-11	9
North Legion St.	N-11	9
Oak Av.	P-11	12A
Oakland Rd.	M-12	10
Oakland Rd.	M-13	10
Oakwood Dr.	P-11	12A
Olive Av.	P-11	12A
Orchard Pl.	N-11	9
Park Pl.	M-12	10
Passaic Av.	N-11	9
Paterson Hamburg Tnpk.	P-11	9
Paterson Hamburg Tnpk.	N-11	12A
Paterson Hamburg Tnpk.	N-11	9
Paterson Hamburg Tnpk.	P-11	12A
Pequannock Av.	P-11	12A
Perrin Av.	N-11	9
Pine St.	P-11	12A
Pompton Av.	N-11	9
Poplar Av.	P-11	12A
Poplar St.	M-11	9
Ramapo Av.	N-11	12A
Ramapo Av.	P-11	9
Ramapo Av.	N-11	9
Ramapo Av.	P-11	12A
Ramapo St.	P-11	12A
Randall Av.	N-11	9
Ringwood Av.	P-11	12A
Ringwood Av.	M-11	12A
Ringwood Ct.	N-11	9
River Edge Dr.	P-11	12A
Rivercrest Dr.	Q-11	12A
Riverdale Blvd.	P-11	12A
Riverside Dr.	P-11	12A
Riverview Rd.	P-11	12A
Romain Av.	N-11	9
Schuyler Av.	N-11	9
Short St.	M-10	9
Spruce Rd.	N-11	9
Stiles Ct.	N-10	9
Stiles Ct.	N-11	9
Stiles Ct. E.	N-11	9
Stiles Ct. N.	N-10	9
Stiles Ct. N.	N-11	9
Stiles Ct. S.	N-11	9
Stiles Ct. W.	N-10	9
Summit Av.	N-11	9
Sunset Rd.	P-11	9
Sunset Rd.	P-11	12A
Sycamore Av.	P-11	12A
Tower Rd.	N-11	9
Tower Rd.	P-11	9
Tower Rd.	N-11	12A
Tower Rd.	P-11	12A
Van Av.	N-11	9
Vanness Av.	P-11	12A
Walnut Av.	P-11	12A
Walnut St.	N-11	9
Wanaque Av.	N-11	9
Washington Av.	P-11	12A
Waterviliet Av.	P-11	12A
West Lenox Av.	N-11	9
White Wy.	M-12	9
White Wy.	N-12	9
Whitney Av.	N-11	9
Willard St.	N-10	9
Willard St.	N-11	9
Willow Av.	P-11	12A
Willow Wood Rd.	P-11	12A
Woodlawn Av.	P-11	12A
Woods Rd.	Q-11	12A

Prospect Park, Borough of

STREET	GRID	MAP
Belle Av.	S-16	13
Brown Av.	S-16	13
Cypress St.	S-16	13
Cyril Av.	S-16	13
E. Main St.	S-17	13
Fairview Av.	S-16	13
Haledon Av.	S-16	13
Hillcrest Dr.	S-16	13
Hopper St.	S-16	13
Jeroloman St.	S-16	13
Kenneth Av.	S-16	13
Lake Shore Dr.	S-16	13
Langlely Pl.	S-17	13
Main St.	S-17	13
Neppel St.	S-16	13
North 10th St.	S-16	13
North 11th St.	S-16	13
North 12th Pl.	S-16	13
North 12th St.	S-16	13
North 13th Pl.	S-16	13
North 13th St.	S-16	13
North 14th St.	S-16	13
North 15th St.	S-16	13
North 16th St.	S-16	13
North 17th St.	S-16	13
North6th St.	S-16	13
North6th St.	S-17	13
North7th St.	S-16	13
North7th St.	S-17	13
North8th St.	S-16	13
North8th St.	S-17	13
North9th St.	S-16	13
Park Av.	S-16	13
Planten Av.	S-16	13
Prescott Av.	S-16	13
Prescott Av.	S-17	13
Prescott Rd.	S-17	13
Savoy Pl.	S-16	13
Shore Dr.	S-16	13
Struyk Av.	S-16	13
Struyk Av.	S-17	13
Struyk Av. Ext.	S-16	13
Wagaraw Blvd.	S-16	13

Ringwood, Borough of

STREET	GRID	MAP
A St.	J-9	6
Algonquin Ter.	G-10	6
Alta Vista Dr.	H-12	7
Anderson Dr.	F-10	3
Apache Tr.	G-13	7
Arcata Pl.	J-11	6
Arrowhead Tr.	G-11	6
Art St.	G-9	6
Ash Ct.	J-12	7
Aspen Pl.	F-12	4
Aspen Rd.	J-12	7
Avery Pl.	J-12	7
Azalea Ct.	J-9	6
B St.	J-9	6
Bear Mountain Rd.	F-13	4
Bearfort Ter.	G-13	4
Beattie Ln.	J-11	6
Beech Ct.	H-12	7
Beech Rd.	D-10	3
Beech Rd.	D-11	3
Bellot Rd.	H-13	7
Bellot Rd.	G-13	7
Betty Ln.	F-13	4
Betty Ln.	E-13	4
Birch Pl.	F-12	4
Birch Rd.	J-12	7
Black Rock Ter.	G-13	7
Black Rock Ter.	G-13	4
Black Rock Ter.	F-13	7
Black Rock Ter.	F-13	4
Boro Pkwy.	E-12	4
Brookside Av.	G-12	7
Buena Vista Dr.	H-12	7
Burnt Meadow Rd.	H-9	6
Burnt Meadow Rd.	G-9	6
C St.	J-9	6
Cable House Rd.	D-12	4
Cannon Mine Rd.	E-12	4
Canterbury Rd.	J-11	6
Carletondale Rd.	F-12	4
Catherine Ct.	F-12	4
Cedar Rd.	F-12	4
Channing Dr.	J-12	7
Cherie La.	G-10	6
Cheshire Ln.	H-13	7
Cheyenne Wy.	H-10	6
Chicken House Rd.	E-12	4
Choctaw Tr.	G-13	7
Chris Ter.	H-12	7
Cliffside Dr.	H-13	7
Club Rd.	G-13	7
Colfax Rd.	G-10	6
Conklintown Rd.	J-12	7
Convent Rd.	E-13	4
Copper Hill Park	H-13	7
Coventry Wy.	J-13	7
Crag Pl.	F-13	4
Cupsaw Av.	G-13	7
Cupsaw Dr.	F-13	4
Custer Dr.	H-10	6
D St.	J-9	6
Dale Rd.	J-9	6
Dan St.	F-10	3
Darmstatter Rd.	F-10	3
Delaware Tr.	F-13	4
Dewey Dr.	H-13	7
Dogwood Ter.	J-12	7
Dolores Dr.	F-12	4
Duffy Rd.	E-13	4
E St.	J-9	6
East Point	E-13	4
Edgewood Ct.	J-11	6
Edgewood Rd.	J-11	6
Edward Dr.	H-13	7
Ellen St.	J-9	6
Erskine Rd.	G-12	7
F St.	J-9	6
Farm Rd.	E-12	4
Fern Pl.	J-11	6
Fieldstone Dr.	H-12	7
Fieldstone Dr.	H-13	7
Forest Rd.	J-11	6
Forsgate Dr.	H-12	7
Fountain Dr.	J-12	7
Foxhill Ln.	H-12	7
Ganz Rd.	G-10	6
Glen Rd.	F-13	4
Greenwood Lake Rd.	G-11	6
Greenwood Lake Rd.	G-12	6
Greenwood Lake Rd.	H-12	7
Greenwood Lake Rd.	J-12	4
Greenwood Lake Rd.	J-12	6
Greenwood Lake Rd.	G-12	7
Greenwood Lake Rd.	G-11	4
Greenwood Lake Rd.	J-11	6
Greenwood Lake Rd.	J-11	4
Greenwood Lake Rd.	G-12	4
Greenwood Lake Tpke.	H-12	7
Hare Pl.	E-13	4
Hare Pl.	F-13	4
Harrison Mountain Lake Rd.	G-10	6
Hemlock Pl.	J-12	7
Hickory Rd.	F-12	4
High Mountain Rd.	J-12	7
High Mountain Rd.	H-12	7
High Point Ln.	G-13	7
Hillside Rd.	F-13	4
Hilltop Rd.	H-12	7
Honeysuckle Ln.	E-13	4
Hope Pl.	G-12	7
Horseshoe Bend Rd.	E-11	3
Howard St.	F-9	3
Industrial Pkwy.	E-11	3
Iroquois Trail	G-10	6
Ivy Pl.	G-12	7
James Dr.	H-13	7
James Dr.	H-12	7
Jayne Ter.	F-13	4
Jayne Ter.	F-12	4
John St.	G-10	6
Joseph Ln.	E-13	4
Judith Ann Dr.	E-13	4
Judith Ann Dr.	E-12	4
Juniper Ter.	J-12	7
Kendall Dr.	F-12	4
Kendall Dr.	F-13	4
Kent Rd.	E-13	4
Kingsley Rd.	G-12	7
Knollwood Dr.	H-12	7

PASSAIC COUNTY

STREET	GRID	MAP
Kozy Ct.	H-12	7
Kraft Pl.	F-13	4
Kraft Pl.	E-13	4
Lake Riconda Dr.	F-10	3
Lakeview Av.	G-13	7
Lakeview Av.	G-12	7
Lakeview Rd.	J-12	7
Laurel Pl.	G-13	7
Le Boun Blvd.	G-10	6
Lenape Rd.	J-12	7
Linnea Pl.	F-12	4
Little Big Horn	G-10	6
Locust Ln.	J-12	7
Longview Ln.	G-13	7
Magee Rd.	H-9	7
Main Beach Rd.	H-12	7
Manning Rd.	J-12	7
Manor Rd.	E-13	7
Manor Rd.	D-13	7
Mansion Rd.	E-13	4
Maple Rd.	G-12	7
Marcia Rd.	F-13	4
Meadow Ln.	J-11	6
Millers Ln.	G-10	6
Milligan Dr.	E-12	4
Millstone Ter.	H-12	7
Mohawk Tr.	G-12	7
Mohawk Tr.	G-13	7
Mohican Ct.	G-10	6
Morris Rd.	E-12	4
Morris Rd.	E-13	4
Mountain Glen Rd.	J-11	6
Nagle Rd.	H-9	6
Nagle Rd.	H-10	6
North Elm Pl.	G-12	7
North Roger Ct.	J-12	7
Northgate Pass	H-12	7
Oak Ln.	J-11	6
Oakwood Dr.	H-12	7
Old Conklintown Rd.	J-12	7
Old Forge Rd.	H-13	7
Old Rd.	F-13	4
Olive Ln.	J-12	7
Oliver Pl.	G-12	7
Orchard Rd.	G-12	7
Overlook Ter.	G-13	7
Palm Ter.	J-12	7
Pequot Rd.	G-13	7
Peter's Mine Rd.	D-12	4
Peter's Mine Rd.	E-12	4
Petzold Av.	E-11	4
Pima Ct.	H-10	6
Pine Pl.	G-12	7
Pinewood Dr.	H-10	6
Pleasant Av.	G-12	7
Point Pl.	G-12	7
Poplar Dr.	J-12	7
Progress Pl.	G-12	7
Ramapo Pl.	G-12	7
Ray Av.	F-9	3
Redwood Ln.	J-12	7
Reiss Rd.	G-10	6
Richard Ct.	J-11	7
Rickers Dr.	F-10	3
Ridge Pl.	J-12	7
Ringwood Av.	E-10	3
Ringwood Av.	E-12	3
Riverview Dr.	E-10	3
Robin Ln.	G-13	7
Russell Rd.	G-12	7
Sally Ct.	F-12	7
Seminole Dr.	G-10	6
Seneca Dr.	J-12	7
Serpentine Rd.	J-12	7
Sharon Ct.	E-13	4
Shepherd Pond Rd.	D-13	4
Shepherd Pond Rd.	E-13	4
Shore Av.	G-10	6
Short Pl.	H-12	7
Sioux Ln.	H-10	6
Skylands Rd.	F-13	7
Skylands Rd.	F-13	4
Skylands Rd.	G-12	7
Skylands Rd.	G-12	4
Skyland Dr.	H-12	7
Skyland Dr.	J-12	7
Skyline Lakes Dr.	J-11	7
Skyline Lakes Dr.	J-12	6
Skyline Lakes Dr.	J-12	7
Skyline Lakes Dr.	J-11	6
Skyline Rd.	H-12	7
Skyline Rd.	K-13	7
Skyline Rd.	K-12	7
Skyline Rd.	H-13	7
Skyview Rd.	F-10	3
Sloatsburg Rd.	E-12	4
Sloatsburg Rd.	F-12	4
Smokey Ridge Rd.	H-12	7
Smokey Ridge Rd.	J-12	7
Snake Den Rd.	J-8	6
Snake Den Rd.	J-9	6
South Elm Pl.	G-12	7
South Roger Ct.	J-12	7
Spruce Pl.	G-13	7
Stetson Rd.	F-13	4
Stonetown Rd.	G-10	6
Stonetown Rd.	H-10	6
Stonewall Ct.	H-12	7
Summit Av.	F-10	3
Summit Pt.	G-13	7
Sunset Rd.	G-13	7
Sweetwater Ln.	H-13	7
Sylvan Ln.	J-11	6
Teak Ct.	J-12	7
Terrace Ln.	J-11	6
The Loop	F-13	4
Tice Pl.	G-12	7
Tomahawk Path	G-11	6
Tulip Av.	J-9	6
Tulip Av.	H-9	6
Underhill Ter.	G-12	7
Upas Ct.	J-12	7
Upper Lakeview Av.	G-13	7
Valley Rd.	F-13	4
Valley Rd.	G-13	4
Valley Rd.	G-13	7
Valley Rd.	F-13	7
Van Dunk Ln.	E-12	4
Van Natta Dr.	E-11	4
Vanessala	H-12	7
Voorhis Pl.	G-12	7
Walker Dr.	F-13	4
Walker Dr.	E-13	4
Wanaque Ter.	F-13	4
Waterford Ct.	H-13	7
Weir Pl.	G-13	7
Welch Rd.	F-12	4
West Brook Rd.	J-11	6
West Brook Rd.	H-9	6
West Brook Rd.	J-10	6
West Cir.	E-13	4
West Roger Ct.	J-12	7
West Shore Ln.	G-9	6
Whaleback Ter.	G-13	7
White Rd.	F-10	3
Wildwood Ter.	H-12	7
Willow Ln.	E-10	3
Willow Pl.	J-12	7
Willow Pl.	H-12	7
Windbeam Av.	F-13	4
Windbeam Ln.	G-10	6
Windbeam Lp.	F-13	4
Windom Wy.	H-13	7
Wood Ter.	H-10	6
Woodland Rd.	F-13	4
Woodside Av.	F-10	6
Woodside Av.	F-10	3
Woodside Av.	G-10	3
Woodside Av.	G-10	6
Yuma Ln.	H-10	6
Zuk Pl.	F-12	4

Totowa, Borough of

STREET	GRID	MAP
Acorn St.	U-14	13
Adams Dr.	V-14	13
Anderson Av.	U-14	13
Anderson Av.	U-15	13
Artillery Park Rd.	U-14	13
Barnert Av.	T-15	13
Barnert Av.	U-14	13
Barnert Av.	U-15	13
Barnert Av.	T-14	13
Battle Ridge Tr.	U-14	13
Battle Ridge Tr.	T-14	13
Bogert St.	U-14	13
Bomont Pl.	V-14	13
Boyle Av.	U-15	13
Briarwood Rd.	V-15	13
Brookmans Ln.	U-14	13
Browne Av.	U-14	13
Cambridge St.	U-15	13
Campus Rd.	U-14	13
Cannon Hill Tr.	T-14	13
Carr Pl.	U-14	13
Carrol Pl.	U-15	13
Catherine St.	U-14	13
Celia St.	U-15	13
Charles St.	U-15	13
Chestnut St.	T-15	13
Church St.	U-15	13
Claremont Av.	U-14	13
Colonial Ct.	U-14	13
Columbus Av.	T-14	13
Columbus Av.	U-14	13
Coolidge Av.	U-14	13
Craig Ct.	U-13	12B
Crescent Av.	V-14	13
Crestwood Ct.	U-14	13
Crews St.	U-14	13
Crosby Av.	U-15	13
Cumberland Av.	T-15	13
Cumberland Av.	U-15	13
Davidson Av.	V-14	13
Denora Dr.	V-14	13
Dewey Av.	U-14	13
Dey Hill Tr.	U-14	13
Duffus Av.	V-14	13
Dunkerly St.	U-14	13
Elizabeth Pl.	U-15	13
Elm St.	T-15	13
Essex Av.	U-14	13
Falls Bridge Dr.	V-13	13
Fellner Pl.	T-15	13
Flint Lock Ct.	T-14	13
Floyd Dr.	V-14	13
Forest Av.	T-15	13
Frances St.	U-14	13
Franklin Pl.	U-15	13
Furler St.	V-14	13
Garfield Pl.	U-14	13
Garreton Av.	U-14	13
Glen Tr.	U-14	13
Gordon Av.	U-15	13
Gordon Av.	U-14	13
Gordon Dr.	U-14	13
Gordon Dr.	V-14	13
Grant Av.	U-14	13
Grant Av.	U-15	13
Greene Av.	U-14	13
Hamilton Dr.	T-15	13
Harding Av.	U-14	13
Haven Av.	U-15	13
Heritage Ct.	T-14	13
Heritage Ct.	T-15	13
Hideaway Dr. E.	U-14	13
Hideaway Dr. N.	U-14	13
Hideaway Dr. S.	U-14	13
Hideaway Dr. W.	U-14	13
Highview Av.	U-14	13
Hillside Av.	U-14	13
Hobart Pl.	U-15	13
Hobart Pl.	U-14	13
Hudson Av.	U-15	13
Hudson Av.	U-14	13
Huizenga Ln.	U-14	13
Huizenga Ln.	T-14	13
Huntington Tr.	T-15	13
Jackson Rd.	U-13	12B
Jefferson Pl.	U-15	13
Killian Av.	U-14	13
King Dr.	V-14	13
Knolwood Dr.	U-14	13
Knox St.	U-14	13
Lackawana Av.	V-14	13
Lewis Pl.	U-15	13
Liberty Ridge Tr.	T-15	13
Liberty Ridge Tr.	T-14	13
Lincoln Av.	U-15	13
Linda Rd.	U-15	13
Linda Rd.	U-14	13
Linden St.	U-14	13
Lookout Point Tr.	U-14	13
Lookout Point Tr.	T-14	13
Madison Rd.	U-13	13
Mair Av.	V-14	13
Maltese Dr.	U-13	13
Maple Ln.	U-13	13
Maple St.	T-15	13
Margaret St.	V-14	13
Meadow Dr.	U-14	13
Melissa Dr.	V-14	13
Minnisink Rd.	U-14	13
Mitchell Av.	U-14	13
Monroe Av.	U-14	13
North Winifred Dr.	U-13	13
Norwood Ter.	V-15	13
Pamela Dr.	U-14	13
Paterson Rd.	U-14	13
Patriots Tr.	T-14	13
Plymouth Tr. Way	V-14	13
Plymouth Way	V-14	13
Raphael Rd.	U-14	13
Redman St.	U-14	13
Riverview Dr.	V-14	13
Riverview Dr.	U-15	13
Riverview Dr.	U-13	13
Roosevelt Av.	U-14	13
Rosalie St.	V-14	13
Roseda Dr.	U-14	13
Roseland Av.	U-14	13
Rosengren Av.	U-14	13
Rutherford Ct.	U-14	13
Saint James Pl.	U-14	13
Sandra Dr.	U-13	12B
Scrivens St.	U-15	13
Shady Ln.	U-13	12B
Shady Pl.	V-14	13
Shepherds Ln.	U-15	13
Shepherds Ln.	T-15	13
South Winifred Dr.	U-13	12B
Stanford Ct.	T-15	13
Stanley St.	U-14	13
Sterling Tr.	T-15	13
Stewart St.	U-14	13
Sutton Av.	U-14	13
Taft Rd.	U-13	12B
Thistle Ct.	U-13	12B
Totowa Rd.	U-15	13
Totowa Rd.	U-14	13
Tow Path Cres.	V-13	13
Tracy Av.	U-15	13
Union Av.	U-15	13
Union Av.	V-15	13
Union Av.	V-14	13
Union Av.	U-14	13
Vita Rd.	U-13	12B
Vreeland Av.	U-14	12B
Vreeland Av.	U-13	13
Vreeland Av.	U-13	12B
Vreeland Av.	U-14	13
Washington Pl.	U-15	13
Washington Pl.	U-14	13
Weldon Ct.	V-13	13
Wentick St.	U-14	13
West End Rd.	U-13	12B
West Winifred Dr.	U-13	13
West Winifred Dr.	U-13	12B
Willard Av.	U-15	13
William Pl.	U-15	13
Willow Ct.	U-13	12B
Wilson Av.	U-14	13
Winifred Dr.	U-13	12B
Young Av.	U-14	13
Young Av.	U-15	13

Wanaque, Borough of

STREET	GRID	MAP
1st Av.	M-10	9
1st St.	K-11	6
2nd Av.	L-11	9
2nd St.	K-11	6
3rd St.	L-11	9
4th Av.	L-11	9
5th Av.	L-11	9
6th Av.	L-11	9
Adams St.	L-11	9
Aldrin Dr.	K-11	6
Alexander Av.	L-10	9
Algonquin Path	M-10	9
Alpha St.	M-10	9
Ann St.	J-11	6
Arcola Pl.	M-11	9
Argyle Rd.	M-11	9
Bartholdi Av.	L-10	9
Beam Av.	K-11	6
Bean Ct.	K-12	7
Bearfort Av.	M-10	9
Belmont Av.	K-11	6
Belvedere Av.	J-11	6
Bergen Av.	L-11	9
Borman Dr.	K-12	7
Boulevard Av.	L-11	9
Brook St.	L-10	9
Brook St.	M-10	9
Burnside Pl.	L-11	9
Butler Pl.	L-11	9
Cannonball Dr.	K-12	7
Carter Rd.	L-11	9
Chestnut St.	K-11	6
Circle Dr.	M-10	9
Clifford Rd.	K-11	6
Clifford Rd.	J-11	6
Coles Av.	M-10	9
Colfax Av.	K-11	6
Conklintown Rd.	J-11	6
Conrad Ct.	J-12	7
Cooper Dr.	J-12	7
Crescent Rd.	K-11	6
Cresente Ln.	M-10	9
Cross Rd.	K-11	6
Cross St.	K-11	6
Cross St.	L-10	9
Dacoata Path	M-10	9
Dardale Ter.	L-10	9
Debow Av.	K-11	6
Decker Rd.	L-11	9
Dee St.	M-10	9
Dena Dr.	K-11	6
Dickens Pl.	M-11	9
Doty Rd.	L-10	9
Dupont Av.	L-10	9
East St.	K-11	6
Eastside Av.	K-11	6
Edgar Pl.	L-11	9
Edgewood Court	K-12	10
Elinora Dr.	K-11	6
Elm St.	M-10	9
Erie Av.	K-11	6
Evergreen Av.	L-10	9
Father Hayes Dr.	L-11	9
Fox Den Rd.	K-11	6
Foxcroft Dr.	L-12	10
Foxcroft Dr.	K-12	10
Foxcroft Dr.	K-12	7
Foxcroft Dr.	L-12	7
Franklin Pl.	M-11	9
Frederiks St.	K-11	6
Furnace Av.	K-11	6
Garbarino Av.	J-11	6
Gardella Pl.	L-11	6
Garden St.	J-11	6
Gary Pl.	J-12	7
George Av.	K-11	6
George Pl.	L-10	9
Glen Ct.	J-12	7
Glenbernie Pl.	L-10	9
Gorge Dr.	M-10	9
Graham Pl.	K-11	6
Greenwood Av.	M-10	9
Greenwood Lake Rd.	K-11	9
Greenwood Lake Rd.	L-11	9
Greenwood St.	L-10	9
Grist Mill Rd.	K-11	6
Gross St.	L-10	9
Grove St.	K-11	6
Guide Pl.	L-10	9
Hannah La.	J-10	6
Hannibal Pl.	L-11	9
Hannibal Pl.	M-11	9
Harriet St.	J-11	6
Haskell Av.	M-10	9
Held Ter.	L-11	6
Henry Pl.	M-11	9
Hickory Dr.	M-10	9
Highland Av.	K-11	9
Highland Av.	K-11	6
Highland Av.	L-11	9
Highland Av.	L-11	6
Hillside Av.	K-11	6
Hillside Rd.	J-10	6
Humbert Pl.	K-12	7
Ivy Ct.	K-11	6
Jackson St.	M-11	9
Jefferson St.	M-11	9
Jenkins Av.	L-11	9
John St.	L-10	9
Kuruc Dr.	K-12	7
Lake Dr.	M-10	9
Lakeside Av.	L-10	9
Lange Av.	L-10	9
Laura Av.	K-11	6
Leonard Pl.	L-11	9
Lettie Ln.	K-12	7
Lily Rd.	J-10	6
Linda Rd.	K-12	7
Lines Av.	K-11	6
Locust St.	L-11	9
Lombardi Pl.	M-10	9
Lovell Dr.	J-12	7
Makemoney Av.	L-10	9
Mann Pl.	M-10	9
Maple Av.	M-11	9
Maple Av.	L-11	9
Margaret Ct.	L-11	9
McAtee Ln.	K-12	7
McKinley St.	M-11	9
McKinnon Pl.	J-11	6
Meadow Brook Av.	K-11	6
Melrose St.	K-11	6
Midvale Av.	K-11	6
Mill St.	K-11	6
Milton Pl.	M-11	9
Molinari Dr.	K-12	7
Monroe St.	M-11	9
Morningside Pl.	K-11	6
Mountain Av.	K-11	6
Mountain Rd.	J-10	6
Mullen Av.	K-11	6
New St.	K-11	6
Norman Ct.	L-11	6
North Gate Park	K-12	7
North Grove St.	K-11	6
North Maple Av.	L-11	6
North Shore Dr.	K-12	10
Northgate	K-11	6
Oak St.	M-10	9
Oak St.	L-10	9
Oak Ter.	J-11	6
Orchard St.	M-11	9
Orchard St.	L-11	9
Orrie Ln.	K-12	7
Park Av.	M-11	9
Paul Pl.	L-11	9
Pellington St.	K-11	6
Phelan Ct.	L-11	9
Pierce Av.	M-10	9
Pocahontas Path	M-10	9
Prospect Park St.	K-11	6
Quarry Rd.	L-10	9
Railroad Av.	K-11	6
Ramapo Mountain Dr.	J-12	7
Red Mine Rd.	J-10	6
Rhinesmith Av.	K-11	6
Rhonda Pl.	K-11	6
Ringwood Av.	K-11	6
Ringwood Av.	L-11	6
Ricker Rd.	L-11	9
Ricker Rd.	L-11	9
Rockhill Dr.	M-10	9
Rockridge Rd.	L-11	9
Roger Av.	M-10	9
Roseland Av.	L-10	9
Schirra Dr.	K-12	7
Schirra Dr.	J-12	7
Scrivani Dr.	K-11	6
Seminole Path	M-10	9
Shady Av.	L-10	9
Shady Av.	M-10	9
Shepherd Dr.	K-12	7
Sherman Av.	K-11	6
Short St.	K-11	6
Skylands Av.	L-10	9
Smith Av.	L-11	9
South Shore Dr.	L-12	10
Specht Dr.	L-10	9
Stafford Dr.	J-12	7
Stafford Dr.	K-12	7
Stephens Av.	K-11	6
Stephens Lake Rd.	K-12	7
Storm Av.	L-10	9
Storm Pl.	L-11	9
Summit Pl.	M-10	9
Susquehanna Av.	M-10	9
Touque St.	L-10	9
Townsend Rd.	J-10	6
Tremont Ter.	K-12	7
Union Av.	M-10	9
Venezia La.	L-11	9
Wabasso Path	M-10	9
Wanaque Av.	L-11	9
War Veterans Pl.	K-11	6
Warsaw Pl.	K-11	6
West Brook Rd.	J-10	6
Whistler Pl.	M-11	9
William Pl.	L-11	9
William St.	L-10	9
Willow Way	K-11	6
Wilson Dr.	K-12	7
Wolfe Dr.	J-12	7
Wolfe Dr.	J-12	7

Wayne, Township of

STREET	GRID	MAP
1st St.	V-12	12B
2nd St.	V-12	12B
3rd St.	V-12	12B
4th St.	V-12	12B
5th St.	V-12	12B
Abbott Rd.	S-12	12B
Aberdeen Av.	S-15	13
Adams Rd.	T-15	13
Adelphia Rd.	Q-11	12A
Adler Av.	N-12	10
Adobe Dr.	N-12	10
Adrian St.	U-12	12B
Agatha La.	R-12	12A
Agawam Dr.	Q-14	11
Agawam Dr.	P-14	11
Alden Pl.	S-14	13
Ales Pl.	T-12	12B
Alexandria Av.	U-12	12B
Algonquin Tr.	N-12	10
Algonquin Tr.	P-12	11
Algonquin Tr.	P-12	10
Algonquin Tr.	N-12	10
Allen Dr.	R-13	12A
Allison Ct.	R-13	12A
Almadera Dr.	S-15	11
Almadera Dr.	S-15	13
Almroth Dr.	S-14	13
Alpine Dr.	S-13	12B
Alps Rd.	T-13	12B
Alps Rd.	R-13	12B
Alps Rd.	T-13	12A
Alps Rd.	R-13	12A
Alps Rd. Ext.	Q-13	12A
Alwood Tr.	Q-12	12A
Ambassador Dr.	V-12	12B
Amboy Rd.	S-14	13
Amherst Ct.	Q-14	11
Amity St.	T-12	12B
Anderson Dr.	S-14	13
Andover Dr.	S-14	13
Angell St.	T-13	12B
Ann St.	V-12	12B
Apache Rd.	N-12	10
Apollo Dr.	S-14	13
Arbor Rd.	P-12	12A
Arcady Pl.	V-12	12B
Archung Rd.	S-12	12B
Armstrong Av.	Q-12	12A
Arnold St.	U-12	12B
Arundel Rd.	T-13	12B
Ashburn Rd.	S-14	13
Ashlyn Ct.	Q-12	12A
Ashwood Ln.	T-13	12B
Ashwood Ln.	T-14	12B
Aspen Ct.	P-12	12A
Atherton Ct.	R-14	11
Atwood Pl.	R-13	12A
Audel Pl.	T-12	12B
Audubon Pkwy.	Q-11	12A
Augusta Dr.	S-14	13
Azusa Ct.	S-14	13
Baker St.	T-13	12B
Baldwin Ter.	R-13	12A
Ballard Rd.	T-14	13
Balsam Rd.	P-12	12A
Barbara Wy.	S-13	12B
Barbour Pond Dr.	Q-14	11
Barge Ln.	R-13	12A
Barker Pl.	T-13	12B
Barnsdale Rd.	U-12	12B
Barton St.	U-12	12B
Basswood Ter.	N-12	10
Baywood Av.	P-12	12A
Beatrice Ln.	R-13	12A
Beaumont Pkwy.	R-15	11
Beech Ter.	N-12	10
Beech Ter.	P-12	11
Beech Ter.	P-12	10
Beech Ter.	N-12	11
Beechwood Dr.	S-12	12B
Beekman Pl.	T-14	13
Belair Ter.	T-13	12B
Bella Ct.	T-14	13
Bella Vista Av.	V-12	12B
Benson Dr.	T-13	12B
Benwell Av.	S-15	13
Berdam Av.	P-13	12A
Berdam Av.	Q-13	12A
Bergan St.	T-12	12B
Berkley Ct.	R-15	11
Berry Dr.	S-13	12B
Bertrand Dr.	S-14	13
Beun Ln.	T-15	13
Beverly Wy.	R-14	11
Bighorn Dr.	N-12	10
Bill Rose La.	T-13	12B
Birch Ln.	S-15	13
Birchwood Ter.	S-14	13
Birchwood Ter.	S-13	12B
Birchwood Ter.	S-14	12B
Birchwood Ter.	S-13	13
Birdseye Cir.	N-12	10
Birkett Ct.	S-13	12B
Birkett Ct.	T-13	12B
Bitola Dr.	S-12	12A
Black Foot Cir.	N-12	10
Black Oak Ridge Rd.	Q-12	12A
Black Oak Ridge Rd.	R-12	12A
Black Oak Ridge Rd.	S-11	12B
Blackbriar La.	T-13	12B
Blanford Ct.	S-14	11
Blanford Ct.	S-14	13
Bobolink Ct.	R-15	11
Bodie Rd.	N-12	10
Bolton Rd.	T-12	12B
Bonita Ter.	R-12	12A
Boonstra Dr.	T-15	13
Boonton Rd.	U-12	12B
Borzotta Blvd.	T-15	13
Bothman St.	U-12	12B
Boulevard Dr.	S-11	12B
Boulevard Dr.	T-11	12B
Bourbon St.	R-12	12A
Bowfell Ct.	R-15	13
Braemar Dr.	R-12	12A
Brandon Av.	T-12	12B
Brandywine Rd.	Q-13	12A
Breen Ter.	R-13	12A
Brentwood Ct.	S-12	12B
Brentwood Rd.	S-12	12A
Briarwood Rd.	Q-12	12A
Brighton Ter.	R-11	12A
Brighton Ter.	R-12	12A
Bristol Pl.	R-12	12A
Brittany Way	Q-13	12A
Broadway	T-12	12B
Brook Ter.	P-12	12A
Brookdale Rd.	P-12	12A
Brookside Rd.	T-12	12B
Brookwood Dr.	S-13	12B
Bryan Ct.	P-12	12A
Budd Wy.	T-13	12B
Bullens Av.	T-15	13
Bundance Dr.	N-12	10
Bunkerhill Rd.	P-12	12A
Burgess Pl.	U-12	12B
Burgundy Way	Q-13	12A
Burke Rd.	R-13	12A
Burnside Pl.	S-14	13
Butternut Dr.	P-13	12A
Buttonwood Av.	U-12	12B
Byrne Ct.	R-13	12A
Cadmus Pl.	R-13	12A
Cambridge Pl.	S-15	13
Camden	S-11	12B
Camillo Dr.	S-14	13
Canterbury Way	S-15	13
Canton Rd.	Q-12	12A
Cardinal Wy.	S-12	12B
Carey Arthur Dr.	P-13	12A
Caribou Cir.	N-12	12
Carlisle Rd.	T-14	13
Carol Pl.	S-14	13
Casey Ln.	T-13	12B
Castles Dr.	S-12	12B
Cathyann Ct.	T-14	13
Cauley Rd.	R-13	12A
Cayuga Tr.	S-13	12B
Cecilia Dr.	T-13	12B
Cedar Pl.	S-12	12B
Cedarcliff Dr.	T-12	12B
Central Av.	S-15	13
Cezar Ct.	T-12	12B
Chadwick Rd.	T-14	13
Chandler Dr.	S-12	12B
Chapel Pl.	T-14	13
Charles St.	U-12	12B
Charlotte Ter.	R-13	12A
Cherokee Tr.	P-12	11
Cherokee Tr.	P-12	10
Cherokee Tr.	N-12	11
Cherokee Tr.	N-12	10
Cherry Wy.	V-13	12B
Cherrywood Dr.	N-12	11
Chestnut Dr.	S-12	12B
Cheyenne Wy.	N-12	10
Chicopee Dr.	Q-14	11
Chimney Ln.	Q-14	11
Chopin Dr.	P-12	12A
Christine Pl.	R-12	12A
Church Ln.	R-13	12A
Church Ln.	R-14	11
Church Ln.	R-13	11
Church Ln.	R-14	12A
Cicone Rd.	S-12	12B
Circle Av.	N-12	10
Claremont Av.	V-12	12B
Claremont Ter.	P-12	12A
Claremont Ter.	Q-12	12A
Clark St.	T-11	12B
Clearwater Dr.	N-12	10
Cliff Rd.	P-12	12A
Clifford Dr.	S-13	12B
Clinton Ln.	S-13	12B
Clove Pl.	R-12	12A
Cobble Stone Ct.	R-13	11
Colburn Ct.	R-12	12A
Cole St.	Q-12	12A
Colfax Rd.	P-12	12A
Colfax Rd.	Q-12	12A
College Dr.	R-15	13
College Dr.	S-15	13
College Rd.	R-15	11
Colombo Ct.	T-14	13
Colonial Rd.	N-12	10
Colonial Rd.	T-14	13
Colville Rd.	Q-12	12A
Commanche Dr.	N-12	10
Concord Pl.	R-12	12A
Coniston Ct.	S-15	13
Continental Dr.	U-13	12B
Cook Rd.	P-12	12A
Copely Ct.	T-13	12B
Corporate Dr.	U-13	12B
Corvair Pl.	S-13	12B
Cosden Ln.	R-12	12A
Cottonwood Rd.	P-12	12A
Cougar Cir.	N-12	10
Court Ln.	S-11	12B
Courter Av.	U-12	12B
Coventry Rd.	R-12	12A
Coyler Ter.	U-12	12B
Cracco Ln.	T-12	12B
Craig Ct.	T-13	12B
Crane Ter.	S-14	13
Cree Ln.	U-12	12B
Crescent Rd.	P-12	12A
Crest Ct.	R-12	12A
Crestwood Dr.	S-13	12B
Crossing Way	U-12	12B
Crow Tr.	S-13	12B
Cyanamid Dr.	Q-12	12A
Dakota Av.	T-13	12B
Dalewood Dr.	Q-12	12A
Dalewood Dr.	R-12	12A
Daly Av.	S-15	13
Danielle Dr.	T-15	13
Darlington Dr.	T-14	13
Dartmouth Rd.	T-13	12B
Dave Espie Wy.	Q-12	12A
David Scott Dr.	R-14	11
Davies Ct.	T-13	12B
Dawn Pl.	T-14	13
Day Pl.	R-12	12A
Debbie Ct.	R-12	12A
Deerfield Rd.	Q-11	12A
Deerfield Rd.	Q-12	12A
Delaware Dr.	T-14	13
Demarest Dr.	U-12	12B
Dey Rd.	U-13	12B
Diagonal Rd.	S-15	13
Diane Ct.	S-15	13
Diane Ct.	S-15	11
Diaz Ct.	R-13	12A
Dillion Rd.	R-14	11
Divan Wy.	Q-12	12A
Dixon Pl.	R-13	12A
Dogwood Ter.	Q-12	12A
Doig Rd.	S-12	12B
Donald Ct.	T-13	12B
Donna Ln.	T-14	13
Doreen Ln.	T-12	12B
Doremus Ln.	T-13	12B
Dorothy St.	Q-12	12A
Dorsa Av.	S-11	12B
Dorsa Av.	T-11	12B
Douglas Wy.	R-14	11
Dowitcher Ct.	R-15	11
Drayton Pl.	R-12	12A
Dubel Rd.	R-14	11
Dudley Ct.	P-14	11
Duncan Ln.	R-15	11
Dupont Ter.	T-11	12B
Dwight St.	S-14	13
Dwyer Rd.	S-14	13
Eagle Dr.	N-12	10
Easdale Rd.	S-15	13
East Rd.	S-15	13
East Wy.	T-14	13
Echo Ct.	R-11	12A
Eden Pl.	R-13	12A
Edgemont Cres.	T-12	12B
Edison Dr.	U-13	12B
Edith Ct.	T-12	12B
Edward St.	V-12	12B
Elder Ct.	R-15	11
Eldorado Dr.	R-12	12A
Eldorado Dr.	R-11	12A
Eleron Pl.	S-13	12B
Ella Ln.	S-14	13
Ellen Ln.	S-11	12B
Ellicott Ln.	R-12	12A
Elmary Pl.	S-13	12B
Elmwood Ter.	S-13	12B
Emanuel Av.	T-12	12B
Emerson	R-13	12A
Erie Av.	U-12	12B
Erli St.	S-13	12B
Ernest St.	V-12	12B
Eros Ct.	R-12	12A
Estate Dr.	Q-13	12A
Eton Ct.	T-12	12B
Evelyn Ter.	S-14	13
Everett Pl.	S-14	13
Evergreen Pl.	S-12	12B
Evers Ct.	R-13	12A
Fair Ridge Ct.	S-15	13
Fairfield Rd.	V-12	12B
Fairfield Rd.	U-12	12B
Fairmount Rd.	Q-11	12A
Fairpark Pl.	U-12	12B
Fairview Pl.	V-12	12B
Fairview Ter.	S-12	12B
Fairway Ln.	R-14	11
Falcon Pl.	S-13	12B
Fargo Pl.	R-11	12A
Farmhouse Rd.	Q-13	12A
Farmingdale Rd.	Q-11	12A
Farmingdale Rd.	R-11	12A
Farmstead La.	Q-12	12A
Fay Ct.	R-11	12A
Fayette Av.	U-12	12B
Fenner Rd.	T-14	13
Fern River Av.	V-13	12B
Fern Ter.	S-13	12B
Ferndale Rd.	S-12	12B
Ferndale Rd.	S-11	12B
Ferrara Av.	T-12	12B
Ferrara Av.	T-11	12B
Ferri St.	T-11	12B
Field Rd.	R-15	11
Fieldstone Pl.	Q-12	12A
Fieldstone Pl.	Q-11	12A
Finley Ln.	S-15	13
Finn's Dr.	V-12	12B
Fir Pl.	S-12	13
Fisk Rd.	R-13	12A
Flynn Pl.	T-13	12B
Ford St.	T-11	12B
Forest Ter.	S-13	12B
Fox Hill Dr.	T-15	13
Fox Hollow Ct.	T-12	12B
Foxboro Rd.	P-14	11
Franklin Av.	T-12	12B
Frederick Ct.	T-14	13
French Hill Rd.	T-13	12B
Friar Wy.	Q-12	12A
Furman Dr.	R-12	12A
Furno Pl.	R-14	11
Gaede Pl.	S-13	12B
Gaede Rd.	S-15	13
Galesi Dr.	V-13	12B
Garden Dr.	Q-12	12A
Garfield Rd.	Q-12	12A
Garside Av.	S-14	13
Garside Av.	T-14	13
Garvey Rd.	R-13	12A
Gates Pl.	Q-13	12A
Geneva Ct.	S-13	12B
Georgia Dr.	S-13	12B
Giannone Rd.	R-14	11
Gibbs Dr.	Q-12	12A
Glen Rd.	N-12	10
Gorge Wy.	P-12	12A
Gorham Ct.	T-12	12B
Gow Rd.	T-14	13
Grace Ct.	S-14	13
Graham Av.	T-14	13
Granada Ln.	R-12	12A
Grand St.	T-12	12B
Grandview Dr.	R-13	12A
Grantwood Rd.	Q-11	12A
Grantwood Rd.	Q-12	12A
Green Knolls Dr.	N-12	10
Greenrale Av.	S-14	13
Greenup Ct.	S-15	13
Greenwood Av.	U-12	12B

PASSAIC COUNTY

STREET	GRID	MAP
Gregory Rd.	R-12	12A
Gressinger Rd.	T-12	12B
Grieves Ter.	T-13	12B
Grove Pl.	Q-12	12A
Grover Dr.	S-13	12B
Haddon Rd.	Q-12	12A
Hadley La.	P-13	12A
Hall St.	S-14	13
Halsey Rd.	S-13	12B
Hamilton Av.	T-14	13
Hampton Ter.	R-12	12A
Hanes Dr.	U-13	12B
Hanover Pl.	R-13	12A
Hansen Pl.	P-12	12A
Hardwick Ln.	S-14	13
Harlan Ter.	Q-13	12A
Harmer Ter.	T-14	13
Harmony Ln.	Q-12	12A
Harrier Ct.	R-15	11
Harrison Rd.	T-13	12B
Harwood Pl.	S-14	13
Haul Rd.	S-11	12B
Hawthorne Rd.	P-12	12A
Hazen Ct.	Q-13	12A
Heights Rd.	T-13	12B
Helene Ct.	T-14	13
Hemlock Ter.	S-13	12B
Henry St.	U-12	12B
Herfort Rd.	S-13	12B
Heritage Manor Dr.	P-12	12A
Herrick Rd.	T-12	12B
Hershey Rd.	S-12	12B
Hickory Pl.	S-12	12B
High Point Dr.	S-12	12B
High Point Dr.	S-12	12A
High St.	U-12	12B
Highland Ct.	T-14	13
Highland Ter.	S-13	12B
Highview Ct.	P-12	12A
Hillcrest Dr.	S-12	12B
Hillside Ter.	S-13	12B
Hilltop Ter.	S-12	12B
Hinchmans Av.	R-14	11
Hobson Av. E.	V-13	12B
Hobson Av. W.	V-13	12B
Hollow Brook Ct.	R-13	12A
Hollow Dr.	Q-13	12A
Hollow Dr.	Q-14	11
Hollow Dr.	Q-13	11
Hollow Dr.	Q-14	12A
Hollywood Av.	V-12	12B
Holmes La.	T-14	13
Holy Cross Way	U-12	12B
Holyoke Ct.	Q-14	11
Holyoke Rd.	Q-14	11
Hoover Pl.	S-14	13
Hopper Ln.	T-13	12B
Horizon Dr.	N-12	10
Howe Av.	T-13	12B
Hubbardton Rd.	R-12	12A
Hudson St.	S-15	13
Huff Rd.	S-14	13
Hunter Pl.	S-14	13
Huron Av.	T-13	12B
Hurst Ter.	R-12	12A
Idependence Av.	P-11	12A
Indian Rd.	N-12	10
Ingraham Ter.	S-13	12B
Iowa Rd.	P-13	12A
Irene Pl.	S-12	12B
Iroquois Tr.	N-12	10
Iroquois Tr.	P-12	11
Iroquois Tr.	N-12	11
Iroquois Tr.	P-12	10
Island St.	U-12	12B
Ivy Pl.	N-12	10
Jackson Av.	Q-12	12A
Jacobus Av.	T-13	12B
James St.	S-11	12B
Jane St.	V-12	12B
Jansen Ln.	T-14	13
Jason Ct.	R-12	12A
Jean Ter.	R-13	12A
Jefferson Pl.	S-13	12B
Jeffrey Rd.	R-12	12A
Jerome Pl.	T-13	12B
Jessica Wy.	R-12	12A
Joan St.	R-13	12A
Joseph Pl.	S-13	12B
Joyce Ln.	R-13	12A
Judith Pl.	T-13	12B
Julie Pl.	T-14	13
Juniper Rd.	P-12	12A
Kane Ct.	R-13	12A
Karen Ct.	R-13	12A
Kassar St.	R-12	12A
Kathleen Ct.	S-13	12B
Kathlyn Av.	V-12	12B
Kathrina Ct.	T-14	13
Keilana Dr.	T-12	12B
Kelly St.	T-11	12B
Kennedy Ct.	R-12	12A
Kenneth St.	T-11	12B
Kent Av.	T-11	12B
Kent Av.	S-11	12B
Kenwood Rd.	R-13	12A
Kevin Pl.	T-12	12B
Kievit Rd.	R-14	11
Kimberly Pl.	S-14	13
Kime Av.	R-11	12A
Kime Av.	R-12	12A
King Ct.	R-13	12A
Kingston Rd.	Q-12	12A
Kipp Ct.	S-13	12B
Kirk Ter.	S-15	13
Kiwanis Dr.	R-12	12A
Knight Rd.	R-12	12A
Knoll Rd.	N-12	10
Knox Ter.	R-14	11
Kossuth Pl.	S-13	12B
Kram Ct.	T-14	13
Kristin Ct.	P-12	12B
Kuiken Ct.	T-14	13
Kurland St.	T-11	12B
Lauwe Av.	S-14	13
Lafayette Ct.	S-14	13
Laguna Dr.	T-12	12B
Lake Dr. E.	S-13	12B
Lake Dr. W.	S-12	12B
Lake Rd.	P-11	12A
Lake Tr. E.	T-13	12B
Lakeside Av.	N-12	10
Lamoreux Rd.	N-12	10
Lancaster Ter.	R-14	11
Langdale Rd.	S-15	13
Larks Meadow Rd.	S-15	11
Larkspur Rd.	T-14	13
Laurel Dr.	T-12	12B
Lauren Ct.	Q-14	11
Lavina Ter.	S-14	13
Lawrence Rd.	S-14	13
Laytham Dr.	S-11	12B
Le Grande Ter.	T-12	12B
Ledge Rd.	N-12	10
Legion Pl.	U-12	12B
Leisure La.	P-11	12A
Lenape Tr.	T-13	12B
Lenox Rd.	S-12	12B
Leo Pl.	T-11	12B
Leonard Ter.	R-14	11
Leslie Dr.	R-13	12A
Lewis St.	U-12	12B
Lexington La.	P-12	12A
Leystar Ln.	T-14	13
Lillian Ct.	T-12	12B
Lilro Ct.	T-12	12B
Lincoln Pl.	S-14	13
Linden Ln.	R-13	12A
Linden Rd.	P-12	12A
Linden Rd.	Q-12	12A
Lindy Rd.	Q-12	12A
Linwood Av.	S-11	12B
Lions Head Blvd.	Q-12	12A
Lions Head Dr. E.	Q-12	12A
Lions Head Dr. W.	Q-12	12A
Lisa Ln.	T-13	12B
Little Pl.	R-14	11
Little Pond Rd.	S-14	13
Littlewood Ct.	S-15	11
Lockley Ct.	S-15	11
Locust Pl.	Q-12	12A
Log Ln.	R-12	12A
Lois Ct.	S-13	12B
Long Pond Rd.	Q-12	12A
Long Pond Rd.	Q-11	12A
Longell Dr.	R-12	12A
Longwood Ct.	T-13	12B
Lorenz Pl.	S-12	12B
Lorrie Ct.	S-14	13
Louisa Ct.	T-14	13
Lowell Dr.	Q-13	11
Lowell Dr.	Q-13	12A
Lucas Ln.	Q-12	12A
Lucille Pl.	Q-12	12A
Ludlum Rd.	P-12	12A
Luke Ln.	R-12	12A
Lulu St.	V-13	12B
Lyle Av.	S-14	13
MacDonald Dr.	T-13	12B
MacDonald Dr.	S-13	12B
Mack St.	S-11	12B
Mader Av.	R-12	12A
Madison St.	T-15	13
Maghee Rd.	T-12	12B
Magnolia Pl.	S-12	12B
Main Av.	V-12	12B
Main Rd.	T-11	12B
Maljin Ct.	S-14	13
Manchester Ct.	R-14	11
Mandeville Dr.	R-12	12A
Mandon Dr.	S-13	12B
Manhatten Av.	T-11	12B
Manitou Pass	N-12	10
Manor Dr.	Q-13	12A
Manor Rd.	S-15	13
Mansard Ct.	T-12	12B
Maple Av.	T-12	12B
Maple Ln.	Q-11	12A
Maplewood Av.	P-12	12A
Maplewood Av.	Q-12	12A
Marc Rd.	S-14	13
Marion St.	V-12	12B
Market St.	V-12	12B
Marling Dr.	R-12	12A
Marlo Rd.	T-12	12B
Marlton Dr.	R-12	12A
Matthew Rd.	T-13	12B
Maybrook Ct.	R-12	12A
Mayfair Dr.	R-13	12A
McClelland Av.	T-12	12B
McDonald Dr.	T-13	12B
McGrogan Ct.	T-14	13
McKennan Ct.	R-12	12A
Mead St.	T-12	12B
Meadow Rd.	T-12	12B
Med Rd.	S-14	13
Medford Pl.	R-12	12A
Melanie Ln.	S-13	12B
Merchant St.	T-12	12B
Meyer La.	R-14	11
Michael Dr.	S-13	12B
Michael Dr.	S-13	12B
Michael Dr.	S-13	13
Michael Dr.	S-14	13
Michardy Pl.	R-12	12A
Micheline Ct.	S-15	13
Midwood Pl.	S-14	13
Miller Rd.	R-13	12A
Minnisink Rd.	V-13	12B
Minns Av.	S-15	13
Miriam Pl.	R-12	11
Mohawk Tr.	P-12	11
Mohawk Tr.	N-12	10
Mohawk Tr.	P-12	10
Mohawk Tr.	N-12	11
Moiyas Rd.	N-12	10
Monhegan Av.	T-13	12B
Monmouth Av.	T-11	12B
Monroe Pl.	S-13	12B
Montauk Tr.	N-12	10
Monterey Dr.	R-12	12A
Morgan Ct.	T-12	12B
Moritz Pl.	P-12	12A
Moritz Pl.	P-11	12A
Morning Watch Rd.	R-15	11
Moro Ter.	T-13	12B
Morris Av.	S-11	12B
Mortimer Rd.	V-12	12B
Mountain Ter.	T-12	12B
Mountain View Blvd.	U-12	12B
Mountainridge Dr.	R-13	12A
Mountainside Dr.	S-13	12B
Mulford Dr.	T-13	12B
Munster Pl.	R-12	12A
Myrtle Av.	T-12	12B
Main Av.	V-12	12B
Nancy Ct.	S-12	12B
Nathan Wy.	R-12	12A
Navajo Av.	T-13	12B
Nellis Dr.	T-13	12B
New St.	T-12	12B
New York Av.	T-12	12B
Newark Av.	T-12	12B
Newark Pompton Tnpk.	S-11	12B
Newton Rd.	U-12	12B
Nimitz Rd.	R-13	12A
Noreen La.	N-12	10
Normandy Dr.	T-14	13
North Jersey Ln.	R-14	11
North Leg	V-13	12B
North Rd.	P-12	12A
North Rd.	P-11	12A
North Rd.	T-11	12B
Nostrand Av.	T-12	12B
North West Rd.	T-11	12B
Nottingham Rd.	Q-13	12A
Nuthatcher Ct.	R-15	11
Oak Hill Dr.	S-12	12A
Oak Hill Dr.	S-12	12B
Oak Ln.	S-14	13
Oak St.	T-12	12B
Oakley Wy.	T-14	13
Oaktree Dr.	S-13	12B
Oakwood Dr.	S-12	12B
Old Homestead Rd.	R-13	12A
Old Turnpike Rd.	V-13	12B
Oldham Rd.	S-15	13
Oldwood Rd.	T-12	12B
Olga St.	R-13	12A
Oliver St.	T-11	12B
Omaha Rd.	P-13	12A
Oneida Tr.	S-13	12A
Orange Pl.	S-12	12A
Orchard Pl.	Q-12	12A
Oriskani Pl.	P-11	12A
Osage Rd.	T-12	12B
Osborne Rd.	S-12	12B
Osborne Rd.	S-13	12B
Osceola Rd.	P-12	12A
Overhill Rd.	P-12	12A
Overlook Av.	T-13	12B
Overlook Av.	S-13	12B
Owens Dr.	R-14	11
Oxbow Pl.	S-14	13
Oxbow Pl.	R-14	11
Packanack Lake Rd.	S-12	12B
Pal Dr.	U-12	12B
Palmer Dr.	S-14	13
Pancake Hollow Dr.	Q-13	12A
Parc Lake Ct.	N-12	10
Parish Dr.	T-13	12B
Parish Rd.	U-12	12B
Park Ln.	V-13	12B
Parker Rd.	U-12	12B
Parkhurst St.	T-12	12B
Parkview Dr.	Q-12	12A
Parkwood Dr.	R-12	12A
Passaic St.	T-12	12B
Paterson Hamburg Tnpk.	Q-12	12A
Paterson Hamburg Tnpk.	P-12	12A
Paterson Hamburg Tnpk.	Q-12	11
Paterson Hamburg Tnpk.	R-13	11
Paterson Hamburg Tnpk.	R-15	11
Paterson Hamburg Tnpk.	R-13	12A
Paterson Hamburg Tnpk.	R-12	11
Paterson Hamburg Tnpk.	R-15	12A
Patricia Ct.	S-12	12B
Patton Ct.	T-14	13
Paul St.	S-12	12B
Pauline Ct.	R-12	12A
Peach Wy.	V-13	12B
Pelham Rd.	T-14	13
Penny Ct.	T-13	12B
Perera Av.	S-13	12B
Perrin Dr.	Q-12	12A
Peslin Ct.	R-12	12A
Peter Pl.	S-13	12B
Peterson Rd.	R-13	12A
Petrie Ln.	T-12	12B
Phyllis Ct.	R-11	12A
Piermont Ter.	R-13	12A
Pike Dr.	R-14	11
Pilgrim Wy.	S-14	13
Pine Ter.	S-13	12B
Pinecrest Ter.	P-12	12A
Pinecrest Ter.	Q-12	12A
Pines Lake Dr. W.	P-12	11
Pines Lake Dr. W.	N-12	11
Pines Lake Dr. W.	P-12	10
Pines Lake Dr. E.	P-12	11
Pines Lake Dr. W.	N-12	10
Pines Lake Dr. E.	N-12	11
Pines Lake Dr. E.	P-12	10
Pines Lake Dr. E.	N-12	10
Pines Lakes Dr.	P-12	12A
Pinetree Dr.	R-12	12A
Pitman Pl.	R-13	12A
Pleasantview Dr.	T-13	12B
Pocahontas Tr.	U-12	12B
Point View Pkwy.	P-14	11
Point View Pkwy.	Q-14	11
Pompton Plains Cross Rd.	Q-11	13
Pompton Rd.	Q-11	13
Pompton Rd.	S-15	13
Pompton Rd.	Q-12	13
Ponds Cir.	T-13	12B
Pontiac Dr.	P-12	12A
Poplar Rd.	P-12	12A
Post Ln.	S-11	12B
Powderhorn Dr.	S-13	12B
Power Av.	R-15	11
Preakness Av.	T-14	13
Preakness Av.	T-15	13
Princton Pl.	P-12	12A
Pueblo Cir.	N-12	10
Queens La.	S-15	13
Quincy Ct.	Q-13	11
Railroad Av.	T-11	12B
Raleigh Ln.	R-12	12A
Ralph Av.	S-15	13
Ramapo Rd.	P-11	12A
Randall Ter.	T-13	12B
Rande Dr.	T-12	12B
Ratcliffe Rd.	S-14	13
Ratzer Rd.	R-14	12A
Ratzer Rd.	R-12	11
Ratzer Rd.	R-12	12B
Ratzer Rd.	R-14	11
Ravine Ln.	Q-14	11
Raymar Ln.	T-12	12B
Rays Ct.	R-14	11
Redwood Av.	Q-12	12A
Redwood Av.	P-12	12A
Reed Ct.	R-12	12A
Reinhardt Rd.	S-15	13
Rene Ct.	P-14	11
Reston Rd.	T-13	12B
Richard Ln.	S-14	13
Ridge Rd.	P-12	12A
Ridgeview Ter.	Q-12	12A
Rigby Ct.	T-13	12B
Rillo Dr.	S-14	13
Rinaldo Ln.	S-14	13
River Lawn Dr.	V-13	13
River Rd. E.	T-12	12B
River Rd. W.	T-11	12B
Riverside Dr.	V-12	12B
Riverview Dr.	U-13	12B
Robin Hood Way	R-12	11
Robin Hood Way	R-12	12A
Robin Rd.	S-14	13
Rock Rd.	S-15	13
Rockledge Ter.	S-13	12B
Roland Pl.	S-14	13
Rolling Hills Dr.	T-14	13
Ronnie Rd.	T-13	12B
Rose Ter.	S-14	13
Rosemount Av.	V-12	12B
Royal Ct.	R-14	11
Rumana Rd.	R-14	11
Runnymeade Dr.	T-14	13
Ruskin Ct.	S-14	13
Russell Ter.	S-13	12B
Rutgers Ct.	T-14	13
Ryder Rd.	S-14	13
Ryerson Av.	T-11	12B
Sagamore Pl.	U-12	12B
Salem Rd.	S-14	13
Salisbury Rd.	R-14	11
Sanderling Rd.	R-15	11
Sandra Ln.	S-11	12B
Saniewski Ln.	T-12	12B
Saratoga Sq.	P-11	12A
Saxon Av.	T-11	12B
Schindler La.	R-14	11
Schumm Sq.	P-11	12A
Schuyler Rd.	Q-12	12A
Scribner Pl.	S-14	13
Sears Pl.	S-14	13
Sell Pl.	R-12	12A
Seminole Av.	T-13	12B
Seneca Tr.	T-13	12B
Sequoia Pl.	P-12	12A
Seth Ct.	R-13	12A
Seven Trails Ln.	Q-14	11
Shadow Ridge Rd.	N-12	10
Shady Ln.	V-12	12B
Shady Ter.	S-13	12B
Shamrock Dr.	V-12	12B
Sharon Ln.	P-12	12A
Shasta Rd.	N-12	10
Shawn Ct.	S-14	13
Shearwater La.	R-15	11
Sheffield Rd.	Q-12	12A
Shepherd Ln.	U-12	12B
Sherman St.	U-12	12B
Sherry Ct.	S-15	11
Sherry Ct.	S-15	13
Sherwood Pl.	R-12	12A
Shesta Dr.	V-12	12B
Shore Rd.	Q-11	12A
Shoshome Tr.	N-12	10
Sierra Ter.	R-11	12A
Siesta Dr.	V-12	12B
Sikkema Av.	S-14	13
Simmons Pl.	S-12	12B
Sinclair Dr.	S-14	13
Sisco St.	R-12	12A
Skyview Rd.	P-12	12A
Sleepy Hollow Dr.	S-12	12B
Sloping Hill Dr.	S-13	12B
Smith Ln.	R-12	12A
Somers Pl.	U-12	12B
South Canal St.	T-12	12B
South Rd.	Q-12	12A
Southhall Ct.	S-14	13
Southhall Ct.	S-14	11
Spring Hill Cir.	P-13	12A
Spring Rd.	T-11	12B
Spruce Ter.	S-13	12B
Squad Pl.	Q-12	12A
Squire Ln.	T-12	12B
Squire Ln.	S-12	12B
St. Moritz Pl.	P-11	12A
Stacy Ct.	R-12	12A
Stagg Rd.	T-13	12B
Stalter Dr.	R-12	12A
Stanford Pl.	R-14	11
Starview Ct.	N-12	10
Stirling Ln.	T-13	12B
Stone Hill Rd.	T-13	12B
Stonycroft Rd.	T-13	12B
Stratton Dr.	T-13	12B
Stuart Ln.	R-14	11
Stuckler Ln.	R-13	12A
Sturbridge Cir.	Q-13	11
Sturbridge Cir.	Q-13	12A
Styles Ter.	U-12	12B
Stylon Rd.	S-11	12B
Summer Hill Rd.	P-13	12A
Summit Dr.	S-13	12B
Sunburst Ln.	N-12	10
Sunny Knolls Ct.	N-12	10
Sunnyridge Rd.	N-12	10
Sunrise Dr.	R-13	12A
Sunset Ter.	S-13	12B
Surrey Dr.	Q-12	12A
Susan Av.	S-13	12B
Sussex Rd.	U-12	12B
Sutter Ln.	T-14	13
Swan Ter.	S-14	13
Swiss Ter.	S-13	12B
Sycamore Ter.	P-12	12A
Sylvan Ter.	S-14	12B
Taft Pl.	S-13	12B
Tall Grass Dr.	R-13	12A
Tall Oaks Dr.	T-12	12B
Tall Oaks Rd.	T-12	12B
Tall Oaks Rd.	T-13	12B
Talsman Ct.	U-13	12B
Tamarack Rd.	Q-12	12A
Tammy Ter.	T-15	13
Tanager Ct.	R-15	11
Taylor Dr.	U-12	12B
Teak Rd.	T-14	13
Terhune Dr.	N-12	10
Terhune Dr.	N-12	12A
Terhune Dr.	P-11	12A
Terhune Dr.	P-11	10
Terhune Dr.	P-12	10
Terhune Dr.	P-12	12A
Terrace Rd.	S-14	13
Teton Cir.	N-12	10
Thomas Ter.	T-13	12B
Thorne Hill	S-15	11
Thorne Hill	S-15	13
Ticonderoga Tr.	P-11	10
Tilghman Dr.	R-12	12A
Timberline Dr.	S-12	12A
Timberline Dr.	S-12	12B
Timothy Rd.	T-13	12B
Todd Ter.	T-12	12B
Tomahawk Dr.	N-12	10
Toms Lake Rd.	Q-12	12A
Toms Lake Rd.	R-12	12A
Torbet Dr.	R-12	12A
Tosch Av.	T-14	13
Totowa Rd.	T-13	12B
Toucan Ct.	S-14	11
Tower Rd.	P-12	11
Tower Rd.	P-12	10
Tower Rd.	N-12	10
Tower Rd.	N-12	11
Towsen Rd.	S-15	13
Traphagen Rd.	R-14	11
Travelo Dr.	V-12	12B
Trenton Ter.	P-12	10
Tripoli St.	T-12	12B
Tudor Ln.	Q-12	12A
Tulip Ter.	P-12	12A
Tuxedo Dr.	S-14	13
Tyler Rd.	V-13	12B
Umberto St.	T-11	12B
Unger Av.	U-12	12B
Upton Ct.	R-12	12A
Urban Club Rd.	R-14	11
Urban Club Rd.	Q-14	11
Vale Rd.	P-12	12A
Valhalla Wy.	Q-12	12A
Valley Hi Rd.	T-14	13
Valley Rd.	T-14	13
Valley Rd.	Q-14	13
Valley Rd.	Q-14	11
Valley Rd.	T-14	11
Valley View Ter.	S-13	12B
Van Allen Ct.	T-13	12B
Van Duyne Av.	U-12	12B
Van Ness Pl.	U-12	12B
Van Riper Rd.	Q-12	12A
Vanderlinde Dr.	Q-12	12A
Vans Ln.	R-12	12A
Varick St.	T-13	12B
Verade Ct.	R-12	12A
Verade Dr.	R-12	12A
Vernon Ct.	R-11	12A
Veteri Pl.	S-13	12B
Veteri Pl.	S-13	13
Veteri Pl.	S-14	13
Veteri Pl.	S-14	12B
Viewpoint Rd.	S-13	12B
Village Dr.	S-14	13
Vincent St.	T-11	12B
Viola Pl.	S-13	12B
Virginia Ct.	S-14	13
Vista Tr.	P-12	12A
Vizcaya Ct.	P-12	12A
Waling Dr.	T-13	12B
Walker Av.	T-11	12B
Wanda Av.	R-12	12A
Warbler Dr.	R-15	11
Warner Wy.	R-12	12A
Warren Pl.	S-13	12B
Water St.	U-12	12B
Waterway Rd.	P-11	12A
Waverly Rd.	T-14	13
Wayne St.	T-11	12B
Webster Dr.	R-12	12A
Wedgewood Dr.	T-12	12B
Weinmanns Blvd.	T-14	13
Wellington Dr.	R-12	12A
Welsh Ct.	P-12	12A
Wendt Ln.	R-11	12A
Wendt Ln.	R-12	12A
West Belt	U-13	12B
West Belt	U-12	12B
West Chester	T-12	12B
West Rd.	R-15	11
West Rd.	R-15	13
West Rd.	S-15	11
West Rd.	S-15	13
West Rd.	T-11	12B
Westervelt St.	U-12	12B
Weston Ct.	R-11	12A
Westview Rd.	P-11	12A
Westview Rd.	P-12	12A
Wheeler Dr.	R-15	11
Whimble Ct.	R-15	11
Whipple Rd.	R-12	12A
White Oak Ln.	T-13	12B
White Oak Ln.	T-13	13
White Oak Ln.	T-14	12B
White Oak Ln.	T-14	13
Whitebirch Ct.	S-13	12B
Whitmore Av.	T-11	12B
Whittaker Ct.	R-12	12A
Widmer Ln.	S-12	12B
Wiessmann Wy.	S-13	12B
William St.	U-12	12B
Williamsburg Ct.	S-14	13
Willis Av.	V-13	12B
Willow Pl.	U-12	12B
Willowbrook Blvd.	V-13	12B
Willowbrook Blvd.	V-13	12B
Wilson Av.	S-13	12B
Winding Wy.	T-12	12B
Windsor Pl.	S-15	13
Winters Dr.	S-13	12B
Witkowski Wy.	T-13	12B
Wittig Ter.	R-12	12A
Wood St.	U-12	12B
Woodhaven Dr.	P-12	12A
Woodhaven Rd.	Q-12	12A
Woodhaven Ct.	S-13	12B
Woodlot Rd.	S-14	13
Woodridge Ter.	T-14	13
Woods Echo Ct.	S-12	12A
Woods Echo Ct.	S-12	12B
Woodstock Dr.	S-14	13
Worcester Dr.	P-13	12A
Yellow Brick Rd.	R-12	12A
Yorktown Rd.	Q-14	11

West Milford, Township of

STREET	GRID	MAP
1st Av.	E-7	3
2nd Av.	E-7	3
3rd Av.	E-7	3
Adams Av.	E-8	3
Adelaide Ter.	E-7	3
Airport Rd.	E-8	3
Albert St.	E-8	3
Albertine Pl.	K-2	8
Albertine Pl.	L-2	8
Albertine Pl.	K-2	5
Albertine Pl.	L-2	5
Algonquin Wy.	K-7	6
Alice Pl.	A-7	1
Allaire Rd.	C-6	1
Allegheny Av.	K-7	6
Allendale Rd.	B-7	1
Allison Av.	K-3	5
Alpine Ct.	B-6	1
Alpine Ln.	G-7	6
Alpine Ridge Rd.	G-7	6
Alps Rd.	A-6	1
Alvin Rd.	H-6	5
Anchor Av.	E-6	2
Ancora Rd.	B-6	1
Andrew Ct.	G-6	5
Anthony St.	A-7	1
Apple Tree Ln.	K-2	5
Applegate Ct.	F-7	3
Apshawa Cross Rd.	M-7	9
Arcata Ln.	E-7	3
Arcola Rd.	C-6	1
Ardena Rd.	B-6	1
Argonne Ter.	B-8	1
Arlington Av.	C-8	1
Arnold Dr.	H-6	5
Arrowhead Dock Rd.	K-7	6
Arundel Rd.	G-6	5
Ash Rd.	E-7	3
Ashbrook Ln.	M-7	9
Ashbury Ct.	B-7	1
Aspen Ln.	D-8	3
Atco Ct.	C-6	1
Atlantic La.	G-5	5
Audubon Rd.	B-7	1
Audubon Rd.	A-7	1
Aura Ct.	A-8	1
Autumn Ct.	F-7	3
Avalon Rd.	B-6	1
Avon Rd.	C-6	1
Awosting Rd.	D-9	3
Baldwin Dr.	J-7	6
Banker Rd.	B-6	1
Barnegat Rd.	B-6	1
Baron Rd.	G-7	6
Bayhead Rd.	A-6	1
Bayonne Dr.	A-6	1
Bayonne Dr.	B-6	1
Beach Haven Rd.	B-6	1
Beacon Hill Rd.	F-6	2
Bear Tr.	F-6	2
Alpine Ct.	B-6	1
Bearford Walk	E-7	3
Bearfort Rd.	E-7	3
Beaver Av.	D-8	3
Beech Av.	D-10	3
Beech Av.	D-11	3
Belcher Av.	D-8	3
Belford Dr.	B-7	1
Belle Av.	B-6	1
Belleau Gateway	E-7	3
Belmar Ct.	B-7	1
Belmont Dr.	D-7	3
Bentley Dr.	C-6	1
Bergen Dr.	G-6	5
Berkley Ct.	B-7	1
Beverly Ct.	B-6	1
Binncale Av.	E-6	2
Birch Av.	D-8	3
Birchwood Pass	E-7	3
Bisset Dr.	H-6	5
Black Walnut Way	F-6	2
Blackfoot Rd.	C-6	1
Blakeley Ln.	L-5	8
Board Rd.	D-8	3
Boat Basin Rd.	D-8	3
Bonter Rd.	J-2	5
Bordeaux Ter.	G-7	6
Bracken Rd.	K-6	5
Bradick Ln.	G-7	5
Bradick Ln.	G-7	6
Bradick Ln.	G-6	5
Bradick Ln.	G-6	6
Bradley Ct.	A-8	1
Brady St.	J-7	6
Briarcliff Dr.	J-7	6
Brielle Ct.	B-7	1
Broad Acres Rd.	D-8	3
Broadway	H-7	6
Broadway	J-7	6
Brook Ln.	C-6	1
Brook Rd.	C-6	1
Brookfield Rd.	D-6	2
Brookfield Rd.	D-5	2
Brookside Dr.	D-6	2
Brown Ct.	F-7	3
Buchanan Rd.	J-7	6
Buck Mountain Ct.	F-8	3
Bunker Hill Rd.	F-6	2
Burlington Dr.	K-7	6
Burnt Meadow Rd.	E-9	3
Burnt Meadow Rd.	E-9	6
Burnt Meadow Rd.	G-9	3
Burnt Meadow Rd.	G-9	6
Burrow Rd.	A-7	1
Bushwick Ln.	E-7	3
Butler Ln.	E-7	3
Cahill Cross Rd.	F-7	3
Caldwell Rd.	C-6	1
Camden Pl.	G-6	5
Camden Pl.	G-5	5
Camelot Dr.	F-6	2
Canistear Rd.	H-2	5
Canistear Rd.	G-2	5
Canistear Rd.	H-1	5
Canistear Rd.	G-1	5
Capstan Rd.	E-6	2
Carmel Rd.	B-6	1
Caro Dr.	L-2	8
Caro Dr.	K-2	8
Caro Dr.	K-2	5
Caro Dr.	L-2	5
Carolyn St.	F-7	3
Carriage Ln.	G-7	6
Carteret St.	G-7	6
Catalpa Dr.	L-6	8
Cedar Ln.	D-8	3
Cedarbrook Rd.	B-6	1
Center St.	F-7	3
Center St.	E-7	3
Central Av.	D-8	3
Charcoal Rd.	J-4	5
Charissa Ct.	C-6	1
Charles St.	E-7	3
Charlottesburg Rd.	L-5	8
Chatham Rd.	A-7	1
Chatham Rd.	B-7	1
Cherbourg Dr.	G-7	6
Cherokee Wy.	M-6	8
Cherry Ridge Rd.	D-5	2
Cherry Ridge Rd.	C-5	2
Cherry Ridge Rd.	C-5	1
Cherry Ridge Rd.	D-5	1
Chester Rd.	A-7	1
Chestnut Dr.	F-7	3
Chickadee Rd.	A-8	1
Chippewa Ter.	G-2	5
Chippy Ln.	K-7	6
Circle Blvd. E.	K-3	5
Circle Blvd. S.	K-3	5
Circle Dr.	K-1	5
Clara St.	H-7	6
Clayton Rd.	B-7	1
Cleer Mountain Rd.	G-8	6
Clermont Rd.	A-6	1
Cleveland Dr.	E-8	3
Cliff Rd.	E-7	3
Cliffside Dr.	J-7	6
Clinton Rd.	J-3	2
Clinton Rd.	E-5	2
Clinton Rd.	G-4	5
Clinton Rd.	G-4	2
Clinton Rd.	E-5	5
Clinton Rd.	J-3	5
Clinton View Ter.	C-6	1
Clover Rd.	J-6	5
Club House Ter.	C-6	1
Club Pl.	C-6	1
Clubhouse Av.	K-7	6
Coal Rd.	F-6	2
Cold Spring Rd.	B-6	1
Commanche Ln.	C-6	1
Community Pl.	K-3	5
Compass Av.	E-7	3
Concord Rd.	F-6	2
Conklin Rd.	J-4	5
Connecting Rd.	C-8	3
Continental Rd.	G-7	6
Cooley Ln.	D-8	1
Cooley Ln.	C-8	1
Cooley Ln.	D-8	3
Cooley Ln.	C-8	3
Coolidge Ter.	E-8	3
Cooper Rd.	K-1	5
Cornelia Av.	D-8	3
Corter Ln.	K-6	5
Cottage Cv.	D-8	3
County R.O.W.	B-9	1
County Rd.	B-6	1
Coventry Rd.	K-3	5
Coventry Rd.	J-3	5
Cozy Lake Rd.	K-3	5
Crabtree Rd.	K-7	6
Crane Ln.	G-1	5
Crawford St.	H-6	5
Crescent Rd.	K-7	6
Crest Lake Dr.	J-2	5
Cross Rd.	F-7	3
Cross Rd.	K-3	5
Croton Rd.	B-6	1
Cudney Rd.	A-6	1
Cumberland Rd.	G-6	5
Curtis Ct.	D-7	3
Cutlass Rd.	C-6	1
Cypress Pl.	L-6	8
Dan Jennings Rd.	K-2	5
Danforth Av.	A-7	1
Daniel St.	K-3	5
Daretown Rd.	A-6	1
Davenport Rd.	L-2	8
Davenport Rd.	K-1	5
Davenport Rd.	K-1	8
Davenport Rd.	L-2	5
Dayton Rd.	C-6	1
DeHart Av.	D-8	3
Deal Rd.	B-7	1
Deborah La.	H-8	6
Deer Path	K-7	6
Deerbrook La.	H-8	6
Dehart Av.	D-8	3
Delaware Rd.	B-6	1
Delmont Rd.	B-6	1
Denville Ct.	A-8	1
Dew Av.	D-8	3
Diane Dr.	G-6	5
Dockerty Hollow Rd.	F-6	5
Dockerty Hollow Rd.	G-6	5
Doe Run	C-6	1
Dogwood Ln.	B-9	1
Dongan Ln.	J-4	5
Doremus Rd.	J-2	5
Dorothy Rd.	A-7	1
Dove Ct.	B-7	1
Dover Rd.	A-7	1
Dover Rd.	A-6	1
Dudley St.	H-7	6
Dunham Rd.	B-7	1
Dunham Rd.	A-7	1
Dunkers Pond Rd.	H-2	5
Dunkirk Ct.	G-7	6
Duralee Ct.	G-5	5
Durant Rd.	D-8	3
Durmont Ct.	B-7	1
Eagle Rock Rd.	G-6	5
Eagle Rock Rd.	G-6	6
Eagle Rock Rd.	G-7	5
Eagle Rock Rd.	G-7	6
East Av.	K-7	6
East Park Dr.	K-7	6
East Shore Dr.	C-9	1
Eastside Rd.	B-8	1
Eatontown Rd.	B-7	1
Echo Lake Rd.	L-5	8

PASSAIC COUNTY

STREET	GRID	MAP
Echo Ln.	E-7	3
Edgar Dr.	E-8	3
Edgecumb Rd.	D-7	3
Edgewater Dr.	D-7	3
Edgewater Dr.	D-8	3
Edgewater Rd.	B-6	1
Edgewater Rd.	C-8	3
Edgewood Rd.	C-8	3
Eisenhower Dr.	E-8	3
Elberon Rd.	B-6	1
Elias La.	G-2	5
Elizabeth Rd.	B-7	1
Ell Rd.	E-7	1
Ellisdale Rd.	A-7	1
Elm St.	D-8	1
Elm St.	D-8	3
Elm St.	C-8	1
Elm St.	C-8	3
Elmer Ct.	B-7	1
Elmwood Ct.	C-6	1
Emerson Rd.	B-7	1
Essex St.	H-7	6
Estelville Ct.	A-8	1
Evanstan Av.	K-7	6
Eve Pl.	D-8	3
Evelyn Dr.	H-6	5
Evergreen Rd.	C-6	1
Ewan Ct.	B-6	1
Fair Pl.	K-3	5
Fairlawn Rd.	A-7	1
Fairview Ct.	B-7	1
Fairview Rd.	F-7	3
Fanwood Ct.	B-7	1
Ferndale Dr.	K-8	6
Fieldstone Ln.	K-6	5
Finderne Ct.	B-6	1
Flanders Rd.	C-7	1
Flanders Rd.	B-7	1
Florence Rd.	B-6	1
Forest Lake Dr.	C-9	1
Forest St.	E-7	1
Forge Rd.	D-9	3
Fountain Rd.	K-6	5
Fox Ct.	G-7	6
Fox Tr.	L-6	8
Foxboro La.	F-6	5
Franklin Ct.	C-6	1
Frederick Dr.	H-6	5
Freehold Ct.	B-7	1
Freemont Ter.	J-3	5
Frontier Tr.	L-6	8
Garfield Rd.	F-8	3
Garret Ct.	G-6	5
Garwood Rd.	A-7	1
Garwood Rd.	A-6	1
George St.	E-8	3
George St.	E-7	3
Germantown Rd.	M-6	8
Germantown Rd.	K-6	5
Germantown Rd.	M-6	5
Germantown Rd.	K-6	8
Gifford Rd.	B-9	1
Gilbert Pl.	H-7	6
Gladstone Rd.	A-7	1
Gleason Rd.	C-8	1
Glen Cross Rd.	D-7	3
Glen Dr.	J-7	6
Glenda Dr.	H-6	5
Glendale Rd.	B-9	1
Glendale Rd.	B-8	1
Glennon Rd.	J-6	5
Glenridge Rd.	B-6	1
Glens Rd.	C-9	1
Glenwood Rd.	B-7	1
Gold Dr.	K-1	5
Gold Finch Ln.	D-6	2
Gold Finch Ln.	D-5	2
Goshen Rd.	B-6	1
Gould Rd.	H-5	5
Graham Dr.	D-8	3
Grandview Ln.	D-7	3
Grant Av.	E-8	3
Green Ln.	K-2	5
Green Terrace Way	J-6	5
Greenbrook Dr.	D-8	3
Greendale Dr.	J-2	5
Greenloch Ct.	B-7	1
Greenwich Rd.	B-7	1
Greenwood Av.	C-9	1
Greenwood Lake Tnpk.	D-9	3
Greenwood Lake Tnpk.	E-9	3
Greenwood Lake Tnpk.	D-8	3
Greenwood Lake Tnpk.	E-8	3
Grove St.	K-2	5
Guy Ln.	E-10	3
Gwyneth Rd.	D-7	3
Haase Rd.	J-7	6
Haddon Rd.	C-6	1
Hamilton Dr.	C-6	1
Hampton Rd.	A-7	1
Hampton Rd.	A-8	1
Hancock Dr.	J-7	6
Hanover Rd.	B-6	1
Harrison St.	K-2	5
Harvey Rd.	B-6	1
Hawthorne Rd.	B-6	1
Hayes Rd.	F-7	3
Hazel Rd.	F-7	3
Heather Ln.	E-7	3
Hemlock Ln.	D-7	3
Henderson Rd.	G-2	5
Henderson Rd.	F-2	5
Henderson Rd.	G-2	2
Henderson Rd.	F-2	2
Henry Rd.	B-6	1
Hewitt Rd.	A-7	1
Hewitt Rd.	B-7	1
Hiawatha Pass	M-6	8
Hickory Av.	E-7	3
High St.	J-7	6
Highcrest Dr.	M-7	9
Highland Av.	L-6	8
Highlander Dr.	H-6	5
Hightop Rd.	J-7	6
Highview Dr.	H-7	6
Hillcrest Dr.	B-6	1
Hillside Ln.	D-7	3
Hilltop Rd.	K-4	5
Hillview Av.	H-6	5
Hilo Ter.	J-4	5
Hilton Ct.	B-7	1
Hirth Dr.	J-5	5
Holiday Ln.	H-7	6
Hollis Ter.	L-6	8
Hollow Rd.	E-5	2
Homestead Rd.	C-7	1
Hoover Rd.	E-7	3
Hopler Pl.	J-4	5
Hudson Dr.	H-7	6
Hunter Blvd.	L-6	8
Hunterton Pl.	G-5	5
Hyde Rd.	F-2	2
Indian Dock Rd.	K-7	6
Indian Tr.	L-6	8
Industrial Rd.	E-8	3
Inez Ct.	F-7	3
Inwood Rd.	K-6	5
Iona Ct.	B-7	1
Irving Pl.	B-6	1
Iselin Rd.	B-6	1
Island Tr.	C-6	1
Ivan Rd.	D-8	3
Ivy Pl.	D-8	3
Jacobs Rd.	K-6	5
James Ln.	E-7	3
Jamesburg Rd.	A-8	1
Janice Ct.	G-6	5
Janvier Rd.	B-6	1
Jefferson St.	K-2	5
Jefferson St.	K-3	5
Jenkins Rd.	B-6	1
Joan Dr.	G-6	5
John St.	D-8	3
Joseph Pl.	J-7	6
Juniata St.	E-7	3
Kanouse Rd.	H-5	5
Kanouse Rd.	K-4	5
Kanouse Rd.	K-5	5
Keel Rd.	E-7	3
Kildeer Path	K-6	5
King Arthur Ct.	F-6	2
Kingsland Rd.	A-7	1
Kingswood Rd.	A-7	1
Kitchell Lake Dr. W.	H-8	6
Kitchell Lake Dr. E.	H-8	6
Kitchell Lake Dr. W.	G-8	6
Knoll Pl.	D-8	3
Krattiger Ct.	J-6	5
Kreson Rd.	B-7	1
Kushaqua Dr. W.	B-8	1
Kushaqua Tr. N.	B-9	1
La Rue Rd.	K-4	5
Lackawanna Tr.	K-8	6
Lafayette St.	E-7	3
Lake Av.	C-9	1
Lake Isle Dr.	J-7	6
Lake Park Ter.	C-9	1
Lake Shore Dr.	C-7	1
Lake Shore Dr.	B-6	1
Lake Shore Dr.	B-7	1
Lakeside Rd.	C-8	1
Lakeview Dr.	J-7	6
Lakeview Dr.	H-7	6
Lakewood Rd.	A-7	1
Lambert Rd.	D-8	3
Lancaster Ln.	G-5	5
Lancelot Ln.	F-6	2
Land of Oaks Dr.	J-2	5
Landing Rd.	B-7	1
Laramie Tr.	C-6	1
Larchmont Dr.	C-6	1
Larsen Rd.	J-7	6
Larve Rd.	K-4	5
Larve Rd.	K-3	5
Laurel Av.	D-8	3
Laurel Hollow	H-7	6
Lawrence Kocher Ln.	D-8	3
Layton Rd.	B-7	1
Lebanon Rd.	B-6	1
Lebanon Rd.	A-6	1
Lee Ct.	B-6	1
Lenape Tr.	E-7	3
Leonard Av.	L-6	8
Leslie Dr.	H-6	5
Lexington Av.	F-6	2
Lincoln Av.	E-8	3
Lincoln Av.	D-8	3
Linden Ct.	C-7	1
Lindsay Rd.	K-2	5
Lindy's Dr.	J-7	6
Lindy's Dr.	H-7	6
Linwood Rd.	A-7	1
Little Pond Ln.	H-7	6
Locust Ct.	F-7	3
Locust Ct.	B-7	1
Logan Av.	H-7	6
Long House Dr.	A-7	1
Long Pond Dr.	C-9	1
Longstreak Rd.	J-4	5
Longview Rd.	M-7	9
Lookout Ln.	L-6	8
Lookover Dr.	D-6	2
Lou Ann Blvd.	D-7	3
Louis Av.	D-8	3
Louise Av.	F-8	3
Lozier Ct.	F-7	3
Lyons Rd.	B-6	1
Ma Donald Dr.	D-8	3
Mac Gregor Rd.	G-6	6
Macopin Rd.	G-7	5
Macopin Rd.	G-6	6
Macopin Rd.	L-7	5
Macopin Rd.	L-7	6
Macopin Rd.	K-6	6
Macopin Rd.	K-6	5
Macopin Rd.	G-6	5
Macopin Rd.	G-7	6
Macopin Ter.	M-7	9
Madelyn Av.	D-8	3
Magnolia Rd.	B-6	1
Maine Rd.	B-6	1
Maine Rd.	A-6	1
Maisie Ln.	F-7	3
Mallard Rd.	J-7	6
Mallory Rd.	M-7	9
Manchester La.	F-6	2
Maple Rd.	J-6	5
Maple Rd.	J-6	6
Maple Rd.	J-7	5
Maple Rd.	J-7	6
Maple Shade Rd.	B-7	1
Marhill Rd.	E-8	3
Marilyn Ct.	B-6	1
Marion St.	E-7	3
Marisa Ct.	H-7	6
Mark Ter.	K-3	5
Marlboro Rd.	C-6	1
Marshall Hill Rd.	E-7	3
Marshall Hill Rd.	E-8	3
Martha St.	K-6	5
Mary St.	J-7	6
Maybelle Ct.	J-4	5
Mayfair Ct.	J-4	5
Mayflower Av.	L-6	8
McCormick Rd.	K-6	5
McKinley Pl.	E-8	3
Meadow Rd.	E-7	3
Meadowview Ct.	J-4	5
Melinda La.	A-7	1
Melody Ln.	F-7	3
Melrose Av.	C-6	1
Mercer Pl.	G-6	5
Metuchen Rd.	A-7	1
Mickens La.	E-7	3
Middlesex Ct.	G-5	5
Midway Tr.	K-7	6
Milford Ln.	E-7	3
Millington Av.	C-8	1
Milton Ct.	B-7	1
Misty La.	K-6	5
Mohawk Tr.	M-6	8
Mohawk Tr.	L-6	8
Mohican Tr.	K-7	6
Monique La.	F-7	3
Monmouth Av.	G-5	5
Monroe Ct.	B-7	1
Moore Rd.	E-8	3
Morris Av.	G-6	5
Morsemere Rd.	B-7	1
Morsemere Rd.	A-7	1
Morsetown Rd.	F-8	3
Morsetown Rd.	H-8	6
Morsetown Rd.	F-8	6
Morsetown Rd.	H-8	3
Mount Hope Av.	C-9	1
Mountain Av.	D-9	3
Mountain Cir. E.	F-8	3
Mountain Cir. N.	F-8	3
Mountain Cir. S.	F-8	3
Mountain Cir. W.	F-8	3
Mountain Rd.	D-7	3
Mountain Side Rd.	J-7	6
Mountain Spring Rd.	L-6	8
Navajo Tr.	L-6	8
Navajo Tr.	M-6	8
Neilson Pl.	J-2	5
Nelson Pl.	L-6	8
Neptune Rd.	B-6	1
Nescoe Ct.	B-7	1
Netcong Rd.	C-6	1
New Bedford Rd.	F-6	2
New City Rd.	M-6	8
New Dockerty Hollow Rd.	G-6	5
New Jersey Av.	E-7	3
Newark Rd.	A-6	1
Newfield Rd.	A-7	1
Newland Dr.	J-2	5
Newton Dr.	K-7	6
Normad Rd.	C-6	1
Norman Av.	K-2	5
North Glenwood Rd.	K-6	5
North Rd.	B-8	1
North Rd.	B-9	1
North Shore Tr.	L-6	8
Northwood Dr.	M-7	9
Norwood Rd.	A-7	1
Nosenzo Pond Rd.	H-6	5
Notch Rd.	E-7	3
O'Leary Rd.	F-7	3
Oak Dr.	K-1	5
Oak Ridge Rd.	L-1	8
Oakley Ct.	B-7	1
Oakwood Av.	L-6	8
Olcott Rd.	D-8	3
Old Echo Lake Rd.	K-6	5
Old Hickory Rd.	G-7	6
Old Hoop Pole Rd.	J-2	5
Old Lakeside Rd. S.	C-8	1
Old Milford Ln.	G-5	5
Old Rd.	E-9	3
Old Route 23	H-1	5
Old Route 23	K-4	5
Olden Av.	C-8	1
Oldwick Ct.	B-7	1
Orange Rd.	D-8	3
Orbit Rd.	D-7	3
Orchard Ln.	E-7	3
Oriole Rd.	D-7	3
Orleans La.	G-7	5
Ormond Rd.	B-6	1
Osage Dr.	S-7	6
Ottenhole Rd.	H-7	6
Ottenhole Rd.	K-7	6
Overlook Rd.	E-7	3
Oxbox Ln.	H-5	5
Palmetto Ln.	D-8	3
Palmyra Rd.	A-7	1
Papscoe Rd.	B-7	1
Papscoe Rd.	A-7	1
Paradise Rd.	K-3	5
Paradise Rd.	H-2	5
Paradise Rd.	G-2	5
Park Ln.	E-7	3
Parlin Ct.	B-7	1
Passaic Dr.	B-7	1
Paterson Rd.	A-7	1
Paterson Rd.	B-7	1
Paul St.	K-2	5
Pawnee Ter.	M-7	9
Peach Tree Ln.	L-6	8
Pecan Pl.	L-6	8
Penmere Rd.	K-8	6
Peter Rd.	F-7	3
Pheasant Ln.	K-7	6
Philips Rd.	B-9	1
Pickwick Ct.	B-7	1
Pickwick Ct.	C-7	1
Pierce Av.	K-1	5
Piermont Ct.	C-6	1
Pilot Av.	E-7	3
Pine Ln.	D-8	3
Pinecliff Lake Dr.	E-7	3
Pinecrest Tr.	G-6	5
Pinehurst Rd.	F-2	2
Pleasant Rd.	A-7	1
Pleasantview Dr.	K-7	6
Pleasantview Dr.	J-7	6
Plumridge Rd.	J-7	6
Plymouth Av.	D-7	3
Plymouth Av.	F-6	2
Point Breeze Dr.	B-7	1
Polk Ct.	B-7	1
Pompton Rd.	Q-12	12A
Pompton Rd.	Q-11	12A
Pond View Dr.	H-3	5
Ponderosa Pl.	D-9	3
Pontiac Ct.	F-7	3
Pool Dr.	J-7	6
Poplar Grove Ter.	K-7	6
Post Brook Rd. S.	J-7	6
Post Brook Rd. N.	J-7	6
Post Pl.	J-4	5
Prescott Av.	D-8	3
Princeton Rd.	B-6	1
Prospect Ln.	E-7	3
Puddinstone Ln.	H-5	5
Quarry Av.	E-7	3
Queens Ct.	F-6	2
Quigley Rd.	B-8	1
Quill St.	E-7	3
Quince Tree Ln.	L-6	8
Quincy La.	F-6	2
Quinton Rd.	B-7	1
Quinty Pl.	D-8	3
Rabbit Run Dr.	J-4	5
Race Track Dr.	B-7	1
Radell Rd.	A-7	1
Ramapo Rd.	C-9	1
Ramsey Ct.	B-7	1
Ramsey Rd.	B-7	1
Raritan Ct.	A-8	1
Raven Ct.	G-7	6
Raymond Blvd.	F-8	3
Red Barn Ln.	H-7	6
Reidy Pl.	C-8	1
Reigler Rd.	B-6	1
Relda Av.	H-6	5
Reservoir Rd.	L-1	8
Rhinesmith Rd.	G-8	6
Richard Dr.	G-6	5
Richmond Rd.	F-7	3
Ricker Rd.	K-3	5
Ridge Rd.	H-7	6
Ridge Rd.	E-7	6
Ridge Rd.	H-7	3
Ridge Rd.	E-7	3
Ridgewood Dr.	L-6	8
Ringwood Ln.	D-8	3
Risley Rd.	A-6	1
Riverside Rd.	A-7	1
Riverview Rd.	K-2	5
Robert St.	E-8	3
Robert St.	E-7	3
Robin Ln.	K-7	6
Rock Rd.	K-7	6
Rock Spring Tr.	L-6	8
Rockburn Pass	G-7	6
Rockledge Rd.	G-6	5
Rocky Point Rd.	C-8	1
Roeblin Rd.	A-7	1
Roger Dr.	H-6	5
Rolling Ridge Rd.	G-7	6
Roosevelt Rd.	E-7	3
Rumson Ct.	B-7	1
Rutgers Av.	E-8	3
Ryan Ct.	G-7	6
Sade Ter.	B-7	1
Saint George St.	D-7	1
Salem Ct.	A-7	1
Salem La.	F-6	2
Sanders Ct.	J-7	6
Sandlor Ter.	J-2	5
Sawmill Rd.	K-6	5
Scenic Dr.	K-2	5
Schmidke La.	B-6	1
Schofield Rd.	J-7	6
School House Cove Rd.	H-3	5
School House Cove Rd.	J-3	5
Seabright Ct.	B-7	1
Secaucus Rd.	B-7	1
Seminole Wy.	L-6	8
Seneca Rd.	J-7	6
Setting Sun Tr.	K-7	6
Sewell Rd.	B-7	1
Seymour Dr.	J-7	6
Seymour Dr.	H-7	6
Shadowy Ln.	D-7	3
Shady Ln.	D-7	3
Shadyside Rd.	C-6	1
Shale Dr.	H-7	6
Shephard Rd.	D-9	3
Sherwood Ct.	J-6	5
Shore Dr.	J-7	6
Silver Ln.	K-1	5
Silverton Walk	B-7	1
Sivertown Rd.	B-7	1
Sisco Rd.	K-4	5
Skyview Rd.	H-8	5
Skyview Rd.	G-8	5
Slater Rd.	D-8	3
Smithville Rd.	C-6	1
Snake Den Rd.	H-8	6
Snake Den Rd.	J-8	6
Somerset Pl.	G-5	5
Sophie Av.	D-8	3
South Rd.	B-8	1
South Richfield Rd.	B-6	1
Spinnler Dr.	J-7	6
Spring Av.	D-8	3
Spruce Point Tr.	C-6	1
Spruce St.	K-2	1
Stainsby Rd.	D-8	1
Stanley St.	K-7	6
Stanton Ct.	B-7	1
Starlight Rd.	H-6	5
Stephens Rd.	E-5	5
Stephens Rd.	G-5	5
Sterling Ct.	B-9	1
Stickle Rd.	H-2	5
Stone Fence Rd.	E-7	1
Stone Hedge Way	H-8	6
Stoney Ln.	K-7	6
Storm Island Rd.	B-9	1
Stowaway Rd.	E-6	2
Struble Ln.	M-7	9
Sugar Maple Av.	J-4	5
Summit Rd.	K-6	5
Sunnyview Dr.	H-7	6
Sunrise St.	K-7	6
Sunset Ln.	E-7	3
Sunset Rd.	D-8	3
Sussex Dr.	G-5	5
Sweet Briar Rd.	K-6	5
Sweetman Ln.	G-6	6
Sweetman Ln.	G-7	6
Sweetman Ln.	G-7	5
Sweetman Ln.	G-6	5
Sycamore Ln.	B-6	1
Sylvan Ln.	E-7	3
Taft Rd.	A-6	1
Tangerine Ct.	D-8	3
Teal Rd.	L-6	8
Tenafly Ct.	A-7	1
Teoter Wy.	K-7	6
Terra Cotta Rd.	B-8	1
Terrace Rd.	E-7	3
Tice Rd.	D-9	3
Timber Ln. E.	H-5	5
Timber Ln. W.	H-5	5
Timberbrook Rd.	L-5	8
Tintle Av.	D-8	3
Tioga Dr.	K-7	6
Toms Rd.	G-6	5
Torne Mountain Rd.	K-7	6
Transboro Rd.	A-7	1
Trenton Rd.	A-6	1
Truro Rd.	K-7	6
Tulip Av.	D-8	3
Twin Oaks Tr.	B-9	1
Ulisses Ln.	J-2	5
Ulisses Ln.	J-1	5
Ulster St.	J-7	6
Umber Rd.	B-6	1
Union Valley Rd.	D-8	3
Union Valley Rd.	K-4	3
Union Valley Rd.	D-7	3
Union Valley Rd.	F-6	3
Upper Greenwood Lake Rd.	A-7	1
Upper Greenwood Lake Rd.	B-7	1
Upper High Crest Rd.	M-7	9
Upper Mount Glen Lake Dr.	J-7	6
Upsula Path	H-7	6
Valley Rd.	B-9	1
Valleyview Ln.	E-7	3
Valleyview Ln.	D-7	3
Van Cleef Rd.	L-7	9
Van Nostrand La.	L-7	9
Van Orden Rd.	J-4	5
Verona Rd.	A-7	1
Viking Rd.	J-7	6
Vine Av.	E-7	3
Vineland Rd.	B-7	1
Vista Rd.	E-7	5
Vreeland Rd.	G-6	5
Vreeland Rd.	G-6	6
Vreeland Rd.	G-7	5
Vreeland Rd.	G-7	6
Walisch Av.	D-8	3
Wallace Cross Rd.	K-2	5
Walnut St.	K-3	5
Wanaque Rd.	C-9	3
Wanaque Rd.	D-9	3
Warren Pl.	G-5	5
Warwick Tnpk.	C-6	1
Warwick Tnpk.	B-6	1
Washington Ln.	E-7	3
Waterford Walk	B-7	1
Wayside Rd.	C-6	1
Weaver Rd.	K-7	6
Weaver Rd.	L-7	9
Weaver Rd.	K-7	9
Weaver Rd.	L-7	6
Weedon Dr.	H-6	5
Wenonah Ct.	B-7	1
Wesley Dr.	H-6	5
West Brook Rd.	H-6	6
West Brook Rd.	H-6	5
West Brook Rd.	H-9	5
West Brook Rd.	H-9	6
West Shore Rd.	E-7	3
West Shore Rd.	E-7	2
Westwood Ct.	C-6	1
White Rd.	D-7	3
Wildwood St.	K-7	6
Wilfred Ln.	K-1	5
Will Ln.	F-7	3
William St.	E-7	3
Wilson Av.	K-2	5
Windbeam Av.	D-9	3
Winding Wy.	G-7	6
Windsor Rd.	D-7	1
Winetka Ln.	E-7	3
Winter Ter.	B-9	1
Witte Rd.	C-6	5
Wolley Rd.	G-6	5
Wolley Rd.	H-5	5
Wolley Rd.	H-6	5
Wolley Rd.	G-5	5
Wood St.	K-6	5
Woodcock La.	L-6	8
Woodcrest Tr.	K-7	6
Woodland Dr.	D-8	3
Woodland Dr.	C-8	3
Woodridge Dr.	J-2	5
Woodside Dr.	J-7	6
Woodside St.	J-7	6
Wykoff Ct.	B-6	1
Wyler Pl.	C-6	1
Yacare Path	K-7	6
Yale Rd.	C-6	1
Yancy Ter.	C-6	1
Yardville Rd.	B-7	1
Yearling Tr.	C-6	1
Yellowstone Av.	D-8	3
Yonder Ln.	D-8	3
Yorkshire Av.	H-6	5
Yorktown Rd.	A-7	1

West Paterson, Borough of

STREET	GRID	MAP
Alcazar Av.	V-15	13
Alexandria Ct.	V-15	13
Andrews Dr.	V-15	13
Arcadia	V-15	13
Bartsch Av.	V-15	13
Bauer's Ln.	V-15	13
Bell Av.	V-15	13
Bergen Blvd.	V-15	13
Bolos La	V-15	13
Borrego Dr.	V-15	13
Borrowski Pl.	V-15	13
Brookview Dr.	V-15	13
Brophy Ln.	V-15	13
Browertown Rd.	V-15	13
Bush Av.	U-15	13
Canger Av.	U-15	13
Caroline St.	V-16	13
Casson Ln.	V-16	13
Cedarhurst Av.	V-15	13
Cedarwood Tr.	W-15	15
Chestnut Grove Av.	U-16	13
Chestnut Grove Av.	U-15	13
Cliffside Dr.	V-15	13
Dogwood Ct.	W-15	15
Dowling Pkwy.	V-15	13
Dulles Dr.	V-15	13
Eben Av.	V-15	13
Elizabeth Ln.	V-15	13
Ferrar Pl.	U-15	13
Filippone Wy.	V-15	13
Garden Av.	U-15	13
Garden Av.	U-16	13
Garret Dr.	V-16	13
Glover Av.	U-15	13
Grandview Dr.	V-15	13
Gray Ter.	W-15	15
Great Notch Rd.	W-15	15
Greenway La.	U-16	13
Harrison Ct.	V-15	13
Haverhill Av.	V-15	13
Hazel St.	V-16	13
Highview Dr.	V-15	13
Hillcrest Av.	V-15	13
Hillery St.	U-15	13
Hillside Ter.	V-16	13
Hobart Av.	V-16	13
Hobart Av.	V-15	13
Hromiak Ter.	V-15	13
Hughs Pl.	V-15	13
Hugo Av.	U-16	13
Irving Pl.	U-15	13
Jackson Av.	U-15	13
Josy St.	U-15	13
Kay Rd.	V-15	13
Kelsey Av.	V-16	13
Leighton Av.	V-16	13
Lincoln Av.	V-15	13
Linden Av.	V-14	13
Lookout Ln.	V-15	13
Lower Notch Rd.	W-15	15
Lozrovich Pl.	V-15	13
Maple Av.	U-15	13
Marcellus Av.	U-15	13
Mary Av.	U-15	13
McBride Av.	V-15	13
McBride Av.	U-14	13
McBride Av.	U-15	13
McBride Av.	V-14	13
McKeown Av.	U-15	13
Memorial Dr.	V-15	13
Merline Av.	V-15	13
Messer Ln.	V-15	13
Miller Pond Rd.	V-15	13
Miller Av.	V-15	13
Morley Dr.	V-15	13
Mount Pleasant Av.	U-15	13
Mount Pleasant Av.	V-15	13
Mountain Av.	U-16	13
Mountain Av.	V-16	13
Mulroony Cir.	V-15	13
New St.	U-16	13
Newby Av.	U-15	13
Oak Dr.	W-13	12B
Oak Hill Rd.	W-15	15
Oak Ridge Rd.	V-15	13
Oak Ridge Rd.	V-16	13
Old Orchard Rd.	V-15	13
Old Rifle Camp Rd.	W-15	15
Overmount Av.	V-15	13
Overmount Av.	V-16	13
Park Dr.	V-16	13
Park Rd.	V-16	13
Park Rd.	U-16	13
Pascale Pl.	V-15	13
Passaic Av.	V-15	13
Pay St.	U-15	13
Peckman Av.	V-15	13
Peckman Av.	V-14	13
Pershing Pl.	V-15	13
Pitts Av.	V-15	13
Poley St.	U-15	13
Pomoton Av.	V-15	13
Pond Rd.	V-16	13
Providence Av.	U-15	13
Radcliff Av.	V-14	13
Ramapo Av.	V-15	13
Randalzo La.	U-15	13
Ray Av.	V-14	13
Reservoir Rd.	W-15	15
Ridgeview Dr.	V-15	13
Rifle Camp Rd.	U-16	13
Rifle Camp Rd.	V-16	13
Rifle Camp Rd.	W-15	13
Rifle Camp Rd.	U-16	14
Rifle Camp Rd.	V-16	14
Rifle Camp Rd.	W-15	14
Robinson Dr.	V-15	13
Rockaway Av.	V-15	13
Rockland Av.	U-15	13
Rose Pl.	V-15	13
Rosina St.	V-16	13
Ryle Park Av.	V-15	13
Short St.	U-15	13
Sibel Ct.	V-15	13
South Dr.	V-16	13
Squirrelwood Rd.	U-15	13
Sunset Dr.	V-15	13
Taft Av.	U-15	13
Taylor La.	V-16	13
Terrace Av.	U-15	13
Thornton Pl.	V-15	13
Tiessen Ter.	V-15	13
Valley Dr.	V-15	13
Van Winkle Ct.	V-15	13
Verbyckas Cr.	V-15	13
Vernon Ct.	U-15	13
Vetrone Dr.	V-15	13
Wallace Ln.	V-15	13
Weaseldrift Rd.	V-16	13
Wedgewood Dr.	V-15	13
West 31st St.	U-15	13
West 32nd	U-15	13
West 34th St.	U-15	13
West 36th St.	U-15	13
Westerholt Av.	V-15	13
Weston Pl.	V-15	13
Whippany Av.	V-15	13
Whitaker Av.	V-15	13
Williams Dr.	V-15	13
Willow Wy.	U-15	13
Wilson Av.	U-16	13
Winslow Pl.	V-15	13
Woodland Dr.	W-15	15
Woodrow Av.	U-15	13
Woodrow Av.	V-15	13
Zambrano Dr.	V-15	13
Zendzian Av.	V-15	13
Zendzian Rd.	V-15	13
Zoar St.	V-15	13

ROCKLAND COUNTY

Town of Clarkstown

STREET	GRID	MAP
1st Av.	M-9	2
1st St.	L-13	2,5
1st St.	L-11	2,5
1st St.	P-12	2
1st St.	M-10	2
1st St.	N-9	2
2nd Av.	M-9	2
2nd St.	N-9	2
2nd St.	L-13	2,5
2nd St.	L-11	2,5
3rd St.	L-11	2,5
3rd St.	M-12	2
Abby Ln.	N-12	2
Aber Ter.	L-11	2,5
Aberdeen Dr.	N-11	2
Acorn Ter.	L-11	2,5
Acres Rd.	P-12	2
Adam Pl.	L-10	2,5
Addison Boyce Dr.	L-10	2,5
Adele Rd.	N-11	2
Adrienne Dr.	K-11	5
Ahearn Av.	M-12	2
Alan Ct.	N-9	2
Alan Dr.	K-10	5
Alan Dr.	L-11	2,5
Albacon Rd.	M-9	2
Albert Ct.	K-13	5
Alcott	L-11	2,5
Aldan Ct.	K-11	5
Aleanne Ter.	N-11	2
Alice Dr.	N-9	2
Alicia Ct.	P-11	2
Allegany Av.	P-12	2
Allen St.	L-13	2,5
Allison St.	M-8	2
Allison Av. E.	P-9	2
Allison Av. E.	P-10	2
Allison Av. W.	P-9	2
Allison Ct. E.	P-10	2
Almond Ct.	J-10	5
Almuth Dr.	J-11	5
Alpine Ct.	K-13	5
Alton Ct.	K-10	5
Alyssa Ct.	M-13	2
Amanda Ln.	K-13	5
Amarilic Dr.	M-10	2
American Legion Way	L-11	2,5
Amethyst Ct.	M-11	2
Amherst Rd.	M-9	2
Amory Dr.	M-13	2
Amsterdam Rd.	L-11	2,5
Amundsen Av.	L-10	2,5
Andover Rd.	M-12	2
Angus Dr.	K-10	5
Ann St.	M-10	2
Annabelle Ln.	K-10	5
Anton Ct.	L-11	2,5
Apollo Ct.	P-9	2
Appleton Rd.	J-11	5
April Ct.	P-10	2
April Ln.	P-9	2
Arbor Ln.	N-10	2
Arcadia Dr.	L-11	2,5
Archdale Av.	N-14	2
Arden Rd.	M-11	2
Ardmore Ln.	M-11	2
Ardsley Dr.	J-11	5
Argow Ct.	P-10	2
Argow Pl.	P-10	2
Arlene Ct.	M-10	2
Arrow Ln.	M-9	2
Ash Ct.	K-11	5
Ash Rd.	N-11	2
Ashland St.	M-13	2
Aspen Ln.	L-10	2,5
Assembly Ct.	K-12	5
Aster St.	N-13	2
Atchison St.	M-13	2
Atlanta Av.	P-9	2
Auburn Dr.	L-11	2,5
Audubon Ct.	P-11	2
Aura Dr.(Vista Rd.)	N-12	2
Avenue C	N-10	2
Avon Ln.	K-11	5
Babbling Brook Ln.	M-12	2
Babcock Av.	N-9	2
Badger St.	L-10	2,5
Badger St.	K-10	5
Baker Ln.	L-10	2,5
Balchen Ter.	L-10	2,5
Baldwin Ct.	L-12	2,5
Baldwin Pl.	M-10	2
Balmoral Dr.	J-10	5
Balsam Ct.	L-11	2,5
Balter Rd.	K-10	5
Baltic Ct.	M-9	2
Banta Pl.	L-11	2,5
Barbara Ln.	N-13	2
Barbara Rd.	K-10	5
Bardonia Rd.	N-10	2
Barnstable Ct.	K-11	5
Barry Ct.	M-12	2
Barry Ln.	N-10	2
Basswood Ct.	M-10	2
Bayberry Ln.	M-12	2
Baylor Rd.	M-9	2
Beacon St.	K-13	5
Beatrice Ln.	K-10	5
Beaumont Dr.	J-11	5
Beauregard Ter.	L-12	2,5
Beaver Ct.	J-12	5
Beech St.	N-10	2
Beechwood Dr.	K-13	5
Belaire Ter.	L-10	2,5
Bellehaven Ct.	M-11	2
Belleville Dr.	M-13	2
Bellows Ln.	L-10	2,5
Bellview Av.	N-12	2
Bellwood Dr.	M-10	2
Ben Wild Rd.	M-9	2
Bender Rd.	L-9	2,5
Benson Av.	P-11	2
Benton Ct.	L-10	2,5
Berkshire Dr.	J-11	5
Berry Ct.	K-13	5
Besso St.	P-12	2
Beth Ln.	K-13	5
Beverly Pl.	K-10	5
Birch Dr.	M-10	2
Birch Dr. N.	M-10	2
Birch Ln.	L-10	2,5
Birchwood Av.	N-8	2
Birchwood Av.	N-13	2
Birchwood Ct.	M-12	2
Bittman Ln.	M-10	2
Blauvelt Av.	P-9	2
Blauvelt Rd.	P-10	2
Blauvelt St.	P-9	2
Bliss Ln.	M-13	2
Blithe Ct.	M-13	2
Blue Willow Ln.	M-10	2
Bluebird Dr.	L-12	2,5
Bluejay Cir.	J-11	5
Bobby Rd.	P-12	2
Bobwhite Ln.	M-11	2
Boecher Ct.	K-10	5
Bonnie Ln.	L-10	2,5
Bontecou Ln.	J-11	5
Bow Ct.	M-12	2
Boxberger Rd.	M-12	2
Bradley Dr.	L-11	2,5
Branchville Rd.	N-12	2
Brenda Ln.	M-10	2
Brenner Dr.	K-13	5
Brentwood Dr.	J-12	5
Brettman Cir.	M-10	2
Brewery Rd.	L-11	2,5
Briar Pl.	M-10	2
Briar Rd.	N-9	2
Briarcliff Rd.	M-9	2
Briarwood Dr.	L-11	2,5
Bridle Ln.	P-10	2
Brighton Ln.	M-10	2
Bristol Ct.	L-10	2,5
Britta Ln.	L-10	2,5
Brittany Ct.	M-13	2
Broadlyn Ct.	M-10	2
Broadway N.	N-14	2
Broadway W.	P-12	2
Brook haven Ct.	Q-8	1,2
Brook Hill Dr.	P-10	2
Brook Ln.	H-11	5
Brook Rd.	J-10	5
Brookdale Ct.	N-11	2
Brookhaven Ct.	P-10	2
Brookline Cir.	J-11	5
Brookline Way	J-11	5
Brookridge Ct.	N-12	2
Brookridge Dr.	N-12	2
Brookside Av.	N-12	2
Brookside Av.	J-12	5
Brookside Dr.	N-10	2
Brookway Av.	M-12	2
Brookwood Ln.	J-10	5
Broome Blvd.	P-12	2
Broward Dr.	M-10	2
Buckingham Rd.	M-10	2
Buena Vista Rd.	K-10	5
Buena Vista Rd.	J-10	5
Bull Run Rd.	P-11	2
Burda Ln.	L-10	2,5
Burda Pl. W.	L-10	2,5
Burda Pl. W.	M-10	2
Burgandy Ln.	L-10	2,5
Burnside Av. S.	L-13	2,5
Burts Rd.	J-13	5
Bush Ct.	K-11	5
Butler Rd.	L-13	2,5
Buttermilk Falls Rd.	P-12	2
Butternut Ln.	P-10	2
Buttonwood Ct.	L-12	2,5
Caesar Ct.	M-13	2
Cairngorm Rd.	K-10	5
Cairnsmuir Ln.	L-11	2,5
Calico Pl.	K-12	5
Camboan Rd.	N-13	2
Candlelight Cir.	K-10	5
Candlewood Ct.	M-10	2
Capital Ct.	L-11	2,5
Capral Ln.	L-11	2,5
Caravella Av.	P-9	2
Cardinal Ct.	M-11	2
Carlann Ln.	M-12	2
Carlisle Ct.	M-11	2
Carlton Ct.	L-11	2,5
Carmen Dr.	N-10	2
Carnaby Ct.	L-9	2,5
Carnation Dr.	M-10	2
Carol Pl.	M-11	2
Carolina Dr.	L-10	2,5
Carriage Ln.	L-10	2,5
Carriage Ln.	N-8	2
Carrie Dr.	L-10	2,5
Carrie Ln.	P-9	2
Casey Ct.	P-10	2
Casper Hill Rd.	N-12	2
Castle Heights Av.	P-13	2
Catalpa Ct.	N-10	2
Catawba Ct.	P-10	2
Catawba Dr.	P-10	2
Cavalry Dr.	K-11	5
Cayuga Ct.	P-12	2
Cedar Av.	N-13	2
Cedar Dr.	M-10	2
Cedarcraft Ln.	P-10	2
Center Av.	N-13	2
Center Ln.	M-10	2
Central Av.	P-13	2
Central Av.	M-10	2
Central Av.	K-13	5
Central Av. S.	N-8	2
Central Dr.	M-10	2
Centre St.	P-9	2
Chaparral Rd.	N-8	2
Charles Blvd.	M-13	2
Charles St.	N-9	2
Charles St.	K-12	5
Chauncy St.	L-13	2,5
Chemong Ct.	P-12	2
Cherry Hill Ln.	P-11	2
Chester Av.	K-13	5
Chestnut	P-12	2
Chestnut Grove Ct.	M-10	2
Chestnut Park Ct.	M-10	2
Chimney Ridge Rd.	P-10	2
Chisholm Ct.	N-9	2
Christian Herald Rd.	N-13	2
Christie Dr.	J-11	5
Christopher Dr.	K-11	5
Church Rd.	M-10	2
Church St.	P-9	2
Cider Mill Ct.	M-10	2
Circle Ct.	K-11	5
Clark Dr.	M-9	2
Clark Pl.	K-11	5
Clarkstown Rd.	M-9	2
Clarkstown Rd. W.	L-9	2,5
Clarkstown Rd. W.	L-10	2,5
Clay St.	M-10	2
Clearview Rd.	M-10	2
Clearwater Ct.	P-9	2
Cleveland St.	P-12	2
Clifford Ct.	P-9	2
Clifton Ct.	L-11	2,5
Clinton Pl.	P-9	2
Clinton St.	M-9	2
Clover Ct.	L-11	2,5
Clover Dr.	P-10	2
Clydesdale Ct.	L-11	2,5
Colgate Dr.	M-11	2
College Av.	P-10	2
Collier Rd.	K-14	5
Collingswood Dr.	K-11	5
Collyer Av.	L-10	2,5
Collyer Av.	L-14	2
Colonial Dr.	L-10	2,5
Colt Ct.	L-11	2,5
Colton St.	L-13	2,5
Columbus Av.	M-13	2
Commonwealth Av.	M-13	2
Concord Dr.	K-11	5
Conger Av.	L-13	2,5
Congers Rd.	K-12	5
Conklin Pl.	L-14	2
Conklin Rd.	J-9	5
Connecticut Ct.	M-13	2
Conrad Ln.	K-12	5
Continental Dr.	P-11	2
Continental Dr.	P-10	2
Convent Rd.	P-9	2
Copper Dr.	M-10	2
Cordes Ln.	K-13	5
Corinthian Rd.	L-9	2,5
Cornell Dr.	M-11	2
Corporate Ct.	M-12	2
Corporate Way	M-13	2
Corral St.	N-9	2
Cortland Dr.	L-11	2,5
Cosmo Ln.	K-12	5
Cottage Av.	P-9	2
Cottage Av.	M-12	2
Cottage Pl.	M-10	2
Cottage Rd.	M-13	2
Cottonwood Ct.	M-10	2
Courtney Dr.	L-11	2,5
Crabapple Ln.	P-10	2
Craftwood Dr.	Q-8	1,2
Cragmere Rd.	K-11	5
Crambrook Rd.	L-11	2,5
Cranford Dr.	K-11	5
Cranford Rd.	N-10	2
Cranford Rd. S.	N-10	2
Crescent Ct.	K-11	5
Crescent Dr.	N-9	2
Crestwood Dr.	L-11	2,5
Cricket Rd.	J-11	5
Crieff Ln.	K-10	5
Crimson Ct.	M-10	2
Crooked Hill	Q-8	1,2
Crosfield Av.	P-11	2
Cross St.	L-11	2,5
Crown Ct.	Q-8	1,2
Crownlyn Ct.	M-10	2
Croyden Ln.	K-11	5
Crum Creek Rd.	J-11	5
Crusher Rd.	N-12	2
Crystal Ct.	N-10	2
Culver Dr.	J-10	5
Cupsaw Ct.	P-10	2
Curtin Dr.	P-10	2
Cypress St.	K-11	5
Cyr Ct.	M-11	2
Dade Rd.	M-10	2
Dahm Rd.	M-12	2
Daisy Ct.	P-10	2
Daisy St.	N-13	2
Daken Ct.	M-13	2
Dalewood Ct.	L-11	2,5
Danlyn Ct.	M-10	2
Danville Ct.	M-11	2
Davenport Ter.	N-11	2
Dean St.	K-13	5
Dearborn Rd.	M-11	2
Debra Ct.	K-12	5
Debra Lee Ct.	P-10	2
Declark Pl.	P-10	2
Deer Meadow Dr.	N-11	2
Deerfield Dr.	L-11	2,5
Deerfoot Ln.	L-12	2,5
Deertrack Ln.	M-12	2
Deerwood Dr.	L-10	2,5
Deforest Av.	K-12	5
Deforest Ct.	L-12	2,5
Deforest Ct.	N-11	2
Della Ct.	K-13	5
Delta Dr.	L-11	2,5
Deltic Rd.	L-9	2,5
Demarest Av.	L-11	2,5
Demarest Av.	N-11	2
Demarest Av.	P-9	2
Demarest Av.	N-9	2
Demarest Mill Ct.	N-11	2
Demarest Mill Rd.	N-10	2
Demarest Mill Rd.	N-11	2
Denver Dr.	H-10	5
Depew Av.	P-13	2
Derby Ln.	L-12	2,5
Derter Pl.	M-12	2
Diane Dr.	K-10	5
Dickenson Av.	P-13	2
Division St.	P-12	2
Dix Ln.	K-11	5
Dixwell Rd.	K-10	5
Doctor Davies Rd.	L-13	2,5
Dogwood Ln.	M-11	2
Dolphin Rd.	K-11	5
Dolton St.	N-13	2
Donna St.	L-11	2,5
Doral Ct.	J-11	5
Dorchester Av.	K-11	5
Dore Ct.	L-12	2,5
Doris Dr.	N-10	2
Doscher Av.	P-11	2
Dover Rd.	L-12	2,5
Down Ct.	P-10	2
Drayton Pl.	M-9	2
Drexler Ct.	M-9	2
Duane Av.	L-11	2,5
Duke Ln.	M-11	2
Dunmore Rd.	J-11	5
Durant Rd.	L-11	2,5
Dustman Ln.	N-10	2
Dutch Ct.	N-11	2
Dutch Glen Dr.	M-10	2
E. Allison Av.	P-10	2
E. Mary La.	M-13	2
Eaders	M-9	2
Eagle Ct.	J-11	5
East Av.	P-10	2
East St.	P-10	2
Eastlyn Ct.	M-10	2
Eastlyn Dr.	M-10	2
Eberling Dr.	K-11	5
Eckerson Rd.	L-9	2,5
Edgebrook Ct.	K-10	5
Edsall Av.	N-9	2
Edsam Rd.	N-12	2
Eileen Av.	K-11	5
Elaine Dr.	K-10	5
Elath St.	L-11	2,5
Eldon Av.	L-10	2,5
Elinor Ln.	L-11	2,5
Elk Dr.	P-10	2
Ellen St.	P-13	2
Ellen St.	M-9	2
Elliot's Alley	M-13	2
Elm St.	N-13	2
Elm St.	J-12	5
Elmsford Rd.	M-11	2
Elmwood Dr.	L-11	2,5
Elon Ct.	L-11	2,5
Elrod Dr.	P-11	2
Elyse Dr.	L-10	2,5
Ember Dr.	K-12	5
Emerald Ct.	L-9	2,5
Emerald Dr.	M-13	2
Endicott St.	L-13	2,5
Englewood Av.	P-9	2
Enterprise Ct.	P-8	2
Erik Ct.	P-10	2
Erskine Ct.	P-10	2
Esquire Rd.	L-11	2,5
Essex Ct.	P-8	2
Esther Av.	K-13	5
Ethel Dr.	K-12	5
Etna Pl.	M-10	2
Evan Dr.	J-10	5
Evergreen Ln.	J-12	5
Executive Blvd.	M-13	2
Fair Haven Dr.	J-11	5
Fairfield Ter.	P-10	2
Fairview Av.	P-13	2
Fairview Av.	P-9	2
Fairview Ct.	K-10	5
Fairview Ct.	P-9	2
Fanley Av.	L-10	2,5
Fanwood Ln.	M-12	2
Farm Ct.	L-11	2,5
Farmhouse Rd.	L-13	2,5
Fawn Ct.	N-11	2
Fawn Hollow Ln.	L-10	2,5
Fay Rd.	L-11	2,5
Featherly Ct.	L-9	2,5
Fenner Ln.	N-9	2
Fenway Ct.	J-11	5
Ferndale Rd.	K-12	5
Fernwood Dr.	L-11	2,5
Fieldcrest Dr.	K-11	5
Fieldstone Ct.	L-12	2,5
Filmont Dr.	J-10	5
Finch Rd.	K-12	5
Findley Ct.	J-11	5
Fir Ct.	P-10	2
Fisher Av.	N-9	2
Fisher Av.	L-13	2,5
Five Oaks Ln.	L-12	2,5
Flint Ct.	N-13	2
Flitt St.	P-10	2
Florence Ct.	M-12	2
Flower Ln.	M-12	2
Floyds Pl.	P-9	2
Forbes Rd.	M-9	2
Forest Av.	N-10	2
Forest Glen Ct.	M-9	2
Forest Glen Rd.	N-12	2
Forest Rd.	M-9	2
Forest View Ct.	M-12	2
Forestbrook Rd.	M-9	2
Foss Dr.	N-13	2
Fouth St.	P-13	2
Fox Rd.	N-11	2
Foxburn St.	M-10	2
Foxcroft Dr.	M-10	2
Foxwood Rd.	P-11	2
Foxwood Rd.	P-10	2
Francis Pl.	P-12	2
Frank St.	K-11	5
Franklin Ln.	L-10	2,5
Fred Hecht Rd.	M-9	2
Frederic St.	N-9	2
Freedman Av.	N-9	2
Fremont Av.	P-9	2
Freund Dr.	N-9	2
Friend Ct.	L-13	2,5
Friend St.	L-13	2,5
Fringe Ct.	K-12	5
Front St.	P-13	2
Frost Ct.	L-11	2,5
Fulle Dr.	N-12	2
Fulton St.	P-11	2
Fulton St.	M-10	2
Gable Rd.	L-11	2,5
Gail Dr.	K-10	5
Gail Dr.	P-13	2
Gallop Ct.	L-12	2,5
Gandy Ln.	M-10	2
Garnet Ln.	L-12	2,5
Garrecht Pl.	P-10	2
Garrett Av.	K-13	5
Gary Dr.	Q-8	1,2
Gate Blvd. W.	J-11	5
Gateway	M-12	2
Gem Ct.	M-9	2
George St.	P-10	2
Georgetown Oval	K-12	5
Gerald St.	M-13	2
Geraldine Pl.	L-10	2,5
Geraldine Rd.	M-9	2
Gerke Av.	M-9	2
Gerken Dr.	L-11	2,5
Gerlack Dr.	M-10	2
Germonds Rd.	M-11	2
Germonds Rd.	M-10	2
Gilchrest Rd.	L-13	2,5
Gilchrest Rd.	M-12	2
Gillis Av.	P-12	2
Glade Ct.	L-9	2,5
Gladys Dr.	K-10	5
Gleeful Ln.	M-13	2
Glen Av.	N-13	2
Glen Ct.	K-13	5
Glen Haven Dr.	L-11	2,5
Glen Ln.	L-10	2,5
Glen Rd.	P-11	2
Glenbrook Rd.	N-13	2
Glenmere Rd.	J-11	5
Glenn Ln.	L-10	2,5
Glenrose Ct.	P-10	2
Glenside Dr.	L-11	2,5
Glenwood Rd.	L-10	2,5
Gloria Ct.	L-11	2,5
Goebel Rd.	K-12	5
Goebel Rd.	J-12	5
Gottlieb Dr.	Q-8	1,2
Grace St.	P-10	2
Grand St.	L-10	2,5
Grandview Av.	P-9	2
Grant Av.	K-13	5
Grant Av.	L-13	2,5
Graphic Ct.	P-10	2
Great Oaks Dr.	M-10	2
Green Av.	M-12	2
Green Hill Ct.	P-9	2
Green Oval	N-9	2
Green Rd.	P-11	2
Greenbower Ln.	L-10	2,5
Greenbush Rd.	P-12	2
Greenbush Rd. N.	P-12	2
Greendale Rd.	M-11	2
Greene St.	L-13	2,5
Greenfield Rd.	J-12	5
Greenfield Ter.	L-12	2,5
Greensward Dr.	M-12	2
Greenwood Dr.	K-10	5
Gregory St.	K-11	5
Grove Ct.	N-11	2
Hacker Pl.	M-10	2
Hague Ct.	N-10	2
Hall Av.	L-11	2,5
Hall Av.	L-10	2,5
Hall Av.	P-13	2
Hall Av. W.	L-10	2,5
Hallmark Dr.	L-10	2,5
Hamden Heights Ct.	K-12	5
Hampshire Ct.	P-10	2
Hancock Av.	N-9	2
Hannah Ln.	N-12	2
Hansen Av.	L-10	2,5
Hansen Ct.	L-10	2,5
Harmon Pl.	M-10	2
Harness Rd.	L-11	2,5
Harrison Av.	L-13	2,5
Harrison Av.	L-13	2,5
Haverhill Rd.	L-10	2,5
Havermill Rd.	L-10	2,5
Haverstraw Rd.	J-11	5
Hazelton Ln.	N-11	2
Hazen Ln.	K-13	5
Hearth Ct.	L-11	2,5
Heather Dr.	K-10	5
Heather Ln.	P-11	2
Hedgerow	L-10	2,5
Hedgerow	K-13	5
Hedgerow Ln.	M-9	2
Helene Rd.	M-13	2
Hemenway Av.	L-13	2,5
Hemingway Av.	L-13	2,5
Hemlock Dr.	K-13	5
Hemlock Rd.	N-11	2
Hemlock Tr.	H-11	5
Hemptor Rd.	K-10	5
Henry Ct.	N-9	2
Henry St.	K-10	5
Herald Ct.	N-13	2
Hereford Ln.	M-11	2
Hess Av.	M-13	2
Hessian Pl.	L-11	2,5
Hickory	N-10	2
High Av.	P-11	2
High S.	P-12	2
High St.	M-13	2
High St.	M-10	2
Highland Av.	P-13	2
Highland Av.	Q-8	1,2
Highland Av.	N-11	2
Highland Av. (Duryea Ln.)	P-8	2
Highland Av. S.	Q-8	1,2
Highmount Av.	P-13	2
Highmount Ter.	P-13	2
Highview Av.	P-9	2
Highway Av.	L-13	2,5
Hilburg	N-10	2
Hill Ln.	N-12	2
Hillcrest Dr.	P-12	2
Hillcrest Rd.	M-11	2
Hillman Rd.	J-11	5
Hillside Av.	P-11	2
Hillside Dr. N.	L-10	2,5
Hillside Dr. S.	L-10	2,5
Hillside Dr. W.	L-10	2,5
Hilltop Dr.	N-13	2
Hilltop Ln.	N-13	2
Hilltop Rd.	L-10	2,5
Hilltop Rd.	L-13	2,5
Hobe St.	P-11	2
Hobert Ct.	K-10	5
Hogenkamp Av.	P-9	2
Holbrook Av.	K-13	5
Holland Dr.	N-11	2
Hollis Ct.	N-10	2
Hollow Dr.	L-10	2,5
Homestead Ln.	K-10	5
Hook Mt. Rd.	N-13	2
Horseshoe Ct.	L-12	2,5
Hortshom Ln.	P-11	2
Howard St.	K-13	5
Hudson View Rd.	N-13	2
Huested Ln.	N-11	2
Huffman Rd.	M-12	2
Hughes St.	K-13	5
Hunter Pl.	N-11	2
Hutton Av.	N-9	2
Independence Ct.	J-12	5
Indian Dr.	P-11	2
Ingalls St.	P-12	2
Inland Rd.	M-10	2
Inverness Dr.	J-11	5
Inwood Dr.	N-11	2
Irion Dr.	L-10	2,5
Ivy Ct.	K-13	5
Ivy Ln.	M-11	2
Ivy St.	P-12	2
J.M. Muller Dr.	M-11	2
Jacqueline Dr.	N-12	2
Jade St.	M-10	2
James Dr.	N-10	2
James St.	K-10	5
Jane Francis Way	L-12	2,5
Jay St.	N-10	2
Jean Ln.	M-10	2
Jeff Ln.	L-12	2,5
Jeffrey Ct.	N-11	2
Jeffrey Pl.	M-12	2
Jennifer Dr.	J-10	5
Jensen Ln.	N-10	2
Jerry's Av.	P-9	2
Jewett Rd.	N-13	2
Jill Dr.	P-11	2
Joan Dr.	K-10	5
Joanne Ln.	L-10	2,5
Jockey Hollow Dr.	P-10	2
Jockey Hollow Ln.	P-10	2
Jockey Ln.	L-12	2,5
Jodi Ln.	M-10	2
John St.	K-10	5
Johnsons Ln.	M-11	2
Jolen Dr.	M-11	2
Jolliffe Av.	K-13	5
Jolliffe St.	L-13	2,5
Joseph Dr.	N-12	2
Joseph Ln.	N-11	2
Joy Dr.	M-13	2
Joyce Dr.	K-11	5
Juanne	L-13	2,5
Judith Ln.	M-10	2
Judith St.	N-9	2
Juniper Ct.	N-10	2
Kakiar Ct.	H-11	5
Karin Ct.	N-12	2
Karl Ct.	K-13	5
Keltz St.	M-9	2
Kelvin Ct.	N-10	2
Kemmer Av.	N-9	2
Kenbar Rd.	M-11	2
Kendall Dr.	L-11	2,5
Kent St.	M-10	2
Kenwood Ln.	M-11	2
Kings Ct.	M-12	2
Kings Highway	M-12	2
Kings Highway	M-10	2
Kings Highway	N-12	2
Kingsgate Parkway	M-9	2
Kingsland Dr.	K-10	5
Kirchner Dr.	P-10	2
Klein Av.	P-11	2
Knapp Ln.	J-12	5
Knollwood Ct.	M-12	2
Kohler Ct.	K-13	5
Kreuz Dr.	P-10	2
Kuyper Dr.	N-13	2
Kuyper Dr. W.	N-13	2
Lady Godiva Way	K-11	5
Lafayette Dr.	M-11	2
Lafayette St.	M-9	2
Lake Dr.	L-10	2,5
Lake Nanuet Dr.	P-10	2
Lake Rd.	L-13	2,5
Lake Rd.	L-14	2
Lake Shore Dr.	M-9	2
Lake St.	M-9	2
Lakeland Av.	K-13	5
Lakeward Av.	L-13	2,5
Lakewood Dr.	L-13	2,5
Lamborn Av.	K-13	5
Lance Ct.	Q-8	1,2
Landing Rd.	K-14	5
Lansdale Rd.	K-11	5
Lansing Ct.	L-11	2,5
Larch Ct.	P-11	2
Lariat Ct.	M-9	2
Larkspur Ct.	K-12	5
Lath Ln.	P-10	2
Laurel Rd.	L-11	2,5
Laurel Rd.	P-12	2
Laurel Rd.	P-12	2
Lauren Dr.	M-9	2
Lawnwood Pl.	L-10	2,5
Lawrence St.	K-13	5
Lawrence St.	M-9	2
Leeland Ct.	L-11	2,5
Lenbar Cir.	L-11	2,5
Lennox Way	H-11	5
Lenox Av.	L-13	2,5
Leona Av.	M-10	2
Lewis Dr.	N-14	2
Lexington Rd.	K-11	5
Lexow Av.	N-13	2
Lexow Av.	P-9	2
Liberty Av.	L-13	2,5
Liberty Cir.	K-11	5
Lillac Ct.	P-10	2
Lily Ln.	M-13	2
Lincoln St.	P-12	2
Linda Ct.	K-13	5
Lindberg Ln.	L-10	2,5
Linden Ct.	J-11	5
Linden St.	K-13	5
Link Ct.	L-10	2,5
Lisa Ct.	K-10	5
Lisa Ln.	K-10	5
Lisa Ln.	M-10	2
Little Tor Rd.	J-10	5
Little Tor Rd.	L-10	2,5
Littlebrook Ln.	K-10	5
Lochness Ln.	L-10	2,5
Locust(Jewel) Dr.	N-13	2
Locust Dr.	N-13	2
Loeser Dr.	P-8	2
Loesher Ln.	Q-8	1,2
Lombardi Dr.	K-10	5
London Ter.	K-11	5
Long Clove Rd.	K-12	5
Long Meadow Dr.	K-11	5
Long St.	L-13	2,5
Loraine Dr.	K-11	5
Loran Ct.	P-10	2
Lori Pl.	L-11	2,5
Lorraine Ct.	M-11	2
Louis Av.	M-13	2
Louis Rd.	K-10	5
Louise Dr.	N-11	2
Louise Pl.	M-9	2
Lowell Dr.	J-11	5
Lower Castle Hts. Av.	P-13	2
Lowerre Pl.	M-13	2
Lucille Blvd.	H-11	5
Ludvigh Rd.	N-10	2
Lupine Ct.	K-12	5
Lyncrest Av.	M-11	2
Lynhaven Dr.	K-10	5
Lynn Ct.	M-9	2
Lynne Dr.	K-10	5
Mace Dr.	M-13	2
Maiden Ln.	L-11	2,5
Maiden Ln.	L-12	2,5
Main Dr.	P-10	2
Main St.	L-11	2,5
Main St.	N-9	2
Main St. N.	K-11	5
Main St. S.	L-11	2,5
Mallard Dr.	M-11	2
Mandarin Ln.	M-11	2
Mandon Ter.	K-10	5
Mannette Ln.	N-12	2
Manor Ct.	J-10	5
Maple Av.	L-11	2,5
Maple Av.	N-13	2
Maple Av.	P-11	2
Maple Rd.	M-12	2
Maplewood Ln.	L-10	2,5
Marcia Ln.	K-11	5
Marcus Rd.	P-11	2
Marie Curie Pl.	L-11	2,5
Marion Ct.	M-11	2
Mark Ln.	L-12	2,5
Marten Dr.	M-11	2
Mary Ln.	M-13	2
Maryann Ln.	K-10	5
Massachusetts Av.	L-13	2,5
Maxine Ct.	M-9	2
May Pl.	P-9	2
Mayfield St.	N-12	2
Mc Carthy Way	M-11	2
Mc Kinley Av.	P-12	2
Mc Leod Ter.	K-10	5
Meadow Ln.	J-11	5
Meadowbrook Ct.	K-11	5
Meadowlark Dr.	M-11	2
Medford Pl.	M-9	2
Medway Av.	L-13	2,5
Mein Dr.	L-11	2,5
Melanie Ct.	N-12	2
Melrose Ln.	M-11	2
Meola Rd.	K-13	5
Meridan Ln.	M-10	2
Mesa Pl.	N-8	2
Meyer Ln.	J-11	5
Mica Ct.	N-13	2
Michelle Av.	K-13	5
Michigan Ct.	M-13	2
Middletown Rd.	P-9	2
Middletown Rd. N.	N-10	2
Midland Av.	N-13	2
Midland Av.	P-13	2
Milich Ln.	L-10	2,5
Mill Creek Rd.	J-12	5
Miller Rd.	M-12	2
Millspaugh Ln.	N-10	2
Milsom Dr.	H-11	5
Minor Ct.	M-11	2
Miriam Ct.	M-11	2
Mirth Ct.	M-13	2
Mitchell Dr.	N-13	2
Moreland Dr.	J-10	5
Morningside Rd.	H-11	5
Morris Dr.	M-11	2
Morton Av.	L-13	2,5
Morton Av.	K-13	5
Morton Pl.	L-12	2,5
Mouacdie Dr.	Q-8	1,2
Mountain Rd. S.	J-12	5
Mountain Rd. S.	H-11	5
Mountain Rd. S.	H-10	5
Mountainview Av.	P-13	2
Muir Ln.	L-12	2,5
Mullberry Rd.	M-13	2
Muller Ct.	L-11	2,5
Murdock Rd.	K-10	5
Murray Hill Rd.	N-8	2
Myrtle Av.	P-9	2
N. Delaware Dr.	P-12	2
N. Midland Av.	M-13	2
N. Midland Av.	N-13	2
Nancy Dr.	K-11	5
Nanuet Av.	P-9	2
Nelson Pl.	N-9	2
New City-Congers Rd.	L-11	2,5
New Haven Av.	N-9	2
New Hempstead Rd.	K-10	5
New Jersey Av.	L-13	2,5
New Pascack Rd.	L-13	2,5
New Lake Rd.	N-12	2
New Valley Rd.	L-10	2,5
New York Av.	L-13	2,5
New York State Thruway	N-9	2
New York State Thruway	N-11	2
Newport Dr.	P-8	2
Nicholas Ct.	N-12	2
Nier Pl.	M-10	2
Nirvana Ct.	M-13	2
Nob Hill Rd.	K-10	5
Norfolk Av.	K-13	5
Norge Av.	N-10	2
Norlen Ln.	L-10	2,5
Norman Pl.	P-10	2
N. Highland Av.	N-13	2
N. Strawberry Hill Ln.	N-12	2
Northlyn Ct.	M-10	2
Norwood Pl.	P-10	2
Nuthatch Ln.	M-11	2
Nyack Av.	P-9	2
Nyack Rd. W.	N-10	2
Nyack Rd. W.	P-11	2
Nyack Turnpike	M-9	2
Oak Ln.	M-10	2
Oak Rd.	L-10	2,5
Oak Rd.	K-13	5
Oak St.	L-11	2,5
Oak St.	N-13	2
Oak Spring Ct.	M-11	2

ROCKLAND COUNTY

ROCKLAND COUNTY

STREET	GRID	MAP
Beckerle Dr.	P-9	2
Beechwood Dr.	R-11	1
Behrendt Dr.	Q-8	1,2
Bell Ln.	S-12	1
Bennett Ln.	T-11	1
Bennington Dr.	T-12	1
Berachan Av.	Q-13	1,2
Bergen Av.	U-12	1
Bergener Ln.	S-12	1
Berry Ct.	S-11	1
Betsy Ross Dr.	S-10	1
Birch Ct.	S-11	1
Birch St.	R-12	1
Birch St.	R-9	1
Birch Tree Rd.	T-12	1
Birchwood Ct.	R-11	1
Blair Ct.	T-12	1
Blaisdell Rd.	S-10	1
Blanch St.	T-12	1
Blauvelt Av.	R-9	1
Blauvelt Rd.	Q-9	1,2
Blauvelt Rd.	Q-10	1,2
Blauvelt Rd.	R-11	1
Blossom Heath Rd.	S-10	1
Blue Hill Rd.	R-10	1
Blue Hill S.	R-10	1
Blue Hill W.	R-10	1
Bluefield Ln.	R-11	1
Bocket Rd.	Q-10	1,2
Bogert Av.	Q-9	1,2
Borger Pl.	P-8	2
Boulevard S.	Q-13	1,2
Bradley Corporate Dr.	Q-12	1,2
Bradley Hill Rd.	S-10	1
Brandt Av.	T-11	1
Brandywine Dr.	S-10	1
Braunsdorf Rd.	Q-9	1,2
Brianbeth Pl.	S-11	1
Bridge Rd.	Q-10	1,2
Bridge St.	S-13	1
Brightwood Av.	Q-9	1,2
Broad Av.	U-12	1
Broadway	P-13	2
Broadway Av.	S-13	1
Broadway Av.	R-12	1
Broadway N.	P-13	2
Broadway S.	Q-13	1,2
Brooks Av.	Q-9	1,2
Brookside Av.	P-13	2
Brown Dr.	Q-9	1,2
Buchanan St.	Q-8	1,2
Buckley St.	P-13	2
Bunker Hill Rd.	S-10	1
Burd St.	P-13	2
Burdick Rd.	Q-8	1,2
Burger Pl.	Q-8	1,2
Burrows Ln.	Q-11	1,2
Buttercup Dr.	R-11	1
Butternut Dr.	Q-8	1,2
Buttonwood Pl.	R-10	1
Campbell Av.	T-12	1
Cara Dr.	Q-10	1,2
Cardean St.	Q-9	1,2
Cardell Av.	R-9	1
Cardinal St.	Q-10	1,2
Carelton Rd.	R-11	1
Carol Ln.	T-12	1
Carroll St.	Q-9	1,2
Carteret Rd.	U-12	1
Castle Rd.	S-13	1
Catherine St.	P-13	2
Cedar Av.	R-9	1
Cazzasa Pl.	Q-10	1,2
Cedar Av.	S-11	1
Cedar Hill Av.	P-13	2
Cedar St.	P-13	2
Cedar St.	T-11	1
Celtic Ln.	Q-11	1,2
Cemetery Ln.	P-13	2
Center St.	Q-8	1,2
Center St.	P-13	2
Central Av.	P-13	2
Central Av.	Q-13	1,2
Central Av.	T-11	1
Central Av. E.	Q-9	1,2
Central Av. W.	Q-8	1,2
Century Rd.	U-13	1
Chamberlain Rd.	R-12	1
Champ Av.	Q-10	1,2
Chapel Ct.	S-11	1
Charles St.	Q-9	1,2
Charles St.	P-13	2
Charles St.	T-11	1
Cherry Ln.	R-9	1
Chestnut Oval	R-11	1
Chestnut Oval E.	R-11	1
Chestnut St.	Q-8	1,2
Chipman Rd.	U-13	1
Christine Ln.	S-11	1
Church	P-13	2
Claudia Ct.	T-11	1
Clausland Mountain Rd.	R-12	1
Cleveland St.	T-11	1
Cleveland St.	Q-10	1,2
Clinton Av.	T-11	1
Clinton Av.	Q-13	1,2
Cobble Pl.	R-10	1
College Av.	Q-13	1,2
Colonial Ct.	Q-9	1,2
Colony Dr.	Q-11	1,2
Concord Dr.	T-12	1
Conklin Av.	T-12	1
Constitution Dr.	S-11	1
Convent Rd.	R-11	1
Convent Rd.	R-10	1
Convent Rd.	P-8	2
Coolidge St.	Q-10	1,2
Cooper Dr.	P-13	2
Corporate Dr.	S-10	1
Cortwood Rd. E.	S-11	1
Cottage Ln.	R-11	1
Court St.	P-13	2
Cowpens Dr.	S-11	1
Crescent Rd.	S-13	1
Crescent Ln.	P-10	2
Crescent St.	S-13	1
Crooked Hill Rd.	Q-9	1,2
Cross St.	P-13	2
Cypress Ln. W.	R-11	1
Cypress Ln. E.	R-11	1
Dakota St.	U-12	1
Dederer St.	S-12	1
Deerpark Rd.	S-12	1
Delo Dr.	T-12	1
Depew Av.	P-13	2
Depew Av.	P-13	2
Derfuss Ln.	R-11	1
Devon Dr.	R-11	1
Dexter Av.	R-8	1
Diane Dr.	Q-11	1,2
Dickenson Av.	P-13	2
Division St.	P-13	2
Dogwood Ln.	S-11	1
Douglas Ct.	Q-9	1,2
Dove St.	Q-9	1,2
Drewry Ln.	S-11	1
Duhane St.	Q-10	1,2
Duryea Pl.	P-13	2
Dutch Hill Rd.	S-11	1
Dutch Hollow Dr.	R-11	1
Dutchess Dr.	S-11	1
E. Carroll St.	Q-9	1,2
E. Park St.	Q-9	1,2
E. Park St.	R-9	1
Eagle Ln.	T-11	1
Earl St. N.	Q-9	1,2
Eastwood Dr.	R-11	1
Edgewater Ln.	Q-13	1,2
Edgewood Cir.	R-11	1
Edgewood Ct.	R-11	1
Edgewood Dr.	R-11	1
Edsall Ter.	Q-10	1,2
Edward St.	S-12	1
Ehrhardt Rd.	Q-10	1,2
Eisenhower Ct.	R-11	1
Elisian Av.	P-13	2
Elissa Ln.	S-11	1
Ellen St.	P-13	2
Ellsworth Dr.	Q-11	1,2
Elm St.	S-13	1
Elm St.	R-10	1
Elmdorf Ln.	Q-9	1,2
Elmendorf Ln.	Q-9	1,2
Elmer St.	S-12	1
Elwin Ln.	Q-9	1,2
Elwin St.	R-9	1
End Av. W.	P-13	2
Eric Dr.	R-9	1
Erie St.	Q-11	1,2
Evergreen Ln. (Aetna Ln.)	S-11	1
Fairmont Av.	R-8	1
Fairview Av.	Q-8	1,2
Fairview Ln.	S-11	1
Ferdon Av.	S-13	1
Fern Av.	Q-13	1,2
Fern Oval E.	S-11	1
Fern Oval W.	S-11	1
Fern Rd.	U-12	1
Ferris Ln.	Q-13	1,2
Ferry Rd.	S-13	1
Fillmore St.	Q-8	1,2
Fisher Av.	Q-8	1,2
Flitt St.	T-12	1
Florence St.	P-13	2
Forest Av.	Q-9	1,2
Forest Dr.	U-12	1
Fort Lee Pl.	S-11	1
Frances Av.	P-13	2
Franklin Av.	Q-9	1,2
Franklin St. N.	P-13	2
Franklin St. S.	P-13	2
Front St.	P-13	2
Gage Ct.	S-11	1
Garber Hill Rd.	S-10	1
Garfield St.	S-11	1
Garfield St.	R-11	1
Gamey Ct.	Q-9	1,2
Garrecht Ln.	R-10	1
Gary Ln.	S-11	1
Gates Pl.	S-11	1
Gatto Ln.(Violet Dr.)	P-8	2
Gedney St.	P-13	2
George Av. E.	Q-9	1,2
Gerson Av.	U-12	1
Gesner Av.	Q-13	1,2
Giadeccka St.	R-11	1
Gilbert Av.	R-9	1
Glenbyron Av.	Q-13	1,2
Glenshaw St.	R-12	1
Gumee Av.	Q-13	1,2
Glenwood Dr.	R-11	1
Glynn Oval	Q-11	1,2
Goehring Curve	R-11	1
Gottlieb Dr.	Q-8	1,2
Grand Av.	P-13	2
Grand Av.	T-11	1
Grand Av.	R-8	1
Graney Ct.	Q-9	1,2
Grant Av.	S-11	1
Greenbush Rd.	Q-12	1,2
Greenbush Rd.	T-11	1
Greenbush Rd.	R-12	1
Greenbush Rd.	S-12	1
Greene Pl.	S-11	1
Greene St.	T-11	1
Greenhedge Ln.	Q-11	1,2
Gregg Ct.	S-11	1
Greywood Dr.	S-11	1
Griffith Pl.	R-9	1
Grove St.	R-9	1
Guterl Ter.	Q-10	1,2
Guttman Ln.	Q-8	1,2
Hale Pl.	S-11	1
Hamilton Av.	S-11	1
Hamilton Pl.	Q-13	1,2
Hancock Pl.	S-11	1
Hansen Av.	Q-8	1,2
Hansen St.	T-12	1
Harding St.	Q-8	1,2
Harding St.	Q-10	1,2
Hardwood Dr.	S-11	1
Haring Av.	S-12	1
Harold St.	P-10	2
Hart Pl.	P-13	2
Haven Ter.	R-10	1
Hawk St.	Q-10	1,2
Hayes St.	R-11	1
Heather Ln.	S-11	1
Helaine Ct.	S-11	1
Henry St.	S-11	1
Hester St.	S-13	1
Hey Hoe Woods Rd.	U-13	1
Hickey St.	S-12	1
Hickory Hill Rd.	T-11	1
Hickory St.	R-12	1
High Av.	P-13	2
High St.	Q-8	1,2
Highland Av.	U-13	1
Highland Av.	T-13	1
Highland Av.	S-12	1
Highland Av.	S-13	1
Highland Av.	P-13	2
Highland Av.	Q-13	1,2
Highland Av.	R-12	1
Highland Av. S.	Q-8	1,2
Highland Av. S.	P-13	2
Highmount Av.	P-13	2
Highview Av.	P-9	2
Highview Av.	R-9	1
Highview Av.	S-11	1
Hillaire Pl.	Q-10	1,2
Hillside Av.	P-13	2
Hillside Av.	Q-9	1,2
Hillside Ter.	P-10	2
Hilltop Dr.	Q-9	1,2
Hobart St.	Q-9	1,2
Hoffman Dr.	R-11	1
Hog Rd.	S-10	1
Hogan Ln.	Q-10	1,2
Hogenkamp Av.	P-9	2
Hollis St.	S-11	1
Holly Ct.	Q-11	1,2
Holt Dr.	Q-9	1,2
Hook St.	S-11	1
Hoover St.	R-11	1
Horan Pl.	T-12	1
Horne Tooke Rd.	U-12	1
Howard Av.	S-11	1
Hudson Av.	P-13	2
Hudson Av.	P-13	2
Hudson Ter.	S-13	1
Hunderfund Ln.	Q-9	1,2
Hunt Av.	Q-9	1,2
Hunt Rd.	S-10	1
Independence Av.	S-11	1
Indian Hill Ln.	U-12	1
Iroquois Av.	U-12	1
Isabel Rd.	S-11	1
J.F. Kennedy Dr.	R-11	1
Jackson Av.	P-13	2
Jackson St.	S-11	1
Jane St.	T-12	1
Jay St.	Q-10	1,2
Jeanne's Pl.	T-12	1
Jefferson Av.	Q-9	1,2
Jefferson St.	P-13	2
Jensen Pl.	Q-9	1,2
Jewett Pl.	P-13	2
John Calvin St.	Q-11	1,2
John St. N.	Q-9	1,2
John St. S.	Q-9	1,2
Johnson Ln.	R-11	1
Jones Pl.	S-11	1
Julia Ct.	S-12	1
Justin Ct.	U-13	1
Kerry Ct.	R-9	1
Kevin Dr.	S-11	1
Key Pl.	S-11	1
Kim Ct.	S-11	1
Kings Highway	S-12	1
Kings Highway	T-11	1
Kingswood Dr.	S-12	1
Kinney St.	S-13	1
Kinsley Grove	R-10	1
Kirchner Dr.	T-12	1
Klee Av.	R-11	1
Knutsen Knoll	S-11	1
La Veta Pl.	P-13	2
Ladik	S-13	1
Lafayette Av.	T-11	1
Lake Dr.	T-12	1
Lang Ter.	Q-9	1,2
Lanram Rd. E.	S-12	1
Lanram Rd. W.	S-12	1
Lapin Ln.	R-11	1
Lark St.	R-10	1
Laurel Rd.	Q-8	1,2
Lawrence Av.	U-13	1
Lawrence St.	P-13	2
Lawrence St.	T-12	1
Leber Rd.	Q-11	1,2
Leber Rd.	Q-12	1,2
Lenape Rd.	R-9	1
Lester Dr.	S-11	1
Lester Dr. W.	S-11	1
Levere Ct.	Q-9	1,2
Lewis Av. E.	Q-9	1,2
Lewis Av. W.	Q-9	1,2
Lexington Av.	T-12	1
Liberty	P-13	2
Liberty Rd.	T-11	1
Liberty St.	S-13	1
Lieutenant Cox Dr.	Q-8	1,2
Lincoln Av.	Q-8	1,2
Lincoln St. N.	Q-8	1,2
Linda Ln.	R-9	1
Livingston St.	T-11	1
Livingston St.	Q-13	1,2
Lockhart Av.	U-12	1
Locust Pl.	Q-13	1,2
Lois Dr.	R-9	1
Lombardi Dr.	Q-9	1,2
Lowe Ln. E.	S-11	1
Lowland Dr.	Q-13	1,2
Lt. Birch Ct.	Q-11	1,2
Ludlow Ln.	U-13	1
Lydecker St.	P-13	2
Maggiola Rd.	Q-8	1,2
Magnolia St. N.	Q-9	1,2
Magnolia St. S.	Q-9	1,2
Main St.	P-13	2
Main St.	T-11	1
Main St.	S-13	1
Main St. N.	Q-9	1,2
Main St. S.	R-9	1
Mallory Ln.	S-11	1
Manor Blvd.	Q-9	1,2
Mansfield St.	Q-13	1,2
Maple Av.	S-11	1
Maple Ln.	Q-11	1,2
Maple St.	P-13	2
Mapleshade Av.	R-10	1
Margaret Keahon Dr.	Q-9	1,2
Marion Pl.	Q-9	1,2
Marion St.	P-13	2
Martha Pl.	Q-8	1,2
Martin Pl.	Q-9	1,2
Mary Jane Av.	Q-11	1,2
Mary St.	T-12	1
Marycrest Rd.	Q-10	1,2
May Rd.	Q-8	1,2
Mc Kenna St.	R-11	1
Mc Kinley St.	Q-10	1,2
Meadow St.	Q-9	1,2
Meadow St.	Q-10	1,2
Mendolia Ct.	Q-8	1,2
Mercury St.	Q-8	1,2
Merritt Dr.	P-10	2
Meyer Oval	R-9	1
Michael Dr.	Q-11	1,2
Middletown Rd. N.	Q-9	1,2
Middletown Rd. S.	R-9	1
Midland Av.	P-13	2
Midland Av.	T-11	1
Midland Av. S.	P-13	2
Mill St. (Not shown-lack space-off MainSt)	P-13	2
Mill St. N.	P-13	2
Mill St. S.	P-13	2
Milton Grant Dr.	Q-11	1,2
Minute Man Cir.	S-11	1
Moehring Dr.	R-11	1
Moison Rd.	R-12	1
Monmouth Ct.	S-11	1
Montgomery Rd.	R-9	1
Moore Av.	Q-9	1,2
Morningside Av.	U-12	1
Morris Pl.	S-11	1
Morristown Dr.	S-11	1
Mountainview Av.	R-9	1
Mountainview Av.	R-11	1
Mountainview Rd.	R-11	1
Muroney Av.	U-12	1
Musket Rd.	T-11	1
N. Center St.	Q-9	1,2
N. Henry St.	Q-9	1,2
N. Highview Av.	P-9	2
N. Mary Francis St.	S-11	1
N. Pearl St.	Q-9	1,2
Nancy Rd.	P-10	2
Naomi Rd.	R-9	1
Nauraushaun Av. E.	R-10	1
Nauraushaun Av. S.	R-10	1
Nauraushaun Av. W.	R-10	1
Neill Ln.	Q-10	1,2
New St.	P-13	2
Newport Av.	S-11	1
Nicole Ter.	Q-9	1,2
North St.	Q-8	1,2
Noyes St.	R-10	1
Oak Ln.	U-13	1
Oak St.	S-11	1
Oak St.	S-13	1
Oak Tree Rd.	T-12	1
Oakland Dr.	P-13	2
Ohio St.	S-13	1
Old Middletown Rd.	R-9	1
Old Mill La.	T-12	1
Old Pascack Rd.	Q-8	1,2
Old Sq. Highland Av.	Q-8	1,2
Old Tappan Rd.	T-11	1
Old Western Highway	Q-11	1,2
Oldert Dr.	R-10	1
Oldert Dr.	R-9	1
Olympic Dr.	S-10	1
Orangeburg Rd.	Q-9	1,2
Orangeburg Rd.	R-10	1
Orangeburg Rd.	S-12	1
Orangeburg Rd.	R-11	1
Orchard Dr.	Q-9	1,2
Orchard Ln.	Q-10	1,2
Orchard Pl.	P-13	2
Orchard Tr.	S-13	1
Orchid St.	Q-9	1,2
Orient St.	T-13	1
Oriole St.	Q-9	1,2
Owen Pl.	Q-9	1,2
P.F.C. Dorset Ct.	Q-11	1,2
Palisades Interstate Parkway	P-10	2
Paradise Av.	S-13	1
Park Av.	Q-9	1,2
Park Av.	U-12	1
Park Pl.	T-12	1
Park Rd.	Q-13	1,2
Park St.	P-13	2
Park St.	Q-9	1,2
Park St. W.	Q-8	1,2
Parker Rd.	Q-12	1,2
Parkway Dr. N.	R-11	1
Parkway Dr. S.	R-11	1
Pascack Rd. S.	Q-8	1,2
Patton Pl.	Q-9	1,2
Paul Ct.	T-12	1
Paulding Pl.	T-12	1
Pauline Ter.	Q-9	1,2
Peach St.	P-10	2
Pear Cir.	Q-10	1,2
Pearce Parkway	Q-9	1,2
Pearl Crest Ct.	Q-9	1,2
Pearl St. S.	R-9	1
Penn Ct.	S-11	1
Perillo Ct.	Q-8	1,2
Peterson Ct.	R-10	1
Pheasant Dr.	T-12	1
Phillips Ln.	R-9	1
Phyllis Dr.	R-9	1
Piermont Av.	Q-13	1,2
Piermont Av.	P-13	2
Piermont Av.	S-12	1
Piermont Pl.	S-13	1
Piermont River Rd.	S-13	1
Piermont St.	T-12	1
Pilgrim Ct.	Q-9	1,2
Pine Glen Dr.	S-10	1
Pinetree Ln.	T-12	1
Pinto Rd.	Q-10	1,2
Piper Ct.	P-11	2
Plum Ct.	P-10	2
Polhemus St.	S-12	1
Post Ln.	U-12	1
Prall Pl.	Q-13	1,2
Prince's Gate	S-12	1
Princeton Dr.	S-11	1
Prior Ct.	U-13	1
Prospect Av.	Q-13	1,2
Prospect Av.	P-13	2
Prospect St.	P-13	2
Prospect St.	Q-13	1,2
Pulaski Ct.	S-11	1
Quake Ln.	R-9	1
Quaspec Rd.	R-10	1
Queens Ct. N.	S-12	1
Queens Ct. S.	S-12	1
Railroad Av.	T-12	1
Railroad Rd.	Q-9	1,2
Ramland Rd.	S-10	1
Red Oak Dr.	T-12	1
Redbud Ln.	Q-11	1,2
Redcoat Ln.	S-11	1
Regal St.	R-11	1
Regina Ct.	Q-11	1,2
Reld Dr.	Q-10	1,2
Reld Dr. E.	Q-10	1,2
Reld Dr. S.	Q-10	1,2
Remson St.	P-13	2
Renee Ln.	Q-8	1,2
Renie Ln.	Q-11	1,2
Resmen St.	P-13	2
Retz	Q-10	1,2
Revere Pl.	S-11	1
Reyerson Pl.	T-11	1
Reynolds Ln.	R-9	1
Ridge St.	R-9	1
Ritie St.	S-13	1
River St.	P-13	2
Riverside Ter.	R-10	1
Riverview Av.	Q-13	1,2
Rizzo Ct.	Q-8	1,2
Robert Ln.	S-11	1
Robertson Dr.	Q-10	1,2
Robin Ct.	Q-10	1,2
Rockland Dr.	P-13	2
Rockland Park	T-12	1
Rockland Rd.	Q-9	1,2
Rockland Rd.	T-13	1
Rolfe Pl.	P-10	2
Rollins Av.	Q-9	1,2
Rolyn Hills Dr.	Q-11	1,2
Roosevelt St.	Q-9	1,2
Roosevelt St.	T-11	1
Ross Av.	P-13	2
Ross Pl.	S-11	1
Rowan Rd.	Q-10	1,2
Rutgers Rd. E.	S-11	1
Rutgers Rd. W.	S-11	1
S. Highland Av.	S-12	1
S. Mary Francis St.	P-11	2
Salina Rd.	Q-8	1,2
Salisbury Pl.	Q-13	1,2
Salmar Dr.	Q-9	1,2
Sandhage Rd.	Q-8	1,2
Sandra Ln.	Q-10	1,2
Saratoga St.	T-12	1
School House Ln.	R-12	1
Schreiber St.	T-11	1
Schuyler Rd.	Q-12	1,2
Schuyler Rd.	S-10	1
Scott Av.	U-12	1
Secor Blvd.	Q-9	1,2
Sergent Amory Av.	P-9	2
Serven St. N.	Q-9	1,2
Serven St. S.	Q-9	1,2
Shadyside Av.	Q-13	1,2
Sherwood Ln.	Q-11	1,2
Sicketown Rd.	Q-11	1,2
Sickles Av.	P-13	2
Sickletown Rd.	Q-10	1,2
Silver Birch Ln.	P-9	2
Sioux St.	U-12	1
Skyview Oval	S-11	1
Slocum Av.	T-12	1
Smith Av.	Q-13	1,2
Smith Ct.	U-12	1
Smith Rd.	T-12	1
Sparkill Av.	T-12	1
Sparrow Ln.	Q-9	1,2
Spear St.	P-13	2
Spencer Ct.	S-10	1
Spreen Av.	Q-9	1,2
Spreen Av.	R-9	1
Spring St.	P-13	2
Springsteen Av.	Q-8	1,2
Spruce St.	R-12	1
Standish Dr.	Q-9	1,2
Station Rd.	R-13	1
Staubitz St.	Q-10	1,2
Stephens Rd.	T-11	1
Sterling Av.	T-11	1
Sterling Pl.	S-10	1
Steuben Av.	T-11	1
Stevenson Av.	R-12	1
Stone Haven Rd.	Q-11	1,2
Strawberry Pl.	Q-10	1,2
Summit Av.	T-11	1
Summit Pl.	P-10	2
Summit St.	Q-9	1,2
Summit St.	P-13	2
Sunrise Ln.	R-10	1
Sunset Rd.	Q-11	1,2
Surrey Ct.	Q-10	1,2
Swannekin Rd.	R-11	1
Sylvanus Ct.	Q-11	1,2
Tallman Av.	P-13	2
Tallman Pl.	P-13	2
Tappan Zee	Q-13	1,2
Tate Av.	S-13	1
Taylor Av.	Q-13	1,2
Tea Pl.	T-11	1
Teema Pl.	T-12	1
Terrace Dr.	P-13	2
Terrace Dr.	R-11	1
Terry Ln.	R-11	1
Theodore Roosevelt Dr.	R-11	1
Thies Ln.	Q-11	1,2
Thomas Cir.	S-11	1
Thomsen Cir.	Q-10	1,2
Tilou Ln.	P-13	2
Tory Cir.	S-11	1
Town Line Rd.	P-9	2
Town Line Rd.	P-10	2
Townsend Av.	Q-13	1,2
Treeline Ter.	R-13	1
Trenton Pl.	S-11	1
Truman Cir.	Q-10	1,2
Tulip Ln.	Q-10	1,2
Turner Rd.	R-9	1
Turner Rd. E.	R-9	1
Twin Ct.	Q-9	1,2
Tygert Rd.	S-10	1
Union St.	T-12	1
Upland Dr.	P-13	2
Upper Ritie St.	S-13	1
Valentine Av.	T-12	1
Valenza Ln.	S-10	1
Valley Forge Pl.	S-11	1
Van Buren St.	Q-8	1,2
Van Ter.	T-12	1
Van Wardt Pl.	T-11	1
Van Wormer Rd.	Q-9	1,2
Van Wyck Rd.	R-11	1
Van Zandt Dr.	P-10	2
Venter Ln.	P-10	2
Veterans Memorial Dr.	R-9	1
Veterans Parkway	Q-9	1,2
Villa Rd.	Q-10	1,2
Violet Dr.	P-9	2
Violet Dr.	P-10	2
Virginia St.	S-12	1
Voorhis Av.	P-13	2
Voorhis Point	Q-13	1,2
W. George Av.	Q-9	1,2
W. Madison Av.	Q-9	1,2
Walnut St.	R-12	1
Warrant Officer Baur Ln.	Q-11	1,2
Washington Av.	Q-13	1,2
Washington Av.	S-11	1
Washington Av. E.	Q-9	1,2
Washington Av. W.	Q-8	1,2
Washington Ln.	T-11	1
Washington Pl.	Q-8	1,2
Washington Spring Rd.	U-13	1
Washington St.	P-13	2
Wayne Ln.	S-11	1
Webster Rd.	S-11	1
Western Highway	T-11	1
Western Highway	Q-11	1,2
Western Highway	R-11	1
Westminster Dr.	R-10	1
White Av.	P-13	2
White Av.	Q-9	1,2
White Oak Rd.	T-12	1
Whittier Rd.	S-10	1
Whittier Rd.	Q-12	1,2
Wildwood Dr.	R-9	1
William St.	T-11	1
William St. N.	Q-9	1,2
William St. S.	R-9	1
Williams St.	T-12	1
Wilson St.	Q-10	1,2
Windsor Brook Ln.	T-12	1
Wisteria Ct.	S-11	1
Woodland Av.	Q-9	1,2
Woodland Ter.	S-11	1
Woods Rd.	U-13	1
Woodway Dr.	Q-10	1,2
Wright St.	Q-9	1,2
Yale Ter.	Q-12	1,2
Yorktown Ct.	T-11	1

Town of Ramapo

STREET	GRID	MAP
1st Av.	M-9	2
1st St.	M-7	3
1st St.	M-4	3
1st St.	M-8	2
1st St.	H-3	4
1st St.	K-3	4
2nd St.	K-3	4
2nd St.	M-7	3
2nd St.	J-9	5
3rd St.	K-3	4
4th St.	L-3	3,4
5th St.	K-3	4
6th St.	L-3	3,4
6th St.	K-3	4
6th St.	J-9	5
7th St.	L-3	3,4
Abbey Rd.	M-6	3
Aberdeen Av.	P-8	2
Academy Rd.	H-3	4
Ace St.	L-9	2,5
Ackerman Av.	M-5	3
Ackerton Rd.	P-7	3
Adam Ct.	H-3	4
Adams Ln.	L-9	2,5
Adams Ln.	M-6	3
Adar Ct.	M-8	2
Adelle Blvd.	K-9	5
Airmont Rd.	L-6	3,4
Airmont Rd. S.	M-5	3
Albert Dr.	M-7	3
Alexander Av.	L-9	2,5
Algonquin Cir.	N-7	3
Allen Dr.	N-7	3
Allen Ln.	H-3	4
Allen Pl.	H-3	4
Alpha Ln.	N-6	3
Alturas Rd.	M-8	2
Amanda Ct.	N-5	3
Amber Ridge Rd.	P-7	3
Amsterdam Av.	J-7	4
Amundsen Ln.	M-5	3
Anchor Rd.	K-9	5
Anders Ln.	J-8	5
Andover Rd.	M-9	2
Andrew Dr.	N-7	3
Angela Ct.	P-7	3
Anjou Ln.	L-7	3,4
Ann Blvd.	N-7	3
Ann St.	M-8	2
Ann St.	H-3	4
Annette Ln.	M-6	3
Anthony Ct.	L-9	2,5
Anthony Dr.	L-8	2,5
Antoinette Ct.	K-7	4
Antrim Av.	L-4	3,4
Apple St.	H-3	4
Appleblossom Ct.	N-6	3
Appledale Ln.	P-8	2
Applegate Ln.	K-9	5
Appleland Rd.	M-6	3
Arcadia Ct.	J-2	4
Arcadian Dr.	J-7	4
Arcadian Dr.	K-8	5
Ardley Pl.	J-7	4
Ari Dr.	J-7	4
Arrowhead Ln.	L-6	3,4
Aselin Dr.	L-8	2,5
Ash Lawn Ct.	K-8	5
Ash St.	K-7	4
Ashel Ln.	L-7	3,4
Ashwood Dr.	L-6	3,4
Aspen Rd.	H-3	4
Astor Pl.	J-7	4
Astri Ct.	L-5	3,4
Atthen Dr.	N-8	2
Auburn Ct.	K-8	5
Augur Dr.	M-5	3
August Av.	M-7	3
Augusta Av.	M-7	3
Avon Ct.	N-6	3
Ayr Ct.	M-6	3
Babbin Rd.	L-8	2,5
Babbling Brook Ln.	K-5	4
Babcock Ln.	J-8	5
Badger St.	P-8	2
Baker Ln.	J-7	4
Balanchine Ct.	N-7	3
Baldwin Ct.	K-8	5
Ballard Av.	H-3	4
Balmoral Dr.	P-8	2
Banker St.	N-8	2
Barbara Ln.	M-7	3
Barnacle Dr.	K-8	5
Barnes St.	M-9	2
Barrie Dr.	K-8	5
Barry St.	H-9	5
Bartlett Rd.	L-7	3,4
Bass Pl.	H-3	4
Bates Dr.	M-7	3
Batrix Rd.	N-5	3
Bay Ct.	L-8	2,5
Bayard Ln.	K-5	4
Bayberry Dr.	M-6	3
Beatrice Rd.	J-8	5
Beatrix Rd.	N-5	3
Beaver Hollow Ln.	N-6	3
Beck Ct.	L-8	2,5
Becketts Ct.	N-7	3
Beaver Ln.	J-8	5
Beckett Ct.	N-7	3
Bedford Ct.	L-8	2,5
Bedford Rd.	K-7	4
Beech Rd.	M-4	3
Beechwood Rd.	M-4	3
Bell Ct.	M-5	3
Bell Ln.	P-8	2
Bella Blvd.	L-6	3,4
Bellows Ln.	P-7	3
Belvedere Path	K-5	4
Berkley Cir.	L-4	3,4
Besen Parkway	M-7	3
Bessie St.	K-9	5
Beth Pl.	K-7	4
Bina Ln.	L-7	3,4
Birch Rd.	N-7	3
Birch Rd.	H-3	4
Bird St.	L-9	2,5
Biret Dr.	M-5	3
Blakslee Pl.	K-4	4
Blauvelt Rd.	M-7	3
Blossom Ct.	M-6	3
Blossom Rd.	M-6	3
Blueberry Hill Rd.	L-8	2,5
Bluebird Rd.	N-7	3
Boar Ct.	H-8	5
Bogart Pl.	L-9	2,5
Bohr Ct.	L-8	2,5
Bolger Ln.	M-6	3
Bon-Aire	M-5	3
Bon-Aire Cir. E.	M-5	3
Bon-Aire Cir. W.	M-5	3
Bonnie Ct.	L-9	2,5
Bonnie Way	N-6	3
Boulder Av.	K-3	4
Boulevard	M-4	3
Boxwood Ln.	M-7	3
Bradley St.	P-7	3
Brewer Rd.	M-7	3
Brian Ln.	P-7	3
Briar Ct.	N-8	2
Briarcliff Dr.	M-7	3
Briarwood Ln.	L-7	3,4
Brice Ct.	K-6	4
Brick Church Rd.	K-8	5
Bridge St.	K-3	4
Bridge St.	L-4	3,4
Bridle Rd.	K-8	5
Brigadoon Dr.	L-5	3,4
Brigitte Ct.	M-5	3
Bristol Ln.	L-9	2,5
Brockton Rd.	L-8	2,5
Brook Av.	L-4	3,4
Brook Hollow Ct.	P-7	3
Brook Ln.	K-10	5
Brook St.	L-4	3,4
Brook St.	J-2	4
Brook St.	L-3	3,4
Brookside Av.	M-5	3
Brookview Blvd.	P-8	2
Bruck Ct.	J-8	5
Buckman Pl.	L-8	2,5
Buena Vista Rd.	L-9	2,5
Buena Vista Rd.	J-8	5
Burlington Av.	M-5	3
Burris Ct.	N-7	3
Burrows Ct.	K-9	5
Bush Av.	H-3	4
Bush Ln.	H-3	4
Bush St.	M-8	2
Buttemut Dr.	K-9	5
Calvert Dr.	L-7	3,4
Cambridge Rd.	K-7	4
Cameo Ridge Rd.	M-7	3
Camp Hill Rd.	H-8	5
Camp Hill Rd.	J-8	5
Campbell Rd.	M-5	3
Cannan Rd.	P-7	3
Canterbury Ln.	L-6	3,4
Cape Ct.	M-7	3
Capri Dr.	P-7	3
Capricorn Ln.	P-7	3
Cardinal Ln.	N-7	3
Carefree Ln.	J-7	4
Carlisle Rd.	P-8	2
Carlton Ln.	L-7	3,4
Carlton Rd.	L-6	3,4
Carmen Ct.	N-7	3
Caroll Dr.	K-6	4
Carpenter Ct.	N-6	3
Carriage Ln.	L-9	2,5
Carter Ln.	J-7	4
Carteret Dr.	J-10	5
Castle Av.	M-8	2
Castle Dr.	P-8	2
Cathrine Ct.	K-5	4
Caville Dr.	M-7	3
Cedar Ln.	L-4	3,4
Cedar Ln.	L-7	3,4
Cedar Ter.	H-3	4

ROCKLAND COUNTY

STREET	GRID	MAP
Celia Ct.	K-7	4
Center Rd.	K-5	4
Center St.	L-4	3,4
Center St.	M-8	2
Central Av.	M-8	2
Central Av. E.	M-8	2
Central Av. S.	N-8	2
Chadwick Pl.	L-4	3,4
Chamberlain Ct.	H-8	5
Chaparral Rd.	N-8	2
Charles Ln.	L-8	2,5
Charles St.	K-9	5
Charlotte Dr.	J-8	5
Charlotte Pl.	M-8	2
Charnwood Dr.	K-6	4
Chatham St.	M-4	3
Chelmsford Ct.	M-7	3
Chelsea Ct.	M-5	3
Cherry Ln.	N-6	3
Cherry Ln.	M-6	3
Cheryl St.	P-8	2
Chestnut Av.	L-3	3,4
Chestnut Ridge Rd.	P-7	3
Chestnut St.	L-4	3,4
Chestnut St.	M-8	2
Christine Dr.	P-8	2
Christmas Hill Rd.	N-6	3
Church Rd.	M-5	3
Church Rd.	N-5	3
Church St.	M-8	2
Cira Dr.	P-7	3
Claremont Ln.	M-5	3
Clayton Dr.	L-8	2,5
Cleveland Pl.	L-9	2,5
Clinton Pl.	L-4	3,4
Clove Rd.	J-2	4
Cloverdale Ln.	L-7	3,4
Clubview Rd.	K-9	5
Cobblestone Rd.	N-6	3
Cobh Ct.	L-9	2,5
Cole Av.	M-8	2
Cole Av. N.	M-8	2
Cole Av. S.	N-8	2
Cole Av. S.	M-8	2
College Rd.	L-7	3,4
Collins Av.	M-8	2
Colonial Av.	J-2	4
Columbus Av.	M-8	2
Commerce St.	M-8	2
Concord Dr.	L-7	3,4
Conklin Rd.	J-9	5
Continental Ct.	P-8	2
Convent Rd.	P-8	2
Cooper Morris Dr.	H-9	5
Copeland Dr.	K-5	4
Cortland Rd.	K-7	4
Cottage Ln.	H-8	5
Council Crest Rd.	J-3	4
Country Club Ln.	M-7	3
Crab Apple Ct.	K-7	4
Cragmere Rd.	M-5	3
Cranberry Rd.	J-2	4
Crane Pl.	L-4	3,4
Crescent Dr.	L-9	2,5
Crest Ct.	L-7	3,4
Crest Rd.	J-3	4
Crestview Ter.	L-8	2,5
Crestwood Dr.	M-4	3
Crocus Ct.	L-6	3,4
Cross St.	L-4	3,4
Crystal St.	M-9	2
Cucolo Av.	M-7	3
Cypress Rd.	M-4	3
Daisy Ct.	N-5	3
Dale Rd.	N-6	3
Dalewood Dr.	L-6	3,4
Dana Rd.	L-8	2,5
Danbury Ct.	M-5	3
Danville Rd.	M-9	2
Darby Rd.	N-7	3
Dashew	M-6	3
David Ct.	M-7	3
Dawn Ln.	M-6	3
De Baum Av.	M-6	3
De Baum Pl.	L-8	2,5
De Salvo Ct.	Q-7	2
Debaum Av.	M-6	3
Debaun Pl.	L-8	2,5
Deborah Ct.	N-7	3
Decatur Av.	M-8	2
Deerwood Rd.	J-8	5
Demarest Rd.	P-8	2
Dennis Ct.	N-7	3
Deronde Rd.	M-7	3
Devon Ct.	N-6	3
Dike Dr.	J-7	4
Dina Dr.	N-8	2
Division St.	N-8	2
Doe Dr.	J-7	4
Dogwood Ln.	J-9	5
Dogwood Ln. N.	J-10	5
Dogwood Ln. S.	J-10	5
Dogwood Pl.	J-9	5
Dogwood Rd.	H-3	4
Dolson Rd.	M-7	3
Donald Rd.	M-5	3
Dorchester Dr.	N-6	3
Dorothy Dr.	K-9	5
Dorset Rd.	L-8	2,5
Dover Ter.	L-7	3,4
Doxbury Ln.	M-5	3
Druid Ct.	L-6	3,4
Dunhill Ln.	L-7	3,4
Dunlop Dr.	M-8	2
Dunn Rd.	M-6	3
Dunnery Ct.	M-4	3
Durante Ct.	L-9	2,5
Durham Ln.	M-4	3
Dusty Rd.	K-10	5
Dutch Ln.	M-8	2
Dwight Av.	L-9	2,5
Dykstra's Way E.	N-7	3
Dykstra's Way W.	N-7	3
E. Castle Av.	M-8	2
Eagle St.	N-7	3
Eagle St.Blvd.	N-7	3
Eagle Valley Rd.	H-2	4
Eagleview Ct.	N-6	3
Earl Ct.	K-8	5
East Ln.	J-8	5
East Pl.	L-5	3,4
Eastborne Dr.	P-8	2
Eastview Rd.	M-7	3
Echo Ridge Rd.	N-6	3
Eckerson Ln.	L-9	2,5
Edgebrook Ln.	N-6	3
Edison Ct.	L-8	2,5
Edward	L-9	2,5
Edwin Ln.	M-7	3
Ehret Dr.	N-7	3
Eileen Ct.	M-6	3
Eisenhower Av.	L-9	2,5
Elaine Pl.	M-8	2
Elber Ct.	N-6	3
Eldorado Dr.	P-8	2
Eleanor Pl.	M-6	3
Elener Ln.	L-8	2,5
Elias St.	M-8	2
Ellington Way	K-8	5
Elliot Ct.	M-7	3
Elliot Pl.	L-9	2,5
Ellish Parkway	M-8	2
Elm St.	L-8	2,5
Elton Ln.	M-9	2
Elyise Rd.	K-7	4
Emerald Dr.	H-8	5
Emes Rd.	M-7	3
Erin Ln.	P-8	2
Eros Dr.	N-5	3
Essex Dr.	M-5	3
Ethan Allen Dr.	J-8	5
Eton Pl.	N-6	3
Ewing St.	M-8	2
Executive Blvd.	L-5	3,4
Fairchild St.	H-3	4
Fairview Av.	M-4	3
Fairview Av.	N-8	2
Fairview Pl.	M-4	3
Fairview Ter.	M-5	3
Fairview Av.	N-7	3
Fairway Oval	K-8	5
Faist Dr.	L-8	2,5
Falcon Ct.	N-8	2
Fanley Av.	M-8	2
Farm Ln.	J-8	5
Farmer Ln.	M-6	3
Fawn Hill Dr.	N-6	3
Fawn Ln.	J-7	4
Feller Ct.	M-6	3
Fernwood Rd.	H-3	4
Ferruza Dr.	P-7	3
Fessler Dr.	K-7	4
Fessler Dr.	L-8	2,5
Fieldcrest Dr.	K-7	4
Firemens Memorial Dr.	J-9	5
Fisher Ct.	L-8	2,5
Flamingo Ln.	K-9	5
Fleetwood Av.	P-7	3
Fletcher Ct.	L-9	2,5
Fletcher Rd.	M-7	3
Flint Dr.	L-8	2,5
Forest Dr.	M-4	3
Forest Glen Ct.	J-8	5
Forest Knoll Dr.	M-4	3
Forest Ln.	J-8	5
Forest Rd.	J-3	4
Forestdale Rd.	M-9	2
Formerly College Rd.	L-7	3,4
Forshay Rd.	K-7	4
Fosse Ct.	N-7	3
Fox Hollow Rd.	L-3	3,4
Fox Ln.	L-8	2,5
Foxhill Rd.	P-7	3
Foxhill Rd.	Q-7	2
Foxwood Av.	M-4	3
Francis Pl.	L-8	2,5
Frank Pl.	M-8	2
Frank Rd.	L-8	2,5
Franklin St.	M-8	2
Fredeller Rd.	M-7	3
Fringe Ct.	N-8	2
Frontier Ln.	N-6	3
Fulton Pl.	L-3	3,4
Funston Av.	M-8	2
Gail Ct.	N-8	2
Galbraith Rd.	K-7	4
Galileo Ct.	J-8	5
Garden Pl.	M-8	2
Garden St.	N-8	2
Garden State Pkwy.	P-8	2
Garfield Rd.	L-9	2,5
Garrett Ct	P-7	3
Gate Dr. S.	L-8	2,5
Gate Rd. E.	K-6	4
Gate Rd. W.	K-6	4
Gate Rd. W.	K-5	4
Gatto Ln.	P-8	2
Gayle Ct.	M-6	3
Gdalin Ct.	K-6	4
George St.	N-8	2
Gerow Av.	N-8	2
Gessner Ter.	J-9	5
Gibbs Ct.	L-7	3,4
Gigi Ct.	K-8	5
Gilda Ct.	L-8	2,5
Gisele Ct.	K-7	4
Gladwyne Ct.	K-8	5
Glasgow Ln.	M-6	3
Glen Brook Rd.	K-7	4
Glen Rd.	H-3	4
Glenmere Ct.	M-6	3
Glode Ct.	M-6	3
Gloria Dr.	L-8	2,5
Grand Park Dr.	K-7	4
Grandview Av.	M-4	3
Grandview Av.	M-5	3
Grandview Av.	K-7	4
Grandview Av.	K-8	5
Grandview Av.	K-6	4
Grandview Rd.	M-7	3
Grant Av.	L-9	2,5
Grant St.	H-3	4
Grant St.	N-8	2
Green Hill Ln.	K-8	5
Greene Rd.	L-9	2,5
Greenridge Way	K-9	5
Greenway E.	H-3	4
Greenway Rd.	H-3	4
Greenway W.	H-3	4
Grosser Ln.	L-7	3,4
Grotke Rd.	P-8	2
Grove St.	M-8	2
Grove St.	M-7	3
Gurnee Ct.	K-9	5
Gwen Ln.	M-8	2
Hadassah Ln.	N-8	2
Halberg Parkway	N-8	2
Hall Av.	M-5	3
Haller Crescent	P-7	3
Hallett Pl.	L-4	3,4
Hamilton Av.	J-2	4
Hamilton Ln.	P-7	3
Hammond St.	M-7	3
Hampton Rd.	M-5	3
Hana Ln.	M-8	2
Hansen Ct.	L-9	2,5
Harlow Ln.	N-6	3
Harriman Av.	J-2	4
Harrison Ln.	L-9	2,5
Harvest Ct.	M-7	3
Harvey Ln.	L-9	2,5
Haskell Av.	M-5	3
Haskell Av. E.	M-5	3
Hastings Rd.	K-7	4
Haven Ct.	N-7	3
Haverstraw Rd.	L-5	3,4
Hawk St.	N-8	2
Hazel Ct.	M-9	2
Hazelwood Rd.	H-3	4
Headden Dr.	L-9	2,5
Heather Dr.	M-6	3
Heather Ln.	M-6	3
Heatherill Ln.	L-5	3,4
Heights Rd.	L-6	3,4
Helen Ct.	L-9	2,5
Helper Ct.	N-7	3
Hemion Rd. N.	L-5	3,4
Hemion Way	M-5	3
Hemlock Ln.	L-4	3,4
Hempstead Rd.	L-8	2,5
Hempstead Rd.	K-9	5
Henry Ct.	K-5	4
Herrick Av.	M-8	2
Hershell Ter.	M-7	3
Hickory Av.	L-3	3,4
Hickory Rd.	H-3	4
Hickory St.	L-8	2,5
Hickory St. E.	L-9	2,5
Hidden Glen Ln.	N-6	3
Hidden Valley Dr.	J-8	5
Highgate Ct.	L-5	3,4
Highland Av.	L-4	3,4
Highridge Rd.	K-9	5
Highview Av.	K-9	5
Highview Av.	M-6	3
Highview Rd.	L-6	3,4
Hilda Ln.	M-7	3
Hillcrest Av.	L-9	2,5
Hillcrest Rd.	M-4	3
Hillman Pl.	M-8	2
Hillside Av.	M-4	3
Hillside Av.	P-6	3
Hillside Ct.	J-8	5
Hillside Ter.	J-8	5
Hilltop Ln.	M-7	3
Hilltop Pl.	L-7	3,4
Hilltop Pl.	M-7	3
Hoffman St.	M-8	2
Holland Ln.	K-7	4
Holly Cir.	M-7	3
Homelawn Ct.	P-8	2
Homer Lee Av.	M-8	2
Homestead Ln.	M-7	3
Hoover Ln.	K-9	5
Horn Ln.	L-9	2,5
Horton Dr.	M-6	3
Howard Dr.	M-8	2
Howell Rd.	K-9	5
Hoyt St.	M-8	2
Hubert Humphrey Dr.	P-8	2
Ida Rd.	M-8	2
Ilana Ln.	K-9	5
Imperial Ln.	P-8	2
Independence Ln.	N-7	3
Interstate St.	M-4	3
Inwood Dr.	M-9	2
Inwood Ln.	L-9	2,5
Iroquois Tr.	N-7	3
Ivy Ln.	K-8	5
Jacaruso Dr.	L-8	2,5
Jackson Av.	L-9	2,5
Jackson St.	M-8	2
Jackson St.	H-3	4
Jacqueline Rd.	P-7	3
Jade Ct.	H-8	5
James Ct.	M-5	3
James St.	M-4	3
Janet Ct.	H-3	4
Janna Ct.	N-8	2
Jasinski Rd.	M-8	2
Jay St.	N-8	2
Jay St.	N-8	2
Jean Ln.	P-7	3
Jeanine St.	M-5	3
Jefferson Av.	L-9	2,5
Jeffrey Pl.	M-8	2
Jeremy Ct.	J-7	4
Jersey Av.	M-4	3
Jill Ln.	L-8	2,5
Joan Ln.	L-7	3,4
Jodi Ct.	J-7	4
Johanna Ln.	M-7	3
John St.	N-8	2
Johnathan Pl.	L-8	2,5
Johnson St.	M-8	2
Johnsontown Rd.	H-3	4
Johnstown Rd.	H-3	4
Jordan Pl.	L-9	2,5
Joseph St.	P-8	2
Joy Rd.	J-7	4
Joyce Dr.	P-7	3
Judith Ln.	K-7	4
Juniper Ter.	J-7	4
Kains Rd.	J-8	5
Kakiat Ln.	L-8	2,5
Karen Dr.	L-8	2,5
Karnell St.	L-9	2,5
Karow Ct.	N-7	3
Karsten Dr.	L-5	3,4
Kathleen Ct.	M-6	3
Kaufman Ct.	M-8	2
Keith Dr.	N-7	3
Kelly Ln.	N-6	3
Kennedy Dr.	N-8	2
Kennedy Parkway	P-7	3
Kennith St.	M-7	3
Kent Rd.	N-6	3
Kentor Ln.	K-8	5
Keri Ln.	K-8	5
Kersing Parkway	L-8	2,5
Kevin Dr.	K-6	4
Kile Ct.	M-7	3
Kim Ln.	K-9	5
King Ter.	L-8	2,5
Kings Ct.	M-6	3
Kings Gate Rd.	K-5	4
Kings Point Ln.	L-7	3,4
Kingston Dr.	J-9	5
Krashes Ct.	M-7	3
Kristoffersen Ct.	M-5	3
Kuperman Ln.	L-7	3,4
Lafayette Av.	L-4	3,4
Lake Av.	L-3	3,4
Lakeview Av.	M-9	2
Lakeview Tr.	M-4	3
Lamplight Ln.	N-6	3
Lancaster Dr.	M-5	3
Lancaster Ln.	N-7	3
Landau Ln.	L-9	2,5
Lane St.	M-7	3
Langeris Dr.	L-8	2,5
Lantern Ct.	J-8	5
Larch Ct.	M-5	3
Larissa Ct.	M-6	3
Lark Ln.	N-7	3
Laura Dr.	M-6	3
Laura Ln.	J-8	5
Laura Pl.	M-8	2
Laurel Ln.	N-8	2
Laurel Rd.	L-3	3,4
Laurel Rd.	H-3	4
Laurie Ln.	L-7	3,4
Lawler Blvd.	M-8	2
Lawrence Pl.	P-8	2
Lawrence St.	M-8	2
Lawrence St.	H-8	5
Leadore Ln.	J-9	5
Leaf Ct.	M-6	3
Ledge Rd.	H-3	4
Lee Dr.	N-7	3
Lenox Ct.	M-5	3
Leon Dr.	M-7	3
Levitsky Ct.	N-8	2
Lexington Av.	L-4	3,4
Liberty Rock Rd.	J-2	4
Lillian Dr.	P-8	2
Lime Kiln Rd.	J-7	4
Lincoln Av.	L-9	2,5
Lincoln St.	M-4	3
Lincoln St.	H-3	4
Lincoln St.	M-8	2
Linda Dr.	K-6	4
Linda Ln.	L-9	2,5
Linden Av.	M-8	2
Linderman Ln.	L-8	2,5
Lisa Ln.	P-8	2
Litchult Ct.	M-5	3
Lochsley Ln.	J-8	5
Locust St.	L-8	2,5
Lodi Ln.	K-7	4
Lois Ln.	K-8	5
Lomond Av.	P-8	2
Lonergan Dr.	M-4	3
Longbow Rd.	L-6	3,4
Longridge Ct.	L-9	2,5
Lorna Ln.	M-6	3
Lorna Ln.	N-6	3
Louis Av.	L-7	3,4
Lyncrest Dr.	K-7	4
Lynhaven Ct.	L-7	3,4
Lynn Dr.	N-8	2
Lynn Dr.	N-7	3
Lynne Ct.	L-6	3,4
Maalot Ct.	L-9	2,5
Macintosh Ln.	K-7	4
Madeline Ter.	N-7	3
Madison Av.	M-8	2
Madison Av. N.	M-8	2
Madison Av. S.	N-8	2
Madison Hill Rd.	M-5	3
Main St.	M-8	2
Main St.	M-7	3
Main St.	L-9	2,5
Main St. S.	M-8	2
Mallory Rd.	L-9	2,5
Maltbie Av.	L-3	3,4
Maltbie Av. E.	L-4	3,4
Maltbie Av. W.	L-4	3,4
Manchester Dr.	L-8	2,5
Manis Av.	P-8	2
Manor Dr.	M-7	3
Mansfield Pl.	L-4	3,4
Maple Av.	M-7	3
Maple Av.	M-8	2
Maple Av. E.	L-4	3,4
Maple Av. W.	L-4	3,4
Maple Leaf Rd.	M-7	3
Maple Pl.	H-3	4
Maplewood Blvd.	M-4	3
Maplewood Ln.	M-7	3
Mar Beth Dr.	M-5	3
Marcia Ln.	L-8	2,5
Marget Ann Ln.	K-6	4
Margetts Rd.	N-7	3
Marian Dr.	L-5	3,4
Marisa Dr.	J-8	5
Marjorie Ct.	N-5	3
Mark Dr.	J-8	5
Marman Pl.	M-8	2
Marrietta Dr.	J-10	5
Martha Rd.	K-7	4
Matson Ct.	P-7	3
Maurice Ln.	J-7	4
Mayer Dr.	L-5	3,4
Mayer Rd.	K-5	4
Mc Kenney Ct.	L-6	3,4
Mc Namara Rd.	K-8	5
Mc Toria Pl.	J-8	5
Meadow Av.	L-4	3,4
Meadow Dr.	N-7	3
Meadowbrook Ln.	L-7	3,4
Meadowbrook Ln.	M-4	3
Medical Park Dr.	J-9	5
Melaney Dr.	K-7	4
Melnick Rd.	M-7	3
Memorial Dr.	L-4	3,4
Memorial Park Dr.	M-8	2
Menocker Rd.	N-7	3
Merrick Dr.	L-8	2,5
Merrick Ln.	M-9	2
Michael St.	L-8	2,5
Michelle Ct.	M-9	2
Midway Rd.	K-5	4
Midway Rd.	P-7	3
Miele Rd.	M-7	3
Mile Rd.	L-5	3,4
Milford Ct.	K-8	5
Milford Ln.	M-5	3
Mill St.	J-3	4
Millbury St.	M-5	3
Mills Rd.	L-5	3,4
Milrose Ln.	N-7	3
Milton Pl.	M-8	2
Miriam Ln.	L-7	3,4
Mirror Lake Rd.	M-9	2
Moccasin Pl.	K-7	4
Monclair Av.	N-6	3
Monroe Ln.	L-9	2,5
Monsey Heights Rd.	M-7	3
Monsey Ladentown Rd.	L-7	3,4
Monsey Rd. S.	N-7	3
Monsey Rd. S.	M-6	3
Montebello Rd.	L-5	3,4
Moriah Ln.	L-5	3,4
Morris Ct.	M-8	2
Morris Rd.	L-8	2,5
Mosier Ct.	L-8	2,5
Mountain Av.	L-3	3,4
Mountain Av.	L-7	3,4
Mountain Rd.	H-8	5
Mountain Rd. S.	H-10	5
Mountain View Av.	M-5	3
Municipal Plaza	J-3	4
Murin St.	M-8	2
Murray Dr.	M-6	3
MuscarellaDr.	M-8	2
Myrtle Av.	M-5	3
Myrtle Av. N.	M-8	2
Myrtle Av. S.	M-8	2
Nancy Ln.	L-8	2,5
Naomi Ln.	L-8	2,5
Navaho Tr.	J-2	4
Neil Rd.	M-8	2
Nelson Pl.	M-7	3
Neptune Ct.	J-9	5
Nesher Ct.	M-8	2
Neva Ct.	K-7	4
New Ackerton Rd.	N-7	3
New County Rd.	M-6	3
New Hempstead Rd.	K-9	5
New York State Thruway	L-5	3,4
Newport Ct.	M-5	3
Nicole Way	P-8	2
Nissan Ct.	M-8	2
Noble Pl.	J-2	4
Noe Av.	M-5	3
Norben Rd.	K-7	4
North Face	J-3	4
North Main St.	M-8	2
Northbrook Rd.	M-9	2
Nottingham Dr.	L-5	3,4
Noyes Av.	N-8	2
Nyack Turnpike	M-5	3
Nyack Turnpike	M-6	3
Oak Ln.	L-4	3,4
Oak Pl.	J-2	4
Oak St.	L-8	2,5
Oak St.	L-9	2,5
Oak St. N.	L-8	2,5
Oak Tr.	J-3	4
Oakdale Manor	M-4	3
Oakwood Ter.	K-9	5
Ohio Av.	M-8	2
Old Cranberry Rd.	J-2	4
Old Mill Rd.	L-5	3,4
Old Nyack Turnpike	M-7	3
Old Nyack Turnpike	N-8	2
Old Pomona Rd.	J-8	5
Old Route 202	H-8	5
Old Schoolhouse Rd.	K-9	5
Olmer St.	L-4	3,4
Olympia Ln.	M-6	3
Onderdonk Rd.	J-8	5
Opal Ct.	H-8	5
Orange Av.	L-4	3,4
Orange Turnpike	K-3	4
Orange Turnpike	J-3	4
Orchard Av.	M-6	3
Orchard Cir.	K-5	4
Orchard Ct.	P-7	3
Orchard Hill Dr.	K-7	4
Orchard Pl.	M-5	3
Orchard Pl.	M-6	3
Orchard St.	M-8	2
Orchard St.	M-7	3
Orchard St.	L-5	3,4
Orchard St.	L-8	2,5
Oriole St.	N-7	3
Overbrook Dr.	N-6	3
Overhill Rd.	M-7	3
Overlook Dr.	H-2	4
Overlook Dr.	K-9	5
Oxford Ct.	M-9	2
Oxford Dr.	L-6	3,4
Oz Ct.	K-8	5
Paddock Ln.	M-5	3
Paikin Dr.	M-8	2
Pamela Dr.	P-7	3
Park Av.	H-3	4
Park Av.	M-8	2
Park Av.	N-7	3
Park Av.	L-4	3,4
Park Ln.	M-8	2
Park Pl.	M-5	3
Park Pl.	K-4	4
Park Pl. E.	L-4	3,4
Park Pl. W.	L-4	3,4
Park St.	M-8	2
Park Ter.	J-8	5
Parker Blvd.	K-7	4
Parker St.	M-8	2
Parkside Dr.	M-4	3
Pasadena Pl.	J-8	5
Pascack Rd.	P-8	2
Pascack Rd.	M-9	2
Pascack Rd.	L-9	2,5
Patricia Ln.	K-8	5
Patriot Dr.	N-7	3
Pauline Ct.	M-9	2
Pavilion Rd. (Oak St.)	L-4	3,4
Peachtree Rd.	K-9	5
Peachtree Ter.	K-9	5
Pearl Dr.	J-8	5
Pennington Way	K-8	5
Perth Av.	P-8	2
Phillips Dr.	M-6	3
Phillis Ter.	M-7	3
Pilgrim Ln.	K-7	4
Pine Brook Rd.	P-7	3
Pine Knoll Ct.	P-7	3
Pine Meadow Rd.	H-5	4
Pine Meadow Rd.	H-6	4
Pine Rd.	L-6	3,4
Pinewood Dr.	M-7	3
Pioneer Av.	L-6	3,4
Plank Rd.	K-8	5
Pleasant Av.	L-4	3,4
Pleasant Ridge Rd.	K-8	5
Plum Rd.	K-7	4
Plymouth Pl.	M-7	3
Pomona Ln.	J-8	5
Pomona Rd.	J-8	5
Pomona Rd.	J-9	5
Post Ln.	M-6	3
Post Ln. S.	M-6	3
Post Rd.	H-2	4
Pothat St.	J-2	4
Potter Ln.	N-5	3
Powder Horn Dr.	J-7	4
Prairie Av.	M-4	3
Private Rd.	L-4	3,4
Private Rd.	L-6	3,4
Prospect Pl.	M-4	3
Prospect St.	M-9	2
Prosperity Dr.	H-7	4
Provost Dr.	M-5	3
Quackenbush Av.	N-7	3
Quaker Rd.	H-8	5
Quince Ln.	K-7	4
Quincy Ct.	M-5	3
Radford Pl.	L-8	2,5
Raina St.	N-8	2
Rainbow Ct.	K-8	5
Ralph Blvd.	L-7	3,4
Ramapo Av.	L-3	3,4
Ramapo Av.	L-4	3,4
Ramapo Cir.	L-5	3,4
Ramapo Ln.	P-6	3
Raoul Ct.	M-6	3
Ravenna Dr.	J-10	5
Raymond Av.	N-7	3
Rayson Ln.	N-6	3
Razel Av.	L-9	2,5
Reeder Pl.	J-7	4
Regina Ct.	N-7	3
Regina Rd.	N-7	3
Reigate Pl.	M-5	3
Remsen Av.	M-7	3
Remsen Av. S.	M-7	3
Renfrew Rd.	P-8	2
Rensselear Dr.	K-9	5
Requa Ln.	M-7	3
Revere Ct.	M-5	3
Rhonda Ln.	N-7	3
Ribier Ct.	L-7	3,4
Richard St.	J-2	4
Ridge Av.	M-8	2
Ridge Av.	L-4	3,4
Ridgeway Ter.	K-8	5
Rigaud Rd.	L-8	2,5
Rita Av.	L-8	2,5
Rita Av.	L-7	3,4
River Rd.	L-5	3,4
Riverside Dr.	L-4	3,4
Robert Pitt Dr.	M-7	3
Roberts Rd.	M-7	3
Robin Rd.	N-7	3
Robin Hill Dr.	J-2	4
Rockingham Rd.	K-8	5
Rockland Av.	L-3	3,4
Rockland Parkway	L-9	2,5
Rockland Ter.	M-4	3
Rockledge Dr.	L-4	3,4
Rocklyn Dr.	L-5	3,4
Rodman Ct.	K-9	5
Rodman Pl.	K-9	5
Roman Blvd.	M-8	2
Ronald Dr.	L-8	2,5
Roosevelt Av.	N-8	2
Roosevelt Av.	L-9	2,5
Rose Av.	M-9	2
Rose Hill Rd.	K-6	4
Rosmel Dr.	K-7	4
Ross Av.	P-8	2
Roven Rd.	J-7	4
Roxbury Ct.	N-8	2
Ruby St.	M-4	3
Rustic Dr.	N-6	3
Ruth Ct.	L-7	3,4
Sabin Dr.	M-5	3
Saddle River Rd.	M-7	3
Saddle River Rd.	N-7	3
Saddle River Rd.	P-7	3
Sagamore Av.	M-4	3
Saint Joan Pl.	J-2	4
Salem Ct.	M-5	3
Salem Ct.	K-8	5
Samego Ct.	J-6	4
Samuel Rd.	P-8	2
Sanatorium Rd.	K-9	5
Sandra Ct.	P-7	3
Sands Point Rd.	L-7	3,4
Sandy Brook Dr.	J-8	5
Sansberry Ln.	K-8	5
Sard St.	H-3	4
Scenic Dr.	J-7	4
Scenic Dr.	J-8	5
Schettic Ct.	L-9	2,5
Schewchenko Pl.	M-8	2
School Dr.	L-8	2,5
School House Rd.	P-8	2
School Tr.	L-7	3,4
Scotland Hill Park	N-8	2
Scotland Hill Rd.	N-8	2
Scotland Rd.	N-8	2
Scott St.	J-2	4
Scottford Ln.	K-9	5
Seabird St.	L-8	2,5
Seabring St.	M-8	2
Sebastian Ct.	J-2	4
Sebec Ln.	M-9	2
Secor	M-7	3
Secora Rd.	M-8	2
Sergio Ct.	N-8	2
Serven Rd.	J-8	5
Seth Ln.	M-6	3
Seven Lakes Dr.	H-3	4
Seven Lakes Rd.	H-3	4
Seven Lakes Rd.	H-4	4
Shavelson Ln.	N-8	2
Shelley Ct.	K-7	4
Sheridan Av.	H-3	4
Sherman St.	N-8	2
Sherman St.	L-9	2,5
Sherman St.	H-3	4
Sherri Ln.	K-8	5
Sherwood	N-8	2
Sherwood Ridge Rd.	J-8	5
Shuart Dr.	L-8	2,5
Shuart Rd.	N-6	3
Shulman Ct.	N-6	3
Sickle Ln.	L-7	3,4
Silver Ln.	N-8	2
Sima Ln.	N-8	2
Sinclair Ct.	M-9	2
Singer Av.	M-8	2
Skokie Ln.	J-10	5
Sky Meadow Rd.	J-6	4
Skye Pl.	P-8	2
Skylark Dr.	K-8	5
Skyline Ct.	M-5	3
Skyline Ter.	J-8	5
Slevin Ct.	M-6	3
Slinn Av.	M-9	2
Smith	M-8	2
Smith Ct.	N-6	3
Smith Hill Rd.	N-6	3
Smith Hill Rd.	N-5	3
Smith House Tr.	J-2	4
Smolley Dr.	L-7	3,4
Sneden Pl.	M-9	2
Sneden Pl. W.	L-8	2,5
Sobrisco St.	M-6	3
Solond Rd.	L-8	2,5
Somerset Dr.	M-5	3
Sonata Dr.	J-10	5
Sonia Ct.	M-6	3
Sophia St.	L-7	3,4
South St.	M-4	3
Sparrow Av.	N-7	3
Spicer Rd.	M-4	3
Spook Rock Rd.	L-6	3,4
Spook Rock Rd.	K-6	4
Spook Rock Rd.	M-6	3
Spring Hill Ter.	P-7	3
Spring Horse Way	J-2	4
Spring Rock Pl.	K-8	5
Springbrook Rd.	M-9	2
Spruce Rd.	K-7	4
Stacie Ln.	L-9	2,5
Stag Ct.	J-8	5
Stage St.	M-5	3
Stanley Pl.	L-8	2,5
Stanley Rd.	J-8	5
State St.	M-4	3
State St.	L-9	2,5
Station Rd.	J-3	4
Station Rd.	J-9	5
Steinway Ct.	J-7	4
Stella Dr.	L-9	2,5
Stemmer Ln.	L-6	3,4
Stemmer Ln. E.	L-6	3,4
Stephens Pl.	M-8	2
Sterling Av.	J-2	4
Sterling Forest Ln.	L-5	3,4
Sterling Mine Rd.	H-2	4
Sterling Rd.	N-8	2
Sterlington Rd.	J-2	4
Stern Dr.	J-8	5
Stetner St.	L-8	2,5
Steward Pl.	L-9	2,5
Stewart Cir.	L-4	3,4
Stockbridge Av.	M-5	3
Stone Dr.	L-8	2,5
Stoneham Ln.	K-9	5
Stonehurst Ct.	J-9	5
Stonehurst Dr.	K-5	4
Stony Brook Rd.	H-3	4
Stysly Ln.	L-8	2,5
Suffern Pl.	L-4	3,4
Suffern Pl.	M-7	3
Suffern Rd.	L-3	3,4
Suhl Ln.	K-7	4
Summit Av.	M-7	3
Summit Av.	M-8	2
Summit Av.	L-3	3,4
Summit Av.	K-9	5
Summit Park Rd.	K-9	5
Summit Park Rd.	J-9	5
Summit Rd.	J-8	5
Summit Rd.	P-7	3
Sumter Dr.	N-6	3
Sunderland Pl.	M-5	3
Sunny Ridge Ct.	L-9	2,5
Sunrise Dr.	M-8	2
Sunset Dr.	L-4	3,4
Sunset Rd.	H-3	4
Sunset Ter.	J-8	5
Surrey Ct.	N-6	3
Sussex Ct.	M-5	3
Sutin Pl.	P-8	2
Sutton Rd.	L-7	3,4
Suzanne Dr.	M-8	2
Suzanne Pl.	M-8	2
Suzie Dr.	K-9	5
Swallow Av.	N-7	3
Sydell Ln.	N-8	2
Sylvan Rd.	M-7	3
Sylvan Way	M-4	3
Taft Ln.	L-9	2,5
Tallman Pl.	M-6	3
Tallman St.	M-8	2
Tammy Rd.	K-8	5
Tara Dr.	J-8	5
Temple Ln.	M-4	3
Tempo Rd.	K-10	5
Ternure Av.	M-8	2
Terrace Av.	L-3	3,4
Terrace Av.	M-4	3
Terrace Rd.	J-8	5
Terrilee Ln.	K-9	5
Thomas Ct.	L-7	3,4
Thomsen Dr.	M-6	3
Thorne Pl.	P-8	2
Tice Ct.	P-7	3
Tiffin Ln.	J-10	5
Tilton Rd.	L-4	3,4
Timber Tr.	J-7	4
Timothy Ct.	L-7	3,4
Tobey Ln.	J-8	5
Todd Ct.	N-6	3
Tokay Ln.	L-7	3,4
Token Rd.	L-9	2,5

ROCKLAND COUNTY

STREET	GRID	MAP
Toni Ct.	K-7	4
Topaz Ct.	L-6	3,4
Tome Brook Rd.	K-3	4
Tome Brook Rd.	K-4	4
Torne Rd. E.	H-3	4
Tower Ln.	M-7	3
Tracey Ct.	L-8	2,5
Trails End	J-9	5
Trailside Ct.	K-10	5
Trailside Pl.	K-10	5
Tranquility Rd.	J-7	4
Treetop Ln.	M-7	3
Trinity Av.	L-9	2,5
Trinity Pl.	L-9	2,5
Truman Av.	L-9	2,5
Trumper Rd.	L-8	2,5
Tulip Ln.	J-8	5
Twin Av.	M-8	2
Twin Lakes Ln.	N-6	3
Twin Pine Dr.	J-9	5
Twinkle Rd.	M-6	3
Ullman Ter.	P-7	3
Underland Pl.	M-5	3
Underwood Rd.	L-7	3,4
Unicorn St.	P-7	3
Union Rd.	K-8	5
Union Rd.	L-8	2,5
Utopian Av.	L-4	3,4
Utopian Pl.	M-5	3
Valencia Dr.	L-7	3,4
Valley View Ter.	L-8	2,5
Van Alstine Av.	M-5	3
Van Gogh Ln.	M-5	3
Van Orden Av.	M-8	2
Van Orden Av.	M-5	3
Van Winkle Rd.	K-7	4
Vanessa Dr.	J-8	5
Vermeer Ct.	N-5	3
Victoria Dr.	M-6	3
Victory Rd.	K-5	4
Villa Ln.	J-7	4
Vincent Rd.	M-8	2
Viola Rd.	K-7	4
Viola Rd.	K-6	4
Viola Rd.	L-8	2,5
Viola Rd. Ext.	L-8	2,5
Violet Ct.	L-6	3,4
Vista Way	L-4	3,4
Vivian Pl.	K-6	4
W. Central Av.	M-8	2
W. Furman Pl.	M-8	2
W. Maple Av.	L-7	3,4
Wagonwheel Dr.	K-9	5
Waldron Ter.	H-3	4
Wallace Dr.	P-8	2
Wallenberg Cir.	M-6	3
Walnut Pl.	M-8	2
Walter Dr.	M-8	2
Wanamaker Rd.	L-5	3,4
Ward Ln.	L-9	2,5
Ward St.	M-4	3
Warren Ct.	M-8	2
Washington Av.	H-3	4
Washington Av.	M-4	3
Washington Cir.	L-4	3,4
Watermill Rd.	P-8	2
Waverly Pl.	M-7	3
Wayne Rd.	K-8	5
Weiss Ter.	N-8	2
Wendover Ln.	L-6	3,4
Wesley Chapel Rd.	J-7	4
West Ln.	J-8	5
West St.	M-8	2
Westside Av.	M-8	2
Westview Rd.	K-9	5
White Birch Dr.	J-8	5
White Pine Rd.	J-2	4
White Pine Rd.	J-3	4
White Rd.	M-6	3
Whitefield Rd.	P-7	3
Whritnour Tr.	H-3	4
Widman Ct.	L-8	2,5
Wiener Dr.	L-7	3,4
Wilbur Rd.	K-6	4
Wilder Rd.	J-7	4
Wildwood Dr.	J-7	4
Williams Av.	L-8	2,5
Williams Rd.	P-8	2
Willow Ct.	J-8	5
Willow Dr.	M-4	3
Willow Tree Rd.	K-7	4
Willow Tree Rd. E.	J-8	5
Wilsher Dr.	L-8	2,5
Wilshire Dr.	P-7	3
Wilson Av.	L-9	2,5
Wilson Ct.	K-8	5
Windmill Dr.	K-8	5
Windsor Ter.	N-7	3
Winesap Ln.	K-7	4
Winston Rd.	K-8	5
Wintergreen Rd.	J-2	4
Wishers Ln.	K-8	5
Witherspoon Dr.	M-9	2
Wits End	M-8	5
Witzel Ct.	M-7	3
Wolfe Dr.	M-8	2
Wood Ln.	J-8	5
Woodcrest Rd.	J-7	4
Woodland Dr.	M-4	3
Woodland Rd.	M-6	3
Woodland Rd.	J-3	4
Woodside Pl.	M-8	2
Woodwind Ln.	K-8	5
Wortman Dr.	N-7	3
Wren St.	N-8	2
Yale Dr.	L-8	2,5
Yale Dr.	M-5	3
Yorkshire Dr.	M-5	3
Youmans Dr.	L-8	2,5
Young Ct.	M-6	3
Zabriskie Ter.	L-8	2,5
Zachary Ct.	N-8	2
Zavatone Rd.	K-8	5
Zeck Ct.	K-5	4
Zeissner Pl.	L-8	2,5
Zuba Ln.	L-8	2,5

Town of Stony Point

STREET	GRID	MAP
2nd St.	F-12	6
3rd St.	F-13	6
4th St.	F-12	6
5th St.	F-12	6
Adams Dr.	E-12	6
Algonquin Dr.	F-10	6
Algonquin Dr.	F-11	6

STREET	GRID	MAP
Allison Av.	F-12	6
Anderson Dr.	F-11	6
Ann Av.	E-11	6
Ann Marie Ct.	E-12	6
Autumn Ln.	F-11	6
Ayers Dr.	C-13	6
Babcock Ct.	F-11	6
Baisley's Farm Ct.	F-11	6
Bay View Dr.	F-12	6
Beach Rd.	F-12	6
Beech Dr.	F-11	6
Bender Ct.	E-11	6
Benson's Point Ct.	F-11	6
Birch Way	F-11	6
Birdhill Rd.	D-12	6
Blanchard Rd.	F-9	6
Bontecou Dr.	F-11	6
Boulderberg Av.	D-12	6
Brainerd Ct.	F-10	6
Brainerd Dr.	F-10	6
Brewster Av.	F-12	6
Brook Pl.	C-12	6
Brooks Ct.	F-11	6
Brooks Dr.	F-11	6
Buckberg Rd.	E-12	6
Bullowa Dr.	E-11	6
Bulsontown Rd.	E-11	6
Bburlingham Ct.	F-11	6
Burres Ct.	F-11	6
Captain Faldermeyer Ct.	F-10	6
Captain Faldermeyer Dr.	F-10	6
Captain McGovern Dr.	F-11	6
Carol Ann Ct.	F-11	6
Cartwright Rd.	F-11	6
Cedar Pond Rd.	D-8	6
Central Dr.	F-11	6
Central Highway	G-11	5,6
Chessecote Ct.	F-9	6
Chestnut St.	E-12	6
Church St.	F-12	6
Church St.	D-12	6
Cinder Rd.	F-11	6
Clark Rd.	F-12	6
Colonel Conklin Dr.	E-10	6
Colonial Rd.	E-12	6
Concord Dr.	E-12	6
Cortlandt Ln.	D-12	6
Covati Ct.	F-11	6
Crestview Dr.	D-12	6
Crickettown Rd.	F-11	6
Cristin Ct.	E-11	6
Cross Creek Ln.	F-10	6
De Halve Dr.	F-11	6
Degan's Ln.	D-12	6
Delaware	F-10	6
Delaware Ct.	F-10	6
Dickens St.	F-11	6
Delaware	F-10	6
Dogwood Ln.	G-11	5,6
Doodletown Rd.	N-2	3
Dunderberg	D-12	6
Dunderberg Tnpk.	N-2	3
E. Main Street	F-12	6
Easton St.	G-11	5,6
Elm Av.	E-12	6
Elm Dr.	F-11	6
Ethan Allen Dr.	F-12	6
Ewald Pl.	F-11	6
Fairview Rd.	D-12	6
Farley Dr.	F-11	6
Fawn Dr.	D-12	6
Filmore Dr.	E-10	6
Filors Ln.	F-11	6
Flora Ct.	F-11	6
Florus Ct.	F-12	6
Fonda Dr.	F-11	6
Fowler Dr.	D-11	6
Foxwood Dr.	E-12	6
Frado Ct.	F-12	6
Franck Rd.	E-11	6
Franklin Dr.	F-12	6
Free Hill Rd.	E-12	6
Funcheon Pl.	F-12	6
Garrison Ln.	F-11	6
Garryann Ter.	F-11	6
Gate Hill Rd.	E-11	6
Gate Hill Rd.	F-9	6
Gays Hill Rd.	D-12	6
Georgian Dr.	E-12	6
Getty Rd.	G-11	5,6
Gilmore Dr.	E-12	6
Govan Dr.	F-12	6
Grant	F-12	6
Grassy Point Rd.	F-12	6
Grassy Point Rd.	G-12	5,6
Griffin Pl.	F-12	6
Gurnee Dr.	F-11	6
Gurran Dr.	F-11	6
Hamilton Dr.	F-12	6
Harrison St.	E-11	6
Hastings Ln.	E-12	6
Hawk Nest Rd.	E-12	6
Hayes Ct.	E-10	6
Heights Rd.	E-11	6
Helen Marie Ct.	F-10	6
Herbert Ct.	D-13	6
Hickory Dr.	F-11	6
Hidden Hill Dr.	F-10	6
High Ridge Rd.	G-11	5,6
Highview Av.	F-12	6
Hill Pl.	F-11	6
Hillside Dr.	D-12	6
Hoke Dr.	G-12	5,6
Hollister Ct.	E-11	6
Hoover Pl.	F-11	6
Hoyt Ct.	E-11	6
Hudson Av.	E-11	6
Hudson Ct.	E-11	6
Hudsonview Dr.	D-12	6
Hunter Pl.	F-12	6
Hurd Ct.	F-11	6
Indian Dr.	F-10	6
Ironwood Ct.	F-11	6
Jackson Dr.	E-12	6
James St.	F-12	6
James St.	D-12	6
Janet Pl.	F-12	6
Jay St.	F-12	6
Jefferson Ct.	E-12	6
Jenkins Av.	F-12	6
Jerben Dr.	G-11	5,6

STREET	GRID	MAP
John F. Kennedy Dr.	E-11	6
John St.	F-12	6
Johnson Dr.	E-10	6
June Ct.	D-12	6
Kay-Fries Dr.	G-12	5,6
Kelly Ct.	D-12	6
Kiefer Ct.	E-11	6
Knapp Rd.	F-10	6
Lake Rd.	G-11	5,6
Lake Welch Parkway	E-8	6
Lakeview Dr.	C-12	6
Lakeview Dr.	D-12	6
Laurel Dr.	F-11	6
Lee Av.	F-12	6
Lemon Rd.	N-2	3
Lenni-Lenape Ct.	F-10	6
Lewis Dr.	F-11	6
Liberty Av.	F-12	6
Lieutenant Fungheon Pl.	F-11	6
Lighthouse Ct.	E-12	6
Lillburn Dr.	F-11	6
Lincoln Oval	F-11	6
Lindberg Rd.	D-11	6
Lindberg Rd.	E-10	6
Lookout Pl.	G-12	5,6
Lookout Rd.	D-12	6
Lowland Hill Rd.	F-12	6
Main St.W.	F-11	6
Main St.E.	F-12	6
Major Andre Dr.	G-11	5,6
Maple Dr.	F-11	6
Maple Pl.	D-12	6
Maple Pl.	E-11	6
Marks Ct.	F-11	6
Maryann Ct.	E-12	6
May Ct.	E-11	6
Miller Ln.	E-12	6
Minnerick Dr.	F-12	6
Mohawk	F-10	6
Mohawk Ct.	E-11	6
Mohawk Ct.	F-10	6
Mott Farm Rd.	D-12	6
Mountainview Dr.	C-12	6
Munn Av.	F-12	6
Munsee Ct.	F-10	6
Nelly Dr.	F-12	6
Nordica Cir.	F-12	6
North Liberety Dr.	N-2	2
North Liberety Dr.	N-2	3
North St.	F-13	6
North St.	F-12	6
Oak St.	F-11	6
Odell Dr.	E-11	6
Old Route 210	E-11	6
Old Route 9W	N-2	3
Old Route 9W	N-2	3
Orchard St.	F-12	6
Osbom Dr.	E-10	6
Overlook Dr.	C-12	6
Park Rd.	E-12	6
Park Rd. N.	E-12	6
Patrick Natale Ct.	E-10	6
Philips Dr.	F-10	6
Pierce Dr.	E-10	6
Pine Dr.	F-11	6
Polk Ct.	F-11	6
Prospect St.	E-12	6
Pyngyp Rd.	D-11	6
Pyngyp Rd.	E-11	6
Queensboro Rd.	D-11	6
Quelch Av.	F-12	6
Regina Ct.	F-11	6
Reservoir Rd.	F-11	6
Richard C. Brown Dr.	E-11	6
Ridge Av.	F-12	6
Ridgetop Dr.	D-12	6
River Rd.	N-2	3
River Rd.	F-13	6
Riverview Ct.	E-12	6
Riverview Dr.	C-12	6
Robin Ln.	G-12	5,6
Rochelle Ct.	F-12	6
Roosevelt Pl.	F-12	6
Rose St.	F-12	6
Rosebud Dr.	G-11	5,6
Rosetown Rd.	D-12	6
Rosewood Dr.	F-11	6
Scandell Ct.	D-12	6
Schassler Pl.	F-12	6
Sengstaken Dr.	F-11	6
Seven Lakes Dr.	M-2	3
Sherwood Farms Ct.	E-10	6
Skerry Rd.	F-12	6
Short Rd.	E-10	6
Skinner Ct.	F-12	6
Slater Dr.	F-12	6
Sloane Ct.	E-11	6
Smith St.	F-12	6
South Entrance Dr.	M-2	3
South Liberty Dr.	F-12	6
South Liberty Dr.	G-12	5,6
Spring Dr.	D-12	6
Spring St.	D-12	6
Spring St.	F-12	6
Springsteen Ct.	F-12	6
Spruce Dr.	F-11	6
Stammers La.	F-11	6
Stella Ct.	F-9	6
Stony Point Av.	E-11	6
Stony Point Av.	F-11	6
Stubee Dr.	F-11	6
Sullivan Dr.	F-11	6
Summit Av.	F-11	6
Sunrise Dr.	F-11	6
Susan St.	F-12	6
Tamarac Ln.	F-11	6
Ten Eyck St.	F-12	6
Termasen Dr.	E-12	6
Thiells Rd.	F-11	6
Thomsen Ct.	F-10	6
Tim Brook Rd.	E-11	6
Tomkins Av.	F-12	6
Tomkins Av. Ext.	F-12	6
Tomkins Dr.	D-12	6
Tomkins Ridge Rd.	D-12	6
Truman Av.	E-10	6
Tyler Pl.	F-11	6
Underhill Rd.	D-12	6
Valley View Rd.	G-11	5,6

STREET	GRID	MAP
Van Buren St.	E-11	6
Van Wort St.	D-12	6
Victor Dr.	E-11	6
Waldron Dr.	F-12	6
Walnut St.	F-12	6
Walter Dr.	E-12	6
Washburns Ln.	F-11	6
Wayne Av.	E-11	6
Wayne Av.	F-12	6
Wenzel Ln.	F-12	6
W. Main St.	F-11	6
White Oak Pl.	D-12	6
Wilderness Rd.	F-11	6
Wiles Dr.	F-11	6
William Rd.	G-11	5,6
William St.	F-10	6
Willow Grove Rd.	F-9	6
Willow Pl.	D-12	6
Wood Av.	F-12	6
Woodrum Dr.	E-11	6
Youngtown Ct.	E-11	6
Zachary Taylor St.	E-10	6

ZIP CODE LISTING
BERGEN, PASSAIC, ROCKLAND COMBINED

LOCALITY	ZIP CODE	MAP PAGE
ALLENDALE	07401	B-12
ALPINE	70620	B-7
BERGENFIELD	70621	B-7
BLOOMINGDALE	07403	P-9
BOGOTA	07603	B-4
CARLSTADT	07072	B-2
CLARKSTOWN	10956	R-5
CLIFFSIDE PARK	07010	B-3
CLIFTON	07015	P-14
CLOSTER	07624	B-8
CRESSKILL	07626	B-7
DEMAREST	07627	B-7
DUMONT	07628	B-7
EAST RUTHERFORD	07073	B-2
EDGEWATER	07020	B-3
ELMWOOD PARK	07407	B-5
EMERSON	07630	B-6
ENGLEWOOD	07631	B-4
ENGLEWOOD CLIFFS	07631	B-4
FAIR LAWN	07410	B-6
FAIRVIEW	07022	B-3
FORT LEE	07024	B-3
FRANKLIN LAKES	07417	B-10
GARFIELD	07026	B-5
GLEN ROCK	07452	B-6
HACKENSACK	07602	B-5
HALEDON	07510	P-13
HARRINGTON PARK	07640	B-8
HASBROUCK HEIGHTS	07604	B-2
HAVERSTRAW	10927	R-5
HAWORTH	07641	B-7
HAWTHORNE	07510	P-11
HILLBURN	10931	R-4
HILLSDALE	07642	B-9
HO-HO-KUS	07423	B-9
LEONIA	07605	B-3
LITTLE FALLS	07424	P-14
LITTLE FERRY	07643	B-2
LODI	07644	B-5
LYNDHURST	07071	B-1
MAHWAH	07430	B-11
MAYWOOD	07607	B-5
MIDLAND PARK	07432	B-9
MONTVALE	07647	B-8
NEW SQUARE	10977	R-5
NORTH HALEDON	07508	P-11
NORWOOD	07648	B-8
NYACK	10960	R-2
OAKLAND	07436	B-10
OLD TAPPAN	07675	B-8
ORADELL	07649	B-6
ORANGETOWN	10913	R-1
PALISADES PARK	07650	B-3
PARAMUS	07652	B-6
PARK RIDGE	07656	B-12
PASSAIC	07055	P-14
PATERSON	07510	P-13
PIERMONT	10968	R-1
POMONA	10970	R-5
POMPTON LAKES	07442	P-9
PROSPECT PARK	07508	P-13
RAMAPO	10901	R-4
RAMSEY	07446	B-11
RIDGEFIELD	07657	B-3
RIDGEFIELD PARK	07660	B-3
RIDGEWOOD	07450	B-9
RINGWOOD	07456	P-7
RIVER EDGE	07661	B-5
RIVER VALE	07675	B-8
ROCHELLE PARK	07662	B-5
ROCKLEIGH	07647	B-8
RUTHERFORD	07070	B-2
SADDLE BROOK	07663	B-5
SADDLE RIVER	07458	B-9
SLOATSBURG	10974	R-4
SOUTH HACKENSACK	07606	B-2
SOUTH NYACK	10960	R-2
SPRING VALLEY	10977	R-2
STONY POINT	10980	R-6
SUFFERN	10901	R-4
TEANECK	07666	B-4
TENAFLY	07670	B-4
TETERBORO	07608	B-2
TOTOWA	07512	P-13
UPPER NYACK	10960	R-2
UPPER SADDLE RIVER	07458	B-12
WALDWICK	07463	B-9
WALLINGTON	07057	B-2
WANAQUE	07465	P-9
WASHINGTON	07675	B-9
WAYNE	07470	P-12B
WEST HAVERSTRAW	10993	R-5
WEST MILFORD	07480	P-1
WEST PATERSON	07424	P-13
WESTWOOD	07675	B-9
WOOD RIDGE	07075	B-2
WOODCLIFF LAKE	07675	B-9
WYCKOFF	07481	B-10

```
                MAP PAGE LOCATION
    B . . . . . . . . . . . . . BERGEN COUNTY MAPS
    P . . . . . . . . . . . . PASSAIC COUNTY MAPS
    R . . . . . . . . . . ROCKLAND COUNTY MAPS
```

Note: Naturally a work of this magnitude and detail will, in spite of our efforts, contain some errors and omissions. We ask your cooperation in calling them to our attention.